# THE ULTIMATE BOOK GUIDE

Edited by Leonie Flynn,
Daniel Hahn & Susan Reuben

A&C Black • London

This book is dedicated to Rosemary Sutcliff (for Aquila)
and to L.M.H. (for everything) – **L.F.**

To Mr Reuben, with love from Mrs Reuben – **S.R.**

...and to Kalina, Lucas, Sebastian, Harry,
Aishwarya and Anjali, Sesha and Olivia. Eventually – **D.H.**

First published 2009 by
A&C Black Publishers Ltd
36 Soho Square, London, W1D 3QY
**www.acblack.com**
**www.ultimatebookguide.com**

ISBN 978-1-4081-0438-5

A CIP catalogue for this book is available from the British Library.

This book is produced using paper that is made from wood grown in managed, sustainable
forests. It is natural, renewable and recyclable. The logging and manufacturing processes
conform to the environmental regulations of the country of origin.

Printed in Great Britain by MPG Books Limited.

# CONTENTS

# INTRODUCTION
## by Anne Fine

How lovely to be invited back to introduce this brand-new edition of *The Ultimate Book Guide*.

What was wrong with the old one? Absolutely nothing – except that it was too great a success. We needed to let you know that over the last five years, these guides have been astonishingly popular, sold thousands of copies and won several awards. Much more importantly, they have helped countless readers discover hosts of new authors to read, and wonderful books to devour.

But there are always fresh surprises on the shelves, and brand-new reading passions. (Just look at how wizards have swept into prominence recently. Historical novels are back in flurries, too.) It seemed important to update the guide with all the new books that we'd like to recommend.

So don't stay stuck on the authors you already know you like. It's time to take the plunge. *The Ultimate Book Guide* works like the perfect librarian – always there, ready to lead you on to something new that you're almost certain to enjoy as much, and perhaps even more. All of the books in here are already someone else's favourite. And the suggestions of where to go for further reading have been designed by people who know their stuff. It's wonderful if you can get your hands on the book that's perfect for you, and everything you need to maximise your chance of doing that is in this guide.

So dip inside. Almost at once, flicking over the pages, you'll notice some books you already know and like a lot. Follow the suggestions beside them. Look for the books in libraries, bookshops, charity shops and on the Internet. (After the first edition came out, I kept bumping into children who kept great lists of 'wanted books' in their pockets, and took enormous satisfaction in ticking off the ones they found. Once, I even met an eight year old who carried his *Ultimate Book Guide* around in a plastic bag. Now that's real commitment!)

There's one more benefit. The more books you find yourself getting through, the easier and faster reading gets, and the wider your interests grow. (Trust me.) So then the range of things that you enjoy reading expands even more, and makes the job of choosing even easier.

This book's designed to be your reading map. You'll find your journey through it is far more twisty and back and forth than any road.

But you will have a brilliant and surprising journey. And that's a promise.

Anne Fine
Children's Laureate, 2001–2003

# HOW TO USE THIS BOOK

Most of this book is self-explanatory, and we hope you'll find it easy to use. But here is a bit of help in case you find any of it confusing.

Most of *The Ultimate Book Guide* is made up of book recommendations. There are over 700 books recommended for you by our team of contributors, and these titles are arranged in alphabetical order to make them easy to find. A useful tip: if you don't find what you're looking for first time, think about where else it might be listed. If you can't find *Northern Lights* under 'N', try looking under 'H' for **His Dark Materials** instead... And this is how the recommendations work:

*This is the book that our contributor has chosen to recommend to you*

*This is who wrote or edited the recommended book*

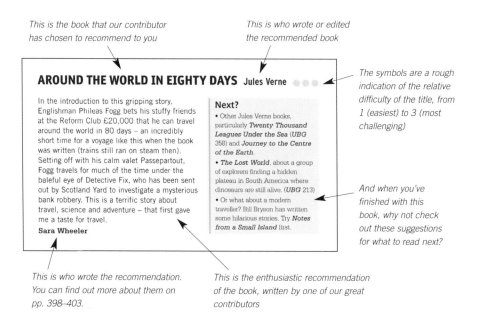

*The symbols are a rough indication of the relative difficulty of the title, from 1 (easiest) to 3 (most challenging)*

**AROUND THE WORLD IN EIGHTY DAYS** Jules Verne

In the introduction to this gripping story, Englishman Phileas Fogg bets his stuffy friends at the Reform Club £20,000 that he can travel around the world in 80 days – an incredibly short time for a voyage like this when the book was written (trains still ran on steam then). Setting off with his calm valet Passepartout, Fogg travels for much of the time under the baleful eye of Detective Fix, who has been sent out by Scotland Yard to investigate a mysterious bank robbery. This is a terrific story about travel, science and adventure – that first gave me a taste for travel.
**Sara Wheeler**

**Next?**
• Other Jules Verne books, particularly *Twenty Thousand Leagues Under the Sea* (UBG 358) and *Journey to the Centre of the Earth*.
• *The Lost World*, about a group of explorers finding a hidden plateau in South America where dinosaurs are still alive. (*UBG* 213)
• Or what about a modern traveller? Bill Bryson has written some hilarious stories. Try *Notes from a Small Island* first.

*And when you've finished with this book, why not check out these suggestions for what to read next?*

*This is who wrote the recommendation. You can find out more about them on pp. 398–403.*

*This is the enthusiastic recommendation of the book, written by one of our great contributors*

The **Next?** box gives you ideas of what you might like to read once you've finished the recommended book. It might include other books by the same author, or books which are funny / exciting / scary in the same way as the book you've just finished, or which deal with a similar subject in a different way. The letters *UBG* mean the book to read next has a recommendation in *The Ultimate Book Guide*, too, which you can find on the page indicated. For example, if you see...

• Or for another book about a wizarding school, try *Harry Potter and the Philosopher's Stone.* (*UBG* 145)

...then you can turn to p. 145 to read about the **Harry Potter** books.

There are also eleven short features, not on particular books but on particular *types* of book – on fantasy books, historical books, school stories, etc. If you have a favourite genre of book, you'll find lots of good suggestions of what to read here. Or if you fancy trying something in a genre you don't know much about ('Hmm, I've never really read much fantasy...'), the features will give you a good idea of where to start. You'll find a list of these features on p. 3.

The features are all written by experts in the field – usually people who write that kind of book themselves (Susan Cooper on fantasy, Dick King-Smith on animals, Joan Aiken on adventure, etc). And next to them, you'll find lists of related titles, too. If any of the titles in the lists sound interesting, you can usually find out more about them by looking them up in this guide. Simple!

Finally, you'll come across reader reviews and the results of our exclusive *UBG* top-ten poll – voted by you! Check out our website at **www.ultimatebookguide.com** for more ways of becoming involved in the future.

# ABOUT THE EDITORS

**LEONIE FLYNN** is a writer and editor. To keep a roof over her head – and because she actually quite likes it – she spends half the week being the librarian at a small prep school in North London. She loves cooking, reading and daydreaming – sometimes she even manages to combine all three! – and hopes one day to have a house big enough for all the books she'd love to own.

**DANIEL HAHN** has been working with Leonie and Susan on the ***Ultimate Book Guides*** since a fateful conversation over dinner in Kentish Town in 2002; and since that first meeting they've produced three *UBG* volumes in the UK and one in the US, and done events and other things related to them, and have now started the process of updating the pesky things (people will insist on publishing new children's books...), which they will all be doing for the rest of their lives. He has done lots of other things since 2002 but, because of the persistent demands of the *UBG*, none of them have been done properly...

**SUSAN REUBEN** co-owns Baobab Editorial and Design Ltd (www.baobabltd.com), a company that carries out freelance work for children's publishers. This allows her to work on a wide variety of projects – most recently concerning food and religion, dinosaurs and insects. Susan enjoys walking, cooking, skiing, talking and, obviously, reading. She has a small son called Isaac and a baby called Emily who educate her daily on which children's books really work.

# THE 7 PROFESSORS OF THE FAR NORTH  John Fardell

Sam Carnabie goes to stay with the eccentric inventor Professor Ampersand and his niece and nephew, Zara and Ben, in Edinburgh. But he isn't there for long before another professor arrives – exhausted and bedraggled, with news of an old enemy...

With Ampersand and his fellow professors kidnapped, it's up to Sam and his new friends to find and rescue them. It's an adventure where the journey is hazardous and exciting – leading to a final showdown with the nasty Professor Roderick Murdo. If the last part of the book seems a bit of a rush, then that just adds to the thrills as plots and their explanations come at Sam with frantic speed.

An exciting 'quest' adventure with helpful illustrations – maps, drawings, pictures – by the author.

**Justin Richards**

## Next?

• Sam, Zara, Ben and their new friend Marcia continue their adventures in *The Flight of the Silver Turtle*.

• Other beautifully illustrated adventure books include *Larklight* by Philip Reeve (*UBG* 196) and *Operation Red Jericho* by Joshua Mowll (*UBG* 253).

• Or try the stunningly inventive and thrilling *The Invention of Hugo Cabret* by Brian Selznick. (*UBG* 175)

★ ★ ★ ★ ★ ★

## A.K.  Peter Dickinson

Paul Kagomi is a young boy, but the guns in his life are not a young boy's toys – they're real. His AK47 assault rifle is his most precious, almost his only, possession. So when the war he has been fighting in for most of his life is over, he doesn't want to give it up. Instead, he buries it carefully in the soil out in the bush, and dutifully heads for school. But peace does not last long, and he knows he will need his AK again.

Though set in a mythical African country, *A.K.* is full of all-too-real experiences of modern African civil wars. More than just a war story, it also shows the emotional and moral struggles Paul faces to find another, more peaceful way of life.

**Marcus Sedgwick**

## Next?

• Try some of Peter Dickinson's other books, such as **The Changes** trilogy (*UBG* 57), or *The Ropemaker*. Another, set in a distant place torn apart by war, is *Tulku*. (*UBG* 356)

• For a book about joining the resistance in a different war, read *Resistance* by Craig Simpson, which is set in World War II Norway.

• Or try *My Brother Johnny*, by Francesco D'Adamo, about a girl whose brother comes home a changed person after flying bombers.

# THE ADVENTURES OF ROBIN HOOD  Roger Lancelyn Green  ●●

### Next?
• Compare this to Marcia Williams's hilarious comic strip, *The Adventures of Robin Hood*.

• Theresa Thomlinson's *The Forest Wife* looks at what might have been the basis for the legend.

• More Roger Lancelyn Green? Read *King Arthur and His Knights of the Round Table*. (*UBG* 189)

My introduction to the tales of Robin Hood was by way of these books, and I've never read better versions. Roger Lancelyn Green went back to the earliest sources he could find – not all of them English – reinterpreted or refocused many of the tales, added his own spin here and there, and bound them together in continuous narratives where they were not always so bound previously. His language and style – dignified and rich, romantic yet business-like – stirred this young reader as much as the tales themselves.

There's chivalry, adventure, romance, skulduggery and cruelty in abundance here, and none of the watering down and pussyfooting you find in some more recent interpretations. I'm glad I came upon R.L.G.'s versions at the age I did, in the age I did, before certain themes, attitudes, manners, customs and tastes were deemed inappropriate or offensive by lofty individuals keen to strip verve, sparkle and humour from stories too rich for their own impoverished sensibilities.

**Michael Lawrence**

★ ★ ★ ★ ★ ★

# THE ADVENTURES OF TOM SAWYER  Mark Twain  ●●●

*Tom Sawyer* is a famous story. A classic. You might already know a bit about the story – Tom lives with his aunt Polly in St Petersburg on the banks of the Mississippi River, and is always getting into trouble. It's also a pretty old story, written (and set) in the nineteenth century.

But here's the thing – this old, famous, classic book is also really, really good! Tom is a great hero and Mark Twain is a very funny writer. Just read a page or two and you'll forget that this is one of those books people keep saying you *ought* to read – once you've met Tom, you'll *want* to keep his company, to meet his friends (especially that other great troublemaker, Huck Finn) and follow their adventures up the Mississippi.

There's a good reason why everyone still talks about this book more than a hundred years on. But don't take my word for it – just give it a try; you'll see why soon enough.

**Daniel Hahn**

### Next?
• More Mark Twain? Try *The Adventures of Huckleberry Finn*, an older and darker story, and *The Prince and the Pauper* (*UBG* 273).

• For characters with something of Tom about them, read *Frindle* (*UBG* 120) and *A Week in the Woods* by Andrew Clements.

• Looking for another high-spirited hero? Try the **Just William** stories – very funny. (*UBG* 186)

## Top Ten Favourite Books

1. **Harry Potter series** by J.K. Rowling

2. **His Dark Materials trilogy** by Philip Pullman

3= **Horrid Henry series** by Francesca Simon

3= **The Lord of the Rings** by J.R.R. Tolkein

5. **Alex Rider series** by Anthony Horowitz

6. **The Story of Tracy Beaker** by Jacqueline Wilson

7. **Artemis Fowl** by Eoin Colfer

8. **Eragon** by Christopher Paolini

9. **Roman Mysteries series** by Caroline Lawrence

10. **A Series of Unfortunate Events** by Lemony Snicket

## AESOP'S FUNKY FABLES
### Vivian French

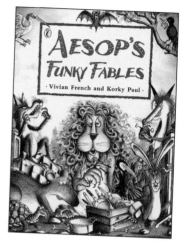

Everyone knows some of these stories off by heart. Aesop wrote them 2,500 years ago. They must be good stories if they're still around after all that time!

Vivian French has taken old favourites like 'The Tortoise and the Hare' and 'The Boy Who Cried Wolf' and made them funky! Yes, funky! Can you hear the bass? Can you hear the drums? Get in the groove and me oh my, that Aesop was a funky guy. And the pictures? Man, they're off the wall. All of them drawn by Korky Paul!

**Shoo Rayner**

### Next?

• If you enjoy these, you'll really like Shoo Rayner's own versions of Kipling's *Just So Stories* – a good one to try is 'How the Whale Got His Throat'.

• What about reading Marcia Williams's *Greek Myths*? (*UBG* 220) Again, stories that you should know, but this time they are in a comic-strip form…

• For more comic-strip action, try the **Asterix** series by René Goscinny and Albert Uderzo. (*UBG* 24)

# AFTER THE DEATH OF ALICE BENNETT
## Rowland Molony

Sam Bennett knows his mum is dead, but he's only a little boy. He just has to try and get through to her, on the other side. So he starts texting his dead mum on her own mobile phone, using a mysterious number he finds. And someone answers...

Sam's story starts slowly, but it draws you in. He's so real, and so are the people around him. If I say this book is about coming to terms with death, it'll sound depressing. If I say it's about anything else, I'd be lying. *After the Death of Alice Bennett* is about ordinary people asking the big, eternal questions and finding big, eternal answers in ordinary places. I've never read anything quite like it. Highly recommended.

**Ann Halam**

### Next?
- Books about death can be hard to read, but some can actually make you feel better. Try Alex Shearer's *The Great Blue Yonder*, about a boy who wishes he wasn't dead.
- Judy Blume's *Tiger Eyes* is about a girl whose father is shot dead and how she copes with the loss.
- Or for something quite different, Katherine Paterson's lyrical *Bridge to Terabithia*. (*UBG* 47)

★ ★ ★ ★ ★ ★

# AIRMAN  Eoin Colfer

Born in a hot-air balloon, Conor Broekhart grows up dreaming of flying. He leads a charmed life in the royal court of an island kingdom, but when he witnesses the murder of the king, the killer imprisons him and tells his parents he is dead. In order to right the injustice, Conor must find a way to escape, but the only way off the island is to fly. The trouble is, the aeroplane hasn't been invented yet. Will Conor be up to the challenge?

A mix of swashbuckling adventure, historical drama and science fiction, *Airman* is fast-paced, witty and full of excitement. If you loved Eoin Colfer's **Artemis Fowl** series but are ready for something a bit more challenging, *Airman* is for you!

**Madelyn Travis**

### Next?
- For other adventures in the skies, try Kenneth Oppel's **Airborn** and its sequel **Skybreaker** – they're very different, but just as enthralling.
- *The Count of Monte Cristo* by Alexandre Dumas is the book that inspired **Airman**. It's a much tougher read (and if you read the full version, very long), but well worth it.
- All of Eoin Colfer's books are great. If you haven't tried his **Artemis Fowl** series (*UBG* 23), then give it a go – there's nothing that quite compares to it, either for adventure or for humour!

# THE ALCHEMIST – THE SECRETS OF THE IMMORTAL NICHOLAS FLAMEL  Michael Scott

● ● ●

What if there had been a time, long ago, when the beings the Greeks, Romans and Egyptians called gods ruled the Earth? This is the central premise of *The Alchemist*, which tells the story of how twins discover that the man they are working for is in fact Nicholas Flamel, who has been engaged in a centuries-long battle with Dr John Dee. Nicholas has been guarding a book known as the Codex, containing several prophecies and spells (such as for the potion of immortality, which Flamel and his wife Perrenelle have been drinking), which are incredibly powerful. Dee then steals this and kidnaps Perrenelle to aid his masters, some of the gods from the ancient times.

While the plot is majestic, the reason I love this book is the detail, the descriptions of the magic and the way each magician has a particular odour in their magic by which you can detect them.

**Tobias Druitt**

### Next?

• There's more Nicholas Flamel in the sequel – *The Magician*.

• And more magic in the **Black Magician** trilogy by Trudi Canavan, which begins with *The Magicians' Guild*.

• Or what about something thrilling and funny and scary and long? Try the **Septimus Heap** books by Angie Sage: *Magyk, Flyte, Physik* and *Queste*. (*UBG* 305)

★ ★ ★ ★ ★ ★

# ALEX RIDER series  Anthony Horowitz

● ●

In the first of this series, *Stormbreaker*, Alex Rider is a normal 14-year-old schoolboy. Normal, that is, until he is recruited by MI6 to investigate the strange goings-on surrounding the famous billionaire, Herod Sayle. Sayle is planning to give a free Stormbreaker computer to every school in Britain, but there's something very suspicious about it all and only Alex Rider can find out what before it's too late.

This gripping adventure story introduces us to brilliant, resourceful Alex Rider, a sort of teenage James Bond – even down to the cunning gadgets! But be warned: the frantic, exciting plot makes this a very hard book to put down.

**Daniel Hahn**

### Next?

• Read them all! After *Stormbreaker* there's *Point Blanc, Skeleton Key, Eagle Strike, Scorpia, Ark Angel* and *Snakehead*.

• More Horowitz? Try his supernatural series, **The Power of Five**. (*UBG* 281)

• Or try the **CHERUB** series – they're more realistic and more grown-up. (*UBG* 60)

• *The Joshua Files: Invisible City* is a stunning adventure story. (*UBG* 183)

# ALICE'S ADVENTURES IN WONDERLAND Lewis Carroll

Alice follows a white rabbit down through a rabbit hole into a strange world inhabited by playing cards. Babies turn into pigs, white roses are painted red, and the Mad Hatter, the March Hare and the Dormouse are involved in an endless tea party. The book is alive with parodies of poems that were well known at the time. By now the original poems are forgotten: it is Lewis Carroll's parodies that we remember. Intelligent and puzzled, Alice moves through Wonderland growing smaller, then taller, then smaller again, until she finally grows so tall she pulls Wonderland into pieces around her.

'Precise, dream-like, subversive' Quentin Blake, Independent on Sunday

Most Victorian stories had stern morals attached to them, but *Alice's Adventures in Wonderland* is told simply for the fun of Alice's adventures and for the fun of the language. Indeed, many of its situations and pronouncements have become part of the language and imagination of the English-speaking world.

**Margaret Mahy**

This is the book that got me hooked on reading. I remember sitting on the stairs, transfixed by the dream-like quality of the story. It seemed, somehow, to be from my own dreams: a mixture of the strange, the funny, the absurd and the frightening. I was especially captured by the illustrations – the original ones by Tenniel, which portrayed Alice as stern and 'unpretty'. The book is a long journey during which she has a series of the most extraordinary encounters with bizarre characters, from the gently eccentric White Rabbit to the terrifying Queen of Hearts. This is a book that stretches your imagination and plays games with all that is logical and sensible, until nothing is what it seems and you start to see the world in a different way!

**Jane Ray**

## Next?

• Alice's next adventures, *Through the Looking Glass*.

• Or what if Alice was a true story? Try Frank Beddor's amazing trilogy – **Alyss of Wonderland**, starting with *The Looking-Glass Wars*.

• Or Neil Gaiman's *Coraline* – also about a girl entering a different world uncannily like her own. (*UBG* 69)

• *The Phantom Tollbooth* by Norton Juster is another surreal story filled with strange events and verbal nonsense. (*UBG* 266)

# ALLIE FINKLE'S RULES FOR GIRLS  Meg Cabot

### Next?

• Try the sequel: *Allie Finkle's Rules for Girls: The New Girl*, then move onto Meg's wonderful **The Princess Diaries** series. (*UBG* 273)

• Or maybe some Judy Blume? Look out for *Tales of a Fourth Grade Nothing*. (*UBG* 341)

• Or try the very funny (and action-packed) **Jane Blonde** series. (*UBG* 180)

Nine-year-old Allie has a rule for every occasion, from never eating anything red or putting a cat in a suitcase, to never, ever sticking a spatula down your best friend's throat. It's a fine set of regulations to live by, even though Allie can't manage it all of the time.

Meg Cabot has created a leading lady with huge appeal. She's fun, sparky, honest, and also has a fierce social conscience (anyone mistreating animals needs to watch out). The first in the series, *Moving Day* is about Allie's determination not to move house. Easy to relate to, it's great fun, very American, and up there with Judy Blume.

**Sarah Ebner**

★ ★ ★ ★ ★ ★

# ALLY'S WORLD: THE PAST, THE PRESENT AND THE LOUD, LOUD GIRL  Karen McCombie

The story of Ally (otherwise known as Alexandra, named after Alexandra Palace) is funny, cheerful and completely absorbing. Her family is mad. Her best friend, Sandie, is sane enough, but their friendship is tested by a new girl at school called Kyra. Kyra is pushy, arrogant and criticises everything. Life is complicated enough with two crazy dogs, one sister who's obsessed with fairy lights and sequins, another sister who's a control freak and a brother who can't understand why everyone doesn't love stick insects as much as he does. When Ally is set to complete a school project with Kyra, it seems things couldn't get worse.

Her dad, who's caring for the family on his own, is great, and he helps Ally to keep her sense of humour as she faces the challenge of Kyra – but what present will be good enough for his birthday?

**Antonia Honeywell**

### Next?

• There are lots more stories about Ally, all with great titles, including *Boys, Brothers and Jelly-Belly Dancing* and *Crushes, Cliques and the Cool School Trip*.

• Then move on to Karen's next series, **Stella Etc**.

• If you enjoyed the close relationship between Ally and her dad, try *The Youngest Girl in the Fifth* by Angela Brazil. (*UBG* 396)

• If you liked reading about the trials of school and family life, try the slightly harder *Are You There, God? It's Me, Margaret*. (*UBG* 22)

# ALONE ON A WIDE WIDE SEA Michael Morpurgo ●●●

Morpurgo is a class act and his work is a timely reminder that fiction for young people need not be 'high-concept' to keep the pages turning. This book opens with a 65-year-old narrator addressing issues of identity and mortality! But it works! Essentially a tale of two journeys, the bulk of the story follows Arthur who, orphaned in England during World War II, is sent to live a challenging new life in Australia. The second journey, much of it told through pleasingly authentic-sounding emails, is that of his daughter, Allie, who sets sail single-handed to England to solve a family mystery. Morpurgo takes the fact of enforced post-war migration and summons an engaging story about family and identity. The author is not afraid to share some difficult truths with his readers, but his work is all the more believable and likeable for that.

**Justin Somper**

### Next?

• Michael Morpurgo has written many wonderful books; try *Kensuke's Kingdom* (*UBG* 187) and *Born to Run*.

• Or something else about immigration? Try Morris Gleitzman's thought-provoking *Boy Overboard*. (*UBG* 46)

• The title of this book is a line from one of the great English poems – 'The Rime of the Ancient Mariner' by Samuel Taylor Coleridge. Try it!

★ ★ ★ ★ ★ ★

# THE AMAZING MAURICE AND HIS EDUCATED RODENTS Terry Pratchett ●●●

### Next?

• This book is set in a world that Pratchett invented. Look out for his **Discworld** books. (*UBG* 68)

• Or for longer books about rodents, try Brian Jacques's **Redwall** series. (*UBG* 282)

• Read about the original Pied Piper, in a poem by Robert Browning, 'The Pied Piper of Hamelin'.

Maurice is a cat who can think and talk, and his educated rodents are rats that can do the same. A change came over them when they ate some rubbish thrown over the wall of a wizard's castle. The rats have adopted names from the tins they find on the dump: Sardines, Hamnpork and Dangerous Beans, to name a few.

This hilarious book turns the story of the Pied Piper on its head. Maurice and the rats team up with a boy who looks stupid (but isn't) and can play a pipe. They travel round the country making money from townspeople who are afraid of rats. But then they reach Bad Blintz, and a terrifying battle begins.

I found this book impossible to put down, and so did my son. We just had to know what would become of Maurice and his wonderful rodents.

**Jenny Nimmo**

# THE AMULET OF SAMARKAND  Jonathan Stroud

● ● ●

What if you had your own genie? Sounds brilliant, doesn't it? But young Nathaniel finds there are drawbacks to becoming a magician. For one thing, it's dangerous, thanks to rival magicians. And a mistake in summoning means your demon-slave can eat you for lunch. The world of *The Amulet of Samarkand* is corrupt. And if it's not as much fun as it sounds being a magic-user, being a djinn like Bartimaeus is even less fun: he's forced to work like a slave for his master, or suffer punishments which destroy his essence. However, he and Nathaniel have a common goal: to stop an evil magician from taking over Britain.

What makes this book and its sequels stand out is the incredible way the world has been developed, with its exploration of the deeds, habits and styles of each djinn, all rounded off with the wonderful footnotes that accompany Bartimaeus's narration. This is a hilarious book with some sombre moments – an adventure which everyone should read.

**Tobias Druitt**

### Next?
• This is the first in the **Bartimaeus** trilogy; read on to *The Golem's Eye* and *Ptolemy's Gate*.

• Another story that involves magic and the crossing of worlds is Garth Nix's **Sabriel** sequence. (*UBG* 292)

• Or what about *Howl's Moving Castle* by Diana Wynne Jones, a book that manages to be tear-inducingly funny and terrifying, too.

★ ★ ★ ★ ★ ★

# ANASTASIA KRUPNIK  Lois Lowry

● ●

Ten-year-old Anastasia Krupnik is bright, precocious and funny (a little like my own heroine, Flavia Gemina – see *The Thieves of Ostia* on p. 288).

Anastasia loves lists and keeps them in her green notebook. Her mother is an artist and her father is a poet. Hers is a family so delightful that you long to be part of it. The first book charts Anastasia's amusing reactions to her mother's pregnancy and the birth of her brother, Sam, who becomes a delightful character in later books in the series.

Lowry never talks down to her readers, which is why it's so much fun to read these books – even for adults!

**Caroline Lawrence**

### Next?
• Other books in the series include *Anastasia at Your Service*, *Anastasia Has the Answers* and *Anastasia on Her Own*.

• Paula Danziger writes great books about families and friends. Try *Everyone Else's Parents Said Yes!*

• You might enjoy *Emily of New Moon* by L.M. Montgomery, about an orphan who is sent to stay with her unwelcoming relations. (*UBG* 99)

# AND THEN THERE WERE NONE  Agatha Christie  ●●●

### Next?

• Everything by Agatha Christie is worth reading. Personally, I tend to prefer the Poirot books, but any will do. Try *Evil Under the Sun* next.

• Arthur Conan Doyle's Sherlock Holmes, of course: *The Hound of the Baskervilles* (*UBG* 160) and *A Study in Scarlet* (*UBG* 335).

• Dorothy L. Sayers wrote many stories about her detective, Lord Peter Wimsey. The first is *Clouds of Witness*, but they're all very good.

This is the best murder-mystery story ever written. (For the record, I've just asked my fellow editors and they agree.) Agatha Christie was the grandmother of this sort of book, and her two regular sleuths, Hercule Poirot and Miss Marple, are among the world's favourites. But this story is different – for one thing there's no detective, just one murderer and nine terrified victims...

It's about the simplest plot you can imagine. Ten people stranded overnight in an isolated house. One is murdered. And then there were nine. Another murder. And then there were eight. And so on...

You'd think that it'd become obvious who the killer is pretty quickly, wouldn't you? Especially as numbers start to dwindle. But try as you might, I'll bet you won't be able to work it out before Agatha Christie reveals her breathtaking ending. I've never yet met anyone who has. Awesome.

**Daniel Hahn**

★ ★ ★ ★ ★ ★

# THE ANGEL FACTORY  Terence Blacker  ●●●

Thomas Wisdom lives a perfect life. Everything, including the dog, is exactly right. But one day, Tom and his friend Gip hack into Tom's father's computer. What they find blows Tom's so-called perfect life apart. Suddenly, he is plunged into a terrifying world where the future of mankind is at stake and treachery is all around him. Tom learns to make some hard choices. And making hard choices when everyone around you seems so kind and caring is particularly difficult. Read this book and you will never look at people you pass on the street in the same way again.

**Karen Wallace**

### Next?

• Try *The Transfer*, also by Terence Blacker (*UBG* 351), about football and a computer program that goes wrong, or his hilarious *The Parent Swap*, about a boy who swaps his boring parents for better ones and ends up reluctantly involved in a reality TV show.

• Or *Hacker* by Malorie Blackman, about a girl who uses her hacking skills to try and save her father from prison. (*UBG* 140)

• Two other children who just might have to save the world appear in Jeanette Winterson's *Tanglewreck*. (*UBG* 343)

# AN ANGEL FOR MAY Melvin Burgess

Tam hates his life. He hates his mum and he hates his dad for not wanting him. To get away from home he takes refuge in a burnt-out old farmhouse in the hills above his house. But the farmhouse is not quite what it seems, and there the hard line between past and present begins to blur, until suddenly Tam finds himself in the ruined house back when it was whole, and lived in by an old man and a strange young girl.

This is a very eerie story. Everything from the stray dog to the smelly old tramp Tam finds in the house have something weird about them. Spending more and more time back in the past, Tam begins to wonder if he wants to return home at all. But he has been taken back in time for a reason, and not all the answers lie in the past.

**Leonie Flynn**

### Next?
• Another great Melvin Burgess book with strange goings-on is *The Ghost Behind the Wall*. (*UBG* 124)
• In Kit Pearson's *A Handful of Time*, a young girl whips back in time and meets her mother as a young girl – and uncovers a secret.
• Or try Pete Johnson's *The Frighteners*, which is very, very scary!

★ ★ ★ ★ ★ ★

# THE ANGEL OF NITSHILL ROAD
## Anne Fine

### Next?
• More Anne Fine? Try *The Chicken Gave it to Me*, about a girl and a heroic chicken. Or *Loudmouth Louis*, about a boy who just can't stop talking, not even in class.
• If you like school stories, try Louis Sachar's quirky *Sideways Stories from Wayside School* and meet Mrs Gorf, a teacher who is also a mean bully! (*UBG* 309)
• Or what about some silly spooky school stories? Try B. Strange's **Too Ghoul for School** series.

There's a bully at Nitshill Road School, and he is making life pretty miserable for the people around him. At least he does until a new girl, Celeste, joins the class. Celeste is not frightened of Barry Hunter – she doesn't seem to be frightened of anything – and the way she deals with him, and changes all the unhappiness he has caused, makes for one of the cleverest books about bullying that you'll ever read.

None of the things Celeste does to the bully are what you'd expect. She doesn't fight him. She doesn't play tricks on him. She doesn't humiliate him. What she does is...

No, I'm sorry... You'll have to read it for yourself!

But I guarantee you won't regret it!

**Andrew Norriss**

# ANGELS UNLIMITED series Annie Dalton ●●

**Next?**

• Sam Hay's *Billy Angel* is the hilarious story of a boy who is visited one night by a hoodie-angel, who reveals his strange destiny.

• *The Lottie Project* is another book about going back into the past – but in a very different way. (*UBG* 213)

• Or try the fabulously funny and exciting *Jane Blonde: Sensational Spylet*, about a mousy girl who becomes a daring super-spy! (*UBG* 180)

What could be better than time travelling with your best friends? That's why fast-talking and totally hip Mel Beeby just *loves* history – because she gets to live it! At the Angel Academy, the students often get pulled out of class to help solve a real-life crisis somewhere in the distant past. In *Flying High*, the angels are off to medieval Jerusalem to help in the Children's Crusade.

Intrigued already? But what *is* the Angel Academy? Well, that's where angels are trained, of course. Angels? Yep – Mel is formerly of this Earth and she has no idea why she was recruited. But her new life and her new friends are fantastic and there's never a dull moment. (There are a few enemies to beware of, too – but aren't there always?) Mel and her friends travel back to sixteenth-century London (*Losing the Plot*) and forwards to Victorian times (*Fogging Over*) and way back to ancient Rome (*Fighting Fit*). And that's just for starters!

**Jon Appleton**

★ ★ ★ ★ ★ ★

# THE ANIMALS OF FARTHING WOOD Colin Dann ●●

Disaster strikes Farthing Wood when the bulldozers crash in and a drought dries up all the water. How can the animals save themselves? They decide to leave their beloved home and take the long journey to White Deer Park, a faraway nature reserve. Under the leadership of Fox, with his trusted deputy, Badger, they follow Toad who has told them stories of this wonderful place.

One of the best things about this book is that it is absolutely action packed. Every single chapter has the animals facing a new danger: a forest fire, a motorway, angry farmers, flooding rivers and a fox hunt. So the story is not only very exciting but easy to read in short chunks. Each episode will keep you on the edge of your seat, wondering how they will ever complete their journey.

**Abigail Anderson**

**Next?**

• The rest of the **Farthing Wood** books! They include *The Fox Cub Bold*, *Strangers in the Park* and *Battle for the Park*.

• *The Wind in the Willows* by Kenneth Grahame is about another group of animals' adventures, but animals who dress and act like humans. (*UBG* 385)

• Colin Dann's written other books about animals, too – try one about a cat, *King of Vagabonds*.

# ANNE OF GREEN GABLES L.M. Montgomery

### Next?
- The story continues in *Anne of Avonlea*, *Anne of the Island*, *Anne of Windy Willows*, *Anne's House of Dreams*, *Anne of Ingleside*, *Rainbow Valley* and *Rilla of Ingleside*.
- And there is a prequel, written by Budge Wilson: *Before Green Gables*.
- You might also like *Little Women* by Louisa M. Alcott. (*UBG* 208)
- Or for another spirited heroine, what about Jacqueline Wilson's *The Story of Tracy Beaker*? (*UBG* 332)

One day, Matthew Cuthbert, a shy and silent man, goes off to the station to pick up an orphan boy to help him on the farm; what he finds instead is a girl – Anne Shirley, an eleven-year-old orphan with bright-red hair, freckles and a hot temper. Anne is desperate for a home, so Matthew quietly persuades his strict sister, Marilla, to let her stay at Green Gables. Anne is a tremendous talker and her imagination is quirky and interesting. It isn't long before she has won Matthew and Marilla's hearts and changed the way they look at the world.

*Anne of Green Gables* has always been my favourite children's book because of Anne herself – she could talk the hind leg off a donkey; she is spirited; she feels different to everyone else; she speaks her mind; and she's very self-conscious about her red hair. Such a brilliant character.

**Jackie Kay**

★ ★ ★ ★ ★ ★

# THE APPRENTICES Leon Garfield

These wonderful tales of London's apprentice children were first published separately, so you had to be patient and wait from one to the next. Now they're collected together and you can choose how to read them: you might read one a day, making friends gradually with trainee undertakers, printers' devils, silver-thread spinners and hangmen, as they serve out their seven-year apprenticeships. But if I were you, I'd read them all in one go, and let the mysterious Link Boy, whose flaming torch lights up every chapter, guide you through Leon Garfield's brilliantly vivid world of eighteenth-century London. And my favourites? 'Mirror, Mirror', which is both terrifying and beautiful, and 'Filthy Beast'.

**Gill Vickery**

### Next?
- Try more Leon Garfield. *Smith* (*UBG* 315) and *Devil-in-the-Fog* are historical adventures. *The Strange Affair of Adelaide Harris* is a hilarious comic romp, about two boys who devise a crazy plan to kidnap a baby. (*UBG* 333)
- For a more light-hearted read, try Penelope Lively's witty and funny *The Revenge of Samuel Stokes*, about a ghost who objects to a modern housing development being built on the site of his beautiful old estate. (*UBG* 284)

# AQUILA  Andrew Norriss

Geoff and Tom are on a school trip when they fall into an old quarry. Inside a cave at the bottom, they find a weird-looking machine. Before they really think about what they're doing, they're climbing into it, pushing a few knobs and suddenly they're in the air.

Aquila is the sort of machine that dreams are made of. It runs on water, it answers questions. It can become invisible and it can immobilise people. Geoff and Tom, once the dunces of the class, suddenly become interested in power-technology, Latin, map reading and maths. Their teachers are naturally suspicious, and it becomes increasingly difficult to keep Aquila a secret.

This story is tremendous fun. The reader is totally absorbed as the boys gradually discover Aquila's amazing powers. And the teachers' reactions are hilarious when you're in on the secret.

**Jenny Nimmo**

### Next?

• You'll need more Andrew Norriss – look out for *The Touchstone*, about a boy who meets an alien. Or *The Unluckiest Boy in the World*, in which Nicholas touches an ancient tomb and finds himself cursed – and terrible things start to happen.

• If you've a taste for ancient Rome, try Theresa Breslin's *Across the Roman Wall*, set in Roman Britain.

• *The Big Bazoohley* by Peter Carey is another wacky, eventful story – about a boy who gets locked out of his room, and then kidnapped!

★ ★ ★ ★ ★ ★

# THE ARABIAN NIGHTS

Genies in lamps! Sparkling treasure! Magic carpets! Ferocious sword fights! Beautiful princesses! You might think you know the stories, but think again. In addition to the favourites, such as 'Aladdin' and 'Ali Baba and the Forty Thieves', there are lots more to discover and many collections to choose from – try Geraldine McCaughrean's *One Thousand and One Arabian Nights*.

The stories are supposed to be those told by Princess Scheherazade to a powerful emperor. The emperor is planning to kill her, but she manages to delay her execution by telling him stories of magic and wonder each night, and in the end he doesn't execute her – he marries her! Her stories certainly do cast a spell over you. They transport you to a hot, exotic world of sights, sounds and smells, far away from rainy old Britain.

**Abigail Anderson**

### Next?

• *The Land of Green Ginger* by Noel Langley – a funny book, set in a fictional land. (*UBG* 195)

• Or look out for P.B. Kerr's **Children of the Lamp** series, which starts with *The Akhenaten Adventure*.

• *The Arthur Rackham Fairy Book* (*UBG* 24) is a great source of classic tales, as is *The Orchard Book of Greek Myths* (*UBG* 254).

# ARAMINTA SPOOK: MY HAUNTED HOUSE Angie Sage

### Next?

- More Araminta Spook? The sequels are *The Sword in the Grotto*, *Frognapped* and *Vampire Bat*.

- For scary children, try the **Edgar and Ellen** series by Charles Ogden, starting with *Rare Beasts*.

- Holly Black and Tony diTerlizzi's **The Spiderwick Chronicles** are deliciously gothic, too; start with *The Field Guide*. (*UBG* 321)

Araminta is a normal goth – oops! I mean girl. Yes, she's a normal girl. A girl who loves her run-down, spider-infested old house, so when her aunt decides to sell (and move to a block of flats!), Araminta comes up with all sorts of Cunning Plans to stop anyone from wanting to buy. And, as Araminta is used to getting what she wants, well … potential buyers had better watch out!

With a feisty heroine, endearing ghosts, spooky goings-on and a lot of really smelly bats, this is a scary story that'll make you laugh as well as shiver.

**Leonie Flynn**

★ ★ ★ ★ ★ ★

# ARE YOU THERE, GOD? IT'S ME, MARGARET
## Judy Blume

Margaret is eleven and just starting at a new school, far away from her beloved grandma in New York. Three girls invite her to join their gang, which meets in secret to discuss 'boys' and 'growing up'. We follow Margaret through Sixth Grade as she worries about her first bra and observes the boys in her class. Her most intimate concerns she addresses directly to God. Nothing much happens, but she learns useful lessons, such as that even the most seemingly confident kids can exaggerate or even lie.

This isn't a book you'll want to reread endlessly, but perfect if you're a ten- to eleven-year-old girl wondering what becoming a teenager is like.

**Jane Darcy**

### Next?

- You might like other books by Judy Blume – try *Iggie's House*.

- My niece recommends **The Princess Diaries** by Meg Cabot. (*UBG* 273) Also, anything by Jacqueline Wilson.

- *Stargirl* by Jerry Spinelli is about what it feels like not to fit in – and what happens when you suddenly do. (*UBG* 324) Or, on the same theme, try *The Wish* by Gail Carson Levine.

# AROUND THE WORLD IN EIGHTY DAYS  Jules Verne ● ● ●

In the introduction to this gripping story, Englishman Phileas Fogg bets his stuffy friends at the Reform Club £20,000 that he can travel around the world in 80 days – an incredibly short time for a voyage like this when the book was written (trains still ran on steam then). Setting off with his calm valet, Passepartout, Fogg travels for much of the time under the baleful eye of Detective Fix, who has been sent out by Scotland Yard to investigate a mysterious bank robbery.

This is a terrific story about travel, science and adventure – which gave me a taste for travel.

**Sara Wheeler**

### Next?
• Other Jules Verne books, particularly *Twenty Thousand Leagues Under the Sea* (*UBG* 358) and *Journey to the Centre of the Earth*.
• *The Lost World*, about a group of explorers finding a hidden plateau in South America where dinosaurs are still alive. (*UBG* 213)
• Or what about a modern traveller? Bill Bryson has written some hilarious stories. Try *Notes from a Small Island* first.

★ ★ ★ ★ ★ ★

# ARTEMIS FOWL  Eoin Colfer ● ●

### Next?
• The sequels so far are *Artemis Fowl and the Arctic Incident*, *Artemis Fowl and the Eternity Code*, *Artemis Fowl and the Opal Deception* and *Artemis Fowl and the Lost Colony*.
• There are also graphic novels based on the **Artemis Fowl** books, written by Eoin Colfer and Andrew Donkin.
• More villains are heroes in *H.I.V.E.* by Mark Walden – the initials stand for Higher Institute of Villainous Education. (*UBG* 154)

I first had to read *Artemis Fowl* when I worked at Puffin. It was late, I was tired and all I thought I wanted to do was watch television. But, in fact, reading *Artemis Fowl* was what I really needed – the closest possible reading experience to watching a big-budget action film.

*Artemis Fowl* is fantasy, but is closer to James Bond than to *The Lord of the Rings*. It is also very funny. In the first book, Artemis Fowl, a 12-year-old criminal mastermind who isn't satisfied with robbing banks, sets his sights on the ultimate treasure – fairy gold. What he doesn't realise is that the fairies he is up against aren't soft and pretty with sparkly wings. These fairies are smart, armed and dangerous, and one of the smartest, Captain Holly Short of the LEPrecon Unit, is going to do everything she can to make sure Artemis doesn't succeed. And so begins a fantastic battle of wits and weapons, with plenty of action and larger-than-life characters, including my favourite, Mulch Diggums, the dwarf with the amazing bum-flap.

**Philippa Milnes-Smith**

# THE ARTHUR RACKHAM FAIRY BOOK Arthur Rackham ● ●

For me, Arthur Rackham was the greatest children's illustrator of them all. He looked like an Edwardian bank clerk – such a contrast to most of the people and creatures depicted in his illustrations. Rackham's astonishing goblins, trees, wizards, genies and giants enthralled the eye and mind of this young lad through childhood. For this particular book, he chose around two dozen popular tales from various countries and illustrated them with line drawings, silhouettes and full-colour paintings.

**Michael Lawrence**

**Next?**

• Some other books brilliantly enhanced by Arthur Rackham illustrations are Kenneth Grahame's *The Wind in the Willows* (*UBG* 385), Charles Dickens's *A Christmas Carol* and Aesop's *Fables* (*UBG* 104).

• There are loads of great versions of classic fairy tales – turn to p. 106 for a selection.

• Or for a more modern take, try *A Necklace of Raindrops* by Joan Aiken. (*UBG* 248)

★ ★ ★ ★ ★ ★

# ASTERIX series René Goscinny and Albert Uderzo ● ●

**Next?**

• Try the **Tintin** series by Hergé. (*UBG* 349)

• Or more by Goscinny? Read the **Nicholas** books, about a schoolboy who somehow never gets things right. (*UBG* 249)

• Jeremy Strong is a writer known for packing his stories with silly jokes and puns. Try *My Mum's Going to Explode!*. (*UBG* 244)

• Or read *The Rotten Romans* in the **Horrible Histories** series, where you get puns, jokes and real history, too! (*UBG* 158)

Adventures, warriors, quests and the funniest bad jokes ever to come out of Gaul. These are the ingredients of this cartoon series. Asterix, a cunning little warrior, and his mountainous best friend, Obelix, are the heroes of over 20 stories about the last Gaulish tribe to remain undefeated by the Roman legions, thanks largely to the magic potion brewed by the druid Getafix.

The heroes' adventures take them to many distant lands, but the recipe remains the same – a fantastic mix of thrills and laughs. Highlights include the fondue orgy scenes in *Asterix in Switzerland*, the constant nose jokes in *Asterix and Cleopatra*, and the great feast at the end of every adventure, when Cacofonix the bard (geddit?) is invariably gagged and tied to a nearby tree to prevent him from performing.

Originally written in French, much effort has been made to ensure that all the jokes and joke names (and there are lots of them) lose nothing in the translation.

You might not learn much (accurate) history reading them, but you'll certainly enjoy the adventures.

**Marcus Sedgwick**

# ASTROSAURS: RIDDLE OF THE RAPTORS
Steve Cole

### Next?
• These stories are addictive, so thankfully, there are a lot of sequels; start with *The Hatching Horror*, *The Seas of Doom*, *The Mind-Swap Menace* and *The Skies of Fear*. There's a second series too, **Astrosaurs Academy**.

• Steve's also written the equally hilarious and exciting **Cows in Action (C.I.A.)** series.

• For more human (sometimes) adventure try Michael Broad's **Jake Cake** series, starting with *The Werewolf Teacher*. Or for more dinosaurs, check out Rex Stone's **Dinosaur Cove** series, starting with *Attack of the Lizard King*.

So you thought the dinosaurs were wiped out when a meteor hit the Earth lots and lots of years ago? Wrong! They, being intelligent, escaped into space and settled in a far part of the galaxy called the Jurassic Quadrant. With space being divided between the Herbivores (our heroes) and the Carnivores (usually the villains!), the stage is set for endless adventures.

The *DSS Sauropod* is on a mission, and its captain, Teggs, and his Astrosaur crew protect the innocent and fight evil. Fast paced, excitingly plotted, full of adventure and mayhem, really, really funny jokes and great illustrations, these books are guaranteed to keep you reading.

**Leonie Flynn**

★ ★ ★ ★ ★ ★

# AT THE SIGN OF THE SUGARED PLUM
Mary Hooper

The turbulent world of 1660s London comes fully to life in this wonderful novel by Mary Hooper. It's a London of excitement and entertainment and sweet shops, but it's also a city quickly being overtaken by the dreaded plague. So when country-girl Hannah chooses this moment to visit the city to stay with her sister, she finds it a quite different place to the one she'd imagined. Though this story is set more than 300 years ago, you'll feel Hannah's world – the good bits and the bad – as though it were your own home, as though her new friends and neighbours were yours. Filled with life and death, this is a thrilling book.

**Daniel Hahn**

### Next?
• Hannah's story continues in *Petals in the Ashes*, which sees the city of London consumed by the Great Fire of 1666.

• Look out for more Mary Hooper. Try *At the House of the Magician*, set in Elizabethan times, and *The Remarkable Life and Times of Eliza Rose*, which involves Charles II and Nell Gwyn.

• Julia Golding's **Cat Royal** is another series with a great female protagonist. (*UBG* 83)

# AUGUST '44 Carlo Gébler

### Next?
• *The Devil's Arithmetic* by Jane Yolen is a deeply moving story set during World War II. (*UBG* 83)

• *The Star Houses* by Stewart Ross is about how one family of Hungarian Jews survived the war.

• Donna Jo Napoli's *Stones in Water* is a beautifully told story of two Italian boys who are taken as slave labourers into Eastern Europe. What happens to them, and how they try and hide the fact that one of them is Jewish, is a moving testament to friendship and is loosely based on a true story. As with many books set around this time, it's once read, never forgotten.

Saul and his family are Jewish. It's World War II and they're hiding out in the forest to escape from the Nazis. Living in a cave, and in constant danger of being found, their lives are harsh and incredibly hazardous. To cheer them all up, Claude, who is a family friend, tells the story of the Golem – a legendary creature created out of clay to help the Jews in Prague, long, long ago.

Carlo Gébler weaves together two amazing stories; both of Jewish people living under terrible persecution, but they are ultimately hopeful. By retelling the legend of the Prague Jews, who at least had the Golem to protect them, he brings to the fore just how vulnerable the Jewish people hiding from the Nazis really were. This is a very powerful and very thoughtful book.

**Susan Reuben**

★ ★ ★ ★ ★ ★

# BADGER ON THE BARGE Janni Howker

In my humble opinion, collections of short stories just don't get enough fuss. They're perfect for reading at bedtime, or on trains and buses, or anywhere where a long story gets interrupted too often. And a good short story can say far more than any three-part epic… especially when that story is written by Janni Howker.

There are five stories in this collection, and each one deals in a different way with a relationship between a child (or children) and a much older person. Do you ever think you know something for *certain* and then find out you've got it all backwards? Well, these stories are about exactly that kind of experience … and they're the kind of stories you can read a zillion times and each time discover something new, profound and mind-stretching. A book to keep for ever.

**Vivian French**

### Next?
• Janni hasn't written a huge number of books, but if you found this as amazing as I hope you will, then you really must read her other longer stories. Try *The Nature of the Beast* first.

• *Flying With Icarus* by Curdella Forbes is a set of short stories all set in the Caribbean.

• Or try David Almond's moving *Counting Stars*. (*UBG* 73)

# THE BAGTHORPE SAGA: ORDINARY JACK

**Helen Cresswell**

If you suffer from low esteem – and who doesn't sometimes? – read this hilarious and uplifting book. Jack Bagthorpe feels low because, unlike the rest of the large Bagthorpe family, who all excel at something, he isn't particularly good at anything. And it's not for want of trying. Uncle Parker, married to ravishingly beautiful Aunt Celia, who typically excels at poetry and pottery and can do *The Times* crossword in ten minutes flat, decides to help Jack out. He says Jack must *pretend* to excel at something and he has a plan to make Jack immortal.

The Bagthorpes are like lots of families, where achievement is the thing; so the story rings true at the same time as being fantastical and farcical, rollicking and rumbustious, and sometimes quite moving.

**Julia Jarman**

**Next?**

• The series continues with *Absolute Zero*, *Bagthorpes Unlimited* and *Bagthorpes v the World*.

• For more boys who outwit most adults, try *Aquila* by Andrew Norriss (*UBG* 21) or Elizabeth Honey's *Don't Pat the Wombat* (*UBG* 90).

• Or for more Helen Cresswell, try *Lizzie Dripping*, about a girl whose best friend is a witch! (*UBG* 208)

★ ★ ★ ★ ★ ★

# BAMBERT'S BOOK OF MISSING STORIES

**Reinhardt Jung**

**Next?**

• *Dreaming in Black and White* is another book by Reinhardt Jung, about a boy who dreams himself back to Nazi-controlled Germany.

• *Love That Dog* by Sharon Creech will keep you thinking long after you've closed it. (*UBG* 214)

• *Where Were You, Robert?* by Hans Magnus Enzenburger is the story of a boy who travels through time, collecting new stories and telling his own.

There is something rather sad about Bambert. A small man, he lives alone in his attic flat. He finds moving around difficult because of the pains in his joints. His only contact is with Mr Bloom, his landlord, who sends food and drink from the ground floor to Bambert in a specially fitted lift. But Bambert's life isn't constrained or lonely – because he writes stories about worlds he imagines and feels he knows. His world is actually as big as his dreams allow, and because he dreams such fabulous dreams, the stories he writes don't reflect his physical life.

This is a book that seems very simple, but long after you've finished it you will still be thinking about Bambert letting his stories float off into the distance in search of their own setting.

**Lindsey Fraser**

# BALLET SHOES Noel Streatfeild

I must have read *Ballet Shoes* at least ten times when I was young. I longed to have ballet lessons myself. I pretended my pink bedroom slippers were real ballet shoes and pranced round our flat, pointing my toes and whirling round and round. I must have looked a total idiot!

*Ballet Shoes* is the story of three adopted girls, Pauline, Petrova and Posy Fossil. They're sent to a London stage school and manage to earn their own livings appearing in plays and films. Pauline is a brilliant actress. Posy is an outstanding dancer. Petrova hates acting and dancing – she loves cars and wants to fly her own aeroplane.

*Ballet Shoes* seems a little old-fashioned now, and you might roll your eyes at the Fossil sisters' idea of their own poverty, given that they live in a big house in London with servants – but it's still a riveting story.

**Jacqueline Wilson**

At the drab end of World War II, ballet exploded across Britain. Before I ever saw a performance I knew it was my thing. The brilliant stage, the stories, the music, the dance, I found them irresistible. Ballet became my passion. When companies came to the Empire Theatre I saw every production, racing from school to queue in a back street and do my homework sitting on the pavement.

The only ballet books I could find were grown-up histories and biographies, and I read them all. *Ballet Shoes* was the exception, a lovely fantasy about three orphans at a stage school, which I read and reread.

I was never teased, but I knew that at that time boys in Sunderland did not become ballet dancers. I didn't know how to go about it. Trying a different form of romanticism, I went to sea instead.

**Alan Temperley**

## Next?

• There are many more Noel Streatfeild 'Shoes' stories – try *Dancing Shoes*, *Theatre Shoes* and *Tennis Shoes*, then look out for all the rest. Her **Gemma** books are about being in the movies; and there's also *White Boots*, which is about ice-skating.

• Another lovely story about wanting to perform on the stage is *The Swish of the Curtain* by Pamela Brown. (*UBG* 337)

• Another girl desperate to escape into the world of the ballet appears in Eva Ibbotson's *A Company of Swans*.

# THE BATTLE OF BUBBLE AND SQUEAK   Philippa Pearce

**Next?**

• More Philippa Pearce!
*A Dog So Small* (*UBG* 88)
is great, as is *The Little
Gentleman*, about a very
ancient talking mole and the
little girl who befriends him.

• Try the fantasy stories of
Hermux Tantamoq the
mouse by Michael Hoeye.
Start with *Time Stops for
No Mouse*. (*UBG* 348)

• For another very short
story of families and pets,
read Anne Fine's *The Diary
of a Killer Cat*.

Philippa Pearce is a brilliant storyteller – she sees and understands real life and knows how to involve her readers in it.

Life for the Sparrow family changes with the arrival of two gerbils: Bubble and Squeak. The Sparrow children, especially Sid, are passionate about the gerbils. Their dad doesn't mind them, but Mrs Sparrow simply wants them out of her house. So the family conflict begins.

The gerbils survive many threats – being returned to the pet shop, being given away, being put out for the dustbin men to collect and being attacked by Ginger the cat. Mr Sparrow tries to keep everyone happy, and of course the story does have a satisfying ending and will leave you smiling.

**Wendy Cooling**

★ ★ ★ ★ ★ ★

# A BEAR CALLED PADDINGTON   Michael Bond

The hapless Paddington is my all-time favourite children's book character. He never fails to make me laugh. This book introduces him and his family, the Browns (having been adopted by them on Paddington Station after his trip from Darkest Peru), as well as the regulars who appear in the series, including grouchy Mr Curry, Paddington's horrible neighbour, and gentle Mr Gruber, his friend from the antiques shop on Portobello Road.

Paddington himself is a walking disaster area, always getting into some desperate scrape or other. Yet, once the mayhem has been sorted out (usually by the long-suffering Browns, or their housekeeper, Mrs Bird), he never fails to come out of it well; often better than he began.

In this book, having a bath, going on the London Underground and visiting the theatre are just some of the events that get the inimitable Michael Bond touch. Timeless, hilarious and essential reading – for all ages!

**Chris d'Lacey**

**Next?**

• There are far too
many books in the
**Paddington** series to
mention them all. If you
liked *A Bear Called...*,
then none of the others
will fail to amuse you.

• Of course another
classic bear book is
*Winnie-the-Pooh* by
A.A. Milne. (*UBG* 387)

• I must also put a word
in here for another of my
favourite authors, Allan
Ahlberg. His young
fiction is brilliant. Read
*Ten in a Bed* – you
won't stop laughing.

# BEAUTY Robin McKinley

When her wealthy family loses all its money, Beauty and her horse, Greatheart, work hard to help out. Having moved far away from their home, the family is just starting to get settled when her father runs foul of a wizardly Beast in an enchanted castle. Beauty and Greatheart go to the castle to live in exchange for her father's life, and find tiny, sly magics everywhere, invisible servants, plenty of books, and a Beast who only distresses her when he asks his nightly question, 'Will you marry me?'.

The story is familiar, but McKinley makes it magical again, with a Beauty who redeems a wistful Beast, a magical library and obliging table settings (created long before the Disney movie), and a hundred grace notes that give this unique retelling a pleasure all its own.

**Tamora Pierce**

## Next?

• If you'd like to see what McKinley does with what happens next, try the dream-like – and tougher – *Rose Daughter*.

• A wonderful story that reads like a fairy tale is Eva Ibbotson's *Secret Countess*. (*UBG* 300)

• 'Sleeping Beauty' has been the starting point for Jane Yolen's *Briar Rose*, Sophie Masson's *Clementine* and Robin McKinley's *Spindle's End*.

• And try the wonderful, older **Egerton Hall** trilogy by Adèle Geras.

★ ★ ★ ★ ★ ★

# BECAUSE OF WINN-DIXIE Kate DiCamillo

## Next?

• Try Kate DiCamillo's next book, *The Tiger Rising*, about a grieving, bullied boy, and *The Tale of Despereaux* (*UBG* 339), the story of a mouse who, despite being the runt of the litter, survives to become a hero.

• Like DiCamillo, Mark Twain writes in the Southern tradition of seeing the adult world through a child's eyes. You might like to try his *The Adventures of Tom Sawyer*. (*UBG* 9)

• A true story of one dog is *Marley: A Dog Like No Other* by John Grogan. (*UBG* 222)

Funny and moving, *Because of Winn-Dixie* tells the story of ten-year-old Opal Buloni, recently arrived with her father, the preacher, at a trailer park in Naomi, Florida. Opal befriends a dog running amok through the local supermarket, calling him Winn-Dixie (like naming a dog Tesco). Winn-Dixie helps Opal and her father deal with the loss of Ruby, Opal's mother, and enables Opal to make friends with many of the town's more interesting citizens, dispelling both their loneliness and her own.

This book deals with big themes: love, loneliness, loss and reconciliation, with a sureness of touch beyond all but a few. The story is told in the absolutely authentic voice of its charming heroine. Every sentence rings true.

**Celia Rees**

# BECKY BANANAS  Jean Ure

### Next?

• Some other 'diary' stories from Jean Ure are *The Secret Life of Sally Tomato*, *Skinny Melon and Me*, *Pumpkin Pie* and *Shrinking Violet*.

• You'll find certain similarities to Jacqueline Wilson's older *Vicky Angel*. (*UBG* 369)

• *Harvey Angell* by Diana Hendry is an upbeat, lighter tale that still makes you think about people. (*UBG* 146)

Don't even think about reading *Becky Bananas* if you're embarrassed when books make you cry. Even the toughest, meanest, most cold-hearted monster among you will be sniffling loudly by the end of this...

And you'll love it, of course. Becky Banaras ('Bananas') is a very loveable character, and the story she's telling you about her own life, and about a girl called Bryony who has leukaemia, is funny, moving, uplifting and lots of other good things.

Of all Jean Ure's great books (and there are loads), this one's definitely my favourite. You'll love all the characters – little brother Danny, Mum, gorgeous Uncle Eddy, but especially the wonderful, lively Becky, of course. And once you've started, you'll probably end up reading it in one sitting as I did. But remember, hankies at the ready...

**Daniel Hahn**

★ ★ ★ ★ ★ ★

# BED-KNOB AND BROOMSTICK  Mary Norton

Have you ever heard about some amazing place and thought, 'I wish I could go there!' but you couldn't, because it was too far away, or too dangerous, too expensive or just plain impossible? Everyone has dreams like that.

Carey and her brothers, summering at their aunt's dull house in Bedfordshire, are given a magic bed-knob by kindly neighbourhood witch-in-training, Miss Price. The bed-knob will take them (and their bed) anywhere they want to go. They can think of loads of places – but which to try first? Should they go to explore a beautiful desert island? Or to London to visit their mother? Or perhaps into the past? But Carey, Charles and Paul soon discover that magical adventures are never as simple as they first seem...

This is 'a classic' – not just because it's very old and your grandparents loved it, but because it's genuinely a brilliant read – exciting, funny, lively – everything you could want in a book.

**Daniel Hahn**

### Next?

• For more sibling adventures, try the enchanting *The Saturdays* by Elizabeth Enright. (*UBG* 295)

• Mary Norton also wrote *The Borrowers*. (*UBG* 43)

• Or try *Mary Poppins* by P.L. Travers, another story of magic intruding on humdrum lives! (*UBG* 223)

# BEOWULF: DRAGONSLAYER  Rosemary Sutcliff

### Next?
• If you want to know more about the original story, try reading some Norse myths (**UBG** 250), or the Icelandic sagas.

• *Hound of Ulster*, about the Celtic hero, Cuchulain, is another Sutcliff based on legend.

• Or for something lighter, try *Fabulous Monsters* by Marcia Williams – monsters can be funny, too!

This is the oldest Anglo-Saxon story in existence. And it might just be the best. It's got everything: Beowulf, a valiant young hero; Grendel, a beast who has been pulling warriors apart for fun; and an even more powerful creature, Grendel's mother, a hideous seahag who lives at the bottom of a lake. Not content with facing these terrors, Beowulf also has a pop at a vicious dragon before he is acclaimed the bravest warrior of all.

Originally written in Old English, the story of Beowulf has been told round the evening fire for generations. Rosemary Sutcliff's retelling brings it to life for our own time, but captures the guts and courage of the dark days that stand at the head of our history.

**Marcus Sedgwick**

★ ★ ★ ★ ★ ★

# BETSY-TACY series  Maud Hart Lovelace

Where were Maud Hart Lovelace's books when I was growing up? I guess they were around, but somehow I missed them. High school would have been so much easier if I'd been prepped for it by reading these books! And even though Betsy, Mrs Lovelace's heroine, went to high school in 1910 Minnesota, things haven't really changed since Betsy's day. There were popular girls who weren't especially nice to her, and cute boys to have huge crushes on, and best friends to fight with, and parties and dances and popular music and pretty new clothes, and even a few things I didn't have growing up – like sleigh rides and onion (blech!) sandwiches.

Start with Betsy's first year in high school – *Heaven to Betsy*. This is the book where she first meets Joe, her one true love... Or *is* he?

Maud Hart Lovelace based the **Betsy** books on her own high-school years. There is even a museum in Minnesota where you can go and see photos of her and her friends and all of the people and places in her stories.

**Meg Cabot**

### Next?
• Look for: *Betsy in Spite of Herself*, *Betsy Was a Junior*, *Betsy and Joe*, *Betsy and the Great World* and *Betsy's Wedding*.

• Laura Ingalls Wilder's **Little House** books (**UBG** 203) is another American series about growing up, starting with *Little House in the Big Woods*.

• For something more modern, try *Simone's Letters* by Helena Pielichaty. (**UBG** 312)

# THE BFG  Roald Dahl

The special friendship between the little orphan girl Sophie and the BFG, and their adventures together as they save the world from less-than-friendly giants (with a little help from the queen), make the most wonderful of stories. It's one of those rare books that sweeps you away from the very beginning of chapter one – 'The Witching Hour' – when the reader immediately knows that magic and mystery are at work. Roald Dahl really does weave his own individual magic in this book, which is also particularly good on tape or read aloud, not least because of the BFG's own delicious (or indeed 'scrumdiddlyumptious') mixed-up language. The story combines excitement, humour and unforgettable characters, including the BFG himself with his trademark ears, sandals and dramatic cloak.

**Philippa Milnes-Smith**

## Next?
• Read all of Roald Dahl's children's books. Try *The Witches* (*UBG* 389) or *The Twits* (*UBG* 359).

• Try Philip Ridley's *Meteorite Spoon* and *Scribbleboy* (*UBG* 298), which also feature extraordinary characters.

• If you want more giants, try Julia Donaldson's *The Giants and the Joneses* – it has a glossary of giant language! (*UBG* 126)

★ ★ ★ ★ ★ ★

# BIGGLES series  Captain W.E. Johns

## Next?
• More flying, but of different sorts? Try Eoin Colfer's *Airman* (with flying machines) (*UBG* 11) or Ken Oppel's *Airborn* (with flying airships).

• For real-life flying adventures, try Roald Dahl's autobiography, *Going Solo*.

• Or try Craig Simpson's *Dogfight*, about two plane-mad boys who get mixed up in World War II.

Flying ace, Squadron Leader James Bigglesworth, ducks and weaves through countless thrilling adventures, invariably escaping disaster by a whisker and leaving his dastardly enemies gasping for mercy. In one book, *Biggles: Foreign Legionnaire*, he enlists in the infamous French Foreign Legion, bravely casting fears aside and plunging in to whatever dangers might present themselves (plenty do). He capers about all over the globe, chomping Chinese fried rice one minute and garlic snails the next.

The author allows him to wander freely through the decades: several of the books are set during the First World War, during which our hero boldly defends the goodies' supply route between Calcutta and China, and on another occasion he scraps with his old German enemy in the wilds of Palestine.

I never tired of Biggles and his breathtakingly hazardous antics, and from him I learnt that with a bit of initiative and a dash of courage, you can think your way out of anything.

**Sara Wheeler**

# BILL'S NEW FROCK  Anne Fine

'When Bill Simpson woke up on Monday morning, he found he was a girl.'

Bill's mother puts a frilly, pink dress over his head, and he is horrified. But there's nothing else for him to wear, so off he goes to school in his frilly, pink dress.

It's the beginning of the worst day of Bill's life, but for the reader it's incredibly funny. Gradually, Bill is made aware of all the injustices a girl has to suffer. The boys won't let him play football, and he has to model for the art class. He is even wolf-whistled. Bill can't help behaving like a boy, and soon the pink dress is in a mess: ripped, muddied and covered in paint. But as the school day draws to a close, we begin to wonder if Bill will ever return to what he was before.

Although this story is about a boy, both boys and girls will find it hilarious. It brings into focus some of the funniest differences between us.

**Jenny Nimmo**

> ### Next?
> • Read some more of Anne Fine's shorter stories: *The Angel of Nitshill Road* for instance (*UBG* 18), and *Ivan the Terrible*. Both are school stories with a difference.
> • Or Allan Ahlberg's *Woof!* about a boy who is transformed into a Norfolk Terrier! (*UBG* 391)
> • Or what about a boy who gets turned into a mouse? Look for Roald Dahl's *The Witches*. (*UBG* 389)

★ ★ ★ ★ ★ ★

# BILLY ELLIOT  Melvin Burgess

> ### Next?
> • For more about boys and ballet, see Alan Temperley's recommendation of *Ballet Shoes* by Noel Streatfeild. (*UBG* 28)
> • What about another book by Melvin Burgess? Try *Kite*. (*UBG* 192)
> • *Cuckoo in the Nest* by Michelle Magorian is about a boy wanting to be an actor.

If you don't know this story, it's about a 12-year-old boy in County Durham who discovers he has a talent for ballet. Not the sort of thing Northern boys are meant to dream about, frankly – just ask Billy's dad, on-strike miner, Jackie. He's not amused. Billy should be boxing or doing something else 'manly' like that. But Billy has a real gift, and his ballet teacher is determined that he shouldn't waste it. It's a story about conflict between what different people think about things; Melvin Burgess dramatises this conflict really effectively by switching between points of view – parts of the story are told by Billy himself, parts by Jackie, Billy's brother Tony, and his friend Michael.

Book adaptations of films are often (usually?) rubbish. But you can trust a writer like Melvin Burgess to produce something this good. Don't read this instead of seeing the film, nor the other way round; both are great.

**Daniel Hahn**

# BLACK BEAUTY  Anna Sewell

Stories can be exciting, mysterious, frightening or funny. But they can also be sad, as much of *Black Beauty* is. One scene in it is among the most moving in all of children's literature.

Cruelty to horses was commonplace in Victorian times, and one thing that Anna Sewell fought against was the use of a bearing rein, a device designed to pull a carriage horse's head right up. It looked smart but it was agony for the animal.

The story isn't all gloom. Admittedly, the black horse with the white star on his forehead has an accident – a fall when driven by a drunkard – but his early life with Squire Gordon, John Manly the coachman and Joe Green the stableboy is a happy one. By the end we can smile, though we may have shed some tears along the way.

**Dick King-Smith**

I read this story often as a child, and whenever I came to a hill (London has plenty), it always made me think of horses carrying heavy loads. And I can't help noticing how horses are treated in, say, Dickens or Sherlock Holmes. I owe this, and much more, to Anna Sewell. But since she died soon after her book's publication, she never knew that she had created a major all-age bestseller, never out of print, still rated as the most influential work of fiction on animal welfare ever written.

*Black Beauty* is the self-told tale of a horse whose many changes of work and owner tell us much. Remember – there was no motorised transport when this was written, but horses were all too cheap and plentiful. There were no traffic rules in the hideously crammed streets, where sick and overworked creatures died daily in harness. The high-bred carriage horses fared no better. Quickly ruined by fashion's cruelties, they were sold off for rough street use. It's all in Anna's book.

**Naomi Lewis**

## Next?

• More books about horses? Try the story of a girl desperate to ride in the Grand National, in Enid Bagnold's *National Velvet*. (*UBG* 247)

• Or maybe a story of wild horses in *The Silver Brumby* by Elyne Mitchell.

• Or try Michael Morpurgo's *Born to Run*, about the life of a greyhound – it'll make you cry, too.

# BLACK JACK Leon Garfield

● ● ●

**Next?**

• Other Leon Garfield books you may enjoy are *Smith* (*UBG* 315) and *Devil-in-the-Fog*.

• For something set at roughly the same time, try Paul Bajoria's *The Printer's Devil*, which is the start of a trilogy – there you'll find kidnap, adventure, disguise and danger. (*UBG* 274)

• *The Ruby in the Smoke* is another detective story set in Victorian times. (*UBG* 289)

A boy, Tolly, is in a moonlit room. With him, the dead body of a huge man who has just been hanged. Then, 'Those eyes! They were wide open! They were moving! They were staring at him!'

So begins an eighteenth-century adventure, with villainy afoot on every page. Interwoven with Tolly's story is that of Belle, a girl who is thought mad and sees visions: 'A tall tower with a golden top – higher than the sky. There are white angels flying with white wings. And all the world's singing a lullaby – for the sun's gone to bed in a blanket.'

Leon Garfield uses words as if they are alive and will draw you into a strange, dangerous world – and it's a sort of love story, too. Read it.

**Helen Cresswell**

★ ★ ★ ★ ★ ★

# BLACK SHIPS BEFORE TROY Rosemary Sutcliff

● ●

Long, long ago, Paris, a Trojan prince, fell in love with Helen, wife of the Greek king Menelaus, and sailed with her back to Troy. Helen's is the famous 'face that launched a thousand ships' – the black ships of the Greeks who set sail for Troy to wreak vengeance on the Trojans and get Helen back.

Nineteen stories, each one ending with a cliffhanger, tell the tale of the ten-year-long war which followed. You'll meet heroes and villains and gods and goddesses in many disguises. There's gruesome realism and there are amazing magical feats. You'll read about a golden apple that could be said to have caused the war, the famous Wooden Horse of Troy that brought it to an end, and what was probably the first cloak of invisibility in literature.

These are some of the oldest stories in the world – and so good that writers have been pinching from them ever since! Rosemary Sutcliff brings them vividly to life in this stunning retelling.

**Julia Jarman**

**Next?**

• Odysseus was one of the bravest and most cunning heroes. His story is told in *The Wanderings of Odysseus*, also by Rosemary Sutcliff, and continues in *The Aeneid*, retold by Penelope Lively.

• Or try a series of adventures based on Greek myth – the **Corydon** books by Tobias Druitt, starting with *Corydon and the Island of Monsters*. (*UBG* 72)

• Or try Diana Wynne Jones's slim but fascinating *The Game* about a mythological treasure hunt.

# BLART: THE BOY WHO DIDN'T WANT TO SAVE THE WORLD

**Dominic Barker**

Blart is a young boy who is destined to be a hero and save the world – or so wizard Capablanca tells him. But Blart doesn't want to be a hero. He wants to stay on his grandfather's farm and look after the pigs. Unwillingly dragged along with wizard, warrior, princess, dwarf and a giant flying horse, to defeat the villainous Zoltab, Blart is forever trying to ditch his comrades and escape his destiny.

The story cracks along with Blart's reluctance and surliness providing much of the abundant humour. It's exciting and well told, with some laugh-out-loud moments as well as a few frights along the way. Will Blart save the world despite himself? You'll have fun finding out!

**Justin Richards**

### Next?

- Blart is back for more – against his wishes – in *Blart 2: The Boy Who Was Wanted Dead Or Alive – Or Both* and in *Blart 3: The Boy Who Set Sail on a Questionable Quest*.
- There are more amusing heroics in *Percy Jackson and the Lightning Thief* (*UBG* 262), or check out the **Edge Chronicles** series. (*UBG* 97)
- Another pig-farming boy who ends up on a huge adventure is Taran in *The Book of Three*. (*UBG* 42)

★ ★ ★ ★ ★ ★

# BLITZCAT  Robert Westall

### Next?

- Robert Westall wrote many acclaimed books about the war; try the classic *The Machine Gunners* (*UBG* 215), or the wonderful *Kingdom by the Sea*.
- Or more animals in war? Try Michael Morpurgo's *War Horse* (*UBG* 373) or Martin Booth's *War Dog*.
- For another look at history through animals' eyes, try Katherine Roberts's *I Am the Great Horse*, about Alexander the Great's horse, Bucephalas. (*UBG* 165)

*Blitzcat* is an animal book with a difference. The heroine is a black cat, Lord Gort, who decides to go in search of her absent person, an RAF pilot. Set in the darkest hours of World War II, Lord Gort's quest takes her first to bomb-torn Dover, then to Coventry, just as the city is being destroyed by fire. The cat then travels across country where she becomes the lucky mascot at an RAF station – and that's just for starters. *Blitzcat* is an exciting, action-packed read, highly realistic and informative about the life of RAF fighter pilots. Be warned – although a cat is the central character, this book is not at all soft or sentimental. It's a breathtaking, vividly told adventure.

**Sherry Ashworth**

# ADVENTURE STORIES
## 'X' Marks the Spot
### by Joan Aiken

When I was a child, my favourite room
was my elder brother John's ground-floor
bedroom. It had a brick floor, a bookcase
full of his books, and an old purple sofa.
John was away at college and I used to
spend hours in there reading those books.
And such books! *The Hound of the
Baskervilles*, *King Solomon's Mines*,
*Kidnapped*, *Treasure Island*, *Around the
World in Eighty Days*, *Dracula*, *The Swiss
Family Robinson*, *The Call of the Wild*,
*The Man in the Iron Mask*, *The Prince and
the Pauper*, *Tom Sawyer*, *Kim*... Not only
those but all the other books by Rudyard
Kipling, Mark Twain, Arthur Conan Doyle,
Robert Louis Stevenson, Jules Verne,
Alexandre Dumas and the rest.

There were a lot of ghost stories, too. From age six to 12, I simply loved being
terrified. I could gulp down books then that I'd
hardly dare open now... Ballantyne's *Coral Island*
had wonderful scenes in underwater coral caves
but also *terrifying* descriptions
of South Sea savages and the things they did to
their prisoners... *The Hound of the Baskervilles*
was fairly hair-raising, too, and so were some of
Kipling's short stories.

Kipling was just about my favourite author
around the age of seven or eight. I knew the
poems in the **Jungle Books** by heart and spent
whole afternoons being Mowgli on the thicketty
South Downs, half a mile away. My favourite
Mowgli story was the one in which he saves his
friends the wolves from an invading pack of
Dholes, wild red dogs ... but there was another
beauty about a wicked old white cobra guarding
a hoard of long-forgotten royal treasure. And
then there was *Kim*, which my mother and I

## Joan Aiken's Top Ten Adventure Stories

- *Captains Courageous* by Rudyard Kipling
- *Kim* by Rudyard Kipling
- *Emil and the Detectives* by Erich Kästner
- *The Hobbit* by J.R.R. Tolkien
- *The Midnight Folk* by John Masefield
- *The Bird of Dawning* by John Masefield
- *She* by H. Rider Haggard
- *The Sword in the Stone* by T.H. White
- *Tom Sawyer* and *Huckleberry Finn* by Mark Twain

read aloud to each other every evening. Meanwhile, I was made to drink a glass of milk every night; I cannot stand the taste of milk, still loathe it to this day, but the story of *Kim* was so marvellous that somehow I managed to get the milk down. I still link the taste of milk with the scene of Kim steering the old llama through the Himalayas and foiling the Russian spies.

A solitary child, I loved the company of those brave characters in my brother's adventure books. They seemed to come in fours: the Four Musketeers (including D'Artagnan), the Walker children in Arthur Ransome's *Swallows and Amazons* books, the four March girls in *Little Women* (that was my sister's); I collected a whole army of my own, using these warriors, and made up new exploits for them, led by me, riding on a white charger... The Psammead's friends were my friends, too.

Now I know that it was not the characters but the books – and their authors – who were my lifelong friends.

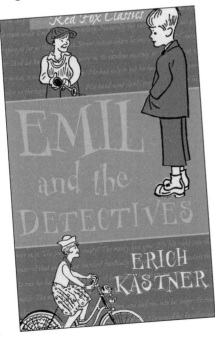

## More Favourites Chosen by the Editors

- **His Dark Materials** trilogy by Philip Pullman
- The *Wolves of Willoughby Chase* by Joan Aiken
- *Go Saddle the Sea* by Joan Aiken
- *The Hound of the Baskervilles* by Arthur Conan Doyle
- *Kidnapped* by Robert Louis Stevenson
- *Treasure Island* by Robert Louis Stevenson
- **Alex Rider** series by Anthony Horowitz; start with *Stormbreaker*
- *Around the World in Eighty Days* by Jules Verne
- *Journey to the River Sea* by Eva Ibbotson
- *Kensuke's Kingdom* by Michael Morpurgo
- *Hatchet* by Gary Paulsen
- *Amazon Adventure* by Willard Price
- *The Joshua Files: Invisible City* by M.G. Harris
- **Biggles** series by Captain W.E. Johns
- *Eagle of the Ninth* by Rosemary Sutcliff
- *Holes* by Louis Sachar
- **Percy Jackson** series by Rick Riordan
- *Gideon the Cutpurse* by Linda Buckley Archer
- *Stone Heart* by Charlie Fletcher
- **Vampirates** series by Justin Somper

# BLOOD RED HORSE K.M. Grant

It is hard to know how to begin describing *Blood Red Horse*. You could see it as a sad story describing the horrors of the Crusades. You could see it as the tale of three boys: Will, Gavin and Kamil. You could see it as the tale of a bond between east and west over a blood-red horse named Hosanna. But in reality it is all of these, intertwining the complex relations of the brothers, Will and Gavin, with a realistic tale of the Crusades and the loss and gain of Hosanna, Will's warhorse, small, spirited and with a white star on his brow, leading the way for the rest of the characters. Unlike most Crusades stories, it does not completely focus on just one side – it focuses on both at different points. All in all, this is the best Crusades story I've had the privilege to read.
**Tobias Druitt**

**Next?**
• This is the first of the **de Granville** trilogy, which continues in **Green Jasper** and **Blaze of Silver**.

• For more K.M. Grant, try *How the Hangman Lost His Heart*, which is set in the 1700s, has a feisty de Granville heroine and is a hilarious, exciting romp that just might make you cry. (*UBG* 161)

• If you want another deeply thought-provoking yet exciting read about the Crusades, try Elizabeth Laird's *Crusade*. (*UBG* 75)

★ ★ ★ ★ ★ ★

# THE BLOOD STONE Jamila Gavin

**Next?**
• Track down some other titles by Jamila Gavin; *The Wheel of Surya* and its sequels are my favourites. (*UBG* 378)

• You might also like William Nicholson's **Wind on Fire** trilogy, another epic adventure. (*UBG* 386)

• There's more unveiling of family secrets in Thomas Bloor's *The Memory Prisoner*.

• Or try something else about a jewel and India, *The Printer's Devil* by Paul Bajoria. (*UBG* 274)

Filippo never knew his father, Venetian jeweller Geronimo Veroneo, who embarked for Hindustan seeking riches before Filippo was born. But Geronimo's presence lingers over the family home, and the dazzling diamond pendant, Ocean of the Moon, remains a token of his adoration for his wife, Theodora.

Now, 12 years have passed. Geronimo has not returned and malevolent merchant, Bernardo Pagliarin, is scheming to destroy the family. When a message arrives that Geronimo has been imprisoned for ransom, Filippo knows he must use the diamond to save him. But as he embarks on a dangerous voyage, whom can he trust?

A marvellous, exotic quest for missing fathers and sons, *The Blood Stone* is a magical story of adventure across continents.
**Helen Simmons**

# THE BOGGART
### Susan Cooper

### Next?
• Try the sequel, *The Boggart and the Monster*.
• If you liked this, why not try Susan Cooper's **The Dark is Rising** sequence? It consists of five books, each one stuffed with ancient magic. (*UBG* 78)
• For stories about more unusual beings, try *The Little Grey Men* by B.B. (*UBG* 203)

Boggarts are invisible most of the time. But just because they can't be seen doesn't mean no one knows they're there. They're mischievous little sprites who love playing tricks on humans, especially ones who don't believe in them.

Emily and Jessup's parents inherit an ancient Scottish castle, but when they pack up the contents, it's more than just a few bits of furniture they take home with them to Canada – for the Boggart, who has been trapped in the castle for centuries, comes along, too.

The children's lives are suddenly intertwined with that of the ancient Boggart, but ironically it's the modern world in the form of computers that comes to their aid.

**Marcus Sedgwick**

★ ★ ★ ★ ★ ★

# THE BOOK OF THE CROW series
### Catherine Fisher

In the first of this series, *The Relic Master*, we meet Raffi, apprentice to the bitter and unpredictable Relic Master, Galen. Outlawed, living on charity and hope, Raffi and Galen wander a hostile and dangerous land, using their magic and their wits to survive. Forced into searching for a Sekoi – one of a race of cat-like people – they begin a journey that takes them deep into terrible danger, but also towards an understanding of what their magic is, why their world is as it is and what the strange relics they hoard really are.

There are four main travellers in these books, and I fell in love with all of them. Following every painful step of their journey, I chewed my nails and urged them on through every page, desperate for them to find some answers – and maybe even some happiness.

**Leonie Flynn**

### Next?
• The other books in the series are *The Interrex*, *Flain's Coronet* and *The Margrave*.
• If you liked the magic here, read **The Dark is Rising** sequence by Susan Cooper. (*UBG* 78)
• Or the **Power of Five** books by Anthony Horowitz.
• Or more Catherine Fisher? Try the **Snow-walker** trilogy (*UBG* 318) or the complex and mysterious *Darkhenge*.

# THE BOOK OF THREE  Lloyd Alexander

**Next?**

• This is book one of the **Chronicles of Prydain**. Look out for the sequels: *The Black Cauldron*, *The Castle of Lyr*, *Taran the Wanderer* and *The High King*.

• For another series full of magic and adventure, try **The Chronicles of Narnia** by C.S. Lewis. (*UBG* 198)

• Or try Christopher Paolini's *Eragon*. (*UBG* 101)

Taran is a very ordinary teenager, dreaming of heroism, swords and magic in the land of Prydain. He works for Dallben, an ancient enchanter given to taking naps. The orphaned Taran yearns for glory, a title and a place in life, but the only title he has is the inglorious one of Assistant Pig-keeper.

Then Dallben's prophetic pig, Henwen, escapes her pen and runs into the forest with Taran trying to catch her. Taran's search introduces him to the heroic Prince Gwydion and the evil sorceress, Achren. He draws companions to him along the way, such as the hapless would-be bard Fflewddur, the chatterbox princess Eilonwy, and the furry, odd Gurgi. Nothing is as it seems: a scruffy stranger can be a prince, a stout, bald smith can be a retired hero, and a pig-keeper may defy the Horned King, who is bent on the conquest of Prydain. Taran is very real, inexperienced, foolhardy, but willing to admit when he makes a mistake. Every reader can identify with him and live with him through his adventures.

**Tamora Pierce**

★ ★ ★ ★ ★ ★

# THE BORRIBLES  Michael de Larrabeiti

Borribles are curious and interesting creatures indeed – humanoid children who live as outcasts and runaways in the dark alleys, disused buildings and overgrown canals of London. They live for ever unless their ears are clipped back to proper shape by the S.B.G. – Special Borrible Group – a London police division bent on unearthing them.

One night, the Battersea Borribles discover that they're under threat from their ancient enemy, the Rumbles. The Borribles' elite fighters set off on what will become The Great Rumble Hunt.

There is so much in this first adventure: a long and dangerous journey, bravery, treachery, violence and devilish cunning – it's got the lot.

**John McLay**

**Next?**

• Read the rest of the trilogy: *The Borribles Go for Broke* and *Across the Dark Metropolis*.

• Try Leon Garfield's *Smith* for another evocative slice of London life in days gone by. (*UBG* 315)

• Or for a more humorous take, try the hilarious *Jammy Dodgers on the Run*, the first in a series about a family of boys and their escapades. (*UBG* 179)

# THE BORROWERS Mary Norton

With wonderful illustrations by Joe and Beth Krush, *The Borrowers* is the story of a family of little tiny people living under the floorboards in a kid's house. They are called 'Borrowers' because they borrow from us, the 'human beans', in order to survive. A spool of thread becomes their table, a sardine can becomes a bed, and crumbs of food provide them with their meals. If you ever wondered why you couldn't find that button you thought you'd left on your desk, or if your pencil is suddenly missing, now you know where everything goes.

When I was a kid, I used to make miniature furniture and leave it around my room for the Borrowers who lived in my house. Maybe you can make stuff for your Borrowers. Read this book and you'll believe they are there.

**Brian Selznick**

This is a must-read. The Clock family – Pod, Homily and their daughter Arriety – are only 13 centimetres high and live under the grandfather clock in the Old Rectory. Their greatest fear (apart from the cat!) is of discovery, or 'being seen'. Pod goes on expeditions to borrow – a silver thimble for a cooking pot, match boxes for chests of drawers, a champagne cork for a stool. When my daughters were small and something went missing they would say, 'The Borrowers have got it!' – and they'd believe it, too.

Arriety is tired of the lonely life under the floorboards and longs to go into the wider world. She breaks the rules by talking to a human bean, a boy, and disaster strikes when the housekeeper sends for the ratcatcher to smoke the Borrowers out. They have to flee their home and set off in search of relatives – Uncle Hendreary, Aunt Lupy, Eggletins, and the others who live in the countryside...

**Helen Cresswell**

### Next?

- You can follow the Clocks' adventures in: *The Borrowers Afield*, *The Borrowers Afloat*, *The Borrowers Aloft* and *The Borrowers Revenged*.
- You might enjoy *The Piemakers* by Helen Cresswell, about the Danby Rollers who make a steak and kidney pie in a dish big enough for them to sail in down the river. (*UBG* 266)
- Try *Charlotte's Web* by E.B. White, a book about a world that is quite impossible and yet entirely real. (*UBG* 59)

# THE BOX OF DELIGHTS   John Masefield   ● ● ●

### Next?

• If you enjoyed this, you will want to read *The Midnight Folk*, also about Kay Harker, who hunts for lost treasure, is bedevilled by a wicked-witch governess, and is helped by his faithful cat, Nibbins.

• You may then want to go on to read Masefield's *The Bird of Dawning*, about a shipwrecked sailor and his mates who find an abandoned ship and sail it home.

• Or what about *Stone Heart* by Charlie Fletcher? Another book in which the ordinary world turns out to be not quite as ordinary as you thought... (*UBG* 326)

Kay Harker is on a train going home for the Christmas holidays. The landscape he sees through the window is snowy and threatening. Two crafty men cheat him out of some money and seem to have bad intentions towards an old Punch-and-Judy showman. Kay helps the showman to escape them, and he gives Kay the Box of Delights, which has magic properties. Wild adventures follow...

This is one of my very favourite books. I read it first when I was 12, on the train, taking it home for the Christmas holidays. Snow was falling outside as I read the first chapter. It was a truly magical experience.

(But I think Masefield should have left off that last paragraph. Do you agree?)

**Joan Aiken**

★ ★ ★ ★ ★ ★

# BOY   Roald Dahl   ● ●

It's clear, even inevitable, from this amazing and eclectic set of real-life memories from his early childhood, how Roald Dahl would grow up to draw on these often grotesque experiences to people his fiction with such quirky and eccentric characters and bizarre situations. Here we meet Mrs Pratchett, the bad-tempered, filthy-fingered sweet-shop lady who gets her comeuppance with a dead mouse surreptitiously placed in her jar of gobstoppers; Corkers, the maths master who hates figures, so teaches his pupils how to solve *The Times* crossword instead; and Dahl's 'ancient half-sister' (aged a mere 21) who nearly caused the young Roald to lose his nose in an accident whilst driving the family's newly acquired car. Weird ... but absolutely wonderful reading.

**Chris d'Lacey**

### Next?

• *Going Solo* is a sort-of sequel.

• There are so many brilliant Roald Dahl books, but among my favourite reads are *Danny, the Champion of the World* (*UBG* 77), *The Twits* (*UBG* 359) because it's so daft, and *Matilda* (*UBG* 224).

• Or for another author's childhood, try *A Vicarage Family* by Noel Streatfeild. (*UBG* 369)

• *My Family and Other Animals* by Gerald Durrell is the wonderful true story of a very unusual childhood. (*UBG* 242)

# THE BOYHOOD OF BURGLAR BILL Allan Ahlberg

**Next?**

• *The Boyhood of Burglar Bill* is the second book about Ahlberg's childhood. Try the first, *My Brother's Ghost*.

• For more football, try *Hot Prospect*, *Long Shot* or *On the Spot* in the **Stadium School** series by Jefferies and Goffe. Or Dan Freedman's **Jamie Johnson** series, starting with *The Kick Off*.

• Other authors who have written about their childhood include David Almond with *Counting Stars* (*UBG* 73) and Roald Dahl with *Boy*. (*UBG* 44)

Allan Ahlberg tells about the best and worst times of his life, aged ten to eleven, growing up in Oldbury. Allan and his friends cobble together a football team, made up of people who did not get into either of his school teams, to enter into the Coronation Cup. Players include the wordless son of an ice-cream salesman, a boy of only seven, and even a girl. While the football provides much of the excitement, it is the industrial backdrop and details about his family life and local characters that make the book such a fantastic read. Then there is the ongoing question of the source of his team's shirts, which turn up on the doorstep of one of his friends. It is an excellent book that changes tone to become unexpectedly moving towards the end.

**Anthony Reuben**

★ ★ ★ ★ ★ ★

# THE BOY IN THE BISCUIT TIN Heather Dyer

Ibby is staying with Francis and Alex, her irritating cousins. Francis finds an old magic set and manages to shrink himself to the size of a small doll, nearly getting trodden on. Luckily, the magic wears off after a bit, and Ibby assumes that will be the end of the story. But no – the magic box contains lots of other tricks: Levitation, the Disappearing Coin, the Vanishing Act and more. The boys can't possibly stop until they've tried them all. And nothing else could possibly go wrong... Could it?

This very entertaining story by the excellent Heather Dyer is great for anyone who has annoying relatives – and for anyone who has ever owned a magic set that they've found just slightly unsatisfying.

**Susan Reuben**

**Next?**

• For more Heather Dyer, read *The Fish in Room 11*, in which a lonely boy meets a stranded mermaid. Or try *The Girl With the Broken Wing*, which actually does feature a girl with a broken wing!

• For another book with magic and adventure, try *Aquila*. (*UBG* 21)

• *Half Magic* by Edward Eager also features a magic coin. (*UBG* 141)

# BOY OVERBOARD Morris Gleitzman

This vivid, comical and lively story details the life of Jamal, an Afghani boy whose undying enthusiasm for football greatly perks up the war-torn life that he leads. As in most of Morris Gleitzman's books, the story is hilarious in places, but the subject of this particular one means that it has a more serious note to it, too.

When Jamal, his rather violent nine-year-old sister and his parents are forced to flee from Afghanistan, they must undertake a dangerous journey that forces them through such horrors as separation, wild seas, corrupt policeman and pirates. The aim is to reach Australia, where they believe they will be able to harvest a share of the never-ending wealth that they have heard about.

The book combines a splendid blend of humour, recent news, football and such issues as war and emigration which together form an action-packed adventure. It gives a real insight into the sort of lives other people lead, and is a must for all young readers!

**Tim Cross**

**Next?**
• More Gleitzman? They all blend serious issues with great humour. Try *Bumface* (*UBG* 49) and *Two Weeks With the Queen* (*UBG* 359).

• For more about looking for a home, try *Give Me Shelter: An Asylum Seeker Anthology* edited by Tony Bradman.

• Or try some of the books Morris Gleitzman has written with Paul Jennings, such as the **Wicked!** (*UBG* 383) and **Deadly!** series.

★ ★ ★ ★ ★ ★

# THE BOY WHO LOST HIS FACE Louis Sachar

**Next?**
• More Sachar! Try *Holes* (*UBG* 155) and *There's a Boy in the Girls' Bathroom* (*UBG* 344).

• *Stargirl* by Jerry Spinelli is another story about wanting to be popular. (*UBG* 324)

• *The Haunting* by Margaret Mahy is seriously spooky (*UBG* 147)

• *The Wish List* by Eoin Colfer is another story that involves the terrible consequences of stealing from the elderly – it also has one of the most unlikely narrators around.

'He only did it to be accepted as part of a gang, but stealing from an old lady? It never seemed right. Especially this cane. From this old lady...'

...because she puts a curse on him. From that day, David cannot do anything right. Everything he does turns into a disaster, and his life turns from sort-of-all-right to completely and utterly miserable. And worse may happen if he can't make things better, because he believes the old lady to be a witch – one who can steal faces to hang on her living-room wall.

Funny, sad, sharp and fast-paced, this is a story about guilt, friendship – and not being rude to your mother.

**Leonie Flynn**

# THE BREADWINNER  Deborah Ellis

### Next?
- In the sequel, *Parvana's Journey*, Parvana becomes separated from her mother and sisters.
- Or read about Shauzia – Parvana's friend – and her struggle to escape from a refugee camp and get to France in *Mud City*.
- For more about the devastating effects of war on young people, read *Zlata's Diary* written by Zlata Filipoviç, a young girl living in Sarajevo during the civil war.
- Or for a graphic novelist's look at oppression, this time in Iran, try Marjane Satrapi's *Persepolis*, a wonderful book that has now been made into a movie.

Parvana is eleven years old and lives in Afghanistan. Under Taliban law, girls are forbidden from going to school and all women must stay at home. For more than a year, Parvana's family has been trapped in their one-roomed flat. But when their father is arrested, the family faces starvation unless Parvana disguises herself as a boy and tries to earn a living. It's a dangerous plan, but it's their only chance of survival.

We've all heard the phrase 'living under the Taliban', but few of us understand what it really means. This book opens our eyes to the chilling truth, but Parvana's courage and determination to survive against all the odds is truly inspiring and there is hope at the end.

**Kathryn Ross**

★ ★ ★ ★ ★ ★

# BRIDGE TO TERABITHIA  Katherine Paterson

I love this book. It's about joy and sorrow, friendship and grief, and it's about learning what really matters in life.

Jess is intrigued by his new neighbour, Leslie. She reads books, doesn't have a television, doesn't give a hoot what the small-town kids think of her, and she can beat them all at running, hands-down.

Soon they're the best of friends, Jess and Leslie, and together they create Terabithia, a secret kingdom in the woods. It becomes their sanctuary until tragedy strikes. But, however sad, Jess knows that Leslie has opened him up to the joys of imagination, learning and true friendship.

My favourite books are the ones that move me – that make me feel deeply sad, deeply happy, and preferably both. This is one of the very best.

**Malachy Doyle**

### Next?
- *The Great Gilly Hopkins* is another wonderful book by Katherine Paterson; or try one of her novels set in Japan, such as *The Master Puppeteer*.
- If you like this sort of book, try *Walk Two Moons* (*UBG* 371) and anything by David Almond – maybe start with *Skellig* (*UBG* 313) or *Kit's Wilderness* (*UBG* 192).

# BROKEN GLASS  Sally Grindley

### Next?

• A classic novel of a child living on the streets, this time in Africa, is Elizabeth Laird's *The Garbage King*.

• Try Sally Grindley's *Spilled Water*, which is about the harshness of a young girl's life in China, or *Saving Finnegan*, which is about a stranded whale and how we deal with death.

• A classic story of survival on the streets is Ian Serrailier's *The Silver Sword*. (*UBG* 310)

*Broken Glass* is set in India and is about two brothers who are forced to leave home. In the big city, they survive – just – by picking through the rubbish for broken glass, which they can sell. They live on a traffic island, and every single day – despite the occasional laughter and the friendship – is a struggle.

This is one of those books that illuminates lives – both of the brothers, Sandeep and Suresh, and of the reader – for no one could read this book and not understand a little more about the reality of how children end up on the streets, or what their lives are like once they are there. There are authors who seem as if they're saying – 'Look, I'm great! I'm writing about an issue!' Sally Grindley isn't one of them. The issue here is vast and important, but it never overshadows the reality of two brothers who just want to survive.

**Leonie Flynn**

★ ★ ★ ★ ★ ★

# THE BROMELIAD trilogy
## Terry Pratchett

For as long as anyone can remember, a race of tiny beings called Nomes has lived under the floors of a huge department store. It is their whole world. As far as they are concerned, there is no Outside, no Night and Day, no Sun or Rain. When they discover the store is going to be demolished, it's up to two of the Nomes, Masklin and Grimma, to use all their ingenuity and help them escape and overcome their fears of the Outside. They get away to a deserted quarry but are forced to leave there, too...

These books are supposed to be children's books, but like so many good books, they can be enjoyed by all ages. I love them now I'm 60 just as much as I did when I first read them.

**Colin Thompson**

### Next?

• The books in the trilogy are *Truckers*, *Diggers* and *Wings*. For more Pratchett, there's the **Johnny Maxwell** trilogy (*UBG* 182) and then the **Discworld** series (*UBG* 68) – there's plenty to enjoy!

• Douglas Adams's *The Hitchhiker's Guide to the Galaxy* has to be one of the funniest books ever. (*UBG* 152)

• More about little people? Try *Mistress Masham's Repose* by T.H. White. (*UBG* 231)

# BUMFACE  Morris Gleitzman  ●●

This novel has the funniest, and to some the most outrageous, opening page in all of today's children's books. It indicates that there is humour to come, but what it doesn't show is that this is also a wonderful and serious story of a young boy forced to take on huge family responsibilities.

Angus is a great character. His mum calls him Mr Dependable and leaves him to care for his brother and sister, and he longs for her to behave like a proper mother. He dreams of being free, wild and bold, but he is caught up in a world of nappies.

Angus's story is a moving one, yet it's told with great humour, making this a book that is impossible to put down. Just open it at the first page, start reading, and you'll see...

**Wendy Cooling**

### Next?

• Humour is Gleitzman's trademark, however serious the subject. *Boy Overboard* is a good one to read next (*UBG* 45), or try *Two Weeks With the Queen* (*UBG* 359). He's good at short stories, too. Look out for *Peas on Earth*.

• At times Angus is very alone, but he is not as alone as Stanley in Louis Sachar's brilliant book *Holes*. (*UBG* 155)

• Elizabeth Honey, also Australian, writes funny books about real things – try *Don't Pat the Wombat*. (*UBG* 90)

★ ★ ★ ★ ★ ★

# BUSTER BAYLISS series  ●●
## Philip Reeve

### Next?

• The rest of the **Buster Bayliss** books! – *The Big Freeze*, *Day of the Hamster* and *Custardfinger*.

• For more puns and daft things, try *Killer Mushrooms Ate My Gran* or the **Jiggy McCue** stories, such as *The Killer Underpants* by Michael Lawrence. (*UBG* 181)

• Another boy often in deep trouble stars in **The War Diaries of Alastair Fury** by Jamie Rix – read *The Revenge Files* first.

Buster Bayliss likes a quiet life; just getting on with his hobbies, like getting out of doing homework and being late for school. But when his mum goes away on a lollipop lady retraining course in Belgium, Buster gets sent to his Fake Aunty Pauline's and life suddenly becomes very busy. You see, there are these plants that are trying to take over. I can hear you thinking – hey! Plants can't do that! But these are no ordinary veg – they eat meat, hypnotise their owners and grow very big very, very fast.

If you want to find out how a French horn and a bathroom sink can save the world, read *The Night of the Living Veg*. Packed with jokes, puns and hilarious happenings, it's a fast, fun read.

**Leonie Flynn**

# THE BUTTERFLY LION  Michael Morpurgo

A lonely boy runs away from boarding school, where he is being bullied. It begins to rain, and the boy notices a car following him. He slips through a gate into the garden of a large house. An old lady appears and invites him in for tea. As the boy eats his scones, he looks out of the window and sees the shape of a white lion, cut into the chalky hillside. The sun comes out and when the lion is suddenly covered in blue butterflies, the old lady begins to tell the boy an extraordinary story. A story about a boy called Bertie who lived in Africa, and the white lion cub he rescued.

This is a beautifully told sad / happy story that makes you think a little deeper about past events every time you read it. It also shows that the end of a story does not always have to be what you expect, in order to be called happy.

**Jenny Nimmo**

### Next?

• Try *The Dancing Bear* or *Why the Whales Came* (*UBG* 382), both by Michael Morpurgo.

• Or for something else set in Africa, look out for *The White Giraffe* by Lauren St John and its sequels *Dolphin Song* and *The Last Leopard*.

• Or try the easy but wonderful **Akimbo** stories by Alexander McCall Smith, starting with *Akimbo and the Crocodile Man*.

• Willard Price wrote brilliant adventure stories about African lions – look out for *Lion Adventure*. His **Adventure** series is recommended on p. 51, and all are worth reading.

★ ★ ★ ★ ★ ★

# CALLING A DEAD MAN
## Gillian Cross

### Next?

• More Gillian Cross books, especially the wonderful **The Lost** series, starting with *The Dark Ground* and continuing in *The Black Room*.

• For a story set in Russia's past, try Marcus Sedgwick's *Blood Red, Snow White*.

• Alison Prince's *Oranges and Murder* is an exciting mystery, set in the London of the early nineteenth century. (*UBG* 253)

Wrap up warm and immerse yourself in this gripping novel, set mostly in a freezing Russian winter. Hayley just wants to see the place where her older brother, John, died suddenly – but when she and John's fiancée, Annie, arrive in Siberia, they find themselves solving the mystery of his disappearance. Meanwhile, in another thread of the story, we meet a man on the run, who has no memory but an awful sense that he is somehow dangerous. He is helped by generous Russian families but he can't get close to any of them. This is a truly tense and unputdownable story.

**Jon Appleton**

# A CANDLE IN THE DARK   Adèle Geras   ● ●

### Next?
• More historical stories in the **Flashbacks** series, such as Linda Newbery's *Blitz Boys*.

• Ann Jungman's *Resistance*, set in occupied Holland, is another short novel which takes an unusual look at wartime.

• *When Hitler Stole Pink Rabbit* is the first in a classic set of stories by Judith Kerr, telling of her wartime childhood when, as a German-Jewish girl, she was forced to flee her native land. (*UBG* 379)

This unusual, moving wartime story tells of Clara, a young German Jewish girl, who is sent to England for safety in 1939. With her five-year-old brother, Maxi, she moves in with Phyllis and her family in a Leicestershire village. It's bad enough leaving her home and parents, but Clara finds that not everyone in Long Easterby is friendly – Phyllis's friend Eileen regards Clara as odd and strange, coming from Germany, the enemy country. Phyllis wants everyone to be friends, but has to cope with Eileen's spitefulness, as well as helping Clara through a dilemma – if she sings 'Stille Nacht' for the nativity play, is she being disloyal to her Jewish parents and upbringing?

Do read the afterword to learn more about what happened to the children sent out of Germany for safety.

**Linda Newbery**

★ ★ ★ ★ ★ ★

# CANNIBAL ADVENTURE   Willard Price   ● ●

Hal and Roger Hunt, two teenage brothers, are off on another of their improbable adventures – this time in pursuit of crocodiles, sharks and death adders for their father's zoo.

Willard Price got me reading when I was eleven, and I think it's just great that his books are still so popular today. They may have aged a little, and capturing animals in the wild may no longer be politically correct, but the stories are action-packed, mixing vicious animals and even more vicious crooks with huge energy and attention to detail. In what other stories would the hero sit down to a meal of 'a large broiled bat garnished with fried beetles'?

The **Adventure** series is a wonderful way to explore the world and to learn about natural history.

**Anthony Horowitz**

### Next?
• There's *African Adventure, Diving Adventure, Volcano Adventure, Whale Adventure* and many more – but not quite as many as you'd like there to be!

• Anthony Horowitz's **Alex Rider** books are some of the most exciting adventure stories of recent years – see *Stormbreaker*. (*UBG* 12)

• Or try the **Hardy Boys** books by Franklin W. Dixon, about a pair of boy detectives. (*UBG* 143)

# THE CANTERVILLE GHOST Oscar Wilde

When an American called Hiram B. Otis buys Canterville Chase, he laughs at the notion that the house is haunted by Sir Simon de Canterville. He uses Champion Stain Remover to get rid of the ghostliest of bloodstains. Then he offers Sir Simon some Rising Sun Lubricator to stop his chains creaking. No matter what the poor ghost gets up to, his new victims are not impressed. This is bad news for a ghost. Soon, he wants Otis out on a permanent basis, but first someone has to take pity on him.

This story is funny and moving, but above all, the writing is elegant and eccentric, and you'll find that each reading reveals something new and exquisite. A true delight.

**Karen Wallace**

### Next?
- You might also like Oscar Wilde's *The Happy Prince and other stories*. (*UBG* 142)
- For modern gothic humour, try Debi Gliori's *Pure Dead Magic* and its sequels. (*UBG* 276)
- If you want good ghostly hilarity, read *Araminta Spook: My Haunted House* by Angie Sage. (*UBG* 22)

★ ★ ★ ★ ★ ★

# CAPTAINS COURAGEOUS
## Rudyard Kipling

This book was written over a hundred years ago and uses words and language that are not always easy to read, but – make no mistake – it's one of the best stories ever written.

Fifteen-year-old Harvey Cheyne is the spoilt son of a multi-millionaire, who accidentally falls off the stern of an ocean liner one night and gets picked up by a fishing boat, the *We're Here*. As a result, he has to spend four months fishing for cod on the Grand Banks in the middle of the Atlantic – an adventure that changes his life for ever.

The work is hard and dangerous, and Harvey has to learn that qualities such as friendship, hard work and courage are needed simply to stay alive. But he does learn, and when the *We're Here* finally returns to America, Harvey is no longer a boy, but a strong and confident young man. Brilliant!

**Andrew Norriss**

### Next?
- Rudyard Kipling wrote several books for children. The most famous are the **Jungle Books**. (*UBG* 185) My favourite is probably *Puck of Pook's Hill*. (*UBG* 275) He also wrote a book of school stories called *Stalky and Co* – you wouldn't believe what school could be like 100 years ago!
- For a story based on the author's own experiences of life on board a sealing ship, look for Jack London's *The Sea-Wolf*.

# CAPTAIN UNDERPANTS series Dav Pilkey

**Next?**
• All **Captain Underpants** books have long, weird and wonderful titles. Try *Captain Underpants and the Invasion of the Incredibly Naughty Cafeteria Ladies from Outer Space* or *Captain Underpants and the Wrath of the Wicked Wedgie Woman*.
• If you've not had enough poo, then try *The Giggler Treatment*. (*UBG* 127)
• Or what about the **Jiggy McCue** books by Michael Lawrence? (*UBG* 181)

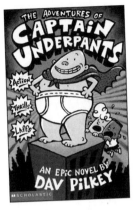

Let's not beat about the bush... If you're the sort of person who thinks it's funny when someone farts during school assembly, then Captain Underpants is for you!

George and Harold use a 3-D Hypno-Ring to hypnotise their mean old head teacher, Mr Krupp, and turn him into the amazing Captain Underpants!

Will the evil Dr Nappy destroy the earth, or will our heroes defeat him? Can you really shoot a pair of underpants? Will a plastic doggy-doo foil Doctor Nappy's plans? I know you want to find out ... so get reading now!

**Shoo Rayner**

★ ★ ★ ★ ★ ★

# CARBONEL Barbara Sleigh

**Next?**
• *Carbonel* is the first in a trilogy. Why not go on to read *The Kingdom of Carbonel* and *Carbonel and Calidor*?
• Adèle Geras is another writer who understands cats. Try her stories told by Ozymandias the cat, in *The Fabulous Fantora Files* and *The Fabulous Fantora Photographs*.
• If you like books about animals, read Dodie Smith's *The Hundred and One Dalmatians*. (*UBG* 164)

Rosemary buys her broom and Carbonel the cat (who costs three precious Queen Victoria farthings) in a London market. Carbonel tells her he is under a binding spell, and she and her friend John race to free him before his kingdom is lost to a vicious rival. But it is silent magic that binds the great cat: no one can tell the children what it is or how to break it. They must discover it for themselves.

When I was small, children were allowed to roam the streets on their own, like Rosemary and John do. In my wanderings, I daydreamed of buying a magic broom, like Rosemary, that would help me talk to the king of cats. It's easy to daydream about *Carbonel*: the story moves along quickly and the characters could – just – be the kind you might meet – even Mrs Cantrip, the retired witch.

**Gill Vickery**

# Top Ten Most Exciting Books

1. Harry Potter series by J.K. Rowling

2. His Dark Materials trilogy by Philip Pullman

3. Alex Rider series by Anthony Horowitz

4. Young Bond series by Charlie Higson

5. Vampirates series by Justin Somper

6. Inkheart by Cornelia Funke

7. Roman Mysteries series by Caroline Lawrence

8. The Saga of Darren Shan by Darren Shan

9. H.I.V.E. by Mark Walden

10. Cry of the Icemark by Stuart Hill

## CARRIE'S WAR   Nina Bawden ●●

When World War II began, thousands of children were moved out of British cities and sent to live with people in small towns or the country, for fear of enemy bombing. Imagine how it would feel, suddenly being dumped among strangers who might or might not want to have you. Actually, most of the children were kindly treated, though they must have missed their homes and families terribly. But some were out of luck and had a miserable time.

Carrie and her younger brother Nick are among the unlucky ones, sent to stay with mean old Councillor Evans ('Up and down the stairs, soon as my back's turned, wearing out the stair carpet,' he complains) and his downtrodden sister, Auntie Lou. Serious, thoughtful Carrie has a hard time, one of her problems being to keep irresponsible Nick out of trouble. But the children survive, find friends in their new surroundings, and even bring about a happy ending for Auntie Lou. *Carrie's War* tells you how they did it. It's a book you'll never forget. And it makes you wonder how you would have managed if all this had happened to you.

**John Rowe Townsend**

### Next?

• *Goodnight Mister Tom* by Michelle Magorian is another evacuee story. (*UBG* 132)

• Or for the story of a girl returning unhappily to England after having spent the war evacuated to America, try Michelle Magorian's *Back Home*.

• Still on the Home Front is *The Machine Gunners* by Robert Westall. (*UBG* 215)

• Other books about a child surviving the war include *Feather Wars* by Sally Grindley and *Doodlebug Summer* by Alison Prince.

# A CASTLE OF BONE  Penelope Farmer ●●

## Next?

• Don't miss Penelope Farmer's other classic, *Charlotte Sometimes* (*UBG* 58), or Diana Wynne Jones's wonderful **The Worlds of Chrestomanci** books (*UBG* 393), which also involve magic that seems remarkably real.

• **The Chronicles of Narnia** by C.S. Lewis have magic, and the world's most famous wardrobe! (*UBG* 198) They also have transformations. Look out for *The Voyage of the Dawn Treader*.

• Or for more stories of transformation and magic, try the classic *Arabian Nights*. (*UBG* 21)

If you buy a cupboard, you don't expect it to change things. But Hugh's new cupboard has amazing powers of transformation. If you place an object inside, out it comes again, altered – changed back into its original elements, or processed further into something new. This is a book full of intriguing ideas about growth and change – in people, not just things. And what is a castle of bone? It lingers throughout the whole story, and it's so satisfying when Penelope Farmer explains just what it is.

Everything makes sense in a Penelope Farmer story, which makes them such a pleasure to read. Above all, this is a gripping story: especially when Hugh's friend, Penn, stumbles into the cupboard himself...

**Jon Appleton**

★ ★ ★ ★ ★ ★

# THE CASTLE OF DARK  Tanith Lee ●●●

Magic comes into lots of fantasy stories, and so do the forces of good and evil. Tanith Lee has them all operating at the same time in this powerfully memorable book.

Lir has the gift of musicianship, and his life is transformed when he fashions a unique, magic harp. The harp leads him from town to town and, as he plays, he earns his keep. But is it only magic that lures him to the Castle of Dark, or something more sinister? There he meets Lilune, the girl in the tower, a prisoner of darkness. Lilune believes Lir has been called to lead her to freedom. Lir wants to oblige, but his pledge to help Lilune may lead to his destruction.

**Jon Appleton**

## Next?

• Want to read another Tanith Lee book? Try *East of Midnight*. (*UBG* 95)

• Jenny Nimmo's *Griffin's Castle* is another eerily atmospheric story.

• **Young Wizards** by Diane Duane is a great series about learning to become a wizard. (*UBG* 396)

• Garth Nix's *Sabriel* is a fabulous mix of fantasy, magic, good and evil. (*UBG* 292)

• For something just as imaginative, try Joanne Harris's *Runemarks*. (*UBG* 291)

# THE CAT ATE MY GYMSUIT

Paula Danziger

## Next?

• Why not try one of Paula's other family stories? Lauren shares her teenage traumas with you in *Can You Sue Your Parents for Malpractice?*

• Helena Pielichaty's **Simone** books look at the problems of starting a new school, parents splitting up, new partners and new babies. (*UBG* 312)

• The **Ally's World** series by Karen McCombie is every bit as enjoyable – all about family and friends. (*UBG* 14)

This isn't a book about cats or about gymsuits, but it is a wonderful feel-good read about a 13-year-old girl called Marcy, who thinks she's hopeless at absolutely everything. She's frightened of her father, convinced she'll never, ever find a boyfriend, bored to death by school... In fact, everything in her life is a big problem ... until she meets the trendy young new teacher, Ms Finney. But just as life starts to look up again, Ms Finney is banned from the school for ever. Does Marcy have the confidence to fight to win her back?

**Eileen Armstrong**

★ ★ ★ ★ ★ ★

# CATHERINE, CALLED BIRDY

Karen Cushman

Birdy is the spirited, inquisitive daughter of a medieval knight, living in England in 1290. She is 13 when she starts to write this diary – and is determined not to let her father marry her off. So what does she do? She blackens her teeth, puts mouse bones in her hair and sets fire to the outside toilet. And that's just the beginning. Her diary romps along, full of details about feasts and horrible medicines and saints like Saint Juthwara, who wore cheeses on her chest.

Birdy's diary gives a rich, funny picture of Birdy's life, but it's not just a joke. As she moans about the tasks she has to do and her father's plans to marry her to the atrocious Shaggy Beard, she is puzzling over life and death as well. And some of the things she learns are just as important now as they were then.

**Gillian Cross**

## Next?

• You might like to try Karen Cushman's *The Midwife's Apprentice*, about a medieval orphan rescued from a dung heap.

• Sue Townsend's hilarious *The Secret Diary of Adrian Mole Aged 13 3/4* is also diary based; it's set in more recent times and is an absolute classic. (*UBG* 301)

• For a medieval fantasy in which a girl disguises herself as a boy so she can become a knight, try the **Protector of the Small** series by Tamora Pierce.

# THE CHANGEOVER

**Margaret Mahy**

Laura Chant is content with her family the way it is – her, her mum, Kate and her little brother, Jacko. She misses the dad who left them, but doesn't want any more changes in their lives. Laura is psychic and, on the morning the book begins, she has a Warning: something is about to change for the worse.

Little Jacko gets his hand branded by the sinister Carmody Braque, owner of a novelty shop that wasn't there before. Jacko falls ill and slips into a coma, the life being drained from him by Braque. Only Laura can save him, with the help of dishy sixth-former, Sorensen Carlisle, who turns out, like her, to be a witch.

An intoxicating mix of magic, danger and romance.

**Mary Hoffman**

### Next?

• You might also like *The Haunting* by the same author. (*UBG* 147)

• For magic, you might enjoy Diana Wynne Jones's books, particularly *Homeward Bounders* (*UBG* 156) and *A Tale of Time City* (*UBG* 340).

• Or try the truly terrifying *Nightmare Stairs* by Robert Swindells or Malorie Blackman's *The Stuff of Nightmares*.

★ ★ ★ ★ ★ ★

# THE CHANGES trilogy

**Peter Dickinson**

### Next?

• Try some of Dickinson's other books, such as *The Gift*, about a boy with second sight, or *A Bone from a Dry Sea*, which mixes the modern day with prehistory in a gripping archaeological adventure.

• Or **The Book of the Crow** series, about a society where there is no technology and machines are seen as magic. (*UBG* 41)

• If you fancy more science fiction, try the unsettling *A Rag, a Bone and a Hank of Hair* by Nicholas Fisk. (*UBG* 278)

These three novels take us into an England in the near future, but one in which something terrible has happened. A strange madness has spread across the country, causing people to hate machines; in fact, any technology invented more recently than the Middle Ages is regarded as evil. As a result, civilisation has come crashing to ruin, and only a handful of children, such as Nicky in the first book, *The Devil's Children*, and Margaret and Jonathan in the second, *Heartsease*, seem to be immune from the machine-hatred. But it is only in the last book, *The Weathermonger*, that Geoffrey and Sally uncover the awful reason underlying The Changes, and only they have the chance to restore England to the way it once was.

**Marcus Sedgwick**

# CHARLIE AND THE CHOCOLATE FACTORY

**Roald Dahl**

Charlie Bucket lives with his parents and grandparents in a tiny wooden house. They are so poor, all they have to eat every day is weak cabbage soup. Then, one day, Charlie finds the last of five golden tickets that allow the winners to spend a whole day inside Willy Wonka's chocolate factory. Apart from Charlie, the other golden ticket winners are either spoilt, greedy or already rich. Only Charlie still has the magical innocence of childhood. And that is what Willy Wonka is looking for...

This is a wonderful book that anyone of any age can enjoy. Read it and then see the first film adaptation starring Gene Wilder as Willy Wonka, which is so good you've probably already seen it three times. I certainly have.

**Colin Thompson**

### Next?

• *Danny, the Champion of the World*, which is wonderful Roald Dahl at his brilliant best. (*UBG* 77)

• Or try Jenny Nimmo's *Midnight for Charlie Bone*, another book about a young boy on a magical adventure. (*UBG* 226)

• Or for another outrageous adult, read Andy Stanton's *You're a Bad Man, Mr Gum!* (*UBG* 397)

• For more realistic, but equally fun, stories try *The Quigleys* by Simon Mason. (*UBG* 277)

★ ★ ★ ★ ★ ★

# CHARLOTTE SOMETIMES  Penelope Farmer

### Next?

• There are lots of excellent time-slip books – one of my favourites is *Playing Beatie Bow* by Ruth Park. (*UBG* 270)

• Berlie Doherty's *Children of Winter* is another gripping time-slip adventure involving surviving a storm in the present day and plague in the seventeenth century, which brings in the true story of the village of Eyam.

• If you like the idea of a magic bed, try *Bed-knob and Broomstick* by Mary Norton. (*UBG* 31)

A famous time-slip story. Charlotte, at boarding school in the 1950s, changes places with Clare, who slept in the same bed towards the end of the First World War. Sometimes, it's just good to feel like a whole person, even if it's the wrong person; other times it's plain confusing. Alarmingly, details of being Charlotte slip away, but she must return to her own time – which becomes even harder when she and her sister, Emily, are sent away from the school and the magic bed. You read this book for its gripping dilemma and when you get to the end, you realise it's about so many other things, and there's an extra, deeper pleasure.

**Jon Appleton**

# CHARLOTTE'S WEB

### E.B. White

### Next?

- E.B. White wrote two other gloriously timeless books for children; *Stuart Little*, about a mouse brought up as a human and *The Trumpet of the Swan*, about a mute swan who learns to express himself.
- Another book about a rather endearing pig is *The Peppermint Pig* by Nina Bawden. (*UBG* 261)
- For something different, and rather harder, but equally lovely, try *Mistress Masham's Repose* by T.H. White, about a lonely girl and the strange creatures she finds. (*UBG* 231)

This is a story about a pig called Wilbur, a rat called Templeton, a spider called Charlotte, plus various other animals. But it is also about a girl called Fern, who saves Wilbur when he is the unwanted runt of the farmyard pig litter, and it is about life on the farm seen from the point of view of the animals. It is funny, and sad, and you become completely involved with all the characters – human and animal. This is a book that I have loved for years and years, and each time I open it I have to read it all through again, from the opening words: '"Where's Papa going with that axe?" said Fern to her mother...'

**Penelope Lively**

★ ★ ★ ★ ★ ★

# CHASING VERMEER

### Blue Balliett

Do you like puzzles? This fascinating story is full of codes, clues and word games used to solve a centuries-old mystery with a modern twist. School friends Calder and Petra are drawn into the hands of a dangerous criminal when they investigate the theft of a priceless painting by Vermeer. Who is sending anonymous letters? Where's Frog? What's happening to Tommy, who is forced to move to New York with his sinister stepfather?

This is a page-turning story, with engaging characters. I also learned more about Vermeer's paintings and how to think laterally. It's inspiring!

**Pauline Chandler**

### Next?

- If you enjoyed *Chasing Vermeer*, look for the sequel *The Wright Three*, set in New York and once again full of puzzles.
- Or try *The London Eye Mystery* by Siobhan O'Dowd. Ted and Kat see their cousin Salim get on board the London Eye, but he does not get off. Where is he? (*UBG* 210)
- Or *Bunker 10* by J.A. Henderson, a thrill-a-minute mystery set in a world from science fiction. Computer games action and the 'real / unreal?' feel of *The Matrix*. A compelling read, but not for the fainthearted.

# CHERUB series Robert Muchamore ● ● ●

### Next?

- Read the whole series, starting with *The Recruit*, then move on to *Class A* – but be careful – the books get darker and more grown-up as James gets older.
- How about more spies? Try the **Spy High** series by A.J. Butcher, starting with *The Frankenstein Factory*. Don't forget (and how could you?) Alex Rider and *Stormbreaker*. (*UBG* 12) For **Young Bond**, read Charlie Higson's *SilverFin*. (*UBG* 311) And for a girl whose father's disappearance makes her become a spy, read Julia Golding's *Ringmaster*.

Kids as spies, a secret organisation to train them, daring and dangerous adventures – sound familiar? Well, it isn't! These books are gritty, exciting and breathtakingly realistic. If you read **Alex Rider** books for the outrageous gadgets and set pieces, don't expect to find the same here, for the **CHERUB** books are all about reality. James is a boy spy, but in a totally imaginable way – complete with missions that don't succeed, tangled emotions and grey-tinged ethics. As the series proceeds, the books get darker and darker, bringing in all the horrors of twenty-first-century life, from terrorism, human trafficking, animal rights and cults, through to drugs. Even as you're frantically reading to find out what happens next, you're also being made to think – quite a trick in a spy series!

**Leonie Flynn**

★ ★ ★ ★ ★ ★

# CHILD X Lee Weatherly ● ● ●

Lots of people dream of being famous, being recognised for doing something brilliantly – singing maybe, or acting. Jules wants to act and when she's given the starring role in a theatre production of *Northern Lights* she's ecstatic, even if she does have to work alongside nerdy Adrian, from whom she'd normally run a mile.

But there's another kind of fame, and when Jules's beloved father, a TV scriptwriter, publicly rejects her and her mother, the paparazzi pursue her everywhere and, despite news reports calling her 'Child X', everyone knows they mean her. Jules quickly learns who her real friends are. What makes Lee Weatherly's book special is that Jules is exactly like you and your friends – a normal, believable school student.

**Gill Vickery**

### Next?

- Look for more Lee Weatherly. *Missing Abby* is about a girl whose ex-best friend goes missing. *Kat Got Your Tongue* is about a girl suffering from amnesia.
- You might also enjoy Linda Kempton's *Who'll Catch the Nightmares?*, in which a girl juggles with a burning ambition to act, whilst dealing with a totally unexpected family crisis.
- If you've been intrigued by Jules's role in *Northern Lights*, you may like to try the novel by Philip Pullman. (*UBG* 151)

# THE CHILDREN OF GREEN KNOWE

## Lucy M. Boston

In this, the first of the **Green Knowe** series, we meet young Toseland (Tolly for short) on his way to live with his great-grandmother, Mrs Oldknow, at her ancient house by the river. Her first greeting to him is: 'So you've come back!' When questioned, she explains that he's very like his grandfather, who bore the same name.

Tolly soon learns that time means little at Green Knowe, and he makes the acquaintance of others who have lived there over the centuries. In the six books, we meet several different children at different time periods. They all have one thing in common: the house itself and their love for it. In one, *The Stones of Green Knowe*, we are present at its construction in the twelfth century.

I didn't discover the series until I was in my 20s. I enjoyed them then, but I'm sure I would have got so much more out of them at the age of nine, ten or eleven. Green Knowe is based on the author's own house, which I have visited several times. Lucy Boston first saw it as a young woman in 1915, and eventually purchased it in 1937. As owner, she at once set about uncovering the various histories of the house, and discovered far more than she had ever imagined. It was these discoveries as much as anything that led to her writing the series.

**Michael Lawrence**

---

### Next?

• Lots of books deal with the possibilities of going back in time – one classic is *A Traveller in Time* by Alison Uttley (*UBG* 352); another is *Tom's Midnight Garden* by Philippa Pearce (*UBG* 351).

• For a more recent take on the idea, try the thrilling *Gideon the Cutpurse* by Linda Buckley-Archer. (*UBG* 126)

• Or look out for Robert Westall's scary *The Windeye*, a time-slip story set around the Farne Islands off the coast of Northumbria.

• *Charlotte Sometimes* by Penelope Farmer is another time-slip story, this one about a girl who finds herself somewhere very different than she expected. (*UBG* 58)

# THE CHILDREN OF THE NEW FOREST  Captain Marryat ●●●

This story is set during the English Civil War. King Charles I has recently escaped from the Parliamentarians who are searching the New Forest, where they believe he is hiding. Edward, Humphrey, Edith and Alice live in a large house in the forest. When Jacob, an elderly forester, overhears the Parliamentarians plotting to burn down the house, he rescues them and takes them to live in his cottage, deep in the forest. Here, they have to hunt, catch wild ponies and grow their own food.

Captain Marryat wrote the book in 1847 when many people considered the Cavaliers to be heroes. Today we have a very different view of the king and his men, but the children themselves are all extremely likeable characters who never fail to engage our sympathy.

**Jenny Nimmo**

### Next?

• You could go on to *Mr Midshipman Easy* and *Masterman Ready*, both written by Captain Marryat but this time set at sea.

• Or try Robert Louis Stevenson's classic adventures, *Treasure Island* (*UBG* 352) and *Kidnapped* (*UBG* 188).

• Rosemary Sutcliff's *Simon* is a historical novel set at around the same time as *The Children of the New Forest*, as is Sally Gardner's *I, Coriander* (*UBG* 166).

★ ★ ★ ★ ★ ★

# CHILDREN ON THE OREGON TRAIL  ●●●
## A. Rutgers van der Loeff

### Next?

• Lots of books deal with what it was like to be a pioneer. Try the true stories by Laura Ingalls Wilder, *Little House on the Prairie* and sequels (*UBG* 203), or hunt out *Sarah, Plain and Tall* by Patricia MacLachlan (*UBG* 294).

• Or what about the same story told from the Native American's point of view? Try Louise Erdrich's *The Birchbark House*.

• A different sort of survival goes on in J.D. Wyss's *The Swiss Family Robinson*, in which a family is shipwrecked. (*UBG* 338)

This book is based on the true story of John Sager, who, in 1844, aged 13, set off with his family to the wild west in America. When his parents die of fever on the gruelling journey, John refuses any easy options. He wants to go the way his father had planned. This is the story of a remarkable journey – crossing rivers with horses, listening to the rumble of thousands of buffalo hooves. The courage of John and his siblings is inspiring. I liked reading this as a child. It was a way of travelling across the frontier towns I'd never seen. It's a great adventure story that perhaps makes uncomfortable reading as an adult when you consider that the land the Sagers went to conquer belonged to the Native Americans...

**Jackie Kay**

# CHINESE CINDERELLA Adeline Yen Mah

### Next?

- Look for the sequel: *Chinese Cinderella and the Secret Dragon Society*, which is more of a story than an autobiography.
- For another true and moving story, try *The Diary of a Young Girl* by Anne Frank. (*UBG* 84)
- For fictional stories of young people coping with difficult times, try Jacqueline Wilson's books, such as *The Illustrated Mum*. (*UBG* 172)
- Or for something else set in China that tells how girls are treated there, try Sally Grindley's *Spilled Water*. (*UBG* 321)

This book, subtitled 'The Secret Story of an Unwanted Daughter', tells the true story of the author's childhood in China in the 1940s. Adeline is considered bad luck because her mother died giving birth to her and she is always made to feel unwanted. Her stepmother is particularly cruel to her; her brothers and sisters are often mean and her father even forgets her real name! But Adeline is a clever girl and does have some happy, and very successful times at school, and strong relationships with her aunt and her grandfather.

This is a moving autobiography, the story of a girl's struggle for acceptance, and it offers a real look at life in another country over 50 years ago. It is unforgettable.

**Wendy Cooling**

★ ★ ★ ★ ★ ★

# CHIPS, BEANS AND LIMOUSINES Leila Rasheed

Take a dip into the diary of child celebrity Bathsheba Clarice de Trop. Find out all about the incredibly glamorous life she leads as the star of a series of successful books. Read about her fantastic best friends, her super-chic home and her fabulous shopping trips.

Then wonder if Bathsheba's diary is all that it seems. Is she really so wonderfully happy as she makes out? Is her life honestly as full of excitement as she claims? And, most importantly of all, is the world really paying her as much attention as she says it is?

This is the kind of satisfying book where you have to work out what's going on behind the words on the page. It's very funny, and in the end, it's quite moving, too.

**Susan Reuben**

### Next?

- Read the next instalment: *Socks, Shocks and Secrets: The Spectacular Second Diary of Bathsheba Clarice de Trop*.
- Jacqueline Wilson writes great books that are narrated by their heroine: try *The Story of Tracy Beaker*, also told by a girl whose life is not all that it seems. (*UBG* 332)
- For another feisty young heroine, read Meg Cabot's **Allie Finkle's Rules for Girls** series (*UBG* 14) or move on to her classic **The Princess Diaries** (*UBG* 273).

# CITY OF GOLD  Peter Dickinson

### Next?

• Dickinson has written too many good books to list them all, but one with an ancient theme is *A Bone from a Dry Sea*.

• *Tales of the Early World* by Ted Hughes is another retelling of early legends. (*UBG* 342) Or try ones from Norse mythology. (*UBG* 250)

• Or for a simply told and beautifully illustrated Bible story, read Jane Ray's *The Story of Christmas*, or the slightly harder *Kings and Queens of the Bible* by Mary Hoffman.

These are no ordinary retellings of Bible stories. Peter Dickinson has a great gift for bringing things to life, and by imagining himself telling the stories before the Bible was ever written down, the tales feel like they happened yesterday. There are 33 stories, full of drama on a big scale as well as the small details of human life that make them utterly convincing. All are from the Old Testament, and are so far removed from the dryness of biblical versions that you will have to remind yourself that's what you're reading. Fantastic stories, wonderfully told, and accompanied by illustrations by acclaimed artist Michael Foreman.

**Marcus Sedgwick**

★ ★ ★ ★ ★ ★

# CLAY  David Almond

David Almond grew up in a very ordinary place called Felling, on the Gateshead side of the River Tyne. Felling pours out in a jumble in his books, true events and people mingling with monsters and magic. Recently I walked in the footsteps of one of his monsters – Clay, in the book of that name which is a brilliant update of the story of Frankenstein's monster. In the novel, the hero, Davie, leads a monster made of clay through the streets of Felling. In the real world, David Almond led me through those same streets and I had the funniest feeling of becoming the thing made of clay. 'This is Felling High Street, which Davie walks with Clay,' David Almond told me, sounding just like Davie in the novel. 'Down here is where *Clay* happens. I imagine Crazy Mary living in one of these houses.'

It is a magical place, Felling. Really. If you don't believe me, read the book.

**Nigel Richardson**

### Next?

• It's worth reading all David Almond's books – go for *Kit's Wilderness* (*UBG* 192) next, then move on to his others, including the brooding, intense *The Fire-Eaters* (*UBG* 113) and his latest, *Jackdaw Summer*.

• Try the original *Frankenstein* story by Mary Shelley and marvel at how fresh it seems, despite having been written nearly 200 years ago.

• *Stone Cold* by Robert Swindells is a hard-hitting book with different sorts of monsters.

# CLEVER POLLY AND THE STUPID WOLF  Catherine Storr

One day, a wolf appears at Polly's front door and quite politely asks if he may eat her. Polly, understandably enough, says: 'No, thank you. I'd rather not be eaten'. It's a simple idea, but this hilarious book spins it out into 12 deliciously intelligent and well-crafted stories. The Wolf's stupidity knows no bounds. He ends up being quite an endearing character and Polly finds it so easy to run rings round him that we enjoy sharing in her cleverness. My favourite bit is the poem Wolf produces as an example of 'proper poetry': 'Monday's child is fairly tough / Tuesday's child is tender enough / Wednesday's child is good to fry...' and so on through the week. This book is pure pleasure.

**Adèle Geras**

**Next?**
• The clever sequel, *Polly and the Wolf Again*.
• Or *A Necklace of Raindrops* by Joan Aiken – a collection of fairy tales where all sorts of weird and wonderful things go on. Look out for the version illustrated by Jan Pienkowski. (*UBG* 248)
• Or try *I Was a Rat!* by Philip Pullman, about a boy who was once a rat! (*UBG* 166)
• Another adventure into the land of fairy stories is *Tom Trueheart* by Ian Beck. (*UBG* 350)

★ ★ ★ ★ ★ ★

# CLIFFHANGER  Jacqueline Wilson

**Next?**
• In the **Ramona** books by Beverly Cleary, Ramona is a bit of a pest, but her mischief makes for fantastic reading! (*UBG* 280)
• *Bill's New Frock* by Anne Fine is a wonderfully funny story of a boy who has to spend a day dressed as a girl. (*UBG* 34)
• Emily Gravett's *Little Mouse's Big Book of Fears* is an amazing book about dealing with your fears. Don't be put off by the picture-book format – it's a book that's for everyone, including grown-ups!

Tim is absolutely hopeless at any kind of sport, so when his dad decides to toughen him up by sending him on a week-long, activity-packed holiday, he just *knows* it'll be hell – and that's before he's even met his big-headed, bullying bunkmate, Giles. But as the week goes on, with the help of his biscuit-chomping friend and his understanding instructor, Jake, he finds he quite enjoys the challenges of canoeing and cliff-climbing and actually excels in the final crazy bucket race. Every chapter ends in a cliffhanger with a clever postcard cartoon from Tim to his parents charting his adventures and new-found confidence. This is an exciting easy-read about facing up to your very worst fears and doing it anyway. Tim is such a likeable, easy-to-understand hero, you'll be dying to see what he and Biscuits get up to in the sequel, *Buried Alive*.

**Eileen Armstrong**

# THE CLOCK TOWER GHOST Gene Kemp

**Next?**

• Track down some other books by Gene Kemp. *The Turbulent Term of Tyke Tiler* is a particular favourite. (*UBG* 357)

• *The Ghost of Thomas Kempe* by Penelope Lively (*UBG* 125) and Helen Cresswell's *Moondial* are other intriguing ghostly novels you might enjoy.

• Or look out for another spooky story that's funny, too, in Julia Jarman's *Ghost Writer*. (*UBG* 125)

You wouldn't exactly call King Cole a contented ghost, but at least he feels at home in the clock tower he haunts: after all, he built it! However, his uneventful routine is shattered when a demon moves in. The demon is Amanda Phillips, who 'from the day she was born, was awful'. As Amanda's family settles into their new home, Amanda becomes increasingly unpopular in her new school *and* with the ghost. Does the family actually belong to Amanda? If so, how come she's a demon?

A tumultuous battle of wills rages between King Cole and Amanda, until Amanda realises how the ghost might find contentment – and how she might lay to rest a few ghosts of her own. This is a funny, quirky ghost story with a difference.

**Helen Simmons**

★ ★ ★ ★ ★ ★

# CLOCKWORK or ALL WOUND UP
## Philip Pullman

This is one of the best-named books ever. It has been put together as carefully as an intricate piece of machinery and even though you could take it apart to see what makes it tick, it's more fun to enjoy the story Pullman has created. He's wound it all up tight, and opening it starts the tale unwinding through the pages.

It's a strange story, with another two or three stories contained within it, and they all have the dark, wintry and Gothic atmosphere associated with European fairy tales: inns, forests, clock towers and a heroine named Gretl.

One of the most original and delightful things about this book is the way the author adds his own commentary to the action. His remarks are presented in capital letters at the side of the page, reminding you that you're reading a story. The act of reading is almost as important as what's being read.

**Adèle Geras**

**Next?**

• Try some other Philip Pullman, for instance *Count Karlstein* or *The Firework-Maker's Daughter* (*UBG* 114).

• Read some much older European fairy tales by the Brothers Grimm – they're terrifying! (*UBG* 107)

• Philip Ridley is a modern storyteller who is quirky enough to be a writer of fairy tales – try *Krindlekrax*.

# CLOUD BUSTING  Malorie Blackman

Supposing your teacher told you to write a poem. Would you groan and moan? Suppose a new kid joined your class, and he or she didn't fit in: too scruffy or too tidy, too dreamy or too clever. Would you make the misfit's life a misery? *Cloud Busting* is a brilliant book about poetry. Every chapter is a different kind of poem, a new way of making words dance to a beat. It's also a wonderful, hard-hitting and moving book about friendship: what a privilege it is to have a true friend, and how terrible it is to lose that privilege. A book to make you think, with ideas that will stay with you for a long time. Dare to be different.

**Ann Halam**

### Next?

• You'll want more Malorie Blackman, and they're all great. She writes for lots of different ages, but ones that might be right after *Cloud Busting* are *Operation Gadgetman!*, *A.N.T.I.D.O.T.E.* and *Hacker* (*UBG* 140).

• There are other novels in verse, too – try *Love That Dog* by Sharon Creech (*UBG* 214) and the slightly older *Locomotion* by Jacqueline Woodson (*UBG* 209).

★ ★ ★ ★ ★ ★

# COLD TOM  Sally Prue

### Next?

• Read Sally Prue's second book, *The Devil's Toenail* – a story of a boy under pressure who turns to something he thinks of as magic for help.

• *Skellig* by David Almond is a wonderful story about a boy who finds a mysterious creature in the broken-down garage at the bottom of his garden. (*UBG* 313)

• For another, gentler story about relating to something alien, try Vivien Alcock's *The Monster Garden*.

• Another novel which is really about love, and what it means, is Alice Hoffman's *Incantation*. (*UBG* 172)

This is a very unusual story. Tom is on the run from his own kind. He takes shelter among the Demons who live alongside the Tribe. One of the best things about the story is the way Prue uses Tom's point of view to show us what our own world might be like to someone who isn't one of our species. Sometimes the effect is very funny. Anna, one of Tom's protectors, has a pet guinea pig called Sophie. Tom thinks 'a sophie' is what she is, and to him, she's no more than meat.

On one level a chilling story of danger and adventure (with a very exciting first chapter), the book is really about love: the different ties that bind us together if we call ourselves human. Prue is a writer of strong but elegant prose. Every word is chosen, thought about, considered and the result is a moving and fascinating novel.

**Adèle Geras**

# THE COLOUR OF MAGIC Terry Pratchett

On the back of four vast elephants standing on a turtle floating through space, sits ... Discworld, whose geography and characters have become more real to millions of readers than most of Earth.

In *The Colour of Magic*, we meet Rincewind, the worst magician ever, who lives in the city of Ankh-Morpork. Rincewind is given the job of looking after a clueless tourist called Twoflower, who is always trying to take pictures with his camera – a box containing a little elf who can draw very quickly. We meet the Luggage, relentlessly following its master on little legs. We meet Death, who rides a horse called Binkie and always talks in capital letters...

I am one of the many people who buy everything Terry Pratchett writes, and one of the best things about discovering this brilliantly funny series is knowing that there are another 36 titles to go (and counting...), and every one of them seems better than the last!

**Andrew Norriss**

**Next?**
• My favourite **Discworld** books include *Mort* and *Guards, Guards!* Well, all of them, really.
• Terry's written some books for children, too, such as *The Carpet People* and *Truckers* – see **The Bromeliad** trilogy. (*UBG* 48)
• For another different and hilarious set of fantasy stories, try Douglas Adams's *The Hitchhiker's Guide to the Galaxy*. (*UBG* 152)

★ ★ ★ ★ ★ ★

# THE CORAL ISLAND R.M. Ballantyne

**Next?**
• Other classic adventures include Robert Louis Stevenson's *Treasure Island* (*UBG* 352) and Daniel Defoe's *Robinson Crusoe*.
• *The Swiss Family Robinson* by J.D. Wyss is a terrific story of a family shipwrecked on a tropical island. (*UBG* 338)
• *Plundering Paradise* by Geraldine McCaughrean is about pirates and the island of Madagascar.

What did we do before TV, radio and cinema? We curled up with a good book – especially one that took us off on exciting adventures in the South Seas.

In the company of Ralph Rover and his friends, Jack and Peterkin, we sail away on a merchant ship. The ship is wrecked on a coral reef, and so begins their Robinson Crusoe-like adventures of survival. And in between times they have many scary encounters with pirates, cannibals and missionaries – who all want bits of their body or their soul.

Though many of the ideas about morality are outdated today, we can still thrill to the adventures and Ballantyne's description of the South Seas. He makes readers wonder how they would fare if they were shipwrecked on an island.

**James Riordan**

# CORALINE  Neil Gaiman

### Next?

• Try the weird world of another London, one where all the broken things go, in China Miéville's *Un Lun Dun*.

• Or John Brindley's *Rhino Boy*, the unusual story of a boy with a rhino horn growing right out of the middle of his head!

• A weird and wonderful tale that always deserves rereading is *Alice's Adventures in Wonderland* by Lewis Carroll. (*UBG* 13)

Coraline is bored. She's just moved into a new house and can't think where to explore next. Then she finds a door in one of the walls. It leads along a dark corridor to another home, almost identical to hers but not quite. It leads her to another mother, almost identical to hers but not quite. What does this other mother want? And why has she got buttons instead of eyes?

This is an imaginative and genuinely scary story that starts off innocently and ends up frightening you half to death.

**Cliff McNish**

★ ★ ★ ★ ★ ★

# CORAM BOY  Jamila Gavin

In her introduction, Jamila Gavin says that 'the highways and byways of England were littered with the bones of little children'. Her book is set in the eighteenth century and is about the 'Coram Man' who toured the country supposedly collecting unwanted babies to take to the Coram Hospital in London. But this newly founded hospital never employed such a man, so exactly what was he doing with all those babies?

This is a thrilling, spellbinding book full of gothic mystery, which had me reading long after I should have been asleep. The historical tone is authentic and the tension is held throughout.

**Mary Hooper**

### Next?

• Other great books by Jamila Gavin include *The Wheel of Surya* (*UBG* 378) and *The Blood Stone* (*UBG* 40).

• Or try her *The Robber Baron's Daughter*, a fast-paced mystery about families and lies.

• For a book that looks at a lot of the same issues, this time in early nineteenth-century London and its black community, try *Jupiter Williams* by S.I. Martin.

• A book that deals with contemporary child trafficking is the deeply unnerving *Bloodchild* by Tim Bowler.

# ANIMAL STORIES
## Two Legs or Four?
### by Dick King-Smith

I like writing books about animals, mostly because I like animals. I'm interested in all the creatures that share this world with us, big or small, feathered or furry or finny. I'm interested in the look of an animal and in its habits. I'm not an expert, but with luck I don't make silly mistakes like one author (I won't tell you her name) who had partridges nesting up in the trees.

I've got favourite animals of course, like pigs, and in the kind of children's books I write, you're allowed to put words into their mouths. There's a posh word for this – anthropomorphism – which means giving human characteristics to what is not human, especially an animal.

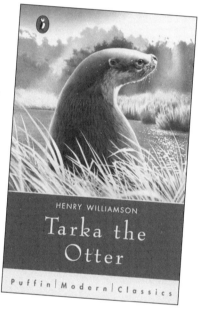

HENRY WILLIAMSON

Tarka the Otter

Puffin | Modern | Classics

So I can make my characters speak the Queen's English. That's all I do, really. I don't dress them up in human clothes (although that can be great fun – think of Beatrix Potter and her rabbits and mice and foxes), and I don't have billy-goats riding bicycles or pussycats playing the piano; I just let them talk. Apart from that, my pigs behave pretty much as all pigs do, and so do my hedgehogs or dogs or frogs or beetles or woodlice, or whatever other creatures I choose to put in my stories.

I think that most children enjoy reading books about animals because most children like animals, and of course there are so many different sorts of creatures, which means there's such a lot of choice, for both writer and reader.

'What shall I write about this time?' I say to myself when I sit down to start a new story.

Often I reply, 'A pig?'

But then I have to give myself a slap on the wrist (not too hard) and say, 'No, no, you've just done one about a pig; choose something else.'

So maybe I'll start thinking about the adventures of a mouse or a rabbit or a pigeon. Once I thought – how about an ostrich story? But then I found out I didn't know enough about ostriches and I didn't want to make silly mistakes (like those partridges nesting up in the trees). So the next time I was in London, I went to the

Natural History Museum and made notes about the ostrich – how tall it is, how fast it can run, what noise it makes and so on. Out of all that came, eventually, a book called *The Cuckoo Child*.

There are all sorts of animal stories. They can be factual, about an animal that behaves completely naturally (no talking, let alone dressing up), like Henry Williamson's *Tarka the Otter*, or Jack London's *White Fang*. Or they can be about animals that behave in many ways exactly like humans (Beatrix Potter's creatures again, or Kenneth Grahame's *The Wind in the Willows*). Or they can be rather crazy stories, where animals do things they couldn't possibly do in real life. And of course there is always magic. Pigs might fly. There's so much to choose from.

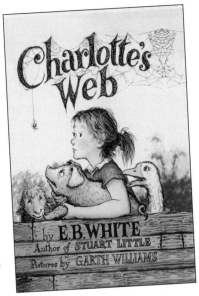

## Some Animal Fantasies in the *UBG*
### (where they might talk, or wear clothes, or drive cars...)

- *The Sheep-Pig* by Dick King-Smith
- *A Dog Called Grk* by Joshua Doder
- *Charlotte's Web* by E.B. White
- *Watership Down* by Richard Adams
- *Silverwing* by Kenneth Oppel
- The **Jungle Books** by Rudyard Kipling
- *The Hundred and One Dalmatians* by Dodie Smith
- *Winnie-the-Pooh* – well, sort of – by A.A. Milne
- *Fantastic Mr Fox* by Roald Dahl
- *The Wind in the Willows* by Kenneth Grahame
- **Paddington** series by Michael Bond
- **Redwall** series by Brian Jacques
- *Varjak Paw* by S.F. Said
- *Doctor Dolittle* by Hugh Lofting
- *Gobbolino the Witch's Cat* by Ursula Moray Williams
- **Spy Dog** series by Andrew Cope
- *The World According to Humphrey* by Betty G. Birney
- *The Tale of Despereaux* by Kate diCamillo
- *Mouse Noses on Toast* by Daren King

# CORBENIC Catherine Fisher ● ● ●

**Next?**

• If you loved the legends hinted at here, read *The Crystal Cave* by Mary Stewart.

• Or Kevin Crossley-Holland's *The Seeing Stone* is another wonderful take on the Arthur legend. (*UBG* 304)

• Try Catherine Fisher's *Darkhenge*, about a boy dealing with his sister being in a coma – will he need myth and magic to save her?

Desperately insecure, unhappy Cal leaves his mother (and her drinking) to go and live with Uncle Trevor, who likes things neat, tidy and the more expensive the better. But Cal gets off the train at the wrong stop and ends up at Corbenic, where there is a castle, in the middle of nowhere. Or does he...?

Finally getting to his uncle's, Cal tries to adjust to his new life. Then he meets up with a group of young travellers, including Arthur, Kai, and the beautiful Shadow – and everything changes again.

Woven through with Arthurian legend, from the Fisher King to the grail itself, this book will keep you guessing and wondering and breathlessly wanting to know more. The story uses real places to make you rethink legend – and if you ever visit the town of Caerleon in South Wales, stand in the centre of the Roman amphitheatre and think of this story.

**Leonie Flynn**

★ ★ ★ ★ ★ ★

# CORYDON AND THE ISLAND OF MONSTERS ● ●
## Tobias Druitt

What do you think of when you see pictures of Greece in holiday brochures? Is your first thought of lying on a beach baking in the sun? Then perhaps this isn't the story to lull you to sleep by the sea! But if those pictures of the ancient temples stir up thoughts of Greek heroes, half-human monsters and battles to stir the dead from their sleep, you'll definitely want to pick up this book!

Join Corydon on his adventures as he befriends wild and wonderful creatures. With suspense and excitement at the turn of every page, this is not a story for the fainthearted.

**Rachel Cole-Fletcher**

**Next?**

• Corydon is up for more tough times in *Corydon and the Fall of Atlantis* and *Corydon and the Seige of Troy*.

• *Snakehead* by Ann Halam is a wonderfully realised reworking of the Perseus myth. (*UBG* 315)

• *Private Peaceful* by Michael Morpurgo is a sensitive and thought-provoking book on the theme of war. (*UBG* 274)

• Or try Diana Wynne Jones's *The Game*, in which the characters are (sort of) Greek gods.

# COSMIC Frank Cottrell Boyce ●●

Well, there's good news and there's bad news. The good news is that 12-year-old Liam gets to go to Infinity Park, the brand-new theme park in China, to go on the biggest thrill ride in the history of the world. The bad news is that he's got to pretend to be Florida Kirby's dad. Oh, and also he's going to be shot into outer space in a big rocket that hasn't been tested yet.

Frank Cottrell Boyce always writes characters you really wish were your friends in real life, and Liam Digby is no exception. An impossible story is filled with real feelings, family and friendships, and real warmth, in this funny, lovely book.

**Daniel Hahn**

### Next?
• Frank Cottrell Boyce has written two other wonderful books that you should try. *Millions* is about two boys trying to spend a lot of money and *Framed* (*UBG* 119), about a plot to make money.

• Another writer who writes funny books with characters you'll love is Andrew Norriss. Try the wonderful *Aquila* (*UBG* 21) or the equally hilarious *The Touchstone*.

• Or for another adventure about space, try Lucy and Stephen Hawking's *George's Secret Key to the Universe*.

★ ★ ★ ★ ★ ★

# COUNTING STARS David Almond ●●●

### Next?
• You might like to see how these true stories develop into David Almond's fiction – try his amazing *Skellig* (*UBG* 313), the deeply unsettling *Clay* (*UBG* 64), or look out for the troubling and tense *Jackdaw Summer*.

• Or see how another great writer's childhood affected his novels, in Roald Dahl's *Boy*. (*UBG* 44)

• Or if it's Almond's spare style you like, or the point where the real slips into the unreal, then you might also enjoy *The Owl Service* by Alan Garner. (*UBG* 258)

If you, like me, prefer to read novels rather than short stories, lay aside your prejudice for Almond's beguiling collection of tales from his Catholic childhood.

Here walks Miss Golightly, the seamstress who keeps her unborn baby in a jar; and David's mam, who strokes behind his shoulder blades to let him know where his angel wings once joined; and David's sister Barbara, who died and really did become an angel, because Mary Byrne, resident of Watermill Lane, saw her out walking, so it must be true.

Almond writes with a brutal beauty and there is real magic in these stories – not the sort to do with wizards but the sort you feel when you look up into a night sky drilled with stars.

**Nicky Singer**

# THE COUNTRY CHILD  Alison Uttley

**Next?**

• You might also enjoy William Mayne's *The Twelve Dancers* or *A Grass Rope* (*UBG* 137) – stories in which the countryside has a powerful presence.

• *The Diddakoi* by Rumer Godden is about an outsider coming to live in a rural community. (*UBG* 85)

• Karen Wallace's *Raspberries on the Yangtze* is about growing up in the wilds of Canada (*UBG* 281), and the sequel is set in England, *Climbing a Monkey Puzzle Tree*.

Susan Garland, the country child, walks through threatening woods on her daily four-mile trek to a village school. This book tells of her childhood and describes not only the woods and the school but also the farmhouse in which Susan lives, and the seasons, festivals, gardens and many other aspects of her life. The book reminds readers that, with the help of a strong imagination, everyday life can become fascinating and mysterious.

Alison Uttley is best known for her **Little Grey Rabbit** stories for young children. However, she also wrote a series of non-fiction books recording a remembered but vanishing British country life, and *The Country Child* is probably the most haunting and unforgettable of these. Certain readers, particularly girls, will enjoy this account of a past life which is made remarkable by the imagination of the writer remembering it.

**Margaret Mahy**

★ ★ ★ ★ ★ ★

# A COYOTE'S IN THE HOUSE  Elmore Leonard

A trot on the wild side of Hollywood Hills, told from the unique viewpoint of Antwan, a wily coyote who knows better than to mix with humans. Antwan knows the score – he can sniff out everything there is to know and he's determined to defend the territory his fellow coyotes have occupied for thousands of years. Antwan takes an unexpected hop into the dangerous world of humans – and showbusiness – when he meets Buddy, a German shepherd who has starred in many movies. That's when the fun begins – and Antwan gets way more than he bargained for. What really makes *A Coyote's in the House* a howl is the way famous crime novelist and screenwriter Elmore Leonard gets up close and personal with real life movie stars – those that walk on four legs, and those that walk on two.

**Rodman Philbrick**

**Next?**

• How about another 'adult' crime author who writes great kids' books? Try Carl Hiaasen's *Hoot* (*UBG* 157) and *Flush*, both have an ecological twist.

• Or what about something by Rodman Philbrick – his books are all great but try *Freak the Mighty* (*UBG* 120) or *Fire Pony* first.

# A CRICKET IN TIMES SQUARE George Selden

When Chester, a cricket from Connecticut, finds himself lost and alone in the subway station of New York's Times Square, he quickly becomes the pet of young Mario Bellini, who helps his parents run a news stall. He also makes friends with Tucker Mouse and Harry Cat, and learns to play the most wonderful music. But cricket, mouse and cat are dogged by disaster!

This is a beautiful story of city life, rich with the sort of detail that comes from good writing. The mix of secondary characters adds extra nooks and crannies to the plot.

**Simon Puttock**

### Next?
• You might like *Charlotte's Web* by E.B. White – another lovely story of eccentric animals and humans. (*UBG* 59)
• For a story of (again, eccentric) characters afloat in a great and unnoticing city, try *The Thief Lord* by Cornelia Funke. (*UBG* 345)
• Similarly, check out the **Hazel Green** books by the wonderfully named Odo Hirsch, starting with … *Hazel Green*!

# CRUSADE Elizabeth Laird

### Next?
• Elizabeth Laird is a wonderful writer. Try *The Garbage King*, about two boys growing up living on the streets of Ethiopia, or *A Little Piece of Ground*, which discusses the whole issue of Israel and Palestine.
• For another book set during the third Crusade, try Elizabeth Jinks's *Pagan's Crusade*, about a streetwise Christian Arab boy who somehow ends up as a servant to one of the Knights Templar, and their unlikely friendship.

When Adam's mother dies without having confessed her sins to a priest, he swears to bring back dust from the Holy Land, as he is told that it will save her soul from Hell. As dog-boy to a knight, he journeys to Acre, and is part of the long, drawn-out and horrific siege that almost destroys the city and its inhabitants. There, by chance, he meets Salim, a boy apprenticed to a doctor. Despite being on different sides of a war, despite differing faiths and beliefs, the boys somehow become friends, and realise how similar they are – not monsters at all.

This is not an original story, but it is told beautifully. Full of heat, dust, blood, excitement and terror, it is a wonderful tale, and one perfectly relevant to today's world.

**Leonie Flynn**

TWO BOYS
TWO FAITHS
ONE UNHOLY WAR

ELIZABETH LAIRD

# THE CRY OF THE ICEMARK  Stuart Hill

### Next?

• You'll need to read the sequel, *Blade of Fire*, and the final volume – *Last Battle of the Icemark*.

• *The Eagle of the Ninth* by Rosemary Sutcliff is a stirring story of soldiers and war. (*UBG* 93)

• Or for another series that has masses of action, try *The Sterkarm Handshake* by Susan Price and its sequel *A Sterkarm Kiss*.

It can be tough being a teenager ... but spare a thought for Thirrin Freer Strong-in-the-Arm Lindenshield who, at the tender age of 14, becomes the monarch of a tiny kingdom called the Icemark and finds herself in charge of defending her country against an undefeated army of tens of thousands of battle-hardened soldiers led by the wiliest general that there has ever been.

Thirrin has plenty of guts. She also has two friends to advise her (her tutor and Oskan, the teenage son of a witch). However, in order to stop the monstrous army from adding the Icemark to its long list of conquered lands, Thirrin must find some allies to join her in expelling it. There's a slight snag, though – the Vampire king and queen, whose help she desperately needs, would rather drink her blood than sign a treaty of alliance.

This is a thrilling, action-packed story crammed with military clashes which are described so vividly that you'll feel in the thick of battle yourself.

**Anna Dale**

★ ★ ★ ★ ★ ★

# CUE FOR TREASON  Geoffrey Trease

The day Peter Brownrigg falls foul of the local squire, his life changes for ever. Forced to go on the run, he joins a company of travelling players and becomes an actor. He proves quite good at it, but there is another boy in the company, Kit Kirkstone, who is totally brilliant and out-acts them all. How does he do it? The scene where Peter discovers Kit's secret used to be one of my all-time favourites when I was young!

Together, the two of them make their way to London, where they bump into William Shakespeare; act in a performance before the Queen; uncover a treasonous plot and are sworn into the Secret Service.

This is a book that brings history vividly to life, complete with romance, intrigue, high adventure – and lots of lovely swashbuckling.

**Jean Ure**

### Next?

• Most of Trease's books are out of print, but worth searching out. Look for *Cloak for a Spy*, about the events leading up to the Spanish Armada.

• Or something else historical? *Sebastian Darke: Prince of Fools* is about a reluctant jester (*UBG* 300) and **The Wickit Chronicles** by Joan Lennon, starting with *Ely Plot*, tell of Pip's adventures (*UBG* 384).

# DADDY-LONG-LEGS  Jean Webster

My father sent me *Daddy-Long-Legs* (I was at boarding school) when I whinged about being miserable and lonely and in bed with chicken pox. The book is a series of letters from an orphan (i.e. more lonely and miserable than me) to the anonymous benefactor who pays for her to go to college on the understanding that she writes to him at least once a month. I was eleven and laughed for three days.

It's a tender tale of growing up, the story of an asylum kid with 'an all-inclusive ignorance', discovering the wider world with an astonished frankness and freshness ('Have you ever read *Hamlet*? It's perfectly corking!') and gradually allowing herself to form a relationship with the man who moves from 'Daddy-Long-Legs' to 'Daddy'. Read it and weep.

**Nicky Singer**

### Next?

• My next chicken-pox read (chicken pox can drag on for weeks) was *The Rose and the Ring* by W.M. Thackeray. Don't be put off by the fact that it was published in 1855. The fantastical tale of Prince Bulbo of Crim Tartary is a 'fireside pantomime' and a good laugh.

• If you want to stay in the family you could try Mark Twain's *The Adventures of Tom Sawyer*. (*UBG* 9) Twain was Jean Webster's great-uncle.

• Another wonderful father / daughter relationship to make you cry is in E. Nesbit's *The Railway Children*. (*UBG* 279)

• There's a few teary moments in *A Little Princess*, too. (*UBG* 205)

\* \* \* \* \* \*

# DANNY, THE CHAMPION OF THE WORLD  Roald Dahl

### Next?

• Try Roald Dahl's *The BFG*, about an orphan girl's adventures with a dream-catching giant. (*UBG* 33)

• Pete Johnson's *Rescuing Dad* is another great book about fathers and sons that manages to be both serious and funny at the same time. (*UBG* 283)

• Or try *Result!* by Neil Arksey – and find out what it's like when your dad is also one of your teachers…

As a boy, what I loved most about this book was the wonderful relationship between Danny and his fabulous father, and the fact that they lived in a gypsy caravan. I stared for a long time at the pictures of the inside of that cosy caravan, and could imagine no better place in the world to live.

Danny discovers his father's deep, dark secret: he loves poaching pheasants from the boorish Victor Hazell's woods. Together, father and son come up with an ingenious scheme to poach every single one of Hazell's pheasants the night before his big pheasant shoot. This book combines thrilling night-time excitement and humour, and is certainly one of Dahl's most realistic and warm-hearted books.

**Kenneth Oppel**

# THE DARK IS RISING sequence
### Susan Cooper

It's almost Christmas, but Will Stanton isn't thinking about presents this year. Radios buzz with static when he goes near them and animals seem afraid of him. On Midwinter's Day, he wakes to find everyone in his house fast asleep. But it is not a normal sleep, and the heavy snow that blankets the surrounding countryside is no ordinary snow. Will is the seventh son of a seventh son, one of the Old Ones, who has come into the world to protect it from an evil force. But time is rapidly running out...

This story is the second book in Susan Cooper's fantasy series, *The Dark is Rising*. Susan Cooper writes brilliantly, contrasting funny scenes with Will's lonely, terrifying struggle against the Dark.

**Annie Dalton**

This sequence is some of the best fantasy ever written, as we are taken from one mystical adventure to another. The first book, *Over Sea, Under Stone*, introduces us to Simon, Jane and Barney, and their great-uncle Merry, around whom strange things seem to happen. Sure enough, the children are swept into a perilous quest for an ancient Grail. *The Dark is Rising*, the second book, is the most haunting, focusing on young Will, the seventh son of a seventh son, who discovers he is the last of the powerful Old Ones. *Greenwitch* moves down to the Cornish coast, and features pagan magic. *The Grey King* takes us to the mountains of North Wales, and a secret lying inside them. It comes to an epic climax in *Silver on the Tree*, when all the threads of the story are finally drawn together.

Susan Cooper drew on many different aspects of British folklore and legend to create this sequence, and the result is worthy of the heritage from which she took inspiration.

**Marcus Sedgwick**

## Next?

• Try **The Changes** trilogy by Peter Dickinson, which travels similar territory with equally powerful writing. (*UBG* 57)

• **The Book of the Crow** by Catherine Fisher is a dark adventure series set in a world that might be the past and might be the future. (*UBG* 41)

• If you'd prefer a more demanding fantasy read, try Alan Garner's **The Owl Service**, a gripping supernatural thriller set in a Welsh village. (*UBG* 258) In fact, anything by Garner is worth reading.

• You might enjoy John Masefield's Christmas fantasy **The Box of Delights**, in which Kay Harker has to protect a wonderful box from evil governess Miss Pouncer and her sinister coven of male and female witches. (*UBG* 44)

# THE DARK HORSE Marcus Sedgwick ● ● ●

## Next?

• If you like the bleak, intriguing setting of this novel, try *Heaven Eyes* by David Almond. (*UBG* 149)

• If you want to read another novel about a young boy forced to become an adult, try *The Sword in the Stone* by T.H. White. (*UBG* 338)

• Marcus Sedgwick has written lots of other novels. Try *Floodland* (*UBG* 116), *Witch Hill* or *The Book of Dead Days*.

• Rosemary Sutcliff is always worth a read; try *Warrior Scarlet* and *Dawn Wind*.

*The Dark Horse* drew me into a strange, primitive world. Sigurd and his adopted sister Mouse (whom he rescued from wolves) are children of the Storn, a tribe led by superstition and fear that is struggling for survival. As the Storn fights within itself, dark forces they know only from legends gather around it. It falls to Sigurd to question his assumptions, rise to the challenge of leadership and face the terrible fate that awaits his people at the hands of the Dark Horse.

This isn't a comfortable novel to read, but I loved it. In most novels, you know that things are going to work out well. In this novel, you can never be sure, so the story is genuinely unpredictable.

It's powerful, too, and made me think about how often we make up our minds without thinking, and about how important it is not to be ruled by fear.

**Antonia Honeywell**

★ ★ ★ ★ ★ ★

# DARKSIDE Tom Becker ● ● ●

Darkside is a place deep under London where nightmares walk the streets. It's ruled by Jack the Ripper's children...

Jonathan Starling is 14. He's an ordinary boy from ordinary London. Ordinary, except that his mother's dead and his father's in an asylum. One day, his home is attacked by kidnappers and he has to go on the run. He runs, and keeps running, until he finds some creepy-looking steps leading down. He follows them and ends up in Darkside. There he finds a whole new world, where some people are friendly and some are ... not. *Darkside* is an unsettling story, full of creepy villains and weird events that intrigue you, scare you and make you really glad there are sequels!

**Max Hart, age 10**

## Next?

• The sequels – *Darkside: Lifeblood* and *Darkside: Nighttrap*, both are terrifically exciting and take Jonathan on more terrifying journeys.

• *Tunnels*, and its sequel *Deeper*, by Roderick Gordon and Brian Williams, are also about a whole separate world that exists under our own. But be warned – these are pretty scary...

• Another boy who ends up in a strange place is the hero of *Tom's Midnight Garden* by Philippa Pearce. (*UBG* 351)

# THE DAY MY BUM WENT PSYCHO  Andy Griffiths

OK, I bet you're thinking – how can a *bum* go psycho? Well, it can ... and when all the bums in the world get fed up with their lot and start the Great Bum Rebellion, someone has to take a stand! Zack is just the guy for the job. His bum has run off, and he doesn't see why he should take that lying down.

To find out about stinks, poos, pongs and how to use a pink, fluffy toilet seat cover as bait for a feral bum – read this book. You'll laugh, you'll cry – you'll probably never look at your bum in the same way again. (And if you've never looked at your bum at all, you'd better get two mirrors and check it's still there...)

**Leonie Flynn**

### Next?
• Finished this book? Don't panic – there's more! The sequels are: *Zombie Bums from Uranus*, *Bumageddon: the Final Pongflict* and *What Bumosaur is That?*
• More toilet humour? Try *The Killer Underpants* by Michael Lawrence (*UBG* 181) or *The Giggler Treatment* by Roddy Doyle (*UBG* 127).
• For more hilarious stories about weird goings-on, try the **Buster Bayliss** books by Philip Reeve. (*UBG* 49)

★ ★ ★ ★ ★ ★

# THE DAY OF THE TRIFFIDS  John Wyndham

### Next?
• John Wyndham wrote lots of other novels, such as *Chocky* and *The Midwich Cuckoos*. They were written for adults, but are worth attempting if you're feeling adventurous.
• If you enjoyed the theme of surviving after a great catastrophe, why not read *Z for Zachariah* by Robert C. O'Brien, or Hugh Scott's *Why Weeps the Brogan?* (*UBG* 383)
• Other science-fiction stories that you might enjoy are Orson Scott Card's **Ender's Saga**, starting with *Ender's Game*.

Ever thought about how the world might end? In this thought-provoking novel, John Wyndham shows us just how quickly civilisation as we know it would fall apart if most of humanity woke up to find that they had gone blind overnight. Throw in man-eating plants walking around and you have the basic premise of the novel.

This book was written at a time when most people were worried about the very real possibility of nuclear war, and you may want to skip the more political bits. What will keep you reading is the way in which it tempts you to imagine how you would cope in such circumstances. If you had to keep a small group of people alive, where would you go and what would you do? From its famous opening line to its nail-biting conclusion, this is a book that will keep you hooked and you'll find yourself thinking about it long after you've finished it.

**Laura Hutchings**

# DEATH AND THE ARROW  Chris Priestley  ●●

### Next?

• Tom Marlowe returns in the sequels, *The White Rider* and *Redwulf's Curse*.

• Chris Priestley also writes unsettling horror. Read *Uncle Montague's Tales of Terror* – if you dare… (*UBG* 361)

• Or what about Sophie Masson's *The Tempestuous Voyage of Hopewell Shakespeare*? Apprenticed to a boring trade, Hopewell envies his distant and famous cousin Will. Given the chance to join the crew of *The Golden Dragon* he jumps at it, and ends up embarking on an adventure that may feel familiar.

It's London, 1715. Another murder has taken place, and again the murder victim is found with a 'death and the arrow' card on him – a card showing the figure of death, pointing, and brandishing an arrow, about to hurl it…

When his friend, Will, becomes involved with these terrible murders, Tom Marlowe just has to do something about it. Tom has some serious sleuthing to do – and fast, before the murderer strikes again… But what do all these victims have in common? And how is Will implicated? And who is the shadowy, caped figure on the roof?

Chris Priestley's detailed creation of eighteenth-century London is totally convincing, and captivating (it's quite a shock to come to the end of the book and find yourself back in the twenty-first century), and the story is absolutely gripping. Thank goodness there are sequels!

**Daniel Hahn**

★ ★ ★ ★ ★ ★

# THE DEATH COLLECTOR  Justin Richards  ●●

A smart, fantasy horror-thriller blending Victorian chills with high-tech thrills, *The Death Collector* takes readers into a dark world of steam-powered monsters, grave-robbing villains and walking cadavers – and provides fun and twists aplenty.

The adventure begins when pickpocket Eddie Hopkins steals the wallet of one George Archer, recently seconded to the Department of Unclassified Artefacts at the British Museum. George's wallet contains a clue to a terrifying mystery, which the cast of likeable, believable characters must unravel if they are to survive… The levels of invention and high-concept intrigue remain potent throughout, as Richards unfolds his tale in assured and page-turning style.

**Steve Cole**

### Next?

• There's a sequel, *The Chaos Code*. You should also check out Richards's **The Invisible Detective** series, or his **Time Runners** series, starting with *The Rewind Assassin*.

• Justin Richards has also collaborated with the adult adventure writer, Jack Higgins, on a new series that starts with *Sure Fire*.

• For further bony adventures, check out Derek Landy's *Skulduggery Pleasant* and its sequels. (*UBG* 314)

# THE DEMON HEADMASTER  Gillian Cross

## Next?

• The series continues with *The Prime Minister's Brain*, *The Revenge of the Demon Headmaster*, *The Demon Headmaster Strikes Again*, *The Demon Headmaster Takes Over* and *Facing the Demon Headmaster*.

• The Demon Headmaster could be a Doctor Who villain. Why not read some of the **Doctor Who** novels by various writers.

• For a more gothic take on the misuse of power, try Stephen Elboz's *The House of Rats*.

'What's the worst thing you can imagine in a school?' For new girl, Dinah Hunter, the answer to this question is as unexpected as it is chilling. She realises something is wrong before lessons have even begun. The pupils stand around in the playground, quietly chanting the times tables and testing one another on geography questions. The prefects' word is law, and they are obeyed without question. A large poster in the corridor proclaims: 'The man who can keep order can rule the world'. And soon she will meet that man, the mysterious and terrifying Demon Headmaster himself. What is the nature of the hold he has over the school? And is there any limit to his craving for power?

**Thomas Bloor**

★ ★ ★ ★ ★ ★

# THE DEPTFORD MICE trilogy  Robin Jarvis

Don't be put off by the fact that the main characters in this trilogy are mice. There's nothing cute about these creatures! In *The Dark Portal*, Arthur and Audrey's father have gone missing in the sewers that lie beyond the grating in the hall. Believing rats have captured him, they go looking for him. But something terrifying dwells deep in the sewers – it's the lair of the evil sorcerer, Jupiter. As the trilogy progresses, the mice battle again and again to repel the dark magic of Jupiter, and in *The Final Reckoning* he returns to exact his revenge.

This is a fantastically exciting trilogy, fast-paced and tense; but there is humour, too, and you'll be kept guessing by the twists in the plot.

**Kathryn Ross**

## Next?

• You'll want to read the prequels, **The Deptford Histories**, which provide fascinating detail about many of the characters in **The Deptford Mice**. Look out also for **The Deptford Mouslets** series.

• Brian Jacques's famous **Redwall** series has a huge fan-base – his heroes are also mice. (*UBG* 282)

• *Silverwing*, *Sunwing* and *Firewing* are the titles of Kenneth Oppel's thrilling series set in the world of silverwing bats. (*UBG* 312)

• Back to mice... Don't miss the adventures of the affable watchmaker mouse, Hermux Tantamoq, hero of Michael Hoeye's original detective story, *Time Stops for No Mouse*. (*UBG* 348)

# THE DEVIL'S ARITHMETIC  Jane Yolen

It is Passover, and Hannah is tired of her family constantly dwelling on the past. What does it mean? What is the point? But then, by some strange twist of time, Hannah finds herself in Poland, in 1942, and on her way to a concentration camp. And much as she tries to remember her 'real' family and the future from which she came, she is soon lost in the awful reality of this new 'now'.

This beautifully told story focuses on a fragment of one of the most despicably vile passages in human history: the Holocaust. But Hannah, out of place, out of time, is not alone. She is bound to those around her through suffering and humanity, and through the devil's arithmetic; counting yourself among the living, one day at a time.

**Simon Puttock**

### Next?
• Something quite different? Something upbeat that'll reassure you that humans can be nice, too… Or maybe just go and talk to someone you really like.
• And if you then want to come back to this subject, try *In My Hands: Memories of a Holocaust Rescuer* by Irene Gut Opdyke.
• Or *The Star Houses* by Stewart Ross, based on the memoirs of a survivor.

★ ★ ★ ★ ★ ★

# THE DIAMOND OF DRURY LANE  Julia Golding

### Next?
• There's more Cat! The sequels are *Cat Among the Pigeons, Den of Thieves, Cat o' Nine Tails* and *Black Heart of Jamaica*. If you read all those, you'll definitely want more Julia Golding – go for *The Ship Between Worlds* next. (*UBG* 308)
• For another story of an orphaned girl with theatrical ambitions who is abandoned on a doorstep as a baby, read *Thursday's Child* and its sequel *Far to Go* by Noel Streatfeild.
• Also set in a theatre, try *The Swish of the Curtain* by Pamela Brown. (*UBG* 337)

You might think that being left on someone's doorstep as a baby would be dreadful but, if you're a character in a children's book, this start in life usually means that you're in for a great adventure. Cat Royal, the heroine of *The Diamond of Drury Lane*, has the good fortune to be deposited on the steps of the Theatre Royal in Drury Lane, where she is welcomed into the rather unorthodox family of actors, stage hands and seamstresses. She is made to sleep on a couch in the costume store and receives no wages for the work she does, but Cat is well-loved and grows into a confident, daring young woman.

This eighteenth-century tale is told in Cat's own words and you will never meet such a lively, dauntless heroine – or read a more thrilling tale.

**Anna Dale**

# THE DIARY OF A YOUNG GIRL  Anne Frank

I first read this as a teenager in South Africa. I knew that Anne's family had been discovered in their hideout in Amsterdam by Nazi soldiers. I knew she had died in a concentration camp. Her diary gripped me because her voice was so alive, so honest. She was also a fantastic observer of people!

This was the first book that told me that literature was real. If I had been born in Europe, I knew that I, too, would probably have been killed because my mother was Jewish. But it was only years later that I realised that my own country was, in many ways, a vast concentration camp for most of its people – black South Africans. I had cried over Anne without seeing the racism all around me.

I still love the freshness of Anne's voice. I am convinced she would have stood up for all people equally – Jews, Muslims, Christians, Arabs, Africans, everyone: 'Why do some people have to starve, while there are surpluses rotting in other parts of the world? Oh, why are people so crazy?'

**Beverley Naidoo**

## Next?

• There is nothing else quite like Anne's diary, but try *Zlata's Diary* by Zlata Filipoviç, written during the war in Bosnia. Like Anne, Zlata sees the madness and stupidity of war.

• Can a cartoon make you cry? Read Art Spiegelman's *Maus*, where the Jews are mice and the Nazis are cats, and see. (*UBG* 225)

• *The Boy in the Striped Pyjamas* by John Boyne is an innocent's-eye-view of the same appalling events.

## Books That Make You Sad – But Happy, Too

• *Goodnight Mr Tom* by Michelle Magorian
• *Charlotte's Web* by E.B. White
• *Journey to Jo'burg* by Beverley Naidoo
• *The Little Prince* by Antoine de Saint-Exupéry
• *Up on Cloud Nine* by Anne Fine
• *The Snow Goose* by Paul Gallico
• *The Iron Man* by Ted Hughes
• *Becky Bananas* by Jean Ure
• *A Little Princess* by Frances Hodgson Burnett
• *The Snowman* by Raymond Briggs

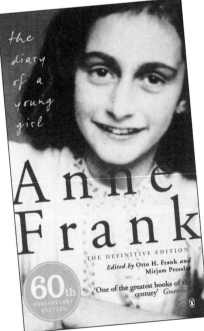

the diary of a young girl

Anne Frank

THE DEFINITIVE EDITION
Edited by Otto H. Frank *and* Mirjam Pressler

'One of the greatest books of the century' *Guardian*

# THE DIDDAKOI  Rumer Godden

## Next?

- Other strong stories that capture the nature of rural England include Philippa Pearce's *Tom's Midnight Garden* (*UBG* 351), the very powerful *Badger on the Barge* (*UBG* 26) and *The Nature of the Beast* by Janni Howker.
- A great story about a boy meeting an outsider is the wonderful *Stig of the Dump* by Clive King. (*UBG* 325)
- Or if you fancy a more hard-hitting, up-to-date story about being an outsider, you could try *The Other Side of Truth* by Beverley Naidoo (*UBG* 255) or *The Frozen Waterfall* by Gaye Hicyilmaz.

Kizzy Lovell and her gran live in a horse-drawn wagon in Admiral Twiss's orchard. When her gran dies, Kizzy has to adapt to living in a house and going to school, where she is bullied mercilessly by the other girls for being a diddakoi – a half-gypsy.

It's a great read, this, and very moving, but it's also an important book, because it shows how very hard it can be to live your life as an outsider. Kizzy is determined not to conform – she is proud of her background, proud of being different. The book gives an insight into the lives of gypsies and travellers and is a plea for tolerance – it asks us to respect and cherish difference, rather than fear and despise it.

**Malachy Doyle**

★ ★ ★ ★ ★ ★

# DIGORY, THE DRAGON SLAYER
## Angela McAllister

'In days of old when knights were bold, there lived a boy called Digory...' So starts this delightful story about, as it says, a boy called Digory, who, as it happens, isn't that bold at all. In fact, he's far more interested in playing his lute, sitting in trees and admiring the clouds than slaying dragons. And the fact that everyone thinks he's a dragon-slaying hero is just an accident ... really it is!

But once he's been called a dragon slayer, then it seems he has to live up to the name. So, knighted and dressed in home-made armour, he leaves his home in Batty-by-Noodle and goes off in search of princesses to rescue and dragons to slay. Except... And... But... Well, telling any more would give far too much away. Instead, I think you should go and read this book (however old you are).

**Leonie Flynn**

## Next?

- Angela McAllister has written many books for kids, including a sequel to this book – look out for *Digory and the Lost King*.
- There are more knightly adventure in Giles Andreae's *Luke Lancelot and the Golden Shield*.
- Or try something else with a gentle sense of humour – Heather Dyer's *The Fish in Room 11*.

# DIMANCHE DILLER series  Henrietta Branford

What a tragic loss to children's literature was the untimely death of Henrietta Branford! She wrote some of the most captivating and original books in the canon. The three **Dimanche Diller** books anticipate the all-the-rage series by Lemony Snicket, **A Series of Unfortunate Events**. A baby, orphaned ('and don't hope her parents will turn up alive at the end') when her rich parents are drowned at sea, is adopted by a ghastly villainess called Valburga Vilemile, posing as her aunt.

VV, who leaves Cruella de Vil at the post, does her best to have the child meet with a fatal accident so she can get her evil hands on her money. Happily, Dimanche – adventurous, sparky and bursting with life – survives, with help from her many friends.

In fact, all who meet her become her devotees, and I greatly hope an endless stream of new readers will feel the same.

**Lynne Reid Banks**

### Next?
• **A Series of Unfortunate Events** by Lemony Snicket, about another three children whom life treats very badly. (**UBG** 306)

• *Harry and the Wrinklies* by Alan Temperley – a story about an orphan, with a wonderfully evil nemesis, Gestapo Lil. (**UBG** 144)

• For a very different story about children being apart from their parents, try *The Owl Tree* by Jenny Nimmo. (**UBG** 259)

★ ★ ★ ★ ★ ★

# THE DIVIDE  Elizabeth Kay

### Next?
• There's more about Felix in *Back to the Divide* and *Jinx on the Divide*.

• *Marianne Dreams* by Catherine Storr is also about dreams, illness and the blurring of the real world. (**UBG** 221)

• For a series of books also about fantasy and reality, try Susan Cooper's **The Dark is Rising** sequence. (**UBG** 78)

• Or for a realistic and terrifying look at life-threatening illness, try Malorie Blackman's *Pig-Heart Boy*. (**UBG** 268)

Elizabeth Kay's first book is a great parallel-world adventure starring Felix, a young boy suffering from a life-threatening illness. As he falls asleep, he is taken to another world where he encounters all sorts of strange and mystical beasts that could only have sprung from the furthest corners of his imagination. Slowly, Felix becomes involved in a race to stop the evil Snakeweed from dominating this fantasy world. With the help of numerous other fantastical beasts, he simultaneously battles evil and manages to find a temporary cure for his illness. The book has a gripping and exciting storyline, the plot is brilliant and the characters are vivid. I certainly haven't read any book quite like it before.

**Tim Cross**

# DOCTOR DOLITTLE Hugh Lofting

### Next?

• More animals? Try the **Jungle Books** by Rudyard Kipling, about a boy brought up by animals. (*UBG* 185)

• Or the delightful *Mr Popper's Penguins* by Richard and Florence Atwater. (*UBG* 238)

• For another series about wonderful goings-on – this time with a tin man, scarecrow and cowardly lion – try L. Frank Baum's *The Wizard of Oz* and its sequels. (*UBG* 390)

Doctor John Dolittle lives in the seaside town of Puddleby-on-the-Marsh. He is not very successful as a 'people' doctor; he prefers looking after his animals. His pet parrot Polynesia persuades him to become a vet and teaches him to talk to his animal patients in their own languages. Gradually his fame spreads, as the animals pass on the good news to one another that at last there is a vet who can understand and treat the needs of his patients!

The doctor's adventures take him all over the world, and even to the moon. His many animal friends, including Polynesia, Jip the dog, Dab-Dab the duck, and a pushmi-pullyu (the rarest animal in all of Africa) are loveable characters in their own right.

There is a whole series of books chronicling the warm and funny adventures of Doctor Dolittle.

**Ian Beck**

★ ★ ★ ★ ★ ★

# A DOG CALLED GRK Joshua Doder

When Tim Malt trips over a dog – the Grk of the title – on his way back from school, he becomes involved in an exciting and dangerous adventure involving the Stanislavian ambassador and his children, Max and Natasha Raffifi (to whom Grk belongs). It is an adventure that will take him jetting off to Eastern Europe (and see him making use of all the hours he has spent playing helicopter games on his computer). This funny, fast-paced story from Joshua Doder is a real page-turner. There is plenty of fun along the way, but there are lots of genuine thrills, too, as Tim and Grk face the sinister and ruthless Major Raki of the Stanislavian Secret Police and attempt to rescue the Raffifi family.

**Chris Priestley**

### Next?

• If you liked this tale of a boy and a dog's exciting adventures, you may well enjoy **Tintin**. Try *King Ottokar's Sceptre* for a start, though to be honest, they're all amazing. (*UBG* 349)

• Or, if you want something a little meatier, try Anthony Horowitz's *Stormbreaker* and all the sequels. (*UBG* 12)

• More spies? Then choose the **Spy Mice** series (yep, the spies are mice, and the books have dreadfully punning titles such as *Goldwhiskers*...)

• Or for some canine spying, *Spy Dog* by Andrew Cope. (*UBG* 322)

# DOGSBODY Diana Wynne Jones

Imagine if stars were living beings! Sirius is the dog-star, and he has a terrible temper. As punishment for apparently killing a lesser star whilst in a rage, he is banished to Earth and reborn as a dog. Once on Earth, he is cared for by Kathleen, a lonely, bullied orphan whom he comes to adore.

*Dogsbody* has wonderfully vivid characters: there are resourceful children like Kathleen; mighty stars like Sol; villains like cruel Aunt Duffy who makes vile ceramics; and hilarious animals like the stupid Hello Dogs.

Best of all is Sirius himself, with his powerful star nature, struggling within his humble dog's body as he tries desperately to prove his innocence and return to his place in the heavens.

**Gill Vickery**

## Next?
• Try *Black Maria*, another of Diana Wynne Jones's books where people are turned into animals. She really makes you understand what it would be like to feel as if you were a wolf or a cat but still thought like a human.

• You will also enjoy Allan Ahlberg's *Woof!*, about a boy who keeps turning into a dog and back again without warning. (*UBG* 391)

• Or for more stars, dogs and dog-stars, try Livi Michael's *The Sky Wolves*, a story that seems to be about an ordinary family pet, but is actually about … no, I can't give the secret away – you'll have to read it and find out!

★ ★ ★ ★ ★ ★

# A DOG SO SMALL Philippa Pearce

## Next?
• Try *The Lady With Iron Bones* by Jan Mark and *The Twelve and the Genii* by Pauline Clarke (*UBG* 358) – terrific stories about the good and bad things that can happen when you really want something to be true.

• *Tom's Midnight Garden* is a wonderful and more challenging story by Philippa Pearce. (*UBG* 351)

• There's another boy who desperately wants a dog in Hilary McKay's delightful *Dog Friday*. There's no magic, just a great story.

Have you ever wanted something so badly it seems to take over your life? Everything that happens in this book is connected with Ben Blewett's wish for a dog. But in a busy family household in busy London, it just isn't possible even to have the smallest dog. At the start of the book, Ben is convinced that his grandparents will give him a dog for his birthday. Instead, he gets a picture of a dog; but not just any old picture. Written on the back are the magic-sounding words *Chiquitito chihuahua* – and magic they are. But Ben discovers that sometimes fantasies can go too far, in this engaging, warm and wonderful book.

**Jon Appleto**

# THE DOLL'S HOUSE Rumer Godden

●●●

This story, by one of the most sensitive of writers, is about a mismatched family of dolls longing for a settled home. Their owners, sisters Emily and Charlotte, restore a house for them, and within its wooden walls unfolds what Godden's biographer Anne Chisholm calls 'a miniature melodrama of love and murder among dolls'. The characters of the dolls are wonderfully described – sensible, loving Tottie, eccentric, vulnerable Birdie and the sinister and manipulative Marchpane. Contrasting with the lives of the dolls is the relationship between Emily and Charlotte themselves.

This is a delightful book – moving, thoughtful and perceptive.

**Jane Ray**

**Next?**

• Another book told from the dolls' point of view is *The Doll People* by Ann Matthews Martin and Laura Godwin, illustrated by Brian Selznick.

• Or try Sylvia Waugh's *The Mennyms*, about another unusual family. (*UBG* 226)

• Or what about Elizabeth Goudge's delightful fantasy, *Henrietta's House*? It's a little older, but well worth reading.

★ ★ ★ ★ ★ ★

# THE DOLPHIN CROSSING Jill Paton Walsh

●●●

**Next?**

• In *Grace*, Jill Paton Walsh explores a true story, this time that of Grace Darling, who became a national heroine after saving some drowning sailors. Or try Paton Walsh's *A Parcel of Patterns*, about when plague visited the Derbyshire village of Eyam. (*UBG* 259)

• Philippa Pearce's *Minnow on the Say* is another story of friendship. (*UBG* 230)

• An unsentimental memoir of growing up during the war is Michael Foreman's *War Boy*.

In 1940, John's comfortable life has been disrupted by the war. His father is in the Merchant Navy and his brother is away in Birmingham. The army has requisitioned their home so he and his mother are living in a gardener's cottage. But at least John is luckier than Pat – an evacuee from London who has to live in a derelict railway carriage with his pregnant stepmother, and is bullied by the local children. John goes out of his way to help Pat, but when John realises the significance of the small boats and pleasure steamers being taken by the navy over the horizon towards Dunkirk in France, he finds it is Pat's turn to help him.

The British evacuation of Dunkirk was one of the turning points of World War II. The little ships helped save 300,000 soldiers. Some of the boats were so small that only a few could be rescued at a time, but because hundreds of boats made the dangerous crossing, thousands of men survived.

**Barbara Wright**

# DON'T PAT THE WOMBAT Elizabeth Honey

This is a funny, rude and sometimes moving book about an Australian school camp. It's told by Mark, one of a group of friends called the Coconuts, who are shocked when the worst teacher of all ('the Bomb' – so-called because you never know when he might explode) suddenly joins them on their annual summer trip. It's full of the gory details of children left almost to their own devices, but has a more serious heart to it – the story of how the Bomb persecutes a strange boy called Jonah, and how Jonah is victorious in the end.

**Marcus Sedgwick**

> **Next?**
> • If you liked this, why not try *45 and 47 Stella Street* or *Fiddleback*, also by Elizabeth Honey?
> • Or some classic stories about young troublemakers, such as *Just William* by Richmal Crompton (*UBG* 186) or the **Jennings** stories by Anthony Buckeridge (*UBG* 181).
> • For more boys in trouble try Franklin W. Dixon's **Hardy Boys** books. (*UBG* 143)

★ ★ ★ ★ ★ ★

# THE DOOMSPELL Cliff McNish

> **Next?**
> • Rachel's battle is continued in two equally readable sequels called *The Scent of Magic* and *The Wizard's Promise*.
> • If you've got the witch twitch, try the most famous witch story of them all, L. Frank Baum's *The Wizard of Oz*. (*UBG* 390)
> • Battling a witch in a faraway land, via the back of an unassuming wardrobe, is the theme of C.S. Lewis's classic *The Lion, the Witch and the Wardrobe*. (*UBG* 198)

When Rachel and her brother, Eric, are sucked unexpectedly through a terrifying portal to the faraway frozen ice world, Ithrea, they know they are in trouble. A seriously unhappy witch called Dragwena – a loathsome creature with blood-red skin, tattooed eyes, four sets of teeth and a writhing snake-mouth filled with purple-eyed, armoured spiders – has been seeking her perfect slave for centuries and thinks Rachel is it.

This book bulges with a classic big battle between good and evil. McNish creates an entertaining story that is by turns magical and gripping, yet full of danger and treachery. It's a page-turner, and sometimes a stomach-churner, and its breakneck excitement never fails to enthral.

**John McLay**

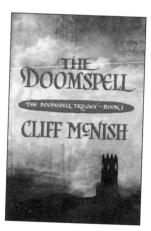

# DOUBLE ACT  Jacqueline Wilson

### Next?

• Try *Lotte and Lisa* by Erich Kästner, another very funny story about identical twins.

• Enid Blyton's **St Clare's** books are stories that feature in *Double Act*.

• *Goggle-Eyes* by Anne Fine is another story about getting used to a step-parent, this time a stepfather. (*UBG* 130)

• *The Prince and the Pauper* by Mark Twain is a classic story about two boys who look like twins. (*UBG* 273)

Ruby and Garnet are identical twins. But although they look exactly alike, Garnet is a lot shyer, so Ruby is used to getting her own way.

When their dad finds a new girlfriend, they're absolutely *disgusted*, and even more so when they all have to move together to the countryside and become a brand-new family. Ruby and Garnet are determined to hate their new life and not make any friends.

This is one of Jacqueline Wilson's most enjoyable books. You'll come to love the twins, even though you'll feel like slapping them sometimes – Ruby for being so bossy and Garnet for being so timid!

**Susan Reuben**

★ ★ ★ ★ ★ ★

# DOWN WITH SKOOL  Geoffrey Willans

The hero of this book is Nigel Molesworth. The first thing you notice is how he spells. Because mostly he doesn't. Also, his world view is refreshingly straightforward. 'My skool is nothing but kanes, lat. French, geog. Hist. Algy, geom., headmasters, skool dogs, skool sossages, my bro molesworth 2 and MASTERS everywhere.' There it is, the world as we all know it (though hopefully not the cane any more!) reduced to essentials: Us (noble, brave, fearless) and Them (oiks et al.).

Political correctness is probably one of the reasons we couldn't create Molesworth these days, as he is very un-PC. He is disrespectful and anarchic to the core, a plotter and troublemaker, over-opinionated, irreligious, mean to his little brother, wily, a smoker, and completely uninterested in that most important thing, Doing Well at School. He is also hilarious – and the illustrations by Ronald Searle are worth the price of the book on their own!

**Diane Duane**

### Next?

• The **Jennings** series by Anthony Buckeridge is a set of very funny stories about boys at boarding school. (*UBG* 181)

• Or try *Three Men in a Boat* by Jerome K. Jerome. This is a humour classic. Just read a bit of it and, if you like it, devour the whole thing.

• Or what about *The Turbulent Term of Tyke Tiler*, for another child who gets into trouble at school? (*UBG* 357)

# DUMB CREATURES  Jeanne Willis

### Next?
- If you like reading about animals, try *Charlotte's Web* by E.B. White. (*UBG* 59)
- *Watership Down* is a longer book about a colony of rabbits and their efforts to survive the dangers of the world. (*UBG* 376)
- *Black Beauty* by Anna Sewell is also more difficult, but a lovely, sad story told in the voice of a horse. (*UBG* 35)

I love this story because it shows that just because animals can't talk, it doesn't mean they can't think and feel. Tom can't talk, either, so people treat him differently. 'Maybe they think that if I can't speak, I have no feelings,' says Tom. 'But I do.' Tom goes to the zoo, and because he is quiet and observant, he notices things that other people don't. Soon he discovers that Zanzi, the female gorilla, can use sign language. Zanzi and Tom sign to each other, and Zanzi tells Tom that she's pregnant. But everything goes wrong when the zoo takes Zanzi's baby away. Only Tom can understand what Zanzi wants – but will anybody hear him? This book is full of lovely observations about animal (and human) behaviour, and shows that we have a lot more in common than some people think.

**Heather Dyer**

★ ★ ★ ★ ★ ★

# EAGER  Helen Fox

*Eager* is a book about a small, experimental robot called EGR3. He's completely new to the world and doesn't really understand what life's about. Does that sound weird? Because surely robots are just robots, and robots aren't alive? But, even in a world where houses talk to you and technology is really advanced, Eager is different. He's been programmed to have feelings, and when he's moved to a new house he's baffled by the strange things he finds there. The Jones family (who buy him) still have their old robot, Grumps, who tries to teach Eager about everything, but Grumps is wearing out, and Eager (who is very bright) finds out what humans do to robots that no longer work...

With fast action, loads of humour and a really good plot, this is an excellent read (I'd give it five stars!). Because Eager thinks about everything, he makes you think, too – though not so much that you don't want to keep reading!

**Eddie Strang, age 10**

### Next?
- There are two sequels so far, *Eager's Nephew* and *Eager and the Mermaid*.
- Another book with a robot – this time a very rude one – is *The Inventors* by Alexander Gordon Smith and Jamie Webb (who are brothers – Jamie was eleven when they wrote this!)
- Something just as funny? Try *Little Darlings* by Sam Llewellyn. (*UBG* 199)

# THE EAGLE OF THE NINTH

## Rosemary Sutcliff

Star Title

A brilliantly exciting story set in Roman Britain. Marcus's father was in the lost Ninth Legion, which marched north and was never seen again. After a serious injury, Marcus has to leave the army, so joins up with his British slave, Esca, and sets off on a quest to retrieve the Ninth's eagle and restore his father's honour. Battles, wild landscapes and strange tribal rituals fill the book with action, and Sutcliff's dense prose makes you feel you're living in Marcus's world.

Two other books continue the story of Marcus's descendants. In *The Silver Branch* the eagle is rediscovered and used against the cruel emperor, Allectus, and in *The Lantern Bearers*, one of Rosemary Sutcliff's best books, Aquila has to choose between leaving Britain with the Roman army or searching for his lost sister.

Sutcliff's books are about friendship and loyalty, about overcoming pain and difficulty. They are not easy, and she doesn't flinch from showing the cruelty and violence of the time. But if you enjoy history and exhilarating adventure, you'll find her books immensely satisfying, and won't rest till you've read them all.

**Catherine Fisher**

If you are having trouble with your Time Machine – and who doesn't from time to time? – and it just will *not* go to Roman Britain, do not despair. Read Rosemary Sutcliff's *The Eagle of the Ninth* from the safety of your own century. You will be transported back in time without any of the usual irritating glitches.

I remember reading this when I was about ten and being entranced by it. Like all wonderful books, this is a story about many things: friendship, the struggles of two cultures to live together, the search for truth about one's family, and growing up and finding your own family in life – the one that is right for you. Plus, it is really exciting. So put that Time Machine back in the garage and read this book!

**Angie Sage**

## Next?

• Try Sutcliff's *Outcast*, a story set in the latter part of the Roman Empire.

• For other, tough history novels, try Henry Treece's *The Horned Helmet* and *The Road to Miklagard*.

• If you like Romans, try Pauline Chandler's *The Mark of Edain*, about Aoife and Madoc, two Roman slaves who dream of escaping to their homeland, Brittania.

• Or for a funny take on the ancient world read Paul Shipton's hilarious *The Pig Scrolls*.

# Top Ten Authors

1. Roald Dahl

2. Jacqueline Wilson

3. Michael Morpurgo

4= Eoin Colfer

4= Anthony Horowitz

6. David Almond

7= Darren Shan

7= Louise Rennison

9. J.K. Rowling

10. Philip Pullman

## EARTHFASTS William Mayne ●●●

Nellie Jack John, the drummer boy, marched into a tunnel in the earth of Yorkshire 200 years ago and was never seen again. So when David and Keith hear the drum and see him emerge into the modern world, they realise something very strange is beginning. A candle that doesn't go out, mysterious moving stones and the theft of all the pigs in the town puzzles them even more. And then David vanishes in a mysterious shaft of lightning, and Keith is left alone.

William Mayne is a wonderful writer, and this has to be one of my favourite books. It's full of loving description of a small rainy Yorkshire town and the fells that surround it, their legends and the area's odd brusque dialect. David and Keith are both very real, and their friendship for each other is clearly conveyed in Mayne's deadpan style. But you'll need to be alert, because this writer often slips things past you without you noticing, and the most astonishing things are told simply. For Mayne the landscape is riddled with its past, and past and present often mesh. This is true also for the two sequels to *Earthfasts* that Mayne wrote many years later.

**Catherine Fisher**

### Next?

• Try the sequels: *Cradlefasts* and *Candlefasts*.

• There are many other great stories by William Mayne; they include *It*, about a girl troubled by a spirit, and *A Grass Rope*, where Mary finds a unicorn's horn which leads her to treasure (*UBG* 137).

• For other time-slip books, try the brilliant *Tom's Midnight Garden* by Philippa Pearce (*UBG* 351) or *A Stitch in Time* by Penelope Lively (*UBG* 325).

# The EARTHSEA trilogy Ursula Le Guin ●●●

Earthsea is a vast group of islands ruled by kings and warlords, but the real power is held by mages – great wizards. These are not beardy types with pointed hats, but immensely wise men who spend years learning their craft. Ged, also known as Sparrowhawk, is a wild and arrogant youth with a gift for magic that he does not understand and cannot control. A dangerous challenge almost costs him his life. Someone else dies in his place and he learns that his gift is also a huge responsibility. As he grows older, he journeys throughout Earthsea meeting with many adventures, and finally becomes Archmage, the supreme wizard. A young prince from a distant kingdom comes to seek his help when a renegade wizard finds a way to cheat death and upsets the balance of nature. Ged must travel to the land of the dead and give up his own powers to make things whole again.

**Jan Mark**

### Next?

• The trilogy consists of *A Wizard of Earthsea*, *The Tombs of Atuan* and *The Farthest Shore*. There are two further novels in the **Earthsea** cycle, *Tehanu* and *The Other Wind*, and a book of Earthsea stories, *Tales from Earthsea*.
• **His Dark Materials** by Philip Pullman is another fantasy trilogy that makes you think. (*UBG* 151)
• *The Blue Hawk* by Peter Dickinson begins with a strange ritual in a far-off land long ago, and tells the story of a boy who dares to break with tradition.

★ ★ ★ ★ ★ ★

# EAST OF MIDNIGHT Tanith Lee ●●●

Tanith Lee's fantasy worlds are so vivid and original that reading her work always feels like an exciting, brand-new experience. This story begins with Zaister, who is the privileged consort to Izvire, the female king. But it's time for someone new to take over, and for Zaister to die. He desperately wants to live and uses magic to swap places with Dekteon, a slave. It seems an easy plan, but the trouble is that Dekteon has kept his own mind, too – and he is stronger than Zaister could ever be. Daringly, he brings huge disruption to Izvire's court. A struggle of identity breaks out between Dekteon and Zaister. Who will triumph, and what will it mean for Izvire's future?

**Jon Appleton**

### Next?

• Look for Tanith Lee's *The Castle of Dark* (*UBG* 55) and the slightly tougher (but utterly brilliant) *Piratica* (*UBG* 270).
• Don't miss Catherine Fisher's books, such as *The Oracle* and the **Snow-walker** trilogy. (*UBG* 318)
• G.P. Taylor's books wrap magic around the battle of good against evil – try *Shadowmancer* first. (*UBG* 307)

# The EDDIE DICKENS trilogy Philip Ardagh

This hilarious series chronicles the bizarre adventures of eleven-year-old Eddie Dickens, and is set in a nineteenth-century world that is a madcap mix of fact and Philip Ardagh's off-the-wall imagination. In *Awful End*, Eddie's parents contract a strange disease that turns them yellow and crinkly round the edges, and he's sent to stay with Mad Uncle Jack (who has a treehouse built of dried fish) and Even Madder Aunt Maud.

Eddie's adventures continue in *Dreadful Acts*, where he narrowly avoids being blown up and arrested, but falls into the clutches of a desperate gang of escaped convicts. Needless to say, he survives, only to be sent to America in the third book to save the family's *Terrible Times* newspaper business – although whether he will actually make it across the Atlantic is another matter...

Philip Ardagh's writing style is unmistakable. He talks directly to you, the reader, and constantly interrupts his own story to tell you amazing facts, awful jokes and share interesting thoughts. Even stranger, his characters know they are in a book and wonder aloud if the author has it in for them. These books are incredibly daft, fantastically funny and completely addictive. You have been warned!

**Kathryn Ross**

## Next?

• Philip Ardagh has also given us **The Further Adventures of Eddie Dickens**, with *Dubious Deeds, Horrendous Habits* and *Final Curtain*.

• Debi Gliori's *Pure Dead Magic* is the first of three very funny books about the Strega-Borgia family, who live in an ancient castle in Scotland. (*UBG* 276)

• And if reading Eddie Dickens has made you want to try some Charles Dickens, then find Marcia Williams's *Mr Charles Dickens and Friends*, a lively comic-strip retelling of five of Dickens's best-known tales. (*UBG* 220)

## Rodent Books

• *Abel's Island* by William Steig
• *The Battle of Bubble and Squeak* by Philippa Pearce
• *The Mouse and His Child* by Russell Hoban
• *Mouse Attack* by Manjula Padma
• *The Song of Pentecost* by W.J. Corbett
• *Mouse Noses on Toast* by Daren King
• *The Mousehunter* by Alex Millway

# The EDGE CHRONICLES Paul Stewart and Chris Riddell

This fabulous fantasy series takes readers into new and amazing worlds. *Beyond the Deepwoods*, the first title, tells the story of Twig, abandoned at birth and brought up by wood trolls, who sets out into the wild world in search of his past.

The story is fast and action-packed and the characters are extraordinary – goblins, trogs, flesh-eating trees and more. The books move on to tell of Twig's dangerous adventures as a sky pirate and of the mysteries, evils and intrigues always to be found in the dangerous floating world of Sanctaphrax.

These books continue to surprise and entertain as new and brilliantly imagined characters join in with the stories. They're given extra wonder by Chris Riddell's intricate and fascinating black-and-white line drawings. The books are a compelling read and great to look at, too!

**Wendy Cooling**

### Next?

• The titles so far include **The Twig Saga** (*Beyond the Deepwoods, Stormchaser* and *Midnight Over Sanctaphrax*), **The Quint Saga** (*The Curse of the Gloamglozer, The Winter Knights* and *Clash of the Sky Galleons*) and **The Rook Saga** (*The Last of the Sky Pirates, Vox* and *Freeglader*).

• If you loved the fantasy element, try *Artemis Fowl* by Eoin Colfer (*UBG* 23) or *Mortal Engines* by Philip Reeve (*UBG* 236), the start of two other brilliant series.

★ ★ ★ ★ ★ ★

# EIGHT DAYS OF LUKE Diana Wynne Jones

### Next?

• This book is based on the Norse legend of Loki, the mischievous trickster god. For another story that uses the same legend, read Patricia Elliott's *The Ice Boy*. (*UBG* 170)

• Joanne Harris's *Runemarks* is another book that takes those legends as inspiration. (*UBG* 291)

• Or try more Diana Wynne Jones. Start with *The Homeward Bounders*. (*UBG* 156)

David's summer holiday looks like it's going to be grim from day one, as he has to spend it with his ghastly relatives who constantly tell him he's horribly ungrateful. Then, accidental magic brings Luke into the picture. Everybody likes Luke, even the ghastly relatives, and David only has to strike a match for Luke to appear. Unfortunately, Luke's family also begins to turn up and events take a sinister turn.

The characters include some seriously eccentric people such as Uncle Bernard and Astrid, who have illness competitions, and Mr Chew, the unnaturally huge gardener with a streak of pure malice.

All Diana Wynne Jones's books are full of humour and this is one of her funniest.

**Gill Vickery**

# THE EIGHTEENTH EMERGENCY Betsy Byars

This American story is set in a landscape of gritty sidewalks, apartment blocks and basketball hoops on walls. Benkie the hero has a habit of labelling things in very small writing. He labels a picture of Neanderthal Man after the school bully. Nobody can help him then – not even his best friend Ezzie, with whom he has already found solutions to 17 life-threatening situations.

Read this book if you have ever been frightened or bullied. You will find it full of useful information and encouragement. Do not read it if you are a bully yourself. It will not increase your self-respect, and you may find yourself having to change your ways.

**Hilary McKay**

### Next?

• Betsy Byars has written dozens of books. Try *The Seven Treasure Hunts* or *The Pinballs*. (*UBG* 268)

• If you like books with an American flavour, you might also enjoy *Dogs Don't Tell Jokes* by Louis Sachar or *The Boy Who Lost His Face* (*UBG* 46).

• Jerry Spinelli is another great American writer; *The Mighty Crashman* is told from a bully's point of view. (*UBG* 228)

★ ★ ★ ★ ★ ★

# ELIDOR Alan Garner

### Next?

• Try Alan Garner's earlier fantasies *The Weirdstone of Brisingamen* (*UBG* 377), *The Moon of Gomrath* or the wonderful *The Owl Service* (*UBG* 258).

• **The Dark is Rising** sequence by Susan Cooper is another brilliant fantasy. (*UBG* 78)

• Or for something really scary, try *The Spook's Apprentice* by Joseph Delaney. (*UBG* 322)

This is a book with fear in it. It's like the dark corner in which something terrible may be lurking; you want to run away, and yet you can't resist having a closer look...

Nicholas, David, Helen and Roland go wandering through Manchester. They find a church that's about to be demolished; hear strange, high music; kick a ball into the church ... and it falls into a different world; a threatened, desperate world called Elidor. The four of them are expected in Elidor, and they save four Treasures, a sword, a spear, a cauldron and a stone, by taking them back into their own world. But danger and sorcery go with them, and the two worlds terrifyingly intermesh. The story leaps between reality and fantasy, as does the magnificent unicorn Findhorn who can save Elidor only through the children, and the climax is as electrifying and heartbreaking as anything you'll ever read.

**Susan Cooper**

# EMIL AND THE DETECTIVES  Erich Kästner

## Next?

• For more child detectives, try Enid Blyton's **The Famous Five** (*UBG* 109), or the stories about her five find-outers in the **Mystery** series.

• *Bambert's Book of Missing Stories* by Reinhardt Jung is another quirky, totally captivating book by a German writer. (*UBG* 27)

• Or there's Chris Riddell's gloriously illustrated story of a girl detective – *Ottoline and the Yellow Cat*. (*UBG* 257)

It all starts because young Emil Tischbein is robbed while he sleeps on board a train. He was right in the middle of a nightmare in which he was facing the consequences of having painted the face on the statue of Grand Duke Charles.

Losing the money is, of course, a disaster, but it's the trigger for the adventure of trying to catch the thief and for us to discover a gangsworth of resourceful young characters setting up the trap. Behind all this, we are treated to an introduction to a Berlin reminiscent of a painter like George Grosz. 'The underground railway rumbled and the noise from the trams and buses and cycles joined together in a wild concert'. Just think, he was celebrating the city even as British children's literature was stuck firmly in Wild Woods, Hundred Acre Woods and Old Brown's Island!

**Michael Rosen**

★ ★ ★ ★ ★ ★

# EMILY OF NEW MOON  L.M. Montgomery

This story is set on an island off the east coast of Canada, about a hundred years ago. Emily, aged ten, is an orphan, taken to live with her relations. They don't particularly want her, but they're stuck with her. Not an unfamiliar plot.

*But* this is a good book! Emily and her wild friend Ilse are a witty, unsentimental pair. The descriptions of the island are vivid. And there's a bit of a tingle, too, an unexplained death and a moment of second sight.

This is a book to read when you are ill, and the weather is bad, and there is nothing but educational documentaries on TV. It is a book to hurl across the floor (Emily's mysterious smile and cloudy hair get a little *too* mysterious and cloudy now and then), but do pick it up again, and straighten out the pages. One rainy day you will want to read more.

**Hilary McKay**

## Next?

• If you want to know what happens to Emily, read *Emily Climbs* and *Emily's Quest* next.

• The **Anne of Green Gables** books are by the same author (but Hilary doesn't think they are as good). (*UBG* 20)

• Try the classic **Katy** books by Susan Coolidge. (*UBG* 378)

• Or for something of Hilary's, try *The Exiles*, which isn't sentimental at all. (*UBG* 104)

# THE ENCHANTED CASTLE  E. Nesbit

Gerald, Kathleen and Jimmy discover a tunnel near the dull town where they are spending the summer holidays. They follow it into mysterious parkland, where statues come alive at night – including a stone dinosaur – and a great house holds a magic ring in a room of jewels.

The ring can grant wishes and make its wearer invisible. But, as the children discover to their cost, it also has a mind of its own...

This story, first published over 100 years ago, may take a little more getting into than stories written today, but it's worth the effort – all E. Nesbit's fantasies sparkle with brilliant, original ideas and unpredictable plots. They are funny as well as magical, and sometimes touched by horror and the surreal. Here, the hideous 'Ugly Wuglies' that come alarmingly to life are amongst the creepiest creations in fiction. And though the children use old-fashioned slang like 'Crikey!' and 'Oh, rot!', they behave just like children nowadays.

**Patricia Elliott**

## Next?
• You might like to try E. Nesbit's *The Phoenix and the Carpet*.
• Or what about *The Cuckoo Clock* by Mrs Molesworth, in which lonely Griselda is taken into strange worlds by the cuckoo from the cuckoo clock?
• Vivien Alcock's *The Stone Walkers* and Jenny Nimmo's *Griffin's Castle* are contemporary novels about statues coming to life.

★ ★ ★ ★ ★ ★

# THE ENDLESS STEPPE  Esther Hautzig

## Next?
• *The Diary of a Young Girl* by Anne Frank, if you haven't read it already. (*UBG* 84)
• *Carrie's War* by Nina Bawden (*UBG* 54) or *When Hitler Stole Pink Rabbit* by Judith Kerr (*UBG* 379), both set during World War II.
• *The Devil's Arithmetic* by Jane Yolen is another moving book on this subject. (*UBG* 83)

Apart from *The Diary of a Young Girl* by Anne Frank, this is probably the finest true account of a war-disrupted childhood ever written. Esther's family lives in happiness and luxury in pre-war Poland, until the Russians take over and banish such 'capitalists' to Siberia. She, her mother, father and grandmother arrive on the Steppe after weeks of comfortless travel by cattle-train. They all have to do hard manual labour in bleak and often freezing conditions, living a life of utter deprivation – yet somehow they survive and retain their humanity. After the Nazis invade Russia, they're no longer prisoners. Esther can go to school, and the totally abnormal somehow comes to seem normal. An astonishing testament to the tenacity and adaptability of human beings, and especially children.

**Lynne Reid Banks**

# ERAGON Christopher Paolini

## Next?

• *Eragon*'s sequels are *Eldest* and *Brisingr*. But you should also try the books where Christopher Paolini found some of his inspiration: J.R.R. Tolkein's *The Hobbit* (*UBG* 154) and *The Lord of the Rings* (*UBG* 211).

• For more thrilling dragon stories try *Dragon Keeper* and its sequels by Carole Wilkinson. There are more thrills in a story set in ancient China, *Dragon Horse* by Peter Ward.

• Or look for Chris d'Lacey's wonderful dragony series, starting with *The Fire Within*. (*UBG* 114)

*Eragon* opens with a storm of magic and mystery involving an Elf, a Shade and a perilous treasure. Then Eragon, an orphan brought up on his uncle's farm, finds a big, beautiful blue stone. The stone, it turns out, is a dragon's egg. When the dragon hatches, she bonds with Eragon. He becomes the first dragonrider to mount the skies since the fall of a mystic warrior brotherhood. Luckily, there's someone watching over him, someone who knows the orphan's true identity and can set him on the path of destiny... If you're a fan of sci-fi and fantasy you'll find this story very familiar, but entertaining. If you're new to dragons, elves, noble gurus and evil empires, it's a good place to start.

**Ann Halam**

★ ★ ★ ★ ★ ★

# ETHEL AND ERNEST Raymond Briggs

Raymond Briggs's strip-cartoon evocation of his parents' life together, from their first meeting in the 1920s when Ethel was a housemaid, through the 1930s, World War II, to their deaths in old age is an extremely touching and warm-hearted story, full of humour and pathos, illustrated with exquisite detail. Let me tell you, it's not often that I finish reading a book hardly able to see it for tears.

Given the popularity and fame of Briggs's other books, I expected to find this in the children's section of my local library when looking for a copy to refresh my memory, but was directed to 'adult autobiographies'. Nothing wrong with that, but I feel children would get just as much out of it as adults. It should definitely be on your shelves, too.

**Michael Lawrence**

## Next?

• For a rather different family story, with more words and fewer pictures, seek out *The Family from One End Street* by Eve Garnett. (*UBG* 109)

• There are other books by Raymond Briggs. Try *When the Wind Blows*, *Fungus the Bogeyman* (*UBG* 121) and *Ug* (*UBG* 360).

• *Farm Boy* by Michael Morpurgo is another book that makes you think about the past.

• Or look for Marjane Satrapi's *Persepolis*, the story in pictures of her life in pre-revolutionary Iran.

# DETECTIVE AND SPY STORIES
## 'I Spy...'
### by Caroline Lawrence

When I was a kid, I was amazed by other people. How did they know how to live in the world? I read books to find out.

My favourite books were detective stories. The detective was an observer – like me – and often a loner. Detectives didn't have to be athletic or good-looking; they just had to be clever.

Sherlock Holmes, for example. He was a brilliant Victorian detective who could look at a person and tell all about them from their gestures, plus the little clues on their hands and clothes.

Or take Nancy Drew, an ordinary American girl who lived in the 1950s and always caught the culprit. I devoured her mysteries. Nancy was clever and brave and could embark on lots of exciting cases because she had no mother and her father was quite absent-minded.

The boy versions of the **Nancy Drew** stories are the **Hardy Boys** or **Biggles** books. Enid Blyton's **Famous Five** books are for boys and girls. The stories in these series are all quite similar, so if you like one you can be sure you'll like the others.

When I decided to write the **Roman Mysteries**, my first thought was: 'The Nancy Drew books meet *Gladiator* the movie'. My girl detective Flavia is clever and brave, with an absent-minded father and no mother, so she can also have exciting adventures. And, like the Famous Five, she has some clever friends and a dog.

Agatha Christie had two great detectives: Miss Marple (an old lady) and Hercule Poirot (a short Belgian). These books are classics and many writers steal from them. Although written for adults they are easy to read and suitable for kids, if somewhat old-fashioned.

### Spies

- *The Recruit* by Robert Muchamore
- Charlie Higson's **Young Bond** series; start with *SilverFin*
- *Nathan Fox: Dangerous Times* by L. Brittney
- Anthony Horowitz's **Alex Rider** series; start with *Stormbreaker*
- **Spy Mice** series by Andrew Cope

For something more modern, try Cornelia Funke's *The Thief Lord*. Or Anthony Horowitz's **Diamond Brothers** series. For a good laugh, try Michael Hoeye's stories about a mouse private eye, starting with *Time Stops for No Mouse*. Or Shoo Rayner's hilarious **The Rex Files**, about a dog detective agency.

Did you know that Philip Pullman has written some historical mysteries with a girl detective? Try *The Ruby in the Smoke*, set in Victorian London. Historical novels (books set in the past) like these make the perfect mystery stories because while the detective is solving the crime, the author is solving the mystery of what it was really like to live in another age.

Then there are spy stories. If the detective is 'the hero who thinks', the spy is 'the hero who acts'. Spies tend to rely on gadgets rather than friends.

The most popular kids' spy series are the **Alex Rider** books by Anthony Horowitz. But there is also a great new series by ex-SAS member Chris Ryan, called **Alpha Force**. Or try the **Outernet** series by Steve Barlow and Steve Skidmore; their space spy stories tie in with a website: you have to go online to get clues and passwords. Finally, there is a good historical novel called *The Spanish Letters* by Mollie Hunter, about a girl spy in sixteenth-century Scotland.

MICHAEL HOEYE

TIME STOPS FOR NO MOUSE

~ A Hermux Tantamoq Adventure ~

## Detectives

- *The Hound of the Baskervilles* by Arthur Conan Doyle
- *The Murder of Roger Ackroyd* by Agatha Christie
- *Emil and the Detectives* by Erich Kästner
- **Nancy Drew Mysteries** by Carolyn Keene
- **The Famous Five** or **The Secret Seven** series by Enid Blyton
- **Hardy Boys** series by Franklin W. Dixon
- **Biggles** series by Captain W.E. Johns
- *Time Stops for No Mouse* by Michael Hoeye
- *The Thief Lord* by Cornelia Funke
- *The Ruby in the Smoke* by Philip Pullman
- **Diamond Brothers** series by Anthony Horowitz
- **Roman Mysteries** series by Caroline Lawrence
- *A Dog Called Grk* by Joshua Doder
- *Chasing Vermeer by* Blue Balliett
- *Half Moon Investigations* by Eoin Colfer

# THE EXILES Hilary McKay

## Next?

• You must read the wonderful books about the Casson family, also by Hilary McKay, starting with *Saffy's Angel* (**UBG** 292); and her book *Dog Friday* – the Robinsons will remind you very much of the Conroys...

• *Little Women* by Louisa M. Alcott is a very different book about four sisters. (**UBG** 208)

• Try the **Ally's World** series by Karen McCombie, for stories about another chaotic family that will make you laugh and cry. **UBG** 14)

Everyone feels sorry for the Conroy sisters. Their parents don't have a car, won't buy a TV and can never afford to go on holiday. But pity is the last thing in the world that Ruth, Naomi, Rachel and Phoebe want. They march defiantly through life, devouring books, arguing constantly and rebelling against every form of authority.

But when they are sent off to stay with Big Grandma for the summer, that is the last straw. 'Big Grandma doesn't like us!' they cry – and they set off mutinously, certain that they're going to have a miserable time.

The Conroy sisters are four of the funniest, most likeable and infuriating characters you're ever likely to read about. And as soon as you've finished *The Exiles*, you'll want to go straight out and find *The Exiles at Home* and *The Exiles in Love*.

**Susan Reuben**

★ ★ ★ ★ ★ ★

# FABLES Aesop

Want to read some of the oldest stories ever told? These fables, written down by Aesop as long ago as the sixth century BC, were probably being told long before that. Ancient they may be, but these stories about the antics of animals and men are every bit as relevant today. Many of them impart a moral, or simple message, usually about foolishness and wisdom. Some of them are amongst the best-known stories of all time: 'The Hare and the Tortoise', 'The Boy who cried Wolf!', 'The Wolf in Sheep's Clothing'. They are all very short – most only a couple of paragraphs, some as short as a line or two – but the best thing about them is their number. There are hundreds of them, and many of the less well-known fables are gems, such as the one about the tortoise who wanted to fly.

**Marcus Sedgwick**

## Next?

• Try a jazzy version of the fables in a retelling by Vivian French called *Aesop's Funky Fables* – it has great illustrations, too! (**UBG** 10)

• Find a good, short version of the oldest written story, the *Epic of Gilgamesh* (try the one by Geraldine McCaughrean, *Gilgamesh the Hero*).

• Or the more modern, and equally wonderful, *How the Whale Became* by Ted Hughes.

# FAERIE WARS  Herbie Brennan

I loved *Faerie Wars* from the first sentence. It starts: 'Henry got up early on the day that changed his life', and just gets better. *Faerie Wars* is a brilliant mixture of fantasy, adventure story and real-life drama.

After being told that his dad's leaving because his mum has met another woman, Henry goes to Mr Fogarty, the cantankerous elderly man he works for, only to find a fairy in the shed. The fairy, Pyrgus, is a full-sized and wingless prince in his own world. He's brave, but never thinks before he acts. (Thankfully, his sister does!) Henry has to defend the faerie world from a diabolical plot, which becomes darker and more sinister as the story unfolds. Henry's parents worry about him, but it's difficult to open up when you've got a world to save, a prince to restore to his throne, and the devil hanging over your very existence.

**Antonia Honeywell**

## Next?

• Try *Mighty Fizz Chilla* by Philip Ridley: a book where, once again, stories interlock and together make something far more exciting. (*UBG* 228)

• Joan Aiken's *Midnight is a Place* is another exciting adventure with more horrible happenings. (*UBG* 227)

• And you have to read the sequels to *Faerie Wars* – *The Purple Emperor*, *Rulers of the Realm* and *Faerie Lord*.

## Witches and Wizards

• **The Worst Witch** series by Jill Murphy
• *Pongwiffy* by Kaye Umansky
• *Lizzie Dripping* by Helen Cresswell
• *Mr Majeika* by Humphrey Carpenter
• *Whispering to Witches* by Anna Dale
• *Witch Child* by Celia Rees
• *The Sword in the Stone* by T.H. White
• **The Dark is Rising** sequence by Susan Cooper
• **Jessica Haggerthwaite** books by Emma Barnes
• **The Worlds of Chrestomanci** series by Diana Wynne Jones

HERBIE BRENNAN

'An astounding blend of fantasy, mythology and science. Brennan is a master of all three' EOIN COLFER

# FAIRY TALES
### Hans Christian Andersen

The fairy tales of Hans Christian Andersen were intensely important to me, and have been a huge influence throughout my life. Mine was a real book: large and heavy with a thick, dark cover and decorative lettering embossed in gold. The pages were thick and creamy white, with clear black print, which seemed to complement the numerous pen-and-ink drawings scattered throughout.

The illustrations by William Heath Robinson were absolutely as much a part of the thrill of this book as the stories themselves. Beneath each illustration, whether a small corner one or a panel in the middle, or a full-scale one in glossy, glorious colour, was always a quote from the story. 'She understood the speech of birds', or '"Yes, I will go with thee," said Tommelise.' These so inspired me, that long before I started writing, I used to draw my own illustrations and write quotes beneath from my non-existent stories.

But it is the power of Andersen's tales which still moves me; I was inspired in childhood to compose an opera about 'The Red Shoes'; I agonised and wept with the Little Mermaid, and was awe-struck by Kay's search for Gerda, which took him to the land of ice and snow and the Northern Lights.

There was never anything cosy about Hans Andersen, but I think he should be a rite of passage that every young reader should experience. It will mark them for life – and for the better.

**Jamila Gavin**

### Next?

• The Puffin edition is probably the best collection of Hans Christian Andersen's tales.

• Try Alan Garner's *Fairy Tales of Gold*.

• Another interesting book to try is *Kate Crackernuts* by K.M. Briggs – a novel based on one of the folk tales in *English Fairy Stories* collected by Joseph Jacobs.

• For a twist on some well-loved tales, try *I Was a Rat!* by Philip Pullman (*UBG* 166), and Roald Dahl's *Revolting Rhymes*.

• You might also enjoy *The Light Princess* (*UBG* 197) and other collections by George MacDonald.

• Oscar Wilde was very influenced by the stories of Hans Christian Andersen. If you like one, you're sure to like the other. Try *The Happy Prince and other stories*. (*UBG* 142)

*Star Title*

## Jacob Ludwig Carl Grimm and Wilhelm Carl Grimm

These are the best-known stories in the history of folk tale and children's reading. Many of the stories, such as 'Rumpelstiltskin' and 'Snow White and the Seven Dwarfs' have become children's classics. People tend to forget that originally the stories were not strictly for children, but belonged to a whole community with connections across Europe and Asia. Among the tales are stories of death and cruelty, but there are also many stories in which the least-regarded child (often a 'simpleton') triumphs through kindness to an old person or an animal, and the simple narratives give power to the good-hearted hero or heroine. By now the tales, often selected and edited, exist in many editions and take many forms.

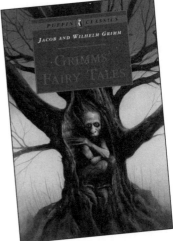

**Margaret Mahy**

## Charles Perrault

Where does the story of 'Cinderella' come from? And what about 'Sleeping Beauty'? From the Disney cartoons? No, long before the Disney versions, these stories came to us from the pen of one Charles Perrault. Perrault was a French writer in the seventeenth century, whose stories would appear in English as the immortal *Mother Goose Tales*. And it isn't just these two classic tales you'll find in Perrault – you'll find canny Puss in Boots here, too, and Bluebeard the wife murderer, trusting Little Red Riding Hood and clever Tom Thumb, as well as many more you've probably never heard of. Tales of ogres and castles and princesses, fairy godmothers and pumpkins and seven-league boots. So much to wonder at, even in the stories you are familiar with. Do you know, for example, what happens *after* the handsome prince wakes up Sleeping Beauty? It gets pretty gruesome, you see, because the handsome prince's mother is an ogress who likes eating beautiful princesses... Brilliant.

**Daniel Hahn**

### And What Else?

• For more folk-tale collections, look at those by Kevin Crossley-Holland, such as *Enchantment: Fairy Tales, Ghost Stories and Tales of Wonder*, or the coloured fairy books by Andrew Lang.

• Or try some new, and very funny, fairy tales by Terry Jones in *Fairy Tales and Fantastic Stories*.

• Other tales that may feel the same are *The Arabian Nights*, and as you read you'll recognise stories that are now used in pantomime. (*UBG* 21)

# THE FALCON'S MALTESER
Anthony Horowitz

## Next?

• There are four more stories about Nick Diamond: *Public Enemy Number Two*, *The French Confection*, *The Blurred Man*, *I Know What You Did Last Wednesday* and *The Greek Who Stole Christmas*.

• Fletcher Moon, who stars in Eoin Colfer's *Half Moon Investigations*, is another schoolboy detective.

• Some more laughs and adventure? Try *Measle and the Wrathmonk* by Ian Ogilvy. (*UBG* 225)

It all begins when a dwarf leaves a package for safe-keeping at the detective agency run by Nick Diamond's extremely dim older brother, Tim. Hours later, the dwarf is dead, Tim is being held at the police station and our hero has to outwit a string of ruthless villains, all in search of the key to Henry von Falkenberg's hidden diamonds.

I can guarantee that you will enjoy this very funny detective thriller in which there is never a dull moment, with laugh-aloud, irreverent jokes on every page. Anthony Horowitz never lets the reader have even the tiniest lull – you really do have to keep turning the page (and laughing).

**Kate Petty**

★ ★ ★ ★ ★ ★

# THE FALL OF FERGAL
Philip Ardagh

Any story that begins with the hero falling out of a window and definitively dying is bound to be a touch different – and this is *very* different. It's one of those books where a lot of the humour lies in the authorial jokes and comments on Fergal's adventures (before he's dead, in case you were wondering); by the end you feel you know Philip Ardagh (and his beard) even better than you know Fergal. (And a very fine thing that is, too.)

The first time I read one of Big Phil's books I got hiccups because I laughed so much. A word of warning, though. This book ends with the hero's brain being... No, read it yourself and find out!

**Vivian French**

## Next?

• When you've chortled your way through *The Fall of Fergal*, there are more **Unlikely Exploits** in *Heir of Mystery* and *The Rise of the House of McNally*. Then read Big Phil's hilariously offbeat **Eddie Dickens** trilogy, beginning with *Awful End*. (*UBG* 96)

• Terry Pratchett is another clever comic writer. Why not try **The Bromeliad** trilogy? (*UBG* 48)

• Enter another world where anything can happen in **The Spiderwick Chronicles** by Holly Black and Tony DiTerlizzi. (*UBG* 321)

# THE FAMILY FROM ONE END STREET  Eve Garnett

The family from One End Street is the Ruggles –
Mum, Dad and seven children: Lily Rose (stout and
helpful), Kate (the brainy one), Jim and John (twins),
Jo, Peg and baby William. With a family as big as that,
it's not surprising they get up to all sort of adventures.

Mr Ruggles is a dustman, Mrs Ruggles is a
washerwoman, and they live in the little town of
Otwell, somewhere between London and the sea.
You'll not only love the characters and the humour
in this classic, but you'll also enjoy finding out about
how ordinary people lived in the 1930s, and the
trouble the children managed to get into. Each chapter
tells a story in itself. Find out what Lily Rose did when
she managed to destroy an artificial silk petticoat, or
what happened when Jim and John join the Gang of
the Black Hand.

**Sherry Ashworth**

### Next?
• There are two more
books about the
Ruggles – *Further
Adventures of the
Family from One End
Street* and *Holiday at
Dew Drop Inn*.

• If you like books set in
the not-too-distant past,
try Bill Naughton's *The
Goalkeeper's Revenge*.

• Or *Stig of the Dump*
by Clive King, which is
a bit less old-fashioned,
and very readable.
(*UBG* 325)

\* \* \* \* \* \*

# THE FAMOUS FIVE series  Enid Blyton

### Next?
• Other Blyton? Along
with **The Famous Five**
and **The Secret Seven**
(*UBG* 303) there is the
**Adventure** series (*UBG*
177), the **Malory
Towers** series (*UBG* 218)
and the **St Clare's**
series.

• Don't miss Louise
Fitzhugh's *Harriet the
Spy* for a different kind
of detective. (*UBG* 144)

• Want a change? *The
Saturdays* by Elizabeth
Enright is perfect.
(*UBG* 295)

It was Enid Blyton who got me hooked on books.
People can be a bit snotty about her, but she helped
me escape from a drab room in a drab house. She
smuggled my imagination down secret passageways.
With her help, I discovered hidden tunnels and
mysterious caves. I spied on robbers and solved
mysteries the grown-ups were too dim to know about!

Her writing might have been awful, repetitive and
clumsy, but I didn't know that back then, and if I
had I wouldn't have cared. She sat down with her
prejudices; her unsophisticated formulae for stories;
her unrealistic, wooden, middle-class characters;
her stereotyped villains; and she did what far better
writers failed to do. She transported us kids beyond
the reaches of school time and bedtime and the thou-
shalt-not world of grown-ups. Would I have become
addicted to books without her? I very much doubt it.

**Brian Patten**

# FANTASTIC MR FOX  Roald Dahl

This book is my favourite Dahl because our children adored it. It's got something very important to the success of any book: a really horrible villain, multiplied by three. Boggis, Bunce and Bean are farmers, and they are truly revolting. They're described in loving detail, right down to things like earwax. Mr Fox, his wife and the small foxes do battle with all three of them, and guess who comes out a winner in the end?

The book finishes with a splendid banquet in which the Foxes invite the other animals to join the feast. The illustrations by Quentin Blake add greatly to the fun and there are many moving and exciting moments along the way. This book is rightly known as a classic.

**Adèle Geras**

### Next?
• *George's Marvellous Medicine* (*UBG* 123) and *The Twits* (*UBG* 359), which are both Dahl classics as well.

• You also might enjoy *How Tom Beat Captain Najork and His Hired Sportsmen* by Russell Hoban.

• Ian Whybrow's *Little Wolf's Book of Badness* is spot-on for laughs and a great story and it has lots of sequels. (*UBG* 207)

\* \* \* \* \* \*

# THE FARTHEST-AWAY MOUNTAIN  Lynne Reid Banks

### Next?
• L. Frank Baum's *The Wizard of Oz* (*UBG* 390) and Lewis Carroll's *Alice's Adventures in Wonderland* (*UBG* 13) both have brave, bright heroines who set out on incredible journeys.

• If tomboys appeal, you may like Princess Amy in M.M. Kaye's *The Ordinary Princess* (*UBG* 254) or Petrova Fossil in *Ballet Shoes* by Noel Streatfeild (*UBG* 28).

• Want to try another story by Lynne Reid Banks? Go for the much-loved *The Indian in the Cupboard* and then track down the sequels. (*UBG* 173)

Dakin is nearly 15 and lives happily with her family in the valley of the Farthest-away Mountain. Dakin is determined to have adventures. From her bedroom the mountain looks quite close, its peaks capped with green, purple and pink snow. No one knows why the snow isn't white, and when the mountain summons her, Dakin does not know why she is wanted. But she understands that the mysterious journey is her destiny, and sets off on a terrifying adventure, encountering trolls, gargoyles and an ogre, before uncovering the evil secret that enslaves the mountain and all who live there...

There are chilling baddies, loveable goodies, passwords and poems, a wicked wood and a sea of spikes. Dakin is a feisty, no-nonsense heroine who embraces her challenges with refreshing good humour.

**Francesca Lewis**

# FATTYPUFFS AND THINIFERS André Maurois

Two brothers discover a secret escalator that takes them to the Country Under The Earth, land of the Fattypuffs and Thinifers. The Fattypuffs are easygoing, lazy and adore food. The Thinifers, on the other hand, are tetchy, hard-working and scarcely eat a thing. Sad to say, these two contrasting nations are both foolish and stubborn enough to let a silly dispute between them develop into a full-scale war. Can Edmund and Terry find a way to bring it to an end?

André Maurois tells a clever, witty and thought-provoking tale, but what makes this book extra special are Fritz Wegner's glorious illustrations which, with their detail, humour and charm, bring alive the eccentric Fattypuffs and Thinifers in a way that means you'll never ever forget them.

**Nick Sharratt**

### Next?

• To see more of Fritz Wegner's wonderful illustrations, try *The Giant Baby* by Allan Ahlberg.

• For something equally hilarious, try the **Professor Branestawm** books by Norman Hunter, about an absent-minded professor who always gets into terrible scrapes. (*UBG* 275)

• Or the totally wild and wacky *The Great Piratical Rumbustification* and *The Librarian and the Robbers*, from the wonderful Margaret Mahy. (*UBG* 138)

• For another librarian, try Eoin Colfer's *The Legend of Spud Murphy*. (*UBG* 197)

★ ★ ★ ★ ★ ★

# FEATHER BOY Nicky Singer

Robert is a tormented boy. In school, the mean and clever bully, Niker, is always on his case. Outside, he's troubled by the ghosts of an old lady's childhood. The ghosts lead Robert and Niker to Chance House, an old haunted ruin, scene of their chilling showdown.

And there are the feathers! If Robert makes a coat of feathers, he thinks the old lady won't die. But life is not that simple.

This book will make you laugh and cry, as well as giving you the creeps. You have to read it, if only to find out what happened during the grape incident! You might end up running to the toilet to be sick!

**Shoo Rayner**

### Next?

• You might like *Skellig* by David Almond. There's a lot going on in Michael's life, too. He's just moved house and found someone strange living in the garage! Angel or devil – who knows? (*UBG* 313)

• There's strangeness, humour and adventure in Henry Porter's *The Master of the Fallen Chairs*. (*UBG* 223)

• For a ghost story with a difference, try Brian Keaney's *The Haunting of Nathaniel Wolfe*.

• Or for another Nicky Singer, try the darker and tougher, *Doll*.

# FERGUS CRANE
## Paul Stewart and Chris Riddell

**Next?**

• *Fergus Crane* is the first in a series of **Far-Flung Adventures**, so why not try *Corby Flood* and *Hugo Pepper* next?

• There are more great books by Stewart and Riddell. Try *Free Lance and the Lake of Skulls* or *Barnaby Grimes: The Curse of the Nightwolf*.

• And if you enjoyed this book then why not try a different kind of illustrated zany adventure: *The Phantom Tollbooth* by Norton Juster. (*UBG* 266)

If you think *your* teachers are strange, you clearly have not met Fergus Crane's. Your school is probably not quite as odd as the school ship *Betty Jeanne*. Fergus's life is set to become stranger still and much more exciting when a flying message box comes to his bedroom window. Soon he is soaring through the air himself, riding a mechanical flying horse over the mountains in search of his long-lost uncle Theo and some very helpful penguins. But can Fergus save his schoolmates from the black-hearted pirate, Captain Claw, and the perils of Fire Island? Beautifully written and wonderfully illustrated as always, this is another lovely book from the Stewart and Riddell partnership.

**Chris Priestley**

★ ★ ★ ★ ★ ★

# FIGHTING FANTASY Steve Jackson and Ian Livingstone

Do you ever wish you could choose the way a story goes? Well, with the **Fighting Fantasy** books you are the main character, and you can do just that – though be warned: although you can decide where to go and what to do next, you can't predict what will happen once you've done it!

In each book you are an explorer, setting off on an intrepid adventure. You have constant choices: 'Will you: Drink the red liquid? Turn to p. 98. Or leave the chamber to continue west? Turn to p. 83.' Each decision could bring instant death, or the accumulation of riches that will help you further along the route.

There are many monsters to battle on the way (with throws of the dice predicting who wins) and only one true path to the end of your quest. You'll have to embark on the adventure again and again before you find the way through!

**Susan Reuben**

**Next?**

• For other books that use gaming as part of their plots, read Diana Wynne Jones's *The Homeward Bounders* (*UBG* 156) and Terry Pratchett's *Only You Can Save Mankind*.

• Or try Alan Gibbons's **Legendeer** trilogy, starting with *The Shadow of the Minotaur*.

• Christopher Paolini's *Eragon* reads like a huge, thrilling adventure game. (*UBG* 101)

# FIRE, BED AND BONE Henrietta Branford

To a fourteenth-century peasant farmer, a dog was a very important possession. Taking one such dog – an old hunting bitch – as its central character, this story views the world from her perspective, as a revolt against the tyranny of the Church and powerful landlords sweeps through England's poorest communities.

The old bitch's faithfulness to the family she grew up with proves stronger than anything circumstance can hurl at her. Her pregnancy, the arrest of her owners, being kidnapped and forced into service by evil people, and much, much more – through it all her instinct and unerring sense of loyalty carries her through. A masterpiece of storytelling – powerful and deeply moving.

**Neil Arksey**

**Next?**
• Henrietta Branford also wrote a book about a wolf: *White Wolf*.
• Melvin Burgess's *The Cry of the Wolf*, in which the hunter and the hunted shift roles, is another brilliant book.
• Or perhaps you want more fantasy mixed with your animals? Try the **Redwall** series by Brian Jacques. (*UBG* 282)

# THE FIRE-EATERS David Almond

**Next?**
• More David Almond, especially *Skellig* (*UBG* 313) and *Kit's Wilderness* (*UBG* 192).
• Stephen Baxter's *The H-Bomb Girl* is set at the same period of history. The author famously writes hard-edged sci-fi for adults, but this time-travel / sci-fi / thriller is great for anyone.
• Lloyd Jones's *Mr Pip* – about the power of books and the terrible consequences of conflict – is a book in which the war has already started.

This is not an easy book. Violence is there on every page: in the imminent threat of nuclear war; in a fawn harried by dogs; in a school where pain and humiliation are everyday; in friendship; in the wheezing breath of Bobby's dad; and most of all in the story of McNulty, who came home from the war in Burma a broken man, and who eats fire, wraps himself in chains and runs skewers bloodily through his own cheeks for money.

Set in October 1962, when the world expected to be blown to smithereens in a single night, this is the story of Bobby and those around him. In some ways it is a history book, but in reality it is timeless. And more harrowing than the printed word has the right to be.

**Leonie Flynn**

THE FIRE EATERS
DAVID 'Masterful' FINANCIAL TIMES
ALMOND

# THE FIRE WITHIN  Chris d'Lacey

Do you believe in dragons? David had never thought that dragons could be real – never in a million years. Not ever. Until he went to live with Mrs Pennykettle and her daughter Lucy and found out that all kinds of things could be true.

The Pennykettles, you see, make pottery dragons. Very beautiful dragons with intelligent faces and spines and wings and big, padded feet. In their house there are dragons everywhere, on every shelf, even on the cistern (David has to turn that one away before he can use the loo). Some of the dragons are very special, as David finds out when the Pennykettles make him his own pottery dragon (whom he calls Gadzooks), and he learns how to find the spark of light in the heart of the dragon that responds to being loved.

**Leonie Flynn**

### Next?
• This series just gets better and better! You have to read on to the rest – *Icefire*, *Fire Star* and *The Fire Eternal*.
• If you liked the idea of something becoming real, try *Manxmouse* by Paul Gallico.
• Or try *Pinocchio*, a very well-known film but an even better book by Carlo Collodi. (*UBG* 269)
• Another great title by Chris d'Lacey is *The Salt Pirates of Skegness*, hilariously funny and very touching, too.

★ ★ ★ ★ ★ ★

# THE FIREWORK-MAKER'S DAUGHTER  Philip Pullman

### Next?
• Read more Philip Pullman – try *Spring-Heeled Jack: a Story of Bravery and Evil*, a fast and funny tale of three defenceless little orphans, or *I Was a Rat!* (*UBG* 166).
• Another spirited character who doesn't give up on her dreams is in *Matilda* by Roald Dahl. (*UBG* 224)
• Another girl on a quest to stay in her family's business is Madeline, daughter of a fan-maker impoverished by a world turned cold. Her adventures are told in Alex Williams's *The Storm Maker*.

Lila lives 'a thousand miles ago, in a country east of the jungle and south of the mountains'. Motherless, she has grown up among the fizz and crackle of her Firework-Maker father's work. Lila's greatest wish is to become a Firework-Maker, too, but her father thinks it's no job for a girl. So Lila must undertake a quest to discover the secrets of the sacred art of firework-making for herself; a difficult, dangerous quest which brings her face to face with Razvani, the terrifying Fire-Fiend...

The world of a Firework-Maker explodes from the page in this exciting story – you can almost smell the gunpowder! Lila's adventure will inspire you to have the courage to fight for the life that you want and to live your own dream.

**Julie Bertagna**

# FISH NOTES AND STAR SONGS  Dianne Hofmeyr  ● ● ●

## Next?

• Dianne Hofmeyr has written several other stories set in Africa. Try *The Waterbearer*, or her more recent novel of ancient Egypt, *Eye of the Moon*.

• For more about the lives of early people, try **The Kin** quartet by Peter Dickinson, about a group of children who must travel to find a home in a new land; or my own story of survival in the Ice Age, *Maroo of the Winter Caves*.

This story, set in Africa, is about the power of the spirit. Four children, each damaged by suffering or loss, must overcome their fear in order to free both themselves and others in the past. In a deep cave, they come upon a chamber full of ancient rock paintings and the body of a man laid to rest there long ago. Jonah, a descendant of this man, helps the others to discover their spirit animals and embark on a challenging journey into the past.

Beautifully written, and full of images of the natural world, this is a story that will make you think and dream. If you fall under its spell, you're sure to want to read it more than once.

**Ann Turnbull**

★ ★ ★ ★ ★ ★

# FIVE CHILDREN AND IT  E. Nesbit  ● ●

E. Nesbit's novels were among the great solaces and imagination-stirrers of my childhood. I read most of her books before the age of 12 (I seem to remember regretting having to put her behind me because I was getting 'too old'). Of all her books, *Five Children and It* and its two sequels, *The Phoenix and the Carpet* and *The Story of the Amulet*, are the ones I loved best. Amongst the most truly 'magical' stories ever written, these three may be read in any order, but they constitute a trilogy, in which five Edwardian siblings embark upon a series of astonishing adventures in time and reality – themes which fascinate me to this day.

E. Nesbit's stories will seem very old-fashioned to modern readers, but they are as much of their time as books currently being produced, which will inevitably seem just as dated a century hence. And those who enjoy eccentric, wholly original characters need look no further than the opinionated Phoenix and Psammead in these three books.

**Michael Lawrence**

## Next?

• *The Story of the Treasure Seekers* is another wonderful E. Nesbit tale. Or if you fancy something with less fantasy, try **The Railway Children** (*UBG* 279).

• C.S. Lewis admired E. Nesbit's work and there are nods to her work in **The Magician's Nephew**. (*UBG* 198)

• Take a look at my **The Griffin and Oliver Pie**. My favourite E. Nesbit stories were very much in mind when I created my griffin (whom I love to bits).

# FLOODLAND  Marcus Sedgwick

### Next?

• *Floodland* was Marcus's first novel. He has gone on to write many other wonderful novels including *The Dark Horse* (*UBG* 79), *My Swordhand is Singing* (*UBG* 245) and *The Book of Dead Days*.

• Try Jill Paton Walsh's *Gaffer Sampson's Luck*, which is set in the same region. (*UBG* 122)

• Or for more global catastrophe, try *Life As We Knew It* by S.B. Pfeffer, which is all about the end of the world as we know it.

In this science-fiction story, a disastrous flood leaves most of England underwater and turns Norwich into an island. Zoe, left behind in the confusion when her parents are rescued, finds an old rowing boat and bravely sets out on a quest to find her lost family. Her journey takes her to Eel Island, run entirely by children, from which she realises she must escape if she is to succeed in her quest.

I first came across this book while judging the Branford Boase Award in 2001 (which it won!), and I was immediately drawn into Zoe's adventure. You'll find a flood story in almost every people's history (there's one in the Bible – Noah's Ark). The difference here is that Zoe's flood happens in our future.

**Katherine Roberts**

★ ★ ★ ★ ★ ★

# FLOUR BABIES  Anne Fine

Simon Martin belongs to class 4C. How to describe class 4C? Let's just say they are the class that has trouble focusing, working, or even listening.

When the science fair arrives, 4C pick the project called 'Flour Babies'. Each child must have his own six-pound flour baby, and care for it at all times. The 'baby' can't get heavier or lighter and must be kept clean. As time goes on Simon (who has never got involved in anything at school before) becomes very attached to his flour baby, and he starts asking his mum questions about himself as a baby. He realises how difficult it must have been for his mum being single with all the responsibility he brought.

*Flour Babies* is riotously funny, perceptive and moving. At the end of the book, my son and I both wanted our own flour baby.

**Jackie Kay**

### Next?

• Anne Fine is one of the best and least compromising writers around. Read a selection; there's bound to be something you'll adore. Start with *The Book of the Banshee* or *Goggle-Eyes* (*UBG* 130).

• You also might enjoy *There's a Boy in the Girls' Bathroom* by Louis Sachar. (*UBG* 344)

• Another boy who finds he has to grow up pretty quickly is Dylan in Frank Cottrell Boyce's funny and endearing *Framed*. (*UBG* 119)

# FLY BY NIGHT Frances Hardinge ● ● ●

Mosca Mye. What a great character. Brought up in the grim, marshy village of Chough, this feisty 12-year-old escapes and finds herself on the road to Mandelion with silver-tongued swindler Eponymous Clent and a homicidal goose called Saracen. And what happens next? Theft, murder, prison breaks, floating coffee houses, secret printing presses, warring factions, a mad duke, locksmiths, Birdcatchers, imaginary marriages, lots of little gods, very dangerous radical books, a crocodile, and much more.

An exciting and original adventure yarn, this is also a beautiful and vivid piece of writing produced by Frances Hardinge in superb and distinctive style; it's been a long time since I've been this sorry for a book to end. I hope we'll see much more of Mosca Mye.

**Daniel Hahn**

## Next?

• Frances Hardinge is also author of the deeply sinister tale of **Verdigris Deep**, in which a minor theft has vast consequences for two friends. (*UBG* 368)

• Another writer who conjures whole worlds intact is Philip Reeve. Try **Larklight** (*UBG* 196) or the fabulous **Mortal Engines** (*UBG* 236) and its sequels.

• Joan Aiken writes in a gentle way about appalling things. She also twists history – try **The Wolves of Willoughby Chase**. (*UBG* 391)

## Ten Books About Animals as Real Animals (not talking, wearing clothes, driving cars, etc)

• *Tarka the Otter* by Henry Williamson
• *The Call of the Wild* by Jack London
• *The Peppermint Pig* by Nina Bawden
• *National Velvet* by Enid Bagnold
• *White Fang* by Jack London
• *The Silver Brumby* by Elyne Mitchell
• *The Midnight Fox* by Betsy Byars
• *My Family and Other Animals* by Gerald Durrell
• *Black Beauty* by Anna Sewell
• *Blitzcat* by Robert Westall

# FOLLOW ME DOWN   Julie Hearn

Tom comes to stay at his grandmother's house by Smithfield Market, in the City of London. Down in the cellar he discovers 'the gap', a way into the past, and when he crosses it he finds himself in eighteenth-century London with a group of people who are exhibited as monsters in a freak show. Although they are wretched and ill-treated, they need Tom's help, not for themselves, but to rescue the bones of a 'Giant' from a doctor who will put them on public display.

Tom's mother is suffering from cancer. She may recover, but not because of anything he can do. Still, he can help his new friends, who may look strange, but are ordinary people – kind and generous.

**Jan Mark**

## Next?

• What about a boy who can travel back to an imaginary Italian city, one very like Venice, called Bellezza, in Mary Hoffman's **Stravaganza** sequence? (*UBG* 334)

• Leon Garfield is a writer who makes you very glad to live now and not then; his books about low-life in eighteenth- and nineteenth-century London include *Smith* (*UBG* 315), *Jack Holborn* and *Mr Corbett's Ghost*.

• Try two of Sally Prue's novels. *Cold Tom* (*UBG* 67) and *Ryland's Footsteps* are both wonderfully strange stories about outsiders.

★ ★ ★ ★ ★ ★

# FOOTBALL FEVER   edited by Tony Bradman

## Next?

• Try other collections of football stories – there are good ones by Gary Lineker, Michael Hardcastle, Alan Durant, Rob Childs and Terence Blacker.

• Try Neil Arksey's *MacB*, in which an old Scottish legend gets re-enacted on the football pitch. (*UBG* 215)

• Or *The Table Football League* by Chris d'Lacey – a light, fun read.

• A series that's about football – and a whole lot of adventure – starts with *The Kick Off* by Dan Freedman.

Here are three volumes of excellent football stories. It is the variety and broad range of authors that makes the **Football Fever** books such a pleasure to read (and I declare an interest here – there's even one by me!). The emphasis is on good, original stories, well told, and in addition to the expected names there are, refreshingly, writers you won't find anywhere else.

Football-mad boys and girls will gobble up this feast of stories about others like them around the world, playing their favourite sport. The variety and power of the stories in these collections is such that even those who do not consider themselves fans of football may find themselves won over by the magical allure of the beautiful game.

**Neil Arksey**

# FRAMED  Frank Cottrell Boyce

Dylan Hughes knows his village of Manod in North Wales is a wonderful place to live. But Manod is in decline, people are leaving, the family's petrol station is losing money, and Dylan has no one to play football with. Then the National Gallery decides to store famous paintings in Manod's disused slate quarry. Can Dylan and his sister save the family business by stealing a painting? What follows is a story full of twists and turns, with some funny and surprising revelations.

I love this book. It's a laugh-out-loud story about community life and the transforming power of art. You'll want to share it with everyone you know. Don't forget to let the adults in your life read it, too.

**Ann Turnbull**

### Next?

• If you liked *Framed*, you're sure to enjoy another Frank Cottrell Boyce book. Try *Cosmic*. (*UBG* 73)

• For a collection of stories about a boy who always does the wrong thing while trying to help, you can't beat *Just William* and the other **William** books by Richmal Crompton. (*UBG* 186)

• Helena Pielichaty and Hilary McKay both write warm and funny stories of everyday life. Try the **After School Club** series by Helena Pielichaty.

★ ★ ★ ★ ★ ★

# FRANK AND THE BLACK HAMSTER OF NARKIZ
## Livi Michael

### Next?

• Frank's story continues in *Frank and the Chamber of Fear* and *Frank and the Flames of Truth*.

• For more rodents, try *The Rescuers* by Margery Sharp. (*UBG* 283)

• Or what about the daring adventures of **Spy Mice** by Heather Vogel Frederick; they start with *The Black Paw*, *Goldwhiskers* and *For Your Paws Only*.

There are all kinds of hamster, just like there are all kinds of person. Some hamsters are friendly, some are fierce, some are courageous and some (like poor, trembling George) are very nervous indeed. Frank is definitely the brave sort of hamster – probably the bravest of the four that live on Bright Street. But will he be able to live up to his motto ('Courage!') when the mysterious Black Hamster starts calling him? Will he be brave enough to follow? Even if it means leaving his cage and venturing out into The Wild?

Livi Michael has a hamster called Frank and wrote this first brilliant book introducing him and his friends to us; she thought Frank's adventures were worth telling us about. Personally, I think she's right and I'm sure you will, too.

**Daniel Hahn**

# FREAK THE MIGHTY Rodman Philbrick ● ● ●

## Next?

• Rodman Philbrick's *The Last Book in the Universe* is set in a post-apocalyptic world and all about an epileptic boy called Spaz.

• In *The Great Harlequin Grim*, Glenn and his father move to the Lake District, and there he meets hostility, a boy giant who lives in a shack, his first love and a great deal of cruelty.

• *The Thing With Finn* is about a boy's journey to find out what happened to his brother. (*UBG* 346)

Kevin (a.k.a. Freak) is very small and sickly and knows lots of big words; Maxwell (a.k.a. Max, or Kicker) is big and strong, and doesn't understand half of what Kevin is saying. Each has his strengths and weaknesses. But together they can be 'Freak the Mighty' – a hybrid eighth-grader who goes on thrilling imaginary quests, and can outrun and outsmart just about anybody. Their first year together is full of adventure and fun. But things are bound to get harder when Maxwell's father gets out of prison...

*Freak the Mighty* is a beautiful laugh-and-cry story of one unique friendship, and a moving and hilarious reminder of why friendship matters. A very special book, about two very special people and how they transform each other's lives.

**Daniel Hahn**

★ ★ ★ ★ ★ ★

# FRINDLE Andrew Clements ● ●

Of all the books I've read this year, *Frindle* is the best. I loved everything about it. It's priceless. It all begins with Nick's school report on how dictionaries are made. He pesters Mrs Granger: 'I still don't get the idea of why words all mean different things. Like, who says that d-o-g means the thing that goes "woof" and wags its tail? Who says so?' She answers: 'Who says dog means dog? You do, Nicholas. You and me and everyone in this class and this school and this town and this country.' And from that moment Nick is determined that he can get people using a new word if he tries. By calling a pen a 'frindle', and persuading his friends to do the same, and more people, and more, he's sure he can do it.

I laughed loads as I read this, and really, really wanted Nick to make it. And I readily confess to a big old lump in my throat at the end... I really can't convey how good, how unique it is in a few words, but just try it and you'll see.

**Daniel Hahn**

## Next?

• *School Story* is another good Andrew Clements title, as is *A Week in the Woods*.

• Or you could try *Loser* by Jerry Spinelli. (*UBG* 212)

• Don't miss my most favourite troublemaker story of them all – *The Turbulent Term of Tyke Tiler*. (*UBG* 357)

# FUNGUS THE BOGEYMAN
## Raymond Briggs

Fungus the Bogeyman lives deep underground in a damp, slimy place called Bogeydom. Bogeys love the things that humans hate. They like to be cold and wet and smelly. They like their bedclothes to be dirty. They eat things like Flaked Corns and Golden Waxy Bits. They brush their teeth with stuff to make them go black and they wear wellies full of dirty water to stop their feet drying out. At night, Bogeymen come up into our world to frighten us. They make tiles fall off the roof, they hide under our beds and pull the covers off.

This is a wonderful picture book that is even *more* wonderful because when it came out, a lot of adults thought it was disgusting and some schools even banned it. Of course, that was a while ago, but it is still a really funny, wonderfully disrespectful book that you should read over and over again.

**Colin Thompson**

### Next?

• There are more Raymond Briggs books to look out for: *Ug* (*UBG* 360), about a caveman, or *Father Christmas* (about Father Christmas – but not as anyone else has ever seen him) are both great.

• Or what about something else wonderfully disgusting? Look for the **Dirty Bertie** series by Alan MacDonald, illustrated by David Roberts.

• Or what about some disgusting trolls? (Well, they do eat toe-cheese!) Try David Melling's brilliantly illustrated *Stone Goblins*.

## The Ultimate Readers' Poll

# Top Ten Sad Books

1. The Diary of a Young Girl by Anne Frank
2. A Series of Unfortunate Events by Lemony Snicket
3. Goodnight Mr Tom by Michelle Magorian
4. Black Beauty by Anna Sewell
5. Vicky Angel by Jacqueline Wilson
6. The Cat Mummy by Jacqueline Wilson
7. Private Peaceful by Michael Morpurgo
8. Born to Run by Michael Morpurgo
9. Call of the Wild by Jack London
10. Knight's Fee by Rosemary Sutcliff

# GAFFER SAMSON'S LUCK

## Jill Paton Walsh

James and his parents have just moved from the Yorkshire Dales to the bleak, flat East Anglian Fens – a contrast that does not at first appeal. But then James makes a friend of Gaffer Samson, an old local man who, believing himself to be on his last legs, asks him to find his 'luck' (an ancient stone) which the Gaffer has lost and without which he feels unable to die peacefully. So James's adventure begins. In the company of village outcast, Angey, he goes in search of Gaffer Samson's luck, and in so doing learns more about the village and the landscape than he thought at the start he would ever want to know. The descriptions of the Fens are evocative, vivid and true. An undervalued classic.

**Michael Lawrence**

### Next?

• I also recommend *Tom's Midnight Garden* by Philippa Pearce. (*UBG* 351) This, too, is set in the Fens and, like *Gaffer Samson's Luck*, includes a visit to Ely.

• Another very good Jill Paton Walsh book is *The Dolphin Crossing*, about two boys and the retreat from Dunkirk. (*UBG* 89)

★ ★ ★ ★ ★ ★

# THE GAUNTLET

## Ronald Welch

### Next?

• For another dream-like time-travelling story, try *Tom's Midnight Garden*. (*UBG* 351) Like *The Gauntlet*, it's a beautiful mixture of feelings of discovery and loss.

• Or try the very spooky **Earthfasts** series. (*UBG* 94)

• If you like feeling as though you're back in time, try *The Wool-Pack* by Cynthia Harnett (*UBG* 392) or *Cue for Treason* by Geoffrey Trease (*UBG* 76).

On holiday in South Wales, Peter Staunton finds a gauntlet which, local legend claims, can raise 600-year-old ghosts. But the gauntlet does more than that; it transports Peter to the fourteenth century, where he is Peter de Blois, son of Lord Roger de Blois, with a lot to learn. (His modern ideas about spelling also leave much to be desired.) As time goes by, it all seems less and less like a dream…

This is a thrilling story, bursting with fascinating medieval detail and great adventure, and seen, often humorously, through the eyes of a twentieth-century boy who cannot help but make the odd comparison and find 'the fourteenth century an evil-smelling world at the best of times'. I loved it as a boy, and still do!

**Simon Puttock**

# GEORGE'S MARVELLOUS MEDICINE

## Roald Dahl

### Next?

• Roald Dahl's funny lists also reminded me of the Emergencies in Betsy Byars's *The Eighteenth Emergency*. (*UBG* 98)

• Something that happens to Grandma may remind you of what happens to Alice in *Alice's Adventures in Wonderland* by Lewis Carroll. (*UBG* 13)

• You'll find a very different (but equally gruesome) sort of gran in Anthony Horowitz's *Granny*.

• When I was young I really loved the **Nurse Matilda** books by Christianna Brand. Nurse Matilda is a stern nanny who comes to look after some very naughty children.

Most grandmothers are lovely, kind and helpful... But not this one.

Poor George, aged eight, is left alone with his 'grizzly grunion of a grandmother'. Hoping to get her to explode, he mixes up his Marvellous Medicine. You'll need to read the book to find out the very funny list of ingredients, but it includes 'NEVERMORE PONKING DEODORANT SPRAY' and horse pills 'FOR HORSES WITH HOARSE THROATS'. The drawings of what happens to Grandma when she drinks the Medicine are hilarious.

And the story doesn't end there. What happens when George tries out his concoctions on the farmyard animals will make you laugh out loud.

**Jane Darcy**

★ ★ ★ ★ ★ ★

# GEORGIE

## Malachy Doyle

Georgie is in care. Life has robbed him of a voice. He shuts people out, shrinking into a brutal world of his own. In the novel, another boarder and a care worker try to get through to Georgie. In other hands this story would sound preachy, but Malachy Doyle pulls it off triumphantly. It is sensitively written and exciting, classic storytelling.

Malachy himself says it was difficult to give a voice to someone who is voiceless. By concentrating on Georgie and allowing the reader to see through his eyes, he succeeds in giving his readers a tautly written, emotional masterpiece.

**Alan Gibbons**

### Next?

• Malachy Doyle's second novel is *Who is Jesse Flood?* (*UBG* 382)

• *Up on Cloud Nine* by Anne Fine is a deeply moving story of two friends. (*UBG* 364)

• Want something very different? Try *Martyn Pig* by Kevin Brooks, about a boy who... No, I can't spoil it for you. Just go ahead and read it – you won't be disappointed.

# THE GHOST BEHIND THE WALL  Melvin Burgess

## Next?

• Try Melvin Burgess's *An Angel for May*, in which Tam is zoomed back in time to World War II. (*UBG* 18)

• You'll find another twist on the classic ghost story in *The Ghost of Grania O'Malley* by Michael Morpurgo.

• Anne Fine's *The Granny Project* is a book that will make you think about your relationship with your grandma and what happens when she can't cope on her own.

It is a Tuesday when 12-year-old David, bored and at home on his own after school, first discovers he can get behind the walls of the very ordinary tower block he lives in with his dad. The ventilation shaft gives him the perfect opportunity to have a bit of fun; from then on, he leads a secret life, getting up to lots of mischief spying on his neighbours and discovering their secrets – old Mr Hadrian, Miss Turner the teacher, baby Georgie and old Mr Alveston who has Alzheimer's and thinks David is a ghost. But when Mr Alveston's flat is vandalised, David gets the blame – and comes face to face with a ghost himself...

This is a gripping, absolutely original page-turner about the developing friendship of a young boy and an old man. It's frightening and funny and makes you understand how people with Alzheimer's must really feel. It'll change the way you look at old people for ever and leave you with plenty to think about.

**Eileen Armstrong**

★ ★ ★ ★ ★ ★

# THE GHOST DRUM  Susan Price

Told almost like a folk tale by a learned storytelling cat, and set in the freezing snow of the far north, this is the story of the young son of the Czar Safa who is kept imprisoned in a tower room. Only the witch-girl Chingis can hear his cries and help him. But two people threaten them: Margaretta, Safa's evil aunt who wants to rule the Czardom herself, and Kuzma, the wicked old shaman who is jealous of Chingis's powers.

Some stories grab you by the collar from the very first page and propel you into an entirely new experience. With this novel you enter a brooding, mysterious world of myth, magic and adventure that's so extraordinarily vivid, you'll feel it's more real than your own.

**Patricia Elliott**

## Next?

• There are two other novels in this trilogy: *The Ghost Song* and *The Ghost Dance*. And look out for Susan's story of two Viking brothers, *Feasting the Wolf*.

• For a similar winter myth-world setting, try Catherine Fisher's atmospheric **Snow-walker** trilogy. (*UBG* 318)

• Alan Garner's *The Weirdstone of Brisingamen* combines myth, magic and desperate danger. (*UBG* 377)

# THE GHOST OF THOMAS KEMPE  Penelope Lively

This is a brilliant story. James and his family move into an old house and things soon start going wrong. Objects are being smashed in the house and everybody blames James. Why is someone advertising as an apothecary? And whose are the broken pipe and spectacles he and Tim the dog dig up in the garden? But it is only when James learns about poltergeists and calls in the local ghost-catcher that things really start to get alarming...

**Catherine Fisher**

### Next?

• Try Penelope Lively's other stories, such as *The Driftway*, about a boy and his sister running away, or *A Stitch in Time*, where a girl staying in Lyme Regis on holiday finds a Victorian sampler and is fascinated to know who sewed it.

• Lively's *The Revenge of Samuel Stokes*, also has an irritable ghost – this time one whose garden is having houses built on it. (*UBG* 284)

• *The Mirror Image Ghost* by Catherine Storr is a deeply atmospheric, and classic, ghost story.

★ ★ ★ ★ ★ ★

# GHOST WRITER  Julia Jarman

### Next?

• Julia Jarman's many books include *Ollie and the Bogle*, about a spiteful sprite and **The Time-Travelling Cat** series, set largely in ancient Egypt. (*UBG* 349)

• *How to Write Really Badly* by Anne Fine (*UBG* 163) is another book about the trials of writing.

• If you're like Frankie, look out for all the books by the publishers Barrington Stoke – they're just for you.

• How about an ADHD kid who has real trouble even sitting still? *Hurricane Wills* by Sally Grindley is all about him and his problems.

You may know someone who struggles with reading and writing, or maybe you have difficulties yourself. Frankie Ruggles knows all too well what it's like. Joining a new village school, he tries to hide his problems by clowning – and always heads straight for the reading group with the thinnest books! It's unlucky for him that his unsympathetic new teacher makes no effort to understand – but there is one person who knows exactly how he feels: the ghostly boy who emerges from the classroom cupboard and leaves messages on the board. What is the boy trying to tell Frankie? In the effort to find out, Frankie makes new friends, learns not to feel left out just because he's new, and ends the story triumphantly D.B.N.T. – Dyslexic But Not Thick! Julia Jarman writes very well about school and village life in this unusual mystery story.

**Linda Newbery**

# THE GIANTS AND THE JONESES  Julia Donaldson

Human children Colette, Stephen and little Poppy are leading a perfectly normal life, when one day they are picked up unceremoniously by a girl giant called Jumbeelia, and taken off up a bimplestonk, away from the land of the iggly plops and into Jumbeelia's home in Groil. Jumbeelia is a keen collector and she is thrilled with her new toys. She gives them a doll's house for a home and feeds them enormous chips, and raisins the size of Christmas puddings.

The three children aren't too thrilled with becoming the toys of a giant, and plot their escape. But they haven't planned for stairs the height of cliffs, a terrifyingly playful giant kitten and, worst of all, Jumbeelia's revolting brother.

This is a fantastically silly story, which includes a Groilish / English dictionary at the back so you can learn to speak Jumbeelia's language.

**Susan Reuben**

### Next?

• For more Julia Donaldson, try the **Princess Mirror-Belle** series.

• Another giant, this time a very young one, stars in *The Giant Baby* by Allan Ahlberg.

• For more extreme silliness and a great story, try *How to Train Your Dragon* by Cressida Cowell. (*UBG* 162)

★ ★ ★ ★ ★ ★

# GIDEON THE CUTPURSE  Linda Buckley-Archer

### Next?

• The sequels: *The Tar Man* and *Lord Luxon*.

• Charlie Fletcher's *Stone Heart* and its sequels also takes a really different look at London. (*UBG* 326)

• Catherine Webb's series that starts with *The Extraordinary and Unusual Adventures of Horatio Lyle* is another historical series that's every bit as exciting as any TV cop show.

I adored this book. I'd like to end the review there, and just say – go and read, but I suspect you might want to know a little bit more... Well, the story is about two kids from now who get catapulted back to the eighteenth century and a villain from the eighteenth century who gets thrown into the London of today. The stories interweave and link seamlessly, with the author never losing her tight hold on the various plots, or letting the excitement levels die down.

Time travel, villainous heroes, heroic villains, mysteries, life-or-death chases, filthily real history, hard science and possibly the end of the world – all that and more is crammed into the pages of this book. If you read it, make sure the sequels are to hand, as otherwise you'll be hot-footing it down to your local bookshop – even if it's the middle of the night!

**Leonie Flynn**

# THE GIGGLER TREATMENT  Roddy Doyle

This is a story all about poo. Honestly. Dog poo, in fact. In this case, a dog called Rover's poo. I'll explain a bit. First, let me introduce you to the Gigglers, baby-sized furry creatures who can change colour. Their job is to look after children and punish adults who treat them unfairly. Their main weapon is dog poo, which they leave in the way of any misbehaving adult. Next, you need to meet the Mack family: there's Mister Mack, a taster in a biscuit factory, his wife Billie Jean, Jimmy, Robbie and little baby Kayla. The book tells the story of why the Gigglers left Rover's poo for Mister Mack on his way to the train station and the heroic efforts of his family, the smaller-than-smallest Giggler and Rover, to save him from his fate.

Even the chapter titles are hilarious. Definitely try this if you like silly jokes and being naughty.

**Abigail Anderson**

## Next?

• There are equally pooey sequels: *Rover Saves Christmas* and *The Meanwhile Adventures*.

• Or for something just as funny, why not try Alan MacDonald's **Troll Trouble** series, starting with *Trolls Go Home*.

• For a story as disgusting as any you can imagine, read Raymond Briggs's *Fungus the Bogeyman*. (*UBG* 121)

• Or look for *Stinky Finger's House of Fun* by Jon Blake, about a world without grown-ups!

★ ★ ★ ★ ★ ★

# THE GIVER

## Lois Lowry

## Next?

• Do you like thinking about the way the future might unfold? Try *Playing the Field* by Neil Arksey, or *A Rag, a Bone and a Hank of Hair* by Nicholas Fisk (*UBG* 278).

• *Mortal Engines* by Philip Reeve is set after the world as we know it has been destroyed. (*UBG* 236)

• *Why Weeps the Brogan?* is another powerful – and disturbing – vision of the future. (*UBG* 383)

• You'll find more haunting visions of the future in Peter Dickinson's **The Changes** trilogy. (*UBG* 57)

This is a powerful story about a future society that has forgotten love. When Jonas reaches the vital age of 12, instead of being assigned a life-task, he finds himself selected to be apprenticed to The Receiver. This old man must pass to Jonas all the memories, beautiful and hideous, of the distant past, a time before the Community found ways to keep the population calm, polite, stable – and heartless. When Jonas learns how unwanted members are 'released', he is driven to try to escape. A gripping, and at times shocking, book, which cries out for a sequel.

**Lynne Reid Banks**

# GLORY GARDENS series  Bob Cattell

## Next?

- The series starts with *Glory in the Cup* and continues with *Bound for Glory*, *The Big Test*, *World Cup Fever*, *League of Champions*, *Blaze of Glory*, *Down the Wicket* and *The Glory Ashes*.
- For more cricket: **Butterfinger** by Bob Cattell and John Agard.
- Or for football, try the **Stadium School** series by Jefferies and Goffe. Also check out *Football Fever* edited by Tony Bradman (*UBG* 118).

Hooker, Azzie, Erica and their friends all love cricket, but it isn't until one of their teachers suggests that they make a team that things get serious. With diagrams, score sheets, tips and tests spread all through the story, you'll follow every twist of every game – and be cheering for our mismatched heroes (and heroines!) to win.

These are some of the best books about cricket you can buy. OK, there may be more serious factual ones about real teams, but if you want sa story that is funny, fast-paced and yet also manages to teach you all about those fiddly field placings and when exactly to get your fast bowler off the field and your spin bowler on, these are the books for you.

**Leonie Flynn**

★ ★ ★ ★ ★ ★

# GO SADDLE THE SEA  Joan Aiken

Meet Felix, otherwise known as Little Tiger, a feisty and mischievous 12 year old living in Spain shortly after the end of the Napoleonic Wars. Since his parents died when he was a baby, Felix has lived on his grandfather's estate with a collection of mean, elderly relatives.

But everything changes drastically the night that Bernardina, the warm-hearted family cook, dies. Just before dying, Bernardina gives Felix a little bundle that once belonged to his father. 'Leave this place and find your father's kin,' she says. 'You know what I always say – go saddle the sea…' And so Felix runs away and starts the long journey to the coast…

This is a high-paced adventure story that you won't be able to put down. Felix forms some wonderful new friendships. He also learns one or two valuable life lessons, and finds out quite a bit about his family. By the time you finish the book, Felix will seem very different from the Felix you met in chapter one, or will he…?

**Candida Gray**

## Next?

- This series of books continues with *Bridle the Wind* and *The Teeth of the Gale*.
- For other Joan Aiken, try her books set at the time of James III, starting with *The Wolves of Willoughby Chase*. (*UBG* 391)
- Why not check out the books Joan Aiken herself recommended for the *UBG*, like John Masefield's *The Box of Delights*. (*UBG* 44)

# GOBBOLINO THE WITCH'S CAT   Ursula Moray Williams

Gobbolino's mother Grimalkin is a witch's cat and his sister, Sootica, promises to be just like her. They are both pure black. But Gobbolino has blue eyes, one white paw and a trace of tabby in his coat. This kitten is no use to a witch, so he's abandoned and has to make his own way in the world.

Each chapter of this enchanting book is a story in itself. Gobbolino is always finding a home, and then losing it because he is a witch's cat. The children he meets always love him because he is playful, kind and selfless, but he will have to prove that he is no longer a witch's cat before he can find the home he deserves, and become the kitchen cat that he has always longed to be.

**Jenny Nimmo**

### Next?
• You might enjoy *The Adventures of the Little Wooden Horse* and *The Further Adventures of Gobbolino and the Little Wooden Horse* by Ursula Moray Williams. Or you could try *The Snow Kitten* by Nina Warner Hooke, another enchanting kitten story.
• Try *The Worst Witch* by Jill Murphy, about a girl who isn't very good at being a witch. (*UBG* 394)
• Or *Taking the Cat's Way Home* by Jan Mark, which is about bullying, a cat and a journey into the unknown.

★ ★ ★ ★ ★ ★

# THE GOD BENEATH THE SEA
## Leon Garfield and Edward Blishen

Beginning with a fiery baby being hurled out of heaven, this book brilliantly retells the legends of the Greek gods, weaving them all together into a continuous story that reads like a novel, and includes the making of the world, the war between the gods and their powerful enemies the Titans, and the creation of mankind.

It's sometimes beautiful, sometimes funny and often really horrific, as the authors don't shy away from the darkness and violence of the original stories. The pictures, by the great illustrator Charles Keeping, fit the words perfectly, and help to make this a book that will linger in your mind for a long time after you've read it.

**Philip Reeve**

### Next?
• You'll find more Greek myths retold in the sequel, *The Golden Shadow*, which deals with the 12 labours of Hercules.
• Look out for Rosemary Sutcliff's *Black Ships Before Troy*. (*UBG* 36)
• Or what about very modern takes on classic myth? Try Rick Riordan's **Percy Jackson** series (*UBG* 262) or Tobias Druitt's **Corydon** series (*UBG* 72) – both about boys who find that they're related to the gods.

# GOGGLE-EYES  Anne Fine

A top story by a top writer who knows how to make you laugh and feel like crying at the same time. 'Goggle-eyes' is what Kitty Killin calls her mum's new boyfriend. She hates him – to start with. Worse, her kid sister Jude seems to like him. Kitty tells the story to her schoolmate, Helly, who's also having problems with her mum's boyfriend, Toad-shoes.

Anne Fine writes brilliantly on family life – the trade-offs, the rows, the jealousies. Everyone who reads this is going to recognise something about their own family. Her characters live and breathe. Kitty's mum is not a cardboard cut-out, as mums so often are in children's books. And you'll love Kitty – she's the least perfect of heroines but one of the funniest and feistiest ever.

**Helen Cresswell**

### Next?
• Read *Madame Doubtfire*, even if you've seen the film – the book's much better. (*UBG* 216) Then go on to discover the rest of Anne Fine's work.

• Or *The Mum-Minder* by Jacqueline Wilson about a girl who is very capable, out of necessity, not out of choice.

• Or try *Indigo Blue* by Anne Cassidy, a darker story about a girl and her family who are hiding from their mum's boyfriend.

★ ★ ★ ★ ★ ★

# GOLD DUST  Geraldine McCaughrean

### Next?
• Try another of Geraldine McCaughrean's books. Start with *Stop the Train*, which is about a character-filled community in the USA. (*UBG* 331)

• If you enjoyed the South American jungle setting, then try *Journey to the River Sea* by Eva Ibbotson – a splendid tale of mistaken identities and inheritance. (*UBG* 184)

• Michael Morpurgo writes terrific adventure stories. Look out for *Kensuke's Kingdom* (*UBG* 187) and *Waiting for Anya*, which is set at the time of the Spanish Civil War.

One day, someone starts digging a hole outside Inez and Maro's home in Serra Vazia, in the forests of Brazil. No one really knows why, but soon a *fofoca* (a rumour) begins, about a seam of gold...

This is a book full of wonderful things – comedy, tragedy, excitement, and a whole community beset by poverty and ambition. As the holes get bigger, and miners, criminals, the teacher, the priest and even Maro fall under the lure of gold, it's only Inez who has the will to put things right. But the football pitch has already been eaten away, and the houses are beginning to tremble. What can Inez do?

An utterly brilliant story, set in an extraordinary and fascinating place.

**Sally Prue**

# THE GOLDEN GOOSE  Dick King-Smith

## Next?

• The **Animal Crackers** series by Rose Impey is charming and funny.

• Or try Dick King-Smith's **Sophie** books, about a young girl determined to grow up to be a farmer. Try *Sophie's Snail* and *Sophie's Lucky*.

• Michael Morpurgo's *The Dancing Bear* is a tear-jerking animal story. For something lighter, try *Harry the Poisonous Centipede* by Lynne Reid Banks, or something emotionally between the two, Harry Horse's *The Last Cowboys*.

Sorrow and Misery, a goose and a gander, belong to Farmer Skint of Woebegone Farm. Just from the name, you can tell at once what kind of a state the farm is in! But one day, Farmer Skint's luck changes. Sorrow lays a golden egg that hatches into a golden goose. She is a beautiful creature who brings happiness and luck to anyone who touches her. Her name is Joy. For all the ways Joy transforms life on Woebegone Farm, you'll have to read the book.

This is a happy story that brings a smile to your face – just as if you had been able to touch Joy in person! It's a lively, quick read and there are some good hidden jokes for on-the-ball readers.

**Abigail Anderson**

★ ★ ★ ★ ★ ★

# GOODKNYGHT!  Steve Barlow and Steve Skidmore

*Goodknyght!* is the first in the **Tales of the Dark Forest** series, and it is a wacky tale about the fantastical city of Dun Indewood, where young Willum the swineherd can only dream of going to the famous knyght school. Life has become one long chore for him, as he must serve as the whipping boy for Symon (the son of the city ruler, Lord Gordin). It's all rather strange, but a great read with a rich plot and a totally original idea.

Alongside our friend Willum, you also meet such bewildering characters as Humphrey the Boggart, Luigi the Pastafarian and the crossbow-toting forest maiden, Rose. They are a stunning group of characters who, coupled with a great storyline, contribute to the amazing atmosphere of the book.

Grab this book if you like a fast and furious read with all the makings of a classic.

**Chris Cross**

## Next?

• The rest of the **Tales of the Dark Forest** series *Trollogy!*, *Whizzard!* and *Knyghtmare!*, so far.

• For another quirky (and funny, and terrifying, and exciting) story that features a forest, try Matt Haig's *Shadow Forest*. (*UBG* 306)

• Or for another wacky and fantastical tale, try Paul Stewart and Chris Riddell's *Muddle Earth*. (*UBG* 240)

• Or look out for Debi Gliori's very funny series that begins with *Pure Dead Magic*. (*UBG* 276)

# GOODNIGHT MISTER TOM  Michelle Magorian

## Next?

• More Michelle Magorian? Try the wonderful **Back Home**, about another evacuee, a young girl called Rusty, who returns home to England after being sent to America for five years – and finds a very different place from the one she left.

• For more stories about children in World War II, you might like to try **Carrie's War** by Nina Bawden (**UBG** 54) and **When Hitler Stole Pink Rabbit** by Judith Kerr (**UBG** 379).

A moving and heart-warming tale about a timid young boy and a gruff old man who form an unlikely bond that transforms both their lives.

At the beginning of World War II, eight-year-old Willie Beech is evacuated to the countryside. He is billeted on the curmudgeonly Mister Tom Oakley, who is less than pleased to be landed with the responsibility of looking after the scrawny, awkward little city boy. However, the old man soon begins to realise that Willie is hiding an unhappy secret. Gradually, under Mister Tom's care, Willie begins to forget his sad, deprived past and grows in strength and confidence. But when a summons comes from London, Willie is forced to leave his new home and return to the war-torn city to face his mother again.

*Goodnight Mister Tom* is one of the most gentle, touching and powerful stories ever written.

**Victoria Webb**

★ ★ ★ ★ ★ ★

# GOOSEBUMPS series  R.L. Stine

'Reader beware – you're in for a scare...' is the slogan on the cover of each of these books, and each spooky story is guaranteed to give you goosebumps...

There's *Monster Blood*, about an evil green slime that grows and grows and sucks up everything in its path; later in the series, you'll meet a new kind of slime that's blue, with eyes and the sharpest teeth...

Or there's a boy who hears voices from another world in *The Haunted School*. Then there's *The Attack of the Mutant*, about Skipper who's obsessed by a comic superhero, The Masked Mutant, and falls into trouble with the most evil superhero of them all...

These ridiculous and spine-tinglingly, hair-raisingly spooky stories are far too silly to be really scary – and the best bit is that there are hundreds of titles to keep you reading – and laughing!

**Eileen Armstrong**

## Next?

• There are lots more tense moments, unguessable plot twists and cliffhangers in store in *Horowitz Horror* by the master of the short-story chiller. (**UBG** 158)

• There's all sorts of spooky stuff in the **Too Ghoul for School** series by B. Strange.

• Or try Darren Shan's funny, freaky, fast-paced vampire saga starting with *Cirque du Freak*. (**UBG** 293)

# GORILLA  Anthony Browne

One of the best things about growing up and becoming a parent is that you get to read all the good children's books you never read when you were a child. When my son was five, we discovered Anthony Browne's amazing surrealistic picture books. *Gorilla* is my favourite.

Gorilla-obsessed Hannah lives alone with her preoccupied father. Things can be scary when you're the only child of an only parent.

She ends up spending the night before her birthday on the town with a gorilla: they go to the zoo, see a film, eat sundaes and dance in the moonlight among gorilla-shaped topiaries. Hannah has never been so happy. Then she wakes up. It was only a dream... Or was it?

Ten years after I first bought this book, I caught my 15-year-old son sitting cross-legged on his top bunk, computer games forgotten, rereading it. *Gorilla* is that kind of book. A classic.

**Caroline Lawrence**

**Next?**
• There are lots of Anthony Browne books to look out for. Two favourites are *My Dad* and *I Like Books*.
• Or what about a boy who thinks he knows what the gorillas in the zoo are saying? Try Jeanne Willis's *Dumb Creatures*. (*UBG* 92)
• Something else quirky? Try *Utterly Me, Clarice Bean*. More words, but they are totally wound up in the pictures. (*UBG* 365)

★ ★ ★ ★ ★ ★

# GRANNY WAS A BUFFER GIRL  Berlie Doherty

**Next?**
• You might also like other books by Berlie Doherty. In *Holly Starcross*, Holly finds out who she really is when she unlocks her family's untold stories.
• Or *Kezzie* by Theresa Breslin, another story of an 'ordinary' family facing hard times, set in Scotland in the 1930s. (*UBG* 188)
• Or, for a very different story, why not try Theresa Tomlinson's *The Herring Girls*? (*UBG* 150)

Jess is off to study in France for a year. Before she goes, her family share the stories that make their history: of Grandma Dorothy dreaming of escaping from her hard, dirty job buffing up Sheffield cutlery; of Grandpa Jack and Grandma Bridie finding love in spite of deeply divided families. And they all have something to add to the story of Danny, Jess's disabled brother, who died.

An ordinary family, perhaps, but *Granny Was a Buffer Girl* quietly proves that behind everyday appearances, nobody's story is really ordinary. Such stories make us who we are, giving us a sense of our past and our place. Knowing these stories makes Jess stronger as she sets off on the next chapter of her family's history. By turns funny, sad and surprising, this is a book you will remember.

**Helen Simmons**

# FANTASY STORIES
## Hobbit Feet and Fairy Dust
### by Susan Cooper

Like a lot of us, I don't write fantasy on purpose, but because it won't go away. Every time I start a story, sooner or later it goes off the tracks of reality into the world of imagination. A realist friend of mine once said, about **The Dark is Rising**: 'This is a very good book until that horse starts to fly'. But in fantasy, the horse of the imagination always flies.

It flies in all the old myths and fairy tales we're told when we're very small; in ancient poems like 'Beowulf' and 'The Faerie Queene' and all the way down to **Harry Potter** (where of course the horse morphs back into a magic broomstick). In the 1800s and early 1900s, only a few writers took off from reality, like Lewis Carroll (*Alice's Adventures in Wonderland*), George MacDonald (*The Princess and the Goblin*) and E. Nesbit (*Five Children and It*). But as the 1900s went on, the two world wars gave everyone such an overdose of reality that fantasy writers have been multiplying ever since. Maybe they took to it, as I did, because it was the kind of thing they loved to read, but couldn't find.

## Susan Cooper's Top Ten Fantasy List
**Take note: these are not the books I think are the best ten fantasies ever written (there are about 30 of those). But they are – in alphabetical order by author – the ten I would certainly take if I had to be marooned on a desert island. In a waterproof bag, please.**

- *Skellig* by David Almond
- *Tuck Everlasting* by Natalie Babbitt
- *The Children of Green Knowe* by L.M. Boston
- *The Owl Service* by Alan Garner
- *The Mouse and His Child* by Russell Hoban
- *A Wizard of Earthsea* by Ursula Le Guin
- *Earthfasts* by William Mayne
- *Tom's Midnight Garden* by Philippa Pearce
- *The Three Little Wolves and the Big Bad Pig* by Eugene Trivizas
- *The Nargun and the Stars* by Patricia Wrightson

In Britain, our imaginations are soaked in history whether we like it or not, so our fantasy novels tend to grow out of it, like amazingly weird trees sprouting out of compost. C.S. Lewis's children go through a wardrobe from real England into Narnia, Philip Pullman's from real Oxford into a parallel world. J.R.R. Tolkien's hobbits start in the extremely English countryside of the Shire and walk off into fantasy. For Alan Garner, William Mayne and others (including me) the unworldly power of magic invades everyday English life, bringing amazement and terror with it.

Other fantasy authors (especially Americans, whose country is so much younger, and lacks compost) invent totally new worlds, like Ursula Le Guin's Earthsea, and Anne McCaffrey's Pern. Tolkien did that once his hobbits had left the Shire, filling his **Lord of the Rings** trilogy with invented geography, creatures and languages. Or there's the type of fantasy story that plays with time, like Philippa Pearce's classic *Tom's Midnight Garden*, or the animal fantasies, such as Kenneth Grahame's *The Wind in the Willows*,

## Cyberfiction

- The **Legendeer** trilogy by Alan Gibbons
- *Hacker* by Malorie Blackman
- The **Johnny Maxwell** trilogy by Terry Pratchett
- *The Transfer* by Terence Blacker
- *Space Demons* by Gillian Rubinstein

## 'Little People' Books

- *The Borrowers* by Mary Norton
- *The Indian in the Cupboard* by Lynne Reid Banks
- *Mistress Masham's Repose* by T.H. White
- *The Mennyms* by Sylvia Waugh
- *The Little Grey Men* by B.B.
- *The Hobbit* by J.R.R. Tolkien

## Books That Slip Between Worlds

- *The New Policeman* by Kate Thompson
- *The Ship Between Worlds* by Julia Golding
- *Piggies* by Nick Gifford
- *Coraline* by Neil Gaiman
- *The Homeward Bounders* by Diana Wynne Jones
- **His Dark Materials** trilogy by Philip Pullman
- **The Chronicles of Narnia** by C.S. Lewis
- **The Dark is Rising** sequence by Susan Cooper
- *Corbenic* by Catherine Fisher
- *The Owl Service* by Alan Garner
- *Elidor* by Alan Garner
- *The BFG* by Roald Dahl
- *Five Children and It* by E. Nesbit
- *The Secret of Platform 13* by Eva Ibbotson
- *Harry Potter and the Philosopher's Stone* (and sequels) by J.K. Rowling
- *Marianne Dreams* by Catherine Storr
- *Midnight for Charlie Bone* by Jenny Nimmo
- *Mary Poppins* by P.L. Travers
- *The Weirdstone of Brisingamen* by Alan Garner
- *Alice's Adventures in Wonderland* by Lewis Carroll
- *An Angel for May* by Melvin Burgess
- *Shadow of the Minotaur* by Alan Gibbons

## Magic!

- *Witch Trade* by Michael Molloy
- *Pure Dead Magic* by Debi Gliori
- *Half Magic* by Edward Eager
- *Carbonel* by Barbara Sleigh
- **The Chronicles of Narnia** by C.S. Lewis
- *The Weirdstone of Brisingamen* by Alan Garner
- *The Book of Three* by Lloyd Alexander
- **Groosham Grange** series by Anthony Horowitz
- *Puck of Pook's Hill* by Rudyard Kipling
- *A Handful of Magic* by Stephen Elboz
- **Septimus Heap** series by Angie Sage
- The **Power of Five** series by Anthony Horowitz
- *The Alchemist* by Michael Scott
- *Measle and the Wrathmonk* by Ian Ogilvy

E.B. White's *Charlotte's Web* or Richard Adams's *Watership Down*.

If you've read a lot of fantasy, you'll know which author belongs in which category. It doesn't matter, of course; all fantasy stories belong to the same family in the end. They're books of escape; books that take you to places you'll never see; books in which the impossible happens, making the hair stand up on the back of your neck. They may not deal with facts and reality, but you know in your heart that they are true.

And d'you know why so many authors write a whole series of fantasy books? Sometimes it's because we know you want to read book after book set in the same imaginary world – but more often, it's because we live there while we're writing about it, and we can't bear to leave.

## Sci-fi books

- *Mortal Engines* by Philip Reeve
- **The Book of the Crow** series by Catherine Fisher
- *A Rag, a Bone and a Hank of Hair* by Nicholas Fisk
- *The Giver* by Lois Lowry
- **The Changes** trilogy by Peter Dickinson
- *Playing on the Edge* by Neil Arksey
- *Why Weeps the Brogan?* by Hugh Scott

## Time-slip Books

- *A Traveller in Time* by Alison Uttley
- *King of Shadows* by Susan Cooper
- *The Children of Green Knowe* by Lucy M. Boston
- *A Stitch in Time* by Penelope Lively
- *Puck of Pook's Hill* by Rudyard Kipling
- *Earthfasts* by William Mayne
- *A Wrinkle in Time* by Madeleine L'Engle
- *The Time-Travelling Cat* by Julia Jarman
- *Charlotte Sometimes* by Penelope Farmer
- *The Ghost of Thomas Kempe* by Penelope Lively

# A GRASS ROPE  William Mayne

### Next?

• You will probably want to read other books by William Mayne. Try *Earthfasts* (scary!) (*UBG* 94), *Cuddy* (yup – scary, too) and *A Year and a Day* (slightly younger and quite magical).

• Helen Cresswell's own *The Night-Watchmen* is along similar lines, and very scary.

• Elizabeth Goudge also writes about a lonely girl, a strange house and a magic horse in *The Little White Horse*. (*UBG* 206)

This is a story from one of our very best writers. Mary lives in a remote Yorkshire dale on a working farm with no neighbours in view. She believes so strongly in the 'legend of the unicorn and the hounds' that she forces them to be real through the sheer power of her imagination. This may be against all known laws of science, but it happens. The plot unfolds slowly, but as you read you will come to share Mary's belief, and be not at all surprised when the unicorn is suddenly there, unmistakably real in that everyday setting.

**Helen Cresswell**

★ ★ ★ ★ ★ ★

# THE GREAT ELEPHANT CHASE  Gillian Cross

Imagine a 2,000-mile journey across America with an elephant! Cissie and Tad, alone in the world and forced together by necessity, have no alternative if they're going to reach the safety of Cissie's only friend, Ketty. Cissie believes the elephant, Khush, belongs to her, but sinister Mr Jackson and his accomplice Esther believe he's theirs and pursue Tad and Cissie all the way.

Khush feels so real you could reach into the book and stroke his long trunk. He's frustrated and playful and totally unpredictable. Unpredictable – that's a good word to describe this heart-stopping story.

**Jon Appleton**

### Next?

• All Gillian Cross's books are good. Try *The Demon Headmaster* (*UBG* 82), or *Wolf*, or the slightly older *A Map of Nowhere* and the heart-stopping *On the Edge*.

• *Black Hearts in Battersea* by Joan Aiken would be a good adventure to move on to. Find out about the book that precedes it, *The Wolves of Willoughby Chase*. (*UBG* 391)

• For another book in which a characterful elephant features, read *Uncle* by J.P. Martin. (*UBG* 361)

# THE GREAT PIRATICAL RUMBUSTIFICATION and THE LIBRARIAN AND THE ROBBERS  Margaret Mahy

Mr and Mrs Terrapin (who are delightfully odd, as parents go) are out for the night – and what a night! All over town, retired pirates are feeling restless – they're longing for a party to steal. Three small boys are restless, too, longing for adventure. All it needs is for the wrong babysitter to arrive, and wild and yo-ho-ho-ish chaos is set to follow.

The second story, *The Librarian and the Robbers*, is one of the funniest I have ever read. It is a tale of Love! Lunacy! Lives of Crime! a Lurgy! and, of course, Librarianship! 'Unglamorous!' do I hear you cry? Nonsense! If all librarians were as quick-witted, daring, delightful and dashing as Miss Laburnum, I for one would set up home on my local library's doorstep.

**Simon Puttock**

**Next?**
• Another wonderfully silly book is *Violet and the Mean and Rotten Pirates* by Richard Hamilton. (*UBG* 370)
• Or try *Urgum the Axeman* by Kjartan Poskitt, all about how stone-age Urgum and his sons cope with a dainty little girl. (*UBG* 365)
• And of course, more Margaret Mahy, especially *The Blood and Thunder Adventure on Hurricane Peak* and *The Riddle of the Frozen Phantom*.

★ ★ ★ ★ ★ ★

# THE GREAT PYRAMID ROBBERY  Katherine Roberts

**Next?**
• The rest of the **Seven Fabulous Wonders** series, each set in a different one of the Seven Wonders of the World: *The Babylon Game*, *The Amazon Temple Quest*, *The Mausoleum Murder*, *The Olympic Conspiracy*, *The Colossus Crisis* and *The Cleopatra Curse*.
• If you liked the strong, clever character of Reonet, try *Faerie Wars* by Herbie Brennan (*UBG* 105) or the **Song of the Lioness** series by Tamora Pierce (*UBG* 319).

This exciting adventure story is set in The Two Lands (ancient Egypt), when the pyramids were being built. Senu longs to work with his father in the temple, but can't pass the tests. He has strange powers that he is forced to face as he is drawn into a dark, secret plot. His father is kidnapped and his tasks become more serious and more deadly than he could ever have guessed.

If you're interested in ancient Egypt, you'll love this novel. The story is based on real history, so although it's fiction, you'll learn a great deal about Egyptian life and beliefs. Senu, his clever friend Reonet, and his mischievous ka, or spirit companion, are wonderful characters – and the story keeps you guessing right to the very end.

**Antonia Honeywell**

# GROOSHAM GRANGE  Anthony Horowitz  ●●

**Next?**

• There's a sequel, *Return to Groosham Grange*. And Anthony's **Diamond Brothers** books (*UBG* 108) are funny, too.

• Want more about wizards? Try **Harry Potter** (*UBG* 145); or for a more serious look at a wizard school, *A Wizard of Earthsea* by Ursula Le Guin. (*UBG* 95)

• For another school that suffers trials and tribulations, try Steve Cole's **One Weird Day at Freekham High** series. (*UBG* 252)

When David Eliot is expelled from Beton College, his cruel and ambitious parents are in despair. Then a prospectus arrives for Groosham Grange: 'an old-fashioned school which still believes in discipline'. Determined to tame David, his parents dispatch him instantly, in the middle of the Christmas holidays.

Groosham Grange is a school for witchcraft. Staff include a vampire, a werewolf, a one-eyed dwarf and a two-headed headmaster. The punishments for non-conformity are dire, but David, a natural rebel, doesn't want to be a witch. Can he outwit the staff, with their supernatural powers? Can he escape before the initiation ceremony on his 13th birthday, which is only days away?

This book is exciting and hilariously funny in lots of different ways. There's satire, witty word play, and larger than life characters. You'll be gripped and grinning from the first page to the last.

**Julia Jarman**

★ ★ ★ ★ ★

# GULF  Robert Westall  ●●●

Robert Westall wrote with power, passion and superb control. You can read this short book in one sitting, yet it might just stay with you for the rest of your life.

Tom, the narrator, watches his extraordinarily sensitive younger brother Andy, a.k.a. Figgis, become more and more strange. Figgis identifies so closely with the suffering of others that he seems to take on their pain. It is the time of the first Gulf War and Tom watches in horror as Figgis starts to live out the life of a young Iraqi soldier, lying in wait for the American onslaught. Can Tom help Figgis back into the real world before it's too late?

Westall had the uncanny ability to tell a rattling good yarn and yet at the same time make you think long and hard about the issues that matter – in this case, the cost of war. Long may his books continue to be read.

**Malachy Doyle**

**Next?**

• Westall's *The Kingdom by the Sea* and *The Machine Gunners* (*UBG* 215) are both exciting and thought-provoking stories about war.

• Other books about war or its effects are the harrowing *The Fire-Eaters* by David Almond (*UBG* 113) and the terrifying *When the Wind Blows* by Raymond Briggs.

# GUMBLE'S YARD  John Rowe Townsend

### Next?

- For a modern child who has problems with her parents, try *The Suitcase Kid* by Jacqueline Wilson.
- For another story about children having to cope alone, read *The Wolves of Willoughby Chase* by Joan Aiken. (*UBG* 391)
- *The Children Who Lived in a Barn* by Eleanor Graham is about five very independent siblings who do actually live in a barn.
- A brother and sister are forced apart in Jacqueline Woodson's *Locomotion*. (*UBG* 209)

Kevin and Sandra have been abandoned by the grown-ups. With no cash, and their two small cousins to look after, they find an old, run-down row of cottages to live in.

They're absolutely determined that no one should find out where they are, as they don't want to be split up and put into care. But when they discover that the cottages they're living in aren't as deserted as they'd thought, things get very hairy indeed...

This book was written 40 years ago, and it was one of the first to talk about children with family difficulties and not much money. Kevin and Sandra's problems are just the same as the problems of some children today – but the way the authorities deal with them is fascinatingly different. It's a really good, gripping read.

**Susan Reuben**

★ ★ ★ ★ ★ ★

# HACKER  Malorie Blackman

Vicky thought she was in trouble when she was threatened with suspension from school for cheating in her maths exam. But this is nothing compared to the trouble her father is in, accused of stealing a million pounds from the bank where he works. Vicky and her half-brother, Gib, know he is innocent – but how do they prove it? Doggedly, they delve into the maze of the bank's computer system to discover an audacious crime – and a shocking surprise!

You don't need to be a computer nut to follow the fast-moving plot: *Hacker* will keep you in suspense and give you a lump in your throat, as Vicky realises that even though she is adopted, this family is where she truly belongs.

**Helen Simmons**

### Next?

- You might also like to try some other books by Malorie Blackman, who often bases her stories around unusual ideas. *Tell Me No Lies* and *Pig-Heart Boy* (*UBG* 268) are well worth a read.
- Check out some novels by Gillian Cross. *The Demon Headmaster* (*UBG* 82) and *The Great Elephant Chase* (*UBG* 137) are both exciting books full of adventure with wonderfully wicked baddies.
- Or try Frank Cottrell Boyce's *Millons* – yes, it's all about money, too.

# HALF MAGIC series Edward Eager

I was nine or ten when I discovered Edward Eager's fantastic books about a group of children's magic adventures. In the first, *Half Magic*, Katharine, Jane, Mark and Martha pick up a coin on the way to the library. They think it's an ordinary nickel, but gradually discover, through a series of misadventures, that it's a magic coin. The catch is, it only grants half your wish. So when the youngest, Martha, is sick of being bossed around by her siblings and wishes she wasn't there, half of her is left behind, while the other half flits about wreaking havoc.

I was intrigued by the idea that magic might not be controllable. I also loved the range of adventures the children have, from fighting pirates to meeting their future offspring.

**Francesca Simon**

**Next?**
• You should try some of the others in the series: *The Knight's Castle*, *Magic by the Lake* and *Time Garden*.
• Beverly Cleary is well known for her great series about Ramona. (*UBG* 280)
• There's more sibling fun in *The Saturdays* by Elizabeth Enright. (*UBG* 295)

★ ★ ★ ★ ★ ★

# A HANDFUL OF MAGIC Stephen Elboz

**Next?**
• *A Land Without Magic* and *A Wild Kind of Magic*, more fast-paced Henry and Kit adventures.
• Also try Stephen Elboz's *The Tower at Moonville*, about orphans who swap places. For a scarier read, try *The House of Rats*, about children trapped in a mysterious house who find help from an unusual place.
• Catherine Webb's *The Extraordinary and Unusual Adventures of Horatio Lyle* is another mystery series that adds science to the mix.
• Or for another boy, a dark mystery and a Dickensian feel, read G.P. Taylor's *Mariah Mundi: The Midas Box*.

Kit lives in a London of magic, wizards and witches. Kit's father is a witch doctor; in fact, the personal witch doctor to Queen Victoria. But Stafford Sparks, 'The Royal Superintendent of Scientific Progress', dislikes magic being used.

Kit's secret friend is Prince Henry, Queen Victoria's grandson. They have adventures all over London using Kit's magic carpet. Queen Victoria discovers their friendship and Kit is sent to live with his aunt. But then children in London start to go missing. Kit goes to the palace to try and help Prince Henry who is still ill, but they get captured and taken underground to dig tunnels. Who is in charge down there? Where are the tunnels going? Will Kit be able to cure Henry from the werewolf poison and save him and all the children? Read on and find out...

**Julia Lytollis**

# THE HAPPY PRINCE AND OTHER STORIES
## Oscar Wilde

I loved these beautiful, tender stories when I was young, and I still do. Stories such as 'The Happy Prince' and 'The Selfish Giant' have stayed with me all my life, and never fail to move me. In them, Oscar Wilde presents us with people who think they are better than everyone else, and then shows us, in wonderfully imaginative ways, how it is the people who are able to show pity, the ones who are better at giving than at taking, who are the truly blessed. In 'The Happy Prince', for example, the statue of a prince is so moved by the human misery in the streets below that he persuades a swallow to take his jewels and gold leaf and give it to the poor.

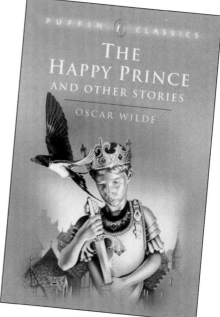

There is much sadness in these stories – they are about beauty and sorrow, friendship and love, pity and suffering – but there is happiness, too, and poetry, wonder and joy. If you like stories that make you think, stories that let your imagination soar, then these are for you.

**Malachy Doyle**

---

## Books About Princesses

- *The Ordinary Princess* by M.M. Kaye
- *The Light Princess* by George MacDonald
- The **Princess Tales** series by Gail Carson Levine
- *The Frog Princess* by E.D. Baker
- *The Princess and the Goblin* by George MacDonald
- *The Princess of the Chalet School* by E.M. Brent-Dyer
- *The Redheaded Princess* by Ann Rinaldi
- *The Two Princesses of Bamarr* by Gail Carson Levine

---

### Next?

- If you loved the magical melancholy of these stories, try Frances Hodgson Burnett's *The Secret Garden* (*UBG* 302); or maybe *Sinbad the Sailor and Other Tales from the Arabian Nights* by N.J. Dawood – there's an entry on the **Arabian Nights** on p. 21.
- For more fairy stories, look on pp. 106–107 for entries about ones by the Brothers Grimm, Hans Christian Andersen and Charles Perrault. .
- Terry Jones is another writer who conjures wonderful stories – look for his *Fairy Tales*.

# The HARDY BOYS series  ●●

## Franklin W. Dixon

**Next?**

• *Emil and the Detectives* by Erich Kästner is a good old-fashioned detective story. (*UBG* 99)

• Two brothers travel the world with their naturalist father and have amazing adventures in Willard Price's **Adventure** books. (*UBG* 51)

• For a girl doing the adventuring, try Carolyn Keene's **Nancy Drew Mysteries**. (*UBG* 246)

Like many teenagers, Frank and Joe Hardy have always fancied the idea of being detectives. Unlike most teenagers, the Hardy Boys get the chance to solve a real mystery when old Mr Applegate's safe is broken into. Once the mystery of their first case, *The Tower Treasure*, is solved, there's another, and another... No sooner have the boys solved a case and returned to the life of normal American schoolboys, something else crops up – another case, another clue...

The **Hardy Boys** books are perhaps a little old-fashioned these days; the plots are all fairly similar, the heroes are a bit too clever, athletic and resourceful and kind-hearted to be true (yeuch); oh, and there are lots and lots of exclamation marks! Yes, lots! Wow!! But they're fun reads, and each will keep you hooked till you find out whodunnit.

**Daniel Hahn**

★ ★ ★ ★ ★ ★

# HAROUN AND THE SEA OF STORIES  ●●●

## Salman Rushdie

Salman Rushdie's career was interrupted when one of his novels caused great offence to sections of the international Muslim community. *Haroun and the Sea of Stories* was his first novel after he was forced to withdraw from public life, and it is about a father – a storyteller in India – who loses his ability to create stories. It is up to his son to help his father, and this novel is all about their struggle to overcome those who want to stop the storyteller sharing his stories. Although it is sad in places, it is also very funny and hugely inventive. If you enjoy complicated, ingenious plots, this is the book for you.

**Lindsey Fraser**

**Next?**

• Try David Almond's collection of short stories, *Counting Stars*. (*UBG* 73)

• *Inkheart* by Cornelia Funke is another book about stories – and their power. (*UBG* 174)

• *Bambert's Book of Missing Stories* by Reinhardt Jung is another captivating book about storytelling. (*UBG* 27)

• Another book that links various short stories into a whole is *Uncle Montague's Tales of Terror* by Chris Priestly. (*UBG* 361)

# HARRIET THE SPY Louise Fitzhugh

## Next?

• If you want to read more about Harriet, track down *The Long Secret*.

• In Lois Lowry's **Anastasia Krupnik** series you can meet another quirky heroine with a mind of her own. (*UBG* 16)

• You might also like *The Eighteenth Emergency* by Betsy Byars, about what happens to Mouse when he gets on the wrong side of the school bully. (*UBG* 98)

Harriet M. Welsch is a New Yorker: her best friends are Sport, who wants to be a famous baseball player, and Janie, who blows things up with her chemistry set. Harriet's passion is her notebook, where she records her innermost thoughts about her friends and her secret life as Harriet the Spy.

After school, in her spy uniform and with notebook in hand, Harriet pounds her spy route, coolly observing the lives of 1960s Manhattan dwellers. Harriet has never been caught – until now. When her friends find her notebook – and read it – Harriet is suddenly totally alone.

I am a big fan of Harriet; she is funny, eccentric and thoughtful, even as she learns some painful truths about herself and friendship.

**Helen Simmons**

★ ★ ★ ★ ★ ★

# HARRY AND THE WRINKLIES Alan Temperley

Harry hates everything about his home and dreads holidays from boarding school when he has to return to his vile nanny (Harry secretly calls her Gestapo Lil), who makes him do all the housework and spends his allowance on herself. Then, one day, he is told that his parents are dead. Orphaned and penniless, Harry is packed off with just a few old clothes in a battered suitcase to live at Lagg Hall with his great-aunts, Florrie and Bridget.

But the sweet old aunts are not your usual knitting-crazy, doddery old ladies. In fact Harry finds himself deep in plots, crime and capers with The Wrinklies, the best band of thieves since Robin Hood and his Merry Men. Like Robin's gang, Florrie and Bridget only steal from those who deserve it. Mostly. And Harry soon discovers that being a Wrinkly is huge fun – but very dangerous, too…

This is a book you'll want to read super-fast. Full of puns and rip-roaring excitement, it'll speed you from page to page faster than Great-Aunt Florrie's Norton Commando.

**Leonie Flynn**

## Next?

• Try the sequel – *Harry and the Treasure of Eddie Carver*.

• If you liked the mad adventures and terrible jokes, try the **Diamond Brothers** books by Anthony Horowitz – see *The Falcon's Malteser*. (*UBG* 108)

• Or for adventures with even stranger adults, look for *7 Professors of the Far North* by John Fardell. (*UBG* 8)

# HARRY POTTER series   J.K. Rowling

**Star Title**

It's hard to believe that when I first started reading *Harry Potter and the Philosopher's Stone*, I didn't know that Harry was a wizard. Now people across the world know about Harry, his miserable early childhood and the exciting new freedom resulting from his enrolment in Hogwarts School of Witchcraft and Wizardry. Harry and his friends are familiar to us all, and their stories are enjoyed by millions of people of all ages throughout the world.

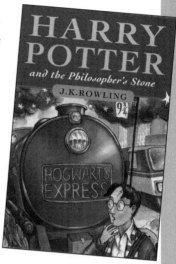

The success of the **Harry Potter** books is due to their popularity with children. Their enthusiastic recommendations to friends in classrooms and playgrounds throughout the country drew the attention of their parents – and the rest, as they say, is history.

**Lindsey Fraser**

## Next?

• Of course, there are the sequels… *HP and the Chamber of Secrets*, *HP and the Prisoner of Azkaban*, *HP and the Goblet of Fire*, *HP and the Order of the Phoenix*, *HP and the Half-Blood Prince* and *HP and the Deathly Hallows*.

• You might enjoy *The Witches* by Roald Dahl. (*UBG* 389)

• *Midnight for Charlie Bone* by Jenny Nimmo is the story of another boy with special powers. (*UBG* 226)

• Debi Gliori has written a series that's just as inventive, which begins with *Pure Dead Magic*. (*UBG* 276)

• Anthony Horowitz's *Groosham Grange* features a school as surprising as Hogwarts. (*UBG* 139)

• Eva Ibbotson's *The Secret of Platform 13* is another fantasy story that features strange goings-on at a railway station. (*UBG* 303)

The trouble with these books is that it's hard to see them clearly any more. Rather than anything about the stories, we see the movies, the hype, the money and the myth. Which is a terrible shame, as Harry's story is one of the most wonderful children's epics ever written, and thoroughly deserving of all the hype, money and myth that's been thrown at it.

Actually, it's quite hard to even sum up the books without, in some way, stumbling over the myth. A young author writing about a long-cherished hero. Rags to riches (or perhaps more Primark to Prada). Midnight queues, stolen volumes, banned books and online fanaticism. Yet, at the heart of it all lies the story of a boy, his friends, his enemies and the triumph of good over evil, of hope over despair. Mostly, though, it's just a great story, simply told. And one I'll always treasure.

**Leonie Flynn**

# HARVEY ANGELL Diana Hendry

This terrific story starts very quietly, but soon explodes into an extravaganza of a book with loads going on.

Let's start with the house. As one of the long-suffering tenants remarks, no one would live at 131 Ballantyre Road unless they had to. Sadly, Henry *does* have to, and must suffer at the hands of miserly Aunt Agatha. Then along comes the irrepressibly cheerful Harvey Angell, who's some sort of electrician (researching energy fields, apparently), and everything changes. Underneath the house's gloomy exterior is the potential for fun – but there's sadness to be revealed and a mystery to be unravelled too, which might just explain why Aunt Agatha is so miserable, and might just tell Henry a thing or two about himself.

**Jon Appleton**

**Next?**
• *MapHead* by Lesley Howarth is another fizzing story about self-discovery. (*UBG* 219)
• One of my favourite fantasy worlds is to be found in Charlotte Haptie's *Otto and the Flying Twins*. (*UBG* 256)
• For books about angels, why not read the **Angels Unlimited** series? (*UBG* 19)

★ ★ ★ ★ ★ ★

# HATCHET Gary Paulsen

**Next?**
• If you want to know what happens to Brian after *Hatchet*, you'll want to get the sequels, starting with *Hatchet: The Return*.
• For another brilliant story of survival, try the classic *I Am David* by Anne Holm, about a boy who escapes from a prison camp and travels across Europe to find his mother. (*UBG* 164)
• Tim Wynne-Jones's *The Survival Game* is about surviving both the wilderness and the cruelty of adults.

A plane has crashed. Brian, a 13-year-old city boy is the sole survivor. But he has landed in the middle of the Canadian wilderness, and no one knows he is there. Brian has only one tool to help him: a hatchet. As the night closes around him on his first day alone, the hatchet seems of little use. How will he eat? How will he keep warm and evade the wild animals all around him?

This is a terrific survival story, simply written, and all the more powerful because the author, Gary Paulsen, has actually lived like Brian. He knows exactly what is required to stay alive in the cruel north.

**Cliff McNish**

# THE HAUNTING  Margaret Mahy  ●●

## Next?

• You might want to read more by Margaret Mahy. She has great insight into the way families work. *Aliens in the Family* has a lot in common with *The Haunting* but *The Changeover* (*UBG* 57) is my favourite.

• Cliff McNish's *Breathe: A Ghost Story* is one of the scariest ghost stories around.

• Or try Charles Butler's deeply frightening *The Lurkers*. Can Verity save her brother from the strange creatures that want to possess him?

Imagine what it would be like to hear a voice in your ear, telling you that you – or someone with your name – is dead. That is what happens to Barney. He even sees the owner of the voice, a golden-haired boy, who he thinks must be a ghost.

At first Barney doesn't tell anyone about his distressing experience, but then the ghost-boy starts to write the chilling message down, and Barney's sister Tabitha notices what's happening. Tabitha wants to be a journalist, and she sets out to find the source of poor Barney's haunting. Gradually we learn the history of Barney's family – a family that hides its strange magical talents.

*The Haunting* is a beautifully written story that never lets you go. You just have to find out who is trying to reach Barney, and why.

**Jenny Nimmo**

★ ★ ★ ★ ★ ★

# THE HAUNTING OF ALAIZABEL CRAY  Chris Wooding  ●●●

Seventeen-year-old Thaniel Fox is the best wych-hunter in London. Every night he prowls the deserted streets in search of the wych-kin – dangerous demons and spirits in every terrifying form imaginable. The city, shaken and shattered after a recent war, is brimming with evil, and the wych-kin are not the only ones to be afraid of. Behind the scenes, a secret powerful cult makes a deadly pact that may have disastrous consequences. But what does the delirious young woman that Thaniel finds in the Old Quarter have to do with this? Who is haunting the mysterious Alaizabel Cray?

There's horror, adventure, suspense and plenty of gore and blood around every corner – the descriptions will make your hair stand on end! You will never walk alone in the dark without thinking of Stitch-face... Read it, and you'll see what I mean.

**Noga Applebaum**

## Next?

• *Poison* also by Chris Wooding. (*UBG* 271)

• Try Justin Richards's scary and thrilling *The Death Collector*. (*UBG* 81)

• You might enjoy Marcus Sedgwick's *The Book of Dead Days* – a chilling novel, set long ago.

• Philip Pullman's **His Dark Materials** trilogy is set in a parallel world. (*UBG* 151)

• Or for something else to keep you awake at night, try *The Watch House* by Robert Westall. (*UBG* 375)

# HAZEL'S PHANTASMAGORIA
## Leander Deeny

Well, this is certainly one of the strangest books I've read in a while. Some of it is tremendously funny – the opening few pages alone have loads of hysterical laugh-out-loud moments – but it's also very dark and creepy and, well, just weird...

Hazel's parents are off on holiday to Egypt for three weeks, so Hazel is going to stay with evil Aunt Eugenia Pequierde and her genius son Isambard. But there are strange goings-on in the Pequierde household, and not just because of the gravy-obsessed cook and the chain-smoking ducks. For wandering in the garden one night, Hazel comes across a group of real, live Nightmares. What's going on? And *why* is Aunt Eugenia just so nasty? If you're in the mood for something utterly peculiar, this brilliant book might just be for you.

**Daniel Hahn**

### Next?

• Philip Ardagh's books are brilliantly funny and quirky (and, like *Hazel's Phantasmagoria*, are illustrated by the wonderful David Roberts) – try *The Fall of Fergal*. (*UBG* 108)

• You don't get more funnier or peculiar than Lemony Snicket's **A Series of Unfortunate Events**. *The Bad Beginning* is the first in the series. (*UBG* 306)

• Or for more of the macabre (and yet more David Roberts illustrations), try Chris Priestley's *Uncle Montague's Tales of Terror*. (*UBG* 361)

• There's more wonderfully outrageous naming going on in *Pure Dead Magic* and its sequels by Debi Gliori. (*UBG* 276)

### So Many Children, So Few Parents

• **Harry Potter** series by J.K. Rowling

• *Harry and the Wrinklies* by Alan Temperley

• *The Silver Sword* by Ian Serrailier

• *I Am David* by Anne Holm

• *The Rinaldi Ring* by Jenny Nimmo

• *Ballet Shoes* by Noel Streatfeild

• *The Thief Lord* by Cornelia Funke

• **The Worlds of Chrestomanci** series by Diana Wynne Jones

• *The Children Who Lived in a Barn* by Eleanor Graham

# HEAVEN EYES

### David Almond

● ● ●

**Next?**

• David Almond has written some of the most unusual and brilliant books for kids ever. Try the disturbing *The Fire-Eaters*. (*UBG* 113)

• *Cold Tom* by Sally Prue is mysterious, haunting and beautifully written. (*UBG* 67)

• Tim Bowler's *Frozen Fire* is another disquieting, gripping story.

Step into a David Almond book and there's no mistaking where you are – there isn't another world like it. The filter through which he sees things is quite unlike anything else you'll ever experience.

Three children run away on a raft and come across Heaven Eyes, an extraordinary girl, and her fierce and protective Grampa. They cannot help but get drawn into the lives of this strange pair, and they find out some extraordinary secrets.

Don't think the story's soppy – it's not. It's quite dark and disturbing in places. It talks of mysteries that you only half understand. It may change, just a little bit, the way you look at the world.

**Susan Reuben**

★ ★ ★ ★ ★ ★

# HEIDI   Johanna Spyri

● ●

Orphaned Heidi is taken to live with her gruff, unfriendly grandfather in an alm hut in the Swiss mountains. Heidi has fears and unhappiness to overcome, yet she transforms the lives of her grandfather and of Peter the goatherd and his blind grandmother with her love and bright spirit. When Heidi is forced to leave and live in a grand house in Frankfurt as a companion to Klara, an invalid girl, she is overcome with homesickness.

*Heidi* was the first book I ever read on my own, and I read it so often I felt as if the characters were my own family. Even now, when I hear the wind in the pine tree outside my bedroom window, I think of Heidi in her hay-loft bed, eating fire-toasted cheese and listening to the music of the mountain pines outside her window. This book gave me a love of lakes and mountains – and toasted cheese!

**Julie Bertagna**

**Next?**

• Read *Heidi Grows Up* to find out what happens next.

• For more fantastic stories of girls who make good, try *Anne of Green Gables* by L.M. Montgomery (*UBG* 20), *Pollyanna* by Eleanor H. Porter (*UBG* 272) and *Rebecca of Sunnybrook Farm* by Kate Douglas Wiggin.

• *Journey to the River Sea* by Eva Ibbotson (*UBG* 184) and *The White Giraffe* by Lauren St John, which is set in Africa, are both stories about orphans sent to live with unwelcoming relatives.

# THE HERRING GIRLS  Theresa Tomlinson

## Next?

• Read more by Theresa Tomlinson. *The Flither Pickers* is also about fisher-girls in the north-east of England. *The Rope Carrier* is set in her hometown of Sheffield.

• *Granny Was a Buffer Girl* is about growing up in a rural community. (*UBG* 133)

• Leon Garfield's *The Apprentices* is about working children. (*UBG* 20)

The setting for this story is the Yorkshire fishing port of Whitby 150 years ago. When her mother falls ill, 13-year-old Dory leaves her small village to live the tough life of a Whitby herring girl, gutting fish from morning till night so she can earn enough money to keep her family from the workhouse. Though the work is gruelling, the fishing community Dory lives in is warm and close-knit. This interesting novel, illustrated with contemporary photographs, shows you what life was like for a teenage girl at that time.

**Kate Petty**

★ ★ ★ ★ ★ ★

# THE HIGHWAYMAN'S FOOTSTEPS  Nicola Morgan

## Next?

• Read the sequel, *The Highwayman's Curse*.

• *Black Jack* by Leon Garfield is another gripping story set in the same period. (*UBG* 36)

• *I, Coriander* by Sally Gardner is clever, exciting and rich in history. (*UBG* 166)

• Linda Buckley-Archer's *Gideon the Cutpurse* has heart-stopping adventure, fearsome villains and romantic heroes. (*UBG* 126)

• Or hunt out the original Alfred Noyes' poem; there's a wonderful version illustrated by Charles Keeping.

Nicola Morgan brings eighteenth-century England brilliantly to life in a book packed with atmosphere and surprise. The story is told by Will, whose father holds an important position in the north of England. When Will meets Bess, a girl experienced in the ways of criminals and fugitives, they embark on a thrilling journey through wild landscapes and squalid towns. Much of the story is based on historical events, and the book is full of vivid detail about life in old times. The best thing of all is the way Will gradually realises that those of high birth, like himself, can sometimes be even more wicked than the people they pursue.

**Paul Bajoria**

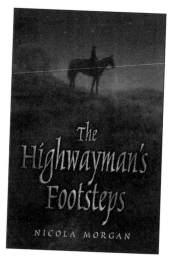

# HIS DARK MATERIALS trilogy

**Star Title**

### Philip Pullman

● ● ●

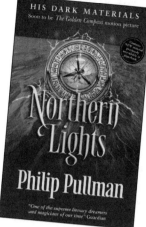

Fantasies don't come more magnificent than this. *Northern Lights*, the first book in Pullman's **His Dark Materials** trilogy, introduces Lyra, an impulsive and adventurous girl, whose search for her missing friend Roger takes her to the far north, and launches her on a quest in which the fate of the human race hangs in the balance.

Pullman has created an alternate world in which magic and technology coexist, and everyone is born with a daemon – an animal familiar that accompanies them through life, and is a sort of manifestation of their soul. The book is thought provoking, fabulously exciting, and chilling. *Northern Lights* is not simply an epic adventure tale, but a reconsideration of good and evil, God and religion.

**Kenneth Oppel**

Lyra, the heroine of the **His Dark Materials** trilogy, lives in Oxford. However, this is not the Oxford we might think we know, because Lyra lives in an alternative world. In her Oxford and her world, you will meet armoured polar bears and flying witches, and everyone has a daemon.

Lyra travels on a huge journey of discovery through these books. She meets the boy Will, who cuts through to her Oxford using the Subtle Knife, which can literally cut holes between the joins of any number of possible worlds. Their adventure eventually takes them into the Land of the Dead, and further.

Inspired by Milton's famous poem *Paradise Lost*, these books are an inspiring and exciting read, full of challenging ideas and unforgettable images. In the end, though, they are simply one enormous and entertaining story told by a master storyteller. They have become modern classics and have captured the imagination of a whole generation of both children and grown-ups.

**Ian Beck**

### Next?

• The next books in the trilogy are *The Subtle Knife* and *The Amber Spyglass*.

• For a fantasy sequence just as powerful in ideas, try Ursula Le Guin's **Earthsea** books. (*UBG* 95)

• *The Owl Service* by Alan Garner works dark mythology into the everyday. (*UBG* 258)

• Or for a huge, sprawling adventure, try J.R.R. Tolkien's *The Lord of the Rings*. (*UBG* 211)

• If you're a fantasy buff, try Kenneth Oppel's brilliant **The Silverwing Saga**. It's about bats. Yes – bats. But don't let that put you off – it's brilliant! (*UBG* 312)

# HISTORICAL HOUSE series

### Adèle Geras, Linda Newbery and Ann Turnbull

**Next?**

• The two series consist of *Lizzie's Wish* by Adèle Geras, *Polly's March* by Linda Newbery, *Josie Under Fire* by Ann Turnbull and *Mary Ann and Miss Mozart* by Ann Turnbull, *Cecily's Portrait* by Adèle Geras and *Andie's Moon* by Linda Newbery.

• You may want to try *Victory* by Susan Cooper, a time-slip adventure about a present-day girl and a boy who is powder-monkey on *HMS Victory*, Nelson's flagship.

What a terrific idea: getting three top authors each to write a book about the same London house and the girls who lived in it over the years. *Lizzie's Wish* is the story of a Victorian girl who wants to become a gardener at a time when career choices for women were limited. The heroine of *Polly's March* is determined to support the suffragettes despite her family's disapproval. And in *Josie Under Fire*, set during World War II, Josie learns to stand up for what's right. Each novel is fairly easy to read, yet full of drama and historical detail that gives a real sense of the times, and the struggles faced by girls living in earlier eras. The second series spans the eighteenth century to the swinging sixties.

**Madelyn Travis**

★ ★ ★ ★ ★ ★

# THE HITCHHIKER'S GUIDE TO THE GALAXY series  Douglas Adams

A few minutes before Earth is destroyed, Arthur Dent, an ordinary, unassuming man, is whisked away to an alien spaceship by his friend, Ford Prefect. Although Ford looks like a human, he comes from a distant planet and had been visiting Earth as a writer for *The Hitchhiker's Guide to the Galaxy*.

What follows is a series of weird adventures where anything can happen and usually does. Our heroes discover that planet Earth was not a planet at all but a giant super-computer built by a race of aliens. They even discover the answer to the meaning of Life, the Universe and Everything.

Once you've read this series and bought the tapes and DVDs, you will find you keep going back to them over and over again for the rest of your life!

**Colin Thompson**

**Next?**

• The 'Trilogy in Four Parts' continues with *The Restaurant at the End of the Universe*; *Life, the Universe and Everything*; *So Long and Thanks for All the Fish* and *Mostly Harmless*.

• Not very much in the human book world comes close to Douglas Adams's series, but try the ones based in Terry Pratchett's Discworld. (*UBG* 68)

# HITLER'S CANARY

### Sandi Toksvig

Mum's a famous actress, Dad makes stage scenery and their family is cosy and secure ... but they are living in 'Hitler's Canary', the nickname for Denmark in World War II. When the German army arrives to 'protect' the locals, life soon gets very nasty. Jews are sent to concentration camps. There are arrests, shootings and amateurish acts of sabotage. The family devises an outrageous scheme to save their Jewish neighbours, and they discover a traitor in their midst, along with some unlikely heroes.

The story is based on true facts and despite some very sad bits, it never gets too heavy. Instead, it's exciting, interesting and, most of all, the funny bits *are* funny. It's the best book I've read for ages.

**Kjartan Poskitt**

### Next?
• **Framed** by Frank Cottrell Boyce is a very funny wartime story set in Wales. (**UBG** 119)
• *Hitler's Daughter* by Jackie French is a thought-provoking time-slip story that looks at the war from a different perspective. (**UBG** 153)
• Or read Michael Morpurgo's **The Mozart Question**, about the horrors of the Holocaust and the power of music.

★ ★ ★ ★ ★ ★

# HITLER'S DAUGHTER

### Jackie French

### Next?
• Everyone should read *The Diary of a Young Girl* by Anne Frank. (**UBG** 84)
• Another book about the war is **Number the Stars** by Lois Lowry, set in Nazi-occupied Denmark.
• Or for another fictional daughter, this time a character from a Shakespeare play, read *Shylock's Daughter* by Mirjam Pressler, which is a slightly tougher read, but well worth trying.

(The author is no relation, although I'd be hugely proud if she was...) This is a bit of a one-off book – I've not read anything quite like it. It's strange and unusual and absolutely fascinating; a story within a story about Hitler's daughter – could it be true? Anna tells Heidi's story to Mark and Little Tracey, and their reactions mirror those of the world at large. If Hitler really had had a daughter, would anybody have ever looked at her as a person in her own right, or would his shadow always have darkened the way she was seen? Could you love a man like that if he was your father? It's a wonderfully thought-provoking idea, and this is genuinely one of the most beautifully written books I've come across... Do, do, *do* try it.

**Vivian French**

# H.I.V.E. Mark Walden

Otto Malpense wakes up one morning to find he is flying in a helicopter to a mysterious island. He has no idea how he got there or why, and neither does his fellow passenger, Wing Fanchu. *H.I.V.E.* is a school-based novel, but like Hogwarts in **Harry Potter**, this is no ordinary school. H.I.V.E. stands for 'Higher Institute of Villainous Education' and this is a school that positively *encourages* bad behaviour. In fact, they actually teach it from books with titles like 'Elementary Evil'. But how did the children get to H.I.V.E. and why do they seem to be prisoners? Otto and his new friends Wing, Shelby and Laura make plans to escape in Mark Walden's clever, action-packed adventure story.

**Chris Priestley**

### Next?
• You'll need the sequels at once – *H.I.V.E: The Overlord Protocol* and *Escape Velocity*.

• For more entertaining evil, try Eoin Colfer's **Artemis Fowl** series. (*UBG* 23)

• Or Stephen Cole's *Thieves Like Us*. Teenage thief – and genius cryptologist – Jonah, gets sprung from a detention centre by a criminal mastermind, and then his adventures really begin.

★ ★ ★ ★ ★ ★

# THE HOBBIT J.R.R. Tolkien

### Next?
• If you're ready to graduate to the grandfather of all fantasy fiction, plunge straight into the massive and magnificent *The Lord of the Rings*. (*UBG* 211)

• You might appreciate Paul Stewart and Chris Riddell's very funny parody fantasy, *Muddle Earth*. (*UBG* 240)

• Or you could try **Fighting Fantasy** (written by Steve Jackson in collaboration with Ian Livingstone). (*UBG* 112)

• Try some Robin Jarvis – fantasy in a rather different vein. There's **The Deptford Mice** trilogy (*UBG* 82) and **The Whitby Witches** trilogy (*UBG* 381).

This was a book that changed my life!

*The Hobbit* was my first introduction to Middle Earth, Tolkien's medieval world of magic, monsters and fantastic quests. Up until then, 'fantasy' had always implied fairy tales – charming bedtime stories for young children. But Tolkien's characters, the stories, the plots, the intrigues, the story of Bilbo's travels, made a huge and lasting impression on me (though when I read the book I was 20 years old!).

Gandalf the Grey, Smaug the Dragon, Shelob the Giant Spider and, of course, Gollum have all become household names. With *The Hobbit* and *The Lord of the Rings*, the whole fantasy genre gained a maturity it never had before. Tolkien's universe was a huge influence over all the role-playing games to come, from 'Dungeons and Dragons' to **Fighting Fantasy**. But let's not forget that *The Hobbit* is also a jolly good read, too!

**Steve Jackson**

# THE HODGEHEG Dick King-Smith

## Next?

• Any other Dick King-Smith book. *The Sheep-Pig* (*UBG* 308) is probably my favourite, but there are lots of other wonderful ones including *The Water Horse* (a story of the Loch Ness Monster) and *Horse Pie*, in which three horses and a donkey have to thwart some rustlers who want to make them into pie!

• Or try Colin Dann's **Animals of Farthing Wood** series. (*UBG* 19)

If you are very lucky, you might have hedgehogs living in your garden. This charming story shows you life from their point of view. The hero is a young hedgehog called Victor Maximilian St George ('Max' for short). After yet another hedgehog's tragic death, brave Max sets out to find a way to cross the road safely. His explorations lead him into great danger, including a close encounter with a bicycle, which gives him a nasty bump on the head and makes him get all his words muddled up. That's when he starts calling himself a 'hodgeheg'. The solution he finally finds will make you laugh and wish you could be there to see it. This is a fun, quick read which will show you familiar things in an unfamiliar way.

**Abigail Anderson**

★ ★ ★ ★ ★ ★

# HOLES Louis Sachar

*Holes* really is a miracle of a book – a fast, involving read that seems very simple on the face of it, but which conceals an incredibly clever structure that's packed with surprises.

It tells the story of the oddly named Stanley Yelnats, who finds himself arrested for stealing a pair of trainers and sent to a terrible American prison, where he is condemned to dig endless holes in a huge, dried-up lake. Stanley comes to realise that there's a reason for this seemingly pointless task. His survival, his friendships and his eventual salvation provide the main thrust of the narrative as secrets, buried in the past, come to the surface in the most unexpected of ways.

I read this short novel in the same week as my 12-year-old son and we both enjoyed it equally. Like all the best children's books, it has enormous adult appeal. I thought it quite simply amazing.

**Anthony Horowitz**

## Next?

• Everything Louis Sachar has written, including the sequel to *Holes, Small Steps*. There's also *The Boy Who Lost His Face* (*UBG* 46) and *There's a Boy in the Girls' Bathroom* (*UBG* 344).

• Jerry Spinelli is another great American writer; try *The Mighty Crashman* (*UBG* 228), about a bully and *Wringer*, about a boy who doesn't want to turn ten, as that's when he has to do something horrible.

• Try Natalie Babbitt's *Tuck Everlasting*. A girl finds herself making an extraordinary decision. (*UBG* 355)

# HOMECOMING   Cynthia Voigt ●●●

### Next?
• There are six more books about the Tillerman family: try *Dicey's Song* and *A Solitary Blue*.

• Another very moving American novel is *Bridge to Terabithia*. (*UBG* 47)

• *Out of the Dust* by Karen Hesse is a wonderful novel set in the middle of nowhere in America.

• Joan Lingard's *Tug of War*, about twins separated as they flee war-torn Latvia.

This is one of those books – the best sort of books – where the author creates real characters that you care about and puts them slap bang in the middle of a crisis. You're willing them to succeed, you're scared stiff they won't, and the book is just about the most important thing in your life until you find out what happens.

Dicey, aged 13, is left in a car park with her younger brothers and sister. When her mentally disturbed mother fails to return, Dicey sees no alternative but to set off across America to try to find a long-lost aunt and a place to call home. The children sleep rough, go hungry, have many near-disasters, and walk, mile after mile after mile.

The characters are beautifully drawn – they're so different and yet so close. There is humour, sadness and wisdom in this story, and my whole family loved it. It's a long book but stick with it, because the ending is tremendous.

**Malachy Doyle**

★ ★ ★ ★ ★ ★

# THE HOMEWARD BOUNDERS   Diana Wynne Jones ●●●

Jamie loves life in his dirty, slummy city. He loves football, and exploring – but one day he blunders into a place where 'They' are playing a game. 'They' make Jamie a Homeward Bounder, fated to be dragged from one world to another until he finds Home again. But there are a multitude of different worlds, and it looks as though Jamie's search will go on for a long, long time.

This is a marvellous adventure, full of extraordinary characters and worlds that you'll remember for a long time. It's perhaps the most powerful and haunting of Diana Wynne Jones's children's books, and Jamie's journey through so many different worlds – some fun to live in and some most definitely not – will keep you transfixed to the end.

**Sally Prue**

### Next?
• Diana Wynne Jones carries the multi-world idea through many books. For a really hilarious story, try *Charmed Life*, or read any of the other **Worlds of Chrestomanci** books. (*UBG* 393)

• Sally Prue's *The Truth Sayer* is another book that slips between worlds. (*UBG* 354)

• *The Wish List* by Eoin Colfer is about struggling with life – and death.

# HOOT  Carl Hiaasen  ●●

Carl Hiaasen has long beguiled older readers with stories about the havoc being wrought by avaricious, land-hungry property developers on the flora and fauna of his beloved Florida. Not an obvious subject for a children's novel, but by bringing into his story pupils from a local school – Dan, the loathsome bully; Roy, his long-suffering victim; an unlikely maiden in shining armour in the Amazonian form of Beatrice Leep; not to mention some burrowing owls – he bridges the gap as though it were the most natural thing in the world.

Exciting and thought provoking from the word go, *Hoot* is full of twists and cliffhangers, spiced overall with Hiaasen's unique brand of humour. It will stay in your mind long after you have finished it.

**Michael Bond**

**Next?**
• More Hiaasen? Read the equally great *Flush*.
• For other books about conserving wildlife, read *Kite* by Melvin Burgess (*UBG* 192), or Julia Golding's **Companions Quartet**.
• Or for the story of a girl – who happens to be very ill – and her new life in Cornwall, try Ann Kelley's *The Burying Beetle*.

★ ★ ★ ★ ★ ★

# HORNBLOWER series  C.S. Forester  ●●●

**Next?**
• Read more of Horatio's adventures in *Hornblower and the Hotspur*. If you're really hooked, you can follow his naval career right up to Admiral!
• There's a story about C.S. Forester himself in Roald Dahl's *The Wonderful Story of Henry Sugar*.
• Or try Michael Molloy's thrilling adventure set during the Napoleonic wars – *Peter Raven Under Fire*. (*UBG* 263)
• For brilliant action at sea, read the **Sharpe** books by Bernard Cornwell, starting with *Sharpe's Rifles*.

Horatio Hornblower is an unlikely hero. He's a 'weedy youth' who is clumsy, stutters, blushes bright pink and gets seasick before his ship has even left the harbour. But he has always dreamed of going to sea. In *Mr Midshipman Hornblower*, Horatio's first trip to sea starts badly. Homesick, seasick and bullied, he challenges his tormentor to a duel, secretly hoping the bully will kill him and end his misery. But the plan doesn't work and Horatio survives. After that, adventures come so fast that he doesn't have time to be homesick. He has lots of challenges to face, from climbing the rigging when he's scared of heights to his first shocking experiences of warfare.

This is a terrific adventure story. But it's more than that. It's the story of a shy, thoughtful teenager who's plunged into nightmare situations and has to grow up, far too quickly, but who discovers qualities in himself he never knew he had.

**Susan Gates**

# HOROWITZ HORROR Anthony Horowitz

If you like sweet, happy stories that ease you to sleep with images of lambs gambolling in the fields and butterflies fluttering – don't read this book!

But ... if you like to be scared, if you like the shivery fear of wondering what might be lurking under the bed or what nasty things might be hiding in the most innocent of objects, then these are the stories for you.

There are nine in the first collection, all short, sharp and shocking. Don't read them if you get nightmares easily – and be careful about lending them to grown-ups – they might not be able to cope!

**Leonie Flynn**

**Next?**
• If you want these stories in handy, bite-sized chunks, each is available as a slim book on its own. And you'll find even more horror from Mr Horowitz in *More Horowitz Horror*.
• If you like being scared, read the spine-chilling **The Saga of Darren Shan** – and try to work out if the story really is true… (*UBG* 293)
• Or for more short stories, try *Uncle Montague's Tales of Terror* by Chris Priestley (*UBG* 361), or Chris Mould's *Dust 'n' Bones*, which has reworkings of classic ghost stories.

★ ★ ★ ★ ★ ★

# HORRIBLE HISTORIES series Terry Deary

**Next?**
• There is also a **Horrible Histories** quiz book: *The Awesome Ancient Quiz Book* and the full-colour *The Horrible History of the World*.
• Or try some of Terry Deary's historical fiction. He writes very funny stories set in the past in his *Tudor Tales, Greek Tales, Egyptian Tales, Roman Tales* and *Knights' Tales*.
• Or the more bloodthirsty among you might like his *The King in Blood Red and Gold* or *The Prince of Rags and Patches*, both in the **Tudor Terror** series.

How could anyone not love Terry Deary's books? The pictures are funny, the puns are awful, the facts are fascinating – and it's all rough, gory and hilarious.

Not that they're not sort-of-serious in their way too, and really well-researched, and all factually correct; it's just that it's really easy to forget that it's all useful and educational (etc, etc) when you're enjoying yourself this much. After all, how many history books do you know that will tell you about glass eyes and earwax and bodysnatchers and lots and lots of toilets?

I think my favourites are *The Measly Middle Ages* and *The Terrible Tudors*, but I've not yet found one that hasn't made me laugh out loud. You can start with *The Savage Stone Age* and work your way through them chronologically, chuckling right up to the twentieth century (I'm sure that if you start, you'll want to read them all...), or just pick one at random and throw yourself in!

**Daniel Hahn**

# HORRID HENRY

**Francesca Simon**

Francesca Simon

Illustrated by Tony Ross

Do you have a brother or sister who is perfect, while you never do anything right? If so, then *Horrid Henry* is for you.

Poor Henry suffers dreadfully. His brother Peter is 'perfect' but Henry somehow manages to get things wrong. It's not Henry's fault that he doesn't tidy up, or that when he wants to buy something he has spent all his money, or that things just seem to 'happen' when he is around.

*Horrid Henry* is a must for everyone. Mum and Dad will enjoy him, too and count their blessings that you are not like Henry (or not very like Henry!). Henry does all the things that you would never dream of doing, but sometimes wish you could.

**Julia Lytollis**

### Next?

- Astrid Lindgren's stories about Emil are just as good; look out for *Emil and the Great Escaper* and *Emil's Clever Pig*. (*UBG* 99)
- Or try *Mr Majeika* by Humphrey Carpenter. Mr Majeika is a schoolteacher who used to be a wizard. (*UBG* 238)
- In *The Worst Witch* by Jill Murphy, Mildred is in her first year at Miss Cackle's Academy for Witches. Like Henry, she can't seem to get anything right. (*UBG* 394)
- Or for another boy who gets into scrapes, try Hilary McKay's **Charlie** series.

## The Ultimate Readers' Poll

# Top Ten Favourite Characters

1 Alex Rider

2 Charlie Bucket (Charlie and the Chocolate Factory)

3 Hermione Granger (Harry Potter series)

4 Horrid Henry

5 Lyra Silvertongue (His Dark Materials trilogy)

6 Tracy Beaker

7 Harry Potter

8 Mia Thermopolis (The Princess Diaries)

9 Montmorency

10 James (CHERUB series)

# THE HOUND OF THE BASKERVILLES

## Arthur Conan Doyle

Try this for size: a vast, deserted moor full of deadly quagmires. The howling of a nightmare beast. A lonely house whose owner has been frightened to death. And two servants who creep about the candle-lit corridors in the dead of night. Dr Watson is left alone to solve the mystery of the Hound of the Baskervilles, while Sherlock Holmes, the greatest detective of all time, is busy on another case.

*The Hound of the Baskervilles* is perhaps the finest detective story ever written. It mingles logic and the supernatural in a bewildering package that even Sherlock Holmes hesitates to unwrap...

**Hugh Scott**

### Next?
- If your hair is not already standing on end after this, maybe you could venture to open *The Collected Ghost Stories* of M.R. James.
- Try Agatha Christie's page-turners, such as *The Pale Horse* and *And Then There Were None* (*UBG* 17).
- Or for a book that involves this story, look for *The Curious Incident of the Dog in the Night-time* by Mark Haddon.
- How about some books about Holmes's Baker Street Irregulars – look out for Anthony Read's **Baker Street Boys** series, and particularly *The Case of the Limehouse Laundry*.

★ ★ ★ ★ ★ ★

# THE HOUNDS OF THE MORRIGAN  Pat O'Shea

One day, Pidge goes into a used bookstore in Galway and finds an old manuscript in which the serpent Olc-Glas lies hidden. And so an amazing adventure begins. Pidge is an ordinary boy, so when the magic starts, it is all the more magical. His relationship with his sister, Brigit, has the same matter-of-fact reality about it, making the dangers they encounter all the more exciting and scary. They're real: you care.

Lots of people help – and hinder – Pidge and Brigit in their battle to help keep the Morrigan from regaining her old power over the world, and probably destroying it in the process.

**Diane Duane**

### Next?
- Something else that weaves Irish legend into the story? Kate Thompson's *The Last of the High Kings* and *The New Policeman* (*UBG* 249) do this to great effect.
- Nicholas Stuart Gray's *The Seventh Swan* is another story that uses an Irish legend. It's out of print, but look for it in your library; it's worth the effort!
- Or try one of the books in Diane Duane's **Young Wizards** series. (*UBG* 396)

# HOW THE HANGMAN LOST HIS HEART K.M. Grant ● ● ●

This novel can only be described as frantically paced, frantically gory, frantically funny and frantically good. The heroine, Alice, after watching the execution of her uncle Frank, decides to rescue his head from where it is being displayed on Temple Bar so that it can be laid to rest with the other parts of his body. But all goes wonderfully awry with vengeful cavalry intent on thwarting the rescue, lots of chasing through the streets of Georgian London, followed by an episode of hiding in bedrooms and then falling in love with a good-looking young captain by the name of Hew French. Things are further complicated when the executioner who originally despatched Uncle Frank then falls in love with Alice and also becomes involved in the rescue attempt.

Confused? You will be, as well as hugely entertained and pumped full of adrenalin. Most definitely *not* a relaxing read.

**Stuart Hill**

### Next?

• Try K.M. Grant's wonderful historical saga that starts with *Blood Red Horse*. (*UBG* 40)

• For another feisty historical heroine, meet Mariane in Pauline Chandler's *Warrior Girl* – a book whose other great female character is Joan of Arc! (*UBG* 375)

• Or what about a bit of a love / hate love story? Read *Dragonfly* by Julia Golding, in which Tashi is sent to marry the totally uncouth heir to a neighbouring throne.

★ ★ ★ ★ ★ ★

# HOW TO EAT FRIED WORMS Thomas Rockwell ●

### Next?

• More Thomas Rockwell! Try *How to Fight a Girl* and *How to Get Fabulously Rich*.

• *Chocolate Fever* by Robert Kimmel Smith or *Freckle Juice* by Judy Blume are also both really good.

• Try Paul Jennings's *Uncanny!* (*UBG* 360) The **Un** books make up a series that is fast, funny and unpredictable.

• Chris d'Lacey's *Shrinking Ralph Perfect*, about a boy who ends up miniaturised and on show in a zoo, is just as funny!

Would you do anything for money? In this delightfully disgusting tale, Billy accepts a bet from his friends to eat 15 worms in 15 days – if he wins, he'll earn enough for a new bike.

When my son was nine, he abandoned 'proper' books for magazines and graphic novels such as **Asterix** and **Tintin**. Then, one day I discovered this book. What nine-year-old boy could resist such a title? I didn't suggest he read it; I merely left it in a prominent position. He read it. I can't swear it was this book that got him reading 'proper' books again, but a year later he had finished the entire **Lord of the Rings** trilogy.

If you think books are boring, this'll definitely change your mind!

**Caroline Lawrence**

# HOW TO LIVE FOREVER   Colin Thompson

I'd already reached the ripe old age of 22 when this book came out, so I didn't get the chance to read it when I was your age. And come to think of it, if someone had given it to me then, I would probably have taken one look at it and said, 'But it's a picture book! That's for babies!'

I would have been so wrong. I loved *How to Live Forever* when I was 22, and still do at an elderly 33 – and if I'm not too old for picture books, then you certainly aren't.

Colin Thompson's pictures are just the cleverest you'll see: chock-full of smart little jokes (and some truly awful puns) hidden away for you to discover. The story itself is lovely, and very simple (a library that comes to life, and a boy who lives there going on a quest for a missing, magical book), but it's really the pictures you'll find delightful and fun, each one jam-packed with brilliant, witty detail. Don't miss out!

**Daniel Hahn**

### Next?

• This is one of those stories that is pretty much unique, but you may find that *The Little Prince* by Antoine de Saint-Exupéry has a similar feel to it. (*UBG* 205)

• Colin Thompson has written and illustrated other books – look out for *Falling Angels*, *The Paperbag Prince*, *Looking for Atlantis* and *The Tower to the Sun*.

• And don't miss our selection of comics and picture books featured on pp. 264–265.

★ ★ ★ ★ ★ ★

# HOW TO TRAIN YOUR DRAGON   Cressida Cowell

### Next?

• Find out what happens next in *How to Be a Pirate*, *How to Speak Dragonese*, *How to Cheat a Dragon's Curse*, *How to Twist a Dragon's Tale* and *How to Ride a Dragon's Storm*.

• Want to find out more about dragons? Seek out *Dragonology*, an amazing book full of everything you ever wanted to know.

• For more humour, read *Urgum the Axeman* (*UBG* 365), or the **Something Wickedly Weird** series by Chris Mould, starting with *The Wooden Mile*.

The answer? Yell at it.

This is the advice given to our young hero, Hiccup Horrendous Haddock III, when he starts his Viking training programme – and things go downhill from there. Ending up with the only toothless dragon in existence, Hiccup is left to defend his people against the most feared sea dragon of them all. And yelling just won't work.

A wonderful book, full of wacky characters (Goober the Belch, Stoick the Vast, and the unforgettable dragon, Toothless), the story bowls along as fast as a Viking longship under full sail, chased by a hoard of Exterminator dragons. Zany illustrations make the pages zing with life.

**Julia Golding**

# HOW TO TRAIN YOUR PARENTS   Pete Johnson

Twelve-year-old Louis (pronounced 'Lou-ee') wants to be a stand-up comic. Trouble is that 'Swotsville', where he lives, is hooked on educational competitiveness – that is, exams! And, worse still, it seems that Louis's parents have caught the bug, even to the extent of removing the telly from his bedroom!

Enter Maddy, his new and resourceful friend and self-styled 'talent scout', who not only guides him along his 'career' path but enrols him in her sure-fire parent-training programme.

Related through the pages of Louis's personal diary, the book is observant and very funny. Pete Johnson has an amazing ability to portray resolutely individual characters, and his story takes a revealing sideways look at over-ambitious and pushy parents. (Your own parents could probably learn something from this book, too...)

**Chris Stephenson**

## Next?
• If you like the diary form, try *Simone's Diary* by Helen Pielichaty. (*UBG* 312)

• Or you might want to follow Louis's example and read the book Todd lends him, *Joy in the Morning*, one of P.G. Wodehouse's funniest stories about Jeeves and Bertie Wooster. Read about the **Jeeves** series on p. 284.

• For something else by Pete Johnson, you can do no better than reading *Rescuing Dad*, another extremely funny and emotionally true novel, and a sort of companion-piece to this one. (*UBG* 283)

★ ★ ★ ★ ★ ★

# HOW TO WRITE REALLY BADLY   Anne Fine

Chester Howard has been to some terrible schools in his time, all of them a thousand times worse than yours; but Walbottle Manor is the most awful of them all. Now he's been buddied up to help the bottom-of-the-class boy who sits next to him.

Joe Gardner isn't a total loser – he can build the most intricate models; he's just hopeless at schoolwork. Until the day Miss Tate sets another one of her 'How to' projects. Wickedly, Chester sets to work with Joe on a project to 'write really badly', something Joe is naturally very good at.

Anne Fine writes the most brilliantly witty, make-you-stop-and-think stories that really keep you reading – and thinking – beyond the last page.

**Eileen Armstrong**

## Next?
• *Joey Pigza Swallowed the Key* by Jack Gantos is about a loveable troublemaker, one who, like Chester, doesn't mean to be. (*UBG* 182)

• *Utterly Me, Clarice Bean* by Lauren Child is a story within a story about a class project that turns out to be more lively than expected! (*UBG* 365)

• Part poem, part story-to-make-you-smile, *Love That Dog* by Sharon Creech is about Jack, who learns that writing poetry isn't difficult after all. (*UBG* 214)

# THE HUNDRED AND ONE DALMATIANS  Dodie Smith

### Next?

• You might also want to read *The Starlight Barking*, Dodie Smith's sequel.

• For a story written from the point of view of a dog, try Henrietta Branford's *Fire, Bed and Bone*. (*UBG* 113) Or for a story that follows the life of one particular dog, try Michael Morpurgo's *Born to Run*.

• Lady Lamorna in Vivian French's wonderful *The Robe of Skulls* is every bit as villainous as Cruella de Vil. (*UBG* 287)

When Pongo and his mate Missis Pongo become the proud parents of 15 dalmatian puppies, they think their happiness is complete. But the sinister Cruella de Vil, lover of all things black and white, also wants their puppies – to make a fur coat! When the puppies are kidnapped, Pongo and Missis set out on a quest to rescue them, helped by the dogs they contact through the mysterious 'Starlight Barking'.

This truly magical story has lingered in my mind since I first read it, aged nine. Cruella de Vil (devil – get it?) makes a wonderful villainess with her half-white, half-black hairstyle and her taste for pepper on everything. But there are tender moments too – my favourite scene is where the Spaniel's old master thinks Pongo and Missis are ghosts of his old dogs, and makes them hot buttered toast over an open fire with his toasting-fork.

**Katherine Roberts**

★ ★ ★ ★ ★ ★

# I AM DAVID  Anne Holm

A boy escapes from a nameless camp in a nameless country. With nothing but a map and a compass, he crosses Europe to find the mother he has never known. He is wary, distrustful, older than his years, and yet in many ways he is an infant. His journey across Europe is a kind of rebirth; he discovers new colours, such as the colour of the sea under a summer sun; new tastes, like the taste of an orange; he learns to trust: people, a dog, God.

This is a timeless story of the triumph of persistence and courage over a truly evil opponent. There is one scene of self-sacrifice which is unforgettable. And the ending is moving beyond belief.

**Caroline Lawrence**

### Next?

• There are a lot of very good stories about children surviving against the odds. Try *Milkweed* by Jerry Spinelli, which is also about appalling events seen through innocent eyes, or *When Hitler Stole Pink Rabbit* by Judith Kerr (*UBG* 379).

• Or look for *Fly Away Home* by Christine Nostlinger, based on the author's own experiences of moving to a house on the outskirts of Vienna and surviving the German and then the Russian armies as they fight their way across country.

• *The Silver Sword* by Ian Serraillier (*UBG* 310) is also about a terrifying wartime journey.

# I AM THE GREAT HORSE

### Katherine Roberts

'I am no black beauty'. So begins the story of Bucephalas, the war stallion of Alexander the Great. Bucephalas is as fierce and uncompromising as the young king who rides him, and his view of Alexander's battles is exciting and vivid. Also, subtly unsettling.

As a stallion, Bucephalas is used to dominating other horses, either by dropping his own dung on top of theirs ('dominating dung') or through shows of strength. How different, we begin to wonder, is Alexander's urge to dominate the world?

There are horse stories aplenty, but this one is out on its own. Katherine Roberts, as usual, has written a well-researched, utterly convincing book with plenty of action and just a dash of the supernatural to round it off. Terrific!

**Katherine Langrish**

### Next?

• More Katherine Roberts? Read her totally fabulous **Seven Fabulous Wonders** series (*UBG* 138) or the magical *Spellfall*, which has no horses, but unicorns instead!

• Or there's Michael Morpurgo's *War Horse*, about a horse who ends up on the battlefields of the First World War. (*UBG* 373)

• Or for other stories based on history, read Geraldine McCaughrean's *Tamburlaine's Elephants* or Susan Cooper's *King of Shadows* (*UBG* 190), which has Shakespeare as a character in it.

### Horse Stories, Old and New

• *Black Beauty* by Anna Sewell
• *National Velvet* by Enid Bagnold
• **Punchbowl Farm** series by Monica Edwards
• **Flambards** series by K.M. Peyton
• *The Silver Brumby* by Mary Elwyn Patchett
• *Blood Red Horse* by K.M. Grant
• *War Horse* by Michael Morpurgo
• *The Little White Horse* by Elizabeth Goudge
• *Ribbons and Rings* by Gillian Baxter

# I, CORIANDER

## Sally Gardner

What a sparkler this is, mixing fairy tale and mystery, in the setting of Oliver Cromwell's London. Daughter of a wealthy Royalist merchant, Coriander Hobie longs to wear the mysterious silver shoes which appear on the doorstep one day. They are her size and they carry the initial 'C' for Coriander, but her mother forbids her to put them on, knowing that they will transport her daughter to another world. When her mother dies, Coriander falls into the hands of a cruel stepmother. When her father is arrested, the wicked preacher, Arise Fell, shuts her into a chest. Can she survive? Can she bring the villains to justice? With an exotic blend of alligators, pearls, fairy tales and time slip, this story is sheer enchantment!

**Pauline Chandler**

### Next?

• *The Red Necklace* is another of Sally Gardner's wonderful historical novels (*UBG* 282); it is about the French Revolution and the sequel, *The Silver Blade*, continues the adventure.

• *The Merrybegot* by Julie Hearn gives us the tale of Nell and her grandmother, wise women and healers, in Tudor England.

• For a heart-wrenching story about unwanted children, read Jamila Gavin's *Coram Boy*. What happens to babies born to the poor, who already have too many mouths to feed? (*UBG* 69)

★ ★ ★ ★ ★ ★

# I WAS A RAT!

## Philip Pullman

### Next?

• Other books that take a different view of fairy stories include *Clever Polly and the Stupid Wolf* by Catherine Storr (*UBG* 65), *Revolting Rhymes* by Roald Dahl, *The Three Little Wolves and the Big Bad Pig* by Eugene Trivizas and Jon Scieszka's *The True Story of the Three Little Pigs*.

• Other Philip Pullmans to find: *Spring-Heeled Jack, Clockwork* (*UBG* 66) and *The Firework-Maker's Daughter* (*UBG* 114).

An absolute must for anybody who has ever considered the implications of the sort of things that fairy godmothers get up to. Our hero is a little boy in a coachman's outfit who is convinced that he used to be a rat. Many people try to use him for their own gain as he tries to sort out what has happened to him and return to the kindly couple who adopted him.

The best thing about the book is the regular use of the front page of the fabulously tabloid *Daily Scourge*, which provides both the voice of the people, and an advertisement for a heavily armed garden gnome, costing only £299.99!

**Anthony Reuben**

# HISTORICAL STORIES
## Past Lives
### by James Riordan

Good writers bring history to life, teach us about the lives of others, and help us to understand ourselves better.

When I was a boy (my children hate me saying that!), I grew up on Stevenson's *Treasure Island*, Ballantyne's *Coral Island*, Rider Haggard's *King Solomon's Mines*, Kipling's *Gunga Din* (it was my grandfather's party piece at Christmas), not to mention Defoe's *Robinson Crusoe*. Even though my childhood years were spent under a chimney-sweep's roof, it never entered my head to ask why all the young heroes of these novels lived in rich and conservative social settings, where women were absent and black people were slaves or servants.

How far we've come in 50 years! There are still historical novels that continue the crusading tradition (where black people and women are second-rate citizens), but they have mostly given way to a view of history that respects girls as well as boys, black as well as white, miners and peasants as well as nobles and kings.

Rosemary Sutcliff was one of the first to set a new standard for history stories by being deeply concerned about ordinary people, especially the Romans and the Britons (in **The Eagle of the Ninth** series). She also brings history vividly to life, as with the Celtic Queen Boudicca (*Song for a Dark Queen*) and the Vikings (*Blood Feud*). Terry Jones is another who gives us a vivid picture of the Vikings (*The Saga of Erik the Viking*).

Although Kevin Crossley-Holland deals with the mythical King Arthur (*The Seeing Stone* and its sequels), he provides a clear and exciting

## Twelve World War II Books

- *Blitzcat* by Robert Westall
- *The Machine Gunners* by Robert Westall
- *Prisoner* by James Riordan
- *The Silver Sword* by Ian Serraillier
- *The Diary of a Young Girl* by Anne Frank
- *Carrie's War* by Nina Bawden
- *Music on the Bamboo Radio* by Martin Booth
- *When Hitler Stole Pink Rabbit* by Judith Kerr
- *Dolphin Crossing* by Jill Paton Walsh
- *August '44* by Carlo Gébler
- *Goodnight Mr Tom* by Michelle Magorian
- *The Snow Goose* by Paul Gallico

insight into British history after the Romans left. The Middle Ages are well covered by Henrietta Branford (*Fire, Bed and Bone*, on the Peasants' Revolt of 1381), Geoffrey Trease (*Bows Against the Barons*), Cynthia Harnett (*The Wool-Pack*) and Geraldine McCaughrean (*A Little Lower than the Angels*), while Susan Cooper sets her *King of Shadows* in Shakespeare's time.

The lives of young people during the Industrial Revolution in both Britain and the United States are amply covered by celebrated writers like Joan Aiken (*Midnight is a Place*), Ann Turnbull (*Pigeon Summer*) and Geraldine McCaughrean (*Stop the Train*), while Theresa Breslin (*Kezzie*) and Robert Swindells (*A Candle in the Night*) recreate the hard lot of child coal miners.

Both Melvin Burgess (*The Copper Treasure*) and Leon Garfield (*Smith* and *The Apprentices*) write of youngsters growing up in Victorian London, while Laura Ingalls Wilder's autobiographical **Little House** books describe her own childhood in the Big Woods of Wisconsin, USA.

## More Brilliant War Books

- *Lord of the Nutcracker Men* by Iain Lawrence
- *War Game* by Michael Foreman
- *War Horse* by Michael Morpurgo
- *Private Peaceful* by Michael Morpurgo
- *Little Soldier* by Bernard Ashley
- *Gulf* by Robert Westall
- **Biggles** series by Captain W.E. Johns
- *I Am David* by Anne Holm
- *Black Ships Before Troy* by Rosemary Sutcliff
- *Crusade* by Elizabeth Laird
- *A.K.* by Peter Dickinson

## Five from Ancient Rome

- *Eagle of the Ninth* by Rosemary Sutcliff
- **Roman Mysteries** series (*The Thieves of Ostia*, etc.) by Caroline Lawrence
- *The Mark of the Horse Lord* by Rosemary Sutcliff
- **Asterix** by René Goscinny and Albert Uderzo
- *Aquila* by Andrew Norriss
- *Minna's Quest* by K.M. Peyton

## Pirate Stories

- *The Last of the Sky Pirates* by Paul Stewart and Chris Riddell (from the **Edge Chronicles**)
- *Plundering Paradise* by Geraldine McCaughrean
- *Treasure Island* by Robert Louis Stevenson
- *The Salt Pirates of Skegness* by Chris d'Lacey
- *Piratica* by Tanith Lee
- *Pirates!* by Celia Rees
- **Vampirates** series by Justin Somper

War is a theme taken up by many authors who have written books dealing with the heroic, and sometimes tragic, lives of children. Nothing, of course, can match Anne Frank's moving *The Diary of a Young Girl*. But books like Anne Holm's *I Am David*, Ian Serraillier's *The Silver Sword*, Jill Paton Walsh's *The Dolphin Crossing*, my own *Match of Death*, Michael Morpurgo's *War Horse* and several others describe war itself; while Robert Westall (*The Machine Gunners* and *Blitzcat*) and Robert Swindells (*Hurricane Summer*) mainly focus on the effects of war on young people at home in Britain. Michelle Magorian (*Goodnight Mr Tom*) and Nina Bawden (*Carrie's War*) write of the lives of children evacuated during the war – the most traumatic years of my own life!

# THE ICE BOY Patricia Elliott

### Next?

• To know more about the mythology the story is based on, try Rodney Matthews's *Norse Myths and Legends* or *Axe-Age, Wolf-Age* by Kevin Crossley-Holland.

• *Eight Days of Luke* by Diana Wynne Jones is very different, but you'll find many of the characters in it familiar. (*UBG* 97)

• *The Weirdstone of Brisingamen* by Alan Garner is an engrossing and exciting story about magic in the everyday and how the ordinary can become extraordinary. (*UBG* 377)

• For ancient evil invading the present, try **The Magician's House Quartet** by William Corlett. (*UBG* 217)

Edward and his brother Matt have always spent summer holidays with their uncle in his seaside home, but this year they are without their father, who drowned at sea the year before. One day, Edward mistakes a stranger for his father. Close to, the man is nothing like him, but he has a job for Edward: to pass on a message to his son. Edward has never met his son, but 'He will know you,' the man tells him.

Edward begins to notice that there are other strangers in town, and even the locals may not be quite what they seem. Something very ancient is being re-enacted and Edward's father is at the heart of it.

**Jan Mark**

★ ★ ★ ★ ★ ★

# ICE CAT Linda Newbery

After a heavy snowfall, Tom begins to make a snowman. Gary, his friend who lives next door, is making one, too, with his father's help. Tom's dad is lying upstairs in the bedroom, and he's very different from the father Tom is used to. He's extremely ill and the book doesn't try to hide from its readers exactly how serious the situation is. Tom's snowman turns out to be a cat, and he's not quite sure how this happened... I won't give away the ending, but the Ice Cat is a personification of Tom's fear and anger at his father's illness. This is an easy book to read on one level, but it talks about complicated feelings of love, resentment and awe very movingly.

**Adèle Geras**

### Next?

• You might also like *Linda's Star Turn* (a touching story about a nativity play) and *Smoke Cat* (a ghost story with a cat in it).

• *The Owl Tree* by Jenny Nimmo is another book about caring. (*UBG* 259)

• Don't miss the wonderful *Storm* by Kevin Crossley-Holland. (*UBG* 331)

• You might also like to try Jacqueline Wilson's **The Cat Mummy**, though beware – it is very sad!

• Raymond Briggs's wordless story, *The Snowman*, is now a classic – even if you've read it, search it out and look again. It's marvellous.

# IGRAINE THE BRAVE  Cornelia Funke

When Sir Lamorak the Wily and his beautiful wife The Fair Melisande accidentally turn themselves into pigs whilst conjuring up a surprise birthday present, there's only one person who can save the day. Step forth, daughter Igraine! Unlike her older brother Albert, Igraine has never wanted to learn magic; instead, she dreams of being a knight. Her quest to find the ingredients that will return her parents to human shape proves just the adventure she's been waiting for. There are dastardly villains to overcome, a three-headed dragon to face and The Sorrowful Knight of the Mount of Tears to cheer up. Highly recommended for readers of all ages – I loved it.

**Laura Hutchings**

### Next?
• For stories of real chivalry read T.H. White's *The Sword in the Stone*. (*UBG* 338)

• Another girl who really is a hero? Try *Alanna, the First Adventure* in **The Immortals** series by Tamora Pierce. Female knights don't turn up often in books; it's worth reading about them when they do.

• Or for something tougher, but worth it, Cornelia's magical *The Thief Lord*. (*UBG* 345)

★ ★ ★ ★ ★ ★

# The ILLMOOR CHRONICLES  David Lee Stone

### Next?
• There are now six in the **Illmoor Chronicles**: *The Yowler Foul-up, The Shadewell Shenanigans, The Dwellings Debacle, The Vanquish Vendetta* and *The Coldstone Conflict*.

• If you enjoyed this, try Garth Nix's adventure series **The Keys to the Kingdom**, starting with *Mister Monday*. (*UBG* 231)

• Brian Jacques's **Redwall** stories are all about talking animals. (*UBG* 282)

• Or try Terry Pratchett's very funny *The Amazing Maurice and His Educated Rodents*. (*UBG* 15)

*The Ratastrophe Catastrophe,* the first in the series, pits mercenaries Groan and Gordo (together with a rather decrepit sorcerer), against an evil pied piper, Diek Wustapha, who leads the children of Illmoor (the fantastical continent in which all of this occurs) down to a series of suitably dank and endless caves for his evil master's gain.

As you may well have guessed from the title, the book features another theme: rodents. In fact, the whole cause of the disappearing children scenario is due to our piper not being paid, owing to deficiencies in the treasuries. The furry beasts completely overcome Illmoor's capital city Dullitch and swiftly become a plague to its inhabitants.

*The Ratastrophe Catastrophe* combines vivid, comic, vibrant characters with a refreshing and original plot. Well, almost original...

**Tim Cross**

# THE ILLUSTRATED MUM  Jacqueline Wilson

Dolphin and Star's mother, Marigold, doesn't behave like other mothers: she spends the food money on ingredients for cakes that go wrong; wears bizarre clothes; and stays out late or lies in bed, drinking vodka. Jacqueline Wilson shows how Marigold's manic depression means she sometimes cannot take care of her daughters and that there are no magic solutions, although Star hopes a boyfriend or her long-lost father will provide one.

An important aspect of this sometimes very sad story is how Dolphin, in particular, still loves her mother and how much she appreciates her creative, playful side, and admires the tattoos that cover her body, each one inspiring its own chapter. Dolphin herself finds refuge in drawing when life gets tough, and Nick Sharratt's artwork is cleverly worked into the structure of the book.

**Geraldine Brennan**

### Next?

• More Jacqueline Wilson? You've probably read many of her books, but it is worth checking that you've found them all. Try *Vicky Angel* (*UBG* 369) and *Secrets*.

• Or how about some Belinda Hollyer? Try *The Truth About Josie Green*, which is about sisters who don't get on and a family secret.

• *The Tulip Touch* is a very disturbing Anne Fine book, about the delicate balance of families and friendship. (*UBG* 355)

• Try Gwyneth Rees's *The Mum Hunt*, about a girl whose mum died when she was a baby. (*UBG* 241)

★ ★ ★ ★ ★ ★

# INCANTATION
## Alice Hoffman

### Next?

• Alice Hoffman writes for adults and young adults. Try *The Foretelling* next, which is a fantasy story about a girl destined to be queen of the Amazons.

• For another story that involves the persecution of the Jews, read *Shylock's Daughter* by Mirjam Pressler.

• Celia Rees's *Witch Child* is also about persecution. Like *Incantation*, it is set in the past, but speaks clearly to us about our own world. (*UBG* 388)

This is a story about love, about betrayal and about persecution. It teaches us that nothing can break the human spirit, but it also teaches us that mankind doesn't change. Set in sixteenth-century Spain and loosely based on fact, *Incantation* tells the story of two friends, Estrella and Catalina, who are as close as sisters – until Andres enters their lives. Jealousy leads to hatred, hatred leads to betrayal and with betrayal comes the destruction of a community. This is a beautifully written book that demonstrates, without preaching, how echoes of the past can be seen in today's troubled times. Truly unforgettable.

**Laura Hutchings**

# INCREDIBLANIA stories

## Norman Hunter

**Next?**

• Read every Norman Hunter book you can find, including all the **Professor Branestawm** books. (*UBG* 275)

• Cressida Cowell's *How to Train Your Dragon* takes a similarly wacky view of the world. (*UBG* 162)

• You could also try *Mrs Pepperpot* by Alf Prøysen (*UBG* 239) and *Vlad the Drac* by Ann Jungman (*UBG* 371).

Welcome to Incrediblania, the wackiest, most eccentric country in nonexistence!

If only our country could be run as well as Norman Hunter's incredible royal family runs theirs. Having fun with disasters is the king and queen's speciality, with a dollop of help from their daughters, Princesses Sonia and Rosy, and their husbands. The despicable gloater, Count Bakwerdz, is always on the carpet for his misdeeds.

I loved illustrating these stories. Norman really was a conjuror and the madness that fizzed out of his pen makes such outrageously funny pictures in your imagination that you will discover the real magic of reading.

**Babette Cole**

★ ★ ★ ★ ★ ★

# THE INDIAN IN THE CUPBOARD   Lynne Reid Banks

This is a classic story of the dangers and temptations that surround magic. Omri is given an old plastic Indian, an old plastic cupboard and an old, strange-looking key. When he decides to put the Indian in the cupboard, the tiny plastic figure comes alive and suddenly, Omri is responsible for the life and safety of a tiny human being. When he lets his best friend, Patrick, in on the secret, things become very complicated.

This story is about temptation, honesty and, above all, the welfare of others. At the end of the book, the two boys have to make a grown-up, selfless decision. Will they be able to do it?

More adventures are in store with *The Return of the Indian* and *The Secret of the Indian*.

**Karen Wallace**

**Next?**

• *The Farthest-Away Mountain* is another great book by Lynne Reid Banks. (*UBG* 110)

• Try *Five Children and It* by E. Nesbit, a classic about the temptations of magic. (*UBG* 115) And *The Phoenix and the Carpet* by the same author – what would happen if a phoenix hatched in your house and took you off on a magic carpet?

• Hans Christian Andersen's fairy tales include lots of stories of toys coming to life. (*UBG* 106)

• *Pinocchio* by Carlo Collodi is another classic in the same vein. (*UBG* 269)

# INGO Helen Dunmore

**Next?**

• You'll want the sequels: *The Tide Knot, The Deep* and *The Crossing of Ingo*.

• If you like the way Helen writes, look out for the harder-to-find *The Lilac Tree* and its sequels, *The Seal Cove* and *The Silver Bead*.

• Try Edith Pattou's *The North Child*, which is based on the old Norse legend.

• *East of the Sun and West of the Moon* by Naomi Lewis is another beautifully written story, full of mystery and yearning.

'I dive, and the current swallows me. Just for a second I feel the terrible python pull of it and I'm scared it's going to crush me … and then I'm part of it.'

When Sapphire's dad is lost at sea, everyone in her tiny Cornish village assumes he's dead – even her mum. But Sapphy remembers the tales he told of the underwater land of Ingo. Could that be where he's gone? Soon she and her brother Conor are drawn after him, exploring the deep sea with the mysterious Mer. But Ingo is dangerous as well as beautiful. It has already torn their family apart. Can Sapphy and Conor resist its lure – even if they try?

This is just the first of a series of books about Ingo. If you've ever longed to know how it might feel to live under the sea, read them!

**Katherine Langrish**

# INKHEART Cornelia Funke

Books can be dangerous things. When they are so vivid that their characters burst out of them into our world, and when those characters are the grimmest, nastiest of evil villains, they can be very dangerous indeed. That's what happens in *Inkheart*, the first marvellously written book in the trilogy by Cornelia Funke, the brilliantly imaginative author of *The Thief Lord*.

Meggie's father Mo is a bookbinder, and he has passed on to her his love of books, though he never reads aloud to her – but why? In *Inkheart*, Funke creates a world very like ours, packed with adventure and rich with stories and lively detail. And packed, too, with just the sort of three-dimensional characters who just might slip out between the pages into your world, if you're not too careful...

**Daniel Hahn**

**Next?**

• The thrilling story continues in *Inkspell* and concludes in *Inkdeath*.

• For more on the amazing power of stories, try *Bambert's Book of Missing Stories* by Reinhardt Jung (*UBG* 27) or Salman Rushdie's *Haroun and the Sea of Stories* (*UBG* 143).

• Or for another perfectly realised magic-packed world, try Diana Wynne Jones's *Homeward Bounders*. (*UBG* 156)

# THE INVENTION OF HUGO CABRET Brian Selznick

*The Invention of Hugo Cabret* opens without any words and continues that way for the first 42 pages. At first you hover above a glowing moon, then you're plunged to Earth, right into the action of a bustling station where, through the crowds, you spot Hugo. He then leads you through a maze of corridors and tunnels in a suspenseful sequence in which eyes become clocks and clocks become eyes. You are reading this in a series of pictures all drawn in graphite pencil and edged in black, that flicker and glow, adding a silvery, silent-film-like quality that is so lovely to look at. You will find yourself pausing the action to look deep into a picture, then racing through the pages to keep pace with a chase scene; sometimes these images are even blurred to speed you along.

The story, set in 1930s Paris, tells of how the lives of a boy and an old toymaker are brought together through the discovery of a mechanical man. Film, time, machinery, invention and dreams are cleverly linked into the plot. The author has even used photographs and film stills as part of the illustration to create an extraordinary and magical book.

**David Roberts**

## Not Quite Human – Or More Than?

- *Eager* by Helen Fox
- *The Indian in the Cupboard* by Lynne Reid Banks
- *The Mennyms* by Sylvia Waugh
- *Cold Tom* by Sally Prue
- *The Doll's House* by Rumer Godden
- *Pinocchio* by Carlo Collodi
- *The Wizard of Oz* by Frank L. Baum
- *Skulduggery Pleasant* by Derek Landy
- *The Borrowers* by Mary Norton
- *Stone Heart* by Charlie Fletcher

## Next?

- There's nothing quite like this book, but Russel Hoban's *The Mouse and His Child* has a similar feel, perhaps? (*UBG* 236)

- Or how about a book without any words at all? Try *Tuesday* by David Wiesner.

- Chris Riddell is best known as an illustrator, but he's a great writer, too – try *Ottoline and the Yellow Cat*, in which he puts both these talents to excellent use! (*UBG* 257)

# THE INVISIBLE MAN H.G. Wells

A gruff stranger arrives at the Coach and Horses, demanding a room, food and warmth. He is an alarming sight, with his head and face completely covered. His name is Griffin, and he's a scientist who has discovered the secret of invisibility and used it on himself. Finding it more of a curse than a triumph, Griffin's temper and sanity unravel and he becomes increasingly violent and dangerous.

Wells's fertile imagination really hit the spot for me, and led me to imaginative works by other writers. This book was intended for adults, but I'm sure that confident young readers who love adventure and unusual goings-on (and don't need their reading to be 'modern') will enjoy this as much as I did.

**Michael Lawrence**

### Next?
• Try *The Time Machine* and *The War of the Worlds* also by H.G. Wells. And his *Short Stories*. (*UBG* 309)

• For a much easier book about the perils of being invisible, try *Invisible!* by Robert Swindells.

• Or for another classic about an experiment gone wrong, try *Dr Jekyll and Mr Hyde* by Robert Louis Stevenson.

★ ★ ★ ★ ★ ★

# THE IRON MAN Ted Hughes

### Next?
• For another creature made of something other than flesh, meet the robot hero of Helen Fox's funny and moving **Eager** series – read *Eager* first, then *Eager's Nephew* and *Eager and the Mermaid*. (*UBG* 92)

• Or look for more by Ted Hughes – try *The Iron Woman*, where the fearsome hero has a just grievance against mankind.

• Malorie Blackman writes up-to-the-moment, cliffhanging thrillers. Check out *Hacker* (*UBG* 140) or *Operation Gadgetman* for starters.

The impact of the first page is instant and unforgettable. 'The Iron Man stepped forward off the cliff into nothingness.' He pieces himself together, most of himself anyway. And then he feels hungry. The problem is, he only eats iron. Understandably, the farmers don't want him eating all their machinery and barbed-wire fences, so they dig a trap for him.

Hogarth, a farmer's son, sees him fall in the trap and takes pity on him. So begins the touching alliance between the two, where trust replaces fear. Wonderfully told by the greatest poet / storyteller of our times, you would think that was good enough. Not for Hughes. From this point on the story takes off, literally, into space, and is transformed into a pulsating battle in which the Iron Man has to save the Earth itself. Yet despite all the frantic cosmic fireworks this remains a story with a heart – the heart of the Iron Man, who proves (as his friend Hogarth knows) that he has a kind and noble spirit.

**Michael Morpurgo**

# THE ISLAND OF ADVENTURE  Enid Blyton  ● ●

**Next?**

• The books in Willard Price's **Adventure** series (*Cannibal Adventure* for instance) have plenty of thrills, too. (*UBG* 51)

• There are so many good adventure stories! Look out for historical ones, such as *Wolf Brother* by Michelle Paver (*UBG* 390), fantasy ones such as *Shadow Forest* by Matt Haig (*UBG* 306) or plain, everyday ones (…well, almost!) like *A Dog Called Grk* by Joshua Doder. (*UBG* 87)

Jack, his parrot Kiki and sister Lucy-Ann are staying for the summer holidays with their new friends, Philip and Dinah, in a rambling, half-ruined house on top of the cliffs. When they spot strange lights at night out at sea on the supposedly deserted Isle of Gloom, they become determined to sail to the island and discover its secret.

Inevitably, they are soon up to their necks in danger – and quite literally – as the old mine tunnels beneath the island, where they have been imprisoned by a gang of criminals, start to flood with sea water…

Enid Blyton was the first professional writer for children, and I think the stories in her **Adventure** series were her best. They crack along at the same amazing pace as her **Famous Five** and **Secret Seven** books, but though they are just as compulsively page-turning, they are longer, more satisfying reads and often have more imaginative settings. *The Island of Adventure* is the first in the series.

**Patricia Elliott**

★ ★ ★ ★ ★ ★

# ISLAND OF THE BLUE DOLPHINS  Scott O'Dell  ● ● ●

This is the story of Karana, a 12-year-old Native American who is abandoned on an island off the coast of California. Alone except for a pack of wild dogs, Karana shows astonishing bravery and resourcefulness.

Scott O'Dell shows us a world of great beauty: otters eating abalone molluscs in their kelp beds, a skirt made of shimmering cormorant feathers, a white dog howling in a grotto, a tidal wave – blood red in the setting sun. And dolphins, of course.

When O'Dell died, his family scattered his ashes over the glittering blue Pacific, and as they turned for home, a dozen leaping dolphins escorted the boat back to shore. A fitting end for the masterful storyteller of this classic.

**Caroline Lawrence**

**Next?**

• *My Side of the Mountain* by Jean Craighead George is the story of a boy living alone in the Catskill mountains, and how he learns to survive.

• *Walk Two Moons* by Sharon Creech has a heroine of Native American descent. (*UBG* 371)

• And *Journey to the River Sea* by Eva Ibbotson is another story about travelling to a strange and exotic place. (*UBG* 184)

# JACKY DAYDREAM

Jacqueline Wilson

### Next?

• More real stories? You might also like **Counting Stars**, David Almond's book of stories about his childhood (**UBG** 73), Allan Ahlberg's autobiography **The Boyhood of Burglar Bill** (**UBG** 46), or **Chinese Cinderella** by Adeline Yen Mah (**UBG** 63), the true story of an unwanted daughter growing up in China.

• Of course, try any of Jacqueline Wilson's many novels. **My Sister Jodie**, about chalk-and-cheese siblings who find that they really do need each other. Or **Secrets**, about two girls from very different backgrounds.

Fans of Jacqueline Wilson will undoubtedly love *Jacky Daydream*, Wilson's autobiography from birth to age eleven. But even if you've never read one of her books before, you're sure to enjoy it, especially if you're a budding writer, or you like reading historical fiction or biography. The author shares the experiences of her own girlhood: the father (who was nasty or distant more often than kind), the hardships of life in post-war England, the personal embarrassments and the disappointments. But despite the difficulties, Wilson writes in her usual warm style without ever sounding sorry for herself. Each chapter ends with a quiz relating an event or character from the author's life to one of her own stories. It's a brilliant finishing touch to a special book.

**Madelyn Travis**

★ ★ ★ ★ ★ ★

# JAKE'S TOWER

Elizabeth Laird

Jake's mother has a very violent boyfriend. Trying to escape from the real world, Jake takes refuge in his imagination. There he creates a fantasy tower on an island where he will have complete control over who is allowed in. But when he and his mother have to escape from the boyfriend, Jake finds that imagination and reality can sometimes meet.

A harrowing and disturbing story that is finally uplifting. It is as compelling as it is distressing to read. Jake is a brave and inspiring boy whose imagination is his saviour.

**Jackie Kay**

### Next?

• Why not try Elizabeth Laird's tough, terrifying story of the African boys, Mamo and Dani, two runaways whose stories are told in **The Garbage King**?

• For the story of two boys who run away from their abusive father, and who end up living on a traffic island, meet Suresh and Sandeep in Sally Grindley's **Broken Glass**. (**UBG** 48)

• For another book about children dealing with the appalling behaviour of adults, read Jerry Spinelli's **Eggs**.

# JAMES AND THE GIANT PEACH  Roald Dahl

Because of a terrible accident (if you can call being eaten by a rhinoceros an accident), James Henry Trotter is left an orphan. One minute he's a happy child with two wonderful parents and a lovely seaside home. The next he's sent to live with his awful aunts, Aunt Sponge and Aunt Spiker. Then one day the aunts are suddenly run over by an enormous peach, as big as a house, and James is free to go on the adventure of his life – with a wonderful group of overgrown garden insects. They travel across the world in the peach, by land and sea and air, always one step ahead of danger.

**Jane Yolen**

### Next?
• Try Roald Dahl's bizarre and wonderful *George's Marvellous Medicine*. (*UBG* 123) Or his seriously hilarious *The Twits*. (*UBG* 359)

• Basil lives in a lighthouse and life is very boring, until a professor turns up at his window in a flying boat, and life changes dramatically. Read about Basil in Wiley Miller's *The Extraordinary Adventures of Ordinary Basil*.

• You'll find another fantastical tale told in Heather Dyer's *The Boy in the Biscuit Tin*. (*UBG* 45)

★ ★ ★ ★ ★ ★

# JAMMY DODGERS ON THE RUN  Bowering Sivers

The Jammy Dodgers are the Perkinski brothers, Jem, Ned and Billy. They live hand-to-mouth in Devil's Acre, one of the least salubrious areas of Victorian London, trying to keep out of the hands of the 'crushers' (the police) and to have adventures as pickpockets, scroungers and villains-in-training.

Very funny, and jam-packed with Victorian slang, this adventure story whizzes along at a breakneck pace. Yet it never lets you forget the realities of dirt, sewers, punishment, chimney sweeps and child snatchers – for all the humour, this is definitely a London that Charles Dickens would recognise.

**Leonie Flynn**

### Next?
• More Jammy Dodgers! They're all great: *Jammy Dodgers Get Filthy Rich*, *Jammy Dodgers Go Underground* and *Jammy Dodgers in Deadly Danger*.

• There are more Dickensian adventures in Paul Stewart and Chris Riddell's **Barnaby Grimes** books; read *The Curse of the Nightwolf* and be thrilled, scared and desperate to read more!

• Or if you're up for a challenge, you could try Mr Dickens himself – start with *Oliver Twist*.

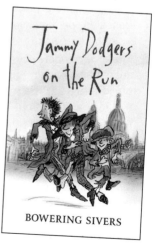

BOWERING SIVERS

# JANE BLONDE: SENSATIONAL SPYLET

## Jill Marshall

**Next?**
• The other **Jane Blonde** books! *Jane Blonde Spies Trouble, Twice the Spylet, Spies on Ice* and *Meet Jane Blonde* – with more to come!

• Or the other girl detective, **Nancy Drew**; her first adventure is *The Secret of the Old Clock.* (*UBG* 246)

• Or what about some history with your mystery? Try the Elizabethan **Lady Grace Mysteries** starting with *A is for Assassin* by Grace Cavendish.

Let's be honest, for a long time the kids' book world has been awash with boy heroes saving the planet, having all the best gizmos and smirking at the girls... Well, if you want an antidote to all that, you have to read this fabulous series, in which skinny, mousey Jane Brown is transformed into super-spy Jane Blonde, and a dull life will never be dull again!

It all begins when her godmother turns up. Not your ordinary godmother – certainly NOT like anyone from fairy stories – but a wacky, bats-in-the-belfry, hip-hop-talking, doughnut-loving godmother who soon sets Jane on the path to spy wow-ness. With a silver cat-suit, gadgets galore – including sparkly hair-clips that help her zoom through the air – Jane is thrown into a fast-paced adventure that hardly lets the reader take breath.

**Leonie Flynn**

★ ★ ★ ★ ★ ★

# JENNIE Paul Gallico

This is, quite simply, absolutely the best book about cats ever written. It is also a story about a great friendship, daring adventures, violent fights and exploring new worlds.

Peter is a lonely boy living in London. One day he is in an accident and when he wakes up he has turned into a cat! He is chased out of the house by Nanny and runs out into what is now a very big, noisy, frightening world. Luckily, he meets Jennie, a kindly stray tabby cat who becomes the kind of best friend everyone wishes they could have. Jennie teaches Peter the rules about being a cat, which everyone who has ever lived with a cat will recognise. Be warned – have hankies ready for the ending; I have never met anyone who didn't cry!

**Abigail Anderson**

**Next?**
• Try other books by Paul Gallico: *The Snow Goose* (*UBG* 317) and *A Small Miracle* tell deceptively simple but deeply moving stories.

• *Old Possum's Book of Practical Cats*! Poetry, yes, but what amazing cats – the poet T.S. Eliot must have known a feline or two.

• *Lionboy* by Zizou Corder is also about a boy befriending cats – big cats! (*UBG* 199)

# JENNINGS series  Anthony Buckeridge  ●●

**Next?**
• The **Just William** stories by Richmal Crompton are in a similar vein of humour. (*UBG* 186)
• Or try *Down With Skool* by Geoffrey Willans and Ronald Searle, which is one of the funniest looks at school life you can find. (*UBG* 91)
• And look out for *My Kind of School* – a collection of short stories covering many different aspects of school life, edited by Tony Bradman.

This classic, much-loved series looks on the sunny side of life at a boys' boarding school. In *Jennings Goes to School*, our young hero goes off (in some trepidation) to Linbury Court Preparatory School, with its traditional dormitories, a common room, tuck boxes, Matron, and squabbles ended by a cry of 'Pax!'

Here, Jennings becomes best friends with the dusty-spectacled Darbishire, and we watch the enthusiastic, and always well-meaning, pair get into one scrape after another and fall in and out of trouble.

One of the joys of this series is the sheer range of language, from the lofty and involuted sarcasm of some of the teachers to the bizarre, invented slang used by the pupils. The stories are varied and extremely well written, offering simple, cheering escapism of the finest sort.

**Anne Fine**

★ ★ ★ ★ ★ ★

# JIGGY MCCUE series  Michael Lawrence  ●●

Jiggy McCue is just an average boy, but he feels like the unluckiest kid in town. Strange things are always happening to him and his best mates, Pete and Angie. He's been haunted by a dead goose, been plagued by a hideous pair of non-removable underpants and fallen foul of a computerised toilet that flushed his life away and gave him another, much worse than his own. When he finally stumbles on a teenage genie willing to grant him three wishes, he thinks his luck has finally changed, but of course nothing could be further from the truth...

With laugh-out-loud humour, wacky plot-lines and a light sprinkling of rudeness, the **Jiggy McCue** books have got the lot.

**Kathryn Ross**

**Next?**
• Read all of Jiggy McCue's hilarious adventures: *The Poltergoose, The Killer Underpants, The Toilet of Doom, Maggot Pie, The Snottle, Nudie Dudie, Neville the Devil, Ryan's Brain, Kid Swap* and *The Iron, the Switch and the Broom Cupboard*.
• For another boy who can't stay out of trouble, try the **Buster Bayliss** stories by Philip Reeve. (*UBG* 49)
• And although he's not as unlucky as Jiggy, strange things certainly happen to Johnny Maxwell in Terry Pratchett's excellent trio of novels beginning with *Only You Can Save Mankind*. (*UBG* 182)

# JOEY PIGZA SWALLOWED THE KEY  Jack Gantos

### Next?
• Read the sequels! *Joey Pigza Loses Control, What Would Joey Do?* and *I Am Not Joey Pigza*.

• For the story of one boy's adventures when he gets sent to a place for 'troublesome kids', read Louis Sachar's *Holes*. (*UBG* 155)

• Or how about a dyslexic, ADHD boy who finds out he's the son of a Greek god? Try *Percy Jackson and the Sea of Monsters* by Rick Riordan. (*UBG* 262)

Joey knows he is 'wired'. When he doesn't take his 'meds' he can't keep still, but must race around frenetically, getting into every kind of trouble. His home life is chaotic, with a 'sometimes' mother, a crazy grandmother and an absent father. The other adults around him try their best to help him overcome his difficulties, but sometimes it seems to Joey that nothing will ever stop his headlong rush to disaster. His adventures are both heartbreaking and horribly funny, like the time he cuts the tip of a girl's nose off by accident... Gantos is a master of mixing misery with bizarre comedy and this is a little masterpiece.

**Lynne Reid Banks**

★ ★ ★ ★ ★ ★

# JOHNNY MAXWELL trilogy  Terry Pratchett

Twelve-year-old worrier Johnny Maxwell is addicted to computer games, especially 'Only You Can Save Mankind' (also the title of the first book in the trilogy), in which an alien fleet from the Mighty ScreeWee empire thunder across the screen to be shot into a million pieces. But one day, the aliens surrender, leaving trigger-happy Johnny and his weird and wonderful friends to save Mankind from the Galactic Hordes – and the Galactic Hordes from Mankind – by getting inside the game and making themselves the targets, which leaves you, the reader, wondering what reality really is!

Pratchett's wickedly funny, completely mad and amazingly imaginative action-packed adventures are easy to get into, but these laugh-a-page stories also make you think, asking important questions about the world and our place in it and our attitudes to the people around us.

**Eileen Armstrong**

### Next?
• The trilogy continues with *Johnny and the Dead* and *Johnny and the Bomb*. For more fabulous Pratchett books, look for the **Discworld** books, starting with *The Colour of Magic* (*UBG* 68).

• Or there's *The Carpet People* – a book Pratchett originally wrote when he was just 17.

• *Space Demons* by Gillian Rubinstein is a fast-paced computer game adventure. (*UBG* 320)

• Or look for Frank Cottrell Boyce's *Cosmic*, in which a boy might just end up in space. (*UBG* 73)

# THE JOSHUA FILES: INVISIBLE CITY  M.G. Harris  ●●

The first thing about this book that grabs you is the cover – orange neoprene that slips off the book like a scabbard baring a blade. Different, intriguing, in-your-face exciting – just like the story that it surrounds.

Invisible City starts as a tragedy, moves into a mystery and ends with you really wanting to read volume two! Josh, only a few pages in, finds out that his archaeologist father's light aircraft has crashed somewhere in Mexico, and that he's dead. Josh's mother can't cope, and Josh's world starts to fall to pieces. But then the mystery kicks in, and Josh ends up in Mexico and the real adventure begins, and it doesn't let up through a jungle chase, near-death, prophecies about the end of the world and, yes, an invisible city.

**Leonie Flynn**

### Next?
• Justin Richards uses similar ingredients in *The Chaos Code*.

• There's more archaeology, mystery and excitement in Philip Caveney's *Alec Devlin: The Eye of the Serpent*, which is set in Egypt in 1923.

• Or for another boy who deals in a real way with death and adventure, try the **Young Bond** series by Charlie Higson starting with *SilverFin*. (*UBG* 311)

★ ★ ★ ★ ★ ★

# JOURNEY TO JO'BURG  Beverley Naidoo  ●●

### Next?
• Other Beverley Naidoo books about children from Africa: *The Other Side of Truth* (*UBG* 255), *Burn My Heart*, *Chain of Fire* and *Out of Bounds*.

• You have to read the heartbreaking and thought-provoking *Roll of Thunder, Hear My Cry* by Mildred D. Taylor and as many sequels as you can find. (*UBG* 287)

• Or for something else set against the same background of apartheid in South Africa, read *Blue Sky Freedom* by Gabrielle Halberstam.

Thirteen-year-old Naledi and her little brother Tiro live in a Tswana village in South Africa. Like most village children, their parents work far away in the city. When their baby sister falls ill, they decide to walk the 300 kilometres to Johannesburg to find their mother. On the way, they discover a land where black people are servants and white people their masters.

They can only travel on a jam-packed bus for 'Blacks Only'; they watch helplessly as police check the passes that all black people must carry; they hear about the shooting of hundreds of black schoolchildren in Soweto as they marched for freedom. Naledi decides to become a doctor, not a maid like her mother.

Nine years after this book was published, Nelson Mandela became President of South Africa and black people were free.

**James Riordan**

# JOURNEY TO THE RIVER SEA  Eva Ibbotson

Maia is unbelievably brave when she discovers that her parents have died and that she must go and live with her aunt and uncle in their home on the banks of the Amazon river. Accompanied by her trusted nanny, she leaves London for South America.

There Maia discovers a completely different world, and tries hard to make her new life work. But she can't ignore the fact that her aunt and uncle, and their horrible daughters, loathe her and will never make her part of the family.

Even so, Maia begins to build friendships with some of the extraordinary people she meets, and through them and her nanny, she finds herself almost enjoying life by the Amazon. Enjoyment, however, is not what her relatives have in mind for the girl, and they try everything they can to ensure that she is as miserable as they are.

**Lindsey Fraser**

### Next?

• Eva Ibbotson is a wonderful writer, so read more of her books! Try *The Star of Kazan* (*UBG* 323) or *The Island of the Aunts*, in which three eccentric, island-dwelling aunts plan to kidnap two children – for the best possible reasons…

• *A Little Princess* by Frances Hodgson Burnett is the story of Sara Crewe who returns from India to go to boarding school. (*UBG* 205)

• In Livi Michael's *The Whispering Road*, a brother and sister try to survive adversity and poverty on a journey to find their lost mother – and each other.

★ ★ ★ ★ ★ ★

# JUDY MOODY series  Megan McDonald

### Next?

• There are lots of books about Judy Moody. Look out for, among others, *Judy Moody Gets Famous*, *Judy Moody Saves the World*, *Doctor Judy Moody* and *Judy Moody Declares Independence*. There is another series of books about Judy's little brother, Stink.

• And try Beverly Cleary's **Ramona** books. (*UBG* 280)

• Julia Donaldson writes very funny books; read about a very mischievous princess in *Princess Mirror-Belle*.

Judy Moody has a mood for every occasion. On the first day of Year 3 her mood is *bad* – so bad, in fact, that she has to resort to using Grouchy Pencils. Things get better, though, when she becomes president of the Toad Pee Club, makes a collage all about herself and brings a Venus flytrap to class. She even makes friends with Frank Pearl, who eats paste. Judy gets into scrapes at school and plays tricks on her little 'bother' Stink, but she's clever and creative, too, and her adventures are always absolutely hilarious. The other books in the series are just as good, and they all have great illustrations. As Judy Moody would say, 'Rare!'

**Madelyn Travis**

# The JUNGLE BOOKS Rudyard Kipling

A tiger springs into the firelight of an Indian woodcutters' camp. The Indians run, but their baby is left behind, and crawls into a wolves' den. When the tiger comes, seeking his dinner, the wolves defend the baby. They adopt him and call him Mowgli – 'little frog'.

Throughout the two **Jungle Books**, short stories tell how Mowgli grows up in the jungle. The tiger Shere Khan hates him, but Mowgli is protected by the wolves, by the great black panther Bagheera, by the wise bear Baloo, and by Kaa, the python. Mowgli himself is no easy prey – he's tough, courageous, resourceful and intelligent. Does Shere Khan kill him? Read the books and find out.

Not all the stories are about Mowgli. Rikki-Tikki-Tavi the mongoose battles cobras in *The Jungle Book*, and Quiquern, a monstrous Arctic ghost, haunts *The Second Jungle Book*. There are other wonderful stories, too, which I leave you to discover for yourself.

My dad loved these books, and bought them for my seventh Christmas. I loved them, too. Still do. If you love them as well, you can pass them on to your children.

**Susan Price**

I don't much care for talking animals, but the book I loved most when I was young is full of them. The jungle creatures in the **Jungle Books** are still real to me: Baloo the wise old bear, Bagheera the beautiful black panther, Hathi the elephant and Kaa the rock python. They all defend Mowgli, the human baby rescued by Mother Wolf, against Shere Khan, the terrifying lame tiger who intends to kill him if he can. From the moment Mother Wolf takes Mowgli to the Council Rock where Akela the Lone Wolf introduces new cubs to the pack with the haunting cry, 'Look. Look well O wolves', this is a marvellously exciting story.

**Nina Bawden**

## Next?

• Anyone who enjoys the **Jungle Books** will almost certainly love the *Just So Stories*, also by Rudyard Kipling. They are funny, extravagant tales told in beautifully rhythmic language. (*UBG* 187)

• Then you could try Kipling's *Puck of Pook's Hill* (*UBG* 275) and *Rewards and Fairies*. In these short stories, the goblin Puck magically summons people from the past to tell the stories of their lives.

• *Stuart Little* by E.B. White is another animal classic, though this time it's about an animal adopted by people, rather than the other way around!

# JUST WILLIAM
### Richmal Crompton

William Brown first appeared in 1922 and has never been out of print since. There has arguably been no greater spirit – celebrated in the most exquisite comic prose – in children's literature.

William is always eleven. At his muddy heel is his ardently faithful dog, Jumble. The Outlaws – Ginger, Henry and Douglas – are William's blood brothers; not scruffy schoolboys, but pirates, cowboys and Indians, ancient Greeks or cannibals. William, with his artist's soul and imagination, his passionate sense of justice, his tactless honesty and clumsy bravery, is their beloved leader.

Through these wonderful stories, peopled by pompous or misguided adults, thwarted sweethearts, baffled teachers and relatives, William stomps with his homemade placards ('RONGS RITED: 1 penny'), his helpful inventions which strew chaos in their wake, his bow and arrow and his catapult – the patron saint of childhood.

**Carol Ann Duffy**

## Next?

• For a more modern story of a child who just can't help getting into trouble, go for *The Turbulent Term of Tyke Tiler* by Gene Kemp. (*UBG* 357)

• Or you could try Anne Fine's own *Flour Babies*, about a school project with a difference. (*UBG* 116)

• Or what about the **Jennings** books by Anthony Buckeridge? They're just as funny. (*UBG* 181)

• Or try the classic, hilarious **Molesworth** books by Geoffrey Willans and Ronald Searle that begin with *Down with Skool*. (*UBG* 91)

William Brown, the eternal eleven-year-old epic hero, never fails to startle with his bold genius at the expense of those grown-ups unlucky enough to cross his path.

William and his three friends call themselves The Outlaws. They meet in a dilapidated old barn where they plan their exploits. These frequently go wrong and get them into hot water. As a result of William having these ideas and doing dreadful things, his long-suffering family are left to pick up the pieces.

Into an orderly world, William brings unexpected, entertaining, never-ending chaos.

**Jan Pienkowski**

# JUST SO STORIES Rudyard Kipling ● ●

**Next?**

• Try *English Folk Tales* by Joseph Jacobs or *A Bag of Moonshine* by Alan Garner – stories based on British folklore and told in an idiomatic storyteller's voice.

• Less direct, rather incoherent at times, yet verbally astonishing, are the *Rootabaga Stories* by Carl Sandburg.

• And, of course, Rudyard Kipling's **Jungle Books**. (*UBG* 185)

• Or try Ted Hughes's *Tales of the Early World* for more newly minted folklore. (*UBG* 342)

This is a collection of 12 short stories, for the most part telling how certain creatures achieved their characteristics: how the leopard got his spots, how the camel got his hump, and so on. What makes the stories outstanding is not only their fantastic inventiveness but also the lively words in which they are told.

Stories read in silence are still heard by the inner ear of the reader, but these stories somehow demand to be heard in the outside world. If you hear them read aloud, the storyteller's voice comes through with humour, excitement and powerful explosions of language (as in 'The Sing-Song of Old Man Kangaroo'). Whether it is through the exclamations of the elephant's child (with a crocodile clinging to his trunk) or through the chanting account of the kangaroo who flees from the dingo and learns to jump in the process, these stories are definitely stories to be heard aloud.

**Margaret Mahy**

★ ★ ★ ★ ★ ★

# KENSUKE'S KINGDOM Michael Morpurgo ● ●

This book has all the best ingredients: a faithful dog, a strange but magical world, hardship and the struggle to survive in an inhospitable place.

Michael is washed overboard and stranded on a desert island with nothing but his dog, Stella, for company. Or so he thinks. The first night he almost gives up hope, and curls up to sleep, not caring if he lives or dies. Then, when he wakes in the morning, he finds a bowl of food by his side...

This is an exciting story that has you reading faster and faster to find out what happens. You might also find yourself with an interest in learning Japanese!

**Caroline Lawrence**

**Next?**

• You'll find *The Last Castaway* by Harry Horse a nice easy read next; it's a very different take on the 'stranded on a desert island' theme.

• For another book about a faithful (and this time real-life) dog, read *Marley: A Dog Like No Other* by John Grogan. (*UBG* 222)

• And of course, you must read more Michael Morpurgo! *Why the Whales Came* (*UBG* 382) and *The Butterfly Lion* (*UBG* 50) are both wonderful stories.

# KEZZIE Theresa Breslin

Set in Scotland in the 1930s, this is a story of 14-year-old Kezzie, and her courage and determination in the face of really tough times.

It's the Depression and jobs are scarce. First Kezzie's mother dies and then her father, leaving her to look after her six-year-old sister Lucy and her crippled grandad. But there's worse to come. When Kezzie becomes ill, Lucy is taken into care and sent to Canada by an adoption agency – a common practice at the time. When she recovers, Kezzie is determined to get Lucy back. Her quest makes for a plot that's moving and thrilling.

This is realistic fiction at its best, mixing powerful ideas with high adventure and a touch of romance.

**Julia Jarman**

## Next?
• There's a sequel: *A Homecoming for Kezzie*.
• For more Theresa Breslin read *The Medici Seal*, an historical adventure that features Leonardo da Vinci. Or try her haunting story of the First World War, *Remembrance*.
• For a gentler story of adoption, try either Hilary McKay's *Saffy's Angel* (*UBG* 292) or Sharon Creech's *Ruby Holler* (*UBG* 288). Both are quite different, but totally wonderful.

★ ★ ★ ★ ★ ★

# KIDNAPPED Robert Louis Stevenson

## Next?
• You've probably already read *Treasure Island*; if not, read it now! (*UBG* 352) You might also like to try Stevenson's scary *Dr Jekyll and Mr Hyde*.
• There are some other old-time adventure stories: R.M. Ballantyne's *The Coral Island* (*UBG* 68) or Rider Haggard's *King Solomon's Mines* (*UBG* 191).
• Or for a book about a different sort of kidnapping, try Tim Bowler's *Storm Catchers*. (*UBG* 332)

Like *Treasure Island*, *Kidnapped* is an adventure story: a classic page-turner. David Balfour is a 17-year-old Scot who, in the year 1751 (his parents being dead), sets out to find his uncle and perhaps his fortune. Before we're into chapter five, his uncle has tried to murder him. Another few chapters, and David has been kidnapped and carried off to sea, has met the most complicated friend of his life, and has killed a man. And we're turning the pages, turning... I remember not being able to understand half the Scottish dialect words in *Kidnapped*, and I still can't. But I've never forgotten the fear and excitement that Stevenson makes us feel along with David, and the brilliant characters, such as weaselly, haunted Uncle Ebenezer and above all David's prickly, arrogant, dangerous companion Alan Breck. This is a story about friendship, and about growing up. And anyone who thinks it's a book just for boys (as its author did) doesn't know much about girls.

**Susan Cooper**

# KING ARTHUR AND HIS KNIGHTS OF THE ROUND TABLE  Roger Lancelyn Green

**Next?**

• There are many versions of these legends; try Marcia Williams's, which are hilarious and brilliantly illustrated. (*UBG* 220)

• For a more challenging read on the same theme, try T.H. White's *The Sword in the Stone*. (*UBG* 338)

• For a more sophisticated look at the Arthurian legend, read Philip Reeve's *Here Lies Arthur*.

I guess I was nine when I tugged this lovely book from my stocking on Christmas morning. It won me over straight away and caused ripples in me that have never settled. Arthur pulls the sword from the stone on the fourth page, he's king by the fifth, and by the time Merlin speaks of Logres, God's Kingdom upon the Earth, I was quite ready to agree that 'all who heard him felt that they were at the beginning of a time of wonders'. Strong and sinewy storytelling. Bloody accounts of heads and limbs being hacked off sit side-by-side with haunting descriptions of magic and miracle. Beautiful illustrations by Lotte Reiniger. A true classic, by a wonderful writer.

**David Almond**

★ ★ ★ ★ ★ ★

# THE KING MUST DIE  Mary Renault

When the Cretans come for the annual tribute that is owed to their god, Theseus, son of the Athenian king, insists on going with them. Among his imprisoned people, he finds strength and the ability to lead, and to keep all of his friends alive. But when the volcano Mount Thera erupts, he must journey into the labyrinth to fight and hopefully kill the Minotaur – a monster: half-man and half-bull.

Mary Renault takes an old Greek myth, set just before the Trojan War, and brings it brilliantly and convincingly to life. But this is more than an adventure story: it's about the responsibilities of power in ancient Pagan religion, for in the last resort, even the king may have to die to save his people.

Following Theseus from childhood, this is a very sophisticated read, but one that really lets you understand the reality behind the myth.

**Patricia Finney**

**Next?**

• Try the sequel, *The Bull from the Sea*.

• For other stories of the ancient world, work your way through Rosemary Sutcliff, especially *The Eagle of the Ninth* (*UBG* 93) and *The Mark of the Horse Lord* (*UBG* 221).

• *The God Beneath the Sea* by Leon Garfield and Edward Blishen is a wonderful collection of retellings of Greek myths. (*UBG* 129)

• For another interpretation of one of the Greek myths, try Adèle Geras's wonderful novel *Troy*. (*UBG* 353)

# Top Ten
# Scary
# Books

★1 The Witches
by Roald Dahl

★2 Point Horror series
by various authors

★3 Goosebumps series
by various authors

★4 Breathe: A Ghost Story
by Cliff McNish

★5 A Series of Unfortunate Events
by Lemony Snicket

★6 Coraline
by Neil Gaiman

★7 The Saga of Darren Shan
by Darren Shan

★8 Horowitz Horror
by Anthony Horowitz

★9 My Swordhand is Singing
by Marcus Sedgwick

★10 The Demonata
by Darren Shan

# KING OF SHADOWS
## Susan Cooper

Nathan Field is a young American actor, who travels to London with his theatre company to stage a version of *A Midsummer Night's Dream* in the newly reconstructed Globe theatre. A few days after his arrival, he is taken seriously ill and when he wakes up, finds himself in a very different London – that of four hundred years earlier. Even stranger is that everyone seems to know him, and is expecting him to play the part of Puck in a special performance at the Globe. Imagine his surprise when he learns who he will be acting alongside none other than William Shakespeare himself.

Susan Cooper weaves past and present together skilfully in this gripping and moving story, rich in the detail of Elizabethan life.

**Marcus Sedgwick**

## Next?

• Why not try Susan Cooper's powerful **The Dark is Rising** sequence (*UBG* 78) or her time-slip story about life in Nelson's navy, *Victory*?

• Or if you like stories that slip between worlds, try *The Truth Sayer* by Sally Prue. (*UBG* 354)

• Or what about L. Brittney's *Nathan Fox: Dangerous Times*, in which a boy actor (who knows fellow-actor, Will Shakespeare) ends up working for Queen Elizabeth's spymaster, Walsingham, and travelling to Venice? There he meets adventure, treachery, racism, jealousy – and the Moor himself, Othello. (*UBG* 247)

# KING SOLOMON'S MINES H. Rider Haggard ● ● ●

### Next?

• There's the sequel *Allan Quartermain*.

• For more swashbuckling manly adventure, try *Treasure Island* by Robert Louis Stevenson (*UBG* 352) or *Beau Geste* by P.C. Wren.

• There's more adventure in all of G.A. Henty's books than in most books around today, so if you fancy an old-fashioned yet thrilling read, hunt out some of his books, including *Under Drake's Flag* and *A Knight of the White Cross*.

Three Englishmen – Allan Quartermain, Sir Henry Curtis and Captain John Good R.N. – guided by a primitive map, set out into an unexplored part of Africa, searching not only for King Solomon's treasure but for Sir Henry's lost brother. They cross a desert and climb a mountain, suffering but surviving, then encounter an unknown tribe and become involved in local wars. They do find treasure … but the discovery is more complicated and dangerous than they had imagined it would be.

While this book is rather more straggling than *Treasure Island*, it is still a classic adventure story. A modern reader may wince at the slaughter of elephants (Quartermain is an ivory hunter, a respectable profession in Rider Haggard's day) but the African characters are imaginatively vital.

**Margaret Mahy**

★ ★ ★ ★ ★ ★

# KISS THE DUST Elizabeth Laird ● ● ●

When this book was first published in 1991, it was right on the button. It is the story of a Kurdish Iraqi family who, in 1984, have to flee their home.

From Sulaimaniya to the mountains, from the mountains to terrible refugee camps in Iran, and from there to England – and a containment centre. It sounds grim. It *is* grim, but there is so much more! From the beautiful descriptions to the uncrushable spirits of the characters, this is a wonderfully life-affirming book.

Sadly, with all that has happened since and the issues over asylum seekers today, this book has not shifted one millimetre from the button. If you are sitting comfortably, then read this story – it is a brilliant insight into a situation no one wants to be in, but so many are.

**Simon Puttock**

### Next?

• Elizabeth Laird has written many other wonderful books; try *The Garbage King* or *Crusade* (*UBG* 75).

• Beverley Naidoo's *The Other Side of Truth* is about two refugees from Nigeria who are abandoned in London. (*UBG* 255)

• *The Night of the Burning* by Linda Press Wulf is based on her family's story and tells of two sisters escaping from the persecution of the Jews in Poland to South Africa and the different sorts of injustice they see there. It's about grief, too, and how hard it can be to find a new life.

# KIT'S WILDERNESS   David Almond

### Next?

• Read *Skellig* and see if you agree with me or Susan. (*UBG* 313)

• Sally Prue's *Cold Tom* is similarly eerie (*UBG* 67); or for something else that's mysterious, try Julie Hearn's *Follow Me Down* (*UBG* 118).

• Tim Bowler also writes uncompromising stories that make you think; try *Bloodchild*. After an accident, Will is left with almost no memory. But he has strange visions that hint at secrets he somehow has to uncover.

For over four years I've had a running argument with Susan (fellow editor) about which David Almond book is best. She thinks it's *Skellig*, I'm sure it's *Kit's Wilderness*. In fact, I think it's one of the best books *anyone* has written in years.

Set in the north-east, it's the story of Kit Watson, and the bonds he forms with classmate Allie Keenan, wild boy John Askew and the spirits of the past, and the game they all play. The game called Death.

This book is just as dark as it sounds, absolutely suffused with death and menace; but there's also great beauty in this wilderness, in Kit's relationship with his old grandfather, his friendships with Askew and Allie, in Kit's storytelling, Allie's acting and Askew's extraordinary drawings.

*Kit's Wilderness* will do something only the greatest books can – it will change the way you see the world. Trust me. Read it.

**Daniel Hahn**

★ ★ ★ ★ ★

# KITE   Melvin Burgess

Taylor Mase is hand-rearing a red kite – a bird of prey. He shouldn't be. They're endangered. And this particular bird is in more danger than most. No one seems to want it to live. The local landowner, the brutal Harris, wants it dead. Even Taylor's own dad wants it dead.

This is a wonderful, nail-biting tale of a bird's incredible will to live and a boy who will do anything to help it.

**Cliff McNish**

*'A writer of the highest quality with exceptional powers of insight' – SundayTimes*

kite

### Next?

• If you enjoyed this, you may like to try another of Melvin Burgess's animal-centred stories, such as *The Cry of the Wolf*.

• Or why not read the brilliant classic *The Call of the Wild* by Jack London – a story of one dog's fight for survival in snowy Alaska?

• *The Midnight Fox* by Betsy Byars is another popular animal story. (*UBG* 227)

# THE KITE RIDER  Geraldine McCaughrean  ● ● ●

To escape from his father's murderer, 12-year-old Gou Hayou joins the travelling Jade Circus, flying high into the skies of medieval China, strapped to gigantic silk and paper kites. But circus master Miao Jie has a deadly secret, and Hayou's scheming Uncle Bo has plans of his own for the kite rider...

This is a rich and exciting book, full of strange sights, sounds, smells and superstitions. The fast-moving story has more twists and turns than a snake doing yoga, and you can never be sure that Hayou and his friends will escape from the terrible predicaments that Geraldine McCaughrean keeps dumping them in.

**Philip Reeve**

### Next?

• Geraldine McCaughrean has written lots of very good books. Try her modern-day gold-rush tale, *Gold Dust* (*UBG* 130) and *A Little Lower than the Angels*, set in the Middle Ages (*UBG* 204).

• For a much tougher sequence set in a semi-mythical Japan, try Lian Hearn's **Tales of the Otori**.

• Linda Sue Park writes about Korea. Try *A Single Shard*, set back in the twelfth century, about a boy who longs to be a potter, or her story of the Japanese occupation, *When My Name Was Keoko*.

★ ★ ★ ★ ★ ★

# THE KNIGHT AND THE SQUIRE  Terry Jones  ● ●

### Next?

• Terry Jones has also written *The Saga of Erik the Viking*, about the voyage of a band of Vikings to the land where the sun sets. (*UBG* 293) His **Fantastic Stories** are also well worth a read.

• If you enjoy fantasy combined with humour, try Eoin Colfer's *Artemis Fowl*. (*UBG* 23)

• Or for a girl who disguises herself in order to become a knight, try the **Song of the Lioness** series by Tamora Pierce, set in a mythical Middle Ages where magic is real. (*UBG* 319)

When Tom decides to run away from home, he knows life won't be easy. Tom lives in the fourteenth century where wolves are on the loose, there are dangerous characters in pursuit and threats all around. But Tom is urged on by his desire for adventure, and he travels across the channel to France and right into the middle of a siege – and that's just for starters. *The Knight and the Squire* is fast-moving, a little bloodthirsty, packed with detail about the past and also – and this is important – very funny. It's not without one final, dramatic twist, too.

Tom's adventures continue in *The Lady and the Squire*, when he travels as the Duke of Lancaster's squire in France and life gets even more exciting – and perilous. If you think you've heard of Terry Jones, it might be because he was also one of the Monty Python team.

**Sherry Ashworth**

# KNIGHT'S FEE Rosemary Sutcliff  ●●●

It could have been the worst day of his life, the day he dropped a half-eaten fig on to the nose of his Lord and Master's horse. For Randall is a dog boy, the lowest of the low, and he knows he is certain to be beaten. But chance intervenes, and after being saved by the castle's minstrel, he ends up packed off as companion to a young Lord, called Bevis.

The Saxon dog boy and the Norman lordling grow up together to become soldiers fighting for King Henry against his brother Robert. It is Bevis's destiny to become a knight, but Randall has no family, land or money – and certainly no way to pay his knight's fee. Can the friendship survive? Set at a time when the Saxons and Normans were just beginning to come together as one people, this is a terrifically exciting story.

**Barbara Wright**

### Next?

• If you fancy another Rosemary Sutcliff about an unlikely friendship, read *The Eagle of the Ninth*. (*UBG* 93) Or for another with a medieval setting, look out for *The Witch's Brat*.

• For another action-packed medieval story, try *Brind and the Dogs of War* by Christopher Russell, about a dog boy, his dog, and a plot that involves the battle of Crécy – there's an evil-soaked sequel, too, in *Plague Sorcerer*.

• What about a fantasy adventure? Try Lloyd Alexander's *The Book of Three*. (*UBG* 42)

★ ★ ★ ★ ★ ★

# KON-TIKI Thor Heyerdahl  ●●●

### Next?

• Other Thor Heyerdahl adventures, such as *The Ra Expeditions* or *Aku Aku* are almost too improbable to be true, but they are!

• If you fancy another true story of suffering, exploration and endurance, read one of the most amazing ever written, *The Worst Journey in the World* by Apsley Cherry-Garrard, about his own experiences on an ill-fated Antarctic journey.

• For a lighter, fictional account of survival, try *The Swiss Family Robinson* by J.D. Wyss. (*UBG* 338)

Sailing on a balsa wood raft across the ocean? Wow! I can still feel the sense of adventure I experienced when reading *Kon-Tiki* as a teenager. The warm Pacific seas, the wind in the sails, even the hardships and relentless sun seemed like exotic fun to me.

Everything from building the boat to planning the journey, along with all of the hardships Heyerdahl and his crew experience, make this more exciting than most works of fiction. Heyerdahl was trying to prove that Polynesian islands could have been settled by sea-faring natives from South America. What he proved to me was that words in a book could take me along as a fascinated member of the crew.

**Jerry Spinelli**

# KRAZY KOW SAVES THE WORLD – WELL, ALMOST

Jeremy Strong

**Next?**
• More good books by Jeremy Strong include *The Indoor Pirates* and *My Mum's Going to Explode!* (*UBG* 244).
• The equally silly *The Adventures of Captain Underpants*, about a very different sort of superhero. (*UBG* 54)
• Or try Jim Benton's **Franny K. Stein, Mad Scientist** series. Start with *Lunch Walks Among Us*.

If you like long and weighty books about serious issues, then this is not for you. However, if you like daft, rollicking reads, preferably involving flying cows and evil villains, then get hold of *Krazy Kow* immediately.

Jamie Frink's great desire in life is to be a film-maker, and when he invents Krazy Kow (a bovine superhero and eco-warrior) there's hope of his dream coming true.

The plot switches constantly between the world of Jamie and his problems, and the world of Krazy Kow and her very different problems. Jeremy Strong whizzes through the story at his usual madcap pace. You won't get bored – I guarantee it!

**Susan Reuben**

★ ★ ★ ★ ★ ★

# THE LAND OF GREEN GINGER   Noel Langley

I love funny books based on traditional tales. This is the story of Aladdin's son, Prince Abu Ali, whose only fault is being too nice. He is sent by the genie of the lamp to free a magician from a nasty spell which has turned him into a button-nosed tortoise. He sets off in search of the flying back garden known as The Land of Green Ginger. On the way, he has some very daft adventures and meets all kinds of weird characters, some good and some Very Bad. They all have wonderfully silly names like Rubdub Ben Thud, Sulkpot Ben Nagnag and Boomalakka Wee. It made me giggle over 30 years ago and it still does now.

Gentle reader, I now leave you with the words of Vapid, Villainous, Vindictive, Vengeful, Wilfully Wicked Prince Tintac Ping Foo: 'Ho there, Slaves! My camels! My retinue! My Magic Sword! My Jellybeans! I leave at once for Samarkand!'

**Kaye Umansky**

**Next?**
• Read more about Aladdin in *The Arabian Nights*. (*UBG* 21)
• Something else just as fantastical? Read Philip Pullman's *The Scarecrow and His Servant*. (*UBG* 295)
• Or for another book about a place that might exist under our noses, try *The Secret of Platform 13* by Eva Ibbotson. (*UBG* 303)
• For a classic, and totally brilliant, weird story, read *The Wind on the Moon* by Eric Linklater. (*UBG* 386)

# LARKLIGHT  Philip Reeve

### Next?

- If you enjoy well-illustrated fantasy, you might enjoy the equally inventive worlds created by Paul Stewart and Chris Riddell. Try their **Edge Chronicles**. (*UBG* 97)
- If you enjoyed Philip Reeve's writing, why not try the **Mortal Engines** quartet, the books are just as imaginative, but darker… (*UBG* 236)
- Or Ken Oppel writes terrific stories, too; try **Airborn** and its sequels, which are about airships.

'I declare Larklight must be the dullest spot in all Creation,' says Myrtle Mumby near the beginning of this book. Well, hardly. For one thing Larklight is a large, Victorian house floating in space. For another, the house is about to be invaded by giant spiders, sending brother and sister, Art and Myrtle, into a wild adventure. This fantastically inventive book is set in a bizarre Victorian, science-fiction universe. You can always count on Philip Reeve for fantastic leaps of imagination and *Larklight* is packed with weird characters and great ideas. It is a nicely designed book too, with lots of wonderful illustrations by David Wyatt that really bring this amazing, eccentric world to life.

**Chris Priestley**

★ ★ ★ ★ ★ ★

# THE LAST VAMPIRE  Willis Hall

Fancy a camping holiday with your parents in the shadow of a mysterious castle in Transylvania? Blood-sucking bats, ravenous wolves and a village full of raging imbeciles who threaten the very lives of you and your family are all part of the fun.

Henry Hollins befriends the unfortunate, misunderstood vegetarian vampire, Count Alucard, who arranges their escape with no help from his own relatives! He accompanies the Hollins family back to England in search of a new home. After trouble with immigration officers, he foxes them by turning himself into a bat and flies off to search for Henry.

A fine romp and a good twist on a vampire story that you can't put down. Stake your heart on it … you'll die laughing!

**Babette Cole**

### Next?

- Do read more of the books about the Hollins family and Count Alucard. Look out for **Vampire Park** and **The Vampire Vanishes**. The Hollins family also feature in **The Inflatable Shop**.
- Try Kaye Umansky's great **Prince Dandypants and the Masked Avenger** – very funny. Or how about her best-loved creation, Pongwiffy (*UBG* 272)?
- For more vampire fun, try Ann Jungman's **Vlad the Drac**, about another vegetarian vampire. (*UBG* 371)
- Or for a boy who really doesn't want to be a vampire, try Michael Lawrence's **Young Dracula**.

# THE LEGEND OF SPUD MURPHY Eoin Colfer

There is a lovely message gently revealed as this tale unfolds, about reading a good story and the joys and escapism that books can offer.

Will and his brother Marty have been forced by their well-meaning mother to spend their holidays not on the computer or out with their mates, but stuck in a library with a dragon of a librarian who won't even let them move off a small square of carpet!

There is a method to the librarian's madness, however, and through her rule, the boys learn to discover the vast and wild world of books and stories and myths and legends, all on their own doorstep. Soon the boys don't want to leave the library – the worlds held between the covers of the books are so enchanting and engrossing they wonder what on earth they were complaining about.

**Rhian Tracey**

**Next?**
• More in the series, of course! There are two so far, *The Legend of Captain Crow's Teeth* and *The Legend of the Worst Boy in the World*.
• What about a boy kidnapped by aliens? Try Sally Prue's very funny *James and the Alien Experiment*.
• Or for another very resourceful librarian, try Margaret Mahy's *The Great Piratical Rumbustification* and *The Librarian and the Robbers*. (*UBG* 138)
• Angela McAllister's *Digory the Dragon Slayer* is about a boy who has trouble living up to his (unearned!) name. (*UBG* 85)

★ ★ ★ ★ ★ ★

# THE LIGHT PRINCESS George MacDonald

**Next?**
• For another unusual fairy tale, try Elizabeth Goudge's *The Little White Horse*. (*UBG* 206)
• For another princess with a strange christening gift, read M.M. Kaye's warm and wonderful *The Ordinary Princess*. (*UBG* 254)
• Or E.D. Baker's *The Frog Princess*, about a clumsy, unhappy princess who hates the prince she is meant to marry. One day she kisses a frog … and is turned into a frog, too!
• Much of the same sort of wonder is imbued in Hilda Lewis's *The Ship That Flew*.
• Or go back to the originals and read the stories by Hans Christian Andersen. (*UBG* 106)

*The Light Princess* has all you'd expect from a fairy story, and more. A king and queen have a much-longed-for daughter. A witch who isn't invited to the christening puts a curse on the baby princess. It's an unusual curse – the witch has taken her sense of gravity. So the baby floats up to the ceiling! The story is funny at the beginning, but grows dark as the princess grows up and the witch's magic grows stronger. But will this fairy tale have a fairy-tale ending?

**Julia Jarman**

# THE LION, THE WITCH AND THE WARDROBE C.S. Lewis

Star Title

When Peter, Susan, Edmund and Lucy stumble through a magic wardrobe into the wondrous world of Narnia, they find themselves caught up in a battle against the White Witch, who has placed a wintry curse on the land. Edmund is separated from his brother and sisters, meets the Witch and, under her spell, makes a secret pact that puts all their lives in danger. Great courage is needed as the other children lead the creatures and talking beasts of Narnia into battle.

Narnia has a long history, told through seven books called **The Chronicles of Narnia**. Each book is a gripping adventure on its own, yet together they make one long and glorious story – a story of brave people and extraordinary creatures struggling to protect Narnia from the evil forces against it; a story of courage and loyalty; of battles and betrayals; of amazing travels and magical places; a story of the wildness and warmth of the lion, Aslan, whose presence shines like a light in all the stories.

**Sherryl Jordan**

I loved the **Narnia** books when I was about your age. But apart from the first two in the series, I hadn't returned to any of them in the 20 years since then. The truth was, I wasn't sure I'd still like them. But I've just been reading them again, and am delighted to discover how wonderful I still think they are!

I'd forgotten how strong the writing and the narrative voice are, and sometimes how funny, too. I'd forgotten about the boy who was called Eustace Clarence Scrubb ('and he almost deserved it'); I'd forgotten the cry of 'Narnia and the North!', and the great lion walking side by side with Shasta silently through the Archenland mountain mist. What a delight to be reminded of it all again! If you haven't read them, read them (yes, *all* of them). If you have, well, like me you can now treat yourself to a bit of rereading...

**Daniel Hahn**

## Next?

• **The Chronicles of Narnia** are best read in the following order: *The Magician's Nephew*, *The Lion, the Witch and the Wardrobe*, *The Horse and his Boy*, *Prince Caspian*, *The Voyage of the Dawn Treader*, *The Silver Chair*, *The Last Battle*.

• And after all that? Try **The Worlds of Chrestomanci** series by Diana Wynne Jones. (*UBG* 393)

• Or **Harry Potter**. You probably know J.K. Rowling's classics already – but if you don't, go and introduce yourself right now. (*UBG* 145)

• Susan Cooper's **The Dark is Rising** sequence deals with magic and mystery in our own world, but it's darker and creepier. (*UBG* 78)

# LIONBOY  Zizou Corder

### Next?
• If you're looking for another epic read to enjoy then try *Dragonrider* by Cornelia Funke: the story of a dragon, a boy and a thrilling journey to try and save the last dragons on Earth.

• If you haven't read the enchanting **Doctor Dolittle** stories by Hugh Lofting, there's a treat in store for you. (*UBG* 87)

• For more fantasy that begins in the real world and sweeps you away, try Alan Garner's brilliant *Elidor*. (*UBG* 98)

Since he was small, Charlie has had the amazing ability to speak Lion. It's not the only unique thing about Charlie, but it stands him in good stead when he needs the lions' help to track down his beloved scientist parents, who have been kidnapped and taken from London to Paris and beyond.

Although it is set in a London of the future, there's something old-fashioned about the feel of the writing and shape of the story that reminded me of classic fantasies I've enjoyed and reread. Maybe *Lionboy*'s magic seeps into everyone who reads it?

This is the first book in a trilogy, and the sequels, *Lionboy: The Chase* and *Lionboy: The Truth*, are just as much fun – while the whole series is hugely imaginative and original.

**Jon Appleton**

★ ★ ★ ★ ★ ★

# LITTLE DARLINGS
## Sam Llewellyn

*Little Darlings* is a hilarious book that anyone would enjoy. With its absurd jokes, it's a must-read for all children. The three Darling children, Daisy, Cassian and Primrose, live with their dad and step-mum (who somehow has managed to remain 26 for the last 20 years!). The kids appear to be very nice, but in reality they are evil… They need a tough babysitter, someone unlike all the others they've driven away. At his wits' end, Papa Darling calls AAA Aardvark's (a nanny agency that so far hasn't struck the Darling family off its books) and a different kind of nanny arrives. Nanny Pete is a huge, bald, kind man with a gruff voice and a pink apron. But when the Darling kids see him looting papa's belongings, the adventures really begin.

**Jonah Freud, age 10**

### Next?
• More **Darlings**! Read *Bad, Bad Darlings* and *Desperado Darlings*.

• For more of Sam Llewellyn's brand of mad humour, try *The Haunting of Death Eric* and *The Return of Death Eric*.

• For something else just as madly hilarious, try *Urgum the Axeman*. (*UBG* 365)

• Or for another really bad boy, try *Artemis Fowl* by Eoin Colfer. (*UBG* 23)

# MYTHS AND LEGENDS
## Legendary!
### by Catherine Fisher

Myths and legends lead us deep into humanity's oldest fears and dreams. We come across them first in fairy tales. Dark forests, third sons, devious dragons, magic swords – such motifs recur throughout this simple, savage world, fascinating in their power over our imagination.

The classic collection is *Grimms' Fairy Tales*, available in many modern versions.

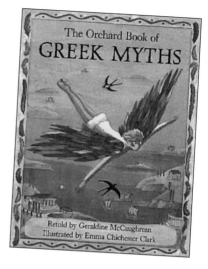

The Orchard Book of GREEK MYTHS

Retold by Geraldine McCaughrean
Illustrated by Emma Chichester Clark

The Grimm brothers collected traditional stories; from their dark forests emerge 'The Frog Prince', 'Rumpelstiltskin', 'Snow White', and from that terrifying house of gingerbread, 'Hansel and Gretel'. Not originally intended for children, they were tales for any age. Hans Christian Andersen may have been the first children's writer to use traditional stories as a basis for his own, to make biting satires like 'The Emperor's New Clothes', 'The Ugly Duckling' and the haunting tale of 'The Little Mermaid'.

Myths are older, and so re-embroidered that no one knows who began them. The ancient tales of Greece and Rome crawl with grotesque creatures and are breathless with epic journeys; they also show us men and women tormented by destiny. Odysseus spends

## Ten Books of (or inspired by) Greek and Roman Myths

- *The God Beneath the Sea* by Leon Garfield and Edward Blishen
- *The King Must Die* by Mary Renault
- *Black Ships Before Troy* and its sequels by Rosemary Sutcliff and Penelope Lively
- *Troy* by Adèle Geras
- *The Orchard Book of Greek Myths* retold by Geraldine McCaughrean
- *Greek Myths for Young Children* by Marcia Williams
- *Tales of the Greek Heroes* by Roger Lancelyn Green
- *Tales of Troy and Greece* by Andrew Lang
- **Corydon** series by Tobias Druitt
- **Percy Jackson** series by Rick Riordan

## Editors' Choices

- *The Just So Stories* by Rudyard Kipling
- *Tales of the Early World* by Ted Hughes
- *The Arthur Rackham Fairy Book* by Arthur Rackham
- *The Snow-walker's Son* by Catherine Fisher
- *Norse Myths*
- *How the Whale Became* by Ted Hughes

years coming home from Troy for offending the wrong god, and Jason searches the world for the Golden Fleece. For modern versions, try *The God Beneath the Sea* by Leon Garfield and Edward Blishen, Geraldine McCaughrean's *The Orchard Book of Greek Myths*, or *Black Ships Before Troy* by Rosemary Sutcliff. For novels set in this world, there is the wonderful *Troy* by Adèle Geras or Mary Renault's fantastic story of Theseus and the Minotaur, *The King Must Die.*

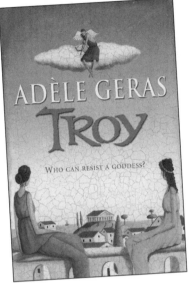

Welsh and Irish stories have a Celtic strangeness that has influenced many modern writers; try *Tales from the Mabinogion* by Gwyn Thomas and Kevin Crossley-Holland for the story of the woman made of flowers, or the crazy list of Arthur's men who help woo the giant's daughter. In *The Owl Service*, Alan Garner makes brilliant use of Welsh myth, as does Susan Cooper in **The Dark is Rising** sequence.

King Arthur is an offshoot of a Welsh story that has electrified the imagination of many. For a good version of the classic, try *King Arthur and the Knights of the Round Table* by Roger Lancelyn Green. Few legends have been retold so often; the powers of Merlin, the search for the mysterious Grail and the betrayal of the perfect court from within are themes that still obsess us. T.H. White's *The Sword in the Stone* explores this world wonderfully; more recently, Kevin Crossley-Holland sets *The Seeing Stone* in medieval Shropshire; and in my own *Corbenic*, the Arthurian legend becomes a struggle of modern times.

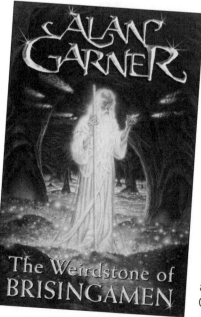

Another fascinating set of myths comes from the North – the Viking stories of Thor and treacherous Loki, of dwarfs, dragons and trolls. Crossley-Holland's *Norse Myths* retells these in jewelled prose. J.R.R. Tolkien uses Norse images and names in *The Hobbit* and *The Lord of the Rings*, as does Alan Garner in *The Weirdstone of Brisingamen.*

Constantly re-interpreted by writers, myths never die. Jenny Nimmo's *The Snow Spider* uses Mabinogion stories, Susan Price's *The Ghost Drum* has Siberian elements, and William Mayne writes of boggarts in **Earthfasts**. Myths remain a haunting backdrop to great stories by Pauline Fisk, Adèle Geras, Peter Dickinson and many, many more.

## Six Arthurian Stories

- *Corbenic* by Catherine Fisher
- *King Arthur and His Knights of the Round Table* by Roger Lancelyn Green
- *King Arthur and the Knights of the Round Table* by Marcia Williams
- **The Dark is Rising** sequence by Susan Cooper
- *The Sword in the Stone* by T.H. White
- *The Seeing Stone* by Kevin Crossley-Holland

## Or Why Not Try a Sort-of Fairy-tale Book?

- *Cold Tom* by Sally Prue
- *Artemis Fowl* by Eoin Colfer
- *Faerie Wars* by Herbie Brennan
- *The Little Grey Men* by B.B.
- *One Thousand and One Arabian Nights* retold by Geraldine McCaughrean
- *I Was a Rat!* by Philip Pullman
- *Clever Polly and the Stupid Wolf* by Catherine Storr
- **Incrediblania** stories by Norman Hunter

# THE LITTLE GREY MEN  B.B.

### Next?

• **Down the Bright Stream** recounts the further adventures of our three heroes, when people invade the secret places that are their home.

• **Brendon Chase**, also by B.B., is the story of three boys who don't want to return to boarding school, and so go to ground in a great forest.

• Or for more about the countryside as it used to be, read Alison Uttley's delightful **The Country Child**. (*UBG* 74)

When spring comes to the Folly Brook, it's time to get moving. Among the animals and birds starting out on the year are Dodder, Baldmoney and Sneezewort, the last gnomes in Britain. Normally they live quiet lives, comfortable in their homes in the roots of an oak tree, but this year is different. Their brother Cloudberry, who went exploring to find the source of the Folly Brook, has gone missing. So they build a boat and set off to find him. It is a dangerous venture, for when you are so small the wilderness has many hazards: weasels, herons, pike and lots of others – including gamekeepers.

This is an adventure story, packed with incident and details of nature. B.B. (Denys Watkins-Pitchford) was art master at Rugby School and illustrated his own book, with colour, scraperboard, and pen-and-ink drawings.

**Alan Temperley**

★ ★ ★ ★ ★ ★

# LITTLE HOUSE ON THE PRAIRIE  Laura Ingalls Wilder

This is the story of a pioneering family in the late nineteenth century. The story centres round Laura, the second daughter and, although her life is sometimes harsh and certainly far removed from our own experiences, it makes you long to be out there, sleeping in a log cabin under the boundless stars and hundreds of miles from anywhere. There are adventures with cowboys, wolves, bears and American Indians. And all the while, Laura's wonderful Pa is sawing and hammering and building, to keep the family and their animals safe and warm.

(A word of warning to fathers: if you fancy yourself as a D.I.Y. specialist, don't read this story to your children. My husband did and he says it left him feeling permanently inadequate.)

**Jenny Nimmo**

### Next?

• Laura Ingalls Wilder wrote six more books about her life in the American West. **Little House in the Big Woods** is the first in the series. For older readers, there's **The First Four Years**, about Laura's early married life.

• For other true stories of people's lives, look for Adeline Yen Mah's **Chinese Cinderella** (*UBG* 63), or **Boy** by Roald Dahl (*UBG* 44).

• **Sarah, Plain and Tall** by Patricia MacLachlan is also set on the American prairies in the nineteenth century. (*UBG* 294)

# LITTLE LORD FAUNTLEROY Frances Hodgson Burnett

This is the story of Ceddie, a seven-year-old American boy, brought back to England at the request of his bad-tempered old grandfather, the Earl of Dorincourt, to become Lord Fauntleroy, heir to a great fortune.

Ceddie is a sweet-natured child who only wants to use his new-found wealth to do good. As a warm relationship develops between the old man and the little boy, the Earl's icy heart gradually thaws. But there are obstacles in the way. The Earl refuses to have anything to do with Ceddie's mother, and when a rival heir appears, it looks as though Ceddie might not be the real Lord Fauntleroy after all...

If you like the idea of being taken back to Victorian times to follow the journey from rags to riches of a character you're bound to love, then look out for this book!

**Gwyneth Rees**

### Next?
• Another classic by the same author is *The Secret Garden* (*UBG* 302) or try *A Little Princess* (*UBG* 205).

• Another book about a child who goes to live with a daunting relative and changes everyone's lives for the better is *Pollyanna*. (*UBG* 272)

• *Rags and Riches* by Joan Lingard is about two children who come from a very poor family, and what happens when they find a coat lined with money.

★ ★ ★ ★ ★ ★

# A LITTLE LOWER THAN THE ANGELS
## Geraldine McCaughrean

### Next?
• Look for other vivid pictures of a medieval England in Kevin Crossley-Holland's *Gatty's Tale*, or Cynthia Harnett's *The Wool-Pack* (*UBG* 392).

• You can find twentieth-century stage-struck characters in Pamela Brown's *The Swish of the Curtain*. (*UBG* 337)

• Or for a story that's about theatre, history and time travel, try Susan Cooper's *King of Shadows*. (*UBG* 190)

'Gabriel jumped into the Mouth of Hell. The smell of burning pricked the back of his nose. He wriggled into the red gullet of Hell. Two hands from beyond reached into his armpits and pulled him through. It was God.' How about that, eh? Well, it's not actually God, it's the leading actor of the Mystery Players, who have turned up in the medieval English town where miserable Gabriel is apprenticed to a bullying mason. Gabriel, instantly stage-struck, runs away with them. He's a natural to play an angel. The peasant audiences think he works miracles, and for a while he thinks so, too – until the mason, the plague and the devil take over his life...

Of all Geraldine McCaughrean's excellent books, this is my favourite, perhaps because I've always been as stage-struck as Gabriel.

**Susan Cooper**

# THE LITTLE PRINCE  Antoine de Saint-Exupéry

**Next?**

• I am supposed to suggest to you what to read next, but I can't. There is no book quite like this. So instead, go outside and feel the wind. Look at the stars if there are any. Make a wish. Wait till tomorrow to start another book. That would be best.

A lone aircraft pilot crashes his plane in a desert, and there he meets a traveller from another world – a little prince. While the pilot struggles to mend his plane, the little prince describes his life.

Read this book! Read the first page, anyway! That will be enough because it is unputdownable. What happens to the little prince an intelligent reader will discover. What happened to the pilot is more of a mystery, because the author, himself a pilot, disappeared. His plane was lost a year after his story was published.

**Hilary McKay**

★ ★ ★ ★ ★ ★

# A LITTLE PRINCESS  Frances Hodgson Burnett

This is the story of Sara Crewe, whose mother died when she was a baby and who has lived in India all her life with her father, Captain Crewe. At the start of the book, Captain Crewe brings Sara to England, to Miss Minchin's Select Seminary for Young Ladies. Sara's papa is very rich, and Sara is very privileged. The other girls call her 'Princess' and Miss Minchin is as nice as pie to her. But when Sara is eleven, tragedy strikes. Her beloved papa dies, and all his money is gone. Poor Sara is left a pauper.

Everyone turns against her. She is put to work as a drudge and sent to live in the attics. Her whole life has collapsed – but Sara is not a girl to give way to despair. She may be cold, and starving, and exhausted, but still she manages to keep her spirits up. And at the end...

This book was written over 100 years ago, but is as magical now as it was then.

**Jean Ure**

**Next?**

• More Frances Hodgson Burnett? Try *The Secret Garden*. (*UBG* 302)

• *The Railway Children* by E. Nesbit is an enchanting story, guaranteed to make you cry! (*UBG* 279)

• Eva Ibbotson's *Star of Kazan* is about an orphan girl and the mystery that surrounds her. (*UBG* 323)

# LITTLE SOLDIER Bernard Ashley

**Next?**

• Other stories about child asylum seekers, such as *The Other Side of Truth* by Beverley Naidoo (*UBG* 255) or Benjamin Zephaniah's *Refugee Boy*.

• *A.K.* by Peter Dickinson is the gripping story of civil war in a fictional African country. (*UBG* 8)

• In *Ruby Tanya* by Robert Swindells, Asra's family is about to be deported, then a bomb goes off at the local school – guess who gets the blame for it?

Kaninda is rescued from a brutal attack in his East African village and joins a rebel army, where he learns to use deadly weapons and vows to take revenge on the enemies that killed his mother, father and sister. Aid workers bring him to London to start a new life with a well-meaning family, but the bullet scar in his arm is a constant reminder of his traumatic past.

His rundown comprehensive school and shabby inner-city estate are rife with violent and dangerous 'tribal' conflicts between rival gangs, and together with his only friend, Laura Rose, Kaninda finds himself drawn into another kind of power struggle which spins out of control.

With its stomach-churning descriptions, street dialogue and fighting, this is not an easy read, but it is exciting, edge-of-the-seat stuff about human conflict, pride and friendship, and a book you just won't be able to put down.

**Eileen Armstrong**

★ ★ ★ ★ ★ ★

# THE LITTLE WHITE HORSE Elizabeth Goudge

Orphan Maria is a rare combination – a practical girl, who is also completely open to magical possibilities.

Sent to the mysterious, beautiful estate of Moonacre, she finds a place where history, myth and fairy tale mingle with her own Victorian world. What is the ancient quarrel that haunts the Merryweather family and makes the vast, dark pine forest so sinister and full of trouble? What is the fatal repeated mistake that has broken so many hearts?

Helped by several animals and humans, not to mention her own true love, Maria must still call on all her own bravery and determination. But then she has glimpsed the magical white horse – the horse with the single silvery horn; to see him again, she will risk almost anything.

**Tanith Lee**

**Next?**

• Tanith Lee has written some wonderfully dark stories. Try *The Castle of Dark*. (*UBG* 55)

• Catherine Fisher's *The Lammas Field* is another fantastical story with a white horse. Magdalen Nabb's *The Enchanted Horse* tells of a wooden horse that comes to life.

• Or *The Enchanted Castle* by E. Nesbit, which has a similar atmosphere of magic. (*UBG* 100)

# LITTLE WOLF series Ian Whybrow

In the *Book of Badness*, Little Wolf is sent to Cunning College. You'll laugh out loud at his letters home. 'I know you want me to be wild and wicked just like Dad, but why do I have to go so far away? I told you I only cleaned my teeth last week for a joke.'

In *Forest Detective*, Little Wolf, Yeller, Normus and Smellybreff start up a detective agency. 'We are good solvers,' he writes, 'but not Smells. His brane is 2 small.'

They locate the 72 missing football boots of Ants United FC: a centipede confesses, 'I just wanted to do loud riverdancing and get faymus.' But Little Wolf's parents don't trust him. They send along Mister Furlock Homes-Wolf, Private Investigator. Whose detection methods will be better?

**Jane Darcy**

## Books that are Funny When You're Eight or 80...

- *Mouse Noses on Toast* by Daren King
- **Araminta Spook** series by Angie Sage
- **Mr Gumm** series by Andy Stanton
- *How to Eat Fried Worms* by Thomas Rockwell
- **Asterix** series by René Goscinny and Albert Uderzo
- *The Legend of Spud Murphy* by Eoin Colfer
- *The Killer Underpants* by Michael Lawrence
- *The Great Piratical Rumbustification* by Margaret Mahy

## Next?

- Some other **Little Wolf** books to look for are: *Little Wolf's Haunted Hall of Horrors, Little Wolf, Pack Leader* and *Little Wolf, Terror of the Shivery Sea.*
- Even though **Little Wolf** can be read by anyone, Ian Whybrow is a bit of a genius when it comes to writing stories for boys, and there's a whole series of them: **Books for Boys**. Look out for, amongst others: *A Footballer Called Flip* and *The Boy Who Had (Nearly) Everything.*
- Eoin Colfer writes very funny stories; try *The Legend of Spud Murphy.* (*UBG* 197)

# LITTLE WOMEN Louisa May Alcott

Ask women writers of 40 or over to name their favourite children's book and you'll find many of them say *Little Women*. This is because they identify closely with Jo, one of the March sisters. She's the tomboyish one, the unconventional one and most importantly, the one who wants to be a writer when she grows up. She also resembles Alcott herself.

The book is about the four sisters and how they cope while their father is away fighting in the American Civil War. Meg, the eldest, is good and domestically competent. Jo is next in age, then Beth, who's dreamy, musical and delicate. Amy, the youngest, is a vain little madam who is also very charming.

I adored *Little Women* because I'm an only child and the idea of having sisters fascinated me. By the time you come to the end of the book, you've made four friends. You live through everything that happens to the March girls, and you really feel you're right there in that house. You will definitely cry during the course of the novel, but you'll laugh as well.

**Adèle Geras**

### Next?
• The story continues in *Good Wives*, *Little Men* and *Jo's Boys*.
• There's more Louisa May Alcott to enjoy, too; read about the orphan girl, Rose, and her struggle to fit in with her uncle's noisy family in *Eight Cousins*, and the sequel, *Rose in Bloom*.
• Try L.M. Montgomery's **Anne of Green Gables** books (*UBG* 20) or the **What Katy Did** books (*UBG* 378).
• *The Exiles* and its sequels are very different stories about four sisters. (*UBG* 104)

★ ★ ★ ★ ★ ★

# LIZZIE DRIPPING Helen Cresswell

### Next?
• Belladonna in Eva Ibbotson's *Which Witch?* longs to be a bad, fiendish old hag instead of a beautiful enchantress.
• Try Jill Murphy's *The Worst Witch* (*UBG* 394), or *Pongwiffy* by Kaye Umansky (*UBG* 272), which has to be the smelliest witch ever!
• If you prefer wizards, Diana Hendry's *Harvey Angell* will have you smiling till the very last page. (*UBG* 146)

Lizzie Dripping is always in trouble and never quite tells the truth, so of course no one believes her when, one day, she says she has seen a witch in the village. Not that this bothers Lizzie – she knows it's true and life is suddenly much more exciting. The witch (who lives in the graveyard) becomes her best friend, and leads her into all kinds of unexpected mischief!

You can follow Lizzie's wonderfully silly and just a little bit spooky adventures in *Lizzie Dripping Again*, *Lizzie Dripping and the Angel*, *Lizzie Dripping and the Witch* and *Lizzie Dripping on Holiday*.

**Eileen Armstrong**

# LOBSTER BOY  Rodman Philbrick  ●●●

## Next?

• More Philbrick? Look out for *Freak the Mighty* (*UBG* 120) and *The Fire Pony*, about a pony, the strange lure of fire and two brothers trying to escape their past.

• Two kids try to deal with some pretty awful stuff in Jennifer Choldenko's *If a Tree Falls in Lunchbreak*.

• Or try Jacques Couvillon's *Chicken Dance*, which is about Don (who used to be Stanley), the mysteries that surround his family, bullying, deceit – and chickens.

This is an involving adventure story, told with great simplicity and immediacy, but it also packs a hefty emotional punch and has you rooting all the way for its 12-year-old hero, Skiff. His first challenge is to raise the family fishing boat, which has sunk into the Maine harbour. Ultimately, in a story that consciously pays homage to Hemingway's *The Old Man and the Sea*, Skiff goes off to hunt a giant tuna. Throughout, Skiff is facing his own internal demons – the death of his mother and the fact that his dad's pretty much given up on life. Rodman Philbrick packs layers of metaphor and emotion into his taut prose and concise chapters. A great boy's-own story but a whole lot more besides.

**Justin Somper**

★ ★ ★ ★ ★ ★

# LOCOMOTION  Jacqueline Woodson  ●●

'So this whole book's a poem because poetry's short,' says Lonnie Collins Motion (Lo Co Motion). Though he's only eleven, he has a lot that needs saying... About his parents, who died in a fire; his sister Lili, who now has a 'new mama'; Miss Edna, with whom he lives; his fellow students.

His teacher's suggestion, writing poetry, releases Lonnie's imagination. Using a variety of forms – sonnets, haiku, free verse – he reveals his story in poetic snapshots expressing his sorrow, hope, fear, pent-up fury and, ultimately, a quiet but barely suppressible joy and confidence.

This is a powerful and gentle novel about the emerging dignity and social awareness of a sensitive boy.

**Chris Stephenson**

## Next?

• Delve into Anne Fine's splendidly personal three-volume collection of her favourite poems, *A Shame to Miss*. The books are full of delights and surprises that'll keep you amused for hours.

• Another story told in verse is LaVaughn's, in Virginia Euwer Wolff's *Make Lemonade*.

• Discover the way another boy handles his troubles at school in Jack Gantos' *Joey Pigza Swallowed the Key*. (*UBG* 182)

• *Georgie* by Malachy Doyle is a tougher read about a boy in care. (*UBG* 123)

# THE LONDON EYE MYSTERY Siobhan Dowd

**Next?**

• For something more challenging, try Mark Haddon's *The Curious Incident of the Dog in the Night-time*; like Ted, Christopher looks at things with an obsessive attention to detail – a skill needed when he tries to solve the mystery of a dog killed with a garden fork.

• Part mystery, part about growing up, *Finding Violet Park* by Jenny Valentine is about a boy who's slightly out of kilter with the world.

• Or for a mystery with added puzzles, try *Chasing Vermeer* by Blue Balliett. (*UBG* 59)

Ted looks at things in a different way to other people. He gathers information, like a computer, paying as much attention to the number of Shreddies in his bowl as to the family's conversation. He knows he annoys people with his obsessions: shaking his hand out, counting things and explaining the weather systems in minute detail. Ted and his sister Kat have to entertain cousin Salim, whose one ambition is to ride the London Eye. Separated in the queue, they watch Salim go on board, but he doesn't return. Where is Salim? With his special powers of observation and logic, Ted takes on the mystery. As well as being a pacy thriller, this book champions people like Ted, who are routinely labelled as having a disability. I loved it!

**Pauline Chandler**

★ ★ ★ ★ ★ ★

# LORD OF THE NUTCRACKER MEN  Iain Lawrence

Johnny Briggs is excited when the First World War starts. His father has carved him wooden soldiers – his Nutcracker Men. Evacuated to his Auntie Ivy's, Johnny turns her garden into a muddy battlefield for them, re-enacting the raids and attacks his father describes in letters home from the trenches.

But the letters become grim. Johnny cannot escape the fact that war is frightening. He learns more from a wounded deserter on the run. He begins to wonder if his mock attacks might be influencing what's really happening in France.

You'll read things that are horrifying, but you'll be fascinated. And there's a cheering side to this story, with a wonderful ending based on the extraordinary real-life truce in Christmas 1914.

**Jane Darcy**

**Next?**

• I don't think you'll find a more brilliant book about the First World War, but *War Game* by Michael Foreman is a moving story of two friends' experiences in the trenches, which also includes the Christmas truce. (*UBG* 373)

• Another brilliant evocation of the same war is Michael Morpurgo's *Private Peaceful*. (*UBG* 274)

• Iain Lawrence also wrote the **High Seas Adventure** trilogy: *The Wreckers*, *The Smugglers* and *The Buccaneers*.

# THE LORD OF THE RINGS
## J.R.R. Tolkien

You've seen the movie – now read the book! This is the story of Frodo the Hobbit's adventures as he struggles to take the terrible Ring to Mount Doom to destroy it, and of his friends as they try to help him. There's Sam, his faithful servant; Merry and Pippin, fellow Hobbits who fight their way through capture by Orcs, sieges and massive battles; Gandalf the wizard, who is a great deal more powerful than he seems; and Aragorn, the warrior and ranger, who must find his own powerful destiny. There are elves, dwarves, hideous Black Riders and the evil all-seeing Sauron who intends to conquer all of Middle Earth.

This is the Big Daddy of all sword-and-sorcery fantasy and it's still one of the best. Tolkien invented an entire world, complete with mythologies and languages. The huge epic sweep of his imagination picks you up and carries you to the final thundering battle of wills on Mount Doom.

**Patricia Finney**

### Next?
- To find out how Bilbo Baggins got the Ring of Power, read *The Hobbit*. (*UBG* 154)
- There are many, many books by Tolkien; try some shorter tales such as *Farmer Giles of Ham* and *Roverandom*, a volume of poetry. Or there's *The Adventures of Tom Bombadil* and *The Silmarillion* – a story of the First Age.
- Or try Philip Pullman's **His Dark Materials** trilogy – a fantasy sequence that really matches *The Lord of the Rings* for scale and epic appeal. (*UBG* 151)
- Or look for *Here There Be Dragons* by James A. Owen, which has Tolkien as one of the characters in it!

This is a tale of mystery, heroism, loyalty, adventure and – against almost impossible hardships – hope. Many years before the story begins, the One Ring of Power was forged in secret by the Dark Lord, Sauron. He meant to use this ring to rule over all of Middle Earth, but lost possession of it in a great war. The ring was thought lost or destroyed, yet it was later found by the Hobbit, Bilbo Baggins, who in turn gave it to his heir, Frodo. But the ring is dangerous, and the safety of all of Middle Earth is under threat. So Frodo volunteers to go on a quest: a quest to destroy the ring; a quest that will change his life out of all recognition.

From the first page, this is a story that holds you and does not let you go. The characters, with their friendships and betrayals, their loves and hatreds, are wonderful and, from the smallest Hobbit to the tallest Ent, I loved them all. Without doubt, this is the best book I've ever read.

**Spencer Johnson, age 10**

# LORNA DOONE R.D. Blackmore

John Ridd is a young man of prodigious strength who lives on Exmoor. It is 1676 and robbers and highwaymen are a part of life. John wanders on to the land of the Doones, a notorious and much-feared family of outlaws. There he meets Lorna, a beautiful little girl who begs him to escape before her violent relatives find him. Years later, John and Lorna meet again and fall in love, but Lorna is now betrothed to the most brutal of all the Doones.

Eventually Lorna discovers her true identity and John rescues her, only to lose her again and again. Published in 1869, the language may seem a little old-fashioned today, but once you get used to it, you'll find it well worth the effort. There are wonderful descriptions of the West Country, great character sketches and brilliantly realised fights where John's great strength proves irresistible.

**Jenny Nimmo**

**Next?**
• You might want to read *Wuthering Heights* by Emily Brontë. Written in 1847, it tells of a passionate and ill-starred relationship, this time set on the Yorkshire Moors.

• *The Last of the Mohicans* by James Fennimore Cooper is a classic adventure, a classic love story and a really exciting read.

• *The Children of the New Forest* by Captain Marryat is another classic story, set during the English Civil Wars. (*UBG* 62)

★ ★ ★ ★ ★ ★

# LOSER Jerry Spinelli

**Next?**
• More from Jerry Spinelli? Try *Stargirl*, a novel as exuberant as a firework display (*UBG* 324), or the darker-toned *Wringer*.

• For a real outsider's impact on everyday family life (in this case, an alien), read about the hilarious complications arising from Pascal's visit with the Castles in Pat Thomson's *Strange Exchange*. It's one of the funniest books around.

'Yahoo!' is Donald Zinkoff's first recorded utterance. Happiness, enthusiasm, laughter – that's his natural habitat. Ever the optimist, he finds pleasure in everything, loves school so much he gets there early, considers his father's job as a mailman the most important in the world, and is friends with everyone (particularly the opposing soccer team).

Trouble is, others don't view it that way; to them he's just a loser, someone you avoid picking to play in your team. But Zinkoff's eternal optimism remains intact, even after narrowly avoiding an unnecessary but characteristically unselfish demise.

The story of the irrepressible Zinkoff's progress through elementary school is funny, warm and occasionally heart-wrenching; a celebration of individuality and non-conformity.

**Chris Stephenson**

# THE LOST WORLD Arthur Conan Doyle ●●●

### Next?

• Try Arthur Conan Doyle's Sherlock Holmes classic, *The Hound of the Baskervilles* (*UBG* 160), or read one of his lesser-known historical novels: *The White Company*, set during the 100 Years War.

• Or what about a world where genetic experimentation has speeded up evolution, and the new species are pretty unfriendly? Try John Brindley's thrilling and thought-provoking *Rule of Claw*.

• Or one of the all-time great dinosaur books, Michael Crichton's *Jurassic Park*, the sequel to which is also called ... *The Lost World*! Both are absolute page-turners!

*The Lost World* was written nearly 100 years ago, and was one of the first books to explore the excitement and possibilities of adventure in encountering dinosaurs. Conan Doyle knew all about telling a story (he was the creator of Sherlock Holmes) and I think the exploits of the extraordinary Professor Challenger and his companions are still gripping today. As a boy's story for men, or a man's story for boys of its time (as the author admits), women hardly get a look-in at all – but perhaps part of the interest of reading the book is also to note the differences of behaviour and expectation between then and now. In that way, too, it is a description of a lost world.

**Quentin Blake**

★ ★ ★ ★ ★ ★

# THE LOTTIE PROJECT Jacqueline Wilson ●●

Have you ever been given a school project that you thought was going to be *really* boring? Well Charlie ('*Don't* call me Charlotte'), the most popular girl in her class, thinks that the project she has to do on the Victorians is going to be deathly dull. But then she dreams up the character of Lottie, a Victorian servant girl the same age as her, and when she starts to write Lottie's diary, a whole new world comes to life in her head.

This book is one of Jacqueline Wilson's very best. It's a sparkling read that deals with friendships, single mums, boyfriends, school and much more as well. Charlie's a great character – she's the sort of girl anyone would want as their best friend, and her only fault is ... she knows it!

**Susan Reuben**

### Next?

• A book about girls, friends and family is Nicola Morgan's equally sparkling *Chicken Friend*.

• Or try *The Story of the Treasure Seekers* by E. Nesbit, about a family of Victorian children.

• In Anne Fine's *A Pack of Liars*, Laura and Oliver are surprised by their new penpals...

• Or look out for Jacqueline Wilson's book about her own childhood, *Jacky Daydream*. (*UBG* 178)

# LOVE THAT DOG  Sharon Creech

This book is very difficult to categorise. It's like a diary that's a collection of poems, which tell a story with some help from William Blake and Robert Frost.

It's just unique. Jack is a boy who thinks poems are for girls until he begins to find his own voice through writing poetry, and starts appreciating the poetry around him. A quick read, this is perfect for those who find big novels hard going, and those who find poetry difficult. Following Jack on his journey is easy, and fun, and as you turn the pages, you get gently drawn into the mind of a little intellectual.

This book is yellow, but it's not afraid to go the way no other book has gone before it. It's a great example of how the rules can be broken by staying true to a simple idea that works.

**Benjamin Zephaniah**

## Pet Dogs, Wild Dogs and Some Not Quite Either!

* *A Dog Called Grk* by Joshua Doder
* *Call of the Wild* by Jack London
* *Dog Friday* by Hilary McKay
* *A Dog So Small* by Philippa Pearce
* *The Hundred and One Dalmatians* by Dodie Smith
* *Marley: A Dog Like No Other* by John Grogan
* *Born to Run* by Michael Morpurgo
* *Woof!* by Allan Ahlberg
* *Dogsbody* by Diana Wynne Jones
* *Fire, Bed and Bone* by Henrietta Branford
* *Greyfriars Bobby* by Eleanor Atkinson

## Next?

* Poetry! You'll get good ideas for a few poets to look for in *Love That Dog*. Or what about the wonderful Mr Zephaniah? Look for *Talking Turkeys*, and his second volume of verse for kids, *Funky Chickens*.
* You might also like collections by Michael Rosen, Roger McGough or *Heard It in the Playground* by Allan Ahlberg.
* Or try the tougher *Locomotion* by Jacqueline Woodson. (*UBG* 209)
* Another Sharon Creech? Try *The Wanderer* for a more challenging read in which you have to piece together the story as you go along. (*UBG* 372)

# MACB

**Neil Arksey**

### Next?

• If it's another grab-you-by-the-throat read you want, then I'd go for *Playing on the Edge*, also by Neil Arksey. (*UBG* 271)

• If you want more ways of finding out about Shakespeare, try the illustrated books by Marcia Williams, starting with *Mr William Shakespeare's Plays*. (*UBG* 220)

• For another boy who finds Shakespeare's stories getting a little too close for comfort, try L. Brittney's *Nathan Fox: Dangerous Times*. (*UBG* 247)

A confession first: I don't like football. So why am I telling you about a book that features football big-time? Because it's such a fantastic story – it's exciting, creepy, fantastically fast-moving – and it gripped me from the first page. I finished it at four in the morning – and when I didn't know what 'Snaking left, then right, he bypassed two' meant it didn't matter a hoot. It's an incredibly clever book because it echoes the story of *Macbeth*, with a fortune-teller promising an unlikely promotion ... but if you don't know any Shakespeare that's fine. And don't think that the Shakespeare connection makes it a 'posh' book; it's full of real kids who chew gum and kick beer cans – and get caught up in a literally deadly rivalry.

**Vivian French**

★ ★ ★ ★ ★ ★

# THE MACHINE GUNNERS

**Robert Westall**

It is 1940, the most dangerous moment of World War II. Britain is alive with rumours of a German invasion. Thirteen-year-old Chas McGill and his friends spend their time scavenging for souvenirs: bits of aircraft and bombs. One day, Chas finds a working machine gun in a crashed bomber. But what happens when he finds a German gun, along with a German gunner, Rudi?

This is a thrilling adventure about outwitting adults, making friends and a war so real you'll imagine you lived through it.

**Alan Gibbons**

### Next?

• Another great book about surviving the war, also by Robert Westall, is *The Kingdom by the Sea*.

• Westall's *Gulf* is set during the first Gulf War in the early nineties. It features the strange relationship between a British boy and an Iraqi soldier far away. (*UBG* 139)

• *Blitzcat* features two of Westall's themes – war and cats – in a terrific adventure. (*UBG* 37)

• Alison Prince's *Doodlebug Summer* is another exciting story set during World War II.

# MADAME DOUBTFIRE  Anne Fine

### Next?
• Or what about Pete Johnson's *Rescuing Dad*, about two kids who try to 'improve' their dad in order to persuade their mum to take him back? (*UBG* 283)

• In Gwyneth Rees's *The Mum Hunt*, a girl tries to find her dad a new girlfriend, with unexpected results. (*UBG* 241)

• *Granny the Pag* by Nina Bawden is a powerful story of a girl's fight to live with whom she chooses.

Out-of-work actor, Daniel Hilliard, is divorced from his businesswoman wife, Miranda; the two of them do not see eye to eye. So in order to spend more time with his children, Daniel disguises himself as a woman and applies for the position as their nanny. And, of course, hilarious situations follow. Will Miranda discover Madame Doubtfire's true identity? As always, Anne Fine resolves the story in an unexpected way.

This clever book is as insightful as it is funny. Out of the misery of an all too common situation – a broken family, and children tugged between warring parents – is plucked love and humour. A well-told tale that is warm and real without sentimentality. A classic with heart.

**Neil Arksey**

# MAGIC FARAWAY TREE series  Enid Blyton

These books were written in 1943. I read them as a child and loved them, my daughter read them (they used to be her favourite books) and you will read them now and enjoy them just as much. Although dated in tone and background (the girls 'help Mother in the house' and the boy, Jo, 'helps his father in the garden'), the stories remain marvellously ingenious and entertaining, combining magic, fantasy, excitement and adventure together with a cosy homeliness. If only life were really like that!

There are several **Magic Faraway Tree** books, all containing lots of adventures. They are quite long, so are not a quick read. Although the content is suitable for those aged eight and upwards, I think you'd find them enjoyable at any age – they are the sort of lovely, comfortable stories you could always turn to if you're feeling frazzled.

**Mary Hooper**

### Next?
• The series consists of: *The Enchanted Wood*, *The Magic Faraway Tree* and *The Folk of the Faraway Tree*. Then you can move on to Enid Blyton's other magical stories such as **The Wishing Chair** series (*UBG* 388). Or try **The Secret Seven** (*UBG* 303), **The Famous Five** (*UBG* 109) and the **Adventure** books (*UBG* 177). And then … but it might take you until you are grown-up to get through them all!

• If you want to try something not by Enid Blyton, read *Half Magic* by Edward Eager. (*UBG* 141)

# THE MAGICIAN'S HOUSE QUARTET  William Corlett

A remote house in a Welsh valley, an Elizabethan alchemist who can travel through time and a villain from the past who wants to control the future – when the Constant children, William, Mary and Alice, spend their holidays at Golden House, in Golden Valley, they suddenly find themselves playing a crucial role in a struggle between the forces of good and evil.

Each book in the series deals with a different threat to Golden Valley. It's only when you reach the end (which isn't entirely happy) and look back, that you realise that slowly the scale of each struggle has been increasing until the children are fighting to save the things that they treasure most.

Not only did I enjoy the time-travelling element of these books, but I also loved the way the children were able to talk to and become one with the animals that helped them.

**Laura Hutchings**

### Next?
• The whole series: *The Steps Up the Chimney*, *The Door in the Tree*, *The Tunnel Behind the Waterfall* and *The Bridge in the Clouds*.

• For another story that brilliantly uses Welsh legend, read Alan Garner's *The Owl Service*. (*UBG* 258)

• Or try Catherine Fisher's *The Relic Master*.

• And for magic, try *The Box of Delights* by John Masefield. (*UBG* 44)

★ ★ ★ ★ ★ ★

# THE MAGIC SHOP series  Bruce Coville

### Next?
• The series starts with *Russell Try, Monster Boy* and continues with *Jeremy Thatcher, Dragon Hatcher*, *Jennifer Murdley's Toad*, *Goblins in the Castle*, *Charlie Eggleston's Talking Skull* and *Juliet Dove, Queen of Love*.

• Or try Patrice Kindl's *Owl in Love*, the story of a young shapeshifter named Owl.

• Patricia Wrede's **Enchanted Forest** books (starting with *Dealing with Dragons*) have more of a fairy-tale setting, but introduce a very practical princess.

Four children – three boys and a girl – find Mr Elives's magic shop with its scary owner, talking owl, magician's tools and books. Each takes one special thing away with them. Russell doesn't read the instructions on his monster ring properly, and it turns him into a winged, clawed, monster. Will he be stuck like that for ever? Jennifer's toad turns out to be embarrassingly talkative. Charlie's skull makes him far too truthful when before he was never honest, and Jeremy's dragon – well, these things *will* eat – and they *are* meat eaters... Each child has to try to pretend that life is normal, and find ways to deal with their very conspicuous new possessions, and some mistakes, once made, can't be erased.

**Tamora Pierce**

# MALORY TOWERS series  Enid Blyton

As a child, I adored Enid Blyton's books and the **Malory Towers** series had two profound impacts on my life: it convinced me to go to boarding school (a mistake) and taught me the value of page-turning narratives (a gift).

The six-book series follows the fortunes of a group of girls from their first to their last term at the school. Even now, 35 years on, when I open a **Malory Towers** book, the characters leap off the page: spoilt and spiteful, golden-haired Gwendoline; sharp-talking Alicia; steadfast Sally; and our brave, hot-tempered heroine, Darryl Rivers.

Blyton's stories follow a strict moral code: they are about owning up to faults, recognising loyalty and kindness, accepting the need for the full and frank apology. Blyton is particularly strong on issues of female peer-group rivalry and the difficulty of changing social allegiances. But her books are also compelling, funny, warm and surprisingly twenty-first-century stories about girls growing up and discovering who and what they are.

**Nicky Singer**

### Next?
• Enid Blyton also wrote about another girls' boarding school in the **St Clare's** series.
• A very modern boarding-school story – with added magic – is the **Charm School** series by Tabitha Black, starting with *The Magic Begins*, *Mona Lisa Mystery* and *Toil and Trouble*.
• For the next stage up girls' rite-of-passage book, try *Daddy-Long-Legs* by Jean Webster. (*UBG* 77)

★ ★ ★ ★ ★ ★

# THE MAN IN THE IRON MASK  Alexandre Dumas

### Next?
• You could try *The Three Musketeers*, also by Alexandre Dumas. It's another enthralling book – and better than the movie!
• Another epic adventure happens in Walter Moers's *The 13 1/2 Lives of Captain Bluebear*.
• Baroness Orczy's *The Scarlet Pimpernel* tells of a band of Englishmen pledged to rescue victims of the post-revolutionary reign of terror in Paris. (*UBG* 298)

The spirit of the Three Musketeers lives on, though wrinkled with the years. Here the story revolves around a mysterious masked prisoner, doomed to a ghastly fate. Who is he?

The 'man in the iron mask' is based on a true character brought to the Bastille in 1698. He was kept masked at all times and never had his name spoken. After his death, five years later, he was buried in an unmarked grave.

Whoever he is, the idea of enclosing a man in an iron mask has its own grisly glamour. But though the purists may carp at Dumas's sprawling unmade bed of a novel (over 600 pages), few storytellers can spin a better yarn or make history come to life so vividly.

**James Riordan**

# MAPHEAD  Lesley Howarth

### Next?

• Another Lesley Howarth? Try *Weather Eye*, about a girl with psychic powers and the effects of environmental change. It's another serious book that manages to be very funny, too.

• Another boy – one made of wood – searching for his mother is Barkbelly in the book of the same name by Cat Weatherill.

• In Pete Johnson's *Eyes of the Alien*, there are two friends; one is obsessed by aliens, while the other is being haunted by them. It's a deeply spooky story with a shocking twist to the tale.

MapHead, who comes from the Subtle World, is facing his 12th birthday – the Dawn Power Year. Usually he roams the world with his dad, but this year they've come to Cornwall to find MapHead's mother, and to find MapHead's own true self.

No one who meets MapHead will ever forget him, and neither will you. He is a true original and his story is one of the sunniest, most cheerful books you'll ever read. It celebrates life – three cheers for Lesley Howarth! Don't forget to look out for the sequel, *MapHead 2*.

**Jon Appleton**

★ ★ ★ ★ ★ ★

# THE MARBLE CRUSHER  Michael Morpurgo

Albert starts a new school when his parents move from the countryside to the town. There, streetwise Sid Creedy takes advantage of Albert's innocence and tells him all sorts of fibs. Without batting an eyelid, Sid informs Albert that their PE teacher Mr Cooper is an escaped monk (bald head: complete giveaway) and that the headmaster has six wives. And Albert believes him. After getting into serious trouble for playing marbles in school, Albert confronts his wicked teachers with their misdeeds and fun and games follow (but sadly, no games of marbles).

I first came across this story when my class and I were feeling particularly fed up at the prospect of the return of our head teacher, Dangerous Doris. Two minutes after starting it we were falling about with laughter and had forgotten all about Doris.

**Michael Cox**

### Next?

• Look for more by Michael Morpurgo. Try *Cool!*, about a boy in a coma – and told by him! Or there's *The Last Wolf*, a tremendous adventure involving a boy, Bonnie Prince Charlie, a wolf cub and a journey to America.

• *Ging Gang Goolie, It's an Alien* by Bob Wilson is a hilarious story about boy scouts encountering an extraterrestrial!

• Anne Fine's *How to Write Really Badly* is a school story with a difference. (*UBG* 163)

• Or what about football and humour? Try Anthony McGown's *The Bare Bum Gang and the Football Face-off*!

# MARCIA WILLIAMS'S COMIC STRIPS

Some of the greatest stories ever told are captured in just a few pages of bright and colourful cartoon strips, packed full of funny details to make you look closer, pull you into the action and really bring the stories alive again. Legend lovers should start with *Greek Myths*, to discover the truth about Pandora's box, meet Theseus and the dreaded Minotaur, daring highfliers Daedalus and Icarus, and many more. For heroes closer to home try *The Adventures of Robin Hood* and meet Little John, Friar Tuck and Maid Marian; or go journeying with *The Iliad* and *The Odyssey*, meeting the lovesick Helen of Troy and the Trojan Horse, the one-eyed Cyclops and the six-headed Scylla, or travel across medieval Spain in *Don Quixote* with the would-be knight and his ever-patient sidekick, Sancho Panza.

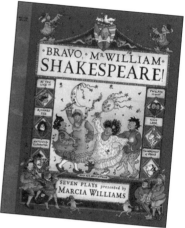

*Charles Dickens and Friends* lets you make friends (or enemies!) of Dickens's colourful goodies and baddies like Mr Fagin, Uriah Heep, Pip and Estella, Tiny Tim, Oliver, Ebenezer Scrooge and many more. Best of all are *Mr William Shakespeare's Plays* and *Bravo, Mr William Shakespeare!* which mix Shakespeare's words with Marcia Williams's cartoon captions to tell the story. The noisy comments of the audience in the clever page borders make you one of the spectators, too, as the curtain goes up on comedies and tragedies like *Hamlet*, *Macbeth*, *Romeo and Juliet*, *A Midsummer Night's Dream* and *The Merchant of Venice*.

And do look out for Marcia's *King Arthur and the Knights of the Round Table*, *Sinbad the Sailor* and *Bible Stories*, too, which use the same winning formula of large-format pages, funny handwritten dialogue based on the words of the original, jokes, bright action-packed frames and easy-to-read captions to capture the sense of the story and all the excitement of the originals.

**Eileen Armstrong**

## Next?

• **The Twisted Tales** series mix Michael Tickner's illustrations, comic strips and comic humour to bring stories to life, and include fascinating fact sections, too – the sort of facts you won't find in history books! The series includes: **Shakespeare Stories** and **Greek Legends** by Terry Deary, **Bible Stories** by Michael Coleman, **Irish Legends** by Margaret Simpson and **Horror Stories** by Michael Cox.

• Geraldine McCaughrean's **The Orchard Book of Greek Myths** is a thrilling retelling of the classic stories. (*UBG* 254)

• Roger Lancelyn Green wrote more expanded versions of **Robin Hood** (*UBG* 9) and **King Arthur** stories (*UBG* 189), and you can try the Lambs' **Tales** (*UBG* 340) or Leon Garfield for more wonderful Shakespeare retellings.

# MARIANNE DREAMS  Catherine Storr

I didn't have my own copy of *Marianne Dreams* when I was a child. I had about 15 scruffy paperbacks on my bedroom shelf in those days – a little different from the 15,000 books crammed into my tiny house now! I borrowed *Marianne Dreams* from the library many times. It was a book that haunted me. Now I've just reread it, I still find it strange, beguiling and frightening, and I'm more aware of the psychological depth of the story.

The plot is simple. Marianne is recovering from a long illness and is confined to bed. She doodles a house in her drawing book and then dreams she is there. She draws a boy looking out of the window and the next night dreams he is there, too. She gets angry with him and scribbles over the window and then in this weird dream-world he is trapped behind bars. She draws eyes on the rocks in the garden and they become real sinister beings, watching the two children… I'm not going to tell you what happens next. Read it yourself!

**Jacqueline Wilson**

### Next?
• Try another Catherine Storr: *The If Game* is a scary story about the blurred edges of reality.

• Another atmospheric and chilling tale of the supernatural is Frances Hardinge's *Verdigris Deep*. (*UBG* 368)

• Or for something that tries to tell the difference between reality and illusion, read Jeanne Willis's *Shamanka* and find out about a girl's quest to learn more about her magician father.

★ ★ ★ ★ ★ ★

# THE MARK OF THE HORSE LORD  Rosemary Sutcliff

### Next?
• More Rosemary Sutcliff? Try *The Eagle of the Ninth*. (*UBG* 93) *Frontier Wolf* is set in Scotland, and brilliant, too.

• More history? Try *The King Must Die* by Mary Renault (*UBG* 189) or *Warrior Girl* by Pauline Chandler, set during the time of Joan of Arc (*UBG* 375). Oh, and have a go at Josephine Tey's *The Daughter of Time*, which looks at how history can be truth, or lies.

This wonderful book is full of classic storytelling devices. There is the gladiator who wins his freedom, the ex-slave who looks enough like a prince to be able to swap roles with him and, of course, a wicked queen.

When Phaedrus the gladiator finally puts life in the arena behind him, he quickly finds himself caught up in a plot to overthrow the treacherous queen of the Dalriad tribes, and to restore the Lord of the Horse People. Phaedrus has to learn how to carry out his new role successfully, and gradually he grows into the part. I won't tell you how the story ends, but be warned – it reduced me to tears!

This is an adventure story, a history lesson and a trip to Scotland all in one. Highly recommended.

**Laura Hutchings**

# MARLEY: A DOG LIKE NO OTHER  John Grogan

### Next?

• Two of the most wonderful stories about dogs ever written have to be Jack London's *The Call of the Wild* and *White Fang* (*UBG* 381).

• For a real-life animal adventure featuring two dogs and a cat, read *The Incredible Journey* by Sheila Burnford.

• For more stories about the havoc that pets can cause, read Gerald Durrell's *My Family and Other Animals*. (*UBG* 242)

Years ago, we had a black Labrador called Shane. One day, he came home, very pleased with himself, carrying a whole joint of beef in his mouth. Someone (we never found out who) had lost their Sunday lunch! Anyone who has ever owned a Labrador knows that they are incorrigible thieves, permanently hungry, and have some disgusting habits. Marley, however, is in a league of his own. During the course of this wonderfully funny book he swallows a precious gold necklace, tows a café table down the street and clears an entire beach in spectacular (and truly revolting) style! John Grogan shared his memories of Marley with the world and his readers responded in their thousands. Check out the website **www.marleyandme.com** and you'll see what I mean.

**Laura Hutchings**

★ ★ ★ ★ ★ ★

# MARTIN FARRELL  Janni Howker

The eponymous hero of *Martin Farrell* is a lad caught between two great feuding families in the north of England. He belongs to both of them, but is loved by neither. They are a fierce, barbaric people, and many of the scenes of the story are truly horrific. But the wicked deeds do not go unobserved. There is a spiritual battle going on for peace in the 'debatable lands', a searching for the time when the killing will cease. And Martin, newly orphaned, is the fulcrum.

Janni Howker's book is a genuine favourite of mine. It ought to be just an historical novel, but it is not. The tale is told as a Border Ballad; the rhythm is perfect, and the lilt of northern speech is interspersed with lovely old dialect words. The proper way to read it is to let the words sing inside your head.

**Sylvia Waugh**

### Next?

• You might also like *The Border Ballads*, a collection of medieval song and verse, all about war, thieving, jealousy and revenge!

• Try reading a version of *Sir Gawain and the Green Knight*; there is a good one by Selina Hastings.

• Janni Howker's other books include *Badger on the Barge* (*UBG* 26) and *The Nature of the Beast*.

• *The Dark Horse* by Marcus Sedgwick deals with an equally barbaric threat. (*UBG* 79).

# MARY POPPINS P.L. Travers

Believe me, the book is far better than the film. It's stranger, and nothing is quite as you expect. Mary Poppins is a governess to Jane and Michael, and a figure with odd, supernatural powers. Whether dining out in a chalk drawing, pasting stars on the sky, having a birthday at the zoo or going Christmas shopping with one of the Pleiades, Mary P. is always starchy and prim, but secretly wise underneath. Hilariously funny, sometimes piercingly sad and full of a surreal magic that is never explained, this is a book you'll never forget.

**Catherine Fisher**

## Next?
• Try others in the series (though I think the first is the best): *Mary Poppins Comes Back* and *Mary Poppins in Cherry Tree Lane*.
• *The Lion, the Witch and the Wardrobe* by C.S. Lewis is a book about the doorways that can lie between worlds. (*UBG* 198)
• Another peculiar nanny? Try the harder, but really great, *Madame Doubtfire* by Anne Fine. (*UBG* 216)
• The classic *The Hundred and One Dalmatians* by Dodie Smith has a similar sense of whimsy. (*UBG* 164)

★ ★ ★ ★ ★ ★

# THE MASTER OF THE FALLEN CHAIRS Henry Porter

## Next?
• Go straight on to the sequel, *The House of Skirt*.
• **The Dark is Rising** sequence by Susan Cooper also starts just before Christmas. (*UBG* 78)
• For another book set at a frozen time, try Marcus Sedgwick's terrifying *The Book of Dead Days*.
• Another strange house with mystery and danger features in Susan Hill's *The Battle for Gullywith*.

This book is set in 1962, just before Christmas. When Kim's mother dies, he is sent from South Africa, where he has lived, to his uncle's large, ramshackle house in dark and chilly England. For Kim, everything in his new life is different from his old one, and to make matters worse, nothing is what it seems. The old house seems haunted, as he keeps hearing ghosts and weird things happen. It all gets even weirder when a stranger arrives at their front door...

If you want an exciting, scary, funny, mysterious book, this is perfect. It's a good long read – great for taking on holiday, too, but beware the cliffhanger – this is the first in a series!

**Nat Phillipps, age 11**

# MATCH OF DEATH   James Riordan

This is based on a true story. And, like many true stories, it is far more shocking and terrifying than anything made up.

Vova is 15 and loves football. He lives in the Ukraine, and is powerless to stop the German army invading his country, although he joins the resistance and fights as best he can. He survives suffering and hardship, until one day he is given the chance to play football again – though the stakes are unbelievably high. Lose and live, or win and die.

Starkly told, and heartbreaking in the way the lives of so many people are shown to be so casually destroyed by war, this book made me cry. I'll always remember Vova, and his choice. And I'll never think of football in quite the same way again.

**Leonie Flynn**

### Next?

• Another James Riordan novel to try is *Rebel Cargo*, an illuminating look at the slave trade. Or *War Games*, another story based on real events; this one on the Christmas football match played in No-man's Land during the First World War.

• For another surprising appearance of football in the midst of war, try Iain Lawrence's *Lord of the Nutcracker Men*. (*UBG* 210)

★ ★ ★ ★ ★ ★

# MATILDA   Roald Dahl

### Next?

• Try *The BFG* (*UBG* 33) and *The Witches* (*UBG* 389), also by Roald Dahl. Or you may prefer his shorter books such as *The Twits* (*UBG* 359) and *George's Marvellous Medicine* (*UBG* 123); both are outrageously funny.

• Another girl with unusual powers appears in Sally Gardner's *The Strongest Girl in the World*, part of the **Magical Children** series.

By the time Matilda is three, she has taught herself to read. She's tiny and extremely brainy, but her awful parents hate her for her cleverness. When she goes to school, she finds that the headmistress, Miss Trunchbull, is even worse than her parents. She's a huge bully, who throws children about whenever she feels like it. One day, Miss Trunchbull goes too far and Matilda is so angry she makes something happen to her. Matilda finds that she has an extraordinary magical power.

Luckily, Matilda is befriended by her teacher, Miss Honey, and when she learns about Miss Honey's sad past, Matilda decides to use her new power to help her. But as well as helping Miss Honey, Matilda changes her own life in a way she never thought possible.

This brilliant story is so entertaining and funny, and so cleverly resolved, that readers of all ages can't fail to enjoy it.

**Jenny Nimmo**

# MAUS  Art Spiegelman  ●●●

### Next?
• *The Diary of a Young Girl* by Anne Frank is a riveting and heartbreaking read. (*UBG* 84)

• Raymond Briggs's *Ethel and Ernest* is a biography of his mum and dad. Although theirs is a more ordinary tale than Spiegelman's, it's a great story, and told in words and pictures with a lot of love and affection. (*UBG* 101)

• *Witnesses to War: Eight True-life Stories of Nazi Persecution* edited by Michael Leapman is a harrowing yet uplifting book.

*Maus* is a survivor's story of life under the Nazis, as told to his son, Art Spiegelman. All the characters, including Art and his dad, are depicted as animals – mice for the Jews, cats for the Germans, and pigs for the Polish. The pictures are tiny and scratchy and look innocent enough, but the story is so overwhelming that even these tiny little characters made me cry at one point. The animal viciousness of the Nazis is worse than any cat-and-mouse game ever was. There are two volumes of this book, both of which are in print and may not be in your library's history section because there are still a few people out there who think anything in comic form isn't a 'proper' book. Wait till you see this.

**Ted Dewan**

★ ★ ★ ★ ★ ★

# MEASLE AND THE WRATHMONK  ●●
## Ian Ogilvy

Things might not appear to be very hopeful for young Measle Stubbs – he's an orphan, he's averse to soap and water, his clothes are rags and he lives with his uncle, a wizard gone bad – but it's all going to get much worse. You see, his uncle has a train set. A wonderful train set that he won't let Measle play with...

Of course, Measle ignores the rule, with awful consequences. He's caught and transformed into a creature only a few centimetres tall. But that's only the beginning, and newly tiny Measle finds fresh allies and plots his revenge – and a way back to his real height – while trying to survive the bats who seem to think a miniature Measle would make a really tasty snack!

**Leonie Flynn**

### Next?
• The sequels. They are: *Measle and the Dragodon*, *Measle and the Mallockee*, *Measle and the Slitherghoul* and *Measle and the Doompit*.

• Chris Mould's **Something Wickedly Weird** series is great, too. Read *The Wooden Mile* first.

• Or for another epic series full of magic and adventure, try Jenny Nimmo's **Children of the Red King** series, starting with *Midnight for Charlie Bone*. (*UBG* 226)

# THE MENNYMS Sylvia Waugh

### Next?

• When *The Mennyms* was published, it reminded people of Mary Norton's classic tale, *The Borrowers*. (*UBG* 43)

• *Mistress Masham's Repose* by T.H. White is a classic tale of discovering a family of strange and different people. (*UBG* 231)

• Or try Rumer Godden's strange and amusing story about the inhabitants of a doll's house – *The Doll's House*. (*UBG* 89)

The Mennyms are a family of human-sized rag dolls, unchanged since life was breathed into them by their maker, 40 years ago. They can deceive the world into thinking they're real people but they can't deceive themselves; they enjoy their 'pretends' but they know their limitations. Suddenly, over the course of a year, the family faces challenges like never before – from both inside and outside their home. You fear for their safety from chapter to chapter and at the end of the book you sigh with delight and trepidation – because there are four more books in this brilliant, compelling series and I guarantee you won't want to leave the Mennyms till you've finished the very last word written about them.

**Jon Appleton**

★ ★ ★ ★ ★ ★

# MIDNIGHT FOR CHARLIE BONE Jenny Nimmo

Charlie is an ordinary boy living with his mum, two grandmas (nice and nasty) and Uncle Paton. Charlie's life changes for ever when, one afternoon, something peculiar happens.

By mistake he gets someone else's family picture from the photo shop and hears the people in the photo talking. He manages to find its owner, Miss Ingledew, who tells him about her niece, Emma Tolly, the baby in the photo. Baby Emma was exchanged for a box and Miss Ingledew has never stopped looking for her since. Charlie decides to try and help Miss Ingledew find Emma (who would now be Charlie's age). In his quest, Charlie makes new friends and enemies.

I didn't want to put this exciting book down. I really wanted to find out what happened to Charlie. Will Miss Ingledew ever see her niece again? You must read it and find out for yourself.

**Julia Lytollis**

### Next?

• Move on to the sequels, *Charlie Bone and the Time Twister*, *Charlie Bone and the Blue Boa*, *Charlie Bone and the Castle of Mirrors*, *Charlie Bone and the Hidden King*, *Charlie Bone and the Wilderness Wolf* and *Charlie Bone and the Shadow of Badlock*. And hopefully there will be more!

• **The Keys to the Kingdom** series by Garth Nix is terrifyingly exciting. Start with *Mister Monday* and work your way through the week from Monday to Sunday. (*UBG* 231)

# THE MIDNIGHT FOX  Betsy Byars

**Next?**
• For a quite different Betsy Byars, read *The Eighteenth Emergency*. (*UBG* 98)
• For a slightly more demanding read, try Matthew Sweeney's *Fox* about a boy who becomes friends with a homeless man and his pet fox.
• Or what about a boy who can turn into a fox? Read Ali Sparkes's *Shapeshifter: Finding the Fox*, which is the first in an exciting supernatural series.

To begin with, Tom is not interested in going to live on a farm for two months – he wants to stay in the city. When his mum tries to entice him with tales of cows and horses, he says: 'Animals hate me'. But then he goes off to his Aunt Millie's farm. Here time slows down for Tom; he's bored and hangs out by the pond. Then, one day, Tom sees a black fox and is absolutely electrified. He is more excited than he has ever been. *The Midnight Fox* follows Tom's sightings of the fox through to him actually fighting to save its life. It is a thrilling adventure story, tense and exciting, that keeps you gripped to the very last page.

**Jackie Kay**

★ ★ ★ ★ ★ ★

# MIDNIGHT IS A PLACE  Joan Aiken

Well, the place is Blastburn, and the hero and heroine are Lucas and Anna-Marie, both beset by wicked relations, lost fortunes and all the trimmings of awful weather and astonishing luck (bad and good). And the time is an industrial age, when children in England worked in dreadful conditions in factories (as they still do in some parts of the world).

All the adventure in this brilliant book is *outrageously* adventurous. The horrible places are about as horrible as they come (wild, pig-infested sewers and the slippery rims of boiling vats of glue). No characters are more likeable than the brave and resourceful Lucas, or the sparkling Anna-Marie. And listen for the song that runs through the story, wistful and beguiling. That's where the title comes from.

**Hilary McKay**

**Next?**
• Now read everything else by Joan Aiken – all her books are superb. Start with *The Wolves of Willoughby Chase* (*UBG* 391) or *The Shadow Guests*.
• *The Midnight Folk* by John Masefield is a classic about magical possibilities. Also look for his *The Box of Delights*, which Joan Aiken recommends on p. 44.
• Another book centred around the mills is *The Cellar Lad* by Theresa Tomlinson.
• Or for something else that teaches you more about sewers than you really needed to know, read Eleanor Updale's *Montmorency*. You might need to go and sniff something fragrant afterwards! (*UBG* 234)

# THE MIGHTY CRASHMAN   Jerry Spinelli

Friendships are forged in the strangest of ways. Crash Coogan is the coolest kid at school. He's the star of the football team; he's big, tough and all the other kids adore him. And then there is Penn Webb. Penn is ... different. He's a vegetarian. His parents are odd. He even wants to be a cheerleader – anybody'd think he *wanted* to be bullied!

And Crash is happy to oblige...

This story, though told through the eyes of a bully, is about a lot more than just bullying. You learn as Crash learns, and when his life takes a dip, and even all his brute strength and football skill can't help him, then you really do take a new look at what it means to be strong.

**Leonie Flynn**

### Next?

• Two other great stories that look at friendship, school and families in a very different way are *Stargirl* (*UBG* 324) and *Loser* (*UBG* 212) both by Jerry Spinelli.

• Also look out for two Louis Sachar books: *Holes* (*UBG* 155) and *The Boy Who Lost His Face* (*UBG* 46). They're both about surviving whatever life throws at you.

• *Cloud Busting* by Malorie Blackman is about an unlikely friendship, and it's written in a very different way. (*UBG* 67)

★ ★ ★ ★ ★ ★

# MIGHTY FIZZ CHILLA
## Philip Ridley

### Next?

• Read more Philip Ridley, such as *Vinegar Street*, *Dakota of the White Flats* and *ZinderZunder*.

• Or try Theresa Breslin's **Dream Master** books, about dreams that can take you back in time.

• Or try something just as offbeat in Jon Berkeley's *The Palace of Laughter*, about a boy who lives in a barrel, a talking tiger, a girl and a very strange circus. There's a sequel, too: *The Tiger's Egg*.

Milo Stick (Ridley names are always tasty) is 13 with sensitive lips and a mohican haircut. His mum, unable to handle him, sends him off to a defunct boarding house by the sea, run by two women: Cressida Bell, who is overweight, blind and emotional, and Dee Dee Six, who is mannish and 'fact-crazy'. Outside, a dangerous Scotsman, Captain Jellicoe, armed with an eye-patch and a kilt, rages and rampages on the shore. Through a set of interlocking stories told by Cressida, Dee Dee and the Captain, an awful lot is concealed and bit by bit things are revealed. These are little masterpieces of weirdness, feeling and suspense. As the book progresses, the tales interweave and by the end magically merge. A clever book from a very clever writer.

**Michael Rosen**

# MILLY-MOLLY-MANDY
## stories Joyce Lankester Brisley

I first read *Milly-Molly-Mandy* when I was a girl and enjoyed the stories then. After rereading them, I can still give them a big thumbs up!

Milly-Molly-Mandy lives with her father, mother, grandma, grandpa, uncle and aunty in a white cottage with a thatched roof. Her real name is Millicent Margaret Amanda, but as that is a real mouthful, her family and friends call her Milly-Molly-Mandy for short. Each chapter in the book tells you about Milly-Molly-Mandy's adventures with her friends Billy Blunt and Susan in the village where she lives.

This is a very enjoyable book to read by yourself or to have read to you. You are sure to have fun with Milly-Molly-Mandy.

**Julia Lytollis**

### Next?

• *My Naughty Little Sister* by Dorothy Edwards is just as charming and funny. (*UBG* 244)

• Another series that was written a long time ago, but is still wonderful, starts with the delightful *Mrs Pepperpot*, written by Alf Prøysen. (*UBG* 239)

• Enid Blyton was another great storyteller; try *Naughty Amelia Jane*, about the naughtiest toy in the nursery, or her **Magic Faraway Tree** series (*UBG* 216).

---

## The Ultimate Readers' Poll

# Top Ten Funny Books

**1** Horrid Henry series
by Francesca Simon

**2** Asterix series
by Goscinny and Uderzo

**3=** My Mum's Going to Explode!
by Jeremy Strong

**3=** How to Train Your Dragon
by Cressida Cowell

**5** The Killer Underpants
by Michael Lawrence

**6** A Series of Unfortunate Events
by Lemony Snicket

**7** Clarice Bean
by Lauren Child

**8=** Little Darlings
by Sam Llewellyn

**8=** You're a Bad Man, Mr Gum!
by Andy Stanton

**10** Astrosaurs
by Steve Cole

# MINNOW ON THE SAY Philippa Pearce

**Next?**

• Another wonderful Philippa Pearce book is *Tom's Midnight Garden*. (*UBG* 351)

• A book with a similar feel is Jan Mark's *Thunder and Lightnings*.

• *The Eagle of the Ninth* by Rosemary Sutcliff is another great adventure story, this time set when the Romans were in Britain. (*UBG* 93)

The *Minnow* is an old canoe which David and Adam restore together to make her riverworthy again. The Say is the river on which they go canoeing. They have a treasure hunt to undertake, a riddle within a riddle to solve, a stranger to name and a home to save, all in a race against time.

This is my favourite Philippa Pearce book. I like the smells of summer that come floating from the pages: clean green river water, flower wine and baking cakes. I like the way the reader solves the puzzle almost side by side with David and Adam. I like the people in the background of the story – they seem so alive. Best of all I like the description of the prickly, stubborn friendship that grows between the boys. It is one of those books that 'feels like real'.

**Hilary McKay**

★ ★ ★ ★ ★ ★

# MISSING series Meg Cabot

Jessica Mastrani is a normal 16-year-old girl living in a town in Indiana – until she gets struck by lightning!

With the electricity comes the sudden ability to dream the whereabouts of missing people, and all of a sudden Jess's life gets really complicated. Not only do the FBI want her to work for them but she also acquires a boyfriend, someone her parents definitely won't approve of, and she finds out the hard way that not everyone who is missing wants to be found.

Jess's abilities help her solve a variety of crimes and each book deals with a different mystery. However, it's the details of life in the very strange Mastrani household and the story of her developing relationship with Rob that will keep you going back for more.

*When Lightning Strikes* is the first book in the **Missing** series. It's fast-paced, funny and full of great dialogue. The sequels are just as good, and I really hope there'll be more!

**Laura Hutchings**

**Next?**

• The series continues with: *Code Name Cassandra*, *Safe House*, *Sanctuary* and *Missing You*.

• Look out for *Jinx*, about a girl who has really bad luck, or *All American Girl*, about Sam, a girl who saves the president's son's life, also by Meg Cabot.

• Or try Cathy Hopkins's **Zodiac Girls** about girls whose lives need a little helpful intervention – from the stars! There's a book for every star sign.

# MISTER MONDAY Garth Nix

*Mister Monday* is the first in a series of ornately and intricately constructed books, **The Keys to the Kingdom**. The central idea is simple: that there is a building named the House that is outside time and space. The House is the centre of everything.

*Mister Monday* is the story of Arthur Penhaligon who is an ordinary boy until he discovers his true identity as heir to the House. But his role has been usurped by the Trustees, who have stolen his inheritance. Put like that, it sounds like a corny rewriting of *Hamlet*. But the universe of the House is so brilliantly realised, filled with such intricacies and ideas that it is impossible not to be amazed and drawn into the story. And of course there is the slight problem that the more Arthur uses the Keys (magical objects of power that were given to the Trustees until the Rightful Heir should come), the less human he becomes...

**Tobias Druitt**

### Next?
• Oh, the rest of the series, for certain! The sequels are *Grim Tuesday*, *Drowned Wednesday*, *Sir Thursday*, *Lady Friday*, *Superior Saturday* and ... one for Sunday, as yet unpublished!

• Garth Nix has written two other great fantasy series: **The Seventh Tower** sequence, starting with *The Fall*, and the older and even more complex **Old Kingdom** trilogy: *Sabriel*, *Lirael* and *Abhorsen* (*UBG* 292).

• Tobias Druitt writes terrific adventure stories too. Try the **Corydon** books. (*UBG* 72)

★ ★ ★ ★ ★ ★

# MISTRESS MASHAM'S REPOSE T.H. White

### Next?
• Terry Pratchett's own *The Amazing Maurice and His Educated Rodents* (*UBG* 15), or *The Wee Free Men* (*UBG* 377) are both about smaller creatures.

• *Harry and the Wrinklies* by Alan Temperley has more chases, wicked villains and hidden secrets. (*UBG* 144)

• Or do you want to read about more 'little people'? Try *The Borrowers* and its sequels by Mary Norton. (*UBG* 43)

I'm amazed to see that *Mistress Masham's Repose* is back in print. Grab it. It's one of my favourites. In this book the events of *Gulliver's Travels* really happened, and some Lilliputians (the small people) are living in secret in England. I thought that was such a great idea when I was a boy. I still do. And there's a huge old stately home where you need a bike to get along the corridors, hidden treasure, artful villains, moonlight chases – it's all there. What more do you need? Some adults think parts of it are too difficult for children. Hah! They really mean that the author sometimes enjoys himself so much that he forgets you don't know as much as him – but he is clever enough to make you think you do.

**Terry Pratchett**

# STORIES FROM OTHER CULTURES
## Out There in the Big, Bad World
### by Elizabeth Laird

Don't tell me – you're a fantasy freak. No? But you love the spooky stuff. Thriller-chillers. Broomsticks and spells. Or is it animal stories you like? What about real life, then? Out there in the big, bad world?

It's the big, bad world, the real one out there beyond our shores, that gets me going. Every day, when I see the TV news, amazing tales unfold: true stories of terror and courage, adventure and survival. But TV only shows the tip of the iceberg. I always want to know more. To feel what it's like for the people to whom momentous things are happening. To climb inside their skins. And when I do, I find stories that are just as exciting as the chilliest thriller or the wildest fantasy.

Novels can transport you to places you're never likely to visit, and let you live, for a little while, the lives of people you'll never meet. Perhaps you've seen short clips about child soldiers in Africa – boys and girls as young as nine or ten, who carry guns, and fight and kill. If you read *Little Soldier* by Bernard Ashley, you'll really

get an idea of how those children feel. Peter Dickinson's wonderful novel, *A.K.*, is on the same theme. Now try to imagine what it's like for two African children, torn away from home, arriving in the chill of London and labelled 'asylum seekers'. If you read *The Other Side of Truth* by Beverley Naidoo, you'll find out what it might really be like.

Tired of Africa? Then let's move on to India, to the enthralling trilogy by Jamila Gavin, beginning with *The Wheel of Surya*. You can travel with two children as they survive a civil war and undertake a daring journey alone, across the sea, to find their father. If you want a gentler tale of India, Anita Desai's beautiful story, *The Village by the Sea*, will fill your mind with new sights and sounds.

It's great to read about distant places, but it's even more fun to write about them. As a writer, I seek people out and immerse myself in their lives. When I lived in Baghdad, I visited the Kurds in their high mountain villages and the story of their struggles gripped me. I wrote about them in *Kiss the Dust*.

Ethiopia's a country I've always loved. I've lived there, and travelled to every corner of it, teaching, writing and collecting folk stories. While I was there, I got to know a gang of kids who lived on the streets of Addis Ababa. They told me about themselves, showed me the place where they sleep and introduced me to their dog. They let me write about their incredible lives in *The Garbage King*.

How did we get back to Africa? I wanted to tell you about Turkey, and Gaye Hiçyilmaz's great book, *Against the Storm* (read it and find out!). And I wanted to tell you something about the host of wonderful books of myths and legends there are to be found, from every part of the world. But I've run out of space – so it's over to you. Find out for yourself. Go on. Try a slice of the big, bad world for a change. You won't be disappointed.

## Eight Very Different Books the Editors Recommend

- *Chinese Cinderella* by Adeline Yen Mah
- *The Village by the Sea* by Anita Desai
- *The Breadwinner* by Deborah Ellis
- *Journey to the River Sea* by Eva Ibbotson
- *Little House on the Prairie* by Laura Ingalls Wilder
- *Journey to Jo'burg* by Beverley Naidoo
- *Flying with Icarus* by Curdella Forbes
- *Roll of Thunder, Hear My Cry* by Mildred D. Taylor

# MOLLY MOON'S INCREDIBLE BOOK
# OF HYPNOTISM Georgia Byng

**Next?**
• Move on to the second book in the series: *Molly Moon Stops the World*.
• For a classic tale of an unhappy orphan, read *A Little Princess* by Frances Hodgson Burnett. (*UBG* 205)
• To read about another girl who gets the better of the adults who are being cruel to her, try *Matilda* by Roald Dahl. (*UBG* 224)

Ten-year-old Molly Moon has a seriously rubbish life. She lives in an orphanage where most of the other children are horrible, and so are the grown-ups. And she isn't very good at anything, either...

Or at least she thinks she isn't, until she discovers a book about how to hypnotise people. She starts off by hypnotising the orphanage dog and then moves on to the cook – and it soon becomes clear that hypnosis is something she's unbelievably talented at. Suddenly, she can make people do anything she wants them to. And if you can make people do anything at all, you can become very powerful very quickly.

This funny and mesmerising story will pull you along with it, as Molly journeys beyond the orphanage to try out her powers in the wider world.

**Susan Reuben**

★ ★ ★ ★ ★ ★

# MONTMORENCY Eleanor Updale

An unnamed robber falls through a glass roof and is terribly injured. But revived and repaired, he is released from prison to become 'Montmorency'. Victorian London is depicted in all its glory and all its unpleasantness, as Montmorency starts a new life, but continues with his former 'career'. He seems to be the epitome of the Victorian gentleman, while at the same time pursuing a life of crime.

From the exclusive Bargles Club to the depths of the Victorian sewer system, Montmorency and his servant Scarper keep readers guessing whether anyone will uncover the truth. This first book in the series takes a little while to set things up, but once it gets going, it's funny, exciting and more than a little macabre...

**Justin Richards**

**Next?**
• The mysterious Montmorency continues his adventures in *Montmorency on the Rocks*, *Montmorency and the Assassins* and *Montmorency's Revenge*.
• A different Scarper appears in Christopher Russell's *Scarper and the Bloodstained Room*.
• For another exciting adventure story with an atmospheric historical setting, try *The Printer's Devil* by Paul Bajoria. (*UBG* 274)
• Something else that takes you down to the sewers is Zizou Corder's thrilling adventure, *Lee Raven, Boy Thief*.

# THE MOOMINS series  Tove Jansson

*A Comet in Moominland* is the very best of the totally brilliant **Moomin** books. They're all excellent but I was only allowed to choose one, and this is it. It's a wonderful introduction to life in Moomin Valley, inhabited by an extraordinary array of creatures, not least the Moomins themselves: large-snouted, silky smooth and brave. I've never read books quite like them. They're funny, sad, exciting and – dare I say it – even make you think. In this race-against-time tale, young Moomintroll and his friend Sniff set off for the Observatory on Lonely Mountain to find out if a comet really is on a collision course with Earth. Along the way, they have some nail-biting adventures, with everything from angry crocodiles to a Snork-eating bush, and they meet some wonderful characters, too.

**Philip Ardagh**

## Next?

• You might enjoy the other full-length **Moomin** books: *Finn Family Moomintroll*, *Moominsummer Madness*, *Moominland Midwinter*, *The Exploits of Moominpappa* and *Moominpappa at Sea*. Younger Moomin fans should look out for the rhyming picture books, *The Book About Moomin, Mimble and Little My* and *Who Will Comfort Toffle?*

• For something different, try *Mr Popper's Penguins* by Richard and Florence Atwater. (*UBG* 238)

★ ★ ★ ★ ★ ★

# MOONFLEET  John Meade Falkner

## Next?

• For more adventures that involve pirates and skulduggery, read Tanith Lee's *Piratica*, about a girl whose mother was a pirate – or was she? (*UBG* 270)

• Robert Louis Stevenson's *Kidnapped* is another classic story of adventure. (*UBG* 188) Or for a scary chase story, read John Buchan's *The Thirty-Nine Steps*.

• There's more adventure, treachery and murder in Christopher Russell's *Smugglers*.

A storm is raging. Smugglers wait with their ponies while a great sailing ship is smashed to pieces by the waves. Worshippers fly in terror as a sound of knocking comes from the crypt beneath the church where the notorious Blackbeard lies in his rotted coffin. Is there any truth in the legend of a priceless diamond with a curse upon it?

This is the village of Moonfleet, where lonely, 15-year-old John Trenchard sits on a gravestone staring out to sea. He is saved from death by Elzevir Block, the brooding, powerful landlord of the Why Not? Inn, who becomes like a father to him.

I love this story: strong characters, powerful action, beautifully written. A classic smuggling adventure!

**Alan Temperley**

# MORTAL ENGINES  Philip Reeve

It's the far future and London is now a Traction City – a seven-tiered metropolis mounted on enormous treads, rolling over the wastes of Europe, searching for smaller cities to gobble up. Fifteen-year-old Tom Natsworthy has his life turned upside down when he stumbles upon a sinister secret concerning the city's beloved hero, Thaddeus Valentine. Left for dead in the barren Out-Country, Tom teams up with Hester Shaw, a disfigured girl who has her own dark reasons for getting back to London.

This is a sensationally exciting book, well written, with a plot that continually surprises. There are airships, cyborg assassins, floating cities, and swashbuckling on a grand scale. Reeve's vision of the future is mesmerising and original, and Tom, in his breakneck quest, is constantly forced to rethink all his beliefs and assumptions about his home, the people and the world around him. A fabulous adventure story.

**Kenneth Oppel**

## Next?
• Tom and Hester's adventures continue in *Predator's Gold*, *Infernal Devices* and *A Darkling Plain*.
• You might also like the series by Joan Aiken, starting with *The Wolves of Willoughby Chase* (*UBG* 391), but in particular *Black Hearts in Battersea* – also about a London that is only just recognisable.
• A boy's adventure set in an alternative past is also in Eoin Colfer's *Airman*. (*UBG* 11)

★ ★ ★ ★ ★ ★

# THE MOUSE AND HIS CHILD  Russell Hoban

## Next?
• The characters in *The Borrowers* also have to struggle in a world dominated by alien giants. (*UBG* 43)
• Why not have a look at *Pinocchio* by Carlo Collodi? There are some surprising connections! (*UBG* 269)
• You might also enjoy *The Glassblower's Children* by Maria Gripe.

When he's wound up, the clockwork mouse of the title tosses his tin child up and down until the clockwork runs down again. Small wonder that they both want to become 'self-winding'. Thrown out when their clockwork breaks down, they are gathered up by the scavenging villain Manny Rat, but they escape and move on through a series of encounters and adventures, with Manny Rat following after them.

This is the sort of book that grows with the reader, who will be able to enjoy it in different ways as he or she gets older. Some of the ideas in it certainly connect with adult literature and one of the final conclusions ('that no one is completely self-winding') is something that adults as well as children can appreciate. A book to reread every now and then for the rest of your life.

**Margaret Mahy**

# THE MOUSEHUNTER  Alex Milway

## Next?

• For more pirates and more magic, try Julia Golding's *The Ship Between Worlds*. (*UBG* 308)

• If you are a literary mousehunter, try Michael Hoeye's *Time Stops for No Mouse* (*UBG* 348) or C.S. Lewis's *The Voyage of the Dawn Treader*, which has one of the best literary mice ever in Reepicheep. (*UBG* 198)

• And don't forget Alex Milway's sequel, *The Curse of Mousebeard*.

Isiah Lovelock is a man who collects mice, and Emiline is his mousekeeper. I know this sounds strange, but in this book the mice are slightly different to ours, and they come in all sorts of varieties and have all sorts of skills. Some can mend frayed ropes, some act as flying messengers, others help load cannons on ships (but then, after a while, they die from breathing in the gunpowder), others are good at fighting, like Sharpclaw.

When Lovelock sets out to kill his hated rival, the pirate Mousebeard (and yes, he has mice living in his beard), Emiline hides on board the privateer and sails with him. She wants adventure, and she gets far more than she could ever have imagined in a story that keeps you urgently turning the pages to find out what happens next!

**Julian Ripley, age 10**

★ ★ ★ ★ ★ ★

# MOUSE NOSES ON TOAST  Daren King

Have you ever been out for dinner and seen mouse noses on toast on the menu? No? Well, then maybe you've heard of a mouse that was allergic to cheese? No again?! Well, you're going to find out all about them in this book, along with a big shaggy dog, a miniature monster named the Tinby and a talking Christmas tree decoration.

If you think this book sounds too young and silly for you, think again. I'm 27 and I found myself chuckling away at the adventures of these miniscule mice. It's hard not to smile at a story of a mouse whose bottom is blue! I challenge you to try and keep a straight face...

**Rachel Cole-Fletcher**

## Next?

• Daren King is a genius. Next, read his crime-noir story *Sensible Hare and the Case of Carrots*, an animal tale that could have been written by Raymond Chandler! Then try *Peter the Penguin Pioneer*. All of them are illustrated by the wonderful David Roberts and all of them are equally amazing.

• A more traditional take on animals as humans is Emily Bearns's *Tumtum and Nutmeg*, about two happy mice who try to improve two unhappy children's lives. (*UBG* 356)

• Or try Betty G. Birney's *The World According to Humphrey*, in which Humphrey (a school hamster) tells his own story. (*UBG* 392)

## MR MAJEIKA  Humphrey Carpenter

**Next?**

• Try Jill Murphy's stories about the **Worst Witch**, who has trouble controlling her magic. (*UBG* 394)

• Or for more classroom mayhem, try the **Pickle Hill Primary** series, each of which has a magic teacher who can explain a subject brilliantly, such as *Miss Nile's Mummy Lessons* about ancient Egypt by Alan MacDonald.

• Try Terence Blacker's *Ms Wiz*. Another magical teacher for another Class Three! (*UBG* 240)

From the very first moment that Class Three see their new form teacher, they know there's something funny about him. For one thing, he arrives through the window on a flying carpet!

Mr Majeika is a wizard – well, he *was* a wizard, but now he's given up magic for good. Now he just wants to be a normal teacher, and never do magic again. Except that sometimes he just can't help himself – especially when class brat, Hamish Bigmore, is involved...

Between the flying potion, the magic carpet and the turn-Hamish-into-a-frog charm, is there any way Mr Majeika will be able to keep his magic a secret from Mr Potter the headmaster?

This book is just the first in a hilarious series of 12. So if you enjoy this one as much as I did – which I'm sure you will – you can read them all!

**Daniel Hahn**

★ ★ ★ ★ ★ ★

# MR POPPER'S PENGUINS
### Richard and Florence Atwater

My battered copy of this book contains an inscription from my grandmother on the occasion of my eighth birthday. Almost 40 years on, I still remember Mr Popper, the house painter (an untidy man, according to his wife), who yearned for a little Arctic excitement and got sent a penguin that obviously had to go in Mrs Popper's fridge. The story tells how one penguin becomes 12 (pressure on the fridge) and the 12 become the performing sensation of America.

All American associations were totally lost on me as a child; I thought it very English. The charm of this book is its deadpan humour, its heartbreaking illustrations (you'd give Mr Popper a penguin, too), and its simple joyfulness.

**Nicky Singer**

**Next?**

• If you like your animals to say a bit more than 'gook', try Hugh Lofting's **Doctor Dolittle** books. (*UBG* 87)

• If you're big on birds, try *Harry's Mad*, Dick King-Smith's heart-warming tale of a parrot.

• If you enjoyed the humour, but prefer it a bit more spiky, try Roald Dahl's *The Twits*. (*UBG* 359)

# MRS FRISBY AND THE RATS OF NIMH   Robert C. O'Brien

I read this to my daughter in 1975 (or thereabouts) at bedtime, and she couldn't wait for the next instalment; she'd hide the book when we finished for the night so I couldn't read ahead. (I wanted to, very badly.) Just recently, I read it again, and it's still great, although I now feel that the boy rats in the story get the best of the action – the girls are more in the background. Still, Mrs Frisby is one fantastically brave and daring mouse mother; she's determined to get help for her son Timothy when he falls dangerously ill – and her bravery opens up the extraordinary world of the rats of NIMH. If you're interested in defending animals from experimentation, you'll be deeply intrigued by this book – and who knows, those rats could well be out there in real life...

**Vivian French**

### Next?

• Robert C. O'Brien is an author who likes to make you think – try his *The Silver Crown*, a dark story of good versus evil.

• Look out for *Watership Down* by Richard Adams if you want a similar kind of book (*UBG* 376), but if you're a rat enthusiast (I am!) then grab Terry Pratchett's *The Amazing Maurice and His Educated Rodents* and enjoy! (*UBG* 15).

• *Mouse Attack* by Manjula Padma is another tale of a mouse – this one likes hot chocolate – and who ends up as a slightly unlikely hero.

★ ★ ★ ★ ★ ★

# MRS PEPPERPOT
## Alf Prøysen

### Next?

• More shrinking and more magic? Read *The Boy in the Biscuit Tin* by Heather Dyer. (*UBG* 45)

• Astrid Lindgren's *Pippi Longstocking*, about a girl with special powers, has the same mix of normal life and weird goings-on. (*UBG* 269)

• *Mrs Pepperpot* and *Pippi Longstocking* are both Scandinavian. The other really great Scandinavian series is the **Moomins** by Tove Jansson. (*UBG* 235)

Mrs Pepperpot is an old lady who lives a quiet life with her husband. She's very ordinary, except for one small thing – she keeps shrinking to the size of a pepperpot! She never knows when it's going to happen, or for how long.

Each story in *Mrs Pepperpot* describes a different day when she shrinks to the size of a pepperpot, and how she does all the things she needs to do. Find out how she delivers a doll she promised to a little girl – when the doll is bigger than she is; and what happens when her husband takes her to the shops in his pocket, and she gets stuck inside a bag of macaroni!

**Susan Reuben**

# MS WIZ series  Terence Blacker

With long, black witchy hair, glossy, black nail polish, a china cat, a magic rat up her sleeve, an owl in her handbag and a vacuum cleaner to travel around on, Ms Wiz isn't your average teacher! She is, in fact, the strangest, cleverest teacher Class Three has ever had, and the minute she walks into St Barnabas' School, they're under her spell – and you will be, too. Weird and wonderful things start happening and life for these pupils will never be boring again. You'll wish she worked in your school!

Scribbly black-and-white sketches add hugely to the fun and excitement in these laugh-out-loud funny reads. They're just the thing to curl up with in winter.

Once you've met Ms Wiz, you'll never want her mad adventures to end – and luckily she has lots more. Try *Ms Wiz Loves Dracula*, *Ms Wiz Smells A Rat*, *Ms Wiz Goes To Hollywood* and *Ms Wiz, Millionaire*: each adventure madder than the one before!

**Eileen Armstrong**

### Next?

• For books about 'real' witches, don't forget *Lizzie Dripping* by Helen Cresswell. (*UBG* 208)

• Another magical teacher is Humphrey Carpenter's *Mr Majeika*. (*UBG* 238)

• The **Marvin Redpost** books by Louis Sachar are about a boy surviving school with no magic at all.

• And though they are very young, go and read the **Meg and Mog** stories by Helen Nicoll. They are wonderful, and the illustrations by Jan Pienkowski are brilliant!

★ ★ ★ ★ ★ ★

# MUDDLE EARTH  Paul Stewart and Chris Riddell

### Next?

• At least have a peek at *The Lord of the Rings* by J.R.R. Tolkien. Yes, it's long, but oh it's good, too. (*UBG* 211)

• Other excellent Stewart / Riddell collaborations include the exciting adventures of hard-bitten, heroic Free Lance, starting with *Free Lance and the Lake of Skulls*, and of course the **Edge Chronicles** (*UBG* 97).

• For another brilliantly realised world of good and evil, try *The Ratastrophe Catastrophe* by David Lee Stone.

Let's get the obvious out of the way first: yes, this epic novel is a bit of a spoof on the legendary world created by J.R.R. Tolkien, but it's absolutely a class act in its own right. Our hero Joe Jefferson is a schoolboy who finds himself transported to Muddle Earth (a world with three moons) by Randalf, the wizard, who requires Joe's services as a warrior hero to help defeat various villainous individuals. There's a particularly nasty spoon to beware of, too.

Yes, it is totally weird, but wonderful and very funny. In the hands of the creators of the superb **Edge Chronicles**, you can't go wrong. And you won't!

**Jon Appleton**

# THE MUM HUNT  Gwyneth Rees

● ●

### Next?

• There are two sequels: *The Mum Detective* and *The Mum Mystery*.

• There's more Gwyneth Rees, too; try *The Making of May*, about a girl and her grown-up brother moving to a mysterious house in the country.

• Cathy Cassidy writes great books about girls and families. Try *Sundae Girl*. (*UBG* 335)

• If you want to read about a family drama, look up *Child X* by Lee Weatherly – a very exciting novel about a complex family situation. (*UBG* 60)

Esmie's dad is a single and overworked police detective, who just seems too busy to date anybody. However, Esmie has other plans! Together with her brother Matthew and Juliette, their French au-pair, she conspires to use a newspaper lonely hearts column to set him up with a new girlfriend. Matthew records the phone message, because he can sound like his dad sometimes, and they wait for the replies to roll in. It's all a disaster, of course, but it helps bring the family back together after a few years of drifting apart.

Everything about this book is warm and well intentioned, confident and easy to read. It's sometimes witty, sometimes sad and sometimes uplifting. Very realistic, too.

**John McLay**

★ ★ ★ ★ ★ ★

# MUSIC ON THE BAMBOO RADIO  Martin Booth

● ● ●

In December 1941, Hong Kong falls to the invading Japanese army. Left alone, English boy Nicholas has no idea where his parents are – or even whether they are alive or dead. All the Europeans are being rounded up and imprisoned, but Nicholas is rescued by the Chinese house servants and smuggled out of the city.

Disguised as a Chinese boy, Nicholas survives as best he can. Looked after by Ah Kwan and Ah Mee, he becomes like their son, but he never forgets his own parents. So, when the chance comes to do something to help the resistance – even though that something is very dangerous – he leaps at it.

Taut and scary, this is an adventure set in a real war. Horrible things happen, and you're never sure – right until the end – if Nicholas's story will end in tragedy or happiness.

**Leonie Flynn**

### Next?

• More from Martin Booth? Try *P.O.W.*, based on a true story about a boy held as a prisoner of war in Germany in 1915, or *War Dog*, set during World War II.

• Another boy whose life is irrevocably changed by war is Billy in James Riordan's *Sweet Clarinet*.

• *Gulf* by Robert Westall is a story about war affecting ordinary people in an extraordinary way. (*UBG* 139)

# MY DARLING, MY HAMBURGER  Paul Zindel

### Next?

• Try the lighter – but just as moving – *Pardon Me, You're Stepping on My Eyeball!* also by Paul Zindel.

• If you want more humour-mixed-with-issues stuff, you can't beat Paula Danziger. Life after your parents' divorce is the subject of *It's an Aardvark-Eat-Turtle World* or try *The Cat Ate My Gymsuit* (*UBG* 56).

• Or try one of Judy Blume's books – like *Are You There, God? It's Me, Margaret.* (*UBG* 22)

Liz is smart, brash and beautiful, and is dating Sean, the coolest boy at school. The two engineer it so that their less beautiful, less cool best mates Maggie and Dennis date each other, too; something Maggie and Dennis aren't happy about – at first.

This is a tale of American teens, peer pressure, rocky relationships and flawed friendships, all wrapped around familiar settings such as the prom and graduation. Yep, there are plenty of movies and books around that cover similar themes, but this was one of the first, and when it comes to describing feelings and emotions, Paul Zindel does it very subtly, and manages to avoid corny clichés. This book deals with tough stuff, and doesn't exactly have a fairy-tale ending, but that makes it all the more realistic.

**Karen McCombie**

★ ★ ★ ★ ★ ★

# MY FAMILY AND OTHER ANIMALS  Gerald Durrell

Probably my favourite book of all time. And it's not even fiction. (Well, maybe just a little...)

Gerald Durrell was ten when his family moved to Corfu. Thanks to a photographic memory, he remembers every detail of each glorious day spent on the colour-saturated, sun-soaked island. Full of the sights, sounds, tastes, smells and animals of a Greek island, this book alternates between being uproariously funny and deliciously descriptive.

Gerald's older brother Lawrence is the one who claims literary greatness, but for my money Gerald beats him hands down! An early scene about the Durrell family's hilarious entry into Corfu town still leaves me helpless with laughter. I steal from this book constantly and unashamedly. Durrell is one of my heroes.

**Caroline Lawrence**

### Next?

• Gerald Durrell's other books about animals are all great. Look out for *Birds, Beasts and Relatives* or *A Zoo in My Luggage*.

• *Chewing the Cud* is Dick King-Smith's story of his own childhood – a must if you like real stories and animals.

• Or *All Creatures Great and Small* by James Herriott, a great book about his life as a vet in Yorkshire.

• Or read Simon Chapman's **Explorers Wanted!** series. Each mixes story and fact – try *In the Jungle* first.

# MY FRIEND FLICKA  Mary O'Hara

Ken McLaughlin lives on his family's ranch in wild and wonderful Wyoming, USA. Ken's a bit of a wimpy daydreamer and his dad would like him to be more like his tough big brother. Ken wants to tame Flicka but the wild and wilful young horse has got other ideas. After all sorts of adventures involving barbed wire and mountain lions and lots more horses, Ken and Flicka become firm friends and Ken's dad realises his son is no wimp after all.

After reading this brilliant horse book I actually became half-boy, half-palomino pony for a while and, as a result, spent many happy afternoons cantering around the streets of Nottingham and being fed sugarlumps by the local shopkeepers.

**Michael Cox**

### Next?
• The follow-up to *My Friend Flicka* about her son, a huge white stallion, is *Thunderhead*. The third book in the **Flicka** trilogy is *The Green Grass of Wyoming*.
• *The Silver Brumby* by Elyne Mitchell – more about horses, this time wild ones in Australia.
• Another author who writes wonderfully about horses is Marguerite Henry, try her classic *Misty of Chincoteague* or *King of the Wind: The Story of the Godolphin Arabian*.

★ ★ ★ ★ ★ ★

# MY FRIEND'S A WEREWOLF  Pete Johnson

### Next?
• *Rescuing Dad* (*UBG* 283) is also by Pete Johnson, but it's very different, as is his sharp and funny adventure, *The Bad Spy's Guide*.
• Try *My Best Fiend* by Sheila Lavelle for a next-door neighbour who isn't as good a friend as she seems.
• For a series about shapeshifting, try Ali Sparkes's **Shapeshifter** series starting with *Finding the Fox*.
• For something gorier, try **The Saga of Darren Shan** by none other than Darren Shan himself! (*UBG* 293)
• Or try *Piggies* by Nick Gifford. Sometimes you can be just too ordinary… (*UBG* 267)

When Simon moves in next door to Kelly, she thinks she has found a new best friend. He is fun to hang out with and brilliant at sport, but why does he always wear those naff black gloves? Does he think they're cool? And what is the truth about the howling from next door at night?

The events that follow are very scary in places, but the scariest thing is that the book is written like a story that could happen to you – or your next-door neighbour. You'll learn a lot about werewolves and about being a true friend. It is also a story about challenging prejudice and learning that being different can be a good thing, and not something of which to be afraid.

**Abigail Anderson**

# MY MUM'S GOING TO EXPLODE!

## Jeremy Strong

What would you do if your mum was expecting a baby, made you and your dad take 'baby lessons' by looking after her old doll (bald and legless), and refused to feed you anything but sausages?

Nicholas is in just this situation. He manages to cope with the help of his dad (who's as fed up about the new baby as he is) and his granny (who's married to a Hell's Angel and has her belly button pierced).

This story is really funny – you'll very probably laugh out loud. But it's quite touching, too – especially as Mum's tummy grows bigger and bigger and Nicholas realises there's soon going to be a real baby in the house. Well – that last bit's not quite accurate – but find out why for yourself!

**Susan Reuben**

## Next?

• Another Jeremy Strong you might like is *The Hundred-Mile-an-Hour Dog*.

• What's it like when your brother or sister is perfect – and you're not? Try Francesca Simon's **Horrid Henry** series. (*UBG* 159)

• Other great tales of mayhem are in David Henry Wilson's *Triple Trouble With Jeremy James*, about a boy who can't quite do the right thing.

• Or try Goscinny's *Nicholas*, a boy who really wouldn't ever do anything wrong! (*UBG* 249)

## London, But Not As We Know It

• *Darkside* by Tom Becker

• *Stone Heart* by Charlie Fletcher

• *Johnny Mackintosh and the Spirit of London* by Keith Mansfield

• *Mortal Engines* by Philip Reeve

• *Black Hearts in Battersea* by Joan Aiken

• *Black Tattoo* by Sam Enthoven

• *Barnaby Grimes* by Paul Stewart and Chris Riddell

• *The Amulet of Samarkand* by Jonathan Stroud

• *The Borribles* by Michael de Larrabeiti

# MY NAUGHTY LITTLE SISTER series

**Dorothy Edwards**

**Next?**

• What about a naughty older brother? Try Francesca Simon's *Horrid Henry* (*UBG* 159); or Sam McBratney's *Jimmy Zest*.

• Alf Prøysen's stories about the small but feisty Mrs Pepperpot are well worth reading. (*UBG* 239)

• Or try one of Megan McDonald's **Judy Moody** books (*UBG* 184) – Judy's perfect, but what about her little brother, affectionately known as Stink!

There are lots of books in this series and it doesn't matter in which order you read them. Each chapter in each book is a self-contained story about something My Naughty Little Sister did. The stories are about everyday things, like your first wobbly tooth, drawing pictures at school, planting an acorn, and are told by the naughty little sister's older sister who half thinks what her sister gets up to is naughty and half thinks it's brilliant fun.

The stories might seem a little old-fashioned at first and our idea of naughty behaviour might be very different now, but there is still something magical about My Naughty Little Sister's way of looking at the world – and there's a lot to learn about how to get your own way!

**Abigail Anderson**

★ ★ ★ ★ ★ ★

# MY SWORDHAND IS SINGING  Marcus Sedgwick

Set in seventeenth-century Romania, this book is about Peter – a woodcutter's son – who finds his life turned upside down as strange events start to take over his small town. Events such as a dead man visiting his wife at night, the arrival of strange gypsies and, worst of all, Peter's father's mysterious past starting to catch up with him.

This is a scary, intense and brilliant book that takes a really unusual approach to vampires, and is a world away from the Dracula 'cape and fangs' type of story. Gothic and wintry, everything in the book is vivid, breathtaking and action-packed – especially the ending which is both blood-soaked and blood-chilling!

**Louis Cross, age 12**

**Next?**

• Peter reappears in Sedgwick's follow-on title, *The Kiss of Death*. If you like the way the author handles tension, menace and gripping fear, try *Witch Hill* and *The Book of Dead Days*, too.

• Try the most famous of vampire stories, complete with cape and fangs: Bram Stoker's *Dracula*.

• *The Lord of the Rings* has even more action-packed adventure – and lots of snow. (*UBG* 211)

• Alexandre Dumas's *The Three Musketeers* has both high adventure and high drama. (*UBG* 347)

# NANCY DREW MYSTERIES Carolyn Keene

**Next?**

• More girl heroes? Where would **Narnia** (*UBG* 198) be without Lucy? Or **The Famous Five** (*UBG* 109) without tomboy, George? Or **Harry Potter** (*UBG* 145) without Hermione? Read about them all!

• Girls are often relegated to being the ones rescued. To put the record straight, read about super-spy Jane Blonde; start with *Sensational Spylet*. (*UBG* 180) Or Grace Cavendish's **Lady Grace Mysteries**; read *Assassin* first.

Nancy Drew is a girl detective with attitude, a real American 'tough cookie' who inherited the mystery-solving gene from her lawyer father and seems to find a brain-bafflingly complicated mystery lurking around every corner of her neighbourhood! It's impossible not to be drawn into the trickiest of situations with her, picking up clues, desperate to solve the case before she does – and until it's solved, you'll find it impossible to put the book down. Nancy herself gets older and wiser the more crimes she solves. Whether you like spooky stories (*The Secret of Candlelight Inn*), scientific crimes (*The Crime Lab Case*), all-action adventure (*The Mystery at the Ski-Jump*), or mind-bogglingly complex thrillers (*The Case of Capital Intrigue*), there's a **Nancy Drew Mystery** to suit you – and another and another!

**Eileen Armstrong**

★ ★ ★ ★ ★ ★

# NATASHA'S WILL Joan Lingard

When a family discovers that they may be thrown out of the house they regard as home, they are shattered. Surely its owner, Natasha, the lady they'd loved and cared for so carefully until her death, wouldn't have left them without a roof over their heads? The search for her will begins, and with it a literary treasure hunt.

In fact, many years previously, Natasha had escaped from St Petersburg at the time of the Russian Revolution and this novel also tells her story, about her daring escape and about the way in which she came to set up home in Scotland.

This is a lovely mixture of mystery, adventure and history. You can enter into the spirit of the story by solving the puzzle of the treasure hunt.

**Lindsey Fraser**

**Next?**

• A story that spans two centuries, involving the French Revolution, is Joan Lingard's *The Sign of the Black Dagger*.

• Another story set around that terrible time is Sally Gardner's *The Red Necklace* (*UBG* 282) and its sequel, *The Silver Blade*.

• *Raider's Tide* by Maggie Prince is set in Elizabethan England and tells of a young girl's fight against the life planned for her by her parents.

• Another book centred on the Russian Revolution is Kate Hubbard's *Rubies in the Snow*.

# NATHAN FOX: DANGEROUS TIMES L. Brittney

Nathan Fox really does live in dangerous times. He's a boy actor at the Globe theatre who gets recruited by Queen Elizabeth I's spy-master to go to Venice and keep an eye on the things happening there; things that involve a general called Othello and a noblewoman, Desdemona.

When I first picked this up, I was a little uncertain, as usually I prefer books set in the present day – books set in the past can be a bit too much like doing history homework. Yet as soon as I read the first few pages, I was hooked. After all, even though this is history, it reads just like an adventure story. In fact it has everything – it's a spy-thriller, a love story, a history, a tragedy, a crib for one of Shakespeare's plays and, above all, it's really entertaining. But the best thing of all, it's the first of a series!

**Tommaso Cunniberti, age 11**

### Next?

• Look out for more about Nathan Fox – the sequel is *Nathan Fox: Traitor's Gold*.

• Cornelia Funke's *The Thief Lord* is another mystery set in Venice. (*UBG* 345)

• Shakespeare's stories creep into other books too – try Neil Arksey's *MacB* (which is sort of *Macbeth* but set in the world of school football). (*UBG* 215)

★ ★ ★ ★ ★ ★

# NATIONAL VELVET Enid Bagnold

### Next?

• *My Friend Flicka* is about a friendship between a horse and a boy. (*UBG* 243)

• Horse stories used to be hugely popular. Try hunting out something by Christine Pullein Thompson, such as the **Phantom Horse** series. Or books by her sisters, Diana and Josephine, too. Harder to find is Ruby Ferguson's **Jill** series. Anything by Monica Edwards is worth reading. Look for her **Punchbowl Farm** stories. (*UBG* 276) And there's **Flambards**, a series about horses, flying and love by K.M. Peyton.

When *National Velvet* was first published, a critic called it 'a super day-dream', but it's much, much more than that. Every time I think about the story, it's as if lightbulbs pop in my head; it's one of those books that lights up your life and makes you truly believe that anything is possible. Basically, it's a thrilling adventure about a girl and a horse, but even if you hate horses you'll still love the story; the world in which Velvet Brown lives is so warm it glows, and so real you can't believe that Edwina, Malvolia, Meredith, Velvet and Donald don't exist.

'The Browns loved Jacob as they loved each other, deeply, from the back of the soul, with intolerance in daily life.' It reads as if it was written yesterday, even though it was first published in 1935; it's so fresh and funny and profound that it'll always be one of my most favourite books of all time.

**Vivian French**

# A NECKLACE OF RAINDROPS
## Joan Aiken

Baby Laura's father finds the North Wind caught in a tree and helps to disentangle him. In return, the North Wind offers to be Laura's godfather and makes the baby a gift of a magic necklace of raindrops. But Meg, a nasty girl from Laura's school, becomes jealous of Laura's special powers and is determined to steal the necklace for herself...

Other stories in this collection feature a cat that swells to an enormous size after eating too much yeast, a giant flying apple pie with a bit of the sky baked into it, and a feathered house that lays an egg.

And in 'The Elves in the Shelves', Janet can't believe it when the characters in her books come to life in the night. This wonderful book will make your imagination soar and may well inspire you to write some stories of your own!

**Francesca Lewis**

### Next?
• You will also love *The Kingdom Under the Sea*, a collection of eleven fairy tales from eastern Europe and the Soviet Union, retold by Joan Aiken.
• Joan Aiken is probably best known for the older *The Wolves of Willoughby Chase*, (*UBG* 391) but her equally wonderful series about Mortimer the raven are worth looking out just as much – try *Arabel's Raven* first.
• Another collection of new stories in the fairy-tale mould is *Singing to the Sun* by Vivian French.

★ ★ ★ ★ ★ ★

# THE NEVERENDING STORY Michael Ende

### Next?
• Another book about being drawn unwillingly into magic is Catherine Fisher's powerful *Corbenic*. (*UBG* 72)
• For a story that leads you into a strange world where colour has to be bought, try Mike Wilks's amazing *Mirrorscape*.
• Or try Cornelia Funke's stunning *Inkheart*, a terrific adventure about stories. (*UBG* 174)

Bastian Balthazar Bux is the sort of boy other kids pick on. One day, he takes a copy of a book called *The Neverending Story* from a second-hand bookshop and, locking himself in a deserted attic above his school, he reads it. It is a story of a fantastical world that is disintegrating. As he reads, he becomes more and more involved in the story until he is part of it. He becomes the hero who alone can save this magical place from destruction.

This is a great storybook full of wonderful ideas and amazing characters. It's a little old-fashioned but well worth reading as it will draw you right into its magic. (Oh, and don't see the movie – it's awful.)

**Colin Thompson**

# THE NEW POLICEMAN  Kate Thompson

### Next?

• Good news: if you're interested in Irish myths and legends, Kate Thompson has provided a reading list at the back of the book.

• Read the sequel to *The New Policeman*, *The Last of the High Kings*, where J.J. Liddy is all grown up with a family of his own and he has a daughter called Jenny, and there's this puca and secrets and … well, more adventure happens! Read it to find out what!

• More Irish myth is woven into *The Hounds of the Morrigan* by Pat O'Shea. (*UBG* 160)

J.J. Liddy is desperately short of time. Maybe it's something to do with the twenty-first century, because everybody's suffering. The village of Kinvara in the sleepy west of Ireland is sleepy through sheer exhaustion these days. Where does the time go? When J.J. finds his way into Tír na n'Óg, the land of the young, he meets a charming trickster, and learns that there are at least two sides to this mystery. But Tír na n'Óg is a perilous place for mortals… Kate Thompson is a brilliant writer and *The New Policeman*, full of timeless music, sly humour, family secrets and real people, is one of her best.

**Ann Halam**

★ ★ ★ ★ ★ ★

# NICHOLAS series  René Goscinny and Jean-Jacques Sempé

Although these stories were written in the 1960s, Nicholas's world of mad teachers, swimming lessons, chaotic school trips and football matches ruined by bossy adults will seem familiar to anyone who's ever suffered the indignity of being a schoolboy.

When the adults aren't creating chaos, Nicholas's gang takes over. From bottom-of-the-class Matthew, and Alec who never stops eating, to the thoroughly spoiled Geoffrey and poor Cuthbert, who regularly gets thumped for being the teacher's pet!

While the heroes of many children's books seek out adventure, Nicholas is an ordinary boy who tries to stay out of trouble. The premise is low-key, but the genius of the series is that the comedy comes from everyday scenarios that you'll find easy to relate to.

**Robert Muchamore**

### Next?

• The **Nicholas** books are: *Nicholas*, *Nicholas Again*, *Nicholas on Holiday* and *Nicholas and the Gang*.

• Goscinny is of course (with Uderzo) famous for his brilliant comic strips about Asterix the Gaul (*UBG* 24), but he also created a great series about a cowboy, this time with illustrator 'Morris', called **Lucky Luke**.

• For another boy trying to stay out of trouble – and failing miserably – you should meet Tintin. There are lots of adventures to chose from: look out for *Tintin and the Red Sea Sharks* first. (*UBG* 349)

# NORSE MYTHS

### Next?

• Kevin Crossley Holland's *Axe-Age, Wolf-Age* is is a great collection of Norse myths.

• Or try stories woven around the myths: *Sea of Trolls* (*UBG* 299) and *The Land of the Golden Apples* by Nancy Farmer are brilliant.

• A story that is based around the god Loki is Diana Wynne Jones's *Eight Days of Luke*. (*UBG* 97)

• Look for the myths of other countries, such as: India – *Seasons of Splendour* by Madhur Jaffrey; Egypt – *Tales from Ancient Egypt* by Roger Lancelyn Green; and China – *Tales from China* by Cyril Birch.

We were pagans in this country once. The stories of the gods we worshipped were common knowledge, but now few remember their names. Only the days of the week give us a clue to how important they were. Tyr's day – Tuesday; Wodin's day – Wednesday; Thor's day – Thursday.

If you like fantasy stories, then you'll love these old tales. It's all there – the dragons and warriors, the elves and dwarfs, the mystery and darkness, the tricks and the treasure, the struggle of good against evil. But on top of that, you have the gods themselves. My favourites are Odin, who loved death and poetry, war and wisdom, and knew how to make the dead speak; and Loki, the model for the Christian devil, who loved to twist things out of shape.

As with all great religious stories, there's something here for everyone.

**Melvin Burgess**

★ ★ ★ ★ ★ ★

# NOTHING TO BE AFRAID OF Jan Mark

No one writes short stories better than Jan Mark, and no one can create more wickedly cunning characters whom you just can't help but like. All the children in these ten stories, which are set in the 1950s, live out their own realities, because they're far more interesting than anything the adults care to tell them. But somehow, each of them gets a little too carried away – with unfortunate consequences for themselves and innocent (and often a bit drippy) bystanders. The results make for cracklingly funny reading. So prepare yourself for Anthea's tales of leopards and fever pits in the local gardens, Alice's dubious potions or Anthony's freakish bonfire guy, and much more. Enjoy!

**Jon Appleton**

### Next?

• Like short stories? Here are some more collections to try: *Badger on the Barge* by Janni Howker (*UBG* 26), *Flying with Icarus* by Curdella Forbes and any of Philippa Pearce's stunning collections: start with *The Shadow Cage* and *The Rope*.

• *The Giant Baby* by Allan Ahlberg is funny, eccentric and all about children getting into scrapes.

# ODIN'S VOICE Susan Price

● ● ●

Spoilt, pretty Affie and her rich friends have been genetically designed for a life of beauty and luxury. Affie even has jellyfish genes to give her flashing, multi-coloured hair! But when her father commits suicide and she's thrown into poverty, her friends abandon her.

Sold as a lowly 'bonder', Affie is miserable. Then she meets charismatic Kylie – once a bonder herself, but now 'Odinstoy', the servant of the god Odin who 'speaks' to his worshippers through her. Affie can hardly believe her luck when Kylie adopts her as a special friend. But Kylie has a secret agenda: soon the two girls are plotting to kidnap a child, go on the run – and escape to Mars…

I loved this book, the first of a trilogy, a riveting blend of fantasy and science fiction with touches of wicked humour.

**Katherine Langrish**

### Next?

• *Odin's Voice* is the first volume in the **Pagan Mars** trilogy – the amazing sequels are *Odin's Queen* and *Odin's Son*.

• Susan Price has the knack of getting inside other worlds. Try her *Ghost Drum*, *Ghost Dance* and *Ghost Song*. (*UBG* 124)

• Set in a deeply unsettling future, Tim Lott's *Fearless* is about a girl daring to speak out against injustice.

★ ★ ★ ★ ★ ★

# THE OGRE DOWNSTAIRS
## Diana Wynne Jones

● ●

### Next?

• If you like magic in a real setting, try *The Indian in the Cupboard* by Lynne Reid Banks. (*UBG* 173)

• I also loved *The Phoenix and the Carpet* and other books by E. Nesbit.

• Heather's own *The Boy in the Biscuit Tin* is about three children who find a conjuring set that does real magic. (*UBG* 45)

This is one of the best magic-in-the-real-world stories I have ever read. Johnny, Caspar and Gwinny are given a chemistry set by their new stepfather (nicknamed 'the ogre'), who has also given an identical set to his own two children, Malcolm and Douglas. But these are no ordinary chemical experiments, and soon the children are doing things like flying through the night wearing diving flippers, or keeping live toffee bars under control. In one experiment, Caspar swaps bodies with his posh Scottish stepbrother and finds out that perhaps it's not so easy being Malcolm, after all. This is a story about magic and also about the difficulties of mixing two families together. It is thrilling and hilarious and the characters are so wonderful that you want to go right inside the book and join in their adventures.

**Heather Dyer**

# ONCE  Morris Gleitzman

After living in an orphanage for three years, Felix still believes his bookseller parents will come back for him. But when he sees soldiers burning books, he worries about his mother and father and sets off in search of them. On the dangerous journey across wartime Poland, he makes new friends who help him keep his spirits up when terrible things happen.

Like Morris Gleitzman's other books, *Once* is funny and exciting, but it is also sadder and more serious than anything else he has written. It's a quick read and written in simple language, but the subject is not for young children. *Once* is a really special book that will stay with you long after you've finished reading it.

**Madelyn Travis**

**Next?**
• You might enjoy another World War II novel, *The Silver Sword* by Ian Serraillier (*UBG* 310), or *The Silver Donkey* by Sonya Hartnett, which takes place during the First World War and is about an army deserter trying to get back to England, where his brother lies dying.
• Or try *Boy Overboard*, also by Morris Gleitzman. (*UBG* 45)

★ ★ ★ ★ ★ ★

# ONE WEIRD DAY AT FREEKHAM HIGH: THUMB
## Steve Cole

**Next?**
• There are four **Freekham High** tales, all about Sam and Sara's increasingly bizarre adventures – the others are *Sock*, *Ouch!* and *Pigeon*.
• To experience life at other very strange schools, try either the **Groosham Grange** series by Anthony Horowitz (*UBG* 139) or the **Stories from Wayside School** from Louis Sachar.
• Try Justin Richards's own unsettling and scary books about a boy who falls through a crack in time and ends up employed to help fix the cracks as they appear – in the **Time Runners** series, starting with *Freeze-Framed*.

Sam and Sara meet on their first day starting at a new school – Freekham High. They have a lot in common – both were born on 29th February for one thing – and soon become friends.

The action of this story all takes place on that single bizarre first day. As Sam and Sara try to settle in, they find they have a few extra-curricular challenges to cope with. Most gruesome of these is the discovery of a severed thumb; and that's only the beginning... Soon, detached thumbs and fingers are cropping up all over the place – even in the school dinners. What is even more unsettling is that the explanation – when Sam and Sara finally discover it – is unpleasantly plausible. Funny, clever, and compelling!

**Justin Richards**

# OPERATION RED JERICHO Joshua Mowll

⬤⬤⬤

**Next?**

• Becca and Doug continue their adventures in *Operation Typhoon Shore* and *Operation Storm City*.

• For more thrilling adventures set before World War II, try Charlie Higson's **Young Bond** series – the first one is *SilverFin*. (*UBG* 311)

• For a classic swashbuckler, try Anthony Hope's *The Prisoner of Zenda*.

A terrific blend of text and illustration, *Operation Red Jericho* is presented as a series of accounts and documents collated by the author and telling the story of Doug and Becca MacKenzie. It's 1920 and the two children are caught up in an exciting adventure with their uncle as they hope to be reunited with their parents. There's intrigue, fights, and secret societies aplenty in this rip-roaring swashbuckler.

The main account is taken from Becca's diary, and illustrated with sketches done by her brother Doug. But there are also fascinating news clippings, maps, diagrams, mini-biographies and detailed background notes... So, as well as a terrific read, you get lots to look at and can explore as much – or as little – of the background to the story as you wish.

**Justin Richards**

★ ★ ★ ★ ★ ★

# ORANGES AND MURDER

⬤⬤⬤

## Alison Prince

Although Joey has always lived with Poll and Curly, he knows they aren't his real parents. At 13, he decides it's time to leave home and become a costermonger, selling fruit and vegetables in Whitechapel market. Life is hard and Joey spends his first few nights in a doss house. Then, just as he is starting to make a life of his own, he is accused of murder!

Joey fights to clear his name and unravels the secret of his birth as well as a web of deceit and corruption. *Oranges and Murder* is packed with the sights, smells and bustle of eighteenth-century London; the pace is fast, the characters are fascinating and there's plenty of mystery.

**Helen Simmons**

**Next?**

• Try some other books by Alison Prince. *The Sherwood Hero* is my favourite: a modern-day take on the Robin Hood story – with a twist!

• You might also like *Coram Boy* by Jamila Gavin, which is set in the same historical period and is another story of lost parents and mystery. (*UBG* 69)

• Or try Paul Bajoria's wonderful trilogy that starts with *The Printer's Devil* – there's everything there, from kidnap, disguise and terror, all the way through to a journey to India and the solving of a deep mystery. (*UBG* 274)

• How about a more modern mystery in *The Secret* by Ellis J. Del Monte?

# THE ORCHARD BOOK OF GREEK MYTHS

## Geraldine McCaughrean

Beautifully and concisely retold, these 16 favourite Greek myths are brought to life with all the excitement, magic, intrigue and drama you could ever hope for: the heroic exploits of Jason; Theseus and Odysseus; Icarus, who flies too close to the sun; Perseus; Heracles and King Midas, whose touch turns everything into gold. All these stories are enhanced by the magnificent illustrations of Emma Chichester-Clark. Lesser known myths are also included: Atlanta the fleet-footed goddess; Arachne the spinner, who boasts so much that she is turned into a spider; and Narcissus, the vain shepherd boy who stares at his own beautiful reflection and pines away in hopeless love until at last he takes root, and all that remains are 'the tissuey petals and a bending stalk'.

**Gervase Phinn**

### Next?

• Try Ted Hughes's colourful collection of creation stories. *Tales of the Early World* is recommended by Geraldine McCaughrean on p. 342.

• For more myths brilliantly retold, read *Black Ships Before Troy – the Story of the Iliad* by Rosemary Sutcliff (*UBG* 36) and *In Search of a Homeland – the Story of the Aeneid* by Penelope Lively.

• Or for an easier, and really funny take on them, try *Helping Hercules* by Francesca Simon. Or Claudia Zeff's *The Amazing Adventures of Hercules*.

★ ★ ★ ★ ★ ★

# THE ORDINARY PRINCESS  M.M. Kaye

### Next?

• If you like Princess Amy's no-nonsense attitude, you might also like Dakin, the heroine of *The Farthest-Away Mountain* (*UBG* 110) or Maria Merryweather in *The Little White Horse* (*UBG* 206).

• Or try Violet Needham's wonderful story of Philippa of Windri and her love for Sigismund, Count of Monte Lucio, in *The Woods of Windri*.

When Princess Amethyst Alexandra Augusta Araminta Adelaide Aurelia Anne is born, excitement is high, for the seventh daughter of a king is the most gifted and beautiful of all. A lavish christening is arranged and all the fairy godmothers in the land are invited. But the fairy Crustacea arrives in a foul mood and gives the baby an unusual gift: that she should be ordinary! So Princess Amy grows up with freckles instead of lily-white skin and prefers climbing trees to attending royal balls. She soon realises that drastic action must be taken to avoid being married to a pompous prince, and that's when her adventures really start.

Princess Amy's story makes you think about what is really important in life, about what you need to make you happy.

**Francesca Lewis**

# ORPHAN OF THE SUN Gill Harvey  ● ●

## Next?

• For a different kind of story set in ancient Egypt, try *The Great Pyramid Robbery* by Katherine Roberts. (*UBG* 138)

• Or for a story set in a world that blends ancient Greece and ancient Egypt, read Catherine Fisher's thrilling trilogy that starts with *The Oracle*.

• For realistic historical stories, look for Jennie Walters's **Swallowcliffe Hall** trilogy about three generations of servants in a great house; or Theresa Tomlinson's *The Herring Girls*.

• Or for more recent history, try Ann Turnbull's own **Historical House** series co-written with Adèle Geras and Linda Newbery. (*UBG* 152)

Orphan Meryt-Re, a 13-year-old girl from a family of tomb builders in ancient Egypt, has all the normal concerns and family problems of a girl her age, plus the threat of an arranged marriage and the feeling that she is not wanted in her uncle's home. Disturbed by mysterious dreams that she feels must have some meaning for her, she turns to the local wise woman for advice – and begins to untangle a web of unsettling events.

If you like realistic stories about ordinary people in the past, don't miss this one. It brings the ancient Egyptians vividly to life and shows how their belief in gods, deified pharaohs and ancestor spirits affected every part of their lives.

**Ann Turnbull**

★ ★ ★ ★ ★ ★

# THE OTHER SIDE OF TRUTH Beverley Naidoo  ● ● ●

After witnessing their mother's murder, 12-year-old Sade and her younger brother Femi are forced to flee Nigeria and are smuggled into England – where they are cruelly abandoned. Penniless and homeless, unsure of where to go or whom they can trust, and at the mercy of the English system for refugees, they make friends and enemies, are forced to move homes, and struggle with official bureaucracy, school bullies and bewildering grief. This is a tense and tragic, gripping but hopeful book, which allows the reader to see the world through Sade and Femi's eyes and share their hopes, fears and troubles. It's about injustice, asylum, bullying and family love – somehow it feels like more than just a good story.

**Eileen Armstrong**

## Next?

• Naidoo's *No Turning Back* tells the story of a street child in Johannesburg; and don't miss the page-turning *Journey to Jo'burg* (*UBG* 183).

• *Abela* by Berlie Doherty is a stunning story of an orphaned Tanzanian girl and her struggle to try and live in the UK.

• *Give Me Shelter: An Asylum Seeker Anthology*, edited by Tony Bradman, tells many stories of children forced from their homes.

• *The Endless Steppe* by Esther Hautzig is another story of children caught up in war. (*UBG* 100)

# THE OTTERBURY INCIDENT  Cecil Day Lewis

### Next?

- For more old-fashioned boy detectives, try **Emil and the Detectives** by Erich Kästner. (**UBG** 99)
- Gillian Avery's **The Elephant War** is slightly old-fashioned but it, too, makes wonderful reading – it's about trying to save Jumbo the elephant from being taken to an American circus.
- Another story of schoolyard conflict is **The War of Jenkins' Ear** by Michael Morpurgo. (**UBG** 374)

When Nick Yates accidentally breaks a school window, he and his friends have to raise the money to pay for the repairs – and so Operation Glazier is born. But it turns out that Operation Glazier is only the beginning of the boys' adventures, which will involve them in some pretty nifty detective work, and end up with a huge pitched battle with air guns, brick throwing, cut-throat razors, and some really nasty villains.

As George (the boy telling us the story) : 'This is a really super story – I should know, I wrote it'. And it *is* a super story – though quite an old-fashioned one. That doesn't mean it isn't every bit as exciting and funny as anything written today; just that the language sounds a bit different (the slang and swearing, especially). You'll get used to it quickly, and soon won't mind at all – and it adds a lot to the atmosphere!

**Daniel Hahn**

★ ★ ★ ★ ★ ★

# OTTO AND THE FLYING TWINS  Charlotte Haptie

Otto lives in a city with bouncing pavements, two-foot-tall butterflies and magical people who can do impossible things. But the city authorities want to control the magic for their own purposes – and they'll stop at *nothing* to achieve this.

Open up this book and get ready to plunge into a world unlike any you've ever dreamed of, peopled with extraordinary characters: Mab, the waif of a girl who travels on a flying carpet; Elfina, cold and arrogant with a bitter past; and Mr Six and Mr Eight – policemen with empty hearts, who seem to be everywhere at once.

This book clings to you after you've reached the end; once you've read it, you'll probably never forget it.

**Susan Reuben**

### Next?

- Read the sequels: *Otto and the Birdcharmers* and *Otto in the Time of the Warrior*.
- Or try J.M. Trewellard's *Butterfingers*, about a clumsy stable boy and his quest to save a stolen princess.
- *Midnight for Charlie Bone* is about a boy who discovers he has magical powers. (**UBG** 226)
- Or what about a world where everyone can fly? *The Wall and the Wing* by Laura Ruby tells of an orphan who can't fly and who thinks she is nothing, until she finds out that she can become invisible.

# OTTOLINE AND THE YELLOW CAT  Chris Riddell

### Next?

• The next in the series!
*Ottoline Goes to School*.

• Or try Chris Riddell and
Paul Stewart's *Fergus
Crane*. It's another book
which tells the story in
pictures and words (though
not so many pictures as
*Ottoline*…). (*UBG* 112)

• Or what about another
girl who has adventures,
with a dog rather than a
cat? Try *Molly Moon's
Incredible Book of
Hypnotism* by Georgia
Byng. (*UBG* 234)

Ottoline is a girl who lives alone. Her parents are travellers, but they make sure that she and her pet, Mr Munroe, are looked after by lots of people, like Jean-Pierre from the Home-Cooked Meal Co., Kate from Smith & Smith Pillow-Plumping and Curtain-Drawing Technicians, Madame Wong from Smiling Dragon Clothes-Folding Co., right through to Big Doug, who's from Door-Handle Shiners Inc. and all the guys from The 1,000-Strong Lightbulb Changing Co.

Oh, and as well as being full of really funny names, and full of strange things that happen to Ottoline and Mr Munroe (who as well as being her pet, is also her best friend), this is also a book full of the most amazing drawings that tell the story, too. In fact it's a bit like a comic, but *so* much better!

**Oli Green, age 10**

★ ★ ★ ★ ★ ★

# THE OUTSIDE CHILD  Nina Bawden

Jane and her friend Plato feel like outside children because they both come from families that are out of the ordinary. Jane's mother is dead and she lives with her two eccentric aunts and only sees her seafaring father occasionally. Then she discovers her father has a whole other family she didn't know about.

Jane's quest to find her half-brother and -sister leads her to uncover some family secrets and, in doing so, come to terms with who she is.

Jane and Plato are very appealing characters and the story has plenty of twists and turns as Jane discovers the truth about her past. This book is a great read – and if you sometimes feel like an outside child yourself, you might enjoy it even more!

**Gwyneth Rees**

### Next?

• Don't miss Nina Bawden's other
story featuring these characters,
*The Real Plato Jones*.

• Two other great Nina Bawden
books are *Carrie's War* (*UBG* 54)
and *The Peppermint Pig* (*UBG*
261).

• The main characters in *The
Pinballs* by Betsy Byars are
a bit like 'outside' children when
they meet at the start of the book.
(*UBG* 268)

• A terrific high-action, seafaring
quest story is Joan Aiken's *Go
Saddle the Sea*. (*UBG* 128) In fact,
all her books are brilliant reads,
you'll enjoy any that you can find.

# THE OWL SERVICE
### Alan Garner

*The Owl Service* is a strange and frightening book about a boy called Gwyn who moves to a remote Welsh valley and finds a stack of plates in the attic. From this unfolds the legend of the woman made out of flowers and turned into an owl. It is a book about the magic that lives inside everything – but that magic might not be the kind you want to let loose.

Brilliant and strange, and for boys and girls alike – but not to be read in the dark on your own.

**Jeanette Winterson**

A very scary and complex fantasy. When Alison's family moves to Wales and she finds the owl-patterned plates in the loft, and when her brother feels the invisible spear whistle past him, they don't know that they have become part of the terrible legend of Blodeuwedd, the woman of flowers, and her ancient destruction. Gwynn, who lives in the valley, is drawn in too, by his resentment and envy of the newcomers.

A book about legend lingering in the soul of a place, about class, and about teenagers becoming adults, *The Owl Service* is a great read for those who like their fantasy full of secrets. Garner teases and riddles with his readers. This is a book that inspires your imagination.

**Catherine Fisher**

## Next?

• Try Alan Garner's *Elidor*, a tale about children bringing the four Hallows from the land of Elidor to urban Manchester. (*UBG* 98)

• If you enjoyed the Welsh legends in *The Owl Service*, read more about them in *The Mabinogion*, available in various retellings. Gwyn Jones and Thomas Jones's version is especially good. Or if you like the idea of something more fanciful, try Lady Charlotte Guest's version.

• Other books using Welsh legend include Susan Cooper's **The Dark is Rising** sequence (*UBG* 78) and most of Catherine Fisher's books, including *The Glass Tower* (three atmospheric and scary stories in one) and *Corbenic* (*UBG* 72).

# THE OWL TREE Jenny Nimmo

Jenny Nimmo is such a wonderful author. Here, in under a hundred pages, she gives us a story of such beauty and wisdom that I find myself close to tears each time I read it.

Joe and Mina go to stay with their great-grandmother while their mother is expecting a baby. Granny Diamond becomes ill because her neighbour wants to cut down the beautiful old tree which overhangs her garden. Joe is terrified of heights, but decides to climb the tree to prove that a rare barn owl is nesting at the top, and then has to convince the crabby old man next door to change his mind.

With echoes of one of my favourite childhood stories, *The Selfish Giant* by Oscar Wilde, Jenny Nimmo gives us an enchanting book that readers of any age will find meaningful.

**Malachy Doyle**

### Next?
• If you want to read a spooky story about the countryside, try *Storm* by Kevin Crossley-Holland. (*UBG* 331)

• Or what about *Ice Cat* by Linda Newbery, about building a snowcat, which is distinctly creepy? (*UBG* 170)

• Have you ever thought about what it is like to be an animal in a cage? In *Countdown* by Anne Fine, Hugo wants a gerbil. His dad agrees, but only if Hugo can spend seven hours alone in his newly painted bedroom, with just three toys for company.

★ ★ ★ ★ ★ ★

# A PARCEL OF PATTERNS Jill Paton Walsh

### Next?
• Try other historical novels by Jill Paton Walsh. *The Dolphin Crossing* (*UBG* 89) and *Fireweed* take place during World War II.

• Berlie Doherty's *Children of Winter* is also concerned with the plague in Derbyshire, as is Linda Kempton's *The Naming of William Rutherford*. Both are time-slip stories, too.

• Or try Mary Hooper's *At the Sign of the Sugared Plum*, set in plague-stricken London. (*UBG* 25)

Like every child growing up in Derby, I knew about what happened in the village of Eyam. It's so peaceful there now it's hard to imagine what it was like when the plague came, and the little grey houses were full of people dying.

Mall tells us how the plague arrived, how the villagers vowed not to leave Eyam until the disease had burnt out, so as not to let it spread any further. And she tells us about these terrified, courageous people – like terrible Marshall Howe, who dragged the dead bodies away with a hook, and Emmot Sydall, who dreamed of her own death.

Mall's story burns as fiercely and relentlessly as the plague she describes with such bitter accuracy while, sometimes one by one, sometimes in dozens, her friends, neighbours and family die around her.

**Gill Vickery**

## The Ultimate Readers Poll

# Top Ten School Books

⭐ **1** Harry Potter series
by J.K. Rowling

⭐ **2** Matilda
by Roald Dahl

⭐ **3** The Demon Headmaster
by Gillian Cross

⭐ **4** The Worst Witch
by Jill Murphy

⭐ **5** The Lottie Project
by Jacqueline Wilson

⭐ **6** Point Blanc (Alex Rider series)
by Anthony Horowitz

⭐ **7** Malory Towers series
by Enid Blyton

⭐ **8** St Clare's series
by Enid Blyton

⭐ **9=** H.I.V.E.
by Mark Walden

⭐ **9=** Midnight for Charlie Bone
by Jenny Nimmo

# THE PENDERWICKS

**Jeanne Birdsall**

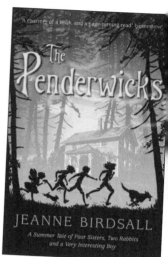

Had enough of dragons? Fed up with spells? This is the book for you. It's really exciting, but nothing happens beyond the fun and heartbreak of an ordinary family summer.

The four motherless Penderwick sisters are just as wildly different from each other as the March girls from *Little Women* are – there's responsible Rosalind, outspoken, football-mad Skye, Jane the writer, and small brave Batty. It's small stuff, but it grips: Batty meets a bull and some rabbits, and later runs away from home; Rosalind falls in love; Skye and Jane befriend Jeffrey, the rich, lonely boy-next-door. They all survive disappointments, and all have a great time. So does the reader.

**Tobias Druitt**

### Next?

• Look out too for more **Penderwick** books – it's going to be a series. Next will be *Penderwicks on Gardam Street*.

• More sisters (and brothers) appear in Eve Garnett's *The Family from One End Street*. (*UBG* 109)

• *All in the Family* is a short-story collection edited by Tony Bradman covering many different aspects of family life.

# THE PENGUIN IN THE FRIDGE  Peter Dixon

Peter Dixon is my favourite children's poet.
I love his humour, cleverness of language
and his brilliantly original verse. Wild,
wonderful and exaggerated characters
abound on page after page. There's Reggie
the Roman, strutting down the street calling,
'Hail Caesar', and Silly Kitty who caught a
condor, and Brett who 'likes being daft and
having laughs'. Some of the poems, such
as 'Hospice', 'Lost Rainbow' and 'Uncle
Charlie', are thoughtful and poignant.

Offbeat, often amusing and great to read
aloud, this collection is enhanced by the
quirky and endearing illustrations of David
Thomas.

**Gervase Phinn**

### Next?

• Try *Ask a Silly Question* by
Irene Rawnsley. I laugh out loud
every time I read her poem, 'Nut
Up My Nose'. *Thawing Frozen
Frogs* by Brian Patten and *Let's
Recycle Grandad* edited by Roger
Stevens are both cracking
collections with much to entertain.

• Michael Rosen is brilliant. Try
his collection of school poems –
*No Breathing in Class*.

• For some more serious poems
try *Under the Moon and Over
the Sea* edited by John Agard and
Grace Nichols. (*UBG* 364)

★ ★ ★ ★ ★ ★

# THE PEPPERMINT PIG  Nina Bawden

### Next?

• More pigs? Try Tanya
Landman's *100% Pig*
and Dick King-Smith's
*The Sheep-Pig* (*UBG*
308).

• Wilbur the pig is the
hero of *Charlotte's Web*
by E.B. White. (*UBG* 59)

• Pigs are also very
important in Lloyd
Alexander's *The Book
of Three*. (*UBG* 42)

• Another story of a
family falling on hard
times and how the
children cope is *The
Silver Skates* by Mary
Mapes Dodge.

The 'peppermint pig' has nothing to do with candy.
He's so-called because he's tiny when he arrives in the
Greengrass household. He's a very real pig; his name is
Johnnie, and Poll Greengrass's
mum is going to rear him.
Dad's gone to America to
seek his fortune, and Mum
and the four children are
having a hard time. Johnnie
grows up clean and well
behaved, and is almost like
one of the family. He can
even be taken out to tea at
the house of a great lady.

This story is set in your
great-grandparents' day, but
it's as bright and fresh as if
it were yesterday.

**John Rowe Townsend**

The
Peppermint
Pig

NINA BAWDEN

# PERCY JACKSON AND THE LIGHTNING THIEF

Rick Riordan

### Next?

• Follow further adventures in *Percy Jackson and the Sea of Monsters*, *Percy Jackson and the Titan's Curse* and *Percy Jackson and the Battle of the Labyrinth*.

• Like your heroes to face powerful creatures with magical powers? Then try *Artemis Fowl* by Eoin Colfer. (*UBG* 23)

• Or Julia Golding's wonderful **Companions** quartet, the first is *Secrets of the Sirens* about a girl who talks to animals.

The gods of Olympus are still running the Earth even in the twenty-first century. Surprised? So is Percy Jackson. And then he finds out that he is the son of one of them – a very powerful god who shouldn't have had him at all. It explains a lot, like why one of his teachers turned into a harpy and tried to kill him. Packed off to Camp Half-Blood to come to terms with his parentage, Percy finds himself plunged into an adventure that takes him across America and into the Underworld on the trail of the lightning thief.

A great hybrid: road movie meets *The Odyssey*. And you'll never look at your teachers in the same way again.

**Julia Golding**

★ ★ ★ ★ ★ ★

# PETER PAN  J.M. Barrie

*Peter Pan* is truly one of the classics – from the original play to the subsequent book, pantomime and film. Ever since Peter first flew in through Wendy Darling's nursery window and took the three children to Neverland, Barrie's story of the boy who never grew up has thrilled young readers – from your great-grandparents to your mum and dad.

Peter loses his shadow, sprinkles fairy dust over the children and flies with them to a magical island. There the real adventures begin: meeting the lost boys and the jealous little fairy Tinkerbell, swimming in the mermaids' lagoon, and fighting pirates led by the evil Captain Hook...

Do you believe in fairies? You must if you are to save Tinkerbell's life... Which brings us to the present: before he died, Barrie gave all future money from *Peter Pan* to saving lives at London's Great Ormond Street Children's Hospital.

**James Riordan**

### Next?

• Geraldine McCaughrean's sequel, *Peter Pan in Scarlet* (*UBG* 263), and Dave Barry's prequel, *Peter and the Starcatchers*.

• For other great adventure stories from a time before radio, TV and cinema, take a look at L. Frank Baum's *The Wizard of Oz* (*UBG* 390) and Lewis Carroll's *Alice's Adventures in Wonderland* (*UBG* 13) – unusually for their times, both have a female hero.

• Another terrific adventure with pirates is Robert Louis Stevenson's *Treasure Island*. (*UBG* 352)

# PETER PAN IN SCARLET  Geraldine McCaughrean  ●●

### Next?

• Check out the previous entry on p. 262 for other *Peter Pan* related books.

• More Geraldine McCaughrean – her books are all wonderful! Try *A Little Lower than the Angels* (*UBG* 204), the fast-paced *Kite Rider* (*UBG* 193), the piratical *Plundering Paradise*, or her superb reworking of *The Odyssey*.

• Or read Linda Buckley-Archer's fantastic adventure series that starts with *Gideon the Cutpurse*. (*UBG* 126)

There are books you return to at different stages of your life, which offer up new treasures with each rereading. I revisited *Peter Pan* recently and was astounded by the strength of Barrie's writing. How courageous, then, for a writer to presume to follow in his well-loved footsteps and write a sequel. But somehow Geraldine McCaughrean manages the impossible and pulls it off. I loved *Peter Pan in Scarlet*. I found it at once brave, subtle and exciting and it remains true to the spirit of J.M. Barrie whilst still being very much McCaughrean's book. And her wonderful prose is sparkling and arch, wise and whimsical. Highly recommended for children and adults alike who long to beach their coracles once more on the shores of Neverland.

**Linda Buckley-Archer**

★ ★ ★ ★ ★ ★

# PETER RAVEN UNDER FIRE  ●●
## Michael Molloy

Cannons, sailing ships, pirates, spies, the high seas – they're all in this brilliant yarn about how young Midshipman Raven gets caught up in a devilish plot involving the French Emperor Napoleon. The details of life in the old navy are fascinating, the action rattles along (and gets quite gory in places!) and the story is packed with a superb range of interesting characters. There's a secret agent who's dead cool until he meets a beautiful, sharp-shooting American heiress; there's a violin player who fights with a blunderbuss, but best of all is the wonderfully horrible archvillain who has a secret hideout in the Caribbean, tons of gold and a mad sister. What more do you need?

**Kjartan Poskitt**

### Next?

• Try Michael Molloy's other books: *The Witch Trade* and its sequels, *The Time Witches* and *The Wild West Witches*, mix wild adventure, magic and time travel; or read *The House on Falling Star Hill*, about a boy who falls into another world and the strange goings-on there.

• A great adventure of ships, danger and suspense is Elizabeth Laird's *The Secrets of the Fearless*.

• Or go further back in time (and add a generous pinch of fantasy) in *Sebastian Darke: Prince of Fools* by Philip Caveney. (*UBG* 300)

# PICTURE BOOKS
## 'No TV for You Any More – From Now On, it's Only Radio!'
**by Ted Dewan**

Imagine what it would be like if a grown-up said this to you: 'Now that you're ten years old, you should stop watching TV and only listen to the radio. You don't need the TV pictures any more... When you listen to the radio, the pictures you make in your head are better anyhow!' This is just what some parents and teachers say about picture books and comics.

When I was about ten years old, I still enjoyed reading picture books long after I could read 'properly'. The school librarian was a bit worried about this, and gently persuaded me to give up the picture books, introducing me to science fiction (which I liked) and some children's classics that just weren't right for me (which misled me into thinking that most books without pictures were boring). Luckily, it didn't work, and I now make and read picture books for a living.

I was also hooked on *MAD* magazine, which, in the 1960s and 1970s, was very political and constantly made fun of advertising. *MAD* was almost entirely comic strips or words and pictures put together. I learned nearly everything I knew about politics, social status, and consumerism by reading it. My mum must be the only mother in the world who didn't throw out my collection of *MAD* magazines; in fact, she went out of her way to preserve them for me, and even rescued them from a cellar flood. They are in my studio to this day.

So why are some people snobby about words? David Fickling, the famous children's book editor, thinks the 'word

## A Few Picture Books Recommended in the *UBG*

- *Fungus the Bogeyman*, *Ethel and Ernest*, *Ug* – all by Raymond Briggs; also look out for his *When the Wind Blows* and *Father Christmas*
- *Maus* by Art Spiegelman
- *Asterix* series by René Goscinny and Albert Uderzo
- *Tintin* series by Hergé
- *Gorilla* by Anthony Browne
- *The Rabbits* by John Marsden, illlustrated by Shaun Tan
- *How to Live Forever* by Colin Thompson; also try his *Falling Angels*
- *Mr William Shakespeare's Plays* and other books by Marcia Williams

snobs' were at their peak in the Middle Ages when most people couldn't read or write. The people in control, the upper classes and especially the Church, kept the secret of written language to themselves (writing in Latin, like a secret code), in order to maintain power over the illiterates. Most people could, of course, understand pictures, which is how the stories of the Bible were told in stained-glass windows for people to 'read' over and over again. But words ruled over pictures, as they still do today in the world of books.

So don't let anyone make you think that learning to read means having to give up the pictures. Nowadays, school librarians are much more aware of good books with words and pictures for older kids. One book you might want to read, *Understanding Comics*, was written by Scott McCloud, a childhood friend of mine who also refused to give up the pictures. It's the best book around that shows how words and pictures work together. After reading it, you'll be able to run rings around any word snob who tries to take your pictures away.

And, of course, it's all done as a comic!

## More Picture Books Not to be Missed

- *Where the Forest Meets the Sea and other torn-tissue collages* by Jeannie Baker
- *Clown* by Quentin Blake
- *The Three Little Wolves and the Big Bad Pig* by Eugene Trivizas, illustrated by Helen Oxenbury
- *The Kiss That Missed* by David Melling
- *Zoo* and *Voices in the Park* by Anthony Browne – in fact, any of Anthony Browne's picture books will delight you and make you think twice
- *Smelly Jelly, Smelly Fish* by Michael Rosen, illustrated by Quentin Blake
- *Where the Wild Things Are* by Maurice Sendak
- *East of the Sun and West of the Moon* by P.J. Lynch
- The **Grinch** books by Dr Seuss – in fact, read everything by Dr Seuss

# THE PHANTOM TOLLBOOTH Norton Juster

I first read this wonderful book when I was nine – then again and again and again... I've since read it to both my children, who loved it (almost) as much as me!

For Milo, 'everything is a waste of time'. This changes when a small car appears, and whisks him away to the Kingdom of Wisdom. He is sent on a quest to rescue the princesses of Rhyme and Reason from the Castle in the Air. On his journey he encounters some of the weirdest characters ever created: Doctor Dischord and the terrible Dynne; Faintly Macabre, the not-so-wicked Witch; the Gelatinous Giant; the Threadbare Excuse, and the Dodecahedron with its 12 faces, each with a different expression – to save wear and tear!

The book has a map, wonderful line drawings by Jules Feiffer and more puns, jokes and brain-teasers than anything I've read before or since.

**Paul Stewart**

**Next?**
• Something else built around puzzles is Blue Balliett's *Chasing Vermeer*. (*UBG* 59)
• Or try Kaye Umansky's delightful *The Silver Spoon of Solomon Snow*, about a boy, lost parents, a silver spoon and ... um ... purple-velvet pantaloons! (*UBG* 310) There's a sequel, too – *Solomon Snow and the Stolen Jewel*.
• Try something by Paul Stewart and Chris Riddell – the **Far-Flung Adventures** are great – read *Fergus Crane* first. (*UBG* 112)

★ ★ ★ ★ ★ ★

# THE PIEMAKERS Helen Cresswell

**Next?**
• Helen Cresswell has a light hand with comedy. You'll also savour the stories about an eccentric family in *The Bagthorpe Saga*. (*UBG* 27)
• I don't always like Roald Dahl's books myself, but *The BFG* is crammed with rich, occasionally slightly rude, humour. (*UBG* 33)
• Michael Rosen's weird *You're Thinking About Doughnuts* (*UBG* 397) will definitely make you smile, as will searching out his poetry.

What a pie! It must be the biggest in the history of the world: a pie to feed 2,000 people. The Roller family, who have been piemakers in Danby Dale for generations, are making it in the hope of winning a prize for the best and biggest pie, awarded by the king. Their daughter Gravella (whose name comes from 'gravy'), is helping.

What a recipe! Two hundred pounds of steak, 75 pounds of kidney, 50 pounds of onions, to say nothing of all those teaspoonfuls of water, pinches of salt and handfuls of herbs. What a voyage, when a pie dish as big as a barge has to be steered down the river! But in the end the pie is a gorgeous, golden-crusted triumph, wheeled out into the sunshine to roars of applause. What a feast!

**John Rowe Townsend**

# PIGEON SUMMER Ann Turnbull

● ● ●

## Next?

• Ann Turnbull has written two more books about the Dyer family. Look out for *No Friend of Mine* and *Room for a Stranger*.

• You might like *The Peppermint Pig* by Nina Bawden; another family story with a determined heroine – and an unlikely animal character. (*UBG* 261)

• Or try one of Michael Morpurgo's books that have animal as well as human characters, such as *Mr Nobody's Eyes*, about a boy who befriends a chimp who has escaped from the circus, or *Why the Whales Came* (*UBG* 382).

You might find the idea of a story about racing pigeons slightly peculiar – but think again! In *Pigeon Summer*, Mary's family are facing hard times. Her father has left home looking for work, her sister's wages help to make ends meet, but whatever Mary herself does is wrong: as her mother says, 'You're that different'. While she is looking after her father's racing pigeons, she thinks of a way to help, even if it means going against her mother – and convention.

Mary is determined to find solutions her way. The pigeons bring dreams of distant places far above the dark mineshafts, and when her father and his winning pigeon finally come home, there is hope of a better future.

**Helen Simmons**

★ ★ ★ ★ ★ ★

# PIGGIES Nick Gifford

● ● ●

Imagine a world where the norm is being a vampire, and humans are seen as nothing more than walking blood-banks. How would you cope if you suddenly found yourself thrust into this parallel universe? In Nick Gifford's original take on traditional vampire stories, this is precisely the situation that his hero, Ben, finds himself in. Victim of a freak accident that transports him to such a place, he quickly finds himself running for his life, desperately searching for fellow humans. The trouble is, once he does find them, they are reluctant to trust him and his problems are far from over…

This clever book is fast-paced and full of suspense (and includes a great surprise ending). Not only that, it makes you think twice about the way our world works, and I guarantee that you'll never look at meat in quite the same way again!

**Laura Hutchings**

## Next?

• If you enjoy reading about vampires then **The Saga of Darren Shan** comes highly recommended. (*UBG* 293)

• For more anarchic adventure, the fabulous *Skulduggery Pleasant* by Derek Landy. (*UBG* 314)

• Marcus Sedgwick writes about yet a different sort of vampire in *My Swordhand is Singing*. (*UBG* 245)

# PIG-HEART BOY Malorie Blackman

### Next?
• Malorie Blackman has written a number of other exciting books for children – try **Thief!** (**UBG** 345), or **Hacker** (**UBG** 140), about a girl determined to prove the innocence of her father.

• Books about illness can be tough, but two others that really aren't are **Big Ben** by Rachel Anderson, about a boy with a Down's Syndrome brother, and Morris Gelitzman's **Two Weeks With the Queen**, about a boy whose brother has cancer (**UBG** 359).

• **Becky Bananas** by Jean Ure is a younger, very moving and unforgettable book about illness that may make you cry. (**UBG** 31)

A viral illness a couple of years ago has left 13-year-old Cameron Kelsey with a failing heart. He's faced with a stark choice – either an early death or a heart transplant, but the only available donor is a pig. Despite his mother's misgivings and his own fear, Cameron opts for the transplant. *Pig-Heart Boy* tells the moving, sometimes funny, and deeply thought-provoking story about a boy who undergoes a pioneering operation. We see his friends' reactions, the stresses and strains on his family and how Cameron bravely tries to cope with the consequences of living with his new heart. This book is an unforgettable 'real-life' read that will keep you thinking long after you've turned the last page.

**Sherry Ashworth**

★ ★ ★ ★ ★ ★

# THE PINBALLS Betsy Byars

Three young people from broken families find themselves in the same foster home. Harvey arrives with two broken legs – he's been run over by his dad driving his new car. Thomas J., abandoned like an unwanted puppy, has been taken in by the 80-year-old Benson twins, until they both break a hip on the same day. The third is a girl called Carlie – cynical, and as hard to crack as a coconut.

But if you think that all sounds a bit heavy, you'd be wrong. The dynamo of the story is wise-cracking Carlie. 'We're just like pinballs,' she tells Mrs Mason, the foster mother. 'Somebody put in a dime and punched a button and out we came, ready or not.'

This is a small treasure that will make you laugh out loud on one page and cry on the next. What else could you possibly want?!

**Rose Impey**

### Next?
• Try others by Betsy Byars: **After the Goat Man**, **The Cartoonist**, **The Midnight Fox** (**UBG** 227), or **The Eighteenth Emergency** (**UBG** 98).

• **Ruby Holler** by Sharon Creech is about two orphaned children adjusting to a new home. (**UBG** 288)

• Morris Gleitzman's **Bumface** (**UBG** 49) and **Two Weeks With the Queen** (**UBG** 359) are both great, and deal with real issues.

# PINOCCHIO Carlo Collodi

Mr Cherry, a carpenter, finds a piece of wood that begs him not to strike it too hard with his axe, and when he planes it, it laughs and says that he's tickling it. The unnerved Mr Cherry gives the wood to his friend Geppetto, who makes a living puppet of it – Pinocchio – who promptly decides that he would like to be a real boy. Pinocchio leaves home to try and find a way to achieve this, and the adventures that follow are many and colourful.

My introduction to this story was the Disney film. On subsequently reading the book, I found that a great deal had been written out of the film, or completely changed. The book tends to moralise, and isn't entirely devoid of sentimentality, but it has a much harder edge than the film, and a far more complex and rewarding storyline.

**Michael Lawrence**

## Next?
- Try Helen Fox's wonderful *Eager*, about a robot boy – there are two sequels, *Eager's Nephew* and *Eager and the Mermaid*. (*UBG* 92)
- Ted Hughes's *The Iron Man* is another fantastic story of a something coming to life. (*UBG* 176)
- Lynne Reid Banks's hugely popular series about something similar starts with *The Indian in the Cupboard*. (*UBG* 173)

★ ★ ★ ★ ★ ★

# PIPPI LONGSTOCKING
## Astrid Lindgren

## Next?
- Look out for *The Amazing Pippi Longstocking*, *Pippi Longstocking in the Park* and *Do You Know Pippi Longstocking?*
- Another really funny series about a wild little girl is *My Naughty Little Sister* by Dorothy Edwards. (*UBG* 245)
- Or there is always Beverly Cleary's **Ramona** series, about a girl who never means to get into trouble, but somehow… (*UBG* 280)

Pippi is a nine-year-old girl with very long feet and bunches that stick horizontally out of her head. She lives in her own house, with a horse and a monkey for company. Although Pippi looks like a scarecrow, she turns out to be very clever, outwitting any adult who crosses her path. During the course of the many **Pippi Longstocking** books, this strange girl wins the battle of wits with lots of grown-ups. I remember being terribly impressed by that, and wondering why I couldn't do the same.

Pippi's friends, Tommy and Annika, envy her as she never has to do boring things like go to school, or go to bed early, or eat vegetables instead of sweets. I envied her, too, as to me she was always so free, especially when she went zipping off to exotic places on her own!

**Sara Wheeler**

# PIRATICA Tanith Lee

For six years, Artemesia (or 'Art') has forgotten everything and in that time has been all that her father wanted her to be – demure, biddable and sweet. But after a crack on the head, her memories come back, and everything changes. Artemesia remembers that her mother was a pirate, so, escaping from a locked room, she flees to 'Lundon'. There, she meets up with her mother's old crew, a shambling bunch of rapscallions. But she soon learns that her memories aren't quite true – her mother was only an actress: one who played the *part* of a pirate queen, Piratica, on the stage.

But that doesn't stifle Art's piratical ambition. She steals a ship, persuades her crew that they can do for real all they acted on stage, and heads out to sea.

Art's adventures bring her to a handsome young man, a parrot, villains, jewels, fights, betrayal and a finale that is so exciting you have to remind yourself to breathe while reading.

**Leonie Flynn**

## Next?

• There's more swashbuckling adventure for Art in *Piratica II: Return to Parrot Island* and in *Piratica III: The Family Sea*.

• Tamora Pierce writes about strong women, too. Read the **Song of the Lioness** series (*UBG* 319) and *Protector of the Small*.

• Or more Tanith Lee? *The Castle of the Dark* (*UBG* 55) and *East of Midnight* (*UBG* 95) are both exciting fantasies.

★ ★ ★ ★ ★ ★

# PLAYING BEATIE BOW Ruth Park

## Next?

• More time slips? Some classics include *Moondial* by Helen Cresswell, *Charlotte Sometimes* by Penelope Farmer (*UBG* 58) and *A Stitch in Time* by Penelope Lively (*UBG* 325).

• Another terrific time slip is *An Angel for May* by Melvin Burgess. (*UBG* 18)

• What about some straight history? Try *The Ruby in the Smoke* by Philip Pullman. (*UBG* 289)

A girl is drawn from the past into modern-day Sydney by children calling her name. They are playing a scary game: Beatie Bow. Fourteen-year-old Abigail Kirk, intrigued by the appearance of this odd-looking child, decides to follow her. She quickly becomes confused by the maze of unfamiliar streets and eventually realises, to her horror, that she is not only lost, but back in another time: the Sydney of 1873.

Abigail's adventures are exciting, heart-warming and terrifying by turns. Her experiences in this strange world turn this shy, prickly, self-centred child into a more mature, generous, tough-minded young woman.

I love the mix of reality, fantasy and history that make up time-slip books. In my opinion, there is no better way of bringing history to life.

**Celia Rees**

# PLAYING ON THE EDGE  Neil Arksey  ● ●

**Next?**
• Neil Arksey's books take a different slant on football. Try *Flint*, about a lad whose dad is a thief. Or *MacB*, a clever twist on *Macbeth*, the Shakespearean drama (*UBG* 215).
• Or what about *The Angel Factory* by Terence Blacker, about a world where nothing is as it seems? (*UBG* 17)
• Or for some real football action, try the **Stadium School** series by Jefferies and Goffe.

Football in 2064 has changed dramatically from today's game. There are now only two leagues playing in Britain – the British Premier League, amalgamations of current top teams, and the Corporates League, owned by the world's biggest companies. However, the underground Unaffiliated Football League is growing in popularity and there is a big swing by the public away from the official teams.

The plot thickens when Todd Linker, a scout for super-team Gunman Reds, finds damning evidence that the performance-enhancing drugs being fed compulsorily to their players are having deadly side-effects. But when Toad is arrested to stop him speaking out, it is left up to his son, Easy, to escape with the evidence and save the day...

**Chris d'Lacey**

★ ★ ★ ★ ★ ★

# POISON  Chris Wooding  ● ● ●

I don't much like fantasy books, frankly. I've never really liked them. All those made-up names and fake maps and languages just annoy me. Am I the only person in the world who just couldn't get into *The Lord of the Rings*? But every once in a while a book comes along that makes me wonder, 'Hmm, maybe there's something in this fantasy stuff after all...' *Poison* is such a book.

It's the sinister story of a girl (Poison) from the Black Marshes, and her quest to rescue her little sister from the Phaerie Lord, facing numerous chilling threats along the way...

But for all the fantasy, the imagined worlds etc., it's really just a great human story, beautifully written, with excitement and emotion and plenty of evil and everything a good story should have. A few pages into it I'd already forgotten that I wasn't meant to be enjoying it, and was hooked.

**Daniel Hahn**

**Next?**
• I suppose you should probably try *The Lord of the Rings* (so should I). (*UBG* 211)
• Try Chris Wooding's bleak, terrifying and very exciting *The Storm Thief*.
• Or how about Lene Kaaberbol's *The Shamer's Daughter*, about a girl who discovers a gift for making others admit their weaknesses.
• Joanne Harris has written a great fantasy in *Runemarks*, about a girl born with the mark of the gods on her hand, and her journey into the World Below. (*UBG* 291)

# POLLYANNA   Eleanor H. Porter

**Next?**

• There is a sequel by Eleanor H. Porter, called *Pollyanna Grows Up*, and several more written by other authors who continue Pollyanna's story.

• Frances Hodgson Burnett's *The Secret Garden* (*UBG* 302) and *A Little Princess* (*UBG* 205) are also classics that feature determined heroines.

If you feel like reading something old-fashioned and heart-warming, you'll enjoy the story of *Pollyanna*. Although her parents have no money, Pollyanna's childhood is full of love. Even when her mother dies, her father manages to keep their spirits up by playing the famous 'glad game'.

Then, when Pollyanna is eleven, her father also dies and she goes to live with cold Aunt Polly, who takes her in simply because she considers it to be her duty. Somehow Pollyanna manages to win over all the eccentric inhabitants of the village, and eventually her aunt, too.

This moving story makes you stop and think about your own life, and your own reasons to be glad.

**Kate Petty**

★ ★ ★ ★ ★ ★

# PONGWIFFY series   Kaye Umansky

Kaye Umansky's madcap stories are always all-singing, all-dancing affairs. Why not try her most famous book of all, and meet her best-loved character, Pongwiffy, 'a witch of dirty habits' (and the star of several books and even a TV show).

Pongwiffy has a bit of a personal hygiene problem, and doesn't always think before she acts, but she's extremely likeable. You'll love her long-suffering friend Sharkadder, too, and even the goblins (although they're quite stupid). In the first story, Pongwiffy finds a new place to live, a new familiar to keep her company, and gets involved in a talent competition and in planning an extra special birthday. Nothing ever quite goes to plan, but it's a lot of fun to read about!

**Jon Appleton**

**Next?**

• If you're into witches and spells, turn immediately to p. 394, and read about Jill Murphy's *The Worst Witch*.

• Or try Kaye Umansky's very funny story of a very different witch, *Clover Twig and the Incredible Flying Cottage*.

• Bruce Coville's *The Magic Shop* books are funny, clever stories that will make you think twice. (*UBG* 217)

# THE PRINCE AND THE PAUPER
**Mark Twain**

● ● ●

Edward Tudor is heir to the throne and spoiled rotten. Tom Canty is poor – a half-starved beggar who, more often than not, gets beaten by his drunken father. The only thing the two boys have in common is they look identical, and that one day, by strange chance, they swap lives.

Written a long time ago, and set even further back in time, this is a classic story of mistaken identity. You'll soon get the hang of the way it is written – words like 'prithee' and 'perchance' crop up a lot – and be reading just to find out what happens to the boys. Will they ever get their own lives back – and will they want to?

**Leonie Flynn**

**Next?**
• Another wonderful Mark Twain story is *A Connecticut Yankee at King Arthur's Court* – one of the first time-travel stories. Twain also wrote *The Adventures of Tom Sawyer*. (*UBG* 9)
• *Lotte and Lisa* by Erich Kästner, about identical twins who play a trick on their separated parents.
• *The Prince of Rags and Patches*, Terry Deary's exciting historical novel, is set in Tudor times, but is about solving a mystery regarding Richard III.

★ ★ ★ ★ ★ ★

# THE PRINCESS DIARIES  Meg Cabot

● ● ●

**Next?**
• Mia's diaries continue in *Take Two*, *Third Time Lucky*, *Mia Goes Fourth*, *Give Me Five*, *Sixational*, *Seventh Heaven*, *After Eight*, *To the Nines*, etc.
• Want to read another story set in New York? Try Louise Fitzhugh's *Harriet the Spy*. (*UBG* 144)
• *A Wrinkle in Time*, one of Mia's own favourites, is recommended on p. 395.
• And look out for everything by Meg Cabot. There's a list of titles that we recommend on p. 409.

Just because you've seen the movie, don't deny yourself this treat. Like all the best children's fiction, this series can be enjoyed by adults as well as kids.

Brilliantly written in the form of an ongoing diary with lots of fun, pop-culture references, these books are delectable! Mia Thermopolis is 14 when she discovers that her Jean-Luc-Picard-lookalike father is really the crowned prince of a small European country. And as his only daughter, she is a princess!

Meg Cabot makes you feel you really know what being a high-school student in New York is like. And besides being funny, well written and totally unputdownable, this book has lots of delightful lists. For example, here is a list of Mia's favourite books: *IQ 83*, *Jaws*, *The Catcher in the Rye*, *To Kill a Mockingbird* and *A Wrinkle in Time* ('only we never get to find out the most important thing: whether or not Meg has breasts...').

**Caroline Lawrence**

# THE PRINTER'S DEVIL  Paul Bajoria

The printer's devil of the title is 12-year-old orphan Mog, who works for printer Mr Cramplock and hangs out round the docks and the inns of London with his dog, Lash. But strange things are happening – and as well as being accused of being in places he wasn't, Mog becomes implicated in a crime.

The story kicks up a gear as Mog meets Nick – a boy who looks very like Mog – and the two of them become involved in a series of dangerous and exciting exploits as they learn more about each other and about themselves…

This top-class adventure story unfolds logically and with style. It has well-defined characters, a likeable hero … and a terrific surprise twist at the end.

**Justin Richards**

### Next?
• Mog and Nick continue their adventures – outside London now – in *The God of Mischief* and *City of Spirits*.

• Other exciting adventures in historic London include Chris Priestley's *Death and the Arrow* (*UBG* 81), Justin's own **Invisible Detective** series, set in the 1930s, and Eleanor Updale's *Montmorency*, set in Victorian times (*UBG* 234).

• Or try *The Highwayman's Footsteps*, which Paul Bajoria has recommended on p. 150.

★ ★ ★ ★ ★ ★

# PRIVATE PEACEFUL  Michael Morpurgo

### Next?
• Read about another young man and his brother in Sonia Hartnett's *The Silver Donkey*, which is also set in France during the First World War.

• Or read the wonderful Marcia Williams's *Archie's War*. It's a boy's scrapbook, kept through the First World War: there are letters, cuttings, diagrams, postcards and doodles. Fictional? Yes. But deeply moving, as well as being a fantastic record of those awful years.

• You could read Michael Morpurgo's collection of short stories about all sorts of different wars, *War: Stories of Conflict*, or try something of his that tackles a different subject, such as *Why the Whales Came*. (*UBG* 382)

Thomas Peaceful is waiting for morning, when something awful will happen. While he waits, he passes the time by remembering his life: his first days at school, his 'special' brother Big Joe, and Molly, his first love. And through it all, Thomas remembers how his older brother Charlie always looked after him. And then the First World War begins. Thomas describes what the war was really like – wet and muddy and cold. The other soldiers were like the boys at home; some shy, some kind – and all of them frightened and wanting to go home. Then, as morning comes, Thomas remembers how he got wounded, and how Charlie disobeyed orders so he could stay with him. There is a gripping twist to this tale, and I read the last few pages with tears in my eyes.

**Heather Dyer**

# PROFESSOR BRANESTAWM  Norman Hunter

## Next?

- You may want to read more **Professor Branestawm** books – like *The Peculiar Triumph of Professor Branestawm*.
- If you like stories that are full of warm and wonderful characters, try *Worzel Gummidge*. (*UBG* 394)
- Or if you really like science, try Russell Stannard's *The Time and Space of Uncle Albert*. (*UBG* 348)

Professor Branestawm is the inventor of, amongst other things, a powerful elixir of life. There are extraordinary results when the potion is accidentally spilt onto the rubbish in his wastepaper bin, culminating in the Professor being chased up into the pear tree by a gigantic postcard.

Illustrated throughout by W. Heath Robinson, an artist whose name has become a byword for outlandish, imaginary inventions, this collection contains 14 stories involving the professor, his housekeeper the often-traumatised Mrs Flittersnoop, and his friend Colonel Dedshott of the Catapult Cavaliers.

There are encounters with screaming clocks, spring-cleaning machines and living photographs and there is a great deal of trouble with the local libraries over a book about lobsters.

**Thomas Bloor**

★ ★ ★ ★ ★ ★

# PUCK OF POOK'S HILL  Rudyard Kipling

The best chapter of all in *Puck of Pook's Hill* is called 'Dymchurch Flit', but to read it you must first read how Una and Dan act their own version of *A Midsummer Night's Dream*, three times running, on Midsummer's Eve, in a field near their Sussex home. Since they happen to be standing inside one of those dark grass circles called a fairy ring, they unwittingly call up Puck, Robin Goodfellow, oldest of the Old Things – and that leads to all kinds of stories from the past, of a kind you don't find in history books. A very English kind of magic echoes through all of them. Kipling was really good at tapping into that, even though he's better known for the **Jungle Books** and his other stories about India.

**Susan Cooper**

## Next?

- Try Kipling's sequel to this, *Rewards and Fairies*. Also his most famous books: the **Jungle Books** (*UBG* 185), and *The Just So Stories* (*UBG* 187).
- Try two other very English fantasies: John Masefield's *The Midnight Folk* and *The Box of Delights* (*UBG* 44).
- A book that tells all sort of intriguing stories from history is H.E. Marshall's *Our Island Story: A History of Britain for Boys and Girls, from the Romans to Queen Victoria*.
- Kevin Crossley-Holland has brought together all sorts of local legends in *The Dark Horseman*, as has Alan Garner with his *Book of British Fairy Tales*.

# PUNCHBOWL FARM stories Monica Edwards

## Next?

• Some others in the series are: *Punchbowl Midnights*, *The Spirit of Punchbowl Farm* and *The Cats of Punchbowl Farm*. Or try Monica Edwards's **Romney Marsh** books, starting with *Wish for a Pony*.

• If you enjoy books about the countryside, try *The Little Grey Men* by B.B.. (*UBG* 203)

• Or look for the delightful *The Children Who Lived in a Barn* by Eleanor Graham.

I loved these books as a child, and read each one several times. Punchbowl Farm seemed so real to me – a feeling helped by the hand-drawn maps inside the book covers – that it was no surprise to learn it was a real place, and that Monica Edwards lived there. Seen mainly from the viewpoint of quiet, animal-loving Lindsey, the stories follow the Thornton family, who first appeared in an early book, *No Mistaking Corker*.

Beginning with *The Black Hunting Whip*, in which the family moves to the derelict farm, the books span several years, and cover various adventures and dilemmas – including fire, a shooting accident, and a conflict when Dion, the schoolboy farmer, wants to fell the ancient yew tree, summoning a warning ghost. Monica Edwards wrote wonderfully about animals, countryside, weather, and all the things that make Punchbowl Farm a living, breathing place.

**Linda Newbery**

★ ★ ★ ★ ★ ★

# PURE DEAD MAGIC Debi Gliori

Any book that has a baddie called Don Lucifer di S'Embowelli has to be pretty extraordinary, and when you throw in a Gothic castle, a hero called Titus Strega-Borgia, a baby called Damp and a spider who *loves* scarlet lipstick, it all adds up to a fantastic package of weird and wonderful plots and counterplots – and a great read. The story rattles along at breakneck speed, and it's completely mad, but there's a really warm heart behind all the activity; the Strega-Borgias may have beasts in the cellars, but they are a gloriously loving and affectionate family when they're not wanting to murder each other – and isn't that just like all the best sorts of families?

**Vivian French**

## Next?

• There are more books about the same family – *Pure Dead Wicked*, *Pure Dead Brilliant*, *Deep Trouble*, *Deep Water* and *Deep Fear*.

• If you like wild and wacky, you could try the **Edgar and Ellen** series, starting with *Rare Beasts* by Charles Ogden.

• Another strange and wild world is that created by Ysabeau S. Wilce in *Flora Segunda: Being the Magickal Mishaps of a Girl of Spirit, Her Glass-Gazing Sidekick, Two Ominous Butlers (One Blue), a House with Eleven Thousand Rooms, and a Red Dog*.

# THE QUIGLEYS
## Simon Mason

Everything we learn in the first few pages of this delightful book makes us think it's going to be fairly ordinary – but that's exactly what makes the book so special! In writing about everyday people and events, Simon Mason shows just how interesting – and funny – family life can be (and he makes a fair case for believing that no one really is 'ordinary' after all).

Here are four stories about the Quigleys: one each about Mum, Dad, Will and Lucy. Lots happens, both planned and unexpected, such as an evening's babysitting which goes disastrously wrong and a wedding in which the bride might be upstaged by a bee!

I loved the humour and observations in this book, but best of all I loved the characters. If you do also (and I think you will) look out for more adventures in the sequel, *The Quigleys at Large*.

**Jon Appleton**

## Next?

• There are more adventures for the Quigleys in *The Quigleys in a Spin* and *The Quigleys Not for Sale*.

• I think you'll enjoy Philippa Pearce's *The Battle of Bubble and Squeak* (*UBG* 29) and also her brilliant set of stories, *Lion at School*.

• Or read Astrid Lindgren's funny stories about Emil, a boy who is always getting into scrapes. (*UBG* 99) Try *Emil's Clever Pig*.

## Happy Families, Sad Families

• *Sundae Girl* by Cathy Cassidy
• **Clarice Bean** series by Lauren Child
• *The Bagthorpe Saga* by Helen Cresswell
• *Saffy's Angel* by Hilary McKay
• *The Family from One End Street* by Eve Garnett
• *The Railway Children* by E. Nesbit
• *The Penderwicks* by Jeanne Birdsall
• *Madame Doubtfire* by Anne Fine
• *The Mum Hunt* by Gwynneth Rhys
• *My Family and Other Animals* by Gerald Durrell
• *The Exiles* by Hilary McKay

# THE RABBITS  John Marsden and Shaun Tan

Australian illustrator Shaun Tan and author John Marsden have created a remarkable story about colonisation and slavery. European rabbits were introduced to Australia centuries ago, and since they had no predators there, the rabbit population went nuts. In this book, the rabbits are dressed as British colonising troops who ride roughshod over the native possums, carving up the land, building cities and displacing the possums.

John Marsden's marvellous storytelling is strangely beautiful and frightening. This amazing book is as visually loaded as a Terry Gilliam film despite its slender 32 pages (no, you're never too old for picture books, especially if they're like this one). *The Rabbits* deserves to become a classroom classic alongside George Orwell's *Animal Farm*.

**Ted Dewan**

## Next?
• Seek out more of Shaun Tan's picture books. You can spend hours searching for different meanings and little stories in the pictures. I've read all his books many, many times and I keep seeing new things. Look especially for **Red Tree**.
• Get a book on the artists Bosch or Brueghel. Both of them lived hundreds of years ago but their paintings are still inspiring today's artists and film-makers.
• *How to Live Forever* by Colin Thompson is another Australian picture book. Only for little kids, eh? Take a good look and see what you think, but be warned, you might get lost in the drawings. (*UBG* 162)

★ ★ ★ ★ ★ ★

# A RAG, A BONE AND A HANK OF HAIR  Nicholas Fisk

## Next?
• Try more of Nicholas Fisk's science fiction, such as *Trillions* or *Grinny*.
• If stories set in the future appeal to you, then Philip Reeve's wonderful *Mortal Engines* is a good choice. (*UBG* 236)
• For a story set in the past, try Nina Bawden's *Carrie's War* which looks back at a child's life in the 1940s. (*UBG* 54)
• *Incarceron* by Catherine Fisher is a brilliantly realised story about the future, one desperately trying to recreate the past.

Brin is 12, and at the end of the twenty-second century that makes him a very important person. The birth rate has plunged following an environmental disaster. The human race could be facing extinction. Brin, with his super-high IQ, receives a request from the Western Council of Seniors to help them with their plans to repopulate the world. His mission is to observe the Reborns, new humans recreated from dead tissue. He meets Brian, Mavis and Mrs Mossop, all Reborns who believe they're still living in 1940. Will they ever be able to adjust to a new world – two centuries on from the one they knew? And why can't Brin shake the feeling there's something he's not being told?

**Thomas Bloor**

## THE RAILWAY CHILDREN  E. Nesbit

Bobbie, Peter and Phyllis have a comfortable suburban life in Edwardian England until their father mysteriously goes away. Nobody will explain where he's gone, or why, and suddenly they find themselves poor, living in a bleak little country house near a railway line. But the chuffing steam trains bring danger and adventure into their lives, and in the end they solve the mystery of where their father's gone, and change their lives again.

Don't be put off by the old-fashioned language of this book; before you know it, you'll be deep inside that family, hardly noticing when Peter calls something excellent 'perfectly ripping'. Edith Nesbit was a crafty storyteller who can make you laugh and cry at the same time – and feel good afterwards.
**Susan Cooper**

Definitely a 'Desert Island' book. You probably know the story already from the film, but you simply must read the book. Then you'll really come to know the family – Roberta (Bobbie) the eldest, and Peter and Phyllis. Their father mysteriously goes away and their mother takes them to Three Chimneys, a tumbledown house in the country.

Suddenly they are poor and have to learn a new, harder way of life. Mother becomes ill and Bobbie is now the carer. They have to discover what poverty, heartbreak and injustice are, but also what kindness and friendship there is in the world. They fight and squabble like any other family, but are brave and honest and funny and never lose hope that one day, if they play their part, everything will come right again. And of course it does, in the most wonderful way possible. I know how this book ends, but every time I read it, I cry. And so will you.
**Helen Cresswell**

### Next?
• You might want to try E. Nesbit's fantasies, *Five Children and It* (*UBG* 115) and *The Phoenix and the Carpet* – same vintage, same engaging kind of family, but with magic thrown in.

• Or try the autobiographical story *A Vicarage Family* by Noel Streatfeild. (*UBG* 369)

• Or what about another family coping while Father is away? Try Louisa M. Alcott's *Little Women*. (*UBG* 208)

# RAMONA THE PEST Beverly Cleary

### Next?
• Read the others, which include: *Ramona Forever*, *Ramona and Her Mother*, *Ramona and Her Father*, *Ramona Quimby, Aged 8*, and *Ramona the Brave*.

• You might also like Judy Blume's *Tales of a Fourth Grade Nothing* (*UBG* 341), *Superfudge* and the rest of the **Fudge** series, and Paula Danziger's **Amber Brown** stories.

Ramona Quimby is one of the most engaging characters in children's fiction. In this book, we follow her through her first days at school, from her joyful start, through her time as a kindergarten drop-out, to her triumphant return. We also get to know the other characters in Ramona's world: her mother and father, her sister Beezus, her friend Howie and her teacher Miss Binney.

Beverly Cleary is an acute observer of ordinary, everyday family and school life. She makes Ramona's world instantly recognisable to anyone under ten (or anyone who remembers being under ten). The books are funny, witty and touching by turns. I read them to my daughter, and we both delighted in them. It is impossible not to share the author's enormous affection for her heroine.

**Celia Rees**

★ ★ ★ ★ ★ ★

# RANGER'S APPRENTICE: THE RUINS OF GORLAN John Flanagan

Will, an orphan, knows only this about his parents: 'His mother died in childbirth, his father died a hero'. When he is not chosen to become an apprentice to any of the Craftmasters on Choosing Day, he cannot help but feel utterly disheartened, especially because all the other wards (also orphans) got chosen for the Crafts they wanted. But then the Ranger hands Baron Arald a sheet of paper concerning Will, and Will has to find out what it says about him...

I loved this book, and when I was reading it I couldn't put it down – I was even reading through meals! John Flanagan has taken the reality of medieval times and mixed it with his imagination, and the result is absolutely thrilling – the best book I've ever read.

**William Ripley, age 12**

### Next?
• The sequels are: *The Burning Bridge*, *The Icebound Land*, *Oakleaf Bearers*, *Sorcerer in the North*, *The Siege of Macindaw* and *Erak's Ransom*.

• For another writer who creates real people, and puts them in terrifying adventures, try Joseph Delaney – read *The Spook's Apprentice* first. (*UBG* 322)

• Or for a book that takes you on a wild adventure into snowbound lands, try Nancy Farmer's *Sea of Trolls*. (*UBG* 299)

# RASPBERRIES ON THE YANGTZE

●●

## Karen Wallace

*Raspberries on the Yangtze* is one of those books that suck you into the story right from the first sentence: 'It all began the day my brother and I decided to poison our mother'. In spite of this promising beginning, it isn't a crime novel. It's a sweet, funny, tender family story about Nancy, her brother Andrew and friends Amy and Clare. They live in the Canadian backwoods and during the summer holidays they're free to roam around all day, swinging on the wire fence, picking wild raspberries, searching for the perfect cave, visiting their kindly neighbour Mr Chevrolet, and peeking at precocious Tracy Wilkins with her boyfriend...

Nancy is lively and funny and wildly imaginative. She's so real you feel she could be your sister or your best friend.

**Jacqueline Wilson**

> **Next?**
> • The sequel, *Climbing a Monkey Puzzle Tree*, in which Nancy has to leave for boarding school in England and her life changes completely.
> • For another book set in the past about a brother and sister, try *Carrie's War* by Nina Bawden. (*UBG* 54)
> • For something else about growing up in the country, try the **Punchbowl Farm** books by Monica Edwards. (*UBG* 276)

★ ★ ★ ★ ★ ★

# RAVEN'S GATE

●●●

## Anthony Horowitz

> **Next?**
> • The series is called **The Power of Five**, so you can guess how many sequels there will be... The second book in the series, *Evil Star*, takes Matt to Peru and the third, *Nightrise*, introduces several new characters and is set mostly in the USA.
> • More Anthony Horowitz? Read *Stormbreaker* (*UBG* 12) or his hilarious **Groosham Grange** series (*UBG* 139)
> • There's more supernatural adventure in Michael Scott's *The Alchemist*. (*UBG* 12)

Matt Freeman is a 14-year-old orphan who discovers that he doesn't just have extraordinary supernatural abilities: he's one of five children who have the power to save the world. When he tries to steal some DVDs from a warehouse, he's caught by the police and sent to a strange kind of foster home in Yorkshire. Soon, he discovers that things are not what they seem...

This novel, the first in a series by Anthony Horowitz, is just as exciting as his **Alex Rider** books, but relies on horror rather than action to provide the thrills. Avoid this book if you don't like being scared. But if you like creepy villains, weird witches and things that go bump in the night, you'll definitely enjoy *Raven's Gate*.

**Joshua Doder**

# THE RED NECKLACE  Sally Gardner

Not a book for the faint-hearted, this tells the story of Yann and Sido, two teenagers caught up in the early days of the French Revolution. Yann is a gypsy with a mysterious past, whilst Sido is the unloved daughter of a French aristocrat. Together with Têtu the dwarf, they battle the evil Count Kalliovski who, rumour has it, has sold his soul to the Devil.

Sally Gardner weaves her story around stunning descriptions of the excesses of the aristocracy and by the end of the book it is all too easy to understand why France descended into the bloodbath that was the Revolution.

**Laura Hutchings**

### Next?
• The sequel, *The Silver Blade*.
• For a classic story of the French Revolution, read Baroness Orczy's *The Scarlet Pimpernel*. (*UBG* 298) Or try Charles Dickens's *A Tale of Two Cities*.
• For another thrilling book that involves gypsies, try Marcus Sedgwick's *My Swordhand is Singing*. (*UBG* 245)
• Or read another Sally Gardner – try *I, Coriander* next. (*UBG* 166)

★ ★ ★ ★ ★ ★

# REDWALL series
## Brian Jacques

### Next?
• Some of the many titles in the series are: *Lord Brockwell*, *Mossflower*, *The Legend of Luke*, *Mariel of Redwall*, *Mattimeo* and *Triss*.
• What about a world where the talking animals believe humankind to be nothing but a myth? Try the *Travels of Thelonious*, first in the **Fog Mound** trilogy by Susan Schade and Jon Buller.
• For animals behaving more like animals, try Kenneth Oppel's bat saga that starts with *Silverwing*. (*UBG* 312)
• Or how about the epic saga of the **Warrior Cats** by Erin Hunter? *Into the Wild* is first. (*UBG* 374)

Brian Jacques's **Redwall** series combines a vivid blend of characters with a fascinating plot to provide an enthralling read. Jacques has incorporated a whole range of songs and poems as well, creating original, lively and hugely enjoyable books.

The series follows the mammalian inhabitants of Redwall Abbey, where a community of animals is entirely self-sufficient and behave in many human ways – cooking, fishing, etc. The book's bad guys are the 'vermin', consisting of foxes, stoats, weasels, polecats, etc.

In *Redwall*, the first book to appear in the series, a young mouse, Matthias, must take up a prophecy of the Abbey's famous warrior and wield his sword in battle against evil. It's a great war / adventure story, but minus most of the gore!

**Tim Cross**

# THE RESCUERS Margery Sharp ●●

### Next?

• Look out for the sequel – *Miss Bianca*. Actually, there are nine sequels, but most of them are very hard to find!

• Try *Mrs Frisby and the Rats of NIMH* by Robert C. O'Brien about a mouse, her family and some very interesting rats. (*UBG* 239)

• Daren King's *Mouse Noses on Toast* is about a mouse discovering a restaurant with a horrifying menu item. (*UBG* 237)

Bernard, Nils and Miss Bianca have been given the terrifying task of rescuing a Norwegian poet imprisoned in the grim, windowless Black Castle. The castle is heavily guarded, and there's no way in or out. Will our heroes be strong enough to overpower the castle jailers? Well, no, actually. The thing is, you see, shy, well-meaning Bernard, unflappable Nils and beautiful (but vain) Miss Bianca are, well, mice. Their only hope is to outwit the jailers instead. But there's another problem, much scarier than the jailers: the biggest test for our friends will be keeping out of the clutches of Mamelouk, the jailers' evil cat, who is 'twice natural size, and four times as fierce!'

I love the Disney version of this, but I do think the book is more exciting, more dangerous, and funnier. The story is quite different, too. Which do *you* prefer?

**Daniel Hahn**

★ ★ ★ ★ ★ ★

# RESCUING DAD Pete Johnson ●●

When Mum and Dad start acting suspiciously nice all of a sudden, Joe knows what's up. Huge smiles, roast chicken and massive slices of chocolate cake can mean only one thing. It's worse than being packed off to boarding school or borstal or the local zoo... Mum is chucking Dad out!

Joe and his sister Claire want life to return to how it used to be when Mum would explode with laughter at Dad's jokes. They have to work fast as Dad's appearance is deteriorating and he needs urgent training for his bad habits, which are too many to be listed. To make matters worse, the slimy Roger Salmon is sniffing around Mum.

Joe and Claire have a matter of weeks to retrain Dad (without him knowing!). All runs relatively smoothly – there's no hitch too big for this determined pair. How will Mum be able to resist 'Dad Mark Two'?

This book tackles a sensitive topic in a humorous and down-to-earth way.

**Elena Gregoriou**

### Next?

• If you enjoyed Pete Johnson's style of writing, why don't you try his other books? There's the scary *My Friend's a Werewolf* (*UBG* 243), or the spooky *Ghost Dog*, and the just plain funny *How to Train Your Parents* (*UBG* 163).

• Karen McCombie's funny and moving **Ally's World** is about a girl living with her dad. (*UBG* 14)

# THE REVENGE OF SAMUEL STOKES  Penelope Lively

### Next?
• You might enjoy Penelope Lively's **The Ghost of Thomas Kempe**, in which the past finds its way into the present. (**UBG** 125)

• How past and present come together is beautifully realised in Philippa Pearce's classic **Tom's Midnight Garden**. (**UBG** 351)

• **Playing Beatie Bow** by Ruth Park tells of a girl who finds herself moving back a century. (**UBG** 270)

When Tim and family move on to a new estate to be near Grandad, it is soon clear that something is not right. The washing machine smells of roast venison, tobacco smoke comes out of the television, cabbage seeds grow into hedges, glass houses turn into Greek temples and then a lake suddenly appears out of nowhere. No one has a clue what it means or what to do. With Grandad's help, Tim and Jane manage to solve the mystery that puzzles the town council and press.

A charming book about how the past can invade the present, the nature of change and progress and how useful a lot of knowledge and 'not thinking in straight lines' can be.

**Ann Jungman**

★ ★ ★ ★ ★

# RIGHT HO, JEEVES  P.G. Wodehouse

Bertie Wooster is an upper-class young gentleman with a man-servant called Jeeves. Bertie, who is not very bright, gets into all sorts of trouble with all sorts of people. He relies on

Jeeves, a solemn man of high intellect, to rescue him. The adventures the pair of them have are hilarious.

Now humour is a personal thing, and what makes me laugh might not make you laugh, but I've never met anyone who didn't find this book funny. It's set in an old-fashioned and out-of-date Britain, but the writing is so smooth and easy, reading it is like getting in a warm bath and just soaking in laughter. Tempting?

**Garry Kilworth**

### Next?
• The 20 or so other **Jeeves** books get better and better!

• Same world as Jeeves? Try the great detective stories written by Dorothy L. Sayers, featuring Lord Peter Wimsey. The first is **Clouds of Witness**.

• Otherwise, there's **The Admirable Crichton** by J.M. Barrie, about a helpless upper-class family shipwrecked with their very capable butler.

# THE RIGHTS OF THE READER
### Daniel Pennac

'You can't make someone read. Just as you can't make them fall in love, or dream...' That's the first sentence of this intelligent, provocative book about the reasons that people read – or don't. Daniel Pennac is a novelist and teacher who knows that people will never read a book unless they want to. If you try to force them to read, they'll throw the book away and do something more interesting instead. He gives a ten-point manifesto which, he suggests, should be granted to every reader. The first is 'the right not to read'. The second is 'the right to skip'. The other eight are equally wise and liberating. This inspiring book isn't just packed with good ideas; it also has fantastic illustrations by Quentin Blake.

**Joshua Doder**

> **Next?**
> • There aren't really any other books quite like this one, but Daniel Pennac has written several novels for children and adults, including *Eye of the Wolf*.
> • Some storybooks that are about books include Cornelia Funke's *Inkheart* (*UBG* 144), *The City of Dreaming Books* by Walter Moers and *Bambert's Book of Missing Stories* by Reinhardt Jung. (*UBG* 27)

★ ★ ★ ★ ★ ★

# THE RINALDI RING
### Jenny Nimmo

> **Next?**
> • Read Caroline Pitcher's powerful and moving novel, *Mine*, in which Shelley finds that she is being haunted by the voices of two girls from the past.
> • Gill Vickery's *The Ivy Crown* is a richly atmospheric novel, set in a strange old house in remote woodland.
> • In Magdalen Nabb's *The Twilight Ghost*, Carrie's attempts to find out the identity of the ghost draw her into time travel.
> • K.M. Peyton's *A Pattern of Roses* is a slightly harder mystery blending past and present.

Eliot is being haunted. Since the death of his mother in America, he has come to stay with his cousins in an English country town. What links his frightening experiences with the mad girl once imprisoned in his room?

To discover the truth about the long-ago tragedy of the Rinaldi ring, Eliot must confront the sinister Freya Greymark. It is only then that his own troubles can come right. But Freya Greymark has guarded her dreadful secret for a long time.

This is a compelling ghost story about loss and redemption, in which events that happened in the First World War cast their shadow over the present day. Eerie and atmospheric, it has plenty of shivery moments...

**Patricia Elliott**

## RIVER BOY  Tim Bowler  ●●●

Jess has a special bond with her grandfather. He is an artist and she is his inspiration, his muse. Jess has her own talent, swimming, and her ambition is to finish a long-distance swim that will really challenge her.

When her grandfather suffers a heart attack and insists on a final holiday in his boyhood home, Jess finally gets her wish. With her grandfather growing weaker every day and struggling to complete his picture of the 'River Boy', she finds herself becoming fascinated by the stranger she keeps glimpsing swimming in the river near their holiday cottage.

This amazing book is about obsession, love and death. The ending is both heartbreakingly sad and yet 'right' at the same time – months after reading it, I'd find myself thinking about Jess and her swim, and what it all meant.

**Laura Hutchings**

### Next?

• *Storm Catchers* (UBG 332), *Dragon's Rock* and *Frozen Fire* are all Tim Bowler books you might like to read.

• *Dirty Angels* by Andrew Clover is a story of illness, family and a really grimy, grittily real London.

• David Almond writes about reality, too: try *The Fire-Eaters*. (UBG 113)

# THE ROBE OF SKULLS  Vivian French ●●

**Next?**

• Try the sequels: *Bag of Bones* and *Heart of Glass*.

• For another woman with a yearning for a nice new coat, read Dodie Smith's classic *One Hundred and One Dalmatians*. (*UBG* 164)

• There are more unusual creatures in Tony DiTerlizzi and Holly Black's **The Spiderwick Chronicles**. (*UBG* 321)

Lady Lamorna needs money for a new robe. Not just any robe, but one that'll make a nice rattling noise as she walks along her cold, stone hallways: one made with skulls. As Lady Lamorna is a witch – and has plenty of henchmen (and hench-creatures) to do her bidding – then it seems quite likely that she'll get exactly what she wants... Except her money-making scheme to kidnap princes and princesses, turn them into frogs and then demand a reward before she'll turn them back, doesn't quite go according to plan.

This is one of those books that you pick up in an idle moment, peruse casually and then end up devouring as fast as you can. The story is delicious, with glorious characters who are either supremely evil or nicely good; there's enchantment, magic, spookiness, a wicked stepsister, a slightly shabby prince and heroic Gracie Gillypot – all of which add up to the funniest of fairy tales.
**Leonie Flynn**

★ ★ ★ ★ ★ ★

# ROLL OF THUNDER, HEAR MY CRY  Mildred D. Taylor ●●●

Nine-year-old Cassie Logan is one of the most feisty characters I know in fiction. She's amazing, and doesn't take any nonsense!

There's a lot of nonsense in Mississippi, America, in the 1930s. The Logans are the only black family who own land in the district. However much Mama, Papa and Big Ma try to protect Cassie and her three brothers from the hateful racism they experience, nothing can stop the children's instinct to fight injustice. And that means trouble.

Mildred D. Taylor is a wonderful storyteller, though she also thanks her father for the gripping family stories he passed down to her. They show the underside of the 'Land of the Free' and show how the human spirit can survive (*has* to survive!) with strong values in a world where powerful people tell so many lies.

**Beverley Naidoo**

**Next?**

• To discover the extraordinary story of how Cassie's grandfather got his own land fifty years earlier, read *The Land*. And there is a sequel, *Let the Circle Be Unbroken*.

• A book that deals with the legacy of slavery is Sarah Mussi's *The Door of No Return*.

• The **My Story** series is excellent for illuminating the past; read *Slave Girl* by Patricia C. McKissack.

# ROMAN MYSTERIES series Caroline Lawrence

**Next?**

• Other titles in this series include *The Secrets of Vesuvius*, *The Pirates of Pompeii*, *The Assassins of Rome* and *The Twelve Tasks of Flavia Gemina* – but there are lots more, too!

• Or try Katherine Roberts's **Seven Fabulous Wonders** books.

• More about Imperial Rome? Try *The Eagle of the Ninth* (*UBG* 93) or K.M. Peyton's **Roman Pony Adventures**, starting with *Minna's Quest*.

In *The Thieves of Ostia*, the first in the **Roman Mysteries** series, the year is 79 AD, and in the port of Ostia, Flavia Gemina is a young Roman girl with an uncanny knack for finding lost objects and a real thirst for mystery. When she sets out to discover who has stolen her father's signet ring, her investigation brings her into contact with Jonathan, a Jewish / Christian boy, Nubia, an African slave-girl, and Lupus, a wild and tongueless street urchin. As they become friends, a new, much more serious mystery begins.

This wonderful series comprises books that can be read entirely separately, but whose plots intertwine and loop back and forth. With each volume, the mysteries become darker and more thrilling, whilst the evocation of Empire life is remarkably vivid.

**Simon Puttock**

★ ★ ★ ★ ★ ★

# RUBY HOLLER Sharon Creech

Florida and Dallas have just about given up hope. Every time they are adopted, their new parents end up deciding they're just too much trouble, and they find themselves thrown back to the Boxton Creek Home for Children, and the custody of not-very-nice Mr and Mrs Trepid. Florida and Dallas don't mean to be 'trouble twins'; they just see the world differently from everyone else!

So when elderly couple Tiller and Sairy ask to have the twins spend the summer with them in their house in Ruby Holler, Florida and Dallas can't help assuming it'll be just another disaster. But they love the magical Holler, and soon discover that Tiller and Sairy are different, too, in their way. Before long all four have become fonder of each other than they'd expected to. And as you read this charming, warm-hearted book, you'll grow fond of them all, too.

**Daniel Hahn**

**Next?**

• For another hard-hitting story of a girl in a children's home, try *Locomotion* (*UBG* 209) or *The Story of Tracy Beaker* (*UBG* 332).

• For something quite different by the wonderful Sharon Creech, try *The Wanderer* (*UBG* 372) or *Walk Two Moons* (*UBG* 371). My favourite is *Love That Dog*. (*UBG* 214)

• Lemony Snicket's **A Series of Unfortunate Events** is a very different story of orphaned siblings! (*UBG* 306)

# THE RUBY IN THE SMOKE Philip Pullman

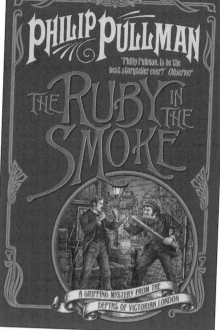

Sally Lockhart is 16 and living on a grudging relative's charity, at a time when middle-class young women were thought incapable of most things and in need of protection. But Sally, being a financial wizard and a sharp-shooter, is spared a future as a governess or lady's companion. Instead, she makes loyal friends, including office-boy Jim and pioneer photographer Fred, joins Fred's ramshackle household and solves the mystery of who killed her father in the South China Sea. The Victorians we meet here are all on the fringes of society because of poverty, criminal tendencies or an interest in stepping outside conventions, and they make intriguing characters.

The later **Sally Lockhart** books, *The Shadow in the North*, *The Tiger in the Well* and *The Tin Princess* might appeal more to older teenage readers, but this one can be read alone, and it will keep you on the edge of your seat.

**Geraldine Brennan**

## Next?

• Philip Pullman is also author of the acclaimed **His Dark Materials** trilogy. (*UBG* 151)

• Another great Victorian detective is Sherlock Holmes. Try Arthur Conan Doyle's *The Hound of the Baskervilles*. (*UBG* 160)

• Julia Golding writes great stories about adventurous girls. Try *The Diamond of Drury Lane*. (*UBG* 83)

## Adventuring with Gutsy Girls

• *The Highwayman's Footsteps* by Nicola Morgan

• *Igraine the Brave* by Cornelia Funke

• *The Secret Countess* by Eva Ibbotson

• *Orphan of the Sun* by Gill Harvey

• *The Diamond of Drury Lane* by Julia Golding

• *Pirates!* by Celia Rees

• *At the Sign of the Sugared Plum* by Mary Hoffman

• *A is for Assassin* by Grace Cavendish

• *Warrior Girl* by Pauline Chandler

# RULES OF THE ROAD  Joan Bauer

● ● ●

In the United States you can get a driving licence at 16. Jenna Boller is still at school but works part-time in a shoe store. One day, the elderly owner, Mrs Gladstone, hires Jenna to drive her from Chicago to company headquarters in Dallas, visiting Gladstone's shops on the way.

As they travel, Mrs Gladstone reveals that her weasel of a son is planning to sell the neighbourhood stores to a giant retail chain. Jenna has plenty of troubles of her own, but she is never afraid to fight for what she believes is right and she soon finds that all the best people are on her side.

If you are tired of drippy girls who whinge and witter about clothes and diets and boys, you will love big, strong, funny Jenna. She could sell shoes to a mermaid – but she wouldn't. That would be cheating, and Jenna never cheats.

**Jan Mark**

**Next?**
• Joan Bauer's *Squashed* is very different but still really great. (*UBG* 323)
• If you would like to meet other strong, intelligent young women, why not try *Breakers* by Julia Clarke, whose heroine has to look after her sister and their actress mother, who still behaves like a teenager.
• Ordinary people take on the big guys in *Stop the Train* by Geraldine McCaughrean. (*UBG* 331)

★ ★ ★ ★ ★ ★

# THE RUNAWAY  Elizabeth Anna Hart

● ● ●

**Next?**
• Brian Fairfax-Lucy's *The Children of the House*, retold by Philippa Pearce: a really good read about the adventures of four children who lived in a great house at the end of the nineteenth century.
• Edith Henrietta Fowler's *The Young Pretenders*, written in 1895, is funny, ironic and still relevant. Two siblings, who have spent their lives running wild in the country, are moved to London where they have to learn to conform. Or do they?
• Or try something by E. Nesbit, such as *The Railway Children*. (*UBG* 279)

This is a delightfully funny story about a lonely girl called Clarice who discovers a girl called Olga – the runaway – and agrees to hide her in her bedroom. The plot is closely woven and reflects the age in which it was written – 1872 – and since the author was a cousin of Lewis Carroll, it is not surprising that there are echoes of *Alice's Adventures in Wonderland* in the writing.

Gwen Raverat says in her preface that this is the sort of book which will always be liked because it is such fun, and she feels that no heroine, however modern, ever climbed trees or walls as well as Olga did. I have only just discovered the book but I was quite captivated by it.

**Anthony Buckeridge**

# THE RUNAWAYS Ruth Thomas ●●●

## Next?

• You could try *Treasure Island* by Robert Louis Stevenson. It's Nathan's favourite book and one of the best books ever about runaways. (*UBG* 352)

• *We Didn't Mean to Go to Sea* by Arthur Ransome is one of my top books about runaways, even though, in this case, they didn't mean to! Very tense and full of excitement. Read about all of Ransome's **Swallows and Amazons** books on p. 336.

• *The Thief Lord* by Cornelia Funke is another excellent book about a gang of runaways in Venice; it's a thriller and a great story about the way an unlikely group of children become friends. (*UBG* 345)

What would you do if you found a stash of money, had no friends at school and were in trouble with your head teacher? Brought together by accident, Nathan and Julia decide the only thing to do is to run. But running away is hard. Where do you go? How do you get there, then fool grown-ups into not noticing you're on your own? How do you become invisible?

An unlikely friendship develops between Nathan and Julia as their roller-coaster journey takes them from Brighton to a dream-like campsite on Exmoor. One minute happy and free, the next scared and running, they can never quite forget their homes and families. This is a novel that keeps you guessing to the very last page!

**Helen Simmons**

★ ★ ★ ★ ★ ★

# RUNEMARKS Joanne Harris ●●●

*Question:* How do you know that a book is really good? *Answer:* Because once it's finished you want to read it again!

*Runemarks* has that quality. Born into a world where imagination and dreams are feared and hated, Maddy Smith has a strange sign on her hand; the locals call it a 'ruin'. A dreamer and teller of tales, Maddy is blamed for anything that goes wrong.

Magic supposedly left the world with the demise of the Old Gods. Now, a priestly 'Order', using the power of the 'Good Book', hopes to keep it at bay for ever. But Maddy's so-called 'ruin' is really a *runemark*, a symbol through which magical power is wielded.

This is an epic tale featuring the Norse gods and a dangerous descent into the underworld. Imaginative, inventive and rich in detail.

**Joseph Delaney**

## Next?

• If you enjoy *Runemarks*, you might also enjoy *Tunnels* by Roderick Gordon and Brian Williams.

• There's more epic Norse-tinged fantasy in Catherine Fisher's the **Snow-walker's** trilogy. (*UBG* 318)

• Edith Pattou's *The North Child* is based on a Norse myth, and has a girl hero, a polar bear and a journey into the other world.

# SABRIEL Garth Nix

**Next?**
• There are two sequels to *Sabriel*: *Lirael* and *Abhorsen*. Garth Nix has also penned *Across the Wall: A Tale of the Abhorsen*.

• You might also love J.R.R. Tolkien's **The Lord of the Rings** (*UBG* 211) and Philip Pullman's **His Dark Materials** trilogy (*UBG* 151). Both are classic fantasy stories, but in very different ways.

• You should also sample **A Wizard of Earthsea** by Ursula Le Guin. (*UBG* 95)

Sabriel is a young woman who lives in Ancelstierre, close to the Old Kingdom. In this mythical world, Charter Magic keeps the inhabitants safe, but Free Magic is an ever-present threat. Sabriel discovers that her father, Abhorsen, is in peril in the Old Kingdom, and she must leave the safety of her boarding school to find him and discover the nature of the danger he is in. Be warned: this unusual and gripping fantasy is quite gruesome in places, and terrifying, too, as the Dead leave their Kingdom to prey on the living. All is so vividly imagined you'll think you're in the midst of battles and fleeing for your life. *Sabriel* is a must, and not just for fans of fantasy.

**Sherry Ashworth**

★ ★ ★ ★ ★ ★

# SAFFY'S ANGEL
## Hilary McKay

This is a far more recent book than my other choices and it was recommended by my ten-year-old daughter – we both loved it. Saffy believes herself to be the second of the four Casson children. The other three are all named after colours on their painter parents' colour charts, and when Saffron realises she is not a colour on the chart, she wants to find out why. When her beloved grandfather dies he leaves Saffy a lost angel in his will. With her friend Sarah, Saffy goes in search of her angel in a journey that takes her from a garden in Italy to a hillside in Wales. And in the course of her search she also comes to understand her place in her chaotic but loving family.

This is a lovely book, funny and moving – a very satisfying read!

**Jane Ray**

**Next?**
• Hurrah, there are sequels! They are *Indigo's Star*, *Permanent Rose*, *Caddy Ever After* and *Forever Rose*.

• If you enjoyed Saffy you might also enjoy **When Marnie Was There** by Joan G. Robinson. This has a similar theme of a lonely child. (*UBG* 379)

• Or try Hilary McKay's **The Exiles** – a series of books which capture exactly what it is like to be part of a big family. (*UBG* 104)

# THE SAGA OF DARREN SHAN  Darren Shan

Darren Shan is not only the author of this horror series – starting with *Cirque du Freak* – but also the main character. A regular kid, Darren likes football, hanging out with his mates, and spiders.

Together with his best friend Steve, Darren sneaks out of his house to visit the mysterious and forbidden Cirque du Freak. Among the many creepy acts in the show is the amazing spider, Madam Octa. Darren cannot resist the temptation – he must have the poisonous creature all to himself, even if that means stealing the spider from her owner, who is (how shall I put it?) a member of the Living Dead. This foolish deed ends in a nightmare and Darren must pay the price with his own blood ... and this is just the first volume!

You certainly need guts to read these books, because many of the characters end up with theirs hanging out of their bodies, half-chewed, if you catch my drift...

**Noga Applebaum**

### Next?

• The saga continues with *The Vampire's Assistant, Tunnels of Blood* and more. Darren Shan has another (gorier, scarier) series, **The Demonata**.

• You might be interested in *The Stuff of Nightmares* by Malorie Blackman, an interlinked series of short, horrific stories.

• *Piggies* by Nick Gifford takes a different look at vampires – and their prey. (*UBG* 267)

★ ★ ★ ★ ★ ★

# THE SAGA OF ERIK THE VIKING  Terry Jones

### Next?

• You could try more books by Terry Jones, including the funny *The Knight and the Squire* (*UBG* 193), and *Fairy Tales*.

• Or for a very funny book, try *How to Train Your Dragon* by Cressida Cowell, in which a young Viking learns everything he can about the care of dragons. (*UBG* 162)

• There are the Norse myths, if you want to read about the gods the Vikings worshipped. A very modern version is *Viking Legends* by Michael Cox in the **Twisted Tales** series.

Erik and his band of loyal followers set sail on an almost impossible quest – to find the land where the sun goes at night. He takes his sword, Blueblade, and his ship, Golden Dragon, and says farewell to his wife and son. What follows is a series of exciting, fantastic and vivid adventures, each one more dramatic than the next.

Travel with Erik and you will meet Enchanters, Dogfighters, the Old Man of the Sea and even see the Edge of the World. But will you find the land where the sun goes at night? And will the crew survive? Anyone who enjoys adventure, fantasy and suspense in equal mixture will love this book and read it again and again.

**Sherry Ashworth**

# SAM PIG   Alison Uttley

My favourite pig. I don't remember when I first came across Sam, but he is as much a part of my childhood as any visit to an aunt in the country or journey into a ditch on the crossbar of my father's bike. Like all the best stories, the sense of place and character in these tales draws the reader in and carries him or her along. Sam's adventures are usually quite slight – writing a letter, going to a country fête, taking a stroll in the moonlight – but always there are incidents and encounters along the way, and the warmth of the language makes the stories a joy to read aloud.

A.E. Kennedy's exquisite illustrations (in early versions) perfectly complement the magical text.

**Michael Lawrence**

**Next?**
• More Alison Uttley? Try *Magic in My Pocket* or *A Country Child* (*UBG* 74).
• If you like *Sam Pig* you have another treat in store in Barbara Euphan Todd's **Worzel Gummidge** series, which is also humorous, inventive and completely original. (*UBG* 394)
• Other great stories about pigs are *100% Pig* by Tanya Landman and *Charlotte's Web* by E.B. White. (*UBG* 59) Or for a different animal, try White's *Stuart Little*, about a mouse.

★ ★ ★ ★ ★ ★

# SARAH, PLAIN AND TALL
## Patricia MacLachlan

**Next?**
• There are two sequels. The first is *Skylark*, in which Anna, Caleb and their parents live through a terrible drought on the prairie. The next is *Caleb*, told from a boy's point of view.
• For stories about growing up at a similar time in America, try Laura Ingalls Wilder's autobiographical **Little House** series (*UBG* 203), starting with *Little House in the Big Woods* or *Children on the Oregon Trail* by Rutgers Van der Loeff (*UBG* 62).
• For a look at country life in Britain, try Berlie Doherty's memorable books, such as *Deep Secret* and *Jeannie of White Peak Farm*. Or look out for Michael Morpurgo's *Farm Boy*.

When Sarah comes as a mail-order bride all the way from Maine to the prairie to marry Anna's father, the motherless Anna isn't at all sure it's a good idea. But her little brother Caleb, whose birth caused their mother's death, has no one to compare Sarah with. Slowly, both children – and their father – come to appreciate Sarah's gentle strength, her good humour and her wisdom. They become a family in the deepest sense of the word.

This gentle, persuasive story is filled with humour, adventure, and an understanding of the practical considerations that made up life on the American prairies in the nineteenth century.

**Jane Yolen**

# THE SATURDAYS  Elizabeth Enright

### Next?
• Well, you won't want to do anything till you've read the sequels: they're *The Four-Storey Mistake*, *Then There Were Five* and *Spiderweb for Two*.

• For another great book about siblings, schemes and friendships, try Hilary McKay's fast and very real *Dog Friday*.

• *Ballet Shoes* by Noel Streatfeild is about three sisters. (*UBG* 28)

• Or read the fun and easy *Tales of a Fourth Grade Nothing* by Judy Blume. (*UBG* 341)

It's Saturday afternoon. It's raining, and the four Melendy children are stuck indoors. None of them has enough pocket money to do anything exciting. The radio's broken, and Mona, Randy and Oliver don't feel like reading or listening to their brother Rush on the piano playing Bach – again. Yawn...

Until Randy has an idea: why don't they pool their pocket money, and take it in turns to spend all of it, one Saturday a month each, doing something really special? Think of all the possibilities! And so begin the adventures of the Saturdays.

Even if you don't have loads of brothers and sisters of your own, Elizabeth Enright makes you feel like you're really part of this family, and that you know them all just as well as any real people. And when it's over you'll be ever so sorry to have to say goodbye to them; but never fear, you won't have to just yet – there are three great sequels!

**Daniel Hahn**

★ ★ ★ ★ ★ ★

# THE SCARECROW AND HIS SERVANT  Philip Pullman

This is the story of a turnip-headed scarecrow, who gets brought to life when he is struck by a bolt of lightning, and of the clever boy Jack, who becomes his servant – though Jack has far more sense than his master (who is, quite literally, pea-brained). Jack frequently has to come to the scarecrow's aid as they set off on an adventure that will see them enlisted in the army, attacked by brigands, shipwrecked on a desert island and much more besides.

Philip Pullman is a master at taking the world of traditional fairy stories and making it his own, and this story is full of fantastic characters and situations, all complemented by Peter Bailey's illustrations.

**Chris Priestley**

### Next?
• If you enjoyed this book, the best thing you can do is try another Philip Pullman. Start with *The Firework-Maker's Daughter* (*UBG* 114) perhaps, or *I Was a Rat*, which has a wonderful twist on a traditional fairy story. (*UBG* 166)

• Another scarecrow stars in L. Frank Baum's wonderful *The Wizard of Oz*. (*UBG* 390)

• *The Mouse and His Child* by Russell Hoban is about a dangerous quest for family and home. (*UBG* 236)

# SCHOOL STORIES
## Top of the Class!
### by Andrew Norriss

School is something we all had to go through, and it's always good to read how other people did it, or how it might have been if your parents had sent you somewhere else! Personally, I always enjoyed reading 'school stories' much more than I enjoyed actually being at school. The children in them seemed to have such a good time. They outwitted sneaky masters, found hidden treasure (there was a lot of it about) and always scored the winning runs in vital cricket matches. But the thing I liked best was the friendship. However bad things were on the outside, the hero had his friends (usually two of them) and together they would battle through. That's the real point of school stories. They're about winning through with your mates.

It's a formula that was begun in the first school story ever written – *Tom Brown's School Days* – and has continued ever since. One of my own favourites was *Stalky and Co* by Rudyard Kipling (written at a time when the older boys had guns and the only subject anyone ever studied was Latin) but I also read several dozen of the books about Billy Bunter at Greyfriars School, and I loved the **Jennings** stories.

The girls had their stories as well, of course, and though I've not read them myself, if you mention the **Chalet School** or Enid Blyton's **Malory Towers** or Angela Brazil, a lot of girls go all misty-eyed at the memory. And one of the nice things about finding you like one of these books is the knowledge that there's a dozen more like it in the same series.

By the time my own children had arrived,

## Twelve Boarding-school Books

- The **Jennings** series by Anthony Buckeridge
- *Boy* by Roald Dahl
- *Point Blanc* (in the **Alex Rider** series) by Anthony Horowitz
- The **Malory Towers** series by Enid Blyton
- The **St Clare's** series by Enid Blyton
- The **Chalet School** series by Elinor Brent-Dyer
- *The Youngest Girl in the Fifth* by Angela Brazil
- *The War of Jenkins' Ear* by Michael Morpurgo
- *Down With Skool / How to Be Topp* by Geoffrey Willans
- *Daddy-Long-Legs* by Jean Webster
- *The Little Princess* by Frances Hodgson Burnett
- *The Time of the Ghost* by Diana Wynne Jones

I noticed that school stories were changing. They weren't all about posh kids sent to boarding school any more, they were about real children in real schools and what really happened to them. I thought it was much more interesting. So Anne Fine writes about bullying in *The Angel of Nitshill Road* (brilliant!) and about understanding other people's viewpoints in *Flour Babies*. Roald Dahl writes about weird teachers in his autobiographical *Boy*, and Gene Kemp describes the trials of a troublemaker in *The Turbulent Term of Tyke Tiler*.

When I wrote *Aquila*, one of the things I wanted to describe was what it was like to be in school when you weren't very clever or good at sport, and how that made you feel. It was a subject I felt I knew something about.

But the old type of school story is still around – though these days it comes in the form of fantasy. **The Demon Headmaster** books by Gillian Cross are great, or there's Bruce Coville's series set in an American high school that begins with *My Teacher is an Alien*. Anthony Horowitz has created Groosham Grange, where the children learn magic, and of course there's the most famous school of them all, Hogwarts, where Harry Potter battles against evil and wins through with his mates: the original magic formula.

## Ten Books About Schools That May Be a Bit Like Yours

- *Frindle* by Andrew Clements
- *Bumface* by Morris Gleitzman
- *The Turbulent Term of Tyke Tiler* by Gene Kemp
- *Flour Babies* by Anne Fine
- *How to Write Really Badly* by Anne Fine
- *The Lottie Project* by Jacqueline Wilson
- *Matilda* by Roald Dahl
- *Aquila* by Andrew Norriss
- *There's a Boy in the Girls' Bathroom* by Louis Sachar
- *My Kind of School* edited by Tony Bradman

## Ten Books About Bullying

- *The Diddakoi* by Rumer Godden
- *Feather Boy* by Nicky Singer
- *The Tulip Touch* by Anne Fine
- *The Eighteenth Emergency* by Betsy Byars
- *Secret Friends* by Elizabeth Laird
- *Step into the Dark* by Bridget Crowley
- *The Present Takers* by Aidan Chambers
- *The Mighty Crashman* by Jerry Spinelli
- *The Angel of Nitshill Road* by Anne Fine
- *Indigo's Star* by Hilary McKay

# THE SCARLET PIMPERNEL Baroness Orczy ●●●

**Next?**

• If you liked the historical and romantic aspect, try books by Georgette Heyer who wrote about Georgian and Regency England. Start with *Powder and Patch*, which has always been my favourite.

• If you like adventurous twists and turns, try Robert Louis Stevenson's *The Master of Ballantrae*, or Alexandre Dumas's classics *The Count of Monte Cristo* or *The Man in the Iron Mask* (*UBG* 218).

Don't worry if you don't know anything about history – this is a fantastic spy story set at the time of the French Revolution, and everything you need to know is explained as part of the action.

A mysterious man, code-named the Scarlet Pimpernel, makes it his task to rescue as many French aristocrats as possible from the deadly peril of the guillotine. Nobody knows the identity of this audacious and cunning Englishman, but this won't deter the evil Chauvelin, who will stop at nothing to hunt him down. Has the Scarlet Pimpernel met his match?

Filled with seemingly impossible escapes, brilliant disguises and twists that keep you guessing right to the end, this book is great fun. And the grand finale leaves you breathless!

**Abigail Anderson**

★ ★ ★ ★ ★ ★

# SCRIBBLEBOY Philip Ridley ●●

Philip Ridley's stories are the most wild and wacky you'll ever see – and see them you must because the wonderfully detailed illustrations, with the words whirling and whizzing and zipping across the pages, are crucial to the way these exciting, sad-but-happy stories work their magic.

Scribbleboy, a magical character we may never actually meet, brightens up his boring, grey, concrete neighbourhood with scribblefabulous scribbles, then mysteriously disappears, leaving Ziggy Fuzz to keep up his good work by starting the Scribbleboy Fan Club.

The racy, pacy adventures of these larger-than-life characters, who somehow manage to make the best of everything, will open your eyes to the magic in the world around you too. Watch out for the breathtakingly inventive twist at the end!

**Eileen Armstrong**

**Next?**

• If you enjoy meeting mad characters, why not try some of Philip's other books? There's Lassiter Peach, who lives behind the barbed wire fortress with its mutant killer eels in *Dakota of the White Flats* for starters!

• Or try *Toonhead* by Fiona Dunbar, a funny adventure about a boy who can predict the future through the cartoons he draws.

• Paul Jennings writes wild and surreal stuff, too – try any of the **Un** books, such as *Uncanny!* (*UBG* 360)

# SEAL SECRET
## Aidan Chambers

William is not having a good holiday. For some unfathomable reason, his parents have decided to rent a farmhouse cottage instead of their usual caravan by the sea. They disappear for hours on end, his father fishing and his mother with her nose in a book, forcing William into an unwilling friendship with Gwyn, the farmer's son. Then Gwyn lets William into his secret – a seal pup kept captive in a cave – and William faces some difficult choices.

Determined and scared at the same time, William learns some hard lessons about speaking up and sticking to his beliefs, whatever the danger. There are wonderful descriptions of the Welsh countryside, the wild cliffs and, of course, the seal!

**Helen Simmons**

### Next?
• Try *A Dog So Small* by Philippa Pearce, about an entirely imaginary animal; one of my favourite animal stories. (*UBG* 88)
• If you liked this, you might also like *Farm Boy* by Michael Morpurgo.
• *The Seal-Singing* by Rosemary Harris is out of print but well worth hunting down, either second hand or from your library. It's wonderfully atmospheric, and deeply moving, too.

★ ★ ★ ★ ★ ★

# THE SEA OF TROLLS   Nancy Farmer

Jack is just an average Saxon boy getting on with life between magical training from the local bard and cold, hard work on the farm. Unfortunately, the Vikings arrive, and Jack and his spoilt baby sister are taken as slaves. It turns out the Vikings aren't so bad, as mad, ruthless killers go. But then the terrifying half-troll wife of Ivan the Boneless loses her hair, and Jack has to fetch water from a magic well, beyond the perilous Sea of Trolls...

Nancy Farmer takes elements from Norse myth, real history, and even (sneakily) the words of a nursery rhyme, and weaves a rich, wise and thrilling saga. This book has unforgettable characters and extraordinary adventures, and it's funny, too: you'll never want it to end.

**Ann Halam**

### Next?
• Read the sequel, *The Land of the Silver Apples*, in which Jack, Thorgil and Lucy have more breathtakingly exciting adventures.
• You could try another hair-raising story of monsters and heroes from Saxon and Norse times: *Beowulf*. There's several versions available; look for those retold by Kevin Crossley-Holland or Rosemary Sutcliff (*UBG* 32).
• Nancy Farmer has also written an amazing, futuristic epic – the unforgettable *House of the Scorpion*. Read it and you might have your world-view challenged.

# SEBASTIAN DARKE: PRINCE OF FOOLS

## Philip Caveney

Sebastian Darke, half-elf, half-man, sets out to seek his fortune, hoping to find employment as a jester at the court of a king.

The bad news...

Sebastian is inept. He can't tell a joke! And there are lots of dangers out there, including murderous brigands and savage, bloodthirsty lupers. But he has companions: Cornelius, a warrior no taller than Sebastian's hip; Max, a very sarcastic talking buffalope; and a spoiled brat of a princess.

This is a book full of adventure, told in humorous prose, with witty dialogue that carries the reader all too quickly towards its exciting conclusion.

**Joseph Delaney**

**Next?**

• The sequel – *Sebastian Darke: Prince of Pirates*.

• Two equally fast-paced and exciting adventures are *Shadow Forest* by Matt Haig (*UBG* 306) and *Blart* by Dominic Barker (*UBG* 37).

• Someone else who carries you through on a wave of excitement is Joseph Delaney. Read *The Spook's Apprentice* and its sequels, but beware, they're much more scary. (*UBG* 322)

★ ★ ★ ★ ★ ★

# THE SECRET COUNTESS

## Eva Ibbotson

**Next?**

• The story of the Tsar's daughter, Anastasia, as it might have been, is told in Kate Hubbard's *Rubies in the Snow*.

• Another rich girl who has to live as a servant is in *A Little Princess* by Frances Hodgson Burnett. (*UBG* 205) Easier? Yes. But if you haven't read it yet, you really should!

• And more of the wonderful Eva Ibbotson? Try *Journey to the River Sea*. (*UBG* 184)

Ibbotson's tale of a young countess, who escapes from revolutionary Russia to find work below stairs in an English country house, is romantic in the best sense of the word. A large and engaging cast of characters from both 'upstairs' and 'downstairs' clamour for the reader's attention as the author deftly brings to life a period from history, warts and all. Indeed, although there is a strong romantic arc at the centre of the story, Ibbotson excels perhaps at depicting the less appetising characters and aspects of life in and around the country house.

I love reading Eva Ibbotson for the detail she weaves into her stories and for her vibrant, and often very funny, dialogue.

**Justin Somper**

# THE SECRET DIARY OF ADRIAN MOLE AGED 13³/₄

## Sue Townsend

### Next?

• There are several follow-ups, written as Adrian grows up. The first and best is *The Growing Pains of Adrian Mole*.

• Do you want more diaries? Try Meg Cabot's **The Princess Diaries** – very different, but very funny. (*UBG* 273)

• Narinder Dhami's *Bend It Like Beckham* is also about the trials of growing up. (You may have seen the movie, but don't let that keep you from trying the book.)

Adrian Mole's diary begins on 1 January with a list of New Year's resolutions, including being kind to the dog, hanging up his trousers and not starting smoking. The final entry, over a year later, tells of being rushed to Casualty with a model aeroplane glued to his nose. What lies between is a hilarious account of a teenage boy's sufferings in an unkind world. What's especially funny is that Adrian takes himself very seriously indeed.

As far as I know, this was the first humorous book written in diary format. There have been many more since, but none appeals right across the age range like **Adrian Mole**. When it first came out, we all read it – children, teenagers, teachers, mums and dads, grandparents, everyone. And, quite rightly, we all loved it. If you like funny books, this is definitely a must-read.

**Kaye Umansky**

★ ★ ★ ★ ★ ★

# SECRET FRIENDS   Elizabeth Laird

Rafaella is a new girl whose ears stick out. Such an easy target. Lucy, who tells us the story, is also nervous on her first day at Dale Road Secondary School when she meets Rafaella. She calls her 'Earwig' and raises a laugh. But the final words of chapter one have an awful ring: 'I'm going to regret that moment till the day I die'.

When I heard that *Secret Friends* had reduced a whole class of children to tears, I wasn't surprised. I cried as well when I read this book. Perhaps our tears were something to do with recognising how easily we, too, might slip...

With its touching illustrations, this short novel is a little gem.

**Beverley Naidoo**

### Next?

• You might also like *Jake's Tower* (*UBG* 178), *Kiss the Dust* (*UBG* 191) and *The Garbage King*, all by Elizabeth Laird.

• Another unsettling book, this time about friendship, is Anne Fine's *The Tulip Touch*. (*UBG* 355)

• Or for something written from the point of view of the bully, try *The Mighty Crashman* by Jerry Spinelli – an easier read. (*UBG* 228)

# THE SECRET GARDEN
## Frances Hodgson Burnett

Unloveable, unhappy little Mary Lennox arrives from India to live in her widowed uncle's huge mansion on the bleak and wind-blown Yorkshire Moors. Orphaned and angry, Mary is incapable of finding any sort of comfort until she stumbles upon a walled garden, hidden in the grounds of the house. Eventually, she also discovers her cousin Colin, an equally lonely child, and along with Dickon, the bright, kindly garden boy, she sets about rescuing the overgrown garden. And in the process she rescues herself and Colin from their unhappiness. I loved this book for its atmosphere, and for the descriptions of the tremendously satisfying rebuilding of the beautiful lost garden.

**Jane Ray**

What drew me to *The Secret Garden* was that I could identify so quickly with the central character, Mary. OK, she was a girl and I was a boy, and I know boys aren't supposed to read books about girls – but who cares? Like Mary, I lived in the countryside and didn't have very many friends. I would often play games by myself, and go on quests around my house and garden in search of adventures and secrets.

### Next?

- *A Little Princess* by the same author is about a little girl who struggles before she finds happiness. (**UBG** 205)
- *Stargirl* by Jerry Spinelli is also about an unlikely friendship. (**UBG** 324)
- Or try *Tom's Midnight Garden* by Philippa Pearce, a magical story about friendship across time. (**UBG** 351)
- *The Children of Green Knowe* by Lucy M. Boston will also prove a satisfying read. (**UBG** 61)

I loved Dickon, the nature-boy, and his whole family. I wasn't too keen on the whining Colin, but through his spiritual and physical growth I came to like him. That's the great thing about *The Secret Garden* – it tells a wonderful, haunting, uplifting story, but it also slips in some important lessons. It shows us that we all have the potential to be better than we are and that we create our own well of happiness or misery. The book deals with childhood and friendship, of course, but so much more as well – death, religion, loneliness, the relationship between humanity and the natural world. But never in a dull, heavy way – it's a joy to read and artfully works its messages into the threads of the story, so that readers learn while they marvel. It's a remarkable, thrilling, mystical coming-of-age tale – no reader should be without it!

**Darren Shan**

# THE SECRET OF PLATFORM 13   Eva Ibbotson

Under Platform 13 at King's Cross Station, there is a 'gump', a secret door that leads to a magical island. Children-in-the-know could tell you all about the gump, and how it opened for exactly nine days every nine years, and not a second longer.

This story begins when Lily and Violet and Rose, the triplet nurses of the young prince, are given permission by the queen to take him on a journey off the island, all because they have become very homesick and want some fish and chips to remind them of their childhood in the shabby streets of North London. But the Prince gets stolen by the vulgarly rich Mrs Trottle and is brought up to be a vulgarly rich little boy called Raymond Trottle, who has no interest in being rescued by anyone, least of all a wizard, an ogre, a fey and a hag. This is an entertaining, witty and wonderful novel, full of surprises, and it's beautifully written.

**Jackie Kay**

### Next?

• Another world reached through a secret entrance at King's Cross Station is of course Hogwarts. Read all about it in the **Harry Potter** series by J.K. Rowling. (*UBG* 145)

• *A Handful of Magic* by Stephen Elboz twists the real London into a world that's quite different. (*UBG* 141)

• There are other magical Eva Ibbotsons, too: *Which Witch* and *The Great Ghost Rescue* are both loads of fun. In fact, look out for anything of hers.

★ ★ ★ ★ ★ ★

# THE SECRET SEVEN series   Enid Blyton

### Next?

• After reading all **The Secret Seven** books, move on to Enid Blyton's **Famous Five** (*UBG* 109) … and then the **Mystery** series, and the **Adventure** series (*UBG* 177). There's enough to keep you going for ages!

• *Swallows and Amazons* by Arthur Ransome is a slightly harder read, also about friends who have fun and solve mysteries. (*UBG* 336)

• Joshua Doder's *A Dog Called Grk* is about a boy and his dog solving crimes and mysteries. (*UBG* 87)

For a really good, gallop-along adventure story, you can't beat Enid Blyton. She may not be recommended by your teacher, and your mum might turn up her nose at her – but her plots are gripping, and once you've got hooked on one book in the series, there's another, and another, and another (and another).

In **The Secret Seven** books, a group of children (you've guessed it – seven of them) form a secret society with a special badge and code. In each story they have a mystery to solve, and they do so bravely and intrepidly, finding themselves in quite a lot of danger on the way and stopping only to drink lemonade.

**Susan Reuben**

# THE SEEING STONE   Kevin Crossley-Holland

Here is a story to sweep you back nearly a thousand years. Arthur is growing up at Caldicot, a medieval manor. He longs to become a knight. Into his hands, his father's wise friend Merlin puts the seeing stone, and in its shining black depths Arthur watches the story of his namesake unfold – King Arthur of England.

We see our hero dealing with his constantly jealous older brother, Serle, his outspoken friend, Gatty, and a host of family and villagers, all the while becoming more and more swept along by the magic and pageantry of the world in his seeing stone.

Through his tale shines what is probably the clearest, most honest, thought-provoking and intelligent view of medieval life yet in a book for the young: it's not just about what people wear and how they speak, but how they think, the things that they believe, and what they know.

**Anne Fine**

## So, You Want A *Really* Long Read?

- *The Lord of the Rings* by J.R.R. Tolkien
- *Midnight for Charlie Bone* by Jenny Nimmo
- **Measle** series by Ian Ogilvy
- **The Keys to the Kingdom** by Garth Nix
- **Septimus Heap** series by Angie Sage
- **The Spiderwick Chronicles** by Holly Black and Tony DiTerlizzi
- *The Spook's Apprentice* by Joseph Delaney
- *Eragon* by Christopher Paolini
- **The Saga of Darren Shan** by Darren Shan
- *The Cry of the Icemark* by Stuart Hill
- **A Series of Unfortunate Events** by Lemony Snicket
- **Roman Mysteries** series by Caroline Lawrence
- **The Worlds of Chrestomanci** by Diana Wynne Jones

## Next?

- Look out for the next two books in the trilogy: *Arthur at the Crossing Places* and *King of the Middle March*. Look out, too, for Crossley-Holland's *Gatty's Tale*, about a field girl with a beautiful singing voice who ends up on a pilgrimage, battling thieves and Saracens!
- *The Sword in the Stone* by T.H. White is the story of the young Arthur (*UBG* 338), which is continued in *The Once and Future King*.
- **The Dark is Rising** sequence by Susan Cooper (*UBG* 78) also explores the Arthur legend in a modern context ... as does *Corbenic* by Catherine Fisher (*UBG* 72).

# SEEKER William Nicholson

Welcome to the **Noble Warriors** trilogy, the story of three young people seeking their way in a world of warlords, monks, bandits and fanatics. This is fantasy on a grand scale by the writer of *The Wind Singer*. It asks the biggest of all questions: who or what is God?

Seeker is a scholar set on joining the mysterious Nomana, or fighter monks, whose powers lie not in weapons but within themselves. Morning Star is a girl who can read the emotions of others by seeing their colours. Wildman is a glorious bandit, blond and brutal, but awed by the unfathomable powers of the monks. All three think joining the Nomana will answer their questions, but instead find this is only the beginning of a startling journey. The reader, too, is taken on a thought-provoking and challenging quest – not one for the fainthearted.

**Julia Golding**

### Next?
• Find out what happens in the rest of trilogy: the other volumes are *Jango* and *Noman*.

• William Nicholson has also written the marvellous **Wind on Fire** trilogy. (*UBG* 386)

• Try Philip Pullman's **His Dark Materials** trilogy, also on the hunt for an elusive god. (*UBG* 151)

• If you like your gods more present, try Tamora Pierce's **Song of the Lioness** series – where the gods just won't leave Alanna alone!

★ ★ ★ ★ ★ ★

# SEPTIMUS HEAP series
## Angie Sage

### Next?
• The whole series – *Magyk*, *Physik*, *Flyte* and *Queste*!

• Try Jonathan Stroud's epic **Bartimaeus** trilogy that begins with *The Amulet of Samarkand* (*UBG* 16) or Stuart Hill's own saga about the struggle to control a land that begins with *The Cry of the Icemark* (*UBG* 76).

• Another wonderful series about magic and destiny is Alison Croggan's **Pellinor**, starting with *The Gift*.

This is a series in the finest tradition of children's storytelling. Wizards and witches do battle with an evil necromancer for the ultimate control of a magical land; a disguised princess and long-lost son appear precisely when they should, and wrongs are ultimately righted with a fine sense of poetic justice.

Angie Sage has a winning style that seizes the reader from the first page and bundles them along on a breathless adventure of brilliant excitement that will enthral its target audience from eight to 80. A superb read that should be enjoyed in a comfortable armchair along with a huge bar of chocolate and a beverage of the reader's choice.

**Stuart Hill**

# A SERIES OF UNFORTUNATE EVENTS  Lemony Snicket  ●●

Are you the kind of reader who likes to read about particularly bad, vicious and unfair things happening to a family of really very nice children, who might, let us say for the sake of argument, be called Violet, Klaus and Sunny Baudelaire? Are you the kind of reader who laughs out loud when truly terrible things happen to such pretty innocents? Are you the kind of reader who delights in identifying with really evil characters who might, say, be called Count Olaf? Then you will laugh and thrill at the sheer spookiness and outrageousness of these wonderfully entertaining books.

Do you like to look closely at spiky drawings made with a meticulous pencil and featuring people with beaky noses and side-whiskers? Do you seriously like to eat cold porridge for breakfast? Then this book and all its wonderfully clammy companion books, with their twisty plots and vile intrigues, are certainly the ones for you, gentle reader.

**Ian Beck**

### Next?

• For more hideous things happening to perfectly nice children, Philip Ardagh's books are always a good bet. Try *Awful End*. (*UBG* 96)

• For something dark, Dickensian and deeply wonderful, read F.E. Higgins's *The Black Book of Secrets*.

• Sam Llewellyn's books are all very funny and very strange. Try *Little Darlings* – I promise you the children are no such thing! (*UBG* 199)

★ ★ ★ ★ ★ ★

# SHADOW FOREST  Matt Haig  ●●

### Next?

•You might also enjoy *Sebastian Darke: Prince of Fools* by Philip Caveney. (*UBG* 300)

• Also, try *Varjak Paw* by S.F. Said, the story of a cat's journey to the Outside. (*UBG* 367)

• *Wolf Brother* by Michelle Paver has danger, superstition and a terrible quest. (*UBG* 390)

A brilliant blend of horror and humour with chills, thrills and blood spills. But don't break the rules!

Samuel and Martha do just that and enter the dreaded Shadow Forest inhabited by trolls, witches, bony-bodied huldres and other nightmare denizens of the dark.

So watch out for flying skullpeckers and give the truth pixie a wide berth! However, some trolls can be friendly and rabbit stew can be very tasty when cooked to perfection. But what if you find yourself changed into a rabbit? What if it's your turn to bubble and boil inside the pot?

Beware the Changemaker! Don't let the witch steal your shadow!

Too late... Now you'll have to read to the end of the book. But it'll be worth it!

**Joseph Delaney**

# SHADOWMANCER G.P. Taylor ●●●

**Next?**
• Try the sequel, *The Curse of Salamander Street*.
• For a series that combines horror, magic and history, try Jonathan Stroud's **Bartimaeus** trilogy, which starts with *The Amulet of Samarkand*. (*UBG* 16)
• Or for something set in a very different world that's terrifying and unique, try Alison Croggon's **Pellinor** series, starting with *The Gift*.

*Shadowmancer* is made up of danger, darkness and the power of belief. Set in the 1700s, it introduces a world both like and unlike our own. The people are recognisable, especially the almost-orphaned Thomas and tomboy Kate, but live in a truly dangerous place. It's not just full of highwaymen and smugglers, but also of a parson who wants to be God and crazed creatures who want to suck the life out of you.

Author G.P. Taylor is a vicar, and says that Philip Pullman inspired him to write. I wonder what Pullman thinks of the result, with its very strong and unapologetic message that following God is the right way, and that superstition and the quest for power are what's wrong with the world. The Christian message is not exactly subtle, but wrapped up in this gripping story of murder, violence, sorcery and the oldest of all battles, between good and evil, it works.

**Sarah Ebner**

★ ★ ★ ★ ★ ★

# THE SHAMAN BOY Caroline Pitcher ●●

Jez and Luka are orphans, victims of a cruel civil war in an imaginary eastern European country which seems locked in perpetual winter. Luka, who is going blind, sees visions of a mysterious Cloud Cat, a snow leopard, and feels compelled to follow it into the mountains. Jez, terrified that he'll lose his brother, struggles to find and save him – but does the real enemy lie elsewhere? And why is the frightening Vaskalia also in search of Luka and using witchcraft to find him?

This is a magical story of courage and love, a mixture of fairy tale and the grim reality of life in a war zone. It's beautifully written, with haunting images of snow, animals and homely village life.

This story was originally published as *Cloud Cat* and *Sky Shifter*.

**Ann Turnbull**

**Next?**
• This story made me think of *The Lion, the Witch and the Wardrobe* by C.S. Lewis. (*UBG* 198) It also has echoes of *Old Peter's Russian Tales* by Arthur Ransome – a wonderful collection of folk tales told by an old man to his grandchildren.
• The **Snow Spider** trilogy by Jenny Nimmo is a fantasy set in Wales, in which Gwyn uses the power of magic against ancient evil. (*UBG* 317)

# THE SHEEP-PIG  Dick King-Smith

### Next?
• Other Dick King-Smith books! Try *Dragon Boy*, about a boy adopted by dragons; or *Martin's Mice*, about a very unusual cat – he keeps mice as pets!

• *I, Jack* by Patricia Finney is a hilarious look at the world through an animal's eyes, as is *The World According to Humphrey* by Betty G. Birney. (*UBG* 392)

• Or try Philippa Pearce's *The Battle of Bubble and Squeak* in which a boy has to try and keep his pet gerbils – even though his mum would do anything to get rid of them. (*UBG* 29)

'"Mum," the little pig said to Fly, the dog who had adopted him and was teaching him the ways of the farm. "If you're a sheep-dog, why can't I be a sheep-pig?"'

There are many reasons: he is fat, he can't run fast enough, he is too polite to bully the sheep. But Babe, the little pig Farmer Hogget won at the fair, is determined.

This is an enchanting book. What I like particularly, though danger and even death are never far off, is the sheer niceness of the storytelling and the main characters. Dick King-Smith has given pigs the credit they deserve and which was long overdue. Basically one simple but brilliant idea, and beautifully written. A modern classic.

**Alan Temperley**

★ ★ ★ ★ ★ ★

# THE SHIP BETWEEN THE WORLDS
## Julia Golding

Anyone with a vivid imagination will identify with David, the young hero of Julia Golding's exciting novel, who finds his wildest dreams coming to life aboard the mysterious ship the *Golden Needle*. David may belong to our own world, and speak and think like a boy in any modern playground, but his adventures take him into the intermingled realms of history and science fiction. He meets an alarming array of crewmen and pirates, humans and aliens, and has a hard time working out whom he can trust. As the threads come together, he begins to believe in himself more, and also finds that his adventures have been leading him closer to his missing father. This is a funny and exciting read, with lots of clever ideas and colourful characters.

**Paul Bajoria**

### Next?
• Julia Golding is always worth reading. Try the **Cat Royal** books, starting with *The Diamond of Drury Lane*. (*UBG* 83)

• Try *Vampirates* by Justin Somper for more gruesome pirate – along with vampire – thrills. (*UBG* 366)

• *Breathe: A Ghost Story* by Cliff McNish is a really chilling story with another believable boy hero.

# SHORT STORIES H.G. Wells

This is a brilliant book full of terrific stories, like 'The Man Who Could Work Miracles'. Many of the stories are what we would call science fiction today, but others, like 'The Country of the Blind', are just very strange tales of men or women who wander into a land where no one has been before. 'The Door in the Wall', for example, is about a man who keeps discovering a door to a beautiful place by accident, but when he purposely tries to find it, he can't.

There's a sort of unusual magic about these stories which you can't define, but which is completely fascinating. I read them when I was about 12 and I'm still rereading them today.

**Garry Kilworth**

**Next?**
• *The Invisible Man* is another excellent H.G. Wells book. (*UBG* 176)
• For something spooky, read M.R. James – if you can do so without being scared, you must have the courage of a cougar. Look for collections of his short stories.
• Try Edgar Allan Poe, an American writer of weird tales from the 1800s. Start with *The Raven*. Very scary!
• Robert Westall was a modern writer of good short stories. Try his collection *Break of Dark*.

★ ★ ★ ★ ★ ★

# SIDEWAYS STORIES FROM WAYSIDE SCHOOL
## Louis Sachar

**Next?**
• Oooh, I hate picking favourites – there are so many great books around – but *Utterly Me, Clarice Bean*, and the whole **Clarice Bean** series by Lauren Child is great. (*UBG* 365)
• More very funny stories are in the **Astrosaurs** books by Steve Cole. (*UBG* 25)
• And if you're feeling very brainy, there's *Sideways Arithmetic from Wayside School: More than 50 Brain-teasing Maths Puzzles*.

All schools are weird. But Wayside School is weirder than most.

Mr Gorf has an unfortunate habit of sucking up pupils' voices with his third nostril. Miss Nogard has three ears and can eavesdrop on kids' brains. And what is that cow doing in Miss Zarves's classroom, particularly when Miss Zarves and her classroom do not really exist?

These laugh-out-loud stories are so funny and cleverly written that my nine-year-old daughter has read and reread them.

(I myself had to read chapter 17 of *Wayside School is Falling Down* THREE TIMES before I realised that it didn't make sense unless you started at the end and read the whole thing backwards.)

Them recommend really I.

**Cressida Cowell**

# THE SILVER SPOON OF SOLOMON SNOW  Kaye Umansky

**Next?**

• *Solomon Snow and the Stolen Jewel* is the sequel.

• *You're a Bad Man, Mr Gum!* by Andy Stanton is the first of a very funny series. (*UBG* 397)

• Araminta Spook meets villains, too – along with spooks, spiders and vampires! Read about her in Angie Sage's *Araminta Spook: My Haunted House*. (*UBG* 22)

Solomon Snow discovers his parents aren't his parents at all and sets out to discover his true identity. He is accompanied by the outspoken and enormously nosed Prudence Pridy, and also by the Prodigy, a little girl who can scream the house down and quite often does. On their way to discovering Solomon's destiny, they have several funny and dangerous adventures. They meet vagabonds and villains galore and get into all sorts of scrapes, yet somehow never manage to rid themselves of the Prodigy.

The story is carried along by sparkling dialogue, witty asides and a vividly vile Victorian atmosphere. (In other words, it's gloomy and raining and their shoes hurt.) Great fun, and with a surprise ending, too!

**Jeremy Strong**

★ ★ ★ ★ ★ ★

# THE SILVER SWORD  Ian Serraillier

**Next?**

• For another brilliant story of wartime survival, try *I Am David* by Anne Holm. (*UBG* 164)

• Esther Hautzig's *The Endless Steppe* is an evocative, memorable depiction of living through a war. (*UBG* 100)

• The short and brilliant *Hatchet* by Gary Paulsen, about survival and hope. (*UBG* 146)

• For a very different kind of survival, try *Broken Glass*. (*UBG* 48)

'The children scrounged what food they could...'

Your dad has been imprisoned. You don't know if your mother is alive. For years you and three other children have been surviving on your own in war-torn Europe. Only sheer courage and resourcefulness have kept you alive. And now, hungry and ill, you have a long journey ahead of you...

This extraordinary and simply written book is based on a true story, and is one of the most powerful novels of its kind ever written.

**Cliff McNish**

# SILVERFIN

### Charlie Higson

Everyone knows about James Bond. But do you know what he got up to at school? Much of *SilverFin* takes place at Eton, but the main action then moves to Loch Silverfin in Scotland where young Bond is pitted against a sadistic – and delightfully bonkers – villain.

The story is realistic and gripping, but with an edge of the bizarre – like the best of the original 007 books and films. James has to rely on his wits and his abilities more than gadgets and luck as he struggles against both the mundane – school bullies – and the fantastic – blood-sucking eels!

Pacy and exciting, the part of the book set at Eton is the most realistic, but it's in the second half where the adrenalin really gets going!

**Justin Richards**

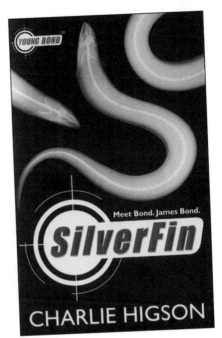

## Boys' Adventures for the Twenty-first Century

- **CHERUB** series by Robert Muchamore
- *Young Samurai* by Chris Bradford
- **Alex Rider** series by Anthony Horowitz
- **Jimmy Coates** series by Joe Craig
- *The Death Collector* by Justin Richards
- **H.I.V.E.** series by Mark Walden
- *GIO: Venom Rising* by Gary Murray
- *Greek Ransom* by Michael Malaghan
- **The Joshua Files** series by M.G. Harris
- *39 Clues: Maze of Bones* by Rick Riordan
- *Code Red: Flash Flood* by Chris Ryan
- **S.T.O.R.M.** series by E.L. Young
- *Thieves Like Us* by Stephen Cole

## Next?

- Young James Bond continues his adventures in *Blood Fever*, *Double or Die*, *Hurricane Gold* and *By Royal Command*.
- Look out for terrific children's novels from top adult thriller writers Chris Ryan, Andy McNab and Jack Higgins. Start with McNab's **Boy Soldier** series.
- Or try Robert Muchamore's compelling **CHERUB** novels, starting with *The Recruit* (*UBG* 60), or Anthony Horowitz's superb **Alex Rider** series (*UBG* 12).

# THE SILVERWING SAGA  Kenneth Oppel

**Next?**

• The saga consists of: *Silverwing*, *Sunwing*, *Firewing* and *Darkwing*. You might like to try *Dead Water Zone*, an earlier, sci-fi-ish novel by Kenneth Oppel, peopled by humans.

• For another unusual animal angle, Morris Gleitzman's *Toad Rage* (and the sequels *Toad Heaven* and *Toad Away*) chronicles the quest of Limpy, the slightly squashed cane toad, to find out whether humans really do hate his species.

Bats have generally had a bad press – think of all those vampires and haunted belfries – but in this gripping trilogy, the story of Shade the Silverwing bat, who begins life as the runt of his colony and finishes as an honoured hero, the balance is powerfully redressed.

The books have cracking stories, brimming with adventures, full of stunningly imaginative flights of invention and fabulously gothic set-pieces, and boasting a truly formidable villain in the mighty Goth. They are based on natural history and bat myths, which Kenneth Oppel plundered and expanded to create his own bat universe and mythology.

As the trilogy progresses, it becomes richer, deeper and fearless in tackling complexities. The writing is of such quality that you share the characters' thoughts, you fly with them – but without ever forgetting they are bats.

**Chris Stephenson**

★ ★ ★ ★ ★ ★

# SIMONE series  Helena Pielichaty

These books are fun because they are not written in a normal storytelling kind of way. Instead, they're made up of Simone's letters to all kinds of people – as well as their replies – extracts from her school diary and questionnaires and entries from her very own website. You get to know Simone very well, in her own words, and she can really make you laugh. Each book tells a story without you noticing, about things which are recognisable and true to life: having divorced parents, changing schools, making new friends, asthma attacks and trips to toffee factories! Sometimes the writing does sound a bit like an adult writing, not that of a ten-year-old, and you might find that a bit annoying – but try them and judge for yourself.

**Abigail Anderson**

**Next?**

• The **Simone** books are: *Simone's Letters*, *Simone's Diary* and *Simone's Website*.

• *Starring Brody as the Model from the States* is another book by the same author, this time in the **After School Club** series.

• Try *The Turbulent Term of Tyke Tiler* for a funny school story. (*UBG* 357)

• *Utterly Me, Clarice Bean* is another great story about a girl. (*UBG* 365)

# SKELLIG  David Almond

I read this story in a day – and it took my breath away. It's a story that picks you up and swirls you around on wings of delight. In other words, it's a terrific read!

Michael's baby sister is ill and she might die. Whilst this family drama is going on, Michael finds Skellig in his garage – a down-and-out creature with a love of Chinese food. But is Skellig good or evil? Is he there to help or harm?

With the help of his friend Mina, Michael learns about life from the creature, who in turn is redeemed through his new friends. The whole story is so unpredictable – which I love. But throughout it all, you're aware that it's a story about the celebration of life, even in the midst of death. The book is moving without being maudlin, and its magic shines off each and every page. *Skellig* really is a book to savour.

**Malorie Blackman**

You'll never forget Skellig. I'm sure you won't. And after you've met him, you may wish to find a creature like him in your garage as well, though the first glimpse Michael gets of him is not very tempting: 'He was filthy and pale and dried out and I thought he was dead'. Well, he isn't. Skellig's wings are covered in cracked and crooked feathers and he likes Chinese food; he eats spiders and has dead bluebottles in his hair.

*Skellig* is one of those stories you want to read aloud to yourself to taste it on your tongue. David Almond paints pictures with just a few words. He paints them onto your skin and into your heart. You'll hear Skellig's croaking voice. You'll see Doctor Death driving up to the house in his car. You'll feel the feverish skin of Michael's little sister under your own fingertips, when he sneaks into his parents' bedroom to look at her. And you'll meet Mina, who knows much about birds and how to be a friend. In short – this book is pure storytelling magic.

**Cornelia Funke**

## Next?

• Read more David Almond: *Kit's Wilderness* (*UBG* 192), *The Fire-Eaters* (*UBG* 113), *Heaven Eyes* (*UBG* 149) and *Counting Stars* (*UBG* 73) are all wonderful.

• *Whistle Down the Wind* by Mary Hayley Bell is about a group of children who find a man they believe is Jesus.

• Another story about what having faith can mean is Michael Morpurgo's *The War of Jenkins' Ear*. (*UBG* 374)

# SKULDUGGERY PLEASANT Derek Landy

## Next?
• The sequels! The first is *Skulduggery Pleasant: Playing with Fire*.

• More horror? Read Darren Shan: either **The Saga of Darren Shan** (*UBG* 293) or the much gorier **The Demonata** series.

• There's more sinister secrets and walking nightmares in Tom Becker's *Darkside*. (*UBG* 79)

• *Triskellion* by Will Peterson is a nail-bitingly thrilling mystery centred on a sinister village.

• Another extraordinary book set in Ireland is Kate Thompson's *The New Policeman*. (*UBG* 249)

The mad cover made me pick it up. The first sentence ('Gordon Edgley's sudden death came as a shock to everyone – not least himself.') reeled me in. This one is really, really different – a cross between a detective thriller, a horror story and a heroic fantasy. The central character's a 12-year-old girl called Stephanie. There's also a private eye who is an animated skeleton. Together they chase the Sceptre of the Ancients, a magical weapon much sought after by the bad guys. The action is fast, the wisecracks are great and the pace never lets up. You'll love it. It's like nothing I've ever read before. I swallowed it whole. Give yourself a treat and do the same.

**Herbie Brennan**

★ ★ ★ ★ ★ ★

# SLEEPOVERS
## Jacqueline Wilson

Daisy loves sleepover parties, and all the other girls in the Alphabet Club (Amy, Bella, Chloe, Daisy and Emily – get it?) are having them on their birthdays.

But Daisy has two big problems. One is that Chloe doesn't like her at all, and she's not the kind of girl who's too shy to say so. The other is that Daisy feels very unsure about whether she wants to have a sleepover party herself when her turn comes around. She has a secret at home that she hasn't told her friends – and she doesn't know what they'll do if they discover it.

You'll find yourself really rooting for Daisy as you read the book. It's a great story for anyone who has ever felt nervous about what other people might think of them – so it's for everyone, in fact!

**Susan Reuben**

## Next?
• Other great Jacqueline Wilson books? Try **The Cat Mummy** and **The Worry Website**.

• A funny series about a girl and her cat starts with **Molly and Mimi** by Sarah Horne.

• Or try Judy Blume's **The Paint and the Great One**, about a brother and sister.

• Anne Fine's **The Angel of Nitshill Road** captures the complications and fun of friendship. (*UBG* 18)

# SMITH  Leon Garfield  ●●

A marvellous book. Garfield-land is nineteenth-century London, and no one knows it better.

Smith is 12, small, filthy, sharp as a needle, top of his trade (he's a pickpocket). Pity he can't read, especially when his latest haul is a document acquired in a dark alley from a confused old gentleman. A minute later, the old man is murdered by two roughs. Enraged by the victim's empty pockets (where's the document?) they glimpse the escaping Smith. Of course! The little rat has not only nabbed the prize – but he has seen the murder. A long hunt for the boy begins...

Meanwhile, a benevolent family offers to teach Smith to read. He's cleaned up; his rags are burnt. But where's the paper? Why is Smith cast into Newgate? And more...

**Naomi Lewis**

### Next?
• More Leon Garfield! Start with *Black Jack* (*UBG* 36) or *The Apprentices* (*UBG* 20).
• For more historical fiction, how about Joan Aiken's *Midnight is a Place*? (*UBG* 227)
• You might enjoy Chris Priestley's *Death and the Arrow*. (*UBG* 81)
• You could also try Charles Dickens – if you want pickpockets, go for *Oliver Twist*, of course.

★ ★ ★ ★ ★ ★

# SNAKEHEAD  Ann Halam  ●●●

### Next?
• Ann Halam's books are always challenging, thought provoking and exciting. They often blend science into the mix. Try *Dr Franklin's Island*, about experimental genetic engineering, or the futuristic *Taylor Five*.
• Rick Riordan's **Percy Jackson** series also brings myth up to date. (*UBG* 262)
• Or look for Katherine Langrish's *Troll Fell*. (*UBG* 353)

If you've been on holiday to the Mediterranean, you'll recognise this world – the little waterfront cafés and restaurants, the ferry boats coming and going between the islands... But this is 2,500 years ago, and the hero is a real hero – the legendary Perseus.

Perseus knows about refugees – he's one himself. When a whole boatload of them disembarks on his little island, he befriends a beautiful girl and gets her a job. But Andromeda is god-touched – a sacrificial victim fleeing her appointed destiny. And Perseus himself, half-divine, is being used by his supernatural relatives, the Achaean gods, for their own mysterious purposes. Soon Perseus, Andromeda and the Yacht Club Boys are on their way to steal the Gorgon's snaky head, whose gaze turns men to stone.

A wonderfully unexpected and vivid makeover of an old legend!

**Katherine Langrish**

# THE SNAKE-STONE Berlie Doherty

Have you ever wondered whether your parents actually wanted you to be born? James has. Although he's always known he's adopted and loves his adoptive parents very much, he can't help wondering about his real mother and why she gave him away, leaving behind only a strange stone wrapped in a tatty old torn envelope with half an almost-illegible address on it.

When he's pushed just too hard in a top-class diving competition and starts quarrelling with his family, James decides he must find out who he really is and why his mother left, using the address as a clue to where he might find her.

All through the book, James's mother tells her own side of the story, making this a gripping read full of people with feelings about what makes us who we are.

**Eileen Armstrong**

### Next?
• In Berlie Doherty's *Holly Starcross*, Holly doesn't know who she is, either, and when her father suddenly comes back into her life she must make hard decisions about where she belongs.

• Anne Fine's *Step by Wicked Step* is a spooky story of five children thrown together in a creepy old castle, who each tell their own stepfamily stories.

• Children who run away from their care home, and survive through their friendship, are the focus of David Almond's *Heaven Eyes*. (*UBG* 149)

★ ★ ★ ★ ★ ★

# SNATCHED!
## Graham Marks

### Next?
• Look for more Graham Marks. Most of his stuff is older, but have a go at *Kai-Ro*, a futuristic thriller set in a city with pyramids.

• There are more startlingly strange circus adventures in Jon Berkeley's *The Palace of Laughter* and Karen Wallace's *The Unrivalled Spangles*.

• Another boy who has adventures with lions can be found in Zouzou Corder's *Lionboy*. (*UBG* 199)

The Time: 1855; the Place: Victorian England, where a travelling circus has taken in an orphan boy who was abandoned in a lion's cage. A boy with both talent and mysterious visions that haunt his dreams. Who is he, really, and why is the truth so dangerous?

A rollicking, grand tale in the richly detailed tradition of Charles Dickens and Robert Louis Stevenson. There are acrobats, equestrians and clowns, there are oddities, animals and strongmen, as well as illustrations to stimulate the imagination. *Snatched!* is a perfect time machine, in that it takes you to a specific place in the past and makes you believe you're really there, sharing the wild, suspenseful adventures.

**Rodman Philbrick**

# THE SNOW GOOSE Paul Gallico ●●●

**Next?**
• Paul Gallico had a knack for writing books that have a huge emotional impact. Try *The Small Miracle* or the slightly longer *Thomasina*, which, if you love animals, will have you entranced; and you can read about his novel *Jennie* on p. 180.

• *The Dolphin Crossing* by Jill Paton Walsh involves the British retreat from Dunkirk. (*UBG* 89)

• And why not try Michael Morpurgo's own *Why the Whales Came*? (*UBG* 382)

I grew up on the wild, marshy east coast where this extraordinary book is set. There was always wind, and the North Sea was always brown and soupy. I remember I used to watch geese fly over, and there was an old man, a recluse, who lived in a shack by the sea wall and who frightened us. Then much later I read *The Snow Goose*. It was as if Paul Gallico had grown up in my place. Here was the same strange landscape, and even a recluse who shunned the world. The story reads like non fiction, and is utterly convincing. It's about a young girl who, in the saving of a wounded snow goose, breaks down the barriers and comes to know and trust the recluse. Here is a tale of tenderness, of friendship and of loss, into which war ultimately intrudes to bring sadness and absence, as it so often does.

**Michael Morpurgo**

★ ★ ★ ★ ★ ★

# THE SNOW SPIDER Jenny Nimmo ●●●

On her brother Gwyn's fifth birthday, Bethan climbed the mountain. She was never seen again. Now, four years later, as Gwyn turns nine, his grandmother announces, 'Time to find out if you are a magician!' The strange collection of objects she gives him includes Bethan's scarf, thought missing since her disappearance. But does he really have the power to get his heart's desire and bring his sister home again?

The appearance of a mysterious silver spider, Gwyn's sudden ability to floor a playground bully without touching him, and the extraordinary visions he sees on the mountain are just the beginning. Gwyn finds he must test his new found powers to the limit as he's drawn into an ancient battle against terrible evil.

**Thomas Bloor**

**Next?**
• Look for the next titles in the trilogy: *Emlyn's Moon* and *The Chestnut Soldier*.

• Alan Garner based his book *The Owl Service* on an old Welsh myth, played out in modern time. (*UBG* 258)

• Kevin Crossley-Holland's *The Seeing Stone*, set in medieval England, depicts a boy who, like Gwyn, has to try to balance the events of his own life with a magical parallel life. (*UBG* 304)

• Or try Thomas Bloor's own terrifically exciting trilogy that starts with *The Worm in the Blood*.

## The Ultimate Readers' Poll

# Top Ten Book Villains

1. **Voldemort**
   (Harry Potter series)

2. **Cruella De Vil**
   (The Hundred and One Dalmatians)

3. **Count Olaf**
   (A Series of Unfortunate Events)

4. **Sauron**
   (The Lord of the Rings)

5. **Mrs Trunchbull**
   (Matilda)

6=. **Mrs Coulter**
   (His Dark Materials trilogy)

6=. **Shere Khan**
   (The Jungle Books)

8. **Captain Hook**
   (Peter Pan)

9. **The Tar Man**
   (Gideon the Cutpurse)

10. **Sidorio**
   (Vampirates series)

## The SNOW-WALKER trilogy  Catherine Fisher

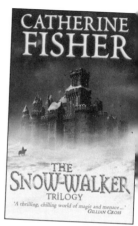

Set in the far North, long ago, these books create a world where the everyday and the fantastic exist side by side.

Jessa's life changes dramatically when she is sent into exile by Gudrun, wicked Queen of the Snow-walker people. The books follow Jessa as she meets Kari, the Snow-walker's son, who is both feared and hated by his mother. Together, Jessa, Kari and a small group of friends battle to defeat Gudrun and free Jessa's people.

These books combine the small details of everyday life in the North with references to the Norse sagas. One moment Jessa and her friends are taking part in a feast in the Jarlshold and the next they are barring the doors in a futile attempt to keep out Gudrun's magic. If you love stories about magic and the struggle of good over evil, then these are just the books for you.

**Laura Hutchings**

### Next?

• The trilogy comprises *The Snow-walker's Son*, *The Empty Hand* and *The Soul Thieves*.

• Catherine Fisher has also written a wonderful quartet called **The Book of the Crow**. (*UBG* 41) These are fantasy books, but if you want something rooted in the real world with a hint of legend about it then try her *Corbenic*. (*UBG* 72)

• Or try the epic series that starts with *The Cry of the Icemark* by Stuart Hill. (*UBG* 76)

# THE SONG OF PENTECOST W.J. Corbett ●●

'An astonishing achievement. I read it with delight.' That's what Roald Dahl said about this book, and he was dead right.

The hero is Pentecost, a small, strange harvest mouse, who has the huge responsibility of leading his tribe away from pollution to a new home in Lickey Top. The individuality and quirkiness of the characters really grab you and won't let you go. There's a lying frog, a highly unreliable snake, a couple of voles and a host of other animals – my favourite is the very fat owl whose life is haunted by a Dreadful Crime. There's a lot of humour, but the story's scary and touching too – and it really makes you think about why folk behave the way they do.

**Vivian French**

> ### Next?
> • There are two sequels: *Pentecost and the Chosen One* and *Pentecost of Lickey Top*.
> • I thought of suggesting Robert C. O'Brien's *Mrs Frisby and the Rats of NIMH*, an older mouse adventure; but maybe they're too alike. What do you think? (*UBG* 239)
> • For more mice and a very involving story, read Russell Hoban's *The Mouse and His Child*. (*UBG* 236)

★ ★ ★ ★ ★ ★

# SONG OF THE LIONESS series Tamora Pierce ●●

> ### Next?
> • The series consists of: *Alanna: the First Adventure, In the Hand of the Goddess, The Woman Who Rides Like a Man* and *Lioness Rampant*. Alanna also appears in **The Immortals** quartet. *Daughter of the Lioness* is about Aly, Alanna's daughter. **Protector of the Small** is another series set in the same world.
> • The **Beca Cooper: A Tortall Legend** books are set at an earlier period of the same history; *Terrier* comes first.
> • Or try Tamora Pierce's books set in a different universe: **The Circle of Magic** quartet.

The second book in the **Song of the Lioness** series, *In the Hand of the Goddess*, continues the story of Alanna of Trebond, a girl who wants to be a knight. She switches places with her brother Thom, and she becomes Alan of Trebond. But it's not easy. To become a knight, Alanna has to learn court manners, history, algebra, how to use magic, how to fight and how to protect herself. In her first year of training she makes new friends – the heir to the throne and the 'King of Thieves' among others – and she makes enemies, too.

It's exciting to read how Alanna proves herself again and again as she struggles to achieve her goal. Then I'm sure you'll want to read the other three books, in which Alanna sees battle as a squire and a knight, lives among desert people and rescues a princess.

**Julia Lytollis**

# SOPHIE AND THE ALBINO CAMEL  Stephen Davies

**Next?**

• Move on to the sequels, *Sophie and the Locust Curse* and *Sophie and the Pancake Plot*.

• Richard Hamilton's books also combine adventure with humour. Try *Violet and the Mean and Rotten Pirates*. (*UBG* 370)

• If you want a more challenging adventure that's lots of fun, read *A Dog Called Grk* by Joshua Doder, about a boy who finds a stray dog that takes him on an adventure to eastern Europe. (*UBG* 87)

Sophie is the only white child in Gorom-Gorom and she feels like an outsider. Then she makes friends with Gidaado the Fourth. Gidaado doesn't go to school; he's a griot – a professional storyteller.

Sophie ignores her father's words: 'Never mess with the Sahara desert!' and sets off with Gidaado on the back of Chobbal, his beautiful white camel. What she doesn't know is that the murderous Moussa ag Litni lurks in the desert. He's a notorious camel stealer who likes chasing his victims before catching them and stealing their camels – so he wears a bell to give them a chance to run away…

This story by the brilliant Stephen Davies is as funny as it is gripping, and Sophie proves herself to be a brave and resourceful heroine.

**Susan Reuben**

★ ★ ★ ★ ★ ★

# SPACE DEMONS  Gillian Rubinstein

It all begins when Andrew's dad comes home from Japan and gives him a prototype of a new computer game…

I love this thriller! When you put it down, don't think you're going to get to sleep. Your palms are sweaty and your heart is beating fast. You're like the kids in the story, so involved with the 'Space Demons' computer game, they can't leave it alone.

The 12-year-old characters seem familiar: cool Andrew, Ben and mad Mario. Through the game you get to know them much better as the unpredictable, sinister force overtakes their lives.

Rubinstein, a masterful writer, was at the cutting edge when she wrote this story in 1986 and it's as strong as ever today. Whether you're a keen reader or not, *read this book*! But first make sure you're not alone in the house.

**Elizabeth Honey**

**Next?**

• The trilogy continues with *Skymaze* and *Shinkei*.

• Or try the **Legendeer** trilogy by Alan Gibbons, another series about gaming and its possibilities!

• A very funny story about two boys who find a spacecraft is *Aquila* by Andrew Norriss. (*UBG* 21)

# THE SPIDERWICK CHRONICLES

Tony DiTerlizzi and Holly Black

Nobody ever asks Jared's opinion about anything, but if they did he'd tell them he didn't think much of leaving New York for his great-aunt's crumbling Gothic mansion in the middle of nowhere. That's even before strange things start happening – sudden disappearances, peculiar noises, mysterious accidents...

The Grace children (all gaunt arms, glaring eyes and sticky-out ears in DiTerlizzi's quirky drawings) are a delicious combination of grumpiness and pluck. They can find a secret room, no problem, and grapple with the issue of their parents' divorce. But they are not impervious to the strains of sibling rivalry – which is what clinches it for me. The bonding is good, but the bickering is even better.

**Sabine Durrant**

**Next?**

• There's a second series by the same authors about Spiderwick: **Beyond the Spiderwick Chronicles**, which begins with *Nixie's Song*.

• Clemency Pogue thinks she loves fairies – until she meets one! Read about her adventures in *Clemency Pogue: Fairy Killer* and its sequels, all by J.T. Petty.

• Or for a book about a boy who finds a magic coin and the adventures that follow, try Edward Eager's *Half Magic*. (*UBG* 141)

★ ★ ★ ★ ★ ★

# SPILLED WATER  Sally Grindley

**Next?**

• Sally Grindley writes books that make you think – and cry – read *Broken Glass* next. (*UBG* 48)

• Adeline Yen Mah's *A Chinese Cinderella* is the story of one unwanted girl. (*UBG* 63) Or look for *First Girl* by Gloria Whelan, which is about 14-year-old Chu Ju, who leaves home rather than allow her baby sister to be given away.

• Women once had a hard time in England, too – read *Emily Davison: The Girl Who Gave Her Life for Her Cause* by Claudia Fitzherbert, to find out about some women who were determined to change that.

Lu Si-yan lives in a tiny village. There's no money for luxuries, like televison or a car, but her father grows the tastiest vegetables, and she has a little brother she loves. When her father dies, everything falls apart, and heartless Uncle Ba decides Si-yan must be sold as a servant. The most painful part of this story is when Si-yan's uncle takes her to market, and she has no idea what's going on. The best part is the kindness and courage that she meets along the way as she struggles to survive. The worst part is that this isn't make-believe. Things like this happen in China, right now. An inspiring story, because Si-yan is a fantastic character. She never gives up.

**Ann Halam**

# THE SPOOK'S APPRENTICE  Joseph Delaney  ● ● ●

The warning on the back of *The Spook's Apprentice*, 'Not to be read after dark', made me smile knowingly until I began reading it one night. Once I'd started, it didn't seem quite so funny any more and I wished I were reading the book in daylight when all seems much safer – but once I had started, I knew I couldn't stop.

As the seventh son of a seventh son, becoming a Spook's apprentice is Thomas's destiny. He takes on a job which is frightening, lonely and very dangerous for a young boy. Thomas moves into the Spook's house, which is protected by curses, run by invisible boggarts and full of horrifying spectres such as the most evil witch in the country, Mother Malkin. The witches prey on Thomas's inexperience, wreaking havoc and causing him a whole world of trouble that he must clear up. But can he do it without the Spook's help?

The stifling atmosphere Delaney creates makes you feel claustrophobic as you witness Thomas trying to deal with boggarts, ghosts, witches and their living graves.
**Rhian Tracey**

**Next?**
• There are more in the **Wardstone Chronicles**: *The Spook's Curse*, *The Spook's Secret*, *The Spook's Battle* and *The Spook's Mistake*.
• Read anything by Marcus Sedgwick, who writes beautifully about the supernatural. My favourites are *My Swordhand is Singing* (*UBG* 245) and **The Dead Days** trilogy.
• Or try the scary, unsettling *The Beguilers* by Kate Thompson.

★ ★ ★ ★ ★ ★

# SPY DOG  Andrew Cope  ●

**Next?**
• The next in the series! *Spy Dog 2* and *Spy Dog Unleashed*.
• Or you can have mice that spy, in Heather Vogel Frederick's very funny and exciting **Spy Mice** series.
• A famous dog and his boy detective appear in Hergé's **Tintin** books. (*UBG* 349)
• Or try the funny adventures in Anthony Horowitz's **Diamond Brothers** detective series. (*UBG* 108)

Lara looks like a normal dog, but she's really a Licensed Assault and Rescue Animal, a top Secret Service agent who can understand five languages, send emails and even drive a car. After she cracks a drug-smuggling ring, Lara turns herself in to the RSPCA, planning to go undercover with an ordinary family until her bosses come to rescue her. But when your instinct is to fight crime and rescue people in trouble, pretending to be a house pet isn't easy.

There's plenty of humour as Ben, Sophie and Ollie try to hide their new dog's amazing abilities, and excitement as the criminal ringleader, Mr Big, comes looking for Lara, intent on revenge...
**Madelyn Travis**

# SQUASHED    Joan Bauer

## Next?

• Read *Rules of the Road* – another great story by Joan Bauer. (*UBG* 290)

• *Ruby Holler* by Sharon Creech will get you laughing, and maybe crying, too. (*UBG* 288)

• If you love *Squashed* as much as I do, then search for Kate DiCamillo's *Because of Winn-Dixie*. (*UBG* 30) They're both American; is there something in the American air that makes for brilliant writers?

This is such a fantastic book that I've never understood why it hasn't won every prize going. It makes me laugh out loud every time I read it, and it also makes me really truly feel good about myself and the world ... and it does it with a pumpkin as the main character! Weird? Yes.

I'd never have believed a story about growing a giant pumpkin to win a competition could be so completely unputdownable, but this is. Ellie, the girl who's doing the growing, is so real – and she's incredibly funny in the way she describes the dreadful Cyril Pool (her rival), her mad-as-a-chair father, her ups and downs with gorgeous Wes ... and the fact that she eats too much ice cream and her jeans are VERY stretched...

READ IT! It's perfect for any reader who's looking for 186 pages packed with zinging humour and a warm glow. (Well, there are 186 pages in my copy...)

**Vivian French**

★ ★ ★ ★ ★

# THE STAR OF KAZAN    Eva Ibbotson

●●

This is one of those books that stays with you long after you've read the last page. It's set in the Vienna of pastries and Lippizaner horses – the ones skilled in dressage – and so full of convincing detail that when I'd read it, I wanted to book my ticket to Austria to see it all for myself!

Annika, abandoned as a baby in a church by her desperate mother, is rescued by Ellie and Sigrid and taken home to their masters, the three professors who live together in a grand house. All through her childhood there, Annika longs to find her real mother. When she befriends an old lady, the owner of a beautiful jewel, the Star of Kazan, Annika is drawn into dangerous adventures, as she explores her own past. I couldn't put it down!

**Pauline Chandler**

## Next?

• Eva Ibbotson's *Secret Countess* is wonderful. (*UBG* 300) As is her *Journey to the River Sea*. (*UBG* 184)

• There's more history and horses in K.M. Grant's *Blood Red Horse*. (*UBG* 40)

• The **Lady Violet Mysteries** by Karen Wallace, starting with *Secret of the Crocodiles*, are about a girl who finds herself involved in strange happenings.

# STARGIRL Jerry Spinelli

## Next?

• Jerry Spinelli has also written a sequel: *Love: Stargirl*, which is a year-long letter from Stargirl to Leo – after she moves away from Arizona. Or try *Loser*, about a boy who's a bit different from the crowd. (*UBG* 212)

• *Firegirl* by Tony Abbott centres on the characters and problems of a typical classroom – with the addition of a girl who has been burned terribly in a fire.

• *Saffy's Angel* by Hilary McKay is a book about finding out who you are – and being happy with it. (*UBG* 292)

Stargirl is different. So different from all the others in her new school that she first attracts everyone's interest and admiration with her outrageous outfits and free-living style. She's everything they're not: genuinely non-conformist (not just a rebel) and a true individual. She's undeniably unique and everyone loves her. Leo Borlock, a classmate, is totally smitten.

However, no one knows what to make of Stargirl, and it doesn't take long for her very differentness to set her apart and for the admiration to turn into something nasty. In desperation and embarrassment at being seen with her, Leo tries to persuade her to become what would ultimately destroy her – a normal girl.

**Chris d'Lacey**

★ ★ ★ ★ ★ ★

# STEP INTO THE DARK Bridget Crowley

Bridget Crowley's brilliant first novel is a spine-tingling ghost story, a touching tale of friendship and a tough, realistic look at bullying.

Beetle (great name) lives with his mother up nine dirty, shadowy flights of tower-block stairs, but spends most of his time down at the Hall with his friends, working the lighting for the community shows. He loves it. Best of all, he gets to light the spellbinding song sung by beautiful Tamar – but his friendship with her gets him into trouble. She's a Kurd, and there are people around who don't appreciate her family settling in their town...

But as if that weren't enough for Beetle to worry about, when he goes up the winding stairs to the balcony to work the lighting rig, he sees a young girl in the gallery, leaning out over the rickety handrail. Every time he goes up to the balcony, she's there, too. Or is she?

**Daniel Hahn**

## Next?

• Bridget Crowley has also written a gripping historical novel entitled *Feast of Fools* and a ballet story with a supernatural twist, *Harriet's Ghost*.

• *The Rinaldi Ring* by Jenny Nimmo is another book in which the past and present blur. (*UBG* 285)

• A gritty, gripping bullying story, *The Present Takers* by Aidan Chambers, makes for unsettling reading.

# STIG OF THE DUMP Clive King

While staying with his grandparents in the country, Barney goes exploring in the off-limits local chalk-pit. He falls over the edge and drops into the world of Stig, a caveboy living amongst the junk that has been dumped in the quarry. Despite their having no shared language, Barney and Stig become instant friends.

Though Barney speaks openly about his new friend in front of his sister and grandparents, his tales are dismissed as the wild imaginings of a young boy. And so Stig remains his secret. Barney feels protective towards him, but more often than not it is the caveboy who comes to the assistance of the contemporary boy. It is a beautifully drawn friendship.

A classic tale in timeless prose, from the very beginning this story takes unexpected twists, and it's packed with adventure and mystery through to the end. If you're anywhere between eight and 12, this book is a must-read for you.

**Neil Arksey**

**Next?**
• For something with a similar feel to it, try Joan Aiken's *The Wolves of Willoughby Chase*. (*UBG* 391)
• Another Clive King, *Me and My Million* (out of print but worth hunting down a copy if you can), is really good, too.
• Or for an hilarious and thought-provoking look at what it must have been like to be a caveman, read *A is for Aarrgh!* by William J. Brooke.

★ ★ ★ ★ ★ ★

# A STITCH IN TIME Penelope Lively

**Next?**
• Try Penelope Lively's other, more famous time-slip story, *The Ghost of Thomas Kempe*. (*UBG* 125)
• Or for more modern ghostly stories, try *The Ghost Behind the Wall* by Melvin Burgess (*UBG* 124) or *Cry in the Dark* by Dee Shulman, a chilling time-slip adventure.
• Or try Henry Chancellor's *The Museum's Secret: The Remarkable Adventures of Tom Scatterhorn*, a fast-paced story that twists time.

A gentle and beautifully written ghost story about a girl called Maria, a quiet and perceptive only child who goes on holiday with her parents to an old – and as it turns out, very unusual – house. At first, Maria is rather overawed by the bouncy family next door. She has acute reasoning, often making the reader pause during the story and think, 'How true that is.' Penelope Lively's prose makes no concession to the fact that she's writing for children, and you finish this book knowing a lot more about trees, fossils, people's characters and life in general than when you started. A lovely book that can be returned to again and again.

**Mary Hooper**

# STONECIPHER

## Judith Heneghan

I've always loved stories that are set in the past and this is one of the best I've ever read. The story takes place in Victorian England and follows the exploits of Jago Stonecipher, a scruffy, parentless urchin and aspiring conjuror, who survives by his wits. In the opening chapter, Jago is travelling with his uncle, a showman who scrapes a living by entertaining crowds with magic tricks. When they arrive at the city of Winchester, it's not long before Jago gets caught up in a swindle and unwisely makes an enemy of wealthy thug, Armbruster. *Stonecipher* is an exciting adventure which takes young Jago on a boneshaking coach ride and onto a steamship where all sorts of hair-raising perils await him. The adventure moves swiftly, is full of twists and turns and it's so brilliantly written that I wanted to read it again as soon as I'd finished it.

**Anna Dale**

### Next?
• *Smith* by Leon Garfield is the story of a young London pickpocket. (*UBG* 315)
• Try *Black Hearts in Battersea* by Joan Aiken, the first in a series of books which feature a cockney waif called Dido Twite.
• Or *The Printer's Devil* by Paul Bajoria – for murder and mayhem in London's criminal underworld. (*UBG* 274)

★ ★ ★ ★ ★ ★

# STONE HEART Charlie Fletcher

### Next?
• The sequels! *Iron Hand* and *Silver Tongue*, for more of the statues' secrets.
• More of Laura Hutching's top five: *Freak the Mighty* by Rodman Philbrick (*UBG* 120), *The Lord of the Rings* by J.R.R Tolkien (*UBG* 211) or *Northern Lights* by Philip Pullman (*UBG* 151).
• And finally (for reasons she can't quite explain) *Stone Heart* always makes her think of John Masefield's *The Box of Delights*. (*UBG* 44)

What I love about good books is their power to make you see the world differently. When *Stone Heart* first came out, it went straight on to my top-five favourites list and I never looked at a statue in the same way again.

*Stone Heart* tells the story of George who, in a moment of bad temper, accidentally awakes the statues in London: both the good (spits) and the bad (taints). Pursued through the streets by the gargoyles of Euston Station, George is helped by the Gunner from the Royal Artillery war memorial and Edie, a young girl with a strange and frightening ability to see into the past.

This is a genuinely gripping story, full of both action and mystery and – best of all – it's the first of a trilogy!

**Laura Hutchings**

# THE STONES ARE HATCHING  Geraldine McCaughrean ● ● ●

**Next?**

• Geraldine McCaughrean's books cover a wide range of subjects. Try *Forever X*, in which it's Christmas every day, *The Kite Rider*, set in China (*UBG* 193), or the historical *Stop the Train* (*UBG* 331).

• Or try D.J. MacHale's epic **Pendragon** series, starting with *Merchant of Death*, about a boy facing magic, danger and time travel.

• Another great magical story is Alan Garner's *The Weirdstone of Brisingamen*. (*UBG* 377)

Phelim is an unusual hero with an unusual name. Living with his bossy sister Prudence, he is not sorry to leave home, but finds himself on an extraordinary quest – a monster, the Stoor Worm, is stirring from its sleep, awakened by the guns of the First World War, and Phelim, it seems, must save the world from it – even though he doesn't think of himself as even a tiny bit heroic. On his way he teams up with helpers – the Maiden, the Fool and the Horse – and encounters a series of horrifying dangers, from the Noonday Twister to the Merrows who trap fishermen's souls in lobster-pots on the seabed.

Geraldine McCaughrean's writing is wonderfully vivid – so good that you will want to dip in again and again once you've finished. Full of twists and surprises, her story makes you feel you've accompanied Phelim on his astonishing journey.

**Linda Newbery**

★ ★ ★ ★ ★ ★

# THE STONES OF MUNCASTER CATHEDRAL  ● ● ●
## Robert Westall

Joe Clarke is a steeplejack, and one thing he isn't afraid of is heights. But when he's called upon to repair the south-west tower of Muncaster Cathedral, he loses his confidence. Why does that gargoyle give him the shivers? Why has the stone it's set in become rotten over the years? Why does his eight-year-old son Kevin start sleepwalking – and heading for the cathedral? There are some jobs, Joe thinks, that try to kill you – and this is one of them. Read this truly chilling story, full of tension and atmosphere, and find out the terrible secret of the south-west tower, hidden since medieval times.

**Linda Newbery**

**Next?**

• If you enjoy this, there are dozens more Westalls to find. He was particularly good at stories set during World War II – try *Blitzcat* (*UBG* 37), *The Machine Gunners* (*UBG* 215) and *The Kingdom by the Sea*. If you like supernatural stories like this one, try the terrifying *Yaxley's Cat*.

• Hugh Scott is another writer who explores supernatural themes in an unusual way; try *The Gargoyle*.

• Or for a series that mixes Celtic legend and drak magic, try Joe Donnelly's *Jack Flint and the Redthorn Sword*.

# REAL LIFE AND FAMILY STORIES
## Parents, Siblings and Other Sorts of Trouble
### by Hilary McKay

Oh, am I a family story writer? I am so sorry to hear that. It sounds so dull. No fantasy. No dragons. No magic. No escape from this place that we call the real world.

Well, although it was never my intention to be such a thing, I suppose it is true. This essay should be entitled 'My Excuse for Inadvertently Writing Family Stories'.

We begin in families. It's the thing we all have in common. A mother figure, adequate or otherwise. A father figure, absent or present. Brothers and sisters, or a lack of them. Some place to sleep at some sort of base. A jumble of people wished upon us from birth.

In fairy stories you get gifts, good or bad.

## Twelve Problem-parent Books

People are always talking about 'problem children'. Well, how about a list of a dozen books about 'problem parents'?

- *Hands Up!* by Paul Magrs
- *The Illustrated Mum* by Jacqueline Wilson
- *Rescuing Dad* by Pete Johnson
- *Madame Doubtfire* by Anne Fine
- *Jake's Tower* by Elizabeth Laird
- *Goodnight Mr Tom* by Michelle Magorian
- *The Mum Hunt* by Gwyneth Rees
- *Jessica Haggerthwaite: Witch Dispatcher* by Emma Barnes
- *Double Act* by Jacqueline Wilson
- *Goggle-Eyes* by Anne Fine
- *Gumble's Yard* by John Rowe Townsend
- *Holly Starcross* by Berlie Doherty

## Ten Books About Dealing With Illness

- *Pig-Heart Boy* by Malorie Blackman
- *Becky Bananas* by Jean Ure
- *Up on Cloud Nine* by Anne Fine
- *Skellig* by David Almond
- *Two Weeks With the Queen* by Morris Gleitzman
- *Pollyanna* by Eleanor H. Porter
- *The Secret Garden* by Frances Hodgson Burnett
- *The Fire-Eaters* by David Almond
- *What Katy Did* by Susan Coolidge
- *Heidi* by Johanna Spyri

Hair as black as ebony, lips as red as blood. A fatal attraction for spinning wheels. The (dubiously useful) talents of being able to detect peas under mattresses and to kiss frogs into handsome princes. In families you get relations. Some of them are blessings, and more of them are curses. You (the hero or heroine of your own epic) must rub along with them as best you can, being (at the start of the story anyway) as helplessly bound to them as any princess to her fate.

That is how it has happened with me. I have given my blessings and curses of human form, bound them as tightly as I could to my principal characters, and written down my observations of the results. And thus (I reluctantly admit) I have created a family story.

It is time I changed all this, but I know it will be hard. I could write about an orphan in an unknown land, but he would inevitably find a fatherly wizard. I could try a love story, but we all know what happens at the end of love stories.

## Real World Stories

- *Goggle-eyes* by Anne Fine
- *The Illustrated Mum* by Jacqueline Wilson
- *Sundae Girl* by Cathy Cassidy
- *My Mum's Going to Explode!* by Jeremy Strong
- *What Katy Did* by Susan M. Coolidge
- *Gumble's Yard* by John Rowe Townsend
- *Swallows and Amazons* by Arthur Ransome
- *Feather Boy* by Nicky Singer
- *Stargirl* by Jerry Spinelli
- *Danny, the Champion of the World* by Roald Dahl
- *The Railway Children* by E. Nesbit
- *The Vicarage Family* by Noel Streatfeild
- And of course Hilary McKay's own *Saffy's Angel* and its four sequels

I could send my heroes and heroines off into the wild, on ships or horses or interstellar spacecraft. They could be shipwrecked on islands, or fight dragons or discover new civilisations. But I know what would come next. They would set up little camps on those islands. They would grow tired of the needless and painful slaughter of endangered species and long for a bed for the night, and someone to admire their wounds. They would look at the civilisations on those distant planets and they would think, how like (or unlike) planet Earth.

So we return. To our blessings and curses. To the ones we love most, and the ones we would obliterate first. To our families. That is the truth of it. We live in our little worlds, spinning our little lives. Hair into rope, straw into gold, dreams into stories.

Personally, I plan to write no more family stories. The next one will be pure fantasy. Battle scenes. Shining friendships. Lonely quests in strange lands. And I will cunningly conceal from my heroes and heroines why they are fighting and what they are searching for. And I will make sure they do not get too close to those shining friends, and I will never, ever, ever, let them come home...

## And We Mustn't Forget Siblings...

- *The Exiles* by Hilary McKay
- *Little Women* by Louisa May Alcott
- *The Cuckoo Sister* by Vivien Alcock
- *Double Act* by Jacqueline Wilson
- *Storm Catchers* by Tim Bowler
- *Ballet Shoes* by Noel Streatfeild
- *Tales of a Fourth Grade Nothing* by Judy Blume
- **Ramona** series by Beverly Cleary
- *My Naughty Little Sister* by Dorothy Edwards
- *The Family from One End Street* by Eve Garnett
- **Horrid Henry** by Francesca Simon

# STOP THE TRAIN  Geraldine McCaughrean

● ● ●

It's 1893 and schoolgirl Cissy Sissney is on a steam train, excited about the new life her family is heading for in Florence, a town yet to be built in the middle of the Oklahoma prairie. They arrive and start to build, but then the railroad company decides that the train won't stop at Florence after all. This means ruin to pioneering families like Cissie's and death to the town, even before it's begun – unless the pioneers can find a way to *stop the train*.

This is a joyous book based on a true story and you'll be gripped, not just by the battle, but by the characters who fought it, and the language of the author as she brings it all to life.

**Julia Jarman**

### Next?
• Try *Little House on the Prairie* by Laura Ingalls Wilder, also about struggling pioneering families. (*UBG* 203)
• More McCaughrean? For something more fantastical, read her brilliant sequel to *Peter Pan* – *Peter Pan in Scarlet*. (*UBG* 263)
• For another family and a train that has a huge impact on their lives, read *The Railway Children* by E. Nesbit. (*UBG* 279)

★ ★ ★ ★ ★ ★

# STORM  Kevin Crossley-Holland

●

### Next?
• Try some of Kevin's retellings of folk tales, such as *Enchantment* and *British Folk Tales*.
• Berlie Doherty has written a book which is totally different from *Storm*, but strangely has two main characters with the same names! It's called *Willa and Old Miss Annie*. (*UBG* 384)
• For more spooky stuff, read *The Haunting of Pip Parker* by Anne Fine or *Ghost Writer* by Julia Jarman (*UBG* 125).

Annie's sister Willa comes home to the marsh to have a baby, but when she goes into labour, a terrible storm blows up and the phone line to the hospital is dead. Young Annie offers to brave the storm and run to the village to fetch the doctor, but she is terrified of the ghost of the ford. And when a strange horseman offers to help her, what will she decide to do?

*Storm* is exciting and haunting, and is beautifully written and illustrated. Kevin Crossley-Holland is a poet and reteller of folk tales, and his work has been a major influence on my own writing.

**Malachy Doyle**

# STORM CATCHERS Tim Bowler ●●●

**Next?**

• Everything by Tim Bowler, but especially *River Boy* (*UBG* 286) and *Dragon's Rock*.

• If you liked this book for its fast-paced adventure, try *Shadow of the Minotaur*, the first of the **Legendeer** books by Alan Gibbons or *The Haunting of Alaizabel Cray* by Chris Wooding (*UBG* 147).

• *Kidnapped* by Robert Louis Stevenson – this time it's the hero who's kidnapped. (*UBG* 188)

Fin should be helping his sister Ella look after their young brother Sam. But their world is safe enough – big house, nice neighbourhood – so without much thought he leaves her to it and goes off to play on his mate's computer. But even the safest-seeming places can be dangerous, and that evening, in the heart of a storm, Ella is kidnapped.

Blamed by everyone including himself for Ella's disappearance, Fin is determined to find her, even though that seems an impossibility. But young Sam is having strange dreams – even when he is awake – and the storm seems to seethe in the air even on quiet sunny days. Somehow, Fin must pull together all the things that are happening and make sense of them – for he is his sister's only real hope. Terrifying, thrilling and heartbreaking, this book is about how secrets and lies can destroy even the happiest of families.

**Leonie Flynn**

★ ★ ★ ★ ★ ★

# THE STORY OF TRACY BEAKER Jacqueline Wilson ●●

Tracy has a glamorous mum who never comes to see her. That's because Tracy lives in a children's home and her mum has disappeared. That doesn't stop Tracy from making up wonderful stories about her, as much to comfort herself as to impress her friends. Tracy is a tough, independent girl who wants to change her situation. She's not going to let anyone see her cry, or almost no one, and taking no prisoners along the way, she tells us her story.

It is a tribute to Jacqueline Wilson that our sympathies are not always with Tracy but our loyalty never waivers. Tracy can be just as mean and jealous as some of her housemates. However, even though the book is very sad in parts, it never loses its humour and tackles a difficult subject with straight-up honesty.

**Karen Wallace**

**Next?**

• Read *The Dare Game* and find out what happens to Tracy when her dream comes true. A lighter and easier Jacqueline Wilson book is *The Lottie Project*. (*UBG* 213)

• If you're interested in the 'children's home' that Tracy has been living in, you can read about a couple of others in *Heaven Eyes* by David Almond (*UBG* 149) and *Ruby Holler* by Sharon Creech (*UBG* 288), and see how they compare.

# THE STRANGE AFFAIR OF ADELAIDE HARRIS

**Leon Garfield**

●●●

Harris and Bostock are the kind of boys you'd go out of your way not to sit next to in class. At their school in nineteenth-century Brighton, this gruesome twosome learn about a famous Greek legend in which a baby is abandoned and brought up by wolves. With a glint in his eye, scheming Harris convinces bumbling Bostock that leaving his new baby sister Adelaide on a nearby hill would be an 'educational' experiment. But instead of wolves, Adelaide is snatched to safety by a courting couple, who then manage carelessly to lose her again. This wickedly funny tale takes in daft duels, silly skullduggery and a deeply creepy detective.

**Karen McCombie**

### Next?

• You might be in the mood for more dark doings set in the past, such as Lemony Snicket's **A Series of Unfortunate Events**, starting with *The Bad Beginning*. (*UBG* 306)

• Theresa Tomlinson's *The Cellar Lad* is another fascinating historical story.

• Or for a historical mystery, try *Oranges and Murder* by Alison Prince. (*UBG* 253)

• Leon Garfield's *Smith* is the exciting tale of a Victorian pickpocket. (*UBG* 315)

★ ★ ★ ★ ★ ★

# STRATFORD BOYS Jan Mark

●●

### Next?

• More Jan Mark? Try *Turbulence*, which is funny and creepy. Or look out for *Something in the Air*, a novel set in the 1920s.

• Sophie Masson's *The Tempestuous Voyage of Hopewell Shakespeare* is a seafaring romp which you may enjoy.

• If you want to begin to discover the joys of Shakespeare's plays, consider first, perhaps, *A Midsummer Night's Dream*, with its own amateur acting company, just like the one in Jan's book.

'The Shakespeares had the builders in again.' The opening sentence sets the tone: here is the domestic Shakespeare, a growing lad at home amongst family and mates, the heady days ahead no more than a half-formed speculation.

Will, his friend Adrian Croft, plus assorted fellow Stratfordians, join together to stage a Whitsuntide play. The subsequent rehearsals – a showcase for personality clashes and for artistic insights and new alliances, described here with relish and affection – culminating in the actual performance of Will's much-amended *Fortune My Foe* – form the backbone of this brilliant, exhilarating tale of comradeship, writing, acting and maturity.

And with writing of this quality you can see, hear and smell Elizabethan Stratford, and pick its muck off your boots.

**Chris Stephenson**

# STRAVAGANZA: CITY OF MASKS  Mary Hoffman  ● ● ●

This book's sumptuous cover – eyes staring from a silver mask, and the Venice waterfront in the background – will attract you across a bookshop. It's a time-slip story in which present-day Lucien, diagnosed with what turns out to be brain cancer, finds that he can 'stravagate' to Bellezza, a place very like Venice – where he meets the spirited Arianna, a girl who doesn't see why being female means she can't be a gondolier (or mandolier, as they're called in Bellezza).

The story switches between past and present, with an intriguing twist when Lucien's parents take him on holiday to the real Venice – complete with McDonalds and the trappings of modern tourism. If you like a story that combines adventure, intrigue, deceptions, gloriously luxurious settings, divided loyalties and a hint of romance, this is for you – and it's only the first of four stories set in Mary Hoffman's fantasy Italy.

**Linda Newbery**

### Next?
• Read the rest of the **Stravaganza** sequence, *City of Stars*, *City of Flowers* and *City of Secrets*.

• Other novels with (almost) Venetian settings include *The Thief Lord* by Cornelia Funke (*UBG* 345), and Kai Meyer's mermaid fantasy, *The Flowing Queen*, with its sequels *The Stone Light* and *The Glass World*.

• For another series where reality and fantasy mix, read **The Dark is Rising** sequence by Susan Cooper. (*UBG* 78)

★ ★ ★ ★ ★ ★

# STRAWGIRL  Jackie Kay  ● ●

### Next?
• The spirited *Stargirl* by Jerry Spinelli is also brilliant. (*UBG* 324)

• Fighting to save something important to you is the theme of *The Summer of Riley* by Eve Bunting. Riley is a loyal and totally housetrained labrador, bought to help William get over his family's traumas and threatened with being put down for a crime he sort-of didn't commit.

• Michael finds a strange, dirty creature living in his garage in David Almond's unique *Skellig*. (*UBG* 313)

Molly (Maybe) MacPherson, so called because she can never answer definitely 'yes' or 'no' to anything, has always felt like an outsider. Her dad is from the Nigerian Ibo tribe which makes her an easy target for the bullies at her school in a tiny remote Scottish village. She wishes she could fit in and make some real friends. When her dad is killed in a car accident, stop-at-nothing businessmen try to buy up her home, Wishing Well Farm, for redevelopment and, because her mum is too depressed to fight back, it's up to Maybe to save the day – and the farm – alone.

**Eileen Armstrong**

# A STUDY IN SCARLET Arthur Conan Doyle ● ● ●

**Next?**

• You may enjoy more of Arthur Conan Doyle's adventures of Sherlock Holmes: *The Sign of Four* and *The Hound of the Baskervilles* (*UBG* 160) are the best known.

• You might like to try books by two authors who inspired Arthur Conan Doyle: Robert Louis Stevenson's *Dr Jekyll and Mr Hyde* and Edgar Allen Poe's *The Murders in the Rue Morgue*.

Introducing ... Mr Sherlock Holmes, the world's most famous detective, and his sidekick Dr Watson. This is their first case. As usual, it starts with a note:

'My dear Mr Sherlock Holmes. There has been a bad business during the night at 3, Lauriston Gardens... Our man on the beat ... found the door open, and in the front room, which is bare of furniture, discovered the body of a gentleman... There had been no robbery, nor is there evidence of how the man met his death.'

This thrilling detective story has Holmes using his amazing powers of deduction to solve the case. How to identify someone by their footprints, long nails and one word written in blood on a wall? Off goes our intrepid detective (equipped with magnifying glass, deerstalker hat and pipe) in pursuit of the cunning villains.

How does he do it? You won't put this book down until you find out. 'Elementary, my dear Watson!' it isn't. But scary and good fun it most certainly is.

**James Riordan**

★ ★ ★ ★ ★ ★

# SUNDAE GIRL Cathy Cassidy ● ● ●

With a title like *Sundae Girl* you'd expect this book to be a frothy, sweet confection, yes? Well, there are funny bits, and places where you laugh out loud – but there are others where you'll want to cry, too, for Jude, the Sundae Girl, has a tough time of it. Her mum's an alcoholic, her gran's got Alzheimer's, her dad dresses like Elvis and there's this floppy-haired boy who's just determined to be nice to her – and she really isn't interested in getting a boyfriend. Not at all. In fact she's too ashamed of her family to let anyone get close enough to find out about them...

Funny, sad, and so real you think you know all of the characters, *Sundae Girl* is less a sundae and more a lemon meringue pie – bitter, sweet, deeply satisfying and definitely moreish.

**Leonie Flynn**

**Next?**

• More Cathy Cassidy! I loved *Scarlett*, which is about an unhappy girl and what happens when she moves from a big city to live with her father and his new wife in rural Ireland.

• Or try Jean Ure's *Gone Missing*, about two girls who decide to run away from home.

• Or Jacqueline Wilson, of course; try *Candyfloss* or *The Illustrated Mum* (*UBG* 172).

# SWALLOWS AND AMAZONS
### Arthur Ransome

'BETTER DROWNED THAN DUFFERS' cables distant father to enquiring mother. 'IF NOT DUFFERS, WON'T DROWN'. So the four Walker children are allowed to sail their little boat *Swallow* across the lake to Wild Cat Island, and camp there, and outwit the pirates in the boat *Amazon* who soon become their friends, and, and...

This is the first in the series of 12 books which were my absolute favourites when I was your age. Arthur Ransome, journalist and sailor, was brilliant at pulling the reader right inside the small adventures of sturdy John, motherly Susan, the imaginative but unfortunately named Titty, and the ship's boy, Roger. Before you know what's happening to you, you're there: sailing a boat in the dark, or trying to tell a secret code-call from the cry of an owl. They're realistic books, but with the classic absent-parents situation of fantasy. Try them. Start with this one.

**Susan Cooper**

### Next?

• Try others in the series, like **The Picts and the Martyrs**, which adds two more nautical kids to the Swallows' and Amazons' adventures in the Lake District. Or **The Big Six**, a kind of detective story which takes you to join Joe, Bill and Pete in the Norfolk Broads.

• Once you've read all the **Swallows and Amazons** stories, move on to **Treasure Island** by Robert Louis Stevenson. (**UBG** 352)

• Or read Philippa Pearce's **Minnow on the Say**, another great adventure that happens over a long summer – with a boat, too! (**UBG** 230)

A series of 12 magical books to savour and love for ever. Start with *Swallows and Amazons* as John, Susan, Titty and Roger set sail for Wild Cat Island and embark on the first of their many adventures with the Amazon pirates. Move on to *Swallowdale*, and then *Peter Duck*, and on through the rest of this classic series of novels.

The adventures will take you from the Lake District to the Norfolk Broads, from the Caribbean to the China Seas – every story packed with adventure and a cast of unforgettable characters. Part of the genius of Arthur Ransome lies in the way he allows the characters themselves to create the world of piracy and adventure through their own imaginations. It's a world so compellingly realised that we're deliciously drawn in. So what are you waiting for? Dive into the books. Soak up the world of the characters. Let the stories enrich your life just as they've enriched mine. Enjoy!

**Tim Bowler**

# A SWARM IN MAY and CHORISTER'S CAKE

**William Mayne**

**Next?**

• You might try *Follow the Footprints* or *Summer Visitors* by the same author. His mysteries aren't of the cops-and-robbers kind and they always lead you back into the past. For very different Maynes, try *Earthfasts* (*UBG* 94) and *A Grass Rope* (*UBG* 137).

• Bridget Crowley's *Feast of Fools* is another gripping, cathedral-school mystery.

Not many people go to boarding school nowadays and even fewer attend choir schools. In these books you can read about the boys who sing in the choir of a cathedral and live in the school which stands in its shadow. Their work in the choir is serious and hard but the rest of the time they are ordinary schoolboys. Sometimes the two halves of their lives are very difficult to fit together.

*A Swarm in May* tells how a cathedral ritual sends John Owen on a quest to solve an ancient mystery at the heart of the great building, involving hidden staircases and forgotten rooms among the stonework.

In *Chorister's Cake*, Peter Sandwell rebels against authority because he thinks it makes everybody the same and gives power to the wrong people. He finds out the hard way that being part of a choir is not about power but co-operation.

**Jan Mark**

★ ★ ★ ★ ★ ★

# THE SWISH OF THE CURTAIN   Pamela Brown

One boring afternoon in sleepy Fenchester, a group of friends discover a disued theatre and decide to bring it back to life. They each have special talents and they write, design and produce every show themselves, with spectacular results.

All the problems of putting on a play are described in hilarious detail, and there are brilliant descriptions of the passion that the actors feel for their job and those special moments when the play takes off and the audience is entranced.

This book will help you believe that dreams can come true. I should know – I now work in the theatre professionally, as a director, and this is the book that started it all off for me!

**Abigail Anderson**

**Next?**

• Look out for *Ballet Shoes* (*UBG* 28) and other Noel Streatfeild books, such as *Dancing Shoes* and *Theatre Shoes*.

• *Billy Elliot* by Melvin Burgess is about a boy who wants to be a ballet dancer. (*UBG* 34)

• Or the very funny *I Am a Tree* by Kaye Umansky – the boy who usually gets the lead role in the school play is cast as a tree...

# THE SWISS FAMILY ROBINSON J.D. Wyss

● ● ●

Abandoned on a sinking ship that is being storm-blown towards destruction, a Swiss pastor, his wife and their children find themselves shipwrecked on a deserted tropical island. Here, through necessity, they make a new life for themselves using what they can salvage from their ruined ship and also all the wonderful things the island has to offer. No spoons to eat your soup? Use oyster shells. No cups? What's wrong with half a coconut shell?

My father read me this book when I was very young, and I can still recall the wonderful illustrations that added to the amazing story. For a long time I wanted to make my own candles and eat an iguana (apparently very tasty), but alas, I had to make do with rereading this story.

**Leonie Flynn**

**Next?**
• If you'd like to read about another shipwreck, try *The Island of Blue Dolphins* by Scott O'Dell. (*UBG* 177)
• If you like adventures in strange and wild places, try *South Sea Adventure* by Willard Price. Or *Cannibal Adventure* in his **Adventure** series. (*UBG* 51)
• If you want to read about a family making a new life somewhere unusual, try *Children on the Oregon Trail* by A.R. van der Loeff. (*UBG* 62)

★ ★ ★ ★ ★ ★

# THE SWORD IN THE STONE

● ● ●

## T.H. White

**Next?**
• Go on to read the sequels which are collected in one volume as *The Once and Future King*.
• And read, if you haven't already, Ursula Le Guin's **Earthsea** sequence. (*UBG* 95)
• Or try *Mistress Masham's Repose* – it's nothing like *The Sword in the Stone*, but interesting as it's by the same author. (*UBG* 231)

How I envy the people who have not yet read this book! They have a present still to unwrap! An unexpected piece of luck! An extra holiday! I wish that I could read this book again for the very first time.

*The Sword in the Stone* is the story of Arthur and his life before he heaved Excalibur from its stone, and thereby brought his fate tumbling down upon his shoulders. It describes his boyhood in a castle deep in a forest, with his foster brother Kay, his guardian Sir Ector, and his tutor, who was (of course) Merlin – the perfect wizard, owner of Archimedes, the perfect owl.

Historians say most of the legends of King Arthur are not true. Definitely, they say, no Merlin, dragons, or talking beasts. However, these are books that ought to be true. I believe them. Right from the first joke, to the last goodbye, they sound like truth to me.

**Hilary McKay**

# THE TAIL OF EMILY WINDSNAP

## Liz Kessler

### Next?

• More Emily in *Emily Windsnap and the Monster of the Deep* and *Emily Windsnap and the Castle in the Mist*.

• For more magic in this vein, there's Philippa Fisher's *Fairy Godsister* – this time with fairies instead of mermaids.

• Or try a different mermaid – **Mermaid Magic** by Gwyneth Rees. There's *Mermaid Magic*, *Rani's Sea Spells* and *Shell Princess*.

Calling all swimmers! This is a fantastical story about mermaids and mermen, proving that love and friendship can conquer the meanest of minds. Emily Windsnap is a scrawny, loveable 13 year old, trying to get along whilst hindered by the school bullies. Fighting her fear of swimming, she discovers she is better at it than she imagines ... when in water she is a mermaid! So begins her journey into discovering a hidden past above and below sea level. A hugely enjoyable read, it carries you along, occasionally with your heart in your mouth.

**Rebecca Le Fevre**

★ ★ ★ ★ ★ ★

# THE TALE OF DESPEREAUX

## Kate diCamillo

This, reader, is the story of a small, small mouse with a French mother and stupendously big ears, and of the princess he falls in love with. You don't believe a mouse could fall in love with a princess? But could you believe, then, in a kingdom where soup has been declared illegal? Oh yes, strange things happen in the kingdom of Dor. How else would a bright, glowing princess called 'The Pea' find herself awoken in the middle of the night by a serving girl called Miggery Sow, with cauliflower ears, a candle in one hand and a kitchen knife in the other, and on her shoulder a rat in a red handkerchief with a soup spoon on his head? How indeed? There's only one way, reader, to find out...

A warm, funny and wise tale of bravery, love and light. And soup.

**Daniel Hahn**

### Next?

• Try the same author's story of a proud rabbit and his journey to find his way home in *The Miraculous Journey of Edward Tulane*.

• Or what about a boy who lives an ordinary life in a lighthouse until... Well, read *The Extraordinary Adventures of Ordinary Basil* by Wiley Miller and find out all about him.

• Or try the story of a girl who wants to be a knight, in Cornelia Funke's funny, exciting and beautifully realised *Igraine the Brave*. (*UBG* 171)

# A TALE OF TIME CITY

Diana Wynne Jones

**Next?**

• You might like to read about Caprona, another city in Diana Wynne Jones's invented world. Try *The Magicians of Caprona*, part of her **The Worlds of Chrestomanci** series. (*UBG* 393)

• You can find Bellezza, another Italianate city, in Mary Hoffman's *Stravaganza: City of Masks*. (*UBG* 334)

• For more magical adventures in real cities, try *The Thief Lord*. (*UBG* 345)

Jonathan and Sam kidnap Vivian Smith, thinking she is the notorious Time Lady, bent on destroying Time City and even history itself. Once they realise their mistake, Vivian helps the boys try to outwit the enemy before time runs out.

Diana Wynne Jones's story ensnares you with a dozen threads of plot all woven into a magic carpet of story that whisks you off to Time City with its habit ghosts, once ghosts and the mysterious Endless ghost who appears every day at midnight, climbing Endless Hill. Like all the author's invented worlds, Time City feels as real and vivid as your own: you will want it to survive just as much as the children who fight desperately to save it.

**Gill Vickery**

★ ★ ★ ★ ★ ★

# TALES FROM SHAKESPEARE Charles and Mary Lamb

In 1807, siblings Charles and Mary Lamb published 20 of Shakespeare's most loved plays in simple prose. Mary wrote the comedies and Charles the tragedies, their intention being to make Shakespeare more accessible and more readily digestible by the young. Wherever possible they have used Shakespeare's original words, and most of his better known lines are quoted.

To the contemporary reader, the language might seem a little old-fashioned. The enduring popularity of the Lambs' *Tales...*, however, is testimony to the writers' skill and judgment in choosing what to extract from Shakespeare's texts and which plays to tackle. They show the bard's genius lay not just in the way he told his tales, but in the tales he picked to tell.

**Neil Arksey**

**Next?**

• Try Marcia Williams's funny and easy-to-follow *Mr William Shakespeare's Plays* (*UBG* 220) and its sequel *Bravo, Mr William Shakespeare!*

• Or for good narrative retellings, try *Macbeth* by Tony Bradman, *Romeo and Juliet* by Michael Cox, or *The Tempest* by Franzeska G. Ewart.

• If you want a novel that uses a story from a Shakespeare play, try Neil Arksey's own *MacB* (*UBG* 215) which is based on *Macbeth*.

# TALES OF A FOURTH GRADE NOTHING
## Judy Blume

Peter Warren Hatcher is nine years old and in the fourth grade. His biggest problem in the whole world is his little brother, Farley Drexel Hatcher, otherwise known as Fudge. Fudge is just two and a half, and is always messing everything up for Peter. If you have a pesky little brother or sister you'll understand – Fudge can be a real pain.

He's moody, noisy, and sometimes just plain weird, and you'll see why Peter finds him really annoying (especially when Fudge eats his turtle...). But you – the reader, who doesn't have him as your brother – will absolutely love him. Because when Fudge is around, everything – going shopping, going to see a movie, having guests for dinner – is a complete riot!

**Daniel Hahn**

## Next?
• More books about Peter and Fudge! Try *Otherwise Known as Sheila the Great*, *Superfudge*, *Fudge-a-Mania* and *Double Fudge*.

• Or something adventurous? *A Dog Called Grk* by Joshua Doder about a boy and his dog who solve crimes. (*UBG* 87)

• Or what about a girl who also often gets it wrong? Beverly Cleary's delightful **Ramona** books. (*UBG* 280)

## Dragons!
• *Dragons of Wayward Crescent* by Chris d'Lacey
• *Eragon* by Christopher Paolini
• *The Hobbit* by J.R.R. Tolkein
• *Dragon Horse* by Peter Ward
• *Dragon Keeper* by Carole Wilkinson
• *How to Train Your Dragon* by Cressida Cowell
• **Dragon Orb** series by Mark Robson
• *The Saint of Dragons* by Jason Hightman
• *Kenny and the Dragon* by Tony diTerlizzi
• *The Fire Within* by Chris d'Lacey
• *Muddle Earth* by Paul Stewart and Chris Riddell
• *Dragon Rider* by Cornelia Funke
• *Green Smoke* by Rosemary Manning

# TALES OF THE EARLY WORLD  Ted Hughes ●●

As a child, I loved mythology: I still do – so gutsy and passionate and communal that no one could ever call it 'kids' stuff'.

I like 'invented' mythology for the same reasons. *Tales of the Early World* and its companion piece *How the Whale Became* are completely amazing, with mesmerising descriptions, clever twists and wonderful jokes. After 45 years of reading stories, I tend to be able to guess where a story is going. But I challenge you to guess where Hughes is taking you in one of his stories. For a long time you can't even be sure who the main character is going to be – whether it's God or his earwax on the mantelpiece. You don't know if you are reading comedy or tragedy, only that the language is sweeping you along too fast for you to grab the bank and pull yourself ashore. Read it and get swept away.

**Geraldine McCaughrean**

**Next?**
• The *Just So Stories* by Rudyard Kipling have more 'origin' stories, such as 'How the Leopard Got His Spots'. (*UBG* 187)
• If you want stories about the early world of humans, try Michelle Paver's *Wolf Brother*. (*UBG* 390)
• Or for other ancient stories, try Geraldine McCaughrean's retelling of the Greek ones in *The Orchard Book of Greek Myths*. (*UBG* 254)

★ ★ ★ ★ ★ ★

# TALES OF TROY AND GREECE  Andrew Lang ●●

**Next?**
• Rosemary Sutcliff wrote *The Truce of the Games*, about how even enemies could be friends for the duration of the Olympic Games – it's hard to find, but worth it!
• *Black Ships Before Troy* by Rosemary Sutcliff tells the Troy story – it has marvellous illustrations, too. (*UBG* 36)
• These stories have been retold many times, look for the feature on pp. 200–202 to discover some more.

The stories and heroes of ancient Greek myth are hugely enjoyable. And a better introduction than Andrew Lang's would be hard to find – he is a master storyteller. Maintaining the classic simplicity of the stories, through his anecdotal style he allows the heroes to become more accessible. They are characters a contemporary audience will readily identify with.

Lang weaves ancient myth with snippets of added historical detail. These condensed stories have freshness and vitality, yet retain the power and drama of their origins. Timeless phrases pop up to remind the reader just how ancient and weighty these stories are. Told at a good pace, with colour and detail to keep things vivid and lively, they will carry you right through to the end.

**Neil Arksey**

# TANGLEWRECK  Jeanette Winterson

### Next?

• Fantasy fans will enjoy *The Tale of Jessica Sweetapple* by Linda Kempton. When the prow of a galleon pushes into her bedroom wall at Apple Manor, Jessica knows that the Ancestors, threatened by dark forces, need her help.

• Or, if you haven't read it yet, you must read *Northern Lights* by Philip Pullman. (*UBG* 151)

• Or try the classic *A Wrinkle in Time* by Madeline L'Engle. (*UBG* 395)

This story explodes like a firework with so many original plot twists and characters that it leaves you breathless. In some places I laughed out loud at the jokes – always a good sign!

Silver River inherits the mansion called Tanglewreck, and lives there with her cold-hearted guardian, Mrs Rockaby. When Time itself is threatened with Time Tornadoes and the world goes out of kilter, only Silver can save it. First she must find the Timekeeper, but two first-class villains are searching for it too: Regalia Mason, head of international corporation, Quantum, seeks world domination, buying and selling Time itself; Abel Darkwater also seeks total power over Time. Can Silver reach the Timekeeper before they do?

**Pauline Chandler**

★ ★ ★ ★ ★ ★

# TARKA THE OTTER  Henry Williamson

As a child, my favourite animal book was *Tarka the Otter*. It still is. I recently reread (for the umpteenth time) Henry Williamson's wonderful story of what the dictionary calls 'an aquatic fish-eating carnivore of the weasel family'. The language the author uses is lyrical, and he paints an unforgettable picture of the beasts and birds of Dartmoor and Exmoor.

I like happy endings and have always wondered about the closing words of Tarka's story. Did Tarka escape the otter-hunters and their hounds by swimming out to sea, and thus to safety?

Read the book and see what you think!

**Dick King-Smith**

### Next?

• Try *Ring of Bright Water* by Gavin Maxwell, a true story of a man's friendship with an otter.

• Or Kenneth Oppel's wonderful stories about bats, beginning with *Silverwing*. (*UBG* 312)

• *Watership Down* is one of the all-time classic adventure stories, even if it is about rabbits. (*UBG* 376)

# THERE'S A BOY IN THE GIRLS' BATHROOM

## Louis Sachar

**Next?**

• Louis Sachar is a wonderful writer, and his other books are all worth a read. Look out for the fabulous *Holes* (*UBG* 155), *The Boy Who Lost His Face* (*UBG* 46) and *Dogs Don't Tell Jokes*.

• Jerry Spinelli is another brilliant American writer; try *Stargirl*. (*UBG* 324)

• For an English boy with school troubles, try Anne Fine's *Flour Babies*. (*UBG* 116)

'There are some kids – you can tell just by looking at them – who are good spitters.' Bradley Chalkers, for example.

I first read this delightful story 15 years ago but it has lost none of its relevance, and, in one chapter, none of its power to make me laugh and cry. Bradley is a bully who finds life less painful if everybody hates him. But the arrival of a new boy Jeff, and a young counsellor Carla, start to change all that. My favourite scenes are the ones Bradley plays out on his bedspread with his collection of little toy animals. Louis Sachar's wife is called Carla. When he first met her, she was a counsellor at an elementary school. That may be why so much of this story rings true.

Louis Sachar's later books – such as *Holes* – have rightly won him critical acclaim, but this one should not be missed.

**Caroline Lawrence**

★ ★ ★ ★ ★ ★

# THEY DO THINGS DIFFERENTLY THERE  Jan Mark

This weird and wonderful book captures the boredom of living in a 'new town', especially for someone as imaginative as Charlotte. She has always suspected, or hoped, that things aren't quite as dull as they seem. But it isn't until she gets to know Elaine that she discovers the bizarre world of Stalemate that lurks under the surface of their blandly uniform town.

From zen yoghurt to the mermaid factory and Dagobert the fishmonger-poet, the girls create a new and much more interesting world – much to the disgust of their classmates, who prefer to talk about diets and cellulite.

There's nothing like a Jan Mark book for giving you a different angle on the world.

**Mary Hoffman**

**Next?**

• Jan Mark's *The Lady With Iron Bones* tells of a close friendship between girls. You may also enjoy her *Handles*.

• Geraldine McCaughrean's clever *A Pack of Lies* will also give you a new slant on fiction.

• Jenna in Joan Bauer's *Rules of the Road* is another interesting and likeable character. (*UBG* 290)

# THIEF!

## Malorie Blackman

Lydia Henson has started at a new school and finds herself accused of being a thief – which is bad enough – but then she's accused of pushing a fellow pupil in front of a car as well. Malorie Blackman's brilliant at describing how angry and frustrated you would feel when everyone thinks you've done something that you haven't. Lydia vows revenge and you can't help hoping she'll get it...

But then the book takes an unexpected turn and Lydia suddenly finds herself blasted into a future where she did do something to get her own back, and it's not as pleasant as she thought.

All Malorie Blackman's books are exciting and thoughtful – and this one's no exception!

**Andrew Norriss**

### Next?

• You'll probably like other books by Malorie Blackman such as the tense and exciting *Hacker* (*UBG* 140) or *Pig-Heart Boy* (*UBG* 268), which looks at what it's like to be made to feel different and excluded.

• Neil Arksey is another writer whose books are full of action and drama. Look out for *Playing on the Edge*, for starters. (*UBG* 271)

★ ★ ★ ★ ★ ★

# THE THIEF LORD

## Cornelia Funke

### Next?

• If you want to read another fantastic story with a Venetian atmosphere, try Mary Hoffman's **Stravaganza** sequence, which begins with *City of Masks*. (*UBG* 334)

• You will probably also like the **Harry Potter** books by J.K. Rowling, if you haven't read them already! (*UBG* 145)

• How about another real place that's just been twisted very slightly out of shape? Try the mysterious, intriguing London of *A Handful of Magic* by Stephen Elboz. (*UBG* 141)

In the misty canals and crumbling alleyways of Venice, two orphans, Prosper and Bo, are on the run. They seek shelter in an old cinema with a gang of children whose mysterious leader, the Thief Lord, provides everything they need. But a detective is on their trail, desperate to find the missing piece of a magical roundabout that can control Time itself.

From the very first page of this book, I was transported to the wonderful city of Venice, and its twisting, fast-moving plot did not let me escape until I had reached the last page. The atmosphere of this book will soon have you wanting to explore the city's secret canals, yet the magical twist to the story is entirely believable. This book is unputdownable!

**Katherine Roberts**

# THE THIEF OF ALWAYS  Clive Barker ● ● ●

### Next?
• Try Clive Barker's new sequence of young-adult fantasies, *Abarat, Days of Magic, Nights of War* and *Absolute Midnight*.

• Philip Pullman's **His Dark Materials** trilogy, starting with *Northern Lights*, will enrapture you with its subtly altered world and sassy heroine. (*UBG* 151)

• Neil Gaiman is another adult author writing chilling fantasy for young people – try *Coraline* (*UBG* 69), or *M for Magic*.

Harvey Swick is bored as only a ten year old can be. So when a stranger appears in his bedroom and offers him a stay at Mr Hood's Holiday House, how can he refuse? Who could turn down a place where all four seasons come every day, where there is nothing to do but eat and play? But the house has a darker face, and for every fantasy, there is a price to be paid...

This is a beautifully unsettling fable, an atmospheric and sinister journey of the imagination. Anyone who has ever daydreamed away an idle hour on a rainy day wishing for the lost magic of summer will find something to identify with here.

**Chris Wooding**

★ ★ ★ ★ ★ ★

# THE THING WITH FINN  Tom Kelly ● ● ●

Ten-year-old Danny and Finn were identical twins in a happy family, but then it all changed; nothing has been the same since the terrible accident... Since then, Danny has stopped talking altogether, he's constantly fretting about his little sister and something terrible happening to her – and now he really just needs to get away from his whole grieving family, to run away ... but where?

On his journey, he meets a poodle that wears pink nail polish, a boy called Tom Thumb who eats all his Cheesy Wotsits, and eventually finds himself on an island with an artist called Nulty and a giant otter.

Danny's voice telling the story is funny, familiar and full of affection; and his story has some very silly fart jokes in it, but real warmth and sadness, too.

**Daniel Hahn**

### Next?
• Death and mourning are hard subjects to tackle, but a book that does so on a massive scale is *The Book Thief* by Marcus Zusak.

• A book written from the point of view of a dead girl is Eoin Colfer's *The Wish List*.

• Another warm-hearted book about running away from your troubles (and how they travel with you) is Nigel Hinton's *Buddy*.

# THE THREE MUSKETEERS Alexandre Dumas ●●●

### Next?

• In the sequel *Twenty Years After*, our heroes fight in France's civil wars.

• Three more exciting books by Dumas are *The Man in the Iron Mask* (*UBG* 218), *The Count of Monte Cristo*, and *The Black Tulip*.

• For more swashbuckling adventure, this time in Wellington's army, try Bernard Cornwell's **Sharpe** books. Try *Sharpe's Rifles* to start with.

• You might also enjoy *The Scarlet Pimpernel* by Baroness Orczy. (*UBG* 298)

'All for one and one for all!' is the famous motto of the Three Musketeers as they swashbuckle their way about seventeenth-century France. The three – the melancholy gentleman Athos, the brave, thick-headed giant Porthos, and the worldly priest Aramis – are each challenged to a duel by an 18-year-old country bumpkin named d'Artagnan from Gascony. After surviving the duels, d'Artagnan becomes firm friends with his three comrades.

The famous four uncover a plot to discredit the queen, and the adventures, skirmishes and sword fights that follow make this book one of the best classic historical romances ever written. Dumas moves us along on a high tide of excitement, devilish plots and counter-plots. We hardly notice time and pages pass.

**James Riordan**

★ ★ ★ ★ ★

# TIGHTROPE Gillian Cross ●●●

Ashley's life isn't easy. Her mum is ill and needs constant looking after. The neighbourhood she lives in is run-down and the kids amuse themselves by tormenting the local shopkeeper. But Ashley has an escape route – she is a graffiti artist. At night she sneaks out, climbs walls and leaves her tag in unexpected places. Only her best friend Vikki knows her secret, or so Ashley believes...

To say any more about this dark, compulsive thriller would be a crime in itself. The ending is bound to surprise you and make you think about when you should ask for help, and when you shouldn't. The characters are strong and the background is utterly believable – *Tightrope* is truly a terrific read.

**Sherry Ashworth**

### Next?

• Gillian Cross's many other books include nail-biting thrillers such as *Calling a Dead Man* (*UBG* 50) and *On the Edge*.

• If you like books about the darker side of life, you'll enjoy Jacqueline Wilson's *Lola Rose*.

• Older readers might like to try Barry Hines's *A Kestrel for a Knave*, about an underprivileged boy in Yorkshire and his pet kestrel.

• *Scribbleboy* by Philip Ridley is a quirkier, younger story about using graffiti to escape from reality. (*UBG* 298)

# THE TIME AND SPACE OF UNCLE ALBERT

Russell Stannard

## Next?

• If you liked this, why not try some of Russell Stannard's other **Uncle Albert** books, such as *Black Holes and Uncle Albert*?

• Or for more about the reality of space and time try *George's Secret Key to the Universe* by Lucy and Stephen Hawking.

• You might also want to read Philip Pullman's intricately constructed story, *Clockwork*. (*UBG* 66)

• The **Horrible Science** series by Nick Arnold has some great titles about real science – all told in a funny way. Look out for *Painful Poison*.

Ever thought physics was boring? This book might just change your mind. It's the story of Gedanken, a bright enough young girl, whose Uncle Albert bears a certain resemblance to another Albert – Albert Einstein. When Gedanken struggles to find an interesting topic for her science project, Uncle Albert proceeds to send her on all sorts of adventures, and she learns amazing facts about physics along the way.

Russell Stannard's great achievement in this book (and its sequels) is not only to make some of the most complex bits of quantum physics easy to understand, but to make them fun and interesting, too.

**Marcus Sedgwick**

★ ★ ★ ★ ★ ★

# TIME STOPS FOR NO MOUSE

Michael Hoeye

The mouse Hermux Tantamoq, a quiet city watch- and clock-mender, falls in love with the beautiful, daredevil aviatrix Linka Perflinger and drops headlong into the most extraordinary adventure, in which he uncovers a quest to find the formula for eternal youth. He unravels great mysteries and, much to his surprise, proves himself to be a very unusual and brave hero.

This is a book of great charm and humour as well as of daring and fearlessness – Hermux, the food- and fashion-conscious mouse is a memorable hero, far too good to miss. With short chapters and a fast-paced story, this really is a page-turningly good read.

**Wendy Cooling**

## Next?

• Look out for the other **Hermux Tantamoq** adventures: *The Sands of Time, No Time Like Show Time* and *Time to Smell the Roses*.

• If you've enjoyed the fantasy, try **Redwall** by Brian Jacques (*UBG* 282) or the **Edge Chronicles** by Paul Stewart and Chris Riddell (*UBG* 97).

• If you want to laugh a lot, read Debi Gliori's *Pure Dead Magic*. (*UBG* 276)

# THE TIME-TRAVELLING CAT Julia Jarman

Topher, who is mourning the death of his mother, finds a cat and takes care of her; or rather, the cat herself decides to be cared for by Topher. He calls her Ka (Egyptian for 'double') as she looks exactly like the carving of a cat that his mother, an Egyptologist, had bought for him. Topher researches ancient Egypt, and he discovers that the ancient Egyptians used to take statues of animals and servants with them when they died. Topher loves Ka and feels that she understands what he is saying. Then one day the most amazing thing happens: he travels back in time to ancient Egypt! But will he be able to get back home?

This book blends adventure with history, and will show you how Topher finds a way to come to terms with his mum's death. It might just make you think a little, too...

**Julia Lytollis**

## Next?

• There are more books about Topher and Ka including *The Time-Travelling Cat and the Roman Eagle*.

• *Carbonel* by Barbara Sleigh is another wonderful book about a magical cat. (*UBG* 53)

• *Over Sea, Under Stone* by Susan Cooper is a brilliant book about magic happening in the everyday world.

★ ★ ★ ★ ★ ★

# TINTIN series Hergé

## Next?

• Try the **Asterix** cartoons by René Goscinny and Albert Uderzo. (*UBG* 24) Or if you think you're a bit old for those, there are many other graphic novels now available.

• What about other boy detectives? Look out for the hilarious **Diamond Brothers** books by Anthony Horowitz. (*UBG* 108)

• Or the classic *Emil and the Detectives* by Erich Kästner. (*UBG* 99)

Who is the most famous Belgian of all time? Easy. Tintin – the boy reporter with the orange quiff, his faithful dog Snowy at his side, and his loyal, if slow-witted, friend Captain Haddock who is never far away.

These stories, originally written 75 years ago, are a wonderful mix of adventure and danger as Tintin gets into and out of perilous predicaments with unerring regularity, and there are a few laughs thrown in for good measure.

One of the most enjoyable things about this series is the huge variety of places Tintin's adventures take him. There's the snow of the Himalayas in *Tintin in Tibet*, the tombs of Egypt in *Cigars of the Pharaoh*, the jungles of Central America in *Tintin and the Picaros*, and even the lunar landscape in *Explorers on the Moon*.

The books feature wonderful characters, such as the bungling detective duo Thomson and Thompson, and crazy Professor Calculus, not to mention Tintin himself.

The stories might be old, but Tintin is as sharp and captivating now as ever he was.

**Marcus Sedgwick**

# TOBY ALONE  Timothée de Fombelle

This is one of those books that has an important message at the heart of it, but which is so wonderfully written and full of character and adventure that you barely notice till it's over. It's set in a tree, inhabited by tiny people – one of whom is young Toby Lolness; the tree is the only world Toby's people have known, but now it's at threat, being plundered and excavated by greedy Joe Mitch and his accomplices. Is it too late for this beautiful place to be saved? Toby's father, a great scientist, is the only man who understands how the tree really works, and what really matters, but the authorities are against him, and it soon falls to Toby to be the hero, against all the odds.

It's a book about friendship and family, and about looking after the only world we've got – beautifully written and translated, and glowing with warmth.

**Daniel Hahn**

### Next?

• Beware, though – this book only tells half the story; you can't read it without its sequel, *Elisha's Eyes*.

• For another tale of ecological threats and young heroism, read Carl Hiaasen's *Hoot*. (*UBG* 157)

• Or for more tiny people, there's Mary Norton's *The Borrowers* (*UBG* 43), or Lynne Reid Banks's *The Indian in the Cupboard* (*UBG* 173) or T.H. White's *Mistress Masham's Repose* (*UBG* 231).

★ ★ ★ ★ ★ ★

# TOM TRUEHEART, BOY ADVENTURER
## Ian Beck

### Next?

• For more of Tom's adventures, read *Tom Trueheart and the Land of Dark Stories*.

• For funny fantasies, you can't beat Eva Ibbotson's *Which Witch?* and *Not Just a Witch* or try her *The Secret of Platform 13* (*UBG* 303).

• Try *Shadow Forest* by Matt Haig for a fairy-tale adventure with darker humour. (*UBG* 306)

Once upon a time, Tom Trueheart lived with his mother and six older brothers – all named Jack – in a little house in the forest.

His brothers work for the Story Bureau, an organisation that writes the beginning of adventures, which the heroes then complete. But someone in the Story Bureau is sabotaging the storylines and Tom's brothers have gone missing, so princesses aren't being saved and beanstalks aren't being chopped down. Can mild-mannered Tom find the courage to rescue his brothers so the stories can end happily ever after?

A clever twist on the familiar world of fairy tales, complete with mystery, adventure, a bit of humour and a really likeable hero.

**Madelyn Travis**

# TOM'S MIDNIGHT GARDEN Philippa Pearce ●●●

**Next?**

• Another wonderful story by Philippa Pearce is *Minnow on the Say*. (*UBG* 230)

• You might also like Penelope Lively's *The Ghost of Thomas Kempe* (*UBG* 125) and *Moondial* by Helen Cresswell, both tales of children who enter mysterious supernatural worlds.

• If you were enchanted by the skating scene, read another of Berlie's favourites, *The Silver Skates* by Mary Mapes Dodge.

Tom has been sent away to stay with his boring aunt and uncle. There's nothing to do, no one to play with, and their small flat doesn't even have a garden. But when one night the clock strikes 13, Tom wanders downstairs to find the furniture in the hall has all changed. And when he opens the back door, he finds the most exciting garden he's ever seen. There are trees to climb, hidden corners to explore ... and a child from another time, Hattie, who has no one to play with either.

Tom's days continue to be boring ... but every night he sneaks outside to the garden, to live a life his aunt and uncle know nothing about. One night Hattie gives him a present: a pair of skates. When the river freezes, they skate together, the boy from now and the girl from then, miles and miles, and for me that scene is one of the most thrilling and wonderful of anything that I've read in any children's book.

**Berlie Doherty**

★ ★ ★ ★ ★ ★

# THE TRANSFER Terence Blacker ●●

Have you ever felt that football is the most important thing in the world? Well, Stanley *knows* it is. Playing, watching, dreaming, thinking, he lives for football and particularly for his team, City. But City are about to be relegated, and Stanley knows he's got to do something, anything. His mum is a computer scientist, and she's working on cybertelekinesis ... and Stanley has a program he's been working on himself: 'TargetMan', with a superhero striker who has the best skills in the world – but who uncannily looks a little like an older version of Stanley. And when he puts these two things together, the strangest things start to happen...

Football, computers and a magic boot-stud take Stanley into an adventure that's more fast-paced and exciting than a cup final in extra time.

**Leonie Flynn**

**Next?**

• More football? Try *Falling 4 Mandy* by Chris d'Lacey or any of Neil Arksey's books: *Brooksie*, *Flint* and *MacB* (*UBG* 215).

• How about a football detective story? Try *Foul Play* by Tom Palmer.

• Two other stories about computers are *Hacker* by Malorie Blackman (*UBG* 140) and Gillian Rubinstein's *Space Demons* (*UBG* 320).

# A TRAVELLER IN TIME  Alison Uttley ●●●

### Next?

• I may well have been influenced by this book when I wrote *Moondial*, also about a girl who finds herself travelling not just to one, but two other periods of time.

• Other time-slip stories are *Charlotte Sometimes* (*UBG* 58) and *A Stitch in Time* (*UBG* 325).

• For another book set during the reign of Elizabeth I, try Geoffrey Trease's *Cue for Treason*. (*UBG* 76)

To be honest, I first read this as a grown-up but was hooked by it. It is a mixture of historical novel and time-slip fantasy. Penelope goes to stay at Thackers, an old manor house in Derbyshire. There she finds she can first hear faint voices calling, see dim figures in the flickering lamplight, and then begins to travel in time, back to a real adventure in the sixteenth century.

This is based on the author's own childhood at Wingfield. I once went to visit Wingfield and half thought I was travelling through time myself. The worlds of Penelope's real life and her experiences in the past are wonderfully woven together. The adventure she finds herself in is the Babington plot to save Mary Queen of Scots and you have a real sense of being involved in history as it unfolds. And Penelope falls in love with Francis Babington, though it is a love doomed from the start.

**Helen Cresswell**

★ ★ ★ ★ ★ ★

# TREASURE ISLAND  Robert Louis Stevenson ●●●

It begins quietly enough for young Jim Hawkins, son of the innkeeper of The Admiral Benbow. An old seaman comes to stay. But, from the first time we hear the refrain – 'Fifteen men on the dead man's chest, Yo-ho-ho and a bottle of rum' – and learn of the mysterious 'black spot', we are hooked.

Once hooked, Stevenson never lets us go, us or Jim Hawkins – we're in this together. He takes us on a giddy journey of twists and turns of fate, through hope, horror and despair and back again. There's violence and blood and treachery (unforgettably embodied in the pirate, Long John Silver) on board ship, the *Hispaniola*, and on Treasure Island itself. And Long John Silver and his friends are no cut-out pirates, these are cut-*throat* pirates, the real thing! We live the adventure with Jim, are terrified with him and for him, all the while urging him on, willing him to win through somehow, anyhow, and bring us safely home.

**Michael Morpurgo**

### Next?

• *Kidnapped* by Robert Louis Stevenson is also a brilliant, classic adventure story. (*UBG* 188)

• More pirates? Try the weirder and scarier *Plundering Paradise* by Geraldine McCaughrean.

• For a very modern, female pirate, read Tanith Lee's *Piratica*. (*UBG* 270)

# TROLL FELL Katherine Langrish ●●

The first book this century to spark a sudden interest in trolls – and possibly its cause – *Troll Fell* begins the story of Peer Ulfsson, the orphan fostered by his hideous uncles, the Grimsson brothers. Peter soon realises that the uncles want to sell him into slavery to the trolls, who inhabit the menacing fell.

Peer has one friend, Hilde, whose family represents normal life, something he feels likely to be shut out from for ever. His uncles Baldur and Grim are implacably cruel to Peer and his dog Loki, but they are the millers of Trollsvik and are proud of it, though chronically short of money.

It is very satisfying when they get their comeuppance and suffer a fitting penalty for dealing with trolls.

**Mary Hoffman**

### Next?

• *Troll Mill* by Katherine Langrish carries on the story, with Peer now living with Gudrun and Ralf and still sweet on their daughter, Hilde. Even more time passes before the action of *Troll Blood*, the magnificent conclusion to the trilogy.

• *Sea of Trolls* by Nancy Farmer has a similar setting, in the frozen North, and has trolls, too. (*UBG* 299)

• Or for some classic stories of trolls, try *The Troll With No Heart in His Body* by Lise Lunge-Larsen.

★ ★ ★ ★ ★ ★

# TROY Adèle Geras ●●●

### Next?

• There is a sequel: *Ithaka*. Or, for other Adèle Geras, try her books in the **Historical House** series. (*UBG* 152)

• You might like to read a translation of Homer's epic poem *The Iliad*, the first story of the fall of Troy; or a simpler retelling like Rosemary Sutcliff's *The Wanderings of Odysseus* and *Black Ships Before Troy* (*UBG* 36).

• Or try another historical mystery with Jamila Gavin's *The Robber Baron's Daughter*.

You may know the story of the Trojan War, the long war caused by Princess Helen, whose legendary beauty 'launched a thousand ships' – but Adèle Geras's *Troy* is no straight retelling of history…

This Trojan tale is told through the eyes of two sisters, Marpessa and Xanthe, who are trapped behind the walls of their city after ten years of siege by the Greek army. Bored by the siege, Aphrodite, goddess of desire, causes Marpessa and Xanthe to fall in love with the same man. A touchingly human story of love and loyalty unfolds against the backdrop of legend, lightened by comic asides from a pair of kitchen 'gossips'. But in keeping with the Greek myths, there is real tragedy here, too. Readers looking for depth and emotion should not miss this powerful book.

**Katherine Roberts**

# TRUE COLOURS  Rhian Tracey

Rosie has discovered that she has an amazing new gift – she can see auras. By reading the colour of the aura glowing around someone's head she can tell what sort of mood that person is in, and also, more interestingly, if they are lying... Rosie can use her new gift to discover whether two of her teachers really are going out, and maybe even to help her win the election to Year Captain. But as she starts to use her powers to try and discover her friends' secrets – and her mother's – things start to get tricky. And will she be able to discover the biggest secret of all? Will she be able – at last – to find out who her dad is?

An entertaining, and often touching, story about friendships and family, with a warming, satisfying ending.

**Daniel Hahn**

### Next?
• Try something else spooky, yet warm and fun – like Cathy Hopkins's **Zodiac Girls** series; try *From Geek to Goddess*. Or her **Mates, Dates...** series.
• Or for a clairvoyant mum and a girl who really starts to see ghosts, try Echo Freer's *Mimosa Fortune*.
• For a girl who's always craved excitement, read about Caitlin, in Rosie Rushton's *Summer of Secrets*.

★ ★ ★ ★ ★ ★

# THE TRUTH SAYER  Sally Prue

### Next?
• If you enjoyed this, you're sure to like the sequel – *Truth Sayer: March of the Owlmen*. Sally's other books are all worth looking out for, too: *The Devil's Toenail* is about a boy desperate to be accepted into a gang and *Cold Tom* is about a stranger who watches us (*UBG* 67).
• Another funny book – this time about the intrusion of someone from the past into the present – is *The Ghost of Thomas Kempe* by Penelope Lively. (*UBG* 125)
• *A Wizard of Earthsea* by Ursula Le Guin is a wonderful story about an apprentice wizard who struggles to control a terrible shadow-beast he has released into the world. (*UBG* 95)

Nian has special powers: he can see into the future and use his mind to move objects or to levitate. Kidnapped and taken to the House of Truth to be indoctrinated with ancient 'Wisdom', he has only one aim: to escape and go home. But his attempt to break free takes him to another world – and into the front room of the house where Jacob Rush lives with his family. The confusion caused as Nian tries to make sense of this extraordinary world will make you laugh, and the events that follow are both exciting and funny. Of course there is more to Nian than first appears. He has a destiny to fulfil, and in the end he must make a difficult choice.

**Ann Turnbull**

# TUCK EVERLASTING Natalie Babbitt

**Next?**

• Something else quite magical is Oscar Wilde's *The Happy Prince and other stories*. (*UBG* 142)

• J.M. Barrie's *Peter Pan* is another book about eternal youth and the price you pay for it. (*UBG* 262)

• Or try the extraordinary picture book *How to Live Forever* by Colin Thompson. (*UBG* 162)

Don't be put off by this book's slow descriptive beginning. You'll be gripped as soon as ten-year-old Winnie is kidnapped – as she's about to drink water from a hidden spring. Scared and angry, she's forced to go home with her kidnappers, the strange Tuck family. They tell her she can choose whether to drink from the spring or not, but if she does she'll live for ever – like them. She must think about it first.

Suddenly the action speeds up with the arrival of the sinister Man in the Yellow Suit. He wants to sell the water and exhibit the Tucks as proof of its magic. Ma Tuck takes drastic action which involves Winnie. Does Winnie drink the water and live for ever? You won't know till the last page.

**Julia Jarman**

★ ★ ★ ★ ★ ★

# THE TULIP TOUCH Anne Fine

This is one of the most chilling books I've ever read. Quite, quite brilliant on the nature and causes of evil.

Natalie finds Tulip exciting, and doesn't care that everyone else is so wary of her. But as Tulip's games become more and more sinister, Natalie realises that her friend will stop at nothing...

Anne Fine is a superb writer, and to my mind this is her best book. Completely unputdownable, you are totally convinced by Natalie, the otherwise friendless narrator, describing how she is drawn into Tulip's dangerous world. The portrait of Tulip is drawn with such acute sensitivity, such understanding; the message is that no one is born evil – that we are all products of our upbringing.

**Malachy Doyle**

**Next?**

• Anne Fine has written many wonderful novels: try *The Book of the Banshee* or the more hard-hitting *The Road of Bones*, about a boy growing up in a terrifyingly brutal society.

• Elizabeth Laird's *Jake's Tower* is another dark and tense story. (*UBG* 178)

• And Robert Cormier's *The Chocolate War* is another book about good, evil and standing up for yourself.

# TULKU  Peter Dickinson

**Next?**

• For other novels which look at what happens when opposing religious views come into contact, try *Between the Moon and the Rock* by Judy Allen or Jan Mark's *The Eclipse of the Century*, a tremendous read which, like *Tulku*, takes you to an unfamiliar part of the world where you cannot take your certainties for granted.

• Or how about something else very different by Peter Dickinson? Try *City of Gold*. (*UBG* 64)

Theo is an English boy who lives in a small Chinese settlement with his missionary parents, until one day they get swept up in a war and Theo is left orphaned and alone. A chance meeting with Mrs Jones, an eccentric English plant hunter, takes Theo on a journey out of China and into Tibet and, eventually, to the Dong Pe monastery.

*Tulku* is a thrilling adventure story with a deeply serious theme. During his perilous journey to Tibet, Theo finds that he is also on a spiritual journey to discover if the religious certainties he grew up with can survive contact with different beliefs. After battling with the terrifying demons of Dong Pe, Theo finds his own truth at last, and learns much about tolerance and compassion.

**Gill Vickery**

★ ★ ★ ★ ★ ★

# TUMTUM AND NUTMEG  Emily Bearn

Tumtum and Nutmeg are husband and wife mice who live in Nutmeg Hall, a beautifully appointed home in the broom cupboard of Rose Cottage. They live in great comfort and want for nothing.

But for the two children who dwell in Rose Cottage itself, the story is very different. Lucy and Arthur live with their eccentric inventor father who isn't very good at running a household. Their house is a mess, their clothes need mending and they are left to fend very much for themselves.

So kind Tumtum and Nutmeg decide to help them, sneaking into their room at night to do little jobs. All goes beautifully until the horrid Aunt Ivy comes to stay – a nasty woman who hates mice and will stop at nothing to get rid of them...

This book is a little gem, as charming and well designed as Nutmeg Hall itself.

**Susan Reuben**

**Next?**

• Move on to the next **Tumtum and Nutmeg** book, *The Great Escape*.

• For another story of a miniature world, try *The Borrowers* by Mary Norton and its sequels. (*UBG* 43)

• Another animal tale, this time about a rat, a mole, a toad and a badger, is *The Wind in the Willows* by Kenneth Grahame. (*UBG* 385)

## THE TURBULENT TERM OF TYKE TILER  Gene Kemp

Are you one of those people who can't seem to do anything right, no matter how hard you try? If so, you'll enjoy reading about Tyke, who can't get it right, either. All Tyke wants to do is climb. The school tower is a terrible temptation; its bell hasn't been rung since 1945. Unfortunately, before there's a chance for Tyke to ring that bell, trouble in the shape of Danny, Tyke's best friend, gets in the way. When Danny innocently takes money from a teacher's bag, Tyke tries to help and ends up being blamed for stealing the money. That problem gets sorted out only to be replaced by another, and another.

Tyke's adventures make you laugh but they also make you think, especially at the end when the author springs an amazing surprise!

**Gill Vickery**

### Next?

• Cricklepit Combined School where Tyke is a pupil has its fair share of students who can't seem to stay out of trouble. Read *Just Ferret* and *Gowie Corby Plays Chicken* to find out what some more of them get up to.

• *The Clock Tower Ghost* is another great book by Gene Kemp. (*UBG* 66)

• You might enjoy reading about Jules in Lee Weatherley's *Child X*. Jules is deeply involved in a school play whilst also juggling with family problems. (*UBG* 60)

## The Ultimate Readers' Poll

# Top Ten Books That Should Be Filmed

1. **The Recruit** by Robert Muchamore

2. **Vampirates** by Justin Somper

3. **The Spook's Apprentice** by Joseph Delaney

4. **Midnight for Charlie Bone** by Jenny Nimmo

5. **All American Girl** by Meg Cabot

6. **The Illustrated Mum** by Jacqueline Wilson

7. **Mortal Engines** by Philip Reeve

8. **Molly Moon's Book of Hypnotism** by Georgia Byng

9. **A Dog Called Grk** by Joshua Doder

10. **Measle and the Wrathmonk** by Ian Ogilvy

# THE TWELVE AND THE GENII  Pauline Clarke

Max finds the 12 toy soldiers wrapped in an old cloth under a loose floorboard in his family's new home. He knows the soldiers' fortunes are always watched over by 'genii', and is more than happy to take on that role for himself, and guide this boisterous troupe through their imagined battles. Before Max, however, the Twelve had some very famous genii (they used to belong to the Brontës), which makes them even more valuable in the eyes of other people. So Max has to help the Twelve solve their own crises – and save them from theft. Some of the language is quite dated, but I promise if you read this book you too will totally believe in the world of the Twelve.

**Jon Appleton**

**Next?**
• A story about real wars? Try **War Horse** by Michael Morpurgo (**UBG** 373) or **The Machine Gunners** by Robert Westall (**UBG** 215).
• And for real battles enacted through toy soldiers, look at Iain Lawrence's **Lord of the Nutcracker Men**, which is set during the First World War.

★ ★ ★ ★ ★ ★

# TWENTY THOUSAND LEAGUES UNDER THE SEA  Jules Verne

**Next?**
• If you want to read about how real submarines were used in wartime, read **Depth Charge Danger** by Jim Eldridge, in the **Warpath** series.
• Another classic Jules Verne book is **Around the World in Eighty Days**. (**UBG** 23)
• If you get the taste for classic adventure, why not try **King Solomon's Mines** by H. Rider Haggard. (**UBG** 191)
• Or for some real-life exploration, read **Kon-Tiki** by Thor Heyerdahl. (**UBG** 194)

This is the story of the mysterious Captain Nemo, an Indian Prince who doesn't much like people, and the self-contained world of his super-sleek submarine, *Nautilus*. When the French naturalist Professor Aronax, his faithful servant Conseil and the Canadian harpooner Ned Land begin a hazardous voyage to rid the seas of a little-known sea-monster, they have no idea that the scary creature will turn out to be *Nautilus* the submarine. Once they have made this discovery, Aronax and the others set out with Nemo to explore the underwater world together. But unbeknownst to the others, Nemo's mission is one of revenge…

**Sara Wheeler**

# THE TWITS  Roald Dahl

### Next?
• You might want to read about other dreadful people and events in Roald Dahl's *George's Marvellous Medicine*. (*UBG* 123)

• More nasty characters abound in Lemony Snicket's more challenging **A Series of Unfortunate Events**. (*UBG* 306)

• Or try Philip Ardagh's *The Fall of Fergal* – it's pretty gruesome, too. (*UBG* 108)

• Or look for Chris Mould's funny series, **Something Wickedly Weird**, starting with *The Wooden Mile*.

This short novel is about a dreadful couple who play appallingly cruel tricks on one another, and are eventually outwitted by a family of acrobatic monkeys. This may not be one of Dahl's best books: the story is thin, and the only sympathetic characters are the monkeys, who don't really come into the story until the second half. But *The Twits* is still tremendous fun, especially to read aloud, and Quentin Blake's illustrations are priceless. The sheer horribleness of Mr and Mrs Twit and their nasty tricks can't help but make you giggle: Mrs Twit plops her glass eye in Mr Twit's mug of beer; Mr Twit puts a frog in her bed ('I'll bet it's that Giant Skillywiggler I saw on the floor just now,' he tells his terrified wife). Nasty, yes, but great fun.

**Kenneth Oppel**

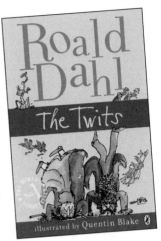

★ ★ ★ ★ ★ ★

# TWO WEEKS WITH THE QUEEN  Morris Gleitzman

Colin Mudford's younger brother Luke is dying of cancer, or so his parents say. They believe the doctors who say Luke can't be cured. Colin doesn't. He's determined to save his brother.

You have to admire Colin. He knows what's important and he never gives up. When his parents send him to stay with his relations in London, to get him out of the way, he has a brilliant idea – to contact the Queen and get her doctor to fly to Australia and cure Luke. Don't let the subject matter of this story put you off. This story is a mix of sad and funny and hilarious, just like real life. You'll laugh and cry but feel strangely better for reading it.

**Julia Jarman**

### Next?
• You might want to read **Bumface** also by Morris Gleitzman. (*UBG* 49)

• *Pig-Heart Boy* by Malorie Blackman tackles illness in a more-serious way. (*UBG* 267)

• Or try *Up on Cloud Nine* by Anne Fine. (*UBG* 364)

# UG: BOY GENIUS OF THE STONE AGE  Raymond Briggs

### Next?

• You might also like other books by Raymond Briggs such as *Fungus the Bogeyman*, which is pure gross-out! (*UBG* 121) Or its complete opposite, *The Snowman*.

• *A is for Aarrgh!* by William J. Brooke is a very funny story set in the Stone Age. Or look for John Grant's wonderful caveboy books, **Littlenose**, starting with *Littlenose the Hero*.

• A really good comic-strip series is **Asterix** by René Goscinny and Albert Uderzo; all are hilarious. (*UBG* 24)

Ug and his parents live in an age when everything is made from stone: stone footballs, stone bedspreads and even stone trousers! But Ug is full of new ideas for a better world: one where food is hot, balls bounce and trousers are soft. Unfortunately not everyone shares Ug's vision of the future. Even Ug's own mother can't understand him.

To make things even worse for Ug, his inventions never seem to serve any practical purpose. His round stone that rolls down the hill is great, but what is it actually for? Perhaps with the help of his father he might actually be able to create the soft trousers he has always dreamed of... This book is humorous, thoughtful and highly original!

**Neal Layton**

★ ★ ★ ★ ★ ★

# UNCANNY!  Paul Jennings

I remember loving *Unreal!* when I read it, Paul Jennings's first collection of twisted, unpredictable tales, and I've been a fan ever since. Paul writes about ordinary kids who have amazing things happen to them – surprising everyone around them. Mostly, his stories are told in the first person, which makes them very engaging – the narrators are the sorts of people you know from school and your local area. And some are real oddballs.

In *Uncanny!* we start with a corpse that's covered in tattoos from head to foot, then we meet a nude store dummy. Things get even more outrageous after that. No two stories are alike, and there's no way in the world you'll be able to guess how each one will end.

**Jon Appleton**

### Next?

• Other great Paul Jennings titles include *Unbearable!*, *Unbelievable!* and *Tongue-tied*.

• You might also enjoy *Seven Spiders Spinning* by Gregory Maguire, which is both spooky and silly.

• *The Day My Bum Went Psycho* by Andy Griffiths might also be up your street. (*UBG* 80) And Paul Jenning's collaboration with Morris Gleitzman, **Wicked!**, will be for sure! (*UBG* 383)

• You'll probably like Susan Gates's *Killer Mushrooms Ate My Gran* and *A Brief History of Slime* as well!

# UNCLE J.P. Martin

Uncle is an enormously rich elephant who normally wears a purple dressing gown. He has many employees and hangers-on and lives in a huge castle of many towers. When I was first asked to draw Uncle, many years ago, I wasn't quite sure how much I liked him; there was no escaping the fact that he was rather pompous. However, I revelled in the extraordinary number of characters in his world, especially the Badfort crowd – a dirty, bristly, badly behaved collection of layabouts with names like Beaver Hateman, Hitmouse and Jellytussle. All the books are being reissued now, and this gallery of eccentrics and their exploits once more put on show. Watch out for that Hitmouse, though – he's a nasty little piece of work.

**Quentin Blake**

### Next?
• Try and find one of the adventures of Babar the Elephant and his family by Jean de Brunhoff. The stories are lovely, and the illustrations are brilliant. They're very young, but who cares when they're this good?

• Or for different (but equally sophisticated) animals, try *Doctor Dolittle* by Hugh Lofting. (*UBG* 87)

• For more (but very different) whimsy, try *Mr Popper's Penguins* by Richard and Florence Atwater. (*UBG* 238)

★ ★ ★ ★ ★ ★

# UNCLE MONTAGUE'S TALES OF TERROR Chris Priestley

### Next?
• More Priestley-esque horror? Read *Tales of Terror from the Black Ship*, if you dare! Or his historical adventures that start with *Death and the Arrow*. (*UBG* 81)

• For another story about stories within stories, try Reinhardt Jung's beautiful (and rather less alarming) *Bambert's Book of Missing Stories*. (*UBG* 27)

• Or for more horror-story nastiness, try Anthony Horowitz's *Horowitz Horror*. (*UBG* 158)

It can't be much fun being a child in one of Uncle Montague's stories. You're liable to be destroyed by an evil elm tree, pushed off a cliff by a hideously maimed version of yourself, pruned by a blind old woman wielding shiny-bladed secateurs, possessed by a demon bench-end or locked in a blanket chest with a sopping-wet girl who's been dead for rather a long time. These are not nice stories. Edgar likes to listen to Uncle Montague tell these stories, but it soon becomes clear that there may be some truth to them...

The atmosphere of Uncle M's room, filled with fascinating objects, and of the tales he tells, is wonderfully captured by Chris Priestley's storytelling skills and David Roberts's superb vignette pictures. A perfect late-night read – ghoulish and gruesome. But you may want to sleep with the lights on...

**Daniel Hahn**

# TIE-INS
## Now, Read the Book!
### by Leonie Flynn

If you visit almost any bookshop in the country you will find, usually in the children's or science-fiction sections, shelves of books that are based on TV programmes or films. These books, whether they're for babies hardly weaned or for adults, come under the heading of 'tie-ins' – a label that tells you exactly what they are, as they 'tie in' with whatever programme they're based on. If something is a success on screen, then more than likely there's a book or ten to go with it (and probably computer games, a soundtrack, action figures and even a fast-food meal!). Should you feel the need – and as long as the show or movie you like is popular enough – you'll find books to tell you about your favourite characters' lives before the series began, after it ended, and at all those moments that happen between episodes when the cameras are turned off.

Sometimes, of course, a film is based on a book, not the other way around. So *Northern Lights* is not the tie-in to *The Golden Compass* movie, though the books about the movie are – as is the book that tells the story of the movie for younger children in words that aren't actually Philip Pullman's. Confused? No need – if the book came first, it's not a tie-in. And, though I may be biased, where movies are concerned, the original book is always better than the film they make of it.

There are novelisations, too. These are just the story of the film, or a TV episode, put into print. Sometimes these will even answer nagging questions that the film / episode has raised but failed to answer. Melvin Burgess's *Billy Elliot* is a good example.

Some tie-ins are worth reading just to find out more about your favourite show. Some are actually good books in their own right. *Stargate: Atlantis* fans are lucky – read any of Martha Wells's tie-in books and you're in for a treat. She's a wonderful writer (of her own worlds, too), but she also brings the TV characters to brilliant life. What about *Star Wars*? Six movies, but a thousand books (well, that might be a small exaggeration, but then again...). Any good? Oh yes – and there's *Star Wars* books for every age and every interest, from the fantastic **Jedi Apprentice** series, to picture books that tell the stories of the movies, to novels that explore everything and anything to do with the worlds George Lucas created.

If you like kids' TV, then there are books to tie in to everything from *In the Night Garden* and *Dora the Explorer* through to *Pokémon* and *Avatar*.

And then there is *Doctor Who*. *Doctor Who* is the UK's all-time favourite sci-fi TV show. For many years it was consigned to the history bin – no new episodes were made, no one wanted to make more – but the show was kept alive through the fans' interest, the video (then subsequently DVD) release of old episodes and the books that were written about the show. Every regeneration of the Doctor had stories written about him, mostly by young authors, many of who went on to be famous in their own right. These books, the ones that helped keep the idea of the show alive, are still around if you hunt in second-hand shops or on eBay – and they're well worth finding too. The books that tie in to the more recent version of *Doctor Who*, the ones starring David Tennant, are much easier to find – and some of them are brilliant stories. Check out the list below for some ideas of which ones to look for.

Most very popular shows have tie-ins for younger as well as older readers. You can usually see which ones will suit you best just by looking at the first page (put very basically, the smaller the print usually means the older the reader the books are meant for).

You'll find that some tie-in authors write in more than one invented world. Catherine Hapka writes *High School Musical*, *Lost*, *Batman*, *Shrek* and *National Treasure* tie-ins. Diane Duane writes *Star Trek* tie-ins as well as her own brilliant **Young Wizards** series. As well as the **Astrosaurs** and **Freekham High** series, Steve Cole has written tie-ins, too – look for his **Doctor Who** books, and his **Mr Bean** stories. Look out for authors you like and remember their names for next time you're book hunting, because as in any genre as huge as this, some writers are bound to be better than others. Be adventurous – and ignore anyone who says these books are rubbish. Read them, then make up your own mind. And if anyone really tries to tell you they are not worth reading, you can tell them that some of the very best authors around have written for *Doctor Who*, *Buffy*, *Star Wars*, *Star Trek*...

## A Few Tie-in Novels

- *Sting of the Zygons* (Doctor Who)
- *The Resurrection Casket* (Doctor Who)
- *The Many Hands* (Doctor Who)
- *The Lost Scrolls: Water* (Avatar)
- *The Best Pokémon Adventures: Red* (Pokémon)
- *Stories from East High: Broadway Dreams* (High School Musical)
- **Jedi Apprentice** series (Star Wars)
- *See No Evil* (Smallville)
- *How I Survived My Summer Vacation* (Buffy)
- *Ishmael* (Star Trek)
- *Yu-Gi-Oh* (Yu-Gi-Oh)

# UNDER THE MOON AND OVER THE SEA: a collection of Caribbean poems
### Edited by John Agard and Grace Nichols

This is a big, bright, lively collection of verse selected by two of my favourite poets: John Agard and Grace Nichols. It is brimming with laughter and fun and delightfully inventive language. Over 50 poems capture the sights and smells, sounds and atmosphere of the Caribbean. There are poems about hurricanes and hummingbirds, crabs and coconuts, clear blue seas and pink coral beaches and much, much more. The collection is divided into five sections, each illustrated by an outstanding artist, including my very favourite, Jane Ray. These musical, haunting poems will excite, challenge and inspire all those who hear them.

**Gervase Phinn**

**Next?**

• More Caribbean poetry is in Agard and Nichols's *A Caribbean Dozen. Everybody Got a Gift* is a collection of Grace Nichols's own poems.

• Try *Island of the Children, an Anthology of New Poems*, compiled by Angela Huth.

• Or for stories about the Caribbean, try Curdella Forbes's *Flying With Icarus*.

• Or for a collection of great, new poems, *The Secret Life of Pants*, chosen by Roger Stevens.

★ ★ ★ ★ ★ ★

# UP ON CLOUD NINE  Anne Fine

**Next?**

• The heroine of Gillian Cross's darker *Tightrope* has trouble fitting in; to create excitement she makes up a sort of double life. (*UBG* 347)

• The story of another of Anne Fine's books, *The Tulip Touch*, is a little bit like this one; but be warned – its main character is a much nastier piece of work than Stolly. (*UBG* 355)

• A girl who yearns for a real friend is Tizzie, in Linda Newbery's *Nevermore* – a story full of mystery, secrets and obsession.

What if your best friend was lying in front of you, unconscious and, perhaps, dying? What if you were afraid his fall wasn't an accident?

Ian's best friend Stolly is the craziest, most entertaining and most maddening friend anyone could have. No one can make up a really convincing story like Stolly. In fact, Stolly's so happy inventing stories, living on cloud nine, that the real world sometimes gets just too boring – and then it's Ian's job to keep Stolly on safe ground.

This marvellous book turns an extraordinary story inside out and tells it with great energy and humour. It is a moving book, but a joyful one, too, with really vivid portraits of many comic characters, and a very special friendship.

**Sally Prue**

# URGUM THE AXEMAN

### Kjartan Poskitt

### Next?

- There are two more books – and I really hope they'll be a fourth. Maybe even a fifth – *Urgum* really is that good! The next are: *Urgum and the Seat of Flames* and *Urgum and the Googoobah*.
- More hilarious happenings happen in Sam Llewellyn's books. Try *The Haunting of Death Eric*, featuring two kids, their ageing rock-star dad and a lot of spookiness. Or try his *Little Darlings*, about the most horrible children in the world. (*UBG* 199)
- Or how about savages, but less humour? Try Michelle Paver's *Wolf Brother*. (*UBG* 390)

This is a weird and utterly wacky book with a wide range of mad and crazy characters. Fall off your seat laughing at every page, as Urgum – the bravest savage in the west – and his seven sons learn to deal with the sudden appearance of a ten-year-old daughter (who is actually a rather wicked gift from the gods). The trouble is she's wittier than all the boys (even Urgum), brings all sorts of girly things into the cave, and wins all the games. How will the boys cope? Will they lose all their killing instincts and become softy girls?

**Jonah Freud, age 10**

★ ★ ★ ★ ★ ★

# UTTERLY ME, CLARICE BEAN

### Lauren Child

Clarice Bean is the third child of a family of four who, along with their mum, dad, grandad, Chirp (Grandad's canary), Cement the dog and Fuzzy the cat, live in a permanent state of pandemonium. The household itself provides many a witty situation and a multitude of clever one-liners, but when Clarice Bean steps outside its confines, the madness does not stop. We meet her utterly best friend Betty Moody, her young neighbour the persistent Robert Granger (whom Grandad calls Shouting Boy) and a further wonderful array of characters at her school, who all lend a hand to make this book one of the funniest (including some great laugh-out-loud moments) and most original I've come across in a long time. Read it – you'll be hooked.

**Chris d'Lacey**

### Next?

- Move on to *Clarice Bean Spells Trouble* and *Clarice Bean, Don't Look Now*.
- And if you like wacky characters, have a look at Debi Gliori's **Pure Dead** series. (*UBG* 276) Or Philip Ardagh's equally strange stories, **Unlikely Exploits**, which start with *The Fall of Fergal*. (*UBG* 108)
- *Fairy Dust* by Gwyneth Rees is a fun look at girls and fairies and not at all what you might expect from the subject.

# VAMPIRATES: DEMONS OF THE OCEAN

## Justin Somper

Meet Connor and Grace Tempest, the twin children of a lighthouse keeper. When the twins are suddenly orphaned under mysterious circumstances, Connor is rescued by a band of cut-throat pirates, including the gorgeous Cheng-Li, who introduces him to a perilous life of adventure. Meanwhile, his sister Grace finds herself aboard a phantom ship with a phantom crew. Only they're not phantoms, exactly, because their fangs are very real!

What follows is a rollicking great sea adventure, with a cast of vivid characters who might just leap out of the book and try to bite you in the throat. And the best thing – this is only the first in a stunningly original series.

**Rodman Philbrick**

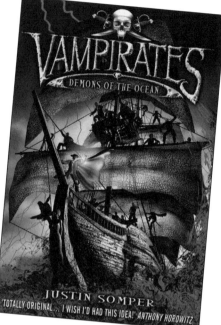

### Next?

• There's more – *Vampirates: Tide of Terror*, *Vampirates: Blood Captain* and *Vampirates: Black Heart*.

• Or for a swashbuckling tale involving a collector of mice, bloody deeds and a heroic girl, read Alex Millway's *The Mousehunter* (*UBG* 237), which comes complete with maps, diagrams and 'The Mousehunter's Almanac'.

• *Pirates!* by Celia Rees is a more traditional tale of piracy on high seas, as is Tanith Lee's *Piratica* (*UBG* 270), though that has a few twists to keep you guessing, too.

### Books With Bite!

• *Dracula* by Mary Shelley
• *Young Dracula* by Michael Lawrence
• *Vlad the Drac* by Anne Jungman
• *The Last Vampire* by Willis Hall
• *Twilight* by Stephanie Meyer
• *My Swordhand is Singing* by Marcus Sedgwick
• **Fang Gang** series by Roy Apps and Sumiko Shimakata
• *Dying to Meet You* by Michael Cox
• *My Sister the Vampire: Switched* by Sienna Mercer
• *Eighth Grade Bites* by Heather Brewer
• **Araminta Spook** series by Angie Sage

# VARJAK PAW S.F. Said

To be a Mesopotamian Blue, Varjak Paw the kitten knows, is to be a very special cat. But his family's exclusive existence in the house on the hill is threatened by the incursion of the menacing gentleman and his two eerie feline sidekicks. Varjak goes over the wall to the Outside, where the cats don't wear collars. His mission: to find help in the shape of that rumoured monster, a dog.

But what do dogs look like? Those four-wheeled speeding objects, perhaps? And what are the Vanishings?

Aided by street-wise cats and edified by his mystical communication with Great Ancestor Jalal who teaches him The Way, Varjak learns survival and how to succeed in this gripping, fast-moving, wise novel.

**Chris Stephenson**

### Next?
- There's a sequel – *The Outlaw Varjak Paw*.
- Look out for Adèle Geras's very funny revelations from Ozymandias the cat in *The Fabulous Fantora Files*.
- Two outstanding animal-based novels are by Henrietta Branford; *Fire, Bed and Bone*, the story of the Peasants'. Revolt as witnessed by a dog (*UBG* 113), and *White Wolf*, about a young wolf's quest to find and run with his own kind in the Canadian wastes.

★ ★ ★ ★ ★ ★

# VENUS SPRING: STUNT GIRL
## Jonny Zucker

### Next?
- Move on to the next Venus Spring titles: *Body Double, Star Turn* and *Face Off*.
- Try Anthony Horowitz's **Alex Rider** books, about a 14-year-old spy. Start with *Stormbreaker*. (*UBG* 12)
- Or what about a female super-spy? Try Jane Marshall's **Jane Blonde** series starting with *Sensational Spylet*, which lives up to its title! (*UBG* 180)

All 14-year-old Venus Spring dreams about is becoming a stunt double in the movies. Her grandfather Dennis is a famous stuntman, and Venus jumps at the chance of taking part in stunt camp, the course that Dennis runs for teenage stunt wannabees.

Events take a dark turn, though, when Franco, one of the boys on the camp, starts behaving in a mysterious way. He keeps sneaking off by himself after the night-time curfew, and when Venus decides to follow him she gets involved in something very sinister indeed. Suddenly she's using her stunt skills not for fun, but to save her own life.

This book is a real page-turner, and just as you think everything's nicely resolved, there's a cliffhanger at the end that will make you feel compelled to carry on to the next in the series.

**Susan Reuben**

# VERDIGRIS DEEP  Frances Hardinge

**Next?**
• More by the same author? Try *Fly by Night*, a very different type of story, this time about a re-imagined Georgian England and featuring a girl, her goose, highwaymen, spies and smugglers. (*UBG* 117)

• There's more supernatural mystery – and a very creepy story – in Celia Rees's *The Ghost Chamber*.

• Or for breathtaking, strange, wonderful adventures, try Philip Reeve's *Larklight* (*UBG* 196) and the sequel, *Starcross*.

What if you and two of your friends stole money from a wishing well, and then had to grant the wishes of the people who had thrown the coins in? This is the story behind *Verdigris Deep*. It sounds fairly impossible, doesn't it? Yet the witch of the wishing well has given the three main characters powers so that they can perform these tasks. One of them has power over electrical appliances, another begins to speak the thoughts of any people who get within a certain radius, and the other has eyes growing in the back of his hand. However, as the wishes continue, two of the friends, Ryan and Chelle, realise that each wish has another hidden within, which is deadly. And they also realise that as they work their way through the coins, their powers should be fading. But instead they are growing stronger...

**Tobias Druitt**

★ ★ ★ ★ ★ ★

# THE VERY PERSISTENT GAPPERS OF FRIP
## George Saunders

Gappers love goats. Each day, the bright-orange, baseball-sized organisms with many eyes, crawl out of the sea to mob the poor animals. The children of Frip have to brush the gappers back into the ocean or else the gappers emit a high-pitched happy shriek of pleasure, causing the goats to stop producing milk. Such is life in the town until, one day, the gappers, led by one with a somewhat larger than average brain, gang up on young Capable's goats because they are closer to the water's edge. See how she manages the problem, through the witty text and lavish illustrations by Lane 'Stinky Cheese Man' Smith. An inspirational fable for readers of all ages – thought provoking and very funny.

**Neal Layton**

**Next?**
• Try another crazy fable, such as André Maurois's *Fattypuffs and Thinifers*. (*UBG* 111)

• What about some Roald Dahl? *Charlie and the Chocolate Factory* is fast, fantastic and utterly delicious. (*UBG* 58)

• Or what about the totally disgusting *Fungus the Bogeyman* by Raymond Briggs? It's wonderful – just don't show it to any adults – they'll think it's too horrible to read. (*UBG* 121)

# A VICARAGE FAMILY  Noel Streatfeild  ●●●

The main character in this book is Noel Streatfeild herself (named Vicky in the story) and this is a warmly told account of her childhood as the daughter of a poor parish vicar in the years leading up to the start of the First World War. Vicky, her two sisters, and favourite cousin John, are growing up in the loving but sometimes oppressive environment of the vicarage where Vicky struggles to be understood. Labelled as the difficult one, she suffers the consequences of a fiery nature and an inability to turn the other cheek as her father would like. This is an entertaining, funny and sad account of the years before the prophecy that 'Vicky is the one who will surprise us all...' came true.

**Gwyneth Rees**

### Next?
• If you want to read more by Noel Streatfeild, I strongly recommend *Ballet Shoes*. (*UBG* 28)
• Why not try another book based on an author's childhood? Look out for *Little House on the Prairie* by Laura Ingalls Wilder (*UBG* 203) or *Little Women* by Louisa May Alcott (*UBG* 208).
• A story of a girl growing up in very different circumstances is *Daddy-Long-Legs*. (*UBG* 77)

★ ★ ★ ★ ★ ★

# VICKY ANGEL  Jacqueline Wilson  ●●

### Next?
• To see the story from the other point of view, try *The Great Blue Yonder* by Alex Shearer.
• Also read the amazing (and very sad) *Bridge to Terabithia* by Katherine Paterson. (*UBG* 47)
• More about angels? Read about the escapades of Mel and her angelic friends in Annie Dalton's **Angels Unlimited** series. (*UBG* 19)
• And there are lots of brilliant Jacqueline Wilsons: try *The Story of Tracy Beaker* (*UBG* 332), *Secrets* and *Double Act* (*UBG* 91).

Do you have a best friend – someone you spend every moment of your day with? Someone you sit next to at school (unless your teacher has already had to separate you ...), and then phone up the moment you get home? And have you ever wondered what you'd do if your friend suddenly wasn't there any more?

That's what happens to Jade, who suddenly loses her best friend, Vicky – beautiful, confident (and sometimes maybe just a bit selfish) Vicky – who's been her best best best friend since nursery school.

What will Jade do? The only person who can help her cope, who can talk to her, is Vicky, and she's gone – or is she?

Jacqueline Wilson never shies away from difficult subjects – yet however sad her stories, somehow her books always leave you feeling a little better, stronger, happier about the world. And *Vicky Angel* is one of her very best.

**Daniel Hahn**

# THE VILLAGE BY THE SEA  Anita Desai

Hari and Lila live with their family in a small fishing town in India. With their mother bedridden and their father always drunk or asleep, Hari and Lila have had to grow up fast. Lila worries about food, she worries about their mother, who doesn't seem to get better, and she worries about her father's next rage. Hari is especially concerned about how he will ever make money to feed the family – he knows they are all counting on him.

Desperation and confusion lead Hari to run away to Bombay, where he is forced to learn how to stay alive in a big city. Lila, as a result, is left to cope with everything at home by herself. But in this heart-warming tale neither child is really alone, for they find valuable friends who help them not only to survive, but to find hope for the future, too.

**Candida Gray**

### Next?
• For another story about adventure in India, try *The Track of the Wind* by Jamila Gavin, from **The Wheel of Surya** trilogy. (*UBG* 378)
• For Indian children in the UK, try Narinder Dhami's *Bindi Babes*, the funny, irreverent story of three sisters living with their dad, and dealing with their mum's death.
• For a very different book about children having to fend for themselves, read *Gumble's Yard* by John Rowe Townsend. (*UBG* 140)

★ ★ ★ ★ ★ ★

# VIOLET AND THE MEAN AND ROTTEN PIRATES
## Richard Hamilton

### Next?
• More Richard Hamilton? Try the story of a boy and his grandfather – both of whom happen to be ghosts – in *Ghostboy and the Moonbalm Treasure*.
• More pirates swagger through the **Pirate Princess** series by Judy Brown. This time they're all female and they're out to save princesses from dull and boring marriages! The books are: *Portia*, *Pandora*, *Pancake* and *Poppy*.
• Another baby that not only turns up in an unexpected place but is also very strange is in Allan Ahlberg's *The Giant Baby*.

The pirates of the *Sleek Sally* have enough trouble, with a captain who can't stand the sight of blood and a distinct shortage of treasure in the hold. Then they board a vessel that's been cleared out by another cut-throat crew. There's nothing left except an abandoned baby. They adopt her, against the captain's advice, name her Violet (Vile for short) and try to bring her up as a proper, mean and rotten pirate. It's not all plain sailing: Vile loves the life, but she has ideas of her own.

A gentle, funny story, with illustrations by Sam Hearn that exactly suit the mood. The best line is probably when the captain tells his crew the awful truth about their new pet. Babies need NAPPIES!

**Ann Halam**

# VLAD THE DRAC  Ann Jungman

## Next?

• Vlad has lots more adventures! For starters, look out for **Vlad the Drac Returns**, and **Vlad the Drac, Superstar**.

• Or what about something really scary and grusome? Try Jamie Rix's **Grizzly Tales** series, starting with *Nasty Little Beasts*.

• For more (slightly older) vampire stories, read **The Last Vampire** by Willis Hall. (*UBG* 196)

• Or try Michael Lawrence's *Young Dracula*.

The hero of this funny book is a little vampire who is squeamish about blood.

Like everyone else, Paul and Judy know that vampires don't exist – until, that is, they come across a baby one on holiday in Romania. The pocket-sized Vlad has slept under a stone for a hundred years and begs to be taken back to London with them.

Luckily, Vlad is a vegetarian, but he still manages to cause chaos (in the way that small aliens do when they're left home alone).

Proud, moody and funny, the tiny Vlad has a larger-than-life personality that is completely endearing without being the least bit soppy. His adventures at a football match, a fancy-dress party, school, not to mention a certain leg-biting episode, are hilarious.

**Kate Petty**

★ ★ ★ ★ ★ ★

# WALK TWO MOONS  Sharon Creech

The books I like best are both funny and deep like this one.

Thirteen-year-old Salamanca has been told by her sorrowing father that her mother, who has disappeared after a bus ride across America, is never coming back.

She refuses to believe this, and her grandparents (a splendidly eccentric and endearing couple) take her on a journey to follow the route her mother took across the heartlands of America – through South Dakota and Wyoming and Yellowstone – to find out what really happened.

As she travels, she tells her grandparents the story of her school friend Phoebe who has a lurid imagination and whose story echoes that of the heroine.

The last chapter, where Salamanca is led to the truth in a valley in Idaho, is so exciting that one finds oneself reading faster and faster – and yet one can't bear to miss a word.

**Eva Ibbotson**

## Next?

• You might enjoy other books by Sharon Creech: try **Absolutely Normal Chaos** and **Chasing Redbird** – both about family life at its oddest, and full of wisdom. Or try her **The Wanderer**. (*UBG* 372)

• **Rules of the Road** by Joan Bauer is another American story full of life and humour. (*UBG* 290)

# THE WANDERER  Sharon Creech

When 13-year-old Sophie signs on for a boat trip across the Atlantic, little does she know what she is letting herself in for.

Not only will this trip be a chance for Sophie to get to know her two cousins, Brian and Cody, but it will also provide an opportunity for her finally to come to terms with a tragedy earlier in her life – something so bad that she has buried all conscious memory of it. It's only when the crew of *The Wanderer* find themselves fighting for their lives in a tremendous storm that Sophie allows herself to remember the past.

I adored this book. I particularly liked the way that Sharon Creech makes you work at having to slowly piece together what has happened to Sophie, rather than telling you straight. In some ways it's a bit like a detective story and, when you've finished it, I guarantee you'll want to start it all over again.

**Laura Hutchings**

## Next?

• Sharon Creech has written lots of books, and they are all worth reading – even if some might be a bit harder than this one. Look out for **Heartbeat**, about a girl coming to terms with her troubled family, **Ruby Holler** (**UBG** 288) and **Bloomability**, about a girl sent to boarding school in Switzerland.

• Try a book by Judy Blume: **Are You There, God? It's Me, Margaret** is brilliant. (**UBG** 22).

• Or read Tim Bowler's haunting **River Boy**. (**UBG** 286)

## Some Carnegie Medal Winners That Are Now Classics

• *The Family from One End Street* by Eve Garnett

• *The Little Grey Men* by B.B.

• *The Little White Horse* by Elizabeth Goudge

• *The Woolpack* by Cynthia Harnett

• *The Borrowers* by Mary Norton

• *Tom's Midnight Garden* by Philippa Pearce

• *The Owl Service* by Alan Garner

• *Watership Down* by Richard Adams

• *The Machine Gunners* by Robert Westall

• *The Ghost of Thomas Kempe* by Penelope Lively

# WAR GAME Michael Foreman

How rare that one person is not only a great artist, but a writer as well. Such is the case with Michael Foreman. He creates in words and pictures the story of a football match on Christmas Day 1914, the first Christmas of the First World War. Standing in the mud and rain of the trenches, faced with gunfire, rats and freezing weather, the soldiers long for home. Yet suddenly someone kicks a football into No Man's Land, and a match begins: England v. Germany. No rules. No referee. Greatcoats and caps for goalposts.

This book is all the more moving when you know that the four English soldiers are really the author's uncles who died in the war, aged between 18 and 24 years.

**James Riordan**

### Next?
• You might like Michael Foreman's personal account of World War II in the prize-winning *War Boy*, with his own wonderful illustrations.
• Ian Serraillier's *The Silver Sword* is about two young children's journey across war-torn Europe. (*UBG* 310)
• Or try Michael Morpurgo's *Friend or Foe*, about two boys who find two downed German airmen.

★ ★ ★ ★ ★ ★

# WAR HORSE Michael Morpurgo

### Next?
• Look out for Michael Morpurgo's *Farm Boy*.
• You may like to read other books about animals. A classic is the horse story *Black Beauty* by Anna Sewell. (*UBG* 35)
• Other animals in war may be found in Martin Booth's *War Dog*, about a poacher's dog trained to track the enemy and rescue the wounded in France during World War II. And don't miss Robert Westall's *Blitzcat*. (*UBG* 37)

In the village hall close to Michael Morpurgo's farm hangs a small, dusty painting of a horse. The inscription says: 'JOEY. Painted by Captain James Nicholls. Autumn 1914'. *War Horse* is Joey's story, told straight from 'the horse's mouth'.

Joey sees all the horrors and cruelty of the First World War, the slaughter of men and of the horses that had to pull the guns, carts and supplies. Yet he makes it through the war, only to be sold at auction in France – and probably to be killed for meat. Will he be saved by his friend, Sergeant Albert?

You'll have to read this book to find out...

**James Riordan**

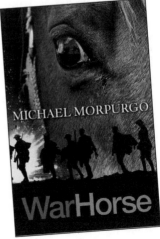

MICHAEL MORPURGO

WarHorse

# THE WAR OF JENKINS' EAR  Michael Morpurgo

### Next?

• For more cheery tales of life in a boarding school, try the **Jennings** books by Anthony Buckeridge; they're all easy to read and extremely funny. (**UBG** 181)

• For old-fashioned girls' school stories, try the **Chalet School** series by Elinor M. Brent-Dyer.

• William Mayne's **A Swarm in May** is an imaginative story set in a choir school. (**UBG** 337)

'Take off your slipper!' demands the headmaster. 'Which one, sir?' answers new boy Christopher coolly.

It begins like a normal, old-fashioned, boarding-school story... Christopher is in trouble for refusing to eat his rice pudding. And yet he is anything but normal. His father is a carpenter and, as he tells his new friend, Toby Jenkins, Christopher can work miracles... We, like Toby, are kept on tenterhooks: can Christopher really be who he says he is?

War breaks out between the 'Toffs' from school and the town boys, the 'Oiks'. Christopher's powers are put to the test as he tries to bring peace. Toby's success – with friends, rugby and Wanda, sister of the chief Oik – all depends on him.

**Jane Darcy**

★ ★ ★ ★ ★ ★

# WARRIOR CATS: INTO THE WILD
## Erin Hunter

The cats in these books are real cats. They don't wear clothes or fight with swords; instead, they use their claws and teeth to fight, and they live in a world that the cats we know would recognise ... except that theirs is a tribal society with clan fighting against clan. These cats aren't cute. They are so real that even though they are cats, you feel for them when they bleed and die, just as if they were people.

The reason I loved these books – and so far I've read 12 of them! – is because they are incredibly exciting. Which on its own wouldn't be enough to make me read so many ... but they are also well written, blood-filled, original, addictive, witty and packed with cliffhangers.

**Jahan Sahni, age 10**

### Next?

• More fearsome creatures appear in Brian Jacques's **Redwall** series. (**UBG** 282)

• There's more blood-soaked heroism in Stuart Hill's **Cry of the Icemark**. (**UBG** 76)

• What about more cats? Try S.F. Said's **Varjak Paw** (**UBG** 367) or Robert Westall's **Blitzcat** (**UBG** 37).

• A series just as complete and exciting, but this time about humans, is D.J. MacHale's **Pendragon** books. Start with **The Merchant of Death**.

# WARRIOR GIRL  Pauline Chandler

In 1429, France and England were at war, and things were desperate for France. Then a young woman, brave and strong, who was sure she had God on her side, told the Dauphin (the heir to the French throne) that he could win, and she led the French to great victories. Her name was Jeanne d'Arc – Joan of Arc. This fantastic true story is told in *Warrior Girl*, through the letters of Joan's cousin, Mariane de Courcey, who has an exciting quest of her own.

I wish Pauline Chandler had provided an afterword, as you just can't help wondering exactly which parts are fiction and which aren't, but this is a gripping and moving adventure that brings medieval wartime powerfully to life. I loved the pet hen!

**Ann Halam**

### Next?

• There's more historical adventure by Pauline Chandler in *Viking Girl*; or try her story set in Roman times: *The Mark of Edain*.

• If you want to know more about Joan of Arc, try *Joan of Arc and Her Marching Orders* by Phil Robins.

• Or for another well known story retold, try Adèle Geras's *Troy* (*UBG* 353) and its sequel, *Ithaca*.

★ ★ ★ ★ ★ ★

# THE WATCH HOUSE
## Robert Westall

### Next?

• Robert Westall wrote many gripping stories of the supernatural. Try *The Stones of Muncaster Cathedral* – terrifying! (*UBG* 327)

• Ann Halam writes wonderfully chilling horror novels, such as *The Haunting of Jessica Raven* and *The Fear Man*.

• Celia Rees has written a scary supernatural trilogy, of which *City of Shadows* is the first title.

• And try John Gordon's ghost story *The Midwinter Watch*, about a train seen travelling – though everyone knows it hasn't run for years...

I've always loved the delicious thrill of a ghost story, but good ones are hard to find. With *The Watch House*, you're in the hands of a master of the macabre.

Anne's mother has dumped her for the summer holidays with an elderly couple living on the cliffs above Garmouth. Bored and lonely, Anne becomes obsessed with the old Watch House nearby, and its store of strange salvage from ships wrecked on the Black Middens. On its dusty shelves are the skulls of drowned sailors.

That is the beginning of an atmospheric and jumpy ghost story that will grip you all the way through, as Anne's frightened attempts to help the ghost of the 'Old Feller' conjure up a far more malevolent force. You probably won't want to read it if you're home alone...

**Patricia Elliott**

# WATERSHIP DOWN
### Richard Adams

I have always loved talking-animal books. This novel is about a 'tribe' of rabbits who have to leave their warren when Fiver, who is a bit of a prophet, foresees a terrible future if they stay. The rabbits go on a long journey, full of incidents and accidents, and finally find a new home. Yet, even as they try to settle peacefully on Watership Down, there is another threat to them, coming from a hostile tribe of rabbits who live not far away.

This is an exciting adventure story that draws you into a world of rabbits who have their own language and religion, their own way of looking at things, their own way of solving tricky problems.

**Garry Kilworth**

> **Next?**
> • The rabbits in this book talk, but they don't wear clothes or fight and play like humans. For books in which the animals do all those things, try the **Welkin Weasels** series by Garry Kilworth or Brian Jacques's **Redwall** series. (*UBG* 282)
>
> • Henry Williamson's **Tarka the Otter** is a classic animal-as-animal story (without any talking). (*UBG* 343)

★ ★ ★ ★ ★ ★

# WAYS TO LIVE FOREVER
### Sally Nicholls

> **Next?**
> • Frank Cottrell Boyce writes lovely and funny first-person heroes; try **Millions** about a boy, his friend, school, nettles, and an awful lot of money.
>
> • For more books about illness and death that are really telling you more about life, you should try the amazing **Freak the Mighty** (*UBG* 120); or for the older among you, the equally life-affirming (but tough) **Before I Die** by Jenny Downham.

Eleven-year-old Sam has leukaemia. He is going to die. *Ways to Live Forever* is his story. It is a happy book.

No, really – this is a wonderfully happy book! Sally Nicholls has managed the amazing feat of producing a book about death that is really about how wonderful life is, a book celebrating the things Sam does, his dreams and memories, his family, the difficult questions he insists on asking, all the things that interest him (Science! Death! Airships!). The voice Nicholls creates for her hero is wonderfully alive, full of charm and humour and never self-pitying. You'll love this book, and although – yes – there will be tears when you say goodbye to Sam, you'll also find to your surprise that you've reached the end of this book about death quite uplifted, a little happier than when you started. Strange, or what?

**Daniel Hahn**

# WEE FREE MEN  Terry Pratchett

### Next?

• Of course there are loads more Terry Pratchetts. Try the first **Discworld**, *The Colour of Magic*. (*UBG* 68) Also read Terry's review of *Mistress Masham's Repose* – his own favourite 'little people' book. (*UBG* 231)

• Eoin Colfer's **Artemis Fowl** is another excellent re-evaluation of the role of elves and pixies. (*UBG* 23)

• Philip Pullman's *I Was a Rat!* questions the fall-out from fairy stories in an original, funny and thought-provoking way. (*UBG* 166)

This is the story of a girl called Tiffany who realises that she can't be the princess because she isn't blonde, so decides to be the witch instead. But when you want to become a witch on Terry Pratchett's Discworld, you can't just enrol in a special boarding school. Still, when her little brother needs rescuing from the evil queen, Tiffany knows it's up to her to save him. She sets out, helped only by a talking frog and the Wee Free Men: a tribe of tiny blue hooligans who speak an incomprehensible Scottish dialect. This is a superb story that keeps as far away from traditional fairy-tale assumptions as the Wee Free Men themselves keep away from the only people they fear: lawyers.

**Anthony Reuben**

★ ★ ★ ★ ★ ★

# THE WEIRDSTONE OF BRISINGAMEN  Alan Garner

This was the first book I ever read that I found totally unputdownable. I was ten at the time, and read it by torchlight under the bedcovers, desperate to discover what would happen at the end.

Colin and Susan are exploring the countryside around Alderley Edge when they are pursued by sinister creatures that are after the strange glowing 'weirdstone' which Susan wears round her wrist. In a breathtaking journey which takes them down claustrophobic mines, over treacherous wintry moorland and a floating island, and through dark, perilous forests, the two children struggle to deliver the stone to Cadellin, the wizard. If they succeed, the evil Morrigan and her deadly morthbrood will be vanquished. If not...

I won't spoil the ending – but if you like stories with powerful magic and ancient legends, wizards, witches and forces of light and darkness, then this is for you.

**Paul Stewart**

### Next?

• Another Alan Garner? *Elidor,* with its oppressive twilight world (*UBG* 98), and *The Owl Service*, where the three protagonists are dragged into an ancient legend (*UBG* 258), are as good, if not better!

• You should also try Susan Cooper's **The Dark is Rising** sequence. Dark, powerful and often deeply disturbing, the whole series is superb. (*UBG* 78)

• Or Catherine Fisher's **The Book of the Crow** series – try and decide if it is fantasy or science fiction. (*UBG* 41)

# WHAT KATY DID  Susan Coolidge  ●●●

### Next?

- To follow, there's *What Katy Did at School* and *What Katy Did Next*.
- In the same genre is *Little Women* by Louisa M. Alcott. (*UBG* 208) Also try *Pollyanna* by Eleanor H. Porter (*UBG* 272) and *Anne of Green Gables* by L.M. Montgomery (*UBG* 20).
- From a later period, and set in the UK, you might enjoy Eve Garnett's *The Family from One End Street*. (*UBG* 109)

This book was first published in 1872 and gives a wonderful picture of American family life at the time. I identified strongly with its heroine, the tearaway Katy Carr, especially when something similar happened to me. She goes on a new swing after being warned not to and injures her spine. At 12, I found myself lying flat in hospital for months, and naturally I reread *What Katy Did*. The world can be a hard place, and there's nothing the matter with going to books for comfort.

Like most of the stories of its time it verges on sentimentality, but I didn't mind that, or probably even notice. I just loved living with this large extended family, with crabby Aunt Izzy and the near-saintly Cousin Helen (I certainly didn't identify with her!). I shared Christmas with them and even cried when someone (I won't tell you who) died... And I much preferred Katy's brothers and sisters, five of them, to my own bossy brother and quarrelsome sister.

**Helen Cresswell**

★ ★ ★ ★ ★ ★

# THE WHEEL OF SURYA  Jamila Gavin  ●●●

Some stories pull you into another time, another place, so completely that you have to shake yourself to come back to the present. *The Wheel of Surya* is like that. From the moment I entered the first chapter, I knew I was on a journey.

It is a terrifying, extraordinary journey for Marvinder and her brother Jaspal. As India moves to Independence in 1947, civil war breaks up the country and the children's family.

Separated from their mother and grandmother, the children escape across India and the ocean to find their father in strange, cold England.

This is the first novel in a trilogy and the ending presents a new challenge for Marvinder and Jaspal.

**Beverley Naidoo**

### Next?

- You will feel drawn to read *The Eye of the Horse* (set in 1948 with Marvinder and Jaspal in England) and *The Track of the Wind* (1951, with the family reunited in India but riven with conflict).
- *Dani's Diary* by Narinder Dhami tells two stories, one of a very modern girl and one of her grandmother, who journeyed from India to England in the 1960s.
- Anita Desai's *The Village by the Sea* is another story set in India. (*UBG* 370)

# WHEN HITLER STOLE PINK RABBIT  Judith Kerr

Anna is nine years old, living comfortably with her mother, her writer father, her brother Max and housekeeper Heimpi. She is happy at school and has plenty of friends. But this is Germany in 1933. Anna and her family are Jewish. Hitler is just about to come to power and Anna's life will be changed for ever.

Judith Kerr's *When Hitler Stole Pink Rabbit* is about her own experiences as a child and this gives the book a fantastic 'being-there' quality. The title expresses the utter destructiveness of Hitler's rise to power: stealing lives, childhoods, invading the everyday securities we all take for granted. Through her poignant and vivid depiction of an ordinary family suddenly overshadowed by history, Judith Kerr makes it possible for us to imagine the impossible: what would it be like if such a thing were to happen to us? The novel is a compelling story of survival and adaptation, of hope, love and loyalty. It eloquently demonstrates the triumph of the human spirit in the face of adversity, the very thing that would eventually cause the Third Reich to fail.

**Celia Rees**

### Next?

• *When Hitler Stole Pink Rabbit* is the first part of an autobiographical trilogy. The other titles are: *Bombs on Aunt Dainty* and *A Small Person Far Away*.

• *Hurricane Summer* by Robert Swindells is also set during World War II.

• Other books about how that war affected the lives of children in Europe include Lois Lowry's *Number the Stars* and Johanna Reiss's *The Upstairs Room*.

★ ★ ★ ★ ★ ★

# WHEN MARNIE WAS THERE  Joan G. Robinson

### Next?

• *Marianne Dreams* is about a girl who, whilst ill in bed, is seemingly drawn into a world she doodles on to paper. (*UBG* 221)

• In *Moondial* by Helen Cresswell, a sundial in the grounds of an old house holds the key to time travel.

• For a girl who has lost her identity, read Tanith Lee's brilliant *Piratica*. (*UBG* 270)

Anna is terrified of letting feelings into her world because she believes that everything she lets in will only be taken away again. She has already lost her family. But when Anna is sent to Norfolk to stay by the sea, she begins to dream of having a secret friend; a friend who doesn't really exist and therefore cannot truly be lost at all.

Then Anna meets Marnie, who becomes the most real thing in Anna's world... But is Marnie real? When Marnie disappears, Anna starts to forget her, as if she really were just a dream, and some very real children help her make the leap into the real, concrete world, and discover her own extraordinary story.

**Simon Puttock**

# WHISPERING TO WITCHES Anna Dale

Joe had been looking forward to a fun Christmas with his dad; but now discovers that instead he's going to be packed off on a train to Canterbury to spend it with his mum, his drip of a stepfather and decidedly odd little sister, Esme. It's not a promising start. But before Joe has even got off the train at Canterbury station, things have got much more interesting. In the days that follow he will have to deal with witches, spells, a new friend called Twiggy, a really nasty (but really glamorous) villain, a suspicious librarian and a few cups of seriously unpleasant dead-nettle tea. An exciting adventure story full of plot-twists, snowy mystery and magic. Also talking rats.

**Daniel Hahn**

### Next?
• Another Anna Dale? Try *Spellbound*, in which a girl really wants to get rid of her annoying brother – until, through magic, she succeeds! Then her world gets far more dangerous as she has to try and get him back.

• There's snow, spells and plot-twists in Susan Cooper's **The Dark is Rising** sequence. (*UBG* 78)

• A girl who finds herself involved in all sorts of strange goings-on is Georgia Byng's Molly Moon – read *Molly Moon's Incredible Book of Hypnotism* first. (*UBG* 234)

★ ★ ★ ★ ★ ★

# WHISPERS IN THE GRAVEYARD
## Theresa Breslin

### Next?
• The harder, and just as scary, *Urn Burial* by Robert Westall, about a megalith, and the disturbing of ancient evils, is a brilliant read. Look for another Westall, *The Watch House*, too. (*UBG* 375)

• Robert Swindells spins a scary story in *The Thousand Eyes of Night*.

• Theresa Breslin also writes **The Dream Master** books, about a boy who slips back in time to the ancient world.

This award-winning story about Solomon, who is trying to come to terms with the bleak cruelties of his life – problems at school, bullying teachers, a drunken father, a runaway mother – is truly poignant. But dyslexia and a disintegrating family life are not the only demons Solomon has to deal with. When workmen dig up the rowan tree that guards the kirkyard where he likes to take refuge, an ancient and hugely malignant force is unleashed...

A scary horror story, but so much more than just that, Solomon's battle to defeat these demons is a gripping, compulsive read. His predicament and suffering are so powerfully evoked, only those with hearts of stone could fail to be moved.

**Neil Arksey**

# THE WHITBY WITCHES Robin Jarvis

### Next?

• You may want to read the rest of Robin Jarvis's trilogy: *A Warlock in Whitby* and *The Whitby Child*. Or try some of his many other books, such as **The Deptford Mice** series. (*UBG* 82)

• Diana Wynne Jones's *Witch Week*, one of **The Worlds of Chrestomanci** books, also explores how the real world can exist alongside a supernatural realm. (*UBG* 393)

• Sally Prue's *Cold Tom* looks at a similar theme from an unusual angle. (*UBG* 67)

Ben and Jennet are sent to live with Alice Boston, a vigorous and eccentric 92-year-old, in the ancient seaside town of Whitby on the Yorkshire coast. But why would an old lady that has never even met the children offer to adopt them, and how will she react to Ben, who is gifted with 'the sight'?

After encountering the mysterious Fisher Folk, Ben, Jennet and Miss Boston are drawn into a desperate struggle against the evil that stalks the dark streets of the town.

Any reader who has visited Whitby, famous for being one of the most haunted towns in Britain, will recognise the various landmarks against which this chilling supernatural adventure is played out.

**Thomas Bloor**

★ ★ ★ ★ ★ ★

# WHITE FANG
## Jack London

This book is the story of White Fang, part dog, mostly wolf. It follows him from his days as a puppy in the wilds of north-west Canada, through his time in an Indian camp and his experiences as a fighting dog in a gold-rush frontier town, to the point where he finally finds a master he can trust.

Jack London's great talent lies in his ability to get inside the heads of the animals that he writes about, and he shows you the world from their point of view. (I guarantee that you'll never look at the family pet in quite the same way again!) He also tells wonderful stories. The opening chapters of this book are about a hungry wolf pack hunting down two men and their team of dogs, and it's one of the most exciting openings to any book I know.

**Laura Hutchings**

### Next?

• If you enjoyed this story then try Jack London's other famous novel about wolves and dogs, *The Call of the Wild*.

• If you enjoy reading about the bond between dogs and their masters, then try **Greatheart** by Joseph E. Chipperfield.

• And for another story of animals surviving in the wild, try Sheila Burnford's *The Incredible Journey*, though this time the two dogs and a cat are the pets that are trying to find their owners, who have moved house.

# WHO IS JESSE FLOOD? Malachy Doyle

### Next?

• Don't miss Malachy Doyle's excellent *Georgie*. (*UBG* 123)

• *Benny and Babe* by Eoin Colfer is also about small-town Ireland and is the sequel to *Benny and Omar*.

• A girl who gets dragged unwillingly to live in rural Ireland is the hero of Cathy Cassidy's *Scarlett*.

• Or what about Jerry Spinelli's *Loser*? You can guess something of what it's about from the title, but as with all Spinelli's books, you can't take anything for granted. (*UBG* 212)

Life in small-town Ireland isn't much fun when you're 14 and your mum's left home. Jesse Flood is good at table tennis, but when it comes to girls he hasn't got a clue. He's bored, he feels different from everyone else and, to make matters worse, he fancies the prettiest girl in Greywater.

However, if you share any of the same problems, I'm certainly not recommending that you try what Jesse does to make life more interesting – the beginning of the book finds him in a railway tunnel waiting for a train to come!

Jesse may be bored but this is a really powerful piece of storytelling. You follow him from his first encounter with a girl, who wants him for more than his amazing skill with a ping-pong bat, through to what is almost a happy ending. And somewhere along the way, Jesse discovers where he fits in.

**Laura Hutchings**

★ ★ ★ ★ ★ ★

# WHY THE WHALES CAME
## Michael Morpurgo

Everyone on the island of Bryher is afraid of the Birdman, a solitary figure who lives on the western shore. He was the last inhabitant of Samson, an island with a terrible curse on it. None of the children are allowed to speak to him but one day Gracie and Daniel find themselves on his beach and meet him face to face. They make a new friend but also begin to discover the awful truth behind the curse.

The beautiful and rugged Isles of Scilly off the coast of Cornwall are the setting for this moving tale of mystery and friendship. The story is told to us directly by Gracie, and vividly conveys her fear, bravery, joy and love at each twist of the tale.

**Abigail Anderson**

### Next?

• *The Wreck of the Zanzibar* is another Michael Morpurgo story set on the Isles of Scilly. (*UBG* 395)

• Try *The Snow Goose* by Paul Gallico, also about a man living alone by the sea and the girl who befriends him. (*UBG* 317)

• Another book about trying to save something you love is Melvin Burgess's *Kite*. (*UBG* 192).

# WHY WEEPS THE BROGAN? Hugh Scott ●●●

Saxon and her younger brother Gilbert have a daily routine – first breakfast and cigars in the coffee shop, then fighting off spiders, after that brushing away the remains of broken heads, and finally feeding the horrifying Brogan. They must stick to this rigid routine, because the existence of their strange world depends on it. But Saxon is troubled. She doesn't know why, but when she hears the Brogan howl, she gets an eerie shiver down her spine.

Are you confused? This book is a real puzzle, one that will have you turning the pages in burning curiosity. But beware – when you reach the conclusion you are in for a real shock.

**Noga Applebaum**

> ### Next?
> • All Hugh Scott's books have a dark and intriguing edge to them. Look out for *Giants* and *The Shaman's Stone*.
> • Try Lesley Howarth's *Ultraviolet* – another puzzling tale, set in the future when the sun's radiation makes it impossible to go outside.
> • Or what about two of Hugh's favourite mysteries? Agatha Christie's *The Pale Horse* and Conan Doyle's *The Hound of the Baskervilles* (*UBG* 160).

★ ★ ★ ★ ★ ★

# WICKED! series Paul Jennings and Morris Gleitzman ●●

> ### Next?
> • Look out for these Australian authors' other series, **Deadly!**. Paul Jennings has also written *Uncanny!* (*UBG* 360)
> • Another author with a great sense of humour is Jeremy Strong. Try *My Mum's Going to Explode!* (*UBG* 244)
> • *Don't Pat the Wombat* by Elizabeth Honey is hilarious – and Australian, too! (*UBG* 90)

Don't you wonder how two authors ever manage to write together? It certainly seems to work, though – the **Wicked!** series is just as good as the title suggests. It was originally published as six separate books – *The Slobberers*, *Battering Rams*, *Croaked*, *Dead Ringer*, *The Creeper* and *Till Death Do Us Part* – and each story led on to the next one. You can tell from the titles the sort of stories they are – creepy, chilling, gruesome and very, very funny. You can also buy them in one book, called *Totally Wicked!*

Incidentally, they're *fantastic* to read out loud; get someone to read them to you at bedtime – you'll all end up under the bedclothes!

**Vivian French**

# THE WICKIT CHRONICLES: ELY PLOT Joan Lennon

Pip is an apprentice in a monastery back in the exciting days when murder plots would just happen on your doorstep and you could have a talking stone gargoyle as a secret pet. The story involves monks, knights, poison and saving a young king, but the best bit is that it's set on the fens in East Anglia. These treacherous swamps around Ely cathedral have their own creepy spirits, such as the Lantern Man, who lures people away to drown. The back pages feature extra facts about the fens and monasteries (for example, why do monks have a bald patch?) that are well worth reading on their own. I loved it!

**Kjartan Poskitt**

**Next?**
• Luckily, there are more **Wickit Chronicles** to look out for: *Fen Gold*, *Ice Road* and *Witch Bell*.
• *A Dog Called Grk* by Joshua Doder has another boy and his pet solving mysteries. (*UBG* 87)
• For more history combined with exciting storytelling read Caroline Lawrence's **Roman Mysteries** series starting with *The Thieves of Ostia*. (*UBG* 288)
• Eva Ibbotson, in *Beasts of Clawstone Castle*, has ghosts helping to save an old stately home.

★ ★ ★ ★ ★ ★

# WILLA AND OLD MISS ANNIE Berlie Doherty

**Next?**
• You might like the **Tilly Mint Tales**, also by Berlie Doherty.
• Other good animal stories? Try *Charlotte's Web* by E.B. White (*UBG* 59) and *Woof!* by Allan Ahlberg (*UBG* 391).
• If you like gentle animal humour, try the **Animal Crackers** series by Rose Impey. Also try *The Golden Goose* (or anything) by Dick King-Smith. (*UBG* 131)

This is a gorgeous little book about a girl called Willa, who makes friends with Old Miss Annie. At first Willa is afraid of her, because she is very old and has twisted hands and a tiny voice, but they become close friends because they share a love of animals. There are three stories in the book, about how Willa and Annie help a goat called Joshua, a pony called Bony and a fox called Vicky.

Berlie Doherty writes with great warmth about the things that matter – sadness and happiness, people and animals and, like all the best stories, her tales stay in the mind long after you've finished them.

**Malachy Doyle**

# THE WIND IN THE WILLOWS
## Kenneth Grahame

Adventure invades the quiet riverside homes of Ratty, Mole and Badger when Mr Toad and his motor car come to visit. Conceited, excitable, swaggering, untrustworthy – yet goodhearted at the core – Mr Toad soon gets himself and all his friends into trouble. Bad trouble indeed. Toad is taken by the police to jail and while he lies in prison, the others try to recover from his mistakes. Will Toad's friends gain the courage they need? Only if they can band together to win back Toad Hall from the weasels and stoats, can they become heroes in spite of themselves.

This book was originally a series of bedtime stories told by Kenneth Grahame to his young son. When the boy went off with his governess to the seaside for a vacation, his father continued to tell him stories by letter. Mrs Grahame saved the letters and they were finally turned into the book.

**Jane Yolen**

### Next?

• Try Rudyard Kipling's **Jungle Books**, which are about more real animals this time, though they still talk to each other. (*UBG* 185)

• For another wild and exciting talking-animal story try Roald Dahl's *James and the Giant Peach*. (*UBG* 179)

• Something more challenging? Try Brian Jacques's **Redwall** series, with fighting mice and a mad, dangerous one-eyed rat as the villain. (*UBG* 282)

• Or something gentler, easier – lovely *Winnie-the-Pooh* by A.A. Milne. (*UBG* 387)

Read *The Wind in the Willows* by Kenneth Grahame – the full version, not the 'retold' versions around now. Sure, it looks like a gentle tale about dressed-up animals, but it is highly strange (a toad is big enough to drive a car but can get down a water-rat hole, and is green and knobbly but can still be disguised as a washerwoman... I mean, you don't have to be a great beauty to wash clothes, but really!) Anyway, that actually makes it far more fun. And don't skip the chapters 'A Piper at the Gates of Dawn' and 'Wayfarers All'.

The best of all animal stories. I read it, aged ten, in the back of a car by passing streetlights and it turned me into a reader overnight.

**Terry Pratchett**

# THE WIND ON THE MOON  Eric Linklater  ●●

**Next?**
• Another Erik Linklater – try *The Pirates in the Deep Green Sea*.
• You probably know Roald Dahl's books already – but perhaps you haven't read *Danny, the Champion of the World*. (*UBG* 77)
• Another fantasy novel with a quest element is Philip Pullman's *The Firework-Maker's Daughter*. (*UBG* 114)

There is wind on the moon, and it has blown straight into the hearts of Dinah and Dorinda, which means they will behave badly for a whole year. And indeed they find themselves in more and more trouble, until finally they run away on a daring mission to rescue their father from captivity in a distant country.

This story is such a wonderful mixture that it's hard to describe. It's a pacy adventure, a magical fantasy – gleeful and inventive, ridiculously zany, yet full of common sense. And I've never been able to see a furniture van without being reminded of it. You'll see what I mean...

**Patricia Elliott**

★ ★ ★ ★ ★ ★

# THE WIND SINGER  William Nicholson  ●●●

This warm-hearted fantasy tells the story of the Hath family, who live in the cramped Orange District of the city of Aramanth in the shadow of an ancient artefact called the 'wind singer'. When baby Pin-Pin makes a mess (literally!) of her first examination, the family is in danger of being demoted to Maroon District. But Kestrel and her brother Bowman rebel against their city's exam culture, and set out on a quest to discover the source of the evil that grips Aramanth.

So begins the first book in a fast-moving fantasy trilogy with the sort of writing that conjures up fantastic scenes in the reader's mind. In it, you will meet the unpopular but brave Mumpo, who becomes Kestrel's friend when she is sent to the bottom of the class, the terrifyingly single-minded Zars, a very sad Emperor, and some unusual pirates. Kestrel, Bowman and Mumpo are endearing characters and Nicholson makes their world come alive without the need for massive amounts of background and detail that can sometimes make books set in such fantastic worlds a bit hard to swallow.

**Katherine Roberts**

**Next?**
• Move on to the sequels, *Slaves of the Mastery* and *Firesong* – though be warned, these are darker and rather gruesome in places. Or read his brilliantly realised **Noble Warriors** trilogy, beginning with *Seeker*. (*UBG* 305)
• For more fantasy, try Katherine Roberts's **Echorium** sequence, beginning with *Song Quest*.
• *The Giver* by Lois Lowry is also about a very controlled future. (*UBG* 127)

# WINNIE-THE-POOH A.A. Milne

Don't be distracted by the Walt Disney versions of these stories. The actual books with pictures by E.H. Shepard are what you should aim for.

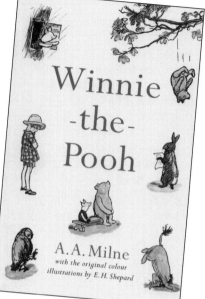

Winnie-the-Pooh (a toy bear) and his owner Christopher Robin are briefly introduced in the first pages of the book, after which the reader plunges into a series of small, comical adventures involving Winnie-the-Pooh, Christopher Robin and a variety of other toys. The characters do not change. Winnie-the-Pooh is always hungry for honey. Piglet is always easily alarmed. Owl is always wise (but in a blundering way) and Christopher Robin is always there to rescue them from any difficulties they might get into. The stories are funny and affectionate but every now and then they can be moving, too.

This book is such a classic that any more comment is probably unnecessary. The stories are wonderful fun to read aloud and the ties of affection and friendship reassure the reader and listener.

**Margaret Mahy**

## Next?

• Read other books by A.A. Milne – there's a sequel, *The House at Pooh Corner*, and two collections of poems: *When We Were Very Young* and *Now We Are Six*.

• It is worth reading the stories about Paddington Bear by Michael Bond, beginning with *A Bear Called Paddington*. (*UBG* 29)

• Readers who have enjoyed this book would probably also enjoy the **Uncle** books by J.P. Martin. (*UBG* 361)

• The **Mary Plain** series by Gwynedd Rae is about 'an unusual first-class bear'!

• Or for something a little harder, try *The Wind in the Willows* by Kenneth Grahame. (*UBG* 385)

## Some Carnegie Medal Classics That Time Forgot

• *Visitors from London* by Kitty Barne

• *We Couldn't Leave Dinah* by Mary Treadgold

• *Sea Change* by Richard Armstrong

• *The Lark on the Wing* by Elfrida Vipont Foulds

• *The Circus is Coming* by Noel Streatfeild

• *Time Trial* by Hester Burton

• *Christmas With the Savages* by Mary Clive

# THE WISHING CHAIR series
## Enid Blyton

Mollie and Peter have a wishing chair that lives in the playroom at the bottom of their garden. On their first adventure in the chair they rescue a pixie called Chinky, and from then on the three have lots of adventures together. It's always exciting and sometimes a little bit scary as the chair flies the children and Chinky up and away to places such as the Land of Spells and the Island of Surprises. There they encounter goodies including the Windy Wizard and Mr Spells, and baddies like the Slipperies, Giant Twisty and the Snoogle.

If you ever dreamed of living in a world that really was full of magic and fairy folk if you only knew where to look, then these are the books for you!

**Gwyneth Rees**

> **Next?**
> • If you liked these then you're bound to like Enid Blyton's stories in the **Magic Faraway Tree** series. (*UBG* 216)
> • Or for more Enid Blyton, this time about an extremely naughty doll, try the **Amelia Jane** books.
> • If you want to read another adventure about children who escape to a magic land, why not try J.M. Barrie's *Peter Pan*. (*UBG* 262)

★ ★ ★ ★ ★ ★

# WITCH CHILD
## Celia Rees

> **Next?**
> • The sequel, *Sorceress*, continues the story of Mary's life in America, seen through the eyes of a Native American girl.
> • Alanna is another feisty, misunderstood heroine – read about her in Tamora Pierce's **Song of the Lioness** series. (*UBG* 319)
> • Elizabeth George Speare's *The Witch of Blackbird Pond* is also set at a time when people feared witches.

This book is in diary form, just as if it had been written by a girl witch in the seventeenth century. So good is the research undertaken, so effortlessly are the ways and language of the century depicted, you really do believe it's all true.

Mary is the witch child. Her grandmother has just been hanged as a witch and Mary knows that she has inherited the same dark powers. It is thought best that Mary should go to America and try to start a new life where no one knows her background (and just who is the mysterious woman who helps with the journey?). But travelling by boat is a perilous process – and the long, tiresome journey must be undertaken without arousing the suspicions of the sullen crowd that Mary must accompany.

**Katherine Roberts**

# THE WITCHES  Roald Dahl

While holidaying at the seaside with his grandmother, our young hero stumbles upon a witches' convention and overhears their plan: to turn the children of England into mice. Unfortunately, before he can escape, the boy is sniffed out by the Grand High Witch, and turned into a mouse himself! Undaunted, the boy-mouse teams up with his grandmother to turn the tables on these child-hating witches.

Parents will find this a much creepier book than children: the idea of witches dressed up as sweet, normal women, preying on unsuspecting boys and girls is terrifying to any mother or father. The story starts off a bit slowly, but once the hero is racing around the hotel as a mouse, plotting to foil the witches, there is all-out excitement. And I loved the book's unusual ending!

**Kenneth Oppel**

Is Roald Dahl the greatest children's writer of all time? Quite possibly. I actually missed out on most of his books when I was a kid. It was only in my teens that I started to read his work – but I soon made up for lost time! I devoured just about everything of his that I could find. He wrote so many classics; but if I had to pick a single favourite, it would have to be *The Witches*.

*The Witches* is a cauldron of sheer, mischievous joy. Whenever I read it I can imagine Dahl as he wrote about the ugly, evil mistresses of mayhem. He must have been laughing his socks off as he went deliciously over the top! These witches have none of the redeeming qualities of many modern-day, watered-down fictional witches. It's all about weird, wicked, wonderful fun!

I can't give away all the secrets, but this is typical Dahl, and sums up what makes him different and gives him an edge. He did what other writers didn't dare, and cocked a snook at the rules. In fact, he behaved pretty much the same way that stubborn, carefree children all around the world behave! That's probably why so many of us love his books – we can see our own dreaming, individual, prankish selves within them.

**Darren Shan**

## Next?

• Other Dahl? They're all good, but start by reading *Matilda* (*UBG* 224) and *The BFG* (*UBG* 33).

• Or Neil Gaiman's very scary *Coraline*. (*UBG* 69)

• Andy Stanton's **Mr Gum** books are brilliantly anarchic, too; try *You're a Bad Man, Mr Gum!* first. (*UBG* 397)

# THE WIZARD OF OZ L. Frank Baum

**Next?**

• L. Frank Baum wrote hundreds of sequels. Well, a dozen or so, at least. Look out for *The Emerald City of Oz* and *Glinda of Oz*.

• Or you could try some other classic fantasy stories, such as *Peter Pan* by J.M. Barrie (*UBG* 262), and *The Box of Delights* by John Masefield (*UBG* 44).

• The best English equivalent of the Oz stories is Lewis Carroll's *Alice's Adventures in Wonderland*. (*UBG* 13)

You have probably seen the classic Judy Garland film version of this book, in which Dorothy flies 'over the rainbow' to the Land of Oz, and finally returns home after triumphing over the Wicked Witches of both East and West. Now don't get me wrong, I do think the film is one of the best ever made. But the book is different. For a start it's longer, and takes us on after the second witchy demise, and we see what becomes of the Scarecrow, the Tin Woodman and the Lion. But the best reason you should read it is for its darkness. There's a menacing vein running through the book that's just not evident in the film. The passage with the flying monkeys is truly chilling, and despite its sometimes quaint language, this is one classic not to overlook.

**Marcus Sedgwick**

★ ★ ★ ★ ★ ★

# WOLF BROTHER Michelle Paver

Six thousand years ago, an ordinary boy called Torak, '12 summers old', sets off on a quest to destroy the bear who killed his father. The world he inhabits is one of deep forests and vicious clans, of floods, prophecies and oaths, of primeval spirits, both good and evil. With the help of the orphaned wolf cub he saves from drowning, Torak lives by his wits and his senses. But often only just – death in this icy world is never far away.

Paver's prose is as stark and urgent as Torak's mission. Sometimes you're in Torak's head, sometimes in Wolf's. They are clan brothers after all.

Fantasy? Adventure? Anthropology? However you choose to define this magical book, you'll devour it.

**Sabine Durrant**

**Next?**

• The **Chronicles of Ancient Darkness** series continues with: *Spirit Walker*, *Soul Eater*, *Outcast*, *Oathbreaker* and *Ghost Hunter*.

• William Nicholson writes wonderfully too; try his **Noble Warriors** series, starting with *Seeker*. (*UBG* 305)

• Or try Beth Webb's series that begins with *Star Dancer*, and tells of ancient druids, magic and a struggle against a powerful enemy.

• Terry Deary's *The Fire Thief* is a thrilling story of early gods and man.

# THE WOLVES OF WILLOUGHBY CHASE  Joan Aiken

Bonnie Green and her loving parents live happily at Willoughby Chase, even though it is a long, cold winter and the wolves are howling all around. When cousin Sylvia comes to stay, Bonnie feels things could not get any better. But Mama is very ill and must go to a warmer climate and so Miss Slighcarp is brought in to look after the two girls.

Once Bonnie's parents are out of the way, Miss Slighcarp and her nasty ally Mr Grimshaw take over the house and send Bonnie and Sylvia to a school where they have their heads shaved, eat next to nothing and work like slaves. However, Bonnie finds she still has friends – Simon the gooseboy, and two faithful servants who help sort the whole wicked mess out.

This is an exciting tale set in an alternative nineteenth century, full of wonderful characters – great villains, enchanting heroines and faithful friends.

**Ann Jungman**

### Next?

• Other rollicking adventures by Joan Aiken set in the imaginary reign of James III include *Black Hearts in Battersea*, *Nightbirds on Nantucket*, *Dido and Pa* and *Cold Shoulder Road*.

• Try *Journey to the River Sea* by Eva Ibbotson, in which our heroine finds herself up the Amazon with as bad a bunch of nasties as you could ever hope to meet. (*UBG* 184)

• *The Secret Garden* by Frances Hodgson Burnett, in which the sour orphan Mary is gradually turned into a happy child again. (*UBG* 302)

★ ★ ★ ★ ★ ★

# WOOF!  Allan Ahlberg

### Next?

• You might like to try *Please Mrs Butler*, a collection of poems by Allan Ahlberg. Or his hilarious novel, *The Giant Baby*.

• And if you enjoyed the story because you liked reading about animals, there are several other writers who follow the same theme. Dick King-Smith is one of the best. He wrote *The Sheep-Pig* (*UBG* 308), which was made into the film *Babe*, and *Harry's Mad*, about a very intelligent parrot.

*Woof!* is the story of a boy who one evening, lying in bed, turns into a Norfolk Terrier. This causes more problems than you might imagine. Like what to do when his parents throw him out of the house, how to get something to eat, and how to find some clothes to put on when he changes back...

This is one of my favourite books. Eric Banks is an ordinary boy in a very un-ordinary situation, and the way he and his friend Roy work out the best way to deal with the problem and find out what is causing it to happen make for a story you can't help but enjoy.

**Andrew Norriss**

# THE WOOL-PACK Cynthia Harnett

It is 1493 and Nicholas Fetterlock is the son of a wealthy wool merchant. His life seems just fine: out in the fields most of the time, a bit of schooling, and a best friend in Hal the shepherd's boy. But Nicholas is growing up, and is soon to be betrothed to Cecily, an eleven-year-old girl he has never met! On top of that, he discovers that his father's business is being ruined by Italian loan sharks, and his uncle wants to beat Columbus to the Indies...

What begins as a pleasing journey through the Cotswolds of lush fifteenth-century England soon grows in pace to become a tense mystery, in which dastardly deeds are afoot. Nicholas, Hal, and Cecily must find a way to unmask the villains and bring them to justice. This wonderful story shows that children have always been ingenious, even if parents have always been slow to believe it.

**Simon Puttock**

### Next?

• *A Little Lower than the Angels* by Geraldine McCaughrean is another story about medieval England. (*UBG* 204)

• A great story of villains and heroes and justice prevailing, set a little later, is Geoffrey Trease's *Cue for Treason*. (*UBG* 76)

• Kate Thompson's *The Alchemist's Apprentice* is a rags-to-riches story set in medieval times about a blacksmith's son and the strange object he finds in the River Thames.

★ ★ ★ ★ ★ ★

# THE WORLD ACCORDING TO HUMPHREY Betty G. Birney

### Next?

• There are sequels, including *Friendship According to Humphrey* and *Trouble According to Humphrey*.

• For another book about pets teaching humans a lesson, try *The Battle of Bubble and Squeak* by Philippa Pearce. (*UBG* 29)

• For another book where the story is told by an animal, try *I, Jack* by Patricia Finney.

• Or look for *I, Houdini* by Lynne Reid Banks, in which a hamster tells the story about his escape to the outside world.

Humphrey the hamster thinks that life can't get any better when he is bought by Ms Mac and becomes the class pet for Room 26. Ms Mac takes him home at night, introduces him to her friends and even takes him for a bike ride. However, Ms Mac is a supply teacher, and when she leaves to go travelling, Humphrey is handed over to the permanent teacher of Room 26, Mrs Brisbane. Life becomes very different for Humphrey and he finds himself being taken home by a different student every weekend. He quickly discovers that everyone has problems and, if only people listen to him, he can help. This is a warm, funny book that teaches you far more about humans than it does about hamsters.

**Laura Hutchings**

# THE WORLDS OF CHRESTOMANCI series

## Diana Wynne Jones

They're set in different places and different times, but these books have one thread in common: sooner or later, the current holder of the title of Chrestomanci will show up, particularly if you speak his name!

The Chrestomanci is a kind of Minister of Magic. He crosses between worlds to sort out magical problems. Magic in worlds overseen by Chrestomanci takes countless forms, from the sort that drags schoolgirls on broomstick rides to the kind that takes you to worlds where mermaids sing and a magical girl priestess wants nothing more than to attend an English boarding school. With cats, witches, music, spell-crafting families who fight like the families of Romeo and Juliet, witch hunts and people being dragged from one world into the next, you never know what interesting new twist Diana Wynne Jones will put into a story. You just have to keep reading her books to see what's new!

**Tamora Pierce**

magic there is.' Neil Gaiman

Magic rules the worlds!

### Next?

• The series comprises: *Charmed Life, The Magicians of Caprona, Witch Week, The Lives of Christopher Chant, Conrad's Fate* and *The Pinhoe Egg.*

• Read anything else by Diana Wynne Jones. You never know what she'll think of next, from a young girl who discovers that being turned into an old woman can be liberating (*Howl's Moving Castle*) to a world where people from our world go on fantasy quest tours, complete with magic (*Dark Lord of Derkholm*), to the trials of a boy who accidentally frees a Norse god (*Eight Days of Luke*) (*UBG* 97).

• Or try Terry Pratchett's *The Amazing Maurice and His Educated Rodents*, which takes the story of the Pied Piper, turns it on its head, bounces it several times and throws it into orbit. (*UBG* 15)

# THE WORST WITCH  Jill Murphy

## Next?

• You will want to move on to *The Worst Witch Strikes Again* straight away, followed by *A Bad Spell for the Worst Witch*, *The Worst Witch All at Sea*, *The Worst Witch Saves the Day*, and *The Worst Witch to the Rescue*.

• Or read about brave Lily Quench. Her first adventure is *Lily Quench and the Dragon of Ashby*.

• For another story of magic, with a cat as well, try *Carbonel* and its sequels by Barbara Sleigh. (*UBG* 53)

Everything goes wrong for Mildred Hubble in her first term at Miss Cackle's Academy for Witches. Even her black cat turns out to be a tabby kitten. Miss Cackle herself is absent-minded, but their form mistress, tall, thin Miss Hardbroom, is scary, especially as she can make herself invisible and is likely to reappear at just the most embarrassing time.

Follow the adventures of Mildred, her best friend Maud and her sworn enemy Ethel Hallow as they learn all about magic spells and chanting and flying on broomsticks.

**Kate Petty**

★ ★ ★ ★ ★ ★

# WORZEL GUMMIDGE  Barbara Euphan Todd

*Worzel Gummidge* was the book chosen for reprinting in a facsimile edition to celebrate 40 years of Puffin Books. I'm not surprised. This is a book for every child. Who wouldn't want Gummidge the scarecrow for a friend? 'He was such a nice sort of betwixt and between person, not quite grown up though he seemed as old as the fields, and yet not quite a child either, though in some ways he seemed as young as they were.' He is funny, unpredictable, and given to fits of the sulks. 'Ooh aye,' he says, 'ooh aye'. He has a comical turn of phrase, and says of his Aunt Sally, 'Ooh aye, I hates her as much as a worm hates ducklings. If I could find a hatchet I'd chop her up.' Then there's his little brown-faced girlfriend Earthy Mangold and all the other scarecrow relations, including a baby. Oh, and he has a robin nesting in his jacket pocket. I read the book from cover to cover yesterday and loved every word of it. So will you. Ooh aye. Trust me.

**Helen Cresswell**

## Next?

• I love the kind of fantasy that weaves into ordinary everyday life, and *Worzel Gummidge* is just that. So is Mary Norton's *The Borrowers* (*UBG* 43) and Clive King's *Stig of the Dump* (*UBG* 325); and so, if I may say so, are most of my own fantasies – *The Night-Watchmen*, *The Bongleweed* and *A Gift from Winklesea*.

• You could also try books by E. Nesbit; *The Phoenix and the Carpet* and *Five Children and It* (*UBG* 115).

# THE WRECK OF THE ZANZIBAR  Michael Morpurgo

This book has the sound of the sea in it. Taking the form of a diary, it covers a few months in the life of a young girl on the Isles of Scilly at the beginning of the twentieth century. Michael Morpurgo's wonderful, lyrical prose depicts the hardship, the joy and the undaunted spirit of those who live by the ocean; and in particular of Laura, whose story this is.

We accompany her through a season of terrifying storms and misfortunes, and see the island and the islanders through her eyes. She writes of her anxiety on finding a dying turtle, her sadness at being separated from her beloved brother, and her excitement at seeing the wrecked sailing ship that may bring salvation to her people.

The text is interspersed with, and enhanced by, Christian Birmingham's atmospheric illustrations. A story to be read aloud, read alone, and shared with others.

**Theresa Breslin**

> **Next?**
> • All books by Michael Morpurgo are worth reading. In particular, try *Twist of Gold* about an Irish family fleeing the famine at home to find a new life in America.
> • If you find yourself interested in the sailing part of this book, try *Swallows and Amazons* by Arthur Ransome, and its sequels. (*UBG* 336)

★ ★ ★ ★ ★ ★

# A WRINKLE IN TIME  Madeleine L'Engle

> **Next?**
> • Try Philip Reeve's wonderful *Mortal Engines* and its sequels. (*UBG* 236)
> • Or the playful *A Handful of Magic* by Stephen Elboz, in which London is almost the same as we know it, but not quite... (*UBG* 141)
> • Or try *Swiftly Tilting Planet*, also by Madeleine L'Engle.
> • And do look out for Penelope Lively's wonderful *A Stitch in Time*. (*UBG* 325)

This wonderfully inventive book is set partly in America and partly in the furthest reaches of the imagination. Meg's father works for the government. When he disappears, Meg and Charles, together with their friend Calvin, set off to find him, with the help of three strange old women who are not what they seem...

In fact, nothing is ever quite what it seems in this fantasy world. The book keeps the reader guessing all the way through, as the children and their three weird companions battle dark forces to rescue Dad from the clutches of a loathsome entity known as IT. IT controls an entire planet – and is casting its evil shadow over Earth. The only way to reach it is through a wrinkle in time. But once the children get there, will they ever be able to get back?

Message to all fans of fantasy, sci-fi and nail-biting excitement: read this book!

**Jean Ure**

# THE YOUNGEST GIRL IN THE FIFTH   Angela Brazil   ● ● ●

Until I read Angela Brazil, I thought a 'wizard wheeze' was Harry Potter with asthma and that a brick was for building walls.

Gwen Gascoyne is poor, plain and awkward, but bright and determined. When she gets moved up to the Fifth Form from the Upper Fourth, she's cut by her classmates, and that unspeakable rotter, Netta Goodwin, is the only person in the Fifth who'll talk to her. Netta lands Gwen into the most frightful hole, leaving Gwen to defend her honour without sneaking, and to win her place in the Fifth.

You don't have to have been in a frightful scrape, or muffed a test, or done an abominable thing to enjoy these stories. You can still find Angela Brazil's books in libraries and second-hand bookshops. She wrote over 40 school stories, between 1906 and 1947, and her novels are still as much fun as ever.

**Antonia Honeywell**

**Next?**
• More old-fashioned school stories? Try the **St Clare's** (*UBG* 218) or **Malory Towers** series by Enid Blyton. Or the **Chalet School** stories by Elinor M. Brent-Dyer.
• If you liked this novel's ending, try *The Story of the Treasure-Seekers* by E. Nesbit, in which six children try to restore their family's fortune.

★ ★ ★ ★ ★ ★

# YOUNG WIZARDS series   Diane Duane   ● ●

**Next?**
• The whole series! *Deep Wizardry*, *High Wizardry*, *Wizard Abroad*, *Wizard's Dilemma* and *Wizard Alone*.
• Diana Wynne Jones's fantasies, particularly *Archer's Goon*, *Witch Week*, one of **The Worlds of Chrestomanci** books (*UBG* 393), and *Howl's Moving Castle*, also present a look at magic as if we could practise it in our world.
• William Nicholson's *The Wind Singer* is about a boy and girl who discover they have special powers and must learn how to use them. (*UBG* 386)

In *So You Want to be a Wizard*, Kit and Nita each find a handbook for wizards, then meet as they try to work its spells. Despite their age they are powerful; due to their age, they make mistakes – big mistakes, which they have to fix. They encounter wonderful things: wizard cats and parrots, a heroic Jaguar automobile, magic as it's practised in outer space or through computers. The boy Kit converses with subway trains, the girl Nita with trees. Duane makes the everyday world magical and heroic at the same time.

But in addition to their magical work, the children also have to deal with everyday family and school problems, and it's this realism that makes these books work, particularly as the series moves on and Kit and Nita grow up.

**Tamora Pierce**

# YOU'RE A BAD MAN, MR GUM! Andy Stanton

This short, silly and hilarious novel features the residents of a small town called Lamonic Bibber. Among them are a little girl named Polly, Jake the dog and Mr Gum, a thoroughly unpleasant man who 'liked snoozing in bed all day, being lonely and scowling at things'. When Mr Gum poisons Jake, who will save him? Polly, of course, with the help of her friend Friday O'Leary and his mysterious catchphrase, 'The truth is a lemon meringue'.

Andy Stanton isn't just a wonderfully imaginative and creative writer; he's also very, very funny. Although aimed at younger readers, the adventures of Mr Gum are guaranteed to make you giggle, whatever your age. Don't miss the 'secret bonus story' at the back.

**Josh Lacey**

## Next?
• There are more books about the residents of Lamonic Bibber – *Mr Gum and the Biscuit Billionaire*, *Mr Gum and the Goblins*, *Mr Gum and the Power Crystals* and *Mr Gum and the Dancing Bear* – and, I hope, there will be many more to come.
• *The BFG* by Roald Dahl has a similar sort of anarchic feel. (*UBG* 33)
• Or for more anarchy, try Eoin Colfer's wonderful *The Legend of Spud Murphy*. (*UBG* 197)

★ ★ ★ ★ ★ ★

# YOU'RE THINKING ABOUT DOUGHNUTS Michael Rosen

## Next?
• Don't miss reading Michael Rosen's poetry – his poems deal with all sorts of subjects and keen readers should enjoy them immensely. There are various collections of his work.
• *Puck of Pook's Hill* (*UBG* 275) and *Rewards and Fairies* by Rudyard Kipling are other stories about being introduced to history in a strange and magical way. They're both quite a bit harder reads, but well worth the effort.

If the title of this book is meant to intrigue the prospective reader and give no clue as to its subject matter, it certainly succeeds. Many children will have experienced the prospect of trying to amuse themselves for a couple of hours in a parent's workplace. In this case the setting is a museum and Frank is accosted by a skeleton who in the course of the story introduces him to characters of history and legend through sequences of fantasy daydreams. Through these, the reader – and Frank – embarks on a journey in which fact has to be sorted out from fiction.

**Anthony Buckeridge**

# ABOUT THE CONTRIBUTORS

**JOAN AIKEN**'s distinguished career spanned 40 years, producing classic books such as *The Wolves of Willoughby Chase*, *Go Saddle the Sea* and *Midnight is a Place*. She died in January 2004.

**DAVID ALMOND** is a highly acclaimed fiction writer. His first novel *Skellig* won the Whitbread Children's Book of the Year and the Carnegie Medal. He lives in the north-east of England – the area he grew up in and loves to write about.

**ABIGAIL ANDERSON** is a theatre director who works all over the country and is a fan of brilliant stories, whether she's reading them on her own or telling them to theatre audiences.

**NOGA APPLEBAUM** completed a PhD in Children's Literature at Roehampton University, soon to be published by Routledge. Twice winner of the London Writers' Competition in the children's fiction category, she now teaches creative writing for children.

**JON APPLETON** worked on the first edition of *The Ultimate Book Guide* at A&C Black and has contributed to its siblings. He now works at Orion Children's Books.

**PHILIP ARDAGH** is a very large man with a very large beard, who has written over 50 children's books; these include the hilarious **Eddie Dickens** trilogy and *The Fall of Fergal*.

**NEIL ARKSEY** has had seven novels published. Of these *MacB* has been by far the best seller but *Flint* has been borrowed from libraries the most. Neil lives in Budapest where he works on a TV soap.

**EILEEN ARMSTRONG** is a secondary school librarian, reviewer and writer. She is currently chair of the National School Library Association and organiser of the UK Kids' Lit Quiz.

**SHERRY ASHWORTH** lives in Manchester and teaches creative writing at Manchester Metropolitan University. She has written extensively for children, her work including the prize-winning novels *Blinded by the Light* and *Paralysed*.

**PAUL BAJORIA** is the author of the **Printer's Devil** trilogy of children's novels. He also writes and produces a wide range of BBC radio programmes, and lives with his family in Northumberland.

**NINA BAWDEN** has written many award-winning children's books, the most famous of which is *Carrie's War*. *The Guardian* has said: 'Nina Bawden's readers should be numbered like the sands of the sea'.

**IAN BECK** is one of the UK's best-loved illustrators. His work includes *Round and Round the Garden*, *Little Brown Bear*, and the novel *The Secret History of Tom Trueheart, Boy Adventurer*.

**JULIE BERTAGNA**'s first paid job was serving in her uncle's ice-cream van, aged seven. She subsequently decided to work as a writer instead, producing many popular novels such as *Exodus*, *The Spark Gap*, *Dolphin Boy* and *Zenith*.

**MALORIE BLACKMAN** was born in London and now lives in Kent. She has written over 50 books, including the **Noughts and Crosses** series, *Pig-Heart Boy*, *Thief* and *Cloud Busting*.

**QUENTIN BLAKE** first had his drawings published when he was just 16. In the years since then, he has grown to become one of this country's best-loved illustrators and authors in his own right (with classic picture books like *Clown* and *Mr Magnolia*). In 1999, he was appointed the first Children's Laureate.

**DAVID BLANCH** was a primary school deputy head teacher until he took early retirement in 1996 to work full time on *Carousel* magazine. He was a founder member of the Birmingham Children's Book Group in 1969.

**JENNY BLANCH** is a former primary school deputy head teacher and an Honorary President of the Federation of Children's Book Groups. In 1995, with her husband David, she launched *Carousel*.

**THOMAS BLOOR** used to be an artificial flower maker, and is now the author of nine children's books, including the cult-hit **Worm in the Blood** trilogy. He also teaches creative writing, part-time.

**MICHAEL BOND** is best known as the author of the hugely popular **Paddington Bear** books, which began with *A Bear Called Paddington* way back in 1958. In 1997 he was awarded the OBE for services to children's literature and in 2008 he brought out a new Paddington book: *Paddington Here and Now*.

**TIM BOWLER** has written eight novels and won 13 awards, including the Carnegie Medal. *The Independent* has described him as 'one of the truly individual voices in British teenage fiction'.

**GERALDINE BRENNAN** is former Books Editor of *The Times Educational Supplement*. She is now a freelance journalist and consultant and has judged literary awards including the Costa Children's Book of the Year.

**HERBIE BRENNAN** published his first book in 1972. It became a specialist best-seller and remains in print to this day. Since then, he has managed to produce more than 108 titles, including the best-selling *GrailQuest* and **Faerie Wars** series.

**THERESA BRESLIN** is a Carnegie Medal winning author whose work has been filmed for television, broadcast on radio, and is read worldwide in a number of languages.

**ANTHONY BUCKERIDGE** was the creator of the **Jennings** books, containing some of the best-loved characters in children's fiction. He died in 2004.

**LINDA BUCKLEY-ARCHER**'s novel *Gideon the Cutpurse*, the first in a time-travelling trilogy which she wrote over a number of years for her own children, was awarded a Highly Commended Distinction by the judges of the 2007 Branford Boase Award. It is currently being published in ten countries, including Russia and Japan.

**MELVIN BURGESS** has received both considerable acclaim and much criticism for his hard-hitting teenage fiction. He has also written less controversial books for pre-teens, including *An Angel for May* and *The Earth Giant*.

**MEG CABOT** has worked as an illustrator and a writer of historical romances. She is the author of the hugely successful **Princess Diaries** books and, for younger readers, the **Allie Finkle's Rules for Girls** series.

**PAULINE CHANDLER** teaches in a school for children with special needs. Her books all have a historical background. *Warrior Girl*, a story of Joan of Arc, met with much critical acclaim. Her most recent title is *The Mark of Edain*.

**BABETTE COLE** published her first picture book in 1976, and has since written and illustrated another 70, including classics like *Mummy Laid an Egg!*, *Drop Dead* and *Princess Smartypants*.

**STEVE COLE**, a former book and magazine editor, has scripted scores of fiction titles for children of all ages, including the **Astrosaurs** and **Cows in Action** series.

**WENDY COOLING** is a children's book expert and creator of Bookstart, the scheme that provides free books for babies and young children. In 2006 she received the Eleanor Farjeon Award for her outstanding contribution to children's literature.

**SUSAN COOPER** lives in the USA and writes fantasies about Britain, probably out of homesickness. They include **The Dark is Rising** sequence, *King of Shadows* and *Victory*.

**CRESSIDA COWELL** is a writer and illustrator who lives in London. Her picture book *That Rabbit Belongs to Emily Brown* won the Smarties Gold Award, and her **Hiccup** fiction series has been translated into over 30 languages.

**MICHAEL COX** is an author and illustrator. After winning the Scholastic / Independent Story of the Year award, he gave up teaching to write full time. His series include **Vampire Vigilantes** and **Action Seeker's Handbooks**.

**HELEN CRESSWELL**'s wonderful television scripts and books earned her huge acclaim. Among her most popular series are the **Lizzie Dripping** stories and *The Bagthorpe Saga*. She died in 2005.

**CHRIS CROSS** is the webmaster behind the book-review website for and by ten to 15-year-olds that he and his brother Tim launched in January 2001 (www.cool-reads.co.uk).

**GILLIAN CROSS** is probably best known as the author of the **Demon Headmaster** series, but has written numerous other wonderful books, including *Wolf* and the **Lost** trilogy. She has won the Carnegie Medal, the Smarties Prize and the Whitbread Award.

**LOUIS CROSS** lives in London. He has enjoyed reading ever since he learned how. His literary obsessions include graphic novels and surreal fiction. His main interests are literature and film. He dreams of becoming a film director for independent cinema.

**TIM CROSS** is in charge of the reviews that appear on www.cool-reads.co.uk. He himself reads at least ten books a week, a habit that he found useful when he was a judge for the 2003 Booktrust Teenage Book Prize.

**TOMMASO CUNIBERTI** is a half-Italian, half-Norwegian boy who lives in London. He loves sport, singing, playing the piano and clarinet, art and history. In particular he enjoys collecting stamps, reading, meeting authors and helping out in the school library.

**ANNA DALE** studied history at university and worked in a bookshop for several years before she became a writer. She has written *Whispering to Witches*, *Dawn Undercover* and *Spellbound*.

**ANNIE DALTON** tried all sorts of jobs, from being a waitress to working in a factory, before she became a writer. She is best known for her hugely popular **Angels Unlimited** series. All of her books have a magical slant.

**JANE DARCY** has worked as an English teacher for over 25 years. She loves books, but can never hope to read as much, or with such pleasure, as she did in childhood.

**JOSEPH DELANEY** was born in Lancashire where his **Wardstone Chronicles** series is located. He used to be an English and Media teacher but now writes full time.

**TED DEWAN** is an author, illustrator, journalist, comedian, musician and cartoonist. He had his first commission when he was 16. He now works in Philip Pullman's old shed, which was passed on to him much in the way of an Olympic torch.

**CHRIS D'LACEY** is a Malteser (he was born in Malta!) but lives in England. His first novel, *Fly, Cherokee, Fly* was highly commended for the Carnegie Medal. His series include **David Rain** and **The Dragons of Wayward Crescent**.

**BERLIE DOHERTY** is a compulsive writer of novels, poems and plays. She has won the Carnegie Medal twice, with *Granny was a Buffer Girl* and *Dear Nobody*. She lives in the Peak District and sometimes writes perched on a stone by the river.

**MALACHY DOYLE** lives on a tiny island off the north-west coast of Ireland. He has written over 60 books, including *The Dancing Tiger*, which won the Smarties Silver Award.

**TOBIAS DRUITT** is the penname of mother and son writing team Michael Dowling and Diane Purkiss, authors of the **Corydon** trilogy. Michael wrote the reviews that appear in this guide.

**DIANE DUANE** is an American who now lives in Ireland. She has written hundreds of books, mainly science fiction and fantasy. Her work includes tie-ins to many television shows, as well as her own creations, like the **Young Wizards** series.

**CAROL ANN DUFFY**'s most recent books for children are *The Hat*, *The Lost Happy Endings*, *The Tear Thief* and *The Princess's Blankets*.

**SABINE DURRANT** is a journalist and novelist. She lives in London with three children, three cats and a dog, and is the author of the **Connie Pickles** novels.

**HEATHER DYER** spent her childhood between Wales and Canada. Her novel *The Girl With the Broken Wing* was featured in the 2007 Richard and Judy Children's Book Club.

**PATRICIA ELLIOTT**'s latest novel for older children is *The Night Walker*. She has worked in publishing, and now runs occasional writing workshops for adults and children.

**ANNE FINE** has written for all ages, from young children to adults, and her amazing books have won her the Carnegie Medal (twice), the Whitbread Award (twice), the Guardian Award and the Smarties Prize. She was elected the second Children's Laureate, serving from 2001–2003.

**PATRICIA FINNEY** had her first novel published while she was still a teenager, and since then has gone on to write many historical novels for adults. In her spare time she takes dictation from her Labrador dog, Jack, so that the world can share his adventures and exploits.

**CATHERINE FISHER** lives in Wales with her two cats. She has won awards for both her fiction and her poetry, and her most famous titles include *The Book of the Crow*, the **Snow-walker** trilogy and the slightly older *Corbenic*. She has recently written *The Pickpocket's Ghost*.

**LINDSEY FRASER** worked as a children's bookseller, and was Executive Director of Scottish Book Trust for eleven years. She is now a partner in Fraser Ross Associates, a literary consultancy based in Edinburgh.

**VIVIAN FRENCH** was an actor and storyteller before becoming a writer. She has written over 200 books, but her favourite is *The Robe of Skulls*, which was Stockport Children's Book of the Year 2008.

**JONAH FREUD** is an eleven-year-old boy who spends most of his time reading. He makes time to do flips on the trampoline and at the weekend he reads on the trampoline. At school, he spends most of his free time in the library looking for new, challenging books.

**CORNELIA FUNKE** is the author of *The Thief Lord*, the **Inkheart** series and other works of brilliant and original fantasy for young readers; born in Germany, she now lives in Los Angeles.

**SUSAN GATES** has taught in Africa and England and has written over 100 books for children. She especially likes writing thrillers and funny books. She now lives in County Durham.

**JAMILA GAVIN** has been writing for children for nearly 30 years. Her books particularly reflect Britain's diverse society. Her novel, *Coram Boy*, won the Whitbread Children's Book Award.

**ADÈLE GERAS** writes for children of all ages and also for adults. Her best-known books are *Troy* and *Ithaka*. She reviews children's books for the *Guardian*.

**ALAN GIBBONS** lives in Liverpool with his wife and four children. He has won The Blue Peter Book Awards and six other literary awards. He has been shortlisted twice for both the Carnegie Medal and the Booktrust Teenage Book Prize.

**JULIA GOLDING** worked as a diplomat and Oxfam policy adviser before writing for children. Her first novel, *The Diamond of Drury Lane*, won the Smarties Gold Medal.

**CANDIDA GRAY** has degrees in theatre, art history and history, but she has always wanted to have one in literature, too! Candida works at a school in New York.

**OLI GREEN** is eleven years old. He's passionate about sport, particularly tennis, cricket, football, rugby, snowboarding and downhill skiing. He also likes his family, adventures and books stored on his iPod.

**ELENA GREGORIOU** is a teacher in London. One of her favourite things is to read to her class – and to listen to them reading to her – which she considers one of the

most valuable learning experiences, for both class and teacher.

**ANN HALAM** writes for teenagers, and also (as Gwyneth Jones) writes science fiction for the young at heart. Her rock-and-roll fantasy *Bold As Love* won the Arthur C. Clarke Award in 2002.

**MAX HART** lives in London and attends Arnold House School. An enthusiastic pianist, he loves his dog 'Bagel' the Beagle and Japanese food. Max is a James Bond fanatic and spends his free time listening to Elvis, exploring at the back of the garden and of course, reading! When he grows up he is considering a career in archaeology or as a magician.

**STUART HILL** was born and brought up in Leicester where he still lives. His first book, *Cry of the Icemark*, won the Waterstones Children's Book Prize in 2005.

**MARY HOFFMAN** has written around 90 books, including the bestselling *Amazing Grace* and its sequels and the *Stravaganza* series for older readers. Her daughter, Rhiannon Lassiter, is also a children's writer. They edit an online magazine together called *Armadillo*.

**ELIZABETH HONEY** grew up on a farm in Victoria, Australia. She studied art, became an illustrator and then a writer. Her 14 titles include picture books, novels and poetry.

**ANTONIA HONEYWELL** is a teacher and writer. She dreams of being a novelist and has even written novels, but until the publishing world catches up with her, she will continue to indulge herself in her favourite pastimes. As these include changing nappies, baking fairy cakes and reading the same book 17 times in a single sitting, her current life as mother to two toddlers and a baby suits her perfectly.

**MARY HOOPER** lives in Oxfordshire. She has written over 70 books and is probably best known for her **Megan** novels. She now mainly writes historical fiction for young adults.

**ANTHONY HOROWITZ** is a writer for TV and cinema, but you'll probably know him best as author of the **Alex Rider** stories (*Stormbreaker*, etc.), **Groosham Grange**, **Horowitz Horror** and the **Power of Five** series.

**LAURA HUTCHINGS** is Head of English at a boys' prep school in London. She freely

admits to finding the Carnegie shortlist more interesting than the Booker. Copious quantities of nephews, nieces and FNRCs (favourite non-related children) have benefited from her avid reading of the *UBG*.

**EVA IBBOTSON** was born in Vienna but came to England when she was eight years old. She has written many books for both children and adults. Her latest is *The Dragonfly Pool*.

**ROSE IMPEY** was born in Cheshire. She has had over 100 books published, from picture books to novels for pre-teens. She is probably best known for creating the popular – now televised – **Sleepover Club** series.

**STEVE JACKSON**, with his collaborator Ian Livingstone, kick-started the gaming phenomenon **Fighting Fantasy**. There are now more than 70 books in the series and they have been sold in over 20 countries.

**JULIA JARMAN** has written many books for children including *Ghost Writer* and the **Time-Travelling Cat** series. All the animals in her books are based on those she has known.

**SPENCER JOHNSTON** has a sister, Isabella, a Tibetan Terrier called Cosmo and a five-year-old goldfish called Caravana. He attends Arnold House School and his favourite food is Sushi. He is a big fan of *The Lord of the Rings* and anything by J.R.R Tolkien.

**SHERRYL JORDAN** lives in New Zealand and is a writer of books mainly for young adults and teens. In 2001, she was awarded the Margaret Mahy Medal for her contribution to children's literature.

**ANN JUNGMAN** is best known as the creator of Vlad the Drac. She was born in London where she still lives, and where she founded and runs the publishing company Barn Owl Books.

**JACKIE KAY** is a poet who has also written widely for stage and screen. She has published various collections of poetry for children, including *Two's Company*, and a novel, *Strawgirl*, for older readers.

**GARRY KILWORTH** is author of the **Welkin Weasels** series and the **Knights of Liofwende** series among many other titles. His work has twice been shortlisted for the Carnegie Medal. He writes for all ages, sometimes as Garry Douglas.

**DICK KING-SMITH** grew up surrounded by pet animals and was a farmer for 20 years. He is one of the best-loved children's writers of today. His many books about animals include *The Sheep-Pig* and *The Hodgeheg*.

**JOSH LACEY's** books include *Bearkeeper* and *God is Brazilian*. Using the name Joshua Doder, he has also written the **Grk** series.

**ELIZABETH LAIRD** has always had a passion for travel, and having lived all over the world and experienced life in many different places, she is amply qualified to write her best-selling, award-winning books, such as *Kiss the Dust* and *Crusade*.

**KATHERINE LANGRISH** always wanted to work with horses and write books. She has lived in France and America, as well as England, and is the author of the historical fantasies *Troll Fell*, *Troll Mill* and *Troll Blood*.

**CAROLINE LAWRENCE** grew up in California but now lives in London. Her best-selling series of novels, the **Roman Mysteries**, is now a glossy BBC TV series.

**MICHAEL LAWRENCE** originally trained as a graphic designer and photographer in London, and worked in several other professions before becoming a full-time author. The books he is most pleased to have written are the three volumes of the **Aldous Lexicon** trilogy.

**NEAL LAYTON** wanted to be an astronaut, then changed his mind and became an artist. He illustrates books, sometimes his own, such as *Oscar and Arabella*, and sometimes other writers', such as *Rover* by Michael Rosen. He won the Smarties Gold Award for *That Rabbit Belongs to Emily Brown* by Cressida Cowell.

**TANITH LEE** was born in 1947, in England. She has written for BBC radio and TV, published almost 100 books, 265 short stories and won many awards.

**REBECCA LE FEVRE** manages the Hampstead branch of Daunt Books alongside her colleagues Zoe and Chris. Like Emily Windsnap, Rebecca enjoys swimming and has even braved the deep, cold waters of her local lido in Tooting.

**FRANCESCA LEWIS** graduated in 1995 and has worked in publishing and public relations. She has two children.

**NAOMI LEWIS** won the Eleanor Farjeon Award for services to children's literature in 1975. She has been the translator for various collections of Hans Andersen's fairy tales and has written introductions to many children's classics.

**PENELOPE LIVELY** is one of Britain's best-loved writers, for both children and adults. She won the Carnegie Medal for *The Ghost of Thomas Kempe* and the Whitbread Award for *A Stitch in Time*.

**JULIA LYTOLLIS** is a teacher currently working, after a long spell abroad, back home in England. As a reader, she enjoys fantasy and science fiction.

**GERALDINE McCAUGHREAN** trained as a teacher, worked in TV and publishing then finally got her lucky break as an author. 140 books later, she is now perhaps best known for *Peter Pan in Scarlet*, official sequel to J.M. Barrie's classic. She won the Carnegie Medal for *Pack of Lies*, and the Whitbread Prize several times.

**KAREN McCOMBIE** lives, just like her heroine Ally, very close to Alexandra Palace in London. Her **Ally's World** series has won her a fanatical following. Other series include **Sadie Rocks** and **Indie Kidd**. Apart from writing, Karen enjoys reading, eating crisps and belly-dancing.

**HILARY McKAY's** *Saffy's Angel* won the 2003 Whitbread Children's Book Award and she has gone on to write four other novels about the Casson family. Her many other titles include the **Exiles** series and the **Charlie** books.

**JOHN MCLAY** is Director of the Bath Festival of Children's Literature and is a children's books literary scout. He also lectures on the MA in Writing for Young People at Bath Spa University.

**CLIFF McNISH's** first series, the **Doomspell** trilogy, is sold in 21 languages. His latest books are the multiple-award-winning 2007 ghost story, *Breathe*, and the spiritual fantasy, *Angel*.

**MARGARET MAHY** has been writing children's books for over 30 years. She has won the Carnegie Medal twice for *The Haunting* and *The Changeover*. Her other novels include *Maddigan's Fantasia* and *Alchemy*.

**JAN MARK** was a highly distinguished children's author. Her first novel, *Thunder and Lightnings*, won the Carnegie Medal and she went on to win it again for *Handles*. Jan died in 2006.

**PHILIPPA MILNES-SMITH** is a literary agent and children's specialist at the agency LAW (Lucas Alexander Whitley). She has worked for many years in children's publishing and has been Managing Director of Puffin Books.

**MICHAEL MORPURGO** is the former Children's Laureate and award-winning author of over 100 books for children including *War Horse*, *Kensuke's Kingdom* and *Private Peaceful*.

**ROBERT MUCHAMORE** always wanted to be a writer, but could never think of a good idea for a novel until he heard his nephew complaining that he couldn't find any decent books to read. The first book in the **CHERUB** series was published in 2004. The series has gone on to sell over 1.5 million copies and is published in more than a dozen languages.

**BEVERLEY NAIDOO** grew up under Apartheid in South Africa and then became a teacher in exile in England. Her many awards include the Carnegie Medal for *The Other Side of Truth*.

**LINDA NEWBERY** writes fiction for children and teenagers. Her books for eight to 12s include *Nevermore*, *Catcall* and *Lost Boy*, and, in the **Historical House** series, *Polly's March* and *Andie's Moon*.

**JENNY NIMMO** is the author of over 40 books for children, including *The Snow Spider* and *The Owl Tree*, both of which won the Smarties Prize, and the **Children of the Red King** series.

**ANDREW NORRISS** lives in Hampshire. He wrote for television (*Woof*, *Bernard's Watch*, *Brittas Empire*) before turning to children's books; his novel *Aquila* won the Whitbread Prize in 1997.

**KENNETH OPPEL** published his first book for children at the age of 17. He lives in Toronto, and is the author of *Silverwing*, *Airborn*, and, most recently, *Dusk*.

**BRIAN PATTEN** is one of the best and most loved poets writing today. Along with Roger McGough and Adrian Henri, he was one of the Liverpool Poets of the 1960s and he has been writing and performing ever since.

**KATE PETTY** was a children's author and editor. She wrote teenage fiction series including **Girls Like You**, and the very successful educational pop-up, *The Terrific Times Table Book*. Most recently she created the children's publishing list at the Eden Project in Cornwall. Kate died in 2007.

**RODMAN PHILBRICK** grew up on the coast of New England, where he worked as a boat builder. His novel *Freak the Mighty* was selected for the first Booked Up! list.

**NAT PHILIPPS** is an eleven-year-old boy who loves his dogs, Minnie and Dido, eating interesting things, watching his dad's bees and reading. He somehow manages to play the saxophone and piano, enjoy football and rugby, hate cricket and art and love libraries, but rarely all at the same time.

**GERVASE PHINN** is an author, poet and broadcaster, and an expert on children and reading. His collections for children, such as *The Day Our Teacher Went Batty*, are hugely popular. He has written several volumes of autobiography, beginning with *The Other Side of the Dale.*

**JAN PIENKOWSKI** was born in Warsaw, arrived in London at the age of nine and went on to read classics at Cambridge. He is the author and / or illustrator of 142 books, most of them for young people.

**TAMORA PIERCE** comes from Pennsylvania, America, and says she was a hillbilly. As a child she loved reading and TV and spent many hours writing fan fiction based on her favourite shows. Now she lives in New York with her husband and four cats, and writes full time in her own wonderful universes.

**KJARTAN POSKITT** is a former schools TV presenter and pub piano player, and is author of the **Murderous Maths** series, the **Urgum the Axeman** series and the musical *Henry the Tudor Dude.*

**TERRY PRATCHETT** published his first story when he was 13 and first got paid for a story four years later. He has written books for younger readers and is most famous for his **Discworld** series, which has sold over 20 million copies and been translated into 27 languages.

**SUSAN PRICE** hated school and for her, reading and writing were an escape. Her first novel was published when she was 16, and since then she has gone on to win the Carnegie Medal for *The Ghost Drum* and the Guardian Award for *The Sterkarm Handshake.*

**SALLY PRUE** has worked in a paper factory and as a piano teacher. She won the Branford Boase Award for *Cold Tom*, and *The Truth Sayer* has been shortlisted for the Guardian Award.

**SIMON PUTTOCK** studied English Literature at university, and since then has lectured in and been a bookseller of children's books. He now lives in Edinburgh and won the Royal Mail Scottish Book Awards and the Highland Book Awards with *Little Lost Cowboy* in 2006.

**SHOO RAYNER** writes tons of fast and funny early readers that children read by the bucket-load.

**CELIA REES** was a teacher before becoming a writer for older children and teenagers. She has written 20 novels and has been shortlisted for the Whitbread Prize, and the Guardian and W.H. Smith Awards.

**GWYNETH REES** is half-English, half-Welsh, now living in London (with cats). Her books include *The Mum Hunt*, *Fairy Dust*, the **Mermaids** series and the **Cosmo** series.

**PHILIP REEVE** is the author of the acclaimed **Mortal Engines** quartet. His novel *Here Lies Arthur* won the Carnegie Medal in 2008.

**LYNNE REID BANKS** was born in London, became an actress and later joined ITN as Britain's first female news reporter. She has written 40 books, mainly for children, including *The Indian in the Cupboard* and *Harry the Poisonous Centipede.*

**ANTHONY REUBEN** writes for the business pages on BBC News online and was economic consultant on the book *Show Me the Money.* He only got to contribute to this guide because he is married to one of the editors.

**JUSTIN RICHARDS** writes exciting novels for children of all ages, and is creative consultant to the BBC Books' hugely successful range of **Doctor Who** novels.

**NIGEL RICHARDSON** lives in London, though people will persist in thinking he lives in Brighton. He has written two novels which feature teenagers (the first was *The Wrong Hands*) and in another life he is a travel writer.

**JAMES RIORDAN** was born in Portsmouth. An expert on Russia, he has written over 20 academic titles, several collections of folk tales and a number of picture books. His stories for children and young adults have won many awards and often deal with difficult subject matter.

**JULIAN RIPLEY** is a pupil of Arnold House School in London. He enjoys reading books a lot, especially action stories. His favourite sport is rugby and the two schools he most wants to go to are Rugby and Westminster.

**WILLIAM RIPLEY** has just completed a year as head boy of his prep school and is soon to be moving on to Westminster school. Like his younger brother, Julian, he is an avid reader.

**DAVID ROBERTS** is an illustrator, much loved for his collaborations with Philip Ardagh (the **Eddie Dickens** trilogy and others), Julia Donaldson (*Tyrannosaurus Drip*) and many more. He has collaborated with his sister on a series of wild retellings of classic fairy tales, and also wrote and illustrated the original *Dirty Bertie* picture book.

**KATHERINE ROBERTS** took a First in Mathematics from Bath University and worked with racehorses for ten years. She won the inaugural Branford Boase Award for her first novel *Song Quest.*

**MICHAEL ROSEN** is one of Britain's best-loved children's poets. Sometimes he lies in bed thinking of all the things he would write if he got up. His many titles include the poetry collections *Quick*, *Let's Get Out of Here* and *You Wait Till I'm Older Than You!*. He was appointed the Children's Laureate in 2007.

**KATHRYN ROSS** is a former English teacher, independent bookseller and Deputy Director of Scottish Book Trust. She is now a partner in the literary consultancy Fraser Ross Associates.

**JOHN ROWE TOWNSEND** is a children's author and academic. He has written a history of children's literature, *Written for Children*, and over 20 children's books, including *Gumble's Yard* and *The Intruder.*

**ANGIE SAGE** lives in Somerset. She studied graphic design and illustration and worked for many years illustrating and writing books for young children before she began writing her best-selling series, **Septimus Heap**.

**JAHAN SAHNI** is a compulsive reader and he combs libraries and bookshops in order to feed his enthusiasm. He also likes sport, friends and family and really without trying has amassed a large collection of bookmarks!

**HUGH SCOTT** is best known for his supernatural and horror novels for young adults. He won the Whitbread Prize in 1989 for *Why Weeps the Brogan?*. He now lectures in creative writing and visits schools regularly.

**MARCUS SEDGWICK** has written several novels for teens, the most recent of which are *My Swordhand is Singing*, winner of the Booktrust Teenage Book Prize, and *Blood Red Snow White*, shortlisted for the Costa Book Award.

**BRIAN SELZNICK** is the illustrator of many books by many different writers, including *The Dinosaurs of Waterhouse Hawkins* and *The Doll People*. He is also the author-illustrator of the extraordinary *Invention of Hugo Cabret*, which won him the 2008 Caldecott Medal.

**DARREN SHAN** lives in Limerick in Ireland, and has written two series: **The Saga of Darren Shan** and **The Demonata**.

**NICK SHARRATT** is the illustrator of Jacqueline Wilson's best-selling novels but he has also produced loads of picture books like *Don't Put your Finger in the Jelly, Nelly!* and *Shark in the Park*.

**HELEN SIMMONS** studied English at university and has spent much of her career working as a children's bookseller; she currently works in Bath in an independent bookshop. She is also a regular reviewer for Booktrust.

**FRANCESCA SIMON** is an American, who now lives in London with her husband and son. She used to be a journalist, but is now a full-time writer, best known for her wonderful **Horrid Henry** books.

**NICKY SINGER's** first published work (aged 16) was a libretto and she is just about to do another for Glyndebourne. In between, she has written ten novels including *Feather Boy*, which won the Blue Peter Book of the Year Award.

**JUSTIN SOMPER** is the author of the bestselling **Vampirates** sequence of adventure novels. He is also a children's book publicist.

**JERRY SPINELLI** isn't always sure how many books he's written, but he knows he has 16 grandkids. And one wife, fellow writer Eileen, with whom he lives in Wayne, Pennsylvania.

**CHRIS STEPHENSON** was a bookseller for 18 years, with a particular interest in children's books. He now works as a freelance writer, frequently contributing to *Carousel*.

**PAUL STEWART** – with his long-time collaborator, the illustrator Chris Riddell – is author of highly popular **Edge Chronicles** and **Barnaby Grimes** books, among others. Paul works every day (apart from Christmas and holidays).

**EDDIE STRANG** is eleven. His hobbies are reading, playing football and climbing trees – though nothing beats a good book. He loves English and hates Maths.

**JEREMY STRONG** lives near Bath with his wife, Gillie, four cats and a lot of frogspawn. He has written over 80 books, won several awards and practises sleeping as his main hobby.

**ALAN TEMPERLEY** lives in Scotland and can often be found on speaking tours of Scottish schools. He has written many books, including *The Magician of Samarkand* and *Harry and the Wrinklies*, which was made into a TV series.

**COLIN THOMPSON** was born in London in 1942 and moved to Australia when he was 52. Since his first book in 1991, he has had over 50 books published around the world and won many awards.

**RHIAN TRACEY** began writing following a career as a secondary school teacher. Her first novel, *When Isla Meets Luke Meets Isla*, was read on the radio by TV presenter Zoe Ball and chosen as one of the 'Top five teen reads of the year' in the *Telegraph*.

**MADELYN TRAVIS** has an MA in children's literature from the University of Roehampton, She is also Website Features Editor for Booktrust and writes articles for publications including *The Horn Book Magazine*.

**ANN TURNBULL** lives in Shropshire and has been writing for children of all ages since 1974. Her novel *No Shame, No Fear* was shortlisted for both the Guardian Award and the Whitbread Prize.

**KAYE UMANSKY** has written over 130 books and is probably best known for the **Pongwiffy** series. She won the 2005 Spoken Word Award for *The Silver Spoon of Solomon Snow*.

**JEAN URE** lives in South London with her husband and their eleven animals. She had her first book published while still at school and has been writing ever since.

**GILL VICKERY's** *The Ivy Crown* won the Fidler Prize. She has stories in the collections *In the Frame* and *Wow! 366*.

She has won an Arts Council England Award to complete her novel *Blood and Roses*.

**KAREN WALLACE** has written award-winning books for all age groups, including *Raspberries on the Yangtze* and *Think of an Eel*. She also writes for television. She firmly believes that all writing is about telling stories.

**SYLVIA WAUGH** was born in the north of England and now lives in Gateshead. She began writing after following a career as a school teacher. Her first book, *The Mennyms*, won the 1994 Guardian Children's Fiction Prize.

**VICTORIA WEBB** studied English and American literature at Exeter University and has worked as an editor for ten years. She lives in Bath with her husband and two young children.

**SARA WHEELER's** books include the bestselling *Terra Incognita: Travels in Antarctica*.

**JACQUELINE WILSON** is one of the most popular writers in the country. Her many titles include *The Lottie Project*, *Double Act*, *Best Friends* and *The Story of Tracy Beaker*. She was the Children's Laureate from 2005–2007.

**JEANETTE WINTERSON** is a highly celebrated writer for adults, with books including *Oranges are not the Only Fruit*; in 2006 she published her first novel for children, *Tanglewreck*.

**CHRIS WOODING** has been a professional author since he was 19, and also works as a screenwriter. His novel *The Haunting of Alaizabel Cray* won the 2003 Smarties Silver Award.

**BARBARA WRIGHT** is a registered Pharmacy Technician who enjoys reading and writing, but doesn't have nearly enough time to do either of them as much as she would like.

**JANE YOLEN**, often called 'the Hans Christian Andersen of America', is the author of over 300 books, ranging from picture books, board books and fiction to poetry, non fiction, novels, graphic novels, and story collections.

**BENJAMIN ZEPHANIAH** is a poet, performer and broadcaster. His books include the poetry collections *Talking Turkeys* and *Funky Chickens*, and the novels *Refugee Boy*, *Face* and *Teacher's Dead*.

# ACKNOWLEDGEMENTS

**For the First Edition**

A book like this is bound to depend on the work of more than just a handful of people, and we have found ourselves enormously lucky to have had the goodwill of so many great people who have put their expertise (and enthusiasm) at our disposal.

Jane Rogers, Ruth Langley and Suzie Dent were all extremely supportive way back when this book was no more than quite a good idea. Adèle Geras and Noga Applebaum offered advice and help early on, too. Geraldine Brennan, Candida Gray, Brenda Marshall of Port Regis School, Jenny Morris, Jane Nissen and Lisa Sainsbury all read our original, and very flawed, provisional list of 'Titles for Possible Inclusion'; their honest and well-informed comments and suggestions were crucial in refining what our book would eventually come to cover.

Thanks to all those many friends who read things for us, suggested titles for inclusion and for exclusion ('Surely you're not going to include X if you're not including Y?'); most helpful / enthusiastic / vehement of these were Abigail Anderson, Jane Darcy, Sarah Eley, Jenni Hicks and Tomaz Sodré Remensnyder.

The process of putting together such a great team of contributors depended largely on the generosity of those willing to open up their address books for our scrutiny. Among those many people who helped us with contacts, and suggested suitable names, we should thank Ann Jungman, Sarah Wilkie and Rosemary Stones. In many cases our contact with our contributors was facilitated by agents, publicists, etc. – thanks to all those who helped. In particular Jo Williamson and Nicola Blacoe at HarperCollins and Alyx Price at Macmillan worked on this far above and beyond. We should also offer warm thanks to Eileen Buckeridge and Robina Masters; sadly Robina's husband Anthony passed away before this book was completed – a great loss to the children's book world.

We must express our huge thanks and admiration to our contributors themselves for a fantastic set of entries and essays; and many of them donated their fees to our designated charity, Hope and Homes for Children.

At various stages we had extremely useful advice on all sorts of subjects from Liz Cross, Elizabeth Hammill, Pam Dix and the Kilburn Bookshop. The all-knowing Julia Eccleshare gave us invaluable advice on many matters, as did Jonathan Douglas, whose enthusiasm for this project seemed very often to exceed our own.

The phenomenal Anne Fine was one of the first people to come on board and express support for the *UBG*, and in those early days carelessly offered to write an introduction – and was then most gracious when many months later we held her to her promise. We are very grateful for her advice back when the idea of this book was still just coming together. It was Anne who introduced us to Eileen Armstrong, who has been absolutely tireless in offering her knowledge and enthusiasm ever since we started discussing this almost two years ago – we are enormously grateful for all the many ways in which she too has helped us over all this time.

Special thanks must also go to Laura Hutchings for working her way pretty much without complaint through hundreds of books on our behalf; and to Anthony Reuben, for support, encouragement, and the mention of *Supergran* at regular intervals.

Araminta Whitley at LAW introduced us to Philippa Milnes-Smith, who bravely agreed to represent this project as our agent. Long after finding us our publisher, Philippa has continued to godmother the project, giving us access to all the things she knows and all the people she knows and her absolutely unwavering enthusiasm for good children's books. She and her assistant Helen Mulligan have always been delighted to help more and yet more, and indeed gave so much of their time and energy that we have now become convinced that we must surely have been the only people they represented...

The publisher that Philippa found us was A&C Black, and the editor there, Jon Appleton, for whom no praise or thanks could be high enough.

**For the Second Edition**

The cover design is by Terry Woodley and the page design by Michelle Canatella – thanks to them, to our proofreaders Nina Randall and Ellen Grace, and to everybody who has contributed entries to this new edition. Huge thanks, as always, to our agent, Philippa Milnes-Smith and her assistant Ayesha Mobin; and, above all, to our editors Susila Baybars and Ruth Dix.

**THE EDITORS**

Versions of the book recommendations by Francesca Simon (p. 141) and Quentin Blake (pp. 213 and 361) have been published previously, the former in *The Guardian*, 28 February 2001, the latter two in *The Laureate's Party* (Red Fox, 2000).

Copyright in all entries belongs to the Editors, with the exception of those by Joan Aiken, Quentin Blake, Susan Cooper, John Rowe Townsend, Brian Selznick, Darren Shan and Jeanette Winterson, where copyright remains with the respective contributors.

For permission to reproduce copyright material in *The Ultimate Book Guide*, the publisher would like to thank the following:

**Andersen Press Ltd** for permission to reproduce the following cover: *Ely Plot* from **The Wickit Chronicles** by Joan Lennon, which appears on p. 384.

**Bloomsbury Publishing Plc** for permission to reproduce the following covers: *My Haunted House* from the **Araminta Spook** series by Angie Sage, which appears on p. 22; *Coraline* by Neil Gaiman, which appears on p. 69; *Faerie Wars* by Herbie Brennan, which appears on p. 105; *Harry Potter and the Philosopher's Stone* from the **Harry Potter** series by J.K. Rowling, cover illustration by Jason Cockroft, which appears on p. 145; *Love That Dog* by Sharon Creech, which appears on p. 214; *Tanglewreck* by Jeanette Winterson, which appears on p. 343; *There's a Boy in the Girls' Bathroom* by Louis Sachar, which appears on p. 297.

**Chicken House** for permission to reproduce the following cover: *Billy Elliot* by Melvin Burgess, which appears on p. 362; *I Am the Great Horse* by Katherine Roberts, cover illustration © Angelo Rinaldi, cover design by Ian Butterworth, 2007, which appears on p. 165.

**Egmont UK Ltd** for permission to reproduce the following covers: *The Little Prince* by Antoine de Saint-Exupéry, which appears on p. 205; the **Snow Spider** trilogy by Jenny Nimmo, which appears on p. 202; *Storm* by Kevin Crossley-Holland, which appears on p. 331; *The Three Little Wolves and the Big Bad Pig* by Eugene Trivizas and Helen Oxenbury, which appears on p. 265; *The Twins at St Clare's* from the **St Clare's** series by Enid Blyton, illustrated by David Roberts, which appears on p. 296; *War Horse* by Michael Morpurgo, which appears on p. 373; *The Wheel of Surya* by Jamila Gavin, illustrated by David Dean, which appears on p. 232; *The Wind in the Willows* by Kenneth Grahame, illustrated by E.H. Shepard, which appears on p. 385; *Winnie-the-Pooh* by A.A. Milne, illustrated by E.H. Shepard, which appears on p. 387; *You're a Bad Man, Mr Gum!* by Andy Stanton, illustrated by David Tazzyman, which appears on p. 397.

**Faber and Faber Ltd** for permission to reproduce the following covers: *The Children of Green Knowe* from the **Green Knowe** series by L.M. Boston, which appears on p. 61; *Awful End* from the **Eddie Dickens** trilogy by Philip Ardagh, which appears on p. 96; *The Turbulent Term of Tyke Tiler* by Gene Kemp, which appears on p. 357.

**HarperCollins Publishers Ltd** for permission to reproduce the following covers: *Charmed Life* from **The Worlds of Chrestomanci** series by Diana Wynne Jones, which appears on p. 393; *The Lion, the Witch and the Wardrobe* from **The Chronicles of Narnia** by C.S. Lewis, which appears on p. 198; *Little Wolf* by Ian Whybrow, which appears on p. 207; *The Lord of the Rings* by J.R.R. Tolkien, which appears on p. 211; *The Owl Service* by Alan Garner, which appears on p. 258; *The Pinhoe Egg* from **The Worlds of Chrestomanci** series by Diana Wynne Jones, which appears on p. 393; *The Sword in the Stone* by T.H. White, which appears on p. 202; *The Weirdstone of Brisingamen* by Alan Garner, which appears on p. 201; *When Hitler Stole Pink Rabbit* by Judith Kerr, which appears on p. 167.

**Hodder Children's Books, a division of Hachette Children's Books, 338 Euston Road, London, NW1 3BH** for permission to reproduce the following covers: *The Fire-Eaters* by David Almond, which appears on p. 113; *Saffy's Angel* by Hilary McKay, which appears on p. 329; *Skellig* by David Almond, which appears on p. 313.

**Macmillan Children's Books, London, UK** for permission to reproduce the following covers: *Crusade* by Elizabeth Laird, which appears on p. 75; *Fly By Night* by Frances Hardinge, which appears on p. 117; *The Garbage King* by Elizabeth Laird, which appears on p. 233; *Hatchet* by Gary Paulsen, which appears on p. 146; *Jammy Dodgers on the Run* by Bowering Sivers, which appears on p. 179; *Just William* by Richmal Crompton, which appears on

# INDEX